The Church
Mystery, Sacrament, Community

The Church
Mystery, Sacrament, Community

A Catechesis on The Creed

Pope John Paul II

With a Foreword
by Francis A. Sullivan, S.J.

BOOKS & MEDIA

Boston

Library of Congress Cataloging-in-Publication Data

John Paul II. Pope, 1920–
    The Church : mystery, sacrament, community / Pope John Paul II;
with a foreword by Francis A. Sullivan.
       p.   cm. — (Catechesis on the creed)
    Reprinted from L'Osservatore romano, English ed.
    Includes index.
    ISBN 0-8198-1546-2 (pbk)
    1. Catholic Church. 2. Mission of the church. 3. Church
I. L'Osservatore romano. II. Title. III. Series: John Paul II, Pope,
1920–   Catechesis on the creed.
BX1751.2.J6244   1998
262'.02—dc21   97-29634
                                                CIP

Reprinted with permission from *L'Osservatore Romano,* English Edition.

Cover Art: Scala/Art Resource, NY
          Early Christian mosaic:
          Lunette with Christ as Good Shepherd.

Printed and published in the U.S.A. by Pauline Books & Media, 50 St. Paul's Avenue, Boston, MA 02130.

http://www.pauline.org

Pauline Books & Media is the publishing house of the Daughters of St. Paul, an international congregation of women religious serving the Church with the communications media.

1 2 3 4 5 6   03 02 01 00 99 98

The following abbreviations are used in the text to indicate certain documents:

AA   *Apostolicam Actuositatem* (Decree on the Apostolate of the Laity)

AAS   *Acta Apostolicae Sedis*

AG   *Ad Gentes* (Decree on the Missionary Activity of the Church)

CCC   *Catechism of the Catholic Church*

CD   *Christus Dominus* (Decree Concerning the Pastoral Office of Bishops in the Church)

CIC   *Codex Iuris Canonici* (Code of Canon Law)

CL   *Christifideles Laici* (The Lay Members of Christ's Faithful People)

DH   *Dignitatis Humanae* (Declaration on Religious Freedom)

DS   *Denzinger-Schönmetzer*

DV   *Dei Verbum* (Dogmatic Constitution on Divine Revelation)

GS   *Gaudium et Spes* (Pastoral Constitution on the Church in the Modern World)

LE   *Laborem Exercens* (On Human Work)

LG   *Lumen Gentium* (Dogmatic Constitution on the Church)

MD   *Mulieris Dignitatem* (On the Dignity and Vocation of Women)

OT	*Optatam Totius* (Decree on Priestly Training)
PC	*Perfectae Caritatis* (Declaration on the Adaptation and Renewal of Religious Life)
PDV	*Pastores Dabo Vobis* (I Will Give You Shepherds)
PO	*Presbyterorum Ordinis* (Decree on the Ministry and Life of Priests)
RD	*Redemptionis Donum* (To Men and Women Religious)
RM	*Redemptoris Missio* (Mission of the Redeemer)
RMt	*Redemptoris Mater* (Mother of the Redeemer)
SC	*Sacrosanctum Concilium* (Constitution on the Sacred Liturgy)
SD	*Salvifici Doloris* (On the Christian Meaning of Human Suffering)
SDO	*Sacrum Diaconatus Ordinem* (General Norms for Restoring the Permanent Diaconate)
UR	*Unitatis Redintegratio* (Decree on Ecumenism)
UUS	*Ut Unum Sint* (On Commitment to Ecumenism)

Contents

The Ministry of Bishops

The Ministry of Priests and Deacons

The Role of the Laity

Consecrated Life

Missionary Activity and Unity among Christians

Foreword

Continuing the publication of the catecheses on the Creed which Pope John Paul II has given during his weekly general audiences, this volume contains the series of his catecheses on the article: "I believe in one, holy, catholic and apostolic Church." This series contains 137 catecheses given between July 10, 1991, and August 30, 1995.

The Second Vatican Council devoted a major share of its attention to explaining what the Catholic Church "has to say of itself," concerning both its own nature, structure and purpose, and its relationship to the world around it. Hence, it is not surprising that in these catecheses on the Church, the Holy Father has chosen to take the teaching of the Council as "his guiding principle," as he says in the catechesis entitled: "God Made a Covenant with Israel."

He also spoke of the "style" of these catecheses as he began his series on the presbyterate, saying: "I will talk about this by adhering strictly to the New Testament texts and by following the approach of the Second Vatican Council, which has been the style of these catecheses." At the same time, he has also used various post-conciliar documents, especially the "post-synodal" apostolic exhortations. For instance, in explaining how he will treat the topic of the laity, he says: "We shall do so by following the lead of the Second Vatican Council, but also by again considering the directives and guidelines in the Apostolic Exhortation *Christifideles Laici.*"

Pope John Paul described the contents of almost all of these catecheses as he began his series on the mission of the Church, to be followed by the concluding series on ecumenism. It seems appropriate to quote his own summary of most of what the reader will find in this volume.

> In the progressive development of the catechesis on the Church, we started with the eternal plan of God who wanted her to be the sacrament, point of convergence and radiating center of the economy of salvation. Having considered the various aspects of the Church's mystery as the People of God, sacrament of the union between humanity and God, bride of Christ and priestly community, we explained the ministries she is called to carry out. Regarding these ministries, we considered the episcopal college's mission in the succession of the apostolic college; the mission of the Pope, Successor of Peter in the Roman episcopate and in his primacy over the universal Church; the mission of priests and its implications for their state of life; the mission of deacons, appreciated today as in early Christian times and rightly considered a fresh leaven of hope for the entire People of God. Further, we spoke of the laity, shedding light on their value and mission as "Christ's faithful" in general, and in their various conditions of personal, family and social life. Lastly, we focused on the consecrated life as a treasure of the Church, in its traditional forms and in its many expressions which are flourishing today.

As we have seen above, when the Holy Father spoke of "the style of these catecheses," he spoke also of "adhering strictly to the New Testament texts." Likewise, when he spoke of "always taking as our guiding principle the teaching of the

Council," he added: "which was wholly inspired by Sacred Scripture." These phrases suggest what is most distinctive of these catecheses, namely, the abundant use which Pope John Paul has made of biblical texts to develop and illustrate each point of the doctrine of Vatican II on the Church.

Their style also corresponds to what Pope John XXIII, in his opening address at Vatican II, described as "a Magisterium which is predominantly pastoral in character." These catecheses are obviously intended not for learned theologians or scripture scholars, but for the ordinary faithful. There are some references to texts of St. Thomas Aquinas, but hardly any to other theologians, whether classical or modern. St. Augustine is the most frequently quoted of the Fathers, but there is nothing here to compare with the wealth of patristic texts with which doctrine has been illustrated in the *Catechism of the Catholic Church*. Perhaps the best way to describe these catecheses is to say that in them Pope John Paul II has given to the faithful a scripturally based and pastoral explanation of that part of the creed in which they profess their faith in the "one, holy, catholic and apostolic Church."

Francis A. Sullivan, S.J.
Boston College

THE MYSTERY OF THE
CHURCH IN THE PLAN OF GOD

Christ Founded the Catholic Church

Today we begin a new cycle of catechetical talks dedicated to the Church, about which the Nicene-Constantinopolitan Creed says: "I believe in one, holy, catholic and apostolic Church." This creed, like its antecedent, the Apostles' Creed, straightaway connects the truth about the Church with the Holy Spirit: "I believe in the Holy Spirit, the holy catholic Church." To go from the Holy Spirit to the Church has its own logic, which St. Thomas explains at the beginning of his catechesis on the Church: "As we see that in man there are one body and one soul, and yet this body has various members, so too, the Catholic Church is one body and has many members. The soul which gives life to this body is the Holy Spirit. For this reason, after expressing our faith in the Holy Spirit, we are commanded to believe in the holy catholic Church" (cf. *In Symbolum Apostolorum Expositio,* art 9, Edit. taur., n. 971).

The Nicene-Constantinopolitan Creed speaks of the Church as "one, holy, catholic and apostolic." These are the so-called "marks" of the Church, which require a certain introductory explanation, even though we will speak about their significance again in later catecheses.

Let us listen to what the last two councils said about this subject.

The First Vatican Council declared the unity of the Church in rather descriptive terms: "The eternal shepherd... decided to establish his holy Church in which the faithful would be united, as in the house of the living God, by bonds of the same faith and charity" (cf. *DS* 3050).

The Second Vatican Council, in turn, states: "Christ, the one Mediator, established and continually sustains here on earth his holy Church, the community of faith, hope and charity, as an entity with visible delineation." It also says: "The earthly Church and the Church enriched with heavenly things...form one complex reality which coalesces from a divine and a human element.... This is the one Church of Christ which in the creed is professed as one, holy, catholic and apostolic" *(LG* 8). The Council teaches us that this Church "...is in Christ like a sacrament or as a sign and instrument both of a very closely knit union with God and of the unity of the whole human race" *(LG* 1).

Clearly, the unity of the Church which we profess in the creed is proper to the universal Church, and the particular (or local) churches are such insofar as they share in this unity. Unity was recognized and preached as a property of the Church from the beginning, that is, from the time of Pentecost. It is a primordial and co-essential reality for the Church, and not merely an ideal which we hope to reach at some unknown point in the future. This hope and search can be valid regarding the historical realization of reuniting believers in Christ, but one cannot nullify the truth enunciated in the Letter to the Ephesians: "...one body and one Spirit, as you were also called to the one hope of your call (Eph 4:3-4). This is the truth of the Church's beginnings, which we profess in the creed: "I believe in *one*...Church."

From the beginning, however, the Church's history has unfolded in the midst of tensions and pressures which compromised unity, even to the point of eliciting appeals and reproofs from the apostles, especially Paul. He exclaimed: "Is Christ divided?" (1 Cor 1:13). It was and is the sign of the human inclination to oppose one another. It is as if one had to—or wanted to—do one's own part in scattering people, as was effectively depicted in the biblical account of Babel.

But the Fathers and pastors of the Church always appealed to unity, to the light of Pentecost which was contrasted with Babel. Vatican II observes: "It is the Holy Spirit, dwelling in those who believe and pervading and ruling over the Church as a whole, who brings about that wonderful communion of the faithful. He brings them into intimate union with Christ, so that he is the principle of the Church's unity" *(UR* 2). It must be a source of joy, hope and prayer for the Church to recognize, especially today, that the honest efforts which aim at overcoming all divisions and reuniting Christians come from the Holy Spirit *(ecumenism).*

The profession of faith contained in the creed also says that the Church is holy. It must be clarified immediately that the Church is such in virtue of her origin and divine institution. The Christ who instituted her is holy and merited for her by the sacrifice of the cross the gift of the Holy Spirit, who is the inexhaustible source of the Church's holiness, as he is the principle and foundation of her unity. The Church is holy because of her purpose, which is the glory of God and the salvation of men; she is holy because of the means used to obtain this purpose, which contain in themselves the holiness of Christ and the Holy Spirit. These means are the teaching of Christ, summed up in the revelation of God's love for us and in the dual commandment of love; the seven sacraments and the entire liturgy, especially the Eucharist; the life of prayer. It is all a divine plan of life, in which the Holy Spirit works through the grace infused and nourished in believers and enriched with manifold charisms for the good of the entire Church.

This, too, is a fundamental truth, professed in the creed and already stated in Ephesians, where the reason for this holiness is explained: "Christ loved the Church and handed

himself over for her to sanctify her" (Eph 5:25-26). He has
made her holy by the outpouring of the Holy Spirit, as Vatican
II says: "The Holy Spirit was sent on the day of Pentecost in
order that he might continually sanctify the Church" *(LG* 4).
This is the ontological basis for our faith in the Church's
holiness. The numerous ways in which this holiness is manifested in the lives of Christians and in the course of the
religious and social facts of history are a continual confirmation of the truth contained in the creed. History is an empirical
way to discover that truth, and in some way to ascertain a
presence in which we believe. Indeed, we can observe that
many members of the Church are saints. Many at least possess
that ordinary holiness which comes from the state of sanctifying grace in which they live. But there is an increasing number
of people who show signs of heroic sanctity. The Church is
very happy to be able to recognize and extol this sanctity of so
many servants of God who remained faithful until death. It is
like a sociological counterbalance to the presence of unfortunate sinners and an invitation to them—and to all of us—to set
out on the path of the saints.

But it is nevertheless true that holiness belongs to the
Church through her divine institution and by the continual
outpouring of gifts which the Holy Spirit accomplishes in the
faithful and in the whole "body of Christ" since Pentecost. This
does not exclude the fact, according to the Council, that each
one must achieve this holiness by following Christ (cf. *LG* 40).

Catholicity is another mark of the Church we profess our
faith in. The Church is "catholic" by divine institution, that is,
"universal" (the Greek *kath'hólon* means "regarding the
whole"). The term was used for the first time by St. Ignatius of
Antioch when he wrote to the faithful of Smyrna: "Where
Jesus Christ is, there is the Catholic Church" *(Ad Smyn.,* 8).
The entire Tradition of the Fathers and doctors of the Church
continues to repeat that definition, which derives from the
Gospel, all the way to Vatican II, which teaches: "This charac-

teristic of universality which adorns the people of God is a gift from the Lord himself. By reason of it, the Catholic Church strives constantly and with due effect to bring all humanity and all its possessions back to its source in Christ, with him as its head and united in his Spirit" *(LG* 13).

This catholicity has a great depth based on the universal power of the risen Christ (cf. Mt 28:18) and on the universal extent of the Holy Spirit's action (cf. Wis 1:7). It is communicated to the Church by divine institution. In fact, the Church was already catholic on the first day of her historical existence on Pentecost morning. Universality for her means being open to all humanity, to all human beings and to all cultures, far beyond the strict spatial, cultural and religious limits to which some of her members could be tied (those called Judaizers). Jesus conferred on the apostles that supreme mandate: "Go...and make disciples of all the nations" (Mt 28:19). He said and promised: "You are to be my witnesses in Jerusalem, throughout Judea and Samaria, yes, even to the ends of the earth" (Acts 1:8). Here too, we face a constitutive element of the Church's mission, and not the simple empirical fact of the Church's spread among the peoples belonging to "every nation," and so, to everyone. Universality is another property which the Church possesses in virtue of her divine institution. It is a constitutive dimension, which she possesses from the beginning as one, holy Church. This property cannot be conceived as the result of a "summation" of all the particular churches. Because of this dimension of her divine origin, she is an object of the faith we profess in the creed.

By the same faith we also profess that the Church of Christ is apostolic, that is, built upon the apostles, from whom she received the divine truth revealed by and in Christ. The Church is apostolic because she preserves the apostolic tradition and guards it as her sacred deposit.

The authoritative guardians appointed to preserve this deposit are the successors of the apostles, assisted by the Holy

Spirit. But without a doubt, all believers, in union with their legitimate pastors, and thus, the whole Church, share in the Church's apostolicity. That is, they share in her bond with the apostles and, through them, with Christ. For this reason the Church cannot be merely reduced to the ecclesiastical hierarchy. The latter is, without a doubt, its institutional foundation. But all the members of the Church—pastors and faithful—belong to her and are called to play an active role in the one People of God, who receive from him the gift of being bound to the apostles and to Christ, in the Holy Spirit. As we read in Ephesians: "You form a building which rises on the foundation of the apostles and prophets, with Christ Jesus himself as the capstone.... You are being built into this temple, to become a dwelling place for God in the Spirit" (Eph 2:20-22).

General audience of July 10, 1991

Christ's Call Establishes the Church

In the present catechesis, which continues our introduction to ecclesiology, we want to analyze briefly the term "Church," which comes to us from the Gospel and from the very word used by Christ. In this way we are following a very classical way of studying things, the first stage of which is to investigate the meaning of terms used to designate those things. For a great and ancient institution such as the Church, which is our concern here, it is important to know what her founder called her, because that name already expresses his thought, his plan, his creative idea.

We are told by the Gospel of Matthew that when Jesus, in response to Peter's confession of faith, announced the establishment of "his Church"—"Upon this rock I will build my Church" (Mt 16:18)—he employed a term whose common usage at the time and in various passages of the Old Testament allows us to discover its semantic value. It must be said that the Greek text of Matthew's Gospel uses here the express *mou ten ekklesían*. This word *ekklesía* was used in the Septuagint (the Greek translation of the Bible dating from the second century B.C.) to translate the Hebrew *qahàl* and the corresponding Aramaic *qahalà*, which Jesus probably used in his response to Simon Peter. This fact is the point of departure for our lexical analysis of Jesus' announcement.

Both the Hebrew term *qahàl* and the Greek *ekklesía* mean "gathering, assembly." *Ekklesía* is etymologically related to the Greek verb *kalein,* which means "to call." In Semitic speech the word meant, in practice, "assembly" ("called together"), and it was used in the Old Testament to designate the "community" of the chosen people, especially in the desert (cf. Dt 4:10; Acts 7:38).

In Jesus' day the word was still being used. One notes, in particular, that in a text from the Qumran sect regarding the war of the sons of darkness, the expression *qehál 'El,* "assembly of God," is used along with others like it on military insignia *(1 QM* 5:10). Jesus, too, used the term to speak of "his" messianic community, that new assembly called together through the covenant in his blood, the covenant proclaimed in the upper room (cf. Mt 26:28).

In both Semitic and Greek usage, the assembly received its character from the will of the one who convoked it and the purpose for which he called it. Both in Israel and in the ancient Greek city-states *(pòleis)* various assemblies were called, those of a profane nature (political, military or professional), as well as those which were religious and liturgical.

The Old Testament also mentions various types of assemblies. But when it speaks of the community of the Chosen People it emphasizes the religious and even theocratic nature of those people who have been called together, by explicitly proclaiming that they belong to the one God. For this reason, it considers the entire people of Israel to be the *qahàl* of Yahweh and calls them such, precisely because they are Yahweh's "special possession, dearer than all other people" (Ex 19:5). It is an altogether special belonging to and relationship with God, based on the covenant made with him and on acceptance of the commandments given to them by intermediaries between God and the people at the moment of their call, which Sacred Scripture designates precisely as "the day of the assembly," *yòm haqqahàl* (cf. Dt 9:10; 10:4). This feeling of belonging spans

Israel's whole history and perdures, in spite of repeated betrayals and the recurrence of crises and defeats. It is a question of a theological truth continued in history, to which the prophets appeal in times of disappointment, like deutero-Isaiah. He said to Israel in the name of God, toward the end of the exile, "Fear not, for I have redeemed you; I have called you by name; you are mine" (Is 43:1). This is an announcement that in virtue of the old covenant he will soon intervene to free his people.

This covenant with God, the result of his own choice, gives a religious character to the entire people of Israel and a transcendent purpose to their whole history, even though its earthly course experiences good times and bad. This fact explains the biblical language which calls Israel "the assembly of God," *qehál Elohim* (cf. Neh 13:1), and more frequently *qehál Yahweh* (cf. Dt 23:2-4, 9). It is the permanent awareness of a belonging based on the election of Israel by God made in the first person: "You shall be my special possession, dearer to me than all other people.... You shall be to me a kingdom of priests, a holy nation" (Ex 19:5-6).

It is scarcely necessary to recall here, still in the context of word analysis, that among the people of the Old Testament, out of great respect for the proper name of God, *qehál Yahweh* was read as *qehál Adonai,* "the assembly of the Lord." For this reason it was also translated in the Septuagint as *ekklesía Kyriou;* we would say "the Church of the Lord."

It should also be noted that the writers of the Greek text of the New Testament followed the Septuagint translation. This fact explains why they call the new People of God (the new Israel) *ekklesía,* just as they refer the Church to God. St. Paul frequently speaks of the "Church of God" (cf. 1 Cor 1:2; 10:32; 15:9; 2 Cor 1:1; Gal 1:13), or the "churches of God" (cf. 1 Cor 11:16; 1 Thess 2:14; 2 Thess 1:4). By this usage he emphasizes the continuity of the Old and New Testaments, even to the point of calling Christ's Church "the Israel of God" (Gal 6:16). However, St. Paul will soon achieve a way to formulate the realities of the Church founded by Christ, as when Paul speaks of the Church "in God the Father and the Lord Jesus Christ" (1 Thess 1:1), or the "Church of God in Jesus Christ" (1 Thess 2:14). In the Letter to the Romans, he even speaks of the "churches of Christ" (Rom 16:16) in the plural, having in mind—and keeping his eye on—the local Christian churches, as in Palestine, Asia Minor and Greece.

This progressive development in language assures us that in the first Christian communities the newness of Christ's words—"Upon this rock I will build my Church" (Mt 16:16)— gradually becomes clearer. The words of Isaiah's prophecy are now applied to this Church in a new sense with greater depth: "Fear not, for I have redeemed you; I have called you by name; you are mine" (Is 43:1). This "divine calling together" is the work of Jesus Christ, the incarnate Son of God; he establishes and builds "his" Church as a "calling together of all people in the new covenant." He chooses a visible foundation for this Church and entrusts to Peter the mandate of governing her. This Church, therefore, belongs to Christ and will always remain his. This is the conviction of the first Christian communities; this is their faith in the Church of Christ.

As one can see, from the terminological and conceptual analysis which can be made of the New Testament texts, there are already results which bear on the meaning of the Church. We can synthesize what we have seen so far in the following assertion: the Church is the new community of individuals, instituted by Christ as a "calling together" of all those called to be part of the new Israel in order to live the divine life, according to the graces and demands of the covenant established by the sacrifice of the cross. This calling together entails for each one a call which requires a response of faith and cooperation in the purpose of the new community, determined by him who gives the call: "It was not you who chose me, but I who chose you and appointed you to go and bear fruit..." (Jn 15:16). This is the source of the Church's connatural dynamism, which has an immense field of activity, because it is a calling to belong to him who wishes to "sum up all things in Christ" (Eph 1:10).

The purpose of this calling together is to be introduced into divine communion (cf. 1 Jn 1:3). The first step in achieving this goal consists in listening to the Word of God which the Church receives, reads and lives in the light which comes from on high, as a gift of the Holy Spirit, according to the promise Christ made to the apostles: "The Holy Spirit that the Father will send in my name will teach you everything and remind you of all that I told you" (Jn 14:26). The Church is called and sent to bring the word of Christ and the gift of the Spirit to everyone: to all the people who will be the "new Israel," beginning with children, about whom Jesus said: "Let the children come to me" (Mt 19:14). But all are called, young and old, and among adults, persons of every condition. As St. Paul says, "There is neither Jew nor Greek, there is neither slave nor freeman, there is neither male nor female; for you are all one in Christ Jesus" (Gal 3:28).

Finally, the goal of this calling together is an eschatological destiny, because the new people are completely oriented toward the heavenly community, as the first Christians knew and felt: "For here we have no lasting city; we are seeking one which is to come" (Heb 13:14). "We have our citizenship in heaven; it is from there that we eagerly await the coming of our Savior, the Lord Jesus Christ" (Phil 3:20).

Our analysis of the name which Jesus gave to his Church has brought us to this transcendent and supernatural summit. It is the mystery of a new community of God's people, which includes, in the bond of the communion of saints, in addition to the faithful on earth who follow Christ along the way of the Gospel, those too who are completing their purification in purgatory, and the saints in heaven. We will discuss all of these points again in subsequent catecheses.

General audience of July 20, 1991

Christic and the Church Are Inseparable

We are continuing our cycle of catecheses devoted to the Church. We have already explained how the profession of this truth in the creed has a specific character, inasmuch as the Church is not only an object of faith, but also its subject. We ourselves are the Church in which we profess our faith; we believe in the Church, while at the same time being the Church which believes and prays. We are the Church in her visible dimension, which expresses her faith in her own reality as Church, a reality which is divine and human. These two dimensions are so inseparable that, if one is missing, the entire reality of the Church, as willed and founded by Christ, is canceled.

This divine and human reality of the Church is organically joined to the divine and human reality of Christ himself. The Church is in a certain sense the continuation of the mystery of the Incarnation. The Apostle Paul actually spoke of the Church as the Body of Christ (cf. 1 Cor 12:27; Eph 1:23; Col 1:24), just as Jesus compared the Christic-ecclesial "whole" to the unity of a vine with its branches (cf. Jn 15:1-5).

From this premise it follows that believing in the Church, stating in regard to her the "yes" of acceptance in faith, is a logical consequence of the entire creed, and especially of our profession of faith in Christ, the God-man. It is a demand resulting from the internal logic of the creed. This should be kept in mind, especially in our time, when we feel that many are separating, and even opposing the Church and Christ, when they say, for example, *Christ—yes, the Church—no.* This opposition is not entirely new, but has been proposed again in certain parts of the contemporary world. So it is good to devote today's catechesis to a calm and accurate examination of the meaning of our *yes* to the Church, even in reference to the opposition just mentioned.

We can admit that this opposition *Christ—yes, the Church—no,* originates within the particular complexity belonging to our act of faith, by which we say: "I believe in the Church." One could ask whether it is legitimate to include among the divine truths to be believed a human, historical, visible reality such as the Church. It is a reality, which like any human thing, has limitations, imperfections and sinfulness on the part of the persons who belong to every level of her institutional structure: lay people as well as ecclesiastics, even among the pastors of the Church, without anyone being excluded from this sad inheritance of Adam.

We must note, however, that Jesus Christ himself wanted our faith in the Church to face and overcome this difficulty, when he chose Peter as "the rock upon which I will build my Church" (cf. Mt 16:18). We know from the Gospel, which reports the very words of Jesus, how humanly imperfect and weak the chosen rock was, as Peter demonstrated at the time of his great test. Nevertheless, the Gospel itself testifies that Peter's triple denial, shortly after he had assured the Master of his fidelity, did not cancel his selection by Christ (cf. Lk 22:32; Jn 21:15-17). Rather, one notices that Peter acquired a new maturity through contrition for his sin, so that after the resurrection he balanced his triple denial with a triple confession: "Yes, Lord, you know that I love you" (Jn 21:15). From the risen Christ Peter received the triple confirmation of his mandate as pastor of the Church: "Feed my lambs" (Jn 21:15-17). Peter then proved that he loved Christ "more than these" (cf. Jn 21:15), by serving in the Church, according to his mandate of apostleship and governance, until his death by martyrdom, his definitive witness for building the Church.

By reflecting on the life and death of Simon Peter, it is easier to move from the opposition *Christ—yes, the Church —no,* to the conviction *Christ—yes, the Church—yes,* as a continuation of our *yes* to Christ.

The logic of the mystery of the Incarnation—synthesized in that *yes* to Christ—entails acceptance of everything that is human in Christ, in virtue of the fact that the Son of God assumed human nature in solidarity with the nature tainted by the sin of Adam's race. Although he was absolutely without sin, Christ took on himself all of humanity's sin—*Agnus Dei qui tollis peccata mundi.* The Father "made him to be sin," the Apostle Paul writes (cf. 2 Cor 5:21). Therefore, the sinfulness of Christians (about whom it is said, and sometimes not without reason, that "they are no better than others"), the sinfulness of ecclesiastics themselves, should not elicit a pharisaical attitude of separation and rejection. Rather, it should compel us to a more generous and trusting acceptance of the Church, to a more convinced and meritorious yes in her regard. This is because we know that precisely in the Church and by means of the Church this sinfulness becomes an object of the divine power of redemption, under the action of that love which makes possible and accomplishes the individual's conversion, the sinner's justification, a change of life and progress in doing good, sometimes even to the point of heroism and holiness. Can we deny that the Church's history is full of converted and repentant sinners who, having returned to Christ, followed him faithfully to the end?

One thing is certain—the life which Jesus Christ, and the Church with him, proposes to man is full of moral demands which bind him to what is good, even to the heights of hero-

ism. It is necessary to observe whether, when one says *no* to
the Church, in reality one is not seeking to escape these demands. Here, more than in any other case, the *no* to the Church
would be the equivalent of a *no* to Christ. Unfortunately, experience shows that this is often the case.

On the other hand, one cannot fail to observe that if the
Church—in spite of all the human weaknesses and sins of her
members—in her entirety remains faithful to Christ and brings
to Christ her many children who have failed in their baptismal
commitments, this occurs because of the "power from on high"
(cf. Lk 24:49), the Holy Spirit, who gives her life and guides
her on her perilous journey through history.

We must also say, however, that the *no* to the Church is
sometimes based, not on the human defects of the Church's
members, but on a general principle of rejecting mediation.
There are indeed people who, although admitting the existence
of God, wish to maintain an exclusively personal contact with
him, without allowing any mediation between their own conscience and God. Therefore, they reject the Church above all.

But be careful. Appreciation of conscience also lies at the
heart of the Church, which claims to be the representative of
God for man's good, both in the moral order as well as on the
more specifically religious level. So the Church gives light,
formation and service to the human conscience. Her job is to
help human minds and consciences to have access to the truth
of God which is revealed in Christ, who entrusted to his
apostles and to his Church this ministry, this *diakonia* of
preaching the truth in love. Every conscience, motivated by a
sincere love for the truth, cannot fail to want to know, and so to
hear—at least the latter—what the Gospel preached by the
Church says to human beings for their own good.

But frequently the problem of *yes* or *no* to the Church
becomes complicated at this point, because it is the very mediation of Christ and his Gospel which is rejected. This means
a *no* to Christ, more than to the Church. This fact must be

seriously considered by anyone who claims and wants to be a Christian. He cannot ignore the mystery of the Incarnation, by which God himself granted man the possibility of establishing contact with him only through Christ, the incarnate Word, of whom St. Paul says: "There is one mediator between God and men, the man Christ Jesus" (1 Tim 2:5). Since the Church's beginning, the apostles preached that "there is no other name [besides Christ's] under heaven given to the human race by which we are to be saved" (Acts 4:12). Christ instituted the Church as a community of salvation, in which his saving mediation is continued to the end of time in virtue of the Holy Spirit whom he sent. The Christian, therefore, knows that according to God's will, man—who, because he is a person, is a social being—is called to be in relationship with God precisely in the community of the Church. It is impossible to separate mediation from the Church which participates in Christ's function as mediator between God and men.

Finally we cannot ignore the fact that the *no* to the Church often has deeper roots, both in individual persons and in human groups and contexts. This happens especially in certain sectors of true or presumed culture—where today, as before or perhaps more than before, it is not difficult to find attitudes of rejection or even hostility. At the bottom of this there is a psychology characterized by the will for total autonomy, originating in a sense of personal or collective self-sufficiency. By this one maintains independence from the superhuman Being which is proposed—or interiorly discovered—as author and Lord of life, of fundamental law, of the moral order, and so, as the ground of the distinction between good and evil. Some pretend to establish on their own what is good or bad, and thus refuse to be directed by another, either by a transcendent God or by a Church which represents him on earth.

This position generally results from a great ignorance of reality. God is conceived as an enemy of human freedom, as a tyrannical master, even though he is actually the one who created freedom and is its most authentic friend. His commandments have no other purpose than to help people to avoid the worst and most shameful form of slavery, that of immorality, and to foster the development of true freedom. Without a trusting relationship with God, it is not possible for the human person to achieve fully his own spiritual growth.

We should not be surprised, then, when we see that an attitude of radical autonomy easily produces a form of subjugation worse than the feared heteronomy: dependence on the opinions of others, on ideological and political ties, on social pressures, or on one's own inclinations and passions. Whenever one believes or boasts that he is independent, free from all servitude, he thus reveals that he is subject to public opinion and to other old and new forms of domination over the human spirit! It is easy to see that the attempt to do without God, or the claim not to need the mediation of Christ and his Church, comes at a high price. It was necessary to recall our attention to this problem in order to conclude our introduction to the cycle of ecclesiological catecheses which we are beginning. Today let us say once again, *yes* to the Church, precisely because of our *yes* to Christ.

General audience of July 24, 1991

God's Plan for the Church Is Eternal

The Church is a historical fact, whose origin can be and has been documented, as we will see later. But as we begin this cycle of theological catecheses on the Church, we want to start from the highest and most authentic source of Christian truth, that is, from revelation, as the Second Vatican Council did. In the Constitution *Lumen Gentium,* the Council considered the Church in her eternal foundation, which is the saving plan conceived by the Father within the Trinity. The Council says precisely: "The eternal Father, by a free and hidden plan of his own wisdom and goodness, created the whole world. His plan was to raise men to a participation of the divine life. Fallen in Adam, God the Father did not leave men to themselves, but ceaselessly offered helps to salvation, in view of Christ, the Redeemer" *(LG 2)*.

In the eternal design of God the Church constitutes, in Christ and with Christ, an essential part of the universal economy of salvation in which the love of God is expressed.

That eternal plan contains the destiny of human beings, who have been created in the image and likeness of God, called to the dignity of children of God and adopted as children of the heavenly Father in Jesus Christ. As we read in Ephesians, God chose us and "destined us for adoption to himself through Jesus Christ in accord with the favor of his will, for the praise of the glory of his grace that he granted us in his beloved Son" (Eph 1:4-6). We read in Romans, "For those he foreknew he also predestined to be conformed to the image of his Son, so that he might be the firstborn among many brothers" (Rom 8:29).

To have a good understanding of the Church's beginning as an object of our faith (the "mystery of the Church"), it is necessary to return to St. Paul's program of "bringing to light for all what is the plan of the mystery hidden from ages past in God...so that the manifold wisdom of God might now be made known through the Church to the principalities and authorities in the heavens. This was according to the eternal purpose that he accomplished in Christ Jesus our Lord" (Eph 3:9-11). As is clear from this text, the Church is part of the Christocentric plan designed by God the Father from all eternity.

The same Pauline texts regard the destiny of the human person, chosen and called to be an adopted child of God, not only in the individual dimension of the human race, but in its community dimension as well. God conceives, creates and calls to himself a community of persons. This divine plan is expressed more explicitly in an important passage from Ephesians: "He has made known to us the mystery of his will in accord with his favor that he set forth in him [Christ] as a plan for the fullness of times, to sum up all things in Christ, in heaven and on earth" (Eph 1:9-10). Therefore, in God's eternal design, the Church, as the unity of humanity in Christ the head, becomes part of a plan which includes all creation. One could say it is a "cosmic" plan, that of uniting everything in Christ the head. The firstborn of all creation becomes the principle of "recapitulation" for this creation, so that God can be "all in all" (1 Cor 15:28). Therefore, Christ is the keystone of the universe. As the living body of those who belong to him by their response to the vocation of being children of God, the

Church is associated with him, as participant and minister, at the center of the plan of universal redemption.

Vatican II explains the "mystery of the Church" against the background of this Pauline conception, in which the biblical vision of the world is reflected and made precise. The Council says: "He [the Father] planned to assemble in the holy Church all those who would believe in Christ. Already from the beginning of the world the foreshadowing of the Church took place. It was prepared in a remarkable way throughout the history of the people of Israel and by means of the old covenant. In the present era of time the Church was constituted and, by the outpouring of the Spirit, was made manifest. At the end of time it will gloriously achieve completion, when, as is read in the Fathers, all the just, from Adam and 'from Abel, the just one, to the last of the elect,' will be gathered together with the Father in the universal Church" *(LG* 2). There is no better way of summarizing in a few lines the history of salvation which unfolds in Sacred Scripture than by focusing on its ecclesiological meaning, which was already formulated and interpreted by the Fathers in accord with the indications given by the apostles and Jesus himself.

When seen in the perspective of the Father's eternal plan, the Church appears from the beginning, in the thought of the apostles and the first Christian generations, as the fruit of the infinite, divine love which unites the Father to the Son within the Trinity. It is actually in virtue of this love that the Father has willed to unite humanity in his Son. The *mysterium ecclesiae* thus finds its origin in the *mysterium Trinitatis.* Here we must use the same exclamation we make at Mass when the renewal of the Eucharistic sacrifice is accomplished, where the Church in turn is gathered: *mysterium fidei!*

The principle of the Church's missionary dynamism is also found in this eternal source. The Church's mission is, as it were, the continuation, or historical expansion, of the mission of the Son and the Holy Spirit, and so one can call it a vital participation, in the form of ministerial association, in the Trinity's activity in human history.

In the Constitution *Lumen Gentium* (cf. nn. 1-4), Vatican II speaks at great length about the mission of the Son and the Holy Spirit. In the Decree *Ad Gentes* it speaks precisely about the communal character of human participation in the divine life, when it says that God's plan "flows from the 'fount-like love' or charity of God the Father, who, being the 'principle without principle' from whom the Son is begotten and the Holy Spirit proceeds through the Son, freely creating us on account of his surpassing and merciful kindness and graciously calling us moreover to share with him his life and his glory, has generously poured out, and does not cease to pour out still, his divine goodness. Thus he who created all things may at last be 'all in all' (1 Cor 15:28), bringing about at one and the same time his own glory and our happiness. But it pleased God to call men to share his life, not just singly, apart from any mutual bond, but rather to mold them into a people in which his sons, once scattered abroad, might be gathered together (cf. Jn 11:52)" *(AG 2)*.

The foundation of the community willed by God in his eternal plan is the work of redemption, which frees human beings from the division and dispersion produced by sin. The Bible teaches us that sin is the source of hostility and violence, as appears in the fratricide Cain committed (cf. Gen 4:8), and as that fragmentation of nations which in its negative aspects finds its paradigmatic expression in the account of the tower of Babel.

God willed to free humanity from this state through Christ. This saving will of his seems to echo in Caiaphas' speech to the Sanhedrin, in regard to which John the evangelist writes: "Since he was high priest for that year, he prophesied that Jesus was going to die for the nation, and not only for the nation, but also to gather into one the dispersed children of God" (Jn 11:51-52). Caiaphas said these words in order to convince the Sanhedrin to condemn Jesus to death, on the pretext that he was causing political danger for the nation in regard to the Romans who were then occupying Palestine. But John knew well that Jesus had come to take away sin from the world and save men (cf. Jn 1:29). So he did not hesitate to give those words of Caiaphas a prophetic meaning, as a revelation of the divine plan. It was written in that plan that Christ, through the redemptive sacrifice accomplished by his death on the cross, would become the source of a new unity for mankind, called in Christ, to regain their dignity as adopted children of God. In that sacrifice on the cross the Church was born as a community of salvation.

General audience of July 31, 1991

The Church in the Old Testament

The revelation of God's eternal plan for the universal community of men, who have been called in Christ to be his adopted children, had its beginnings in the Old Testament, the first phase of the divine word to the human race and the first part of Sacred Scripture for us Christians. For this reason, catechesis on the historical genesis of the Church should first of all search in the sacred books which we have in common with ancient Israel for the foreshadowings of the future People of God. Vatican II shows us the path to follow when it says that the Holy Church, in which the Father determined to call together those who should believe in Christ, was "prepared in a remarkable way throughout the history of the people of Israel and by means of the old covenant" *(LG* 2). In this catechesis we shall see how the Father's eternal plan is recognized especially as the revelation of a future kingdom of God, which will come to pass in the messianic and eschatological phase of the economy of salvation.

"The Lord must rule over you," we read in the Book of Judges (Jgs 8:23). After his victory over the Midianites, Gideon addressed these words to the Israelites living in the region of Shechem who wanted him to rule over them and even to found a dynasty (cf. Jgs 8:22). Gideon's response in which

he refused to be their king perhaps should be seen in relationship to the antimonarchical currents of another section of the
people (cf. 1 Sam 8:4-20). But it remains an eloquent expression of his thought, and that of a large part of Israel, regarding
the unique kingship of God: "I will not rule over you, nor shall
my son rule over you. The Lord must rule over you" (Jgs 8:23).

This double tendency is found later in Israel's history,
when there were groups who wanted a king in an earthly and
political sense. After the attempt of Gideon's sons (cf. Jgs
9:1ff.), we know from the First Book of Samuel that the elders
of Israel asked the judge who by now was advanced in age:
"Appoint a king over us to judge us" (1 Sam 8:5). Samuel had
appointed his sons as judges, but they abused the power they
received (cf. 1 Sam 8:1-3). However, Samuel was especially
displeased because he saw in their request another attempt to
take away from God his exclusive kingship over Israel. For this
reason Samuel turned to God, consulting him in prayer. It is
written: "The Lord said in answer: 'Grant the people's every
request. It is not you they reject, they are rejecting me as their
king'" (1 Sam 8:7). This is probably another example of a
confrontation between the two tendencies—monarchical and
antimonarchical—which belong to that period of Israel's formation as a politically united and established people. But it is
interesting to note Samuel's partially successful effort, no
longer as a judge but as a prophet, at reconciling the demand
for a profane monarchy with the prerogatives of God's absolute kingship, which at least some of the people had forgotten.
He anointed the kings given to Israel as a sign of their religious
role, besides their political one. David would be the king who
symbolizes this reconciliation of aspects and roles, and because of his great personal authority he will even become the
anointed *par excellence,* a figure of the future Messiah and
king of the new people, Jesus Christ.

One must note, however, this intersection of the two
dimensions of kingship and rule: the temporal and political

dimension, and the transcendent and religious one, which is already present in the Old Testament. The God of Israel is a king in the religious sense, even when those who rule the people in his name are the political heads. The idea of God as king and Lord of all, inasmuch as he is the Creator, appears in the historical and prophetic books of the Bible, as well as in the psalms. In the Book of the Prophet Jeremiah God is called three times "the king whose name is Lord of hosts" (Jer 46:18; 48:15; 51:57). Several psalms proclaim, "The Lord is king" (Ps 93:1; 96:10; 97:1; 99:1). This transcendent and universal kingship was first expressed in the covenant with Israel, the true act which established the proper and original identity of this people whom God chose and with whom he made a covenant. This is what we read in the Book of Exodus: "Therefore, if you hearken to my voice and keep my covenant, you shall be my special possession, dearer to me than all other people, though all the earth is mine. You shall be to me a kingdom of priests, a holy nation" (Ex 19:5-6).

Israel's belonging to God as his people demands obedience and love in an absolute sense: "You shall love the Lord, your God, with all your heart, and with all your soul, and with all your strength" (Dt 6:5). This first and supreme commandment represents the true constitutive principle of the old covenant. This commandment defines the destiny and vocation of Israel.

Israel is aware of this fact and experiences her relationship with God as a type of submission to her own king. Psalm 48 says: "Mount Zion...is the city of the great king" (Ps 48:3). Even when Yahweh allows the establishment in Israel of a king and dynasty in a political sense, Israel knows that this institution retains a theocratic character. By divine inspiration the prophet Samuel designates Saul as the first king (cf. 1 Sam 10:24), and later David (cf. 1 Sam 16:12-13), from whom the Davidic dynasty descended. As we know from the books of the Old Testament, the kings of Israel, and later of Judah, often transgressed the commandments which were the fundamental principles of the covenant with God. The prophets intervened against these transgressions with their warning and reproaches. The history of these interventions shows clearly that there are divergences and conflicts between the demands of God's reign and the kingdom in an earthly and political sense. This explains the fact that, although Yahweh maintains his faithfulness to the promises made to David and his descendants (cf. 2 Sam 7:12), history also describes cases of plotting in order to rule over "the kingdom of the Lord commanded by the sons of David" (cf. 2 Chr 13:8). It is a conflict which continues to clarify the messianic meaning of the divine promises.

In fact, almost as a reaction to the disappointment experienced in regard to the political kings, there was a growing hope in Israel for a messianic king, an ideal sovereign, about whom we read in the prophets, especially in Isaiah, that "his dominion is vast and forever peaceful, from David's throne, and over his kingdom, which he confirms and sustains by judgment and justice, both now and forever" (Is 9:6). Isaiah dwells on his prediction of this sovereign, to whom he gives the names of "Wonder-Counselor, God-Hero, Father-Forever, Prince of peace" (9:5), and describes his kingdom as an earthly and utopian paradise: "Justice shall be the band around his waist, and faithfulness a belt upon his hips. Then the wolf shall be a guest of the lamb, and the leopard shall lie down with the kid.... There shall be no harm or ruin...for the earth shall be filled with knowledge of the Lord, as water covers the sea" (11:5-6, 9). These metaphors are intended to bring out the essential element of the prophecies regarding the messianic kingdom: a new covenant which God will make with man for his benefit and salvation.

After the exile and the Babylonian captivity, the vision of a "messianic" king takes on even more clearly the sense of a direct kingship on God's part. Almost as if to overcome all the disappointments which the people experienced with their political sovereigns, Israel's hope, nourished by the prophets, turns toward a reign in which God himself will be the king. It will be a universal kingdom: "The Lord shall become king over the whole earth; on that day the Lord shall be the only one, and his name the only one" (Zech 14:9). However, even in its universality this kingdom will retain a connection with Jerusalem. Isaiah predicts: "The Lord of hosts will reign on Mount Zion and in Jerusalem" (Is 24:23). "On this mountain he will provide for all peoples a feast of juicy, rich food and pure, choice wines" (Is 25:6). Here, too, one sees a metaphor for the new joy in the fulfillment of ancient hopes.

The eschatological dimension of God's kingdom is accentuated more and more as the time of Christ's coming approaches. In particular, the Book of Daniel emphasizes this aspect of the future age in the visions which it describes. We read: "As the visions during the night continued, I saw one like a son of man coming on the clouds of heaven; when he reached the Ancient One and was presented before him, he received dominion, glory and kingship; nations and peoples of every language serve him. His dominion is an everlasting dominion that shall not be taken away; his kingship shall not be destroyed" (Dan 7:13-14).

Thus, according to Daniel the future kingdom is closely connected with a person who is presented as one like a "son of man"; this is the origin of the title which Jesus will attribute to himself. At the same time Daniel writes that "the kingship and dominion and majesty of all the kingdoms under the heavens shall be given to the holy people of the Most High" (Dan 7:27). This text recalls another one in the Book of Wisdom which says: "The just...shall judge nations and rule over peoples, and the Lord shall be their king forever" (Wis 3:1, 8).

These sayings are all glances into the future, glimpses of the mystery toward which the history of the old covenant is heading, a history which now appears ready for the coming of the Messiah, who will bring it to completion. Beyond the enigmas, dreams and visions, a "mystery" continues to be more clearly delineated. Every hope is directed to this mystery, even in the darkest hours of defeat, captivity and exile.

That which arouses our interest and admiration in these texts is the fact that the hope for the kingdom of God continues to be clarified and purified in terms of a direct reign by the transcendent God. We know that this kingdom, which includes the person of the Messiah and the multitude of believers in him, as foretold by the prophets, has found on earth an initial realization. It is imperfect in its historical dimensions but is continually striving toward a full and definitive completion in the eternity of God. The Church of the new covenant moves toward this final fullness and all are called to take part as the children of God, heirs of the kingdom and co-workers of the Church which was founded by Christ as the fulfillment of the ancient prophecies and promises. All are called to participate in this kingdom which is intended for them and, in a certain sense, is realized by means of them. Therefore, all of us are called to build up the body of Christ (cf. Eph 4:12). It is a great mission!

General audience of August 7, 1991

The Kingdom of God, the Kingdom of Christ

We read in *Lumen Gentium* that God "planned to as-semble in the holy Church all those who would believe in Christ.... [The Church] was prepared in a remarkable way throughout the history of the people of Israel and by means of the old covenant. In the present era of time the Church was constituted and, by the outpouring of the Spirit, was made manifest" *(LG* 2). We dedicated the preceding catechesis to this preparation of the Church in the old covenant. We saw that in Israel's progressive awareness of God's plan through the revelations of the prophets and the facts of her history, the concept of a future kingdom of God gradually became clearer. This concept was loftier and more universal than anything foreseen regarding the fate of the Davidic dynasty. Today we will consider another historical fact, one which is rich in its theological significance. Jesus Christ began his messianic mis-sion with the proclamation: "This is the time of fulfillment. The kingdom of God is at hand" (Mk 1:15). Those words indicate the start of "the fullness of time," as St. Paul says (cf. Gal 4:4). They prepare the way for the new covenant, which is based on the mystery of the Son's redemptive Incarnation and destined to be an eternal covenant. In Jesus Christ's life and mission the kingdom of God is not only "at hand" (Lk 10:9), but is already present in the world, already at work in human history. Jesus himself said: "The kingdom of God is among you" (Lk 17:21).

The difference in standard and quality between the time of preparation and that of fulfillment—between the old and new covenant—was made known by Jesus himself when he spoke about his precursor, John the Baptist, saying: "Amen, I say to you, among those born of woman there has been none greater than John the Baptist; yet the least in the kingdom of heaven is greater than he" (Mt 11:11). From the banks of the Jordan (and from prison), John certainly made a greater contribution than anyone else, even more than the ancient prophets (cf. Lk 7:26-27), in preparing the immediate way for the Messiah. Nevertheless, in a certain sense he still remained on the threshold of the new kingdom which entered the world with Christ's coming and became manifest through his messianic ministry. Only through Christ do individuals become true "children of the kingdom," that is, children of the new kingdom which is superior to the one to which Jews at the time considered themselves the natural heirs (cf. Mt 8:12).

The new kingdom has an eminently spiritual character. To enter it, it is necessary to repent and believe in the Gospel, to be freed from the power of the spirit of darkness, to submit to the power of God's Spirit, which Christ brings to human beings. As Jesus says: "But if it is by the Spirit of God that I drive out demons, then the kingdom of God has come upon you" (Mt 12:28; cf. Lk 11:20).

The spiritual and transcendent nature of this kingdom is also expressed in the equivalent term we find in the Gospel texts: "kingdom of heaven." It is a wonderful image which allows us to glimpse the origin and purpose of the kingdom—"heaven"—and the same divine-human dignity of him in whom the kingdom of God is made historically concrete through the Incarnation: Christ.

The transcendence of God's kingdom results from the

fact that it takes its origin not only from human initiative, but from the plan, design and will of God himself. Jesus Christ, who makes it present and realizes it in the world, is not merely one of the prophets sent by God, but the consubstantial Son of the Father, who became man in the Incarnation. The kingdom of God is thus the kingdom of the Father and his Son. The kingdom of God is the kingdom of Christ; it is the kingdom of heaven which has begun on earth to allow men to enter this new world of spirituality and eternity. Jesus stated, "All things have been handed over to me by my Father.... No one knows the Father except the Son and anyone to whom the Son wishes to reveal him" (Mt 11:27). "For just as the Father has life in himself, so also he gave to his Son the possession of life in himself. And he gave him power to exercise judgment, because he is the Son of Man" (Jn 5:26-27).

Along with the Father and the Son, the Holy Spirit is also at work, realizing the kingdom in this world. Jesus himself reveals this. The Son of Man "drives out demons by the Spirit of God," and for this reason "the kingdom of God has come upon you" (Mt 12:28).

But although the kingdom of God is realized and develops in this world, it has its purpose in "heaven." It is transcendent in its origin and also in its goal, which is reached in eternity, on condition that one is faithful to Christ in this life and throughout the course of time. Jesus informed us of this when he said that, in conformity with his power of "judging" (Jn 5:27), at the end of the world the Son of Man will give the command to collect "out of his kingdom all who cause others to sin," namely, all the iniquities committed even in the confines of Christ's kingdom. Jesus added: "Then the righteous will shine like the sun in the kingdom of their Father" (Mt 13:41, 43). Then the full and definitive realization of the "kingdom of the Father" will occur, to whom the Son will hand over the elect who have been saved by him in virtue of the redemption and by the work of the Holy Spirit. The messianic

kingdom will then reveal its identity with the kingdom of God
(cf. Mt 25:34; 1 Cor 15:24).

There is, then, a historical cycle to the kingdom of Christ,
the incarnate Word. But the alpha and omega of this kingdom, and one would even say, the basis on which it begins,
lives, develops and reaches its fulfillment, is the *mysterium
Trinitatis*. We have already said, and we will see again later,
that the *mysterium ecclesiae* takes root in this mystery.

The point of transition and connection from one mystery
to the other is Christ, who was already predicted in the old
covenant and awaited as a Messiah-King with whom the kingdom of God is identified. In the new covenant Christ identifies
the kingdom of God with his own person and his own mission.
He not only proclaims the fact that with him the kingdom of
God is in the world, but he teaches that one should give up
everything which is humanly most valuable "for the kingdom
of God" (cf. Lk 18:29-30), and at another point, to leave all
this "for the sake of my name" (cf. Mt 19:29) or "for my sake
and for the sake of the Gospel" (Mk 10:29).

The kingdom of God is thus identified with the kingdom
of Christ. It is present in him; it is realized in him. It passes
from him, on his own initiative, to the apostles, and through
them to all those who will believe in him: "I confer a kingdom
on you, just as my Father has conferred one on me" (Lk 22:29).
It is a kingdom which consists in the spread of Christ himself
through the world, through human history, as a new life which
comes from him and is communicated to believers in virtue of
the Holy Spirit, the Paraclete, whom he sends (cf. Jn 1:16;
7:38-39; 15:26; 16:7).

The messianic kingdom realized by Christ in the world
is revealed and shows its precise and definitive meaning in
the context of his passion and death on the cross. During
Christ's entrance into Jerusalem an event occurred, which
he had planned and which Matthew presents as a fulfillment
of a prophetic prediction made by Zechariah about the "king

who comes to you riding on an ass, and on a colt, the foal of a beast of burden" (Zech 9:9; Mt 21:5). In the prophet's mind, in Jesus' intention and in the evangelist's interpretation, the ass means meekness and humility. Jesus was the meek and humble king who entered the city of David, where he fulfilled the prophecies about the true messianic kingship by his own sacrifice.

This kingship is clarified during the questioning Jesus underwent before the judgment seat of Pilate. The accusations made against Jesus were that "He misleads the people; he opposes the payment of taxes to Caesar and maintains that he is the Messiah, a king" (Lk 23:2). Therefore, Pilate asked the accused if he was a king. Jesus replied: "My kingdom does not belong to this world. If my kingdom did belong to this world, my attendants would be fighting to keep me from being handed over to the Jews. But as it is, my kingdom is not here." The evangelist states: "So Pilate said to him, 'Then you are a king?' Jesus answered, 'You say I am a king. For this I was born and for this I came into the world, to testify to the truth. Everyone who belongs to the truth listens to my voice'" (Jn 18:36-37).

This declaration concludes all the ancient prophecies which flow through Israel's history and which become a fact and a revelation in Christ. The words of Jesus enable us to catch the flashes of light which streak through the darkness of the mystery condensed in the three terms: kingdom of God, messianic kingdom, People of God called together in the Church. Along this path of prophetic and messianic light, we can better understand and repeat, with clearer comprehension of the words, the prayer Jesus taught us (Mt 6:10): "Thy kingdom come." It is the kingdom of the Father, which entered the world with Christ; it is the messianic kingdom which develops through the work of the Holy Spirit in man and in the world, in order to return to the heart of the Father in the glory of heaven.

General audience of September 4, 1991

The Church Is Also a Historical Fact

In the Father's eternal plan the Church was conceived and desired as the kingdom of God and of his Son, the incarnate Word, Jesus Christ. The Church is realized in the world as a historical fact. Although she is certainly full of mystery and accompanied by miracles at the time of her birth, and one could say throughout her long history, she nevertheless exists in the sphere of observable, experimental and documentable facts.

In this regard, the Church began with the group of twelve disciples whom Jesus himself chose from among the multitude of his followers (cf. Mk 3:13-19; Jn 6:70; Acts 1:2) and who are called apostles (cf. Mt 10:1-5; Lk 6:13). Jesus called them, formed them in a particular way and finally sent them into the world as witnesses and preachers of his message, his passion and death, and his resurrection. On this basis, he sent them as founders of the Church, the kingdom of God which, however, always has her foundation in him, Christ (cf. 1 Cor 3:11; Eph 2:20).

After the ascension, a group of disciples gathered around the apostles and Mary as they waited for the Holy Spirit promised by Jesus. Truly, they were faced with the "promise of the Father" which had been stated once more by Jesus while they were at table, a promise which concerned a "baptism in the Holy Spirit" (Acts 1:4-5). Then they asked the risen Master, "Lord, are you at this time going to restore the kingdom of Israel?" (Acts 1:6). Evidently, they were still psychologically influenced by the hope of a messianic kingdom consisting of a temporal restoration of the Davidic kingdom, which was an expectation of Israel (cf. Mk 11:10; Lk 1:32-33). Jesus dissuaded them from this expectation and reconfirmed his promise: "You will receive power when the Holy Spirit comes upon you, and you will be my witnesses in Jerusalem, throughout Judea and Samaria, and to the ends of the earth" (Acts 1:8).

On the day of Pentecost, which for Israel had been a harvest feast (cf. Ex 23:16) but had also become a feast of renewing the covenant (cf. 2 Chr 15:10-13), the promise of Christ was fulfilled in the way which is now well known. Under the action of the Holy Spirit the group of apostles and disciples was strengthened, and the first people converted by the preaching of the apostles, and especially of Peter, were gathered around the apostles. The growth of the first Christian community began in this way (Acts 2:41) and the church of Jerusalem was established (cf. Acts 2:42-47). It quickly grew and extended to other cities, regions and nations—even to Rome! This happened both in virtue of her own internal dynamism, inspired by the Holy Spirit, as well as by the circumstances which compelled Christians to flee from Jerusalem and Judea and to be scattered in different localities, and by the commitment with which the apostles in particular wanted to fulfill Christ's command regarding a universal evangelization.

This is the historical fact concerning the origins Luke described in the Acts of the Apostles and confirmed by other Christian and non-Christian texts. These texts document the spread of Christianity and the existence of various churches throughout the Mediterranean basin and beyond by the last decades of the first century.

The mysterious element of the Church is contained in the historical context of this fact. Vatican II speaks about this: "To carry out the will of the Father, Christ inaugurated the kingdom of heaven on earth and revealed to us the mystery of that kingdom. By his obedience he brought about redemption. The Church, or, in other words, the kingdom of Christ now present in mystery, grows visibly through the power of God in the world" *(LG* 3). These words are the synthesis of the preceding catechesis on the beginning of the kingdom of God on earth in Christ and through Christ. At the same time they indicate that the Church is called into existence by Christ, so that this kingdom may last and develop in her and through her during the course of human history on earth.

From the beginning of his messianic mission Jesus Christ preached conversion and called his listeners to faith: "Repent, and believe in the Gospel" (Mk 1:15). He entrusted to the apostles and the Church the task of joining people together in the unity of this faith, by inviting them to enter the community of faith which he founded.

The community of faith is at the same time a community of salvation. Jesus repeated many times: "The Son of Man has come to seek and to save what was lost" (Lk 19:10). He knew and declared from the beginning that his mission was to "bring glad tidings to the poor, to proclaim liberty to captives and recovery of sight to the blind" (cf. Lk 4:18). He knew and declared that he had been sent by the Father as the Savior (cf. Jn 3:17; 12:47). This is the reason for his special concern for the poor and for sinners.

Consequently, the Church too is meant to begin and develop as a community of salvation. The Second Vatican Council emphasized this in the Decree *Ad Gentes:* "But what the Lord preached that one time, or what was wrought in him for the saving of the human race, must be spread abroad and published to the ends of the earth (cf. Acts 1:8), beginning from Jerusalem (cf. Lk 24:27), so that what he accomplished at that one time for the salvation of all, may in the course of time come to achieve its effect in all" *(AG 3)*. The Church's mission and her missions throughout the world originate from this requirement of spreading salvation, which was expressed in the Gospel and the Acts of the Apostles.

The Acts of the Apostles attest that in the early Church, the Jerusalem community, there was a fervent prayer life and that Christians came together for the "breaking of the bread" (Acts 2:42ff.), a phrase that in Christian language meant an early Eucharistic rite (cf. 1 Cor 10:16; 11:24; Lk 22:19; etc.).

Jesus actually wanted his Church to be the community in which God would be worshipped in Spirit and truth. This was the new meaning of worship which he taught: "But the hour is coming, and is now here, when true worshippers will worship the Father in Spirit and truth, and indeed the Father seeks such people to worship him" (Jn 4:23). Jesus said this in his conversation with the Samaritan woman. But this worship in Spirit and truth does not exclude a visible element; it does not exclude liturgical signs and rites, for which the first Christians gathered both in the temple (cf. Acts 2:46) and in homes (cf. Acts 2:46; 12:12). In speaking to Nicodemus, Jesus himself alluded to the rite of Baptism: "Amen, amen, I say to you, no one can enter the kingdom of God without being born of water and Spirit" (Jn 3:5). This was the first sacrament of the new community. It brought rebirth through the Holy Spirit and entrance into the kingdom of God, signified by the visible rite of washing with water (cf. Acts 2:38, 41).

The highest expression of the new worship—in Spirit and truth—was the Eucharist. The institution of this sacrament was the pivotal point in the Church's formation. In relationship to Israel's Passover meal, Jesus conceived it and instituted it as a banquet in which he gave himself under the appearance of food and drink: bread and wine, signs of sharing divine life— eternal life with those who participate in the banquet. St. Paul expresses this ecclesial aspect of participation in the Eucharist quite well when he writes to the Corinthians: "The bread that we break, is it not a participation in the body of Christ? Because the loaf of bread is one, we, though many, are one body, for we all partake of the one loaf" (1 Cor 10:16-17).

Since the beginning the Church has understood that the institution of this sacrament at the Last Supper signified the entrance of Christians into the very heart of God's kingdom, which Christ began through his redemptive Incarnation and established in human history. Christians realized from the beginning that this kingdom continues in the Church, especially through the Eucharist. The Eucharist—as a sacrament of the Church—was and is the highest expression of that worship in Spirit and truth which Jesus spoke of in his conversation with the Samaritan woman. At the same time, the sacrament of the Eucharist was and is a rite which Jesus instituted so that it would be celebrated by the Church. In fact, he said at the Last Supper: "Do this in memory of me" (Lk 22:19; cf. 1 Cor 11:24-25). These words were spoken on the eve of his passion and death on the cross, in the context of a discourse to the apostles in which Jesus instructed them and prepared them for his own sacrifice. They understood these words in this sense. From these words the Church derived the doctrine and practice of the Eucharist as an unbloody renewal of the sacrifice of the cross. This fundamental aspect of the Eucharist was expressed by St. Thomas Aquinas in the famous antiphon: *O sacrum convivium, in quo Christus sumitur, recolitur memoria passionis eius.* He adds what the Eucharist produces in those who participate in the banquet, according to Jesus' preaching of eternal life: *mens impletur gratia, et futurae gloriae nobis pignus datur.*

Vatican II summarizes the Church's doctrine on this point in the following way: "As often as the sacrifice of the cross in which Christ our Passover was sacrificed (cf. 1 Cor 5:7), is celebrated on the altar, the work of our redemption is carried on, and, in the sacrament of the Eucharistic bread, the unity of all believers who form one body in Christ (cf. 1 Cor 10:17) is both expressed and brought about" *(LG* 3).

According to the Council, the Last Supper was the moment in which Christ, anticipating his death on the cross and his resurrection, started the Church. The Church was begotten together with the Eucharist, inasmuch as she was called "to this union with Christ, who is the light of the world, from whom we go forth, through whom we live, and toward whom our whole life strains" *(LG* 3). Christ is such above all in his redemptive sacrifice. It was then that he fulfilled the words he once said: "The Son of Man did not come to be served but to serve and to give his life as a ransom for many" (Mk 10:45; Mt 20:28). At that moment Christ brought about the Father's plan, by which he "had to die to gather into one the dispersed children of God" (Jn 11:51-52). Therefore, in his sacrifice on the cross Christ is the center of the Church's unity, as he had predicted: "When I am lifted up from the earth, I will draw everyone to myself" (Jn 12:32). In his sacrifice on the cross, renewed on the altar, Christ remains the perennial source of life for the Church, in which all are called to share in his eternal life in order one day to be able to share in his eternal glory. *Et futurae gloriae nobis pignus datur.*

General audience of September 11, 1991

The Church Is Revealed in Parables

The Gospel texts document Jesus' teaching about the kingdom of God in relation to the Church. They also document how the apostles preached this teaching and how it was understood and believed in the early Church. The mystery of the Church as the kingdom of God is revealed in these texts. Vatican II says: "The mystery of the holy Church is manifest in its very foundation. The Lord Jesus set it on its course by preaching the Good News, that is, the coming of the kingdom of God.... In the word, in the works, and in the presence of Christ, this kingdom was clearly open to the view of men" *(LG* 5). In addition to everything we said in this regard during the preceding catecheses, today we will reflect further on the teaching that Jesus gave about the kingdom of God in his parables, especially in those which are especially concerned about explaining its significance and essential value.

Jesus said: "The kingdom of heaven may be likened to a king who gave a wedding feast for his son" (Mt 22:2). The parable of the wedding feast presents the kingdom of God as a royal—and therefore *sovereign*—undertaking by God himself. It also includes the theme of love, and precisely of spousal love: the son for whom the father is preparing the wedding feast is the bridegroom. The circumstances indicate his presence and allow us to understand who he is. This will appear clearly in other New Testament texts which identify the Church as the bride (cf. Jn 3:29; Rev 21:9; 2 Cor 11:2; Eph 5:23-27, 29).

In this parable instead, there is a clear indication of who the bridegroom is. It is Christ, who establishes the Father's new covenant with humanity. This is a covenant of love, and the kingdom of God itself appears as a communion (community of love), which the Son establishes through the Father's will. The feast is the expression of this communion. In the context of the economy of salvation described by the Gospel, it is not difficult to see in this wedding feast a reference to the Eucharist: the sacrament of the new and eternal covenant, the sacrament of the marriage of Christ and humanity in the Church.

Although the Church is not mentioned as the bride in this parable, other elements in the context recall what the Gospel tells us about the Church as the kingdom of God. Thus, the divine invitation is universal: "The king said to his servants, 'Invite to the feast whomever you find'" (Mt 22:9). Among those invited to the Son's wedding feast some of those who were chosen first are missing. Those were to have been guests according to the tradition of the old covenant. They refused to go to the feast of the new covenant, giving various excuses. Then Jesus had the king, the master of the house, say: "Many are invited, but few are chosen" (Mt 22:14). Many others are invited in their place and they fill the banquet hall. This detail makes us think of another parable of warning which Jesus taught: "I say to you, many will come from east and west, and will recline with Abraham, Isaac and Jacob at the banquet in the kingdom of heaven, but the children of the kingdom will be driven out into the outer darkness" (Mt 8:11-12). Here one clearly sees how the invitation becomes universal. God intends to make a new covenant in his Son not only with the Chosen People, but with all humanity as well.

The next part of the parable indicates that definitive participation in the wedding feast is tied to certain essential conditions. Entering the Church is not enough to guarantee eternal salvation: "My friend, how is it that you came in here without a wedding garment?" (Mt 22:12), the king asks one of the guests. At this point the parable seems to pass from the people of Israel's historical refusal of their election to the personal conduct of anyone who is invited and to the judgment which will be made in his regard. The parable does not give a precise meaning to this "garment." But it can be said that the explanation is found in all of Christ's teaching. Especially in the Sermon on the Mount, the Gospel speaks of the commandment of love which is the principle of divine life and perfection, modeled on the Father: "Be perfect, just as your heavenly Father is perfect" (Mt 5:48). It is a matter of that new commandment which, as Jesus taught, consists in this: "As I have loved you, so you also should love one another" (Jn 13:34). Therefore, it seems possible to conclude that the wedding garment, as a condition for participating in the feast, is precisely this love.

This fact is confirmed by another great parable which concerns the final judgment and so has an eschatological character. Only those who practice the commandment of love through the spiritual and corporal works of mercy toward their neighbor can take part in the feast of the kingdom of God: "Come, you who are blessed by my Father. Inherit the kingdom prepared for you from the foundation of the world" (Mt 25:34).

Another parable helps us understand that it is never too late to enter the Church. God's invitation can be addressed to a person even at the last moment of life. This is the well-known parable of the workers in the vineyard: "The kingdom of heaven is like a landowner who went out at dawn to hire laborers for his vineyard" (Mt 20:1). He later went out several times at different hours of the day, until the last hour. Each of them was given a salary in which, beyond the limit of what was owed in strict justice, the landowner wished to show all his generous love.

In this regard, the moving episode comes to mind which was recounted by the evangelist Luke about the "good thief" who was crucified next to Jesus on Golgotha. The invitation was given to him as an act of mercy by God, as the thief said, almost breathing his last: "Jesus, remember me when you come into your kingdom." He heard from the mouth of the Redeemer and bridegroom, who had been condemned to death on a cross: "Amen, I say to you, today you will be with me in Paradise" (Lk 23:42-43).

Let us cite another one of Jesus' parables: "The kingdom of heaven is like a treasure buried in a field, which a person finds and hides again, and out of joy goes and sells all that he has and buys that field" (Mt 13:44). Analogously, there is the merchant in search of fine pearls: "When he finds a pearl of great price, he goes and sells all that he has and buys it" (Mt 13:45). This parable instills a great truth in those who are invited: to be worthy of the invitation to the bridegroom's royal feast it is necessary to show that one understands the supreme value of what is being offered. Hence, there must be a willingness to sacrifice everything for the kingdom of heaven, which is worth more than everything. No earthly good is comparable to it in value. One can abandon everything, without loss, in order to take part in the feast of Christ the bridegroom.

Jesus indicated the essential condition of detachment and poverty, with all the other conditions, when he called blessed "the poor in spirit," "the meek," "those who are persecuted for the sake of righteousness," for "theirs is the kingdom of heaven" (cf. Mt 5:3, 10). He also indicated this when he presented a child as "the greatest in the kingdom of heaven." He said: "Unless you turn and become like children, you will not enter the kingdom of heaven. Whoever humbles himself like this child is the greatest in the kingdom of heaven" (Mt 18:2-4).

Along with Vatican II, we can conclude that in the words and actions of Christ, especially in his teaching through parables, the "kingdom was clearly open to the view of men" *(LG* 5). In preaching the coming of that kingdom, Christ founded his Church and showed her inner, divine mystery (cf. *LG 5*).

General audience of September 18, 1991

Parables Reveal the Church's Growth

As we said in the preceding catechesis, it is not possible to understand the origin of the Church without considering everything which Jesus preached and did (cf. Acts 1:1). On this theme he gave his disciples and all of us a basic teaching in the parables he preached about the kingdom of God. Among these parables, those which declare and reveal to us the nature of the historical and spiritual development which is proper to the Church according to her Founder's plan have particular importance.

Jesus says: "The kingdom of God is like the case of a man who scatters seed on the land and then sleeps and rises night and day. The seed sprouts and grows, but he doesn't know how. Of its own accord the land yields fruit, first the blade, then the ear, then the full grain in the ear. When the grain is ripe, he wields the sickle, for the harvest has come" (Mk 4:26-29). The kingdom of God, then, grows here on earth in human history by virtue of an initial seed, that is, a foundation which comes from God, and a mysterious work of God himself, which the Church continues to cultivate through the centuries. In God's activity for the kingdom, the "sickle" of sacrifice is also present, for the development of the kingdom does not occur without suffering. This is the meaning of the parable recorded in Mark's Gospel.

We find the same idea in other parables, too, especially in those collected in Matthew's text (13:3-50). "The kingdom of heaven," we read in this Gospel, "is like a mustard seed that a man took and sowed in a field. It is the smallest of all the seeds, yet when full-grown it is the largest of plants. It becomes a large bush, and the birds of the sky come and dwell in its branches" (Mt 13:31-32). This is the growth of the kingdom in an extensive sense.

Another parable, however, shows the kingdom's growth in an intensive or qualitative sense, comparing it to "yeast that a woman took and mixed with three measures of wheat flour until the whole batch was leavened" (Mt 13:33).

In the parable of the sower and the seed, the growth of the kingdom of God certainly appears as the result of the sower's work, but the seed produces a harvest in relation to the soil and climatic conditions: "a hundred or sixty or thirty-fold" (Mt 13:8). The soil signifies a person's interior receptivity. According to Jesus, then, the growth of the kingdom of God is also conditioned by man. Human free will is responsible for this growth. Therefore, Jesus urges everyone to pray, "Your kingdom come" (cf. Mt 6:10; Lk 11:2). This is one of the first petitions of the *Pater noster*.

One of the parables told by Jesus about the growth of the kingdom of God on earth reveals to us in a very realistic way the type of struggle which the kingdom entails, due to the presence and action of an "enemy," who "sowed weeds all through the wheat." Jesus says: "When the crop grew and bore fruit, the weeds also appeared." The slaves of the householder wanted to pull them up, but the householder does not allow them to do this: "No, if you pull up the weeds you might uproot the wheat along with them. Let them grow together until harvest; then at harvest time I will say to the harvesters, 'First collect the weeds and tie them in bundles for burning, but gather the wheat into my barn'" (Mt 13:24-30). This parable explains the co-existence and the frequent mingling of good and evil in the world, in our lives and in the very history of the Church. Jesus teaches us to see these things with Christian realism and to handle every problem with clear principles, but also with prudence and patience. This presupposes a transcendent vision of history, in which one knows that everything belongs to God and every final result is the work of his Providence. However, the final destiny—in its eschatological dimension—of the good and bad is not hidden. It is symbolized by the gathering of the wheat into the barn and the burning of the weeds.

Jesus himself gave an explanation of the parable of the seed at the request of his disciples (cf. Mt 13:36-43). Both the temporal and the eschatological dimensions of God's kingdom appear in his words.

He said to his own: "The mystery of the kingdom of God has been granted to you" (Mk 4:11). He instructed them in this mystery and, at the same time, by his words and actions, he conferred a kingdom on them, just as the Father has conferred one on him (cf. Lk 22:29). This conferral was taken up again after his resurrection. We read in the Acts of the Apostles that "He appeared to them during forty days and spoke about the kingdom of God" (cf. Acts 1:3), up to the day when he "was taken up into heaven and took his seat at the right hand of God" (Mk 16:19). These were the last instructions and arrangements given to the apostles about what they were to do after the ascension and Pentecost in order to give a concrete beginning to the kingdom of God at the Church's birth.

The words addressed to Peter at Caesarea Philippi are also situated within the context of his preaching about the kingdom. Jesus said to Peter: "I will give you the keys to the kingdom of heaven" (Mt 16:19), immediately after having called him the *rock*, on which he would build his Church. This Church will be invincible in regard to the "gates of hell" (cf. Mt 16:18). This promise was expressed at the time by a verb in the future tense, "I will build," because the definitive establishment of the kingdom of God in this world was to be accomplished by the sacrifice of the cross and the victory of the resurrection. Afterward, Peter and the other apostles will be intensely aware of their call to "announce the praises of him who called them out of darkness into his wonderful light" (cf. 1 Pet 2:9). At the same time, all of them will also be aware of the truth which appears in the parable of the sower: "Neither the one who plants nor the one who waters is anything, but only God, who causes the growth," as St. Paul will write (1 Cor 3:7).

The author of the Book of Revelation expresses this same awareness of the kingdom when he refers to the hymn addressed to the Lamb: "You were slain and with your blood you purchased for God those from every tribe and tongue, people and nation. You made them a kingdom and priests for our God" (Rev 5:9-10). The Apostle Peter explains that they were appointed to "offer spiritual sacrifices acceptable to God through Jesus Christ" (cf. 1 Pet 2:5). These are all expressions of the truths taught by Jesus. In the parables about the sower and the seed, the wheat and the weeds, and the mustard seed which is sown and then becomes a large bush, these truths speak of the kingdom of God. Through the action of the Spirit the kingdom grows in souls by the vital force coming from Jesus' death and resurrection. The kingdom continues to grow until the time foreseen by God himself.

"Then comes the end," St. Paul proclaims, "when he [Christ] hands over the kingdom to his God and Father, when he has destroyed every sovereignty and every authority and power" (1 Cor 15:24). "When everything is subjected to him, then the Son himself will also be subjected to the one who subjected everything to him, so that God may be all in all" (1 Cor 15:28).

From beginning to end, the Church is situated within this marvelous eschatological perspective of God's kingdom, and here her history unfolds from the first day to the last.

General audience of September 25, 1991

The Birth of the Church at Pentecost

During the preceding catecheses we have often referred to the Holy Spirit's intervention in the Church's origins. Now it is time for us to devote a special catechesis to this beautiful and important topic.

Before ascending to heaven, Jesus said to the apostles, "I am sending the promise of my Father upon you, but stay in the city until you are clothed with power from on high" (Lk 24:49). Jesus intended to prepare the apostles directly for the fulfillment of "the promise of my Father." The evangelist Luke repeats the same final exhortation of the Teacher in the first verses of the Acts of the Apostles: "While meeting with them, he enjoined them not to depart from Jerusalem, but to wait for the promise of the Father" (1:4).

During all of his messianic activity, Jesus preached about the kingdom of God and prepared for the "time of the Church," which was to begin after his departure. When his departure was close, he announced that the day was soon coming when this time was to begin (cf. Acts 1:5), that is, the day of the descent of the Holy Spirit. Looking to the future, he added, "But you will receive power when the Holy Spirit comes upon you, and you will be my witnesses in Jerusalem, throughout Judea and Samaria, and to the ends of the earth" (Acts 1:8).

When the day of Pentecost came the apostles were gathered together in prayer with the Mother of the Lord. They saw proof that Jesus Christ acted in conformity with what he had announced; the "promise of the Father" was being fulfilled. The first of the apostles, Simon Peter, proclaimed this when he spoke to the assembly. Peter spoke by first recalling Jesus' death on the cross, and then he witnessed to the resurrection and the outpouring of the Holy Spirit: "God raised this Jesus; of this we are witnesses. Exalted at the right hand of God, he received the promise of the Holy Spirit from the Father and poured it forth" (Acts 2:32-33).

From the first day Peter asserted that the "promise of the Father" has been fulfilled as a result of the resurrection, because it is in virtue of his cross and resurrection that Christ, the Son who has been exalted "at the right hand of God," sends the Spirit, as Christ had announced even before his passion during the farewell in the upper room.

The Holy Spirit thus initiated the mission of the Church, which was established for all people. But we cannot forget that the Holy Spirit was at work as an "unknown God" (cf. Acts 17:23) even before Pentecost. He was at work in a special way in the old covenant, enlightening and leading the Chosen People on the way which brought ancient history to the Messiah. He was at work in the messages of the prophets and in the writings of all the inspired authors. He was especially at work in the Incarnation of the Son. The Gospel of the annunciation witnesses to this, as does the history of the subsequent events connected with the incarnate Word's coming into the world and assuming human nature. The Holy Spirit was at work in the Messiah and surrounded the Messiah from the moment when Jesus began his messianic mission in Israel. One can see this in the Gospel texts about the theophany at the time of his baptism in the Jordan and his declarations in the synagogue of Nazareth. But from that time and throughout Jesus' whole life, expectations were heightened and promises renewed for the future definitive coming of the Holy Spirit. John the Baptist tied the mission of the Messiah to a new baptism "in the Holy Spirit." Jesus promised "streams of living water" to those who would believe in him. This promise is mentioned in John's Gospel, which explains it this way: "He said this in reference to the Spirit that those who came to believe in him were to receive. There was, of course, no Spirit as yet, because Jesus had not yet been glorified" (Jn 7:39). On the day of Pentecost, Christ, who was now glorified after completing his mission, made "streams of living water" well up from within himself. He poured out the Spirit to fill the apostles and all believers with divine life. They were thus able to be "baptized in one Spirit" (cf. 1 Cor 12:13). It was the beginning of the Church's growth.

The Second Vatican Council teaches: "Christ sent from the Father his Holy Spirit, who was to carry on inwardly his saving work and prompt the Church to spread out. Doubtless, the Holy Spirit was already at work in the world before Christ was glorified. Yet on the day of Pentecost, he came down upon the disciples to remain with them forever (cf. Jn 14:16). The Church was publicly displayed to the multitude, the Gospel began to spread among the nations by means of preaching, and there was presaged that union of all peoples in the catholicity of the faith by means of the Church of the new covenant, a Church which speaks all tongues, understands and accepts all tongues in her love, and so supersedes the divisiveness of Babel" *(AG* 4).

The conciliar text indicates what constitutes the Holy Spirit's action in the Church, beginning with the day of Pentecost. It is an interior, saving work which is also expressed externally in the birth of a community and institution of salvation. This community—the community of the first disciples—was permeated with love, which overcomes all differences and divisions of an earthly nature. A sign of this is the Pentecost event with an expression of faith in God which is understandable to all, despite the differences in language. The Acts of the Apostles attests that the people who gathered around the apostles at the first public manifestation of the Church said in amazement: "Are not all of these men who are speaking Galileans? How is it that each of us hears them in his native tongue?" (Acts 2:7-8).

The Church, which had just been born in this way on the day of Pentecost by the work of the Holy Spirit, was immediately revealed to the world. It is not a closed community, but an open one—it could be called a community thrown wide open—to all the nations "even to the ends of the earth" (Acts 1:8). Those who enter this community through Baptism become, by virtue of the Holy Spirit of truth, witnesses of the Good News and are ready to pass it on to others. It is therefore a dynamic, apostolic community, the Church "in a state of mission."

The Holy Spirit first "bears witness" to Christ (cf. Jn 15:26) and this witness pervades the heart and soul of those who participate in Pentecost. They in turn become witnesses and proclaimers. The "tongues of fire" (Acts 2:3) which appeared over the head of each one present are the external sign of the enthusiasm enkindled in them by the Holy Spirit. The apostles extended this enthusiasm to their listeners, as already happened after Peter's discourse on the first day: "Some three thousand were added" (Acts 2:41).

The entire Acts of the Apostles is a grand description of the Holy Spirit's work at the beginning of the Church, which— as we read—"was being built up and was making steady progress in the fear of the Lord; at the same time it enjoyed the increased consolation of the Holy Spirit" (Acts 9:31). We know that it had internal difficulties and persecutions, and there were the first martyrs. But the apostles were certain that

the Holy Spirit was there to guide them. This awareness
of theirs would in some way be formalized in the concluding decision of the Council of Jerusalem, whose resolutions
began with the words: "It is the decision of the Holy Spirit, and
ours too..." (Acts 15:28). In this way the community gave
evidence of its own awareness of being moved by the action of
the Holy Spirit.

General audience of October 2, 1991

The Church Lives in the Trinity's Love

The Second Vatican Council concludes the first part of its exposition on the Church in the Constitution *Lumen Gentium* with a concise and profound phrase taken from St. Cyprian: "The universal Church has been seen as 'a people made one with the unity of the Father, the Son and the Holy Spirit'" *(LG* 4). According to the Council, then, the Church in her very essence is a mystery of faith, which is intimately joined to the infinite mystery of the Trinity. We must now turn our thoughts to this mystery within the mystery, following our previous catecheses on the Church in the teaching of Jesus and the *opus paschale* which he accomplished by his passion, death and resurrection, and crowned on the day of Pentecost with the descent of the Holy Spirit on the apostles. According to the teaching of Vatican II, which was the heir of Tradition, the mystery of the Church is rooted in God the Trinity, and therefore has this trinitarian dimension as its first and fundamental dimension, inasmuch as the Church depends on and lives in the Trinity from her origins to her historical conclusion and eternal destination (cf. St. Cyprian, *De Oratione Dominica,* 23: *PL* 4, 553).

This trinitarian perspective on the Church was revealed by Jesus in his final words to the apostles before his definitive return to the Father: "Go, therefore, and make disciples of all nations, baptizing them in the name of the Father, and of the Son, and of the Holy Spirit" (Mt 28:19). "All nations," which have been invited and called to be united in one faith, are marked by the mystery of the triune God. They are all invited and called to Baptism, which means being brought into the mystery of the Holy Trinity's divine life, through the Church of the apostles and their successors, the visible foundation of the community of believers.

This trinitarian perspective, indicated by Christ when he sent the apostles to preach the Gospel to the whole world, is expressed in Paul's greeting to the community of Corinth: "The grace of the Lord Jesus Christ and the love of God [the Father] and the fellowship of the Holy Spirit be with all of you" (2 Cor 13:13). This is the same greeting which, in the liturgy of the Mass as renewed after Vatican II, the celebrant addresses to the assembly, just as the Apostle Paul once did to the faithful of Corinth. It expresses the wish that Christians may all become sharers in the gifts which are ascribed to the Father, the Son and the Holy Spirit: the love of the Creator Father, the grace of the Redeemer Son, the unity in communion of the Holy Spirit, the Trinity's bond of love, in which the Church shares.

This same trinitarian perspective is found again in another Pauline text which has great importance from the standpoint of the Church's mission: "There are different spiritual gifts but the same Spirit; there are different forms of service but the same Lord; there are different workings but the same God who produces all of them in everyone" (1 Cor 12:4-6). Without a doubt the Church's unity reflects the unity of God, but at the same time it receives its vitality from the Trinity of the Father, the Son and the Holy Spirit, which is reflected in the richness of ecclesial life. This unity produces many signs of life. The sovereign mystery of the triune God extends over the whole mystery of the Church's very rich unity.

In the Church's life one can discover reflections of the divine unity and trinity. At the source of this life one especially sees the love of the Father, who takes the initiative, both in creation and redemption, whereby he gathers individuals together as his children in his only-begotten Son. Therefore, the Church's life is the life of Christ himself who lives in us by giving us a share in his own divine sonship. This sharing is accomplished by the Holy Spirit, who enables us to say to God, like Christ and with Christ: "Abba, Father!" (Rom 8:15).

In this cry the new awareness of human sharing in the sonship of God's Son, through the Holy Spirit who gives grace, finds a formulation of its divine—and trinitarian—origin. By grace the same Spirit fulfills Christ's promise about the indwelling of God the Trinity in the children of divine adoption. In fact, the promise made by Jesus: "Whoever loves me will keep my word, and my Father will love him, and we will come to him and make our dwelling with him" (Jn 14:23), is elucidated by an earlier promise: "If you love me, you will keep my commandments. I will ask the Father, and he will give you another Advocate to be with you always" (Jn 14:15-16). A similar teaching has been given to us by St. Paul, who tells Christians that they are "the temple of God" and explains this marvelous privilege by saying: "The Spirit of God dwells in you" (1 Cor 3:16; cf. Rom 8:9; 1 Cor 6:19; 2 Cor 6:16).

This is the great truth which we learn from these texts: the human person is, in the Church, the dwelling place of God the Trinity, and the whole Church, composed of persons in whom the Trinity dwells, is in its entirety the temple of the Trinity.

The essential source of the Church's unity is also found in God the Trinity. This is indicated in the "priestly" prayer of Jesus in the upper room: "...so that they may all be one, as you, Father, are in me and I in you, that they also may be one in us, that the world may believe that you sent me. I have given them the glory you gave me, so that they may be one, as we are one, I in them and you in me, that they may be brought to perfection as one, that the world may know that you sent me, and that you loved them even as you loved me" (Jn 17:21-23). Here is the source and also the model of the Church's unity. Jesus prayed, "May they be one, as we are one." But the achievement of this divine likeness occurs within the unity of the Trinity: "they in us." The Church abides in this trinitarian unity and lives in the truth and love of the Father, the Son and the Holy Spirit. The source of all the efforts for the reunion of Christians in the unity of the Church, wounded in the human and historical dimension of unity, is always in the one and undivided Trinity. At the foundation of true ecumenism we find this truth of ecclesial unity which the priestly prayer of Christ reveals to us as deriving from the Trinity.

The holiness of the Church—and all holiness in the Church—has its source in the holiness of God the Trinity. The movement from trinitarian holiness to ecclesial holiness occurs above all in the Incarnation of God's Son, as is clear from the words at the annunciation to Mary: "The child to be born will be called holy" (Lk 1:35). This "holy one" is Christ, the Son who was consecrated by the anointing of the Holy Spirit (cf. Lk 4:18), the Son who consecrates himself by his sacrifice to be able to communicate to his disciples his own consecration and his own holiness: "I consecrate myself for them, so that they also may be consecrated in truth" (Jn 17:19). Glorified by the Father through this consecration (cf. Jn 13:31; 17:1-2), the risen Christ communicates the Holy Spirit to his Church (cf. Jn 20:22; 7:39), who makes her holy (cf. 1 Cor 6:11).

I want to conclude by emphasizing that our one and holy Church is called to be, and is placed in the world as, a revelation of that love which is God: "God is love," St. John writes (1 Jn 4:8). If God is Father, Son and Holy Spirit, then the divine Persons' infinite life of knowledge and love is the transcendent reality of the Trinity. Precisely this "love of God has been poured out into our hearts through the Holy Spirit that has been given to us" (Rom 5:5).

The Church—"a people made one with the unity of the Father, the Son and the Holy Spirit," as St. Cyprian has told us—is thus the "sacrament" of trinitarian love. Her most profound mystery consists precisely in this love.

General audience of October 9, 1991

God Made a Covenant with Israel

According to the Second Vatican Council, which quotes St. Cyprian's text which we reflected on during the preceding catechesis, "The universal Church is seen to be 'a people made one with the unity of the Father, the Son and the Holy Spirit'" *(LG* 4; cf. St. Cyprian, *De Oratione Dominica,* 23: *PL* 4, 553). As we have explained, in these words the Council teaches that the Church is above all a mystery rooted in the triune God; the Church is a mystery whose primary and fundamental dimension is trinitarian. It is in relationship to the Trinity, the eternal source from which she arises, that the Church "is seen to be a people" *(LG* 4). Thus she is the people of God—of the triune God. We wish now to devote this catechesis and the following ones to this theme, always taking as our guiding principle the teaching of the Council, which was wholly inspired by Sacred Scripture.

The Council states precisely: "God, however, does not make men holy and save them merely as individuals, without bond or link between one another. Rather has it pleased him to bring men together as one people, a people which acknowledges him in truth and serves him in holiness" *(LG* 9). This plan of God began to be revealed in the history of Abraham by the first words God spoke to him: "The Lord said to Abram:

'Go forth from the land of your kinsfolk...to a land that I will show you. I will make of you a great nation and I will bless you'" (Gen 12:1-2).

This promise was then confirmed by a covenant (Gen 15:18; 17:1-4) and solemnly proclaimed after the sacrifice of Isaac. Following God's request, Abraham was ready to sacrifice his only son whom the Lord had given to him and his wife Sarah in their old age. But God only meant to test his faith. In this sacrifice, then, Isaac did not die, but continued living. However, Abraham had consented in his heart to the sacrifice and this sacrifice of the heart, the proof of a magnificent faith, obtained for him the promise of innumerable descendants: "I swear by myself, declares the Lord, that because you acted as you did in not withholding from me your beloved son, I will bless you abundantly and make your descendants as countless as the stars of the sky and the sands of the seashore" (Gen 22:16-17).

The fulfillment of this promise was to take place in different stages. Abraham was destined to become "the father of all who have faith" (cf. Gen 15:6; Gal 3:6-7; Rom 4:16-17). The first stage was achieved in Egypt where "the Israelites were fruitful and prolific. They became so numerous and strong that the land was filled with them" (Ex 1:7). By now Abraham's stock had become "the Israelite people" (Ex 1:9). However, they were in the humiliating condition of slavery. Faithful to his covenant with Abraham, God called Moses and said, "I have witnessed the affliction of my people in Egypt and have heard their cry.... I have come down to rescue them.... Come, now! I will send you...to lead my people, the Israelites, out of Egypt" (Ex 3:7-10).

So, Moses was called to lead that people out of Egypt. However, Moses was only God's agent in fulfilling his plan, the instrument of his power, for according to the Bible, God himself led Israel out of slavery in Egypt. "When Israel was a child I loved him; out of Egypt I called my son," we read in the

Book of the Prophet Hosea (11:1). Israel, then, is the people of God's favor: "It was not because you are the largest of all nations that the Lord set his heart on you and chose you, for you are really the smallest of all nations. It was because the Lord loved you and because of his fidelity to the oath he had sworn to your fathers" (Dt 7:7-8). The Israelites were not chosen to be the People of God because of their human qualities, but solely by God's initiative.

The divine initiative, the Lord's sovereign choice, assumed the form of a covenant. This occurred in regard to Abraham. It occurred after the deliverance of Israel from slavery in Egypt. Moses was the mediator of this covenant at the foot of Mt. Sinai. "When Moses came to the people and related all the words and ordinances of the Lord, they all answered with one voice, 'We will do everything that the Lord has told us.' Moses then wrote down all the words of the Lord and, rising early the next day, he erected at the foot of the mountain an altar and twelve pillars for the twelve tribes of Israel." Then sacrifices were offered and Moses splashed half of the blood of the sacrifice on the altar. "Taking the book of the covenant, he read it aloud to the people," once again receiving from those present the promise to obey the words of God. Finally, he sprinkled the people with the other half of the blood (cf. Ex 24:3-8).

The Book of Deuteronomy explains the significance of this event: "Today you are making this agreement with the Lord: he is to be your God and you are to walk in his ways and observe his statutes, commandments and decrees, and to hearken to his voice. Today the Lord is making this agreement with you: you are to be a people peculiarly his own" (Dt 26:17-18). The covenant with God is a special "promotion" for Israel. In this way Israel becomes "a people sacred to the Lord [their] God" (cf. Dt 26:19). This means that they belong to God in a special way. Even more it is a reciprocal belonging: "Then I will be your God and you shall be my people" (Jer 7:23). This is the divine arrangement. God commits himself to the covenant. All the infidelities on the people's part at the various stages of their history do not affect God's fidelity to the covenant. One can say at most that in a certain sense these infidelities open the way to the new covenant foretold in the Book of the Prophet Jeremiah: "But this is the covenant which I will make with the house of Israel after those days, says the Lord. I will place my law within them, and write it upon their hearts" (Jer 31:33).

In virtue of the divine initiative taken in the covenant, a people becomes the People of God, and as such they are holy, that is, sacred to the Lord God: "For you are a people sacred to the Lord, your God" (Dt 7:6; cf. Dt 26:19). The meaning of this consecration also clarifies the words of Exodus: "You shall be to me a kingdom of priests, a holy nation" (Ex 19:6). Even though during the course of their history this people would commit many sins, they did not cease being the People of God. For this reason, Moses appealed to the Lord's fidelity to the covenant which he himself had established, and addressed a moving petition to him: "Destroy not your people, your heritage," as we read in Deuteronomy (9:26).

For his part, God did not cease addressing his word to the Chosen People. He speaks to them many times through the prophets. The principal commandment continues to be to love God above all things: "You shall love the Lord, your God, with all your heart, with all your soul, and with all your strength" (Dt 6:5). This commandment is joined to the commandment of love for one's neighbor: "I am the Lord. You shall not defraud or rob your neighbor.... Take no revenge and cherish no grudge against your fellow countrymen. You shall love your neighbor as yourself" (Lev 19:13, 18).

Another element appears in the biblical texts: the God who made a covenant with Israel wants to be present among his people, present in a particular way. During the pilgrimage in the desert this presence was shown by the meeting tent.

Later it was expressed by the temple which King Solomon built in Jerusalem.

In regard to the meeting tent, we read in Exodus: "Whenever Moses went out to the tent, the people would all rise and stand at the entrance of their own tents, watching Moses until he entered the tent. As Moses entered the tent, the column of cloud would come down and stand at its entrance while the Lord spoke with Moses. On seeing the column of cloud stand at the entrance of the tent, all the people would rise and worship at the entrance of their own tents. The Lord used to speak to Moses face to face as one man speaks to another" (Ex 33:8-11). The gift of this presence was a special sign of divine election, which is revealed in symbolic ways and almost as the omen of a future reality: God's covenant with his new people in the Church.

General audience of October 20, 1991

The Church Is the New People of God

We can also begin this catechesis, following the program and method which we have chosen, by reading a passage from the Council's Constitution *Lumen Gentium,* which says: "God, however, does not make men holy and save them merely as individuals, without bond or link between one another. Rather has it pleased him to bring men together as one people, a people which acknowledges him in truth and serves him in holiness. He therefore chose the race of Israel as a people unto himself. With it he set up a covenant. Step by step he taught and prepared this people, making known in its history both himself and the decree of his will and making it holy unto himself" *(LG* 9). The subject of the preceding catechesis was this People of God of the old covenant. But the Council immediately adds: "All these things, however, happened as a preparation and figure of that new and perfect covenant which was to be ratified in Christ, and of the fuller revelation which was to be given through the Word of God made flesh" *(LG* 9). The entire passage quoted from *Lumen Gentium* is found at the beginning of chapter II, entitled "The People of God." According to the Council, the Church is the People of God of the new covenant. This is the idea already expressed by St. Peter to the first

Christian communities: "Once you were 'no people,' but now you are God's people" (1 Pet 2:10).

In her historical reality and theological mystery the Church comes from the People of God of the old covenant. Although designated by the term *qahàl* (i.e., assembly), from the New Testament it is clear that the Church is the People of God established in a new way through Christ and in virtue of the Holy Spirit.

St. Paul writes: "For we are the temple of the living God, as God said: 'I will live with them and move among them, and I will be their God and they shall be my people'" (2 Cor 6:16). The People of God is established in a new way, because all those who believe in Christ are part of it, with "no distinction" between Jew and non-Jew (cf. Acts 15:9). St. Peter says this clearly in the Acts of the Apostles when he describes "how God first concerned himself with acquiring from among the Gentiles a people for his name" (Acts 15:14). St. James declares: "The words of the prophets agree with this" (Acts 15:15).

During his first stay in the pagan city of Corinth, St. Paul was given another confirmation of this perspective when he heard these words of Christ: "Do not be afraid. Go on speaking...for I have many people in this city" (Acts 18:9-10). Lastly, there is a proclamation in the Book of Revelation: "Behold, God's dwelling with men. He will dwell with them and they will be his people and God himself will always be with them" (Rev 21:3).

All this clearly shows that from the beginning the Church was conscious of the continuity and, at the same time, the newness of her own reality as the People of God.

In the Old Testament, Israel already owed its existence as the People of God to God's choice and initiative. However, this people was limited to a single nation. The new People of God goes beyond this limitation. It includes people of all nations, languages and races. It has a universal character; it is catholic. As the Council says: "Christ instituted this new covenant, the new testament, that is to say, in his blood (cf. 1 Cor 11:25), calling together a people made up of Jew and gentile, making them one, not according to the flesh but in the Spirit. This was to be the new People of God" *(LG 9)*. The basis of this newness—universalism—is the redemption accomplished by Christ. He "also suffered outside the gate, to consecrate the people by his own blood" (Heb 13:12). "Therefore, he had to become like his brothers in every way, that he might be a merciful and faithful high priest before God to expiate the sins of the people" (Heb 2:17).

Thus the people of the new covenant was formed. This covenant was proclaimed by the prophets of the Old Testament, especially Jeremiah and Ezekiel. We read in Jeremiah: "The days are coming, says the Lord, when I will make a new covenant with the house of Israel and the house of Judah" (Jer 31:31). "This is the covenant which I will make with the house of Israel after those days, says the Lord. I will place my law within them, and write it upon their hearts; I will be their God, and they shall be my people" (Jer 31:33).

The prophet Ezekiel more clearly reveals the prospect of an outpouring of the Holy Spirit in which the new covenant will be fulfilled: "I will give you a new heart and place a new spirit within you, taking from your bodies your stony hearts and giving you natural hearts. I will put my spirit within you and make you live by my statutes, careful to observe my decrees" (Ez 36:26-27).

The Council especially draws on the First Letter of Peter for its teaching about the People of God of the new covenant, which is the heir of the people of the old one: "For those who believe in Christ, who are reborn not from a perishable but from an imperishable seed through the word of the living God (cf. 1 Pet 1:23), not from the flesh but from water and the Holy Spirit (cf. Jn 3:5-6), are finally established as 'a chosen race, a royal priesthood, a holy nation, a purchased people...who in times past were not a people, but are now the people of God'"

(LG 9). As you see, this teaching of the Council emphasizes, with St. Peter, the continuity of the People of God with that of the old covenant. But it also brings out what in a certain sense is the absolute newness of the new people who are established in virtue of Christ's redemption, set apart (purchased) by the blood of the Lamb.

The Council describes this newness of the "messianic people," which "has Christ for its head, 'who was delivered up for our sins, and rose again for our justification' (Rom 4:25), and now, having won a name which is above all names, reigns in glory in heaven. The state of this people is that of the dignity and freedom of the sons of God, in whose hearts the Holy Spirit dwells as in his temple. Its law is the new commandment to love as Christ loved us (cf. Jn 13:34). Its end is the kingdom of God, which has been begun by God himself on earth, and which is to be further extended until it is brought to perfection by him at the end of time, when Christ, our life (cf. Col 3:4), shall appear, and 'creation itself will be delivered from its slavery to corruption into the freedom of the glory of the sons of God' (Rom 8:21)" *(LG* 9).

This is how the Church is described as the People of God of the new covenant (cf. *LG* 9), the nucleus of the new human-ity which has been called in its entirety to be part of the new people. The Council adds: "That messianic people, although it does not actually include all men, and at times may look like a small flock, is nonetheless a lasting and sure seed of unity, hope and salvation for the whole human race. Established by Christ as a communion of life, charity and truth, it is also used by him as an instrument for the redemption of all, and is sent forth into the whole world as the light of the world and the salt of the earth (cf. Mt 5:13-16)" *(LG* 9).

We will devote the next catechesis to this basic and fasci-nating topic.

General audience of November 6, 1991

The Church Is Universal by Nature

The Church is the People of God of the new covenant, as we saw in our previous catechesis. The topic of today's catechesis is the universal dimension of the People of God. According to the teaching of the Second Vatican Council, "Although it does not actually include all men, and at times may look like a small flock, [the Church] is nonetheless a lasting and sure seed of unity, hope and salvation for the whole human race" *(LG* 9). Such a universality of the Church as the People of God is in close relation to the revealed truth about God as Creator of all that exists, Redeemer of all mankind, author of holiness and life in every person through the power of the Holy Spirit.

We know that the old covenant was established with only one people chosen by God, the people of Israel. However, the Old Testament is not lacking in texts which foretell this future universality. This is indicated in the promise God made to Abraham: "All the communities of the earth shall find blessing in you" (Gen 12:3), a promise renewed several times and extended to "all the nations of the earth" (Gen 18:18). Other texts specify that this universal blessing would be communicated by the offspring of Abraham (cf. Gen 22:18), Isaac (cf. Gen 26:4) and Jacob (cf. Gen 28:14). The same concept is repeated in other expressions by the prophets, especially in the Book of Isaiah: "In days to come," he writes, "the mountain of the Lord's house shall be established as the highest mountain and raised above the hills. All nations shall stream toward it; many peoples shall come and say 'Come, let us climb the Lord's mountain, to the house of the God of Jacob, that he may instruct us in his ways and we may walk in his paths'.... He shall judge between the nations and impose terms on many peoples" (Is 2:2-4). "On this mountain the Lord of hosts will provide for all peoples a feast of rich food and choice wines.... On this mountain he will destroy the veil that veils all peoples, the web that is woven over all nations" (Is 25:6-7). From Second Isaiah come the predictions concerning the "servant of the Lord": "I, the Lord...formed you and set you as a covenant of the people, a light for the nations" (Is 42:6). The Book of Jonah is also significant when it describes the prophet's mission to Nineveh, which was outside Israel's sphere (cf. Jon 4:10-11).

These passages, and others too, help us to understand that the Chosen People of the old covenant was a foreshadowing of and preparation for the future People of God, which would be universal in breadth. Therefore, after Christ's resurrection, the "Good News" was first proclaimed to Israel (cf. Acts 2:36; 4:10).

Jesus Christ was the founder of this new people. When Jesus was a mere infant the aged Simeon saw in him the "light" coming "for revelation to the Gentiles," as Isaiah's prophecy had foretold (cf. Is 42:6). Christ opened the way for people to attain to the universality of the new People of God, as St. Paul writes: "For he is our peace, he who made both one and broke down the dividing wall of enmity" (Eph 2:14). "There is neither Jew nor Greek...for you are all one in Christ Jesus" (Gal 3:28). The Apostle Paul was the principal spokesman of the universal extension of the People of God. Especially from his teaching and action, derived from that of Jesus himself, the Church reached the firm conviction that in Jesus Christ all are called, without distinction of nation, language or culture. As the Second Vatican Council says, the messianic people which is born of the Gospel and redemption through the cross, is a *firmissimum germen* ("most firm seed") of unity, hope and salvation for the whole human race (cf. *LG* 9).

Enlightened from on high, this affirmation of the universality of the People of God of the new covenant coincides with the aspirations and efforts with which, especially in our day, people seek unity and peace, working most of all in the domain of international life and its vital institutions. Because of her very vocation and original mission the Church cannot fail to be involved in this historic moment.

In fact, the Council continues by stating that the messanic people, the Church, "established by Christ as a communion of life, charity and truth...is also used by him as an instrument for the redemption of all, and is sent forth into the whole world as the light of the world and the salt of the earth (cf. Mt 5:13-16)" *(LG* 9). This openness to the whole world, to all peoples and to everything human, belongs to the Church's nature. It flows from the universality of the redemption earned through Christ's cross and resurrection (cf. Mt 28:19; Mk 16:15). It finds its consecration on Pentecost in the descent of the Holy Spirit upon the apostles and the Jerusalem community, the Church's first nucleus. Since that time the Church has always been aware of the universal call to all people to be part of the people of the new covenant.

God has called the entire community of those who look with faith upon Jesus, author of salvation and source of peace and unity, to be part of his people. This "community which has been called" is the Church, established that "for each and all it may be the visible sacrament of this saving unity. While it transcends all limits of time and confines of race, the Church is destined to extend to all regions of the earth and so enters into the history of mankind" *(LG* 9). The Council's teaching continues: "Israel according to the flesh, which wandered as an exile in the desert, was already called the Church of God (Neh 13:1; cf. Num 20:4; Dt 23:1ff.). Likewise the new Israel which while living in this present age goes in search of a future and abiding city (cf. Heb 13:14) is called the Church of Christ (cf. Mt 16:18). For he has bought it for himself with his blood (cf. Acts 20:28), has filled it with his Spirit and provided it with those means which befit it as a visible and social union" *(LG* 9).

The Church's universality therefore corresponds to the transcendent plan of God, who works in human history through his mercy, willing "everyone to be saved" (1 Tim 2:4).

From the beginning God the Father's saving will has been the reason and purpose for the Church's activity in response to her vocation to be the messianic people of the new covenant, with a dynamism that is open to universality. Jesus himself indicated this in the mandate and assurance he gave to Paul of Tarsus, the Apostle to the Gentiles: "I shall deliver you from this people and from the Gentiles to whom I send you, to open their eyes that they may turn from darkness to light and from the power of Satan to God, so that they may obtain forgiveness of sins and an inheritance among those who have been consecrated by faith in me" (Acts 26:17-18).

The new covenant to which humanity is called is also an eternal covenant (cf. Heb 13:20) and therefore the messianic people is marked by an eschatological vocation. This is attested to especially in the last book of the New Testament, the Book of Revelation, which highlights the universal nature of a Church extended in time and, beyond time, into eternity. In the great heavenly vision which follows the letters addressed to the seven churches in the Book of Revelation, the Lamb is solemnly praised because he was sacrificed and with his blood he purchased for God "those from every tribe and tongue, people and nation" and made them a kingdom of priests for our

God (cf. Rev 5:9-10). In a later vision John sees "a great multitude, which no one could count, from every nation, race, people and tongue. They stood before the throne [of God] and before the Lamb" (Rev 7:9). The earthly Church and the heavenly one; the Church of the apostles and their successors and the Church of the blessed; the Church of the children of God in time and eternity—it is the single reality of the messianic people which extends beyond all limits of space and historical time, in accord with the divine plan of salvation which is mirrored in her catholicity.

General audience of November 13, 1991

The Church Is the Body of Christ

St. Paul uses the metaphor of the body to represent the Church. He says: "For in one Spirit we were all baptized into one body, whether Jews or Greeks, slaves or freemen, and we were all given to drink of one Spirit" (1 Cor 12:13). It is a new image. While the concept of the "People of God" which we explained in the preceding catecheses belongs to the Old Testament and is taken up again and enriched in the New Testament, the image of the body of Christ, which Vatican II also used in speaking about the Church, has no precedents in the Old Testament. It is found in the Pauline letters, which we shall especially refer to in this catechesis. This concept has been studied by exegetes and theologians of our century in its Pauline origin, in the patristic and theological tradition which derives from it, and in the validity which it also possesses for presenting the Church today. It was also employed by the papal Magisterium. Pope Pius XII devoted a memorable encyclical to it, with the title of *Mystici Corporis Christi* (1943).

We must also note that in the Pauline letters we do not find the adjective "mystical," which only appears later; the letters speak of the body of Christ simply and with a realistic comparison to the human body. The Apostle writes: "As a body is one though it has many parts, and all the parts of the body, though many, are one body, so it is with Christ" (1 Cor 12:12).

With these words the Apostle intends to highlight both the unity and multiplicity which is proper to the Church. "For as in one body we have many parts, and all the parts do not have the same function, so we, though many, are one body in Christ and individually parts of one another" (Rom 12:4-5). It may be said that, although the concept of People of God highlights the multiplicity, that of body of Christ emphasizes the unity within this multiplicity, pointing out especially the principle and source of this unity: Christ. "You are Christ's body, and individually parts of it" (1 Cor 12:27). "We, though many, are one body in Christ" (Rom 12:5). Therefore, this concept highlights the unity of Christ and the Church, and the unity of the Church's many members among themselves, in virtue of the unity of the entire body with Christ.

The body is an organism which, precisely as an organism, expresses the need for cooperation among the individual organs and parts in the unity of the whole, which is put together and structured in such a way, according to St. Paul, "that there may be no division in the body, but that the parts may have the same concern for one another" (1 Cor 12:25). "Indeed, the parts of the body that seem to be weaker are all the more necessary" (1 Cor 12:22). We are, the Apostle adds, "individually parts of one another" (Rom 12:5) in the body of Christ, the Church. The multiplicity of the members and the variety of their functions cannot damage this unity, just as, on the other hand, this unity cannot cancel or destroy the multiplicity and variety of the members and their functions.

The need for "biological" harmony in the human organism is applied analogously in theological language to indicate the necessity of solidarity among all the members of the Church community. The Apostle writes: "If one part suffers, all the parts suffer with it; if one part is honored, all the parts share its joy" (1 Cor 12:26).

Thus, the concept of Church as the body of Christ can be said to complement the concept of People of God. The same reality is expressed according to the two aspects of unity and multiplicity by two different analogies.

The analogy of the body especially highlights the unity of life: the Church's members are united with one another through the principle of unity in an identical life which comes from Christ. "Do you not know that your bodies are members of Christ?" (1 Cor 6:15). It is a spiritual life; in fact, it is life in the Holy Spirit. We read in *Lumen Gentium:* "By communicating his Spirit, Christ made his brothers, called together from all nations, mystically the components of his own body" *(LG* 7). In this way, Christ himself is "the head of the body, the Church" (Col 1:18). The condition for participating in the life of this body is the bond with the head, that is, with him "from whom the whole body, supported and held together by its ligaments and bonds, achieves the growth that comes from God" (Col 2:19).

The Pauline concept of the head (Christ, the head of the body which is the Church) signifies first of all the power which he possesses over the whole body. It is a supreme power, in regard to which we read in Ephesians that God "put all things beneath his feet and gave him as head over all things to the Church" (Eph 1:22). As head, Christ fills the Church, his body, with his divine life, so that all may grow "into him who is the head, Christ, from whom the whole body, joined and held together by every supporting ligament, with the proper functioning of each part, brings about the body's growth and builds itself up in love" (Eph 4:15-16).

As head of the Church, Christ is the principle and source of cohesion among the members of his body (cf. Col 2:19). He is the principle and source of growth in the Spirit: from him the entire body grows and "builds itself up in love" (Eph 4:16). This is the reason for the Apostle's exhortation to live "the truth in love" (Eph 4:15). The spiritual growth of the Church's body and its individual members is a growth "from Christ" (the principle) and also "into Christ" (the goal). The Apostle tells us this when he finishes his exhortation with these words: "Living the truth in love, we should grow in every way into him who is the head, Christ" (Eph 4:15).

We must add that the doctrine of the Church as body of Christ, the head, has a close connection with the Eucharist. The Apostle asks: "The cup of blessing that we bless, is it not a participation in the Blood of Christ? The bread that we break, is it not a participation in the Body of Christ?" (1 Cor 10:16). Obviously, this refers to the personal Body of Christ which we receive in a sacramental way in the Eucharist under the appearance of bread. But St. Paul continues his discourse in answer to the question raised: "Because the loaf of bread is one, we though many, are one body, for we all partake of the one loaf" (1 Cor 10:17). This "one body" comprises all the members of the Church who are spiritually united to the head, who is the Person of Christ.

The Eucharist, as the sacrament of the personal Body and Blood of Christ, forms the Church, which is the social body of Christ in the unity of all the members of the ecclesial community. We will have to be content for now with the taste of a wonderful Christian truth, which we will speak about again when, God willing, we discuss the Eucharist.

General audience of November 20, 1991

The Church Has a Sacramental Nature

According to Vatican II, "The Church is in Christ like a sacrament or as a sign and instrument both of a very closely knit union with God and of the unity of the whole human race" *(LG* 1). This doctrine, which is presented from the very beginning of the *Dogmatic Constitution on the Church,* requires some clarifications, which we will make in this catechesis. Let us begin by noting that the text just quoted about the Church as "sacrament" is found in the first chapter of *Lumen Gentium,* which is entitled: "The Mystery of the Church" *(De ecclesiae mysterio).* Therefore, the explanation of this sacramentality which the Council attributes to the Church must be sought in the context of mystery *(mysterium)* as it is understood in the first chapter of the constitution.

The Church is a divine mystery because the divine design (or plan) for humanity's salvation is realized in her, namely, "the mystery of the kingdom of God" revealed in the word and very life of Christ. This mystery was revealed by Jesus first of all to the apostles: "The mystery of the kingdom of God has been granted to you. But to those outside everything comes in parables" (Mk 4:11).

The meaning of the parables of the kingdom, to which we devoted an earlier catechesis, is first realized in a fundamental way through the Incarnation and finds its fulfillment in the period between the Passover of Christ's cross and resurrection and Pentecost in Jerusalem, where the apostles and the members of the first community received the Baptism of the Spirit of truth. At the same time the eternal mystery of the divine plan for the salvation of humanity was given its visible form as the Church, the new People of God.

The letters of Paul express this in an especially explicit and effective way. In fact, the Apostle proclaims Christ "according to the revelation of the mystery kept secret for long ages but now manifested" (Rom 16:25-26). "The mystery hidden from ages and from generations past, but now manifested to his holy ones, to whom God chose to make known the riches of the glory of this mystery among the Gentiles; it is Christ in you, the hope of glory" (Col 1:26-27). This is the mystery revealed to comfort hearts, to give instruction in love, to achieve a full understanding of the richness which it contains (cf. Col 2:2). At the same time the Apostle asks the Colossians to pray "that God may open a door to us for the word, to speak of the mystery of Christ," hoping for himself "that I may make it clear, as I must speak" (Col 4:3-4).

If this divine mystery, or the mystery of humanity's salvation in Christ, is above all the mystery of Christ, it is intended "for human beings." Indeed, we read in Ephesians: "This mystery was not made known to human beings in other generations as it has now been revealed to his holy apostles and prophets by the Spirit, that the Gentiles are coheirs, members of the same body, and co-partners in the promise in Christ Jesus through the Gospel. Of this I became a minister by the gift of God's grace that was granted me in accord with the exercise of his power" (Eph 3:5-7).

This teaching of Paul is taken up again and reproposed by Vatican II, which said: "Christ, having been lifted up from the earth has drawn all to himself (cf. Jn 12:32). Rising from the dead (cf. Rom 6:9), he sent his life-giving Spirit upon his disciples and through him has established his body which is the Church as the universal sacrament of salvation" *(LG* 48). And again: "God gathered together as one all those who in faith look upon Jesus as the author of salvation and the source of unity and peace, and established them as the Church that for each and all it may be the visible sacrament of this saving unity" *(LG* 9).

Therefore, the eternal initiative of the Father, who conceives the saving plan which was revealed to humanity and accomplished in Christ, is the foundation of the Church's mystery. In the Church, through the work of the Holy Spirit, the mystery is shared with human beings, beginning with the apostles. By this sharing in the mystery of Christ, the Church is the body of Christ. The Pauline image and concept of body of Christ express at the same time the truth of the Church's mystery and the truth of her visible character in the world and the history of humanity.

The Greek word *mysterion* was translated into Latin as *sacramentum.* The Council's teaching uses the word in this sense in the passages cited above. In the Latin Church the word *sacramentum* has acquired the more specific meaning of designating the seven sacraments. Obviously, applying this meaning to the Church can be done only in an analogous way.

According to the teaching of the Council of Trent, a sacrament "is a sign of a sacred reality and the visible expression of invisible grace" (cf. *DS* 1639). Without a doubt, this definition can only refer to the Church in an analogical sense.

However, it should be noted that this definition does not suffice to express what the Church is. She is a sign, but not only a sign; in herself she is also the fruit of redemption. The sacraments are means of sanctification; the Church, instead, is the assembly of the persons sanctified; thus, she constitutes the purpose of the saving action (cf. Eph 5:25-27).

With these clarifications, the term "sacrament" can be applied to the Church. The Church is indeed the sign of the salvation accomplished by Christ and meant for all human beings through the work of the Holy Spirit. The sign is visible; the Church, as the community of God's people, has a visible character. The sign is also efficacious, inasmuch as belonging to the Church obtains for people union with Christ and all the graces necessary for salvation.

When sacraments are spoken of as efficacious signs of the saving grace instituted by Christ, the analogy of sacramentality in relation to the Church remains valid for the organic connection between the Church and the sacraments. But one must keep in mind that it is not a matter of a substantial identity. One cannot attribute the divine institution and effectiveness of the seven sacraments to the whole of the Church's functions and ministries. Moreover, there is a substantial presence of Christ in the Eucharist, and certainly that cannot be extended to the whole Church. We will postpone to another time a more complete explanation of these differences. But we can conclude this catechesis with the joyous observation that the organic connection between the Church as sacrament and the individual sacraments is especially close and essential in regard to the Eucharist. Actually, inasmuch as the Church (as sacrament) celebrates the Eucharist, the Eucharist realizes the Church and makes her present. The Church is expressed in the Eucharist, and the Eucharist makes the Church. Especially in the Eucharist the Church is and becomes ever more fully the sacrament "of communion with God" (cf. *LG* 1).

General audience of November 27, 1991

Mary's "Yes" Is the Start of the New Covenant

The Old Testament already spoke of a type of spousal relationship between God and his people Israel. We read in the third part of Isaiah's prophecy: "For he who has become your husband is your Maker; his name is the Lord of hosts; your redeemer is the Holy One of Israel, called God of all the earth" (Is 54:5). Our catechesis on the Church as "sacrament of communion with God" *(mysterium ecclesiae,* cf. *LG* 1), takes us back to the ancient reality of God's covenant with Israel, the Chosen People, which was the preparation for the basic mystery of the Church, a prolongation of the very mystery of the Incarnation. We saw this in the preceding catecheses. Today we wish to highlight the fact that God's covenant with Israel was presented by the prophets as a marital bond. This particular aspect of God's relationship with his people also has value as a symbol and a preparation for the nuptial bond between Christ and the Church, the new people of God, the new Israel established by Christ through the sacrifice of the cross.

In the Old Testament, in addition to the text of Isaiah quoted above, we find other texts, especially in the books of Hosea, Jeremiah and Ezekiel, in which God's covenant with Israel is interpreted by analogy with the matrimonial pact between spouses. On the strength of this comparison, these

prophets accuse the Chosen People of being like an unfaithful
and adulterous wife. Hosea says: "Protest against your mother,
protest! For she is not my wife, and I am not her husband"
(Hos 2:4). Jeremiah says the same: "But like a woman faithless
to her lover, even so have you been faithless to me, O house of
Israel" (Jer 3:20). Again, looking at Israel's infidelity to the
law of the covenant, especially her repeated sins of idolatry,
Jeremiah adds the rebuke: "But you have sinned with many
lovers, and yet you would return to me, says the Lord" (Jer
3:1). Ezekiel says: "But you were captivated by your own
beauty; you used your renown to make yourself a harlot, and
you lavished your harlotry on every passerby" (Ez 16:15; cf.
16:29, 32).

However, it must be said that the words of the prophets
do not contain an absolute and definitive rejection of the adulterous wife, but rather an invitation to conversion and a
promise to take back the repentant spouse. Hosea says: "I will
espouse you to me forever; I will espouse you in right and in
justice, in love and in mercy; I will espouse you in fidelity, and
you shall know the Lord" (Hos 2:21-22). In analogous terms
Isaiah says: "For a brief moment I abandoned you, but with
great tenderness I will take you back. In an outburst of wrath,
for a moment I hid my face from you, but with enduring love I
take pity on you, says the Lord, your Redeemer" (Is 54:7-8).

These prophetic proclamations go beyond the historical
boundaries of Israel and beyond the ethnic and religious dimension of a people who did not maintain the covenant. They
should be seen in the perspective of a new covenant, pointed
out as something which will come in the future. This can be
seen especially in Jeremiah: "This is the covenant which I will
make with the house of Israel after those days.... I will place
my law within them, and write it upon their hearts; I will be
their God, and they shall be my people" (Jer 31:33). Ezekiel
announces something similar, after promising the exiles that
they would return to their homeland: "I will give them a new

heart and put a new spirit within them; I will remove the stony heart from their bodies, and replace it with a natural heart, so that they will live according to my statutes, and observe and carry out my ordinances; thus they shall be my people and I will be their God" (Ez 11:19-20).

The realization of this promise of a new covenant began with Mary. The annunciation is the first revelation of this beginning. Indeed, at that moment we hear the Virgin of Nazareth respond with the obedience of faith to God's eternal plan for human salvation through the Incarnation of the Word. The Incarnation of God's Son means the fulfillment of the messianic prophecies, as well as the dawning of the Church as the people of the new covenant. Mary is aware of the messianic dimension of the message she receives and of the *yes* she gives in response. The evangelist Luke appears to highlight this dimension with a detailed description of the dialogue between the angel and the Virgin, and then with the formulation of the Magnificat.

Mary's humility appears in the dialogue and in the canticle, but so does the intensity with which she spiritually lived in expectation of the fulfillment of the messianic promise made to Israel. The prophets' words about God's spousal covenant with the Chosen People, which she kept and meditated on in her heart, resound in the same heart during the decisive moments reported by Luke. She herself wanted to be the personal image of that absolutely faithful bride, totally devoted to the divine bridegroom, and therefore she became the beginning of the new Israel (that new people willed by the God of the covenant) in her spousal heart. Both in the dialogue and the canticle, Mary does not use terminology characterized by analogy with a marital relationship, but goes much further. She confirms and strengthens a consecration already in effect, which becomes the abiding condition of her life. She replies to the angel of the annunciation: "I have no relations with a man" (Lk 1:34), as if to say: I am a virgin devoted to God, and I do not intend to leave my spouse, because I do not think that God wills it—he who is so jealous of Israel, so severe with anyone who betrays him, so persistent in his merciful call to reconciliation!

Mary is well aware of her people's infidelity and she wants personally to be a bride who is faithful to her most beloved divine spouse. The angel announces to her the fulfillment in her of God's new covenant with humanity in an unexpected dimension, as a virginal motherhood through the work of the Holy Spirit. "The Holy Spirit will come upon you, and the power of the Most High will overshadow you" (Lk 1:35). By the work of the Holy Spirit the Virgin of Nazareth becomes the mother of God's Son in a virginal way. The mystery of the Incarnation encompasses this motherhood of Mary, divinely accomplished by the power of the Holy Spirit. This, then, is the beginning of the new covenant, in which Christ, as the divine bridegroom, joins humanity to himself and calls it to be his Church, as the universal people of the new covenant.

At the moment of the Incarnation, Mary as Virgin-Mother becomes a figure of the Church in both her virginal and maternal character. Vatican II explains: "For in the mystery of the Church, which is itself rightly called mother and virgin, the Blessed Virgin stands out in eminent and singular fashion as exemplar both of virgin and mother" *(LG 63)*. With good reason the messenger sent by God greets Mary from the start with the word *chaïré* ("rejoice"). This greeting echoes so many prophetic words of the Old Testament: "Rejoice heartily, O daughter Zion; shout for joy, O daughter Jerusalem! See, your king shall come to you; a just savior is he" (Zech 9:9). "Be glad and exult with all your heart, O daughter Jerusalem!... The Lord is in your midst.... Fear not, O Zion...a mighty savior...will renew you in his love; he will sing joyfully because of you" (Zep 3:14-17). "Fear not, O land! Exult and rejoice! For the Lord has done great things.... O children of Zion, exult and rejoice in the Lord your God!" (Joel 2:21, 23).

Mary and the Church are thus the fulfillment of these prophecies, on the threshold of the New Testament. One can even say that on this threshold the Church is found in Mary, and Mary is in the Church and like the Church. It is one of those wondrous works of God which are the object of our faith.

General audience of December 4, 1991

Jesus Is the Bridegroom of His People

"For he who has become your husband is your Maker; his name is the Lord of hosts; your redeemer is the Holy One of Israel" (Is 54:5). Once again we quote these words of Isaiah to recall that the prophets of the Old Testament saw God as the spouse of the Chosen People. Israel was depicted as a bride, often an unfaithful one due to her sins, especially her falling into idolatry. However, the Lord of hosts remained faithful to his Chosen People. He continued to be their Redeemer, the Holy One of Israel.

On the groundwork laid by the prophets, the New Testament presents Jesus Christ as the spouse of the new People of God. He is that "redeemer, the Holy One of Israel" who was foretold and announced from afar; in him the prophecies were fulfilled. Christ is the bridegroom.

The first one to present Jesus in this light was John the Baptist, in his preaching on the banks of the Jordan: "I am not the Messiah," he told his listeners, "but I was sent before him. The one who has the bride is the bridegroom; the best man, who stands and listens for him, rejoices greatly at the bridegroom's voice" (Jn 3:28-29). As is apparent, the spousal tradition of the Old Testament is reflected in the awareness that this austere messenger of the Lord had of his mission in relationship to Christ's identity. He knew who he was and "what had been given him from heaven." His entire service among the people was directed to the bridegroom who was to come. John presented himself as "the best man," and confessed that his greatest joy was to have been allowed to hear Jesus' voice. Because of this joy he was ready to accept his own "decrease," that is, to make room for him who was to be revealed, who was greater than he, and for whom he was ready to give his life. He knew that according to the divine plan of salvation the bridegroom, the Holy One of Israel, must "increase." "He must increase; I must decrease" (Jn 3:30).

Therefore, Jesus of Nazareth was brought into the midst of his people as the bridegroom who had been announced by the prophets. He himself confirmed this when, in answer to the question raised by John's disciples, "Why do...your disciples not fast" (Mk 2:18), he said: "Can the wedding guests fast while the bridegroom is with them? As long as they have the bridegroom with them they cannot fast. But the days will come when the bridegroom is taken away from them, and then they will fast" (Mk 2:19-20). With this answer Jesus made it clear that the prophetic message about God the Spouse, about the "Redeemer, the Holy One of Israel," was fulfilled in himself. He revealed his awareness of being the bridegroom among his disciples, from whom at the end, however, "the bridegroom will be taken away." He was aware of both his messiahship and the cross on which he accomplished his sacrifice in obedience to the Father, as foretold by the prophets (cf. Is 42:1-9; 49:1-7; 50:4-11; 52:13-53, 12).

What appears from John's declaration on the banks of the Jordan and from Jesus' answer to the question raised by the Baptist's disciples, namely, that the bridegroom announced by the prophets had already come, is also confirmed by the parables. In them the spousal motif is indirect, but obvious enough. Jesus said, "The kingdom of heaven may be likened to a king who gave a wedding feast for his son" (Mt 22:2).

Everything in the parable makes it clear that Jesus is speaking of himself, but he does so in the third person, which is a feature of his discourse in the parables. In the context of the parable about the king who invites guests to his son's wedding feast, Jesus used the analogy of a wedding banquet to highlight the truth about the kingdom of God, which he himself brings to the world, and God's invitation to the bridegroom's feast. This involves the acceptance of Christ's message in communion with the new people whom the parable presents as being called to a wedding. But he also added a reference to the refusals made to the invitation, which Jesus observed in the situation of many of his listeners. He also added that all those invited in his time and at all times must have an attitude worthy of the calling received, symbolized by the "wedding garment" which is to be worn by those who intend to participate in the banquet. Whoever does not wear it is sent away by the king, that is, by God the Father who invites us to his Son's feast in the Church.

It seems that in Israel's world on the occasion of great banquets the clothes to be worn were made available to the guests in the banquet hall. This fact makes the meaning of that detail in Jesus' parable even clearer: the responsibility not only of the person who rejects the invitation, but also of those who claim to attend without fulfilling the necessary conditions for being worthy of the banquet. This is the case of those who maintain and profess that they are followers of Christ and members of the Church, without obtaining the "wedding garment" of grace, which engenders a living faith, hope and love. It is true that this "garment"—more internal than external—is given by God himself, the author of grace and of every good which the soul possesses. But the parable emphasizes the responsibility that every guest has, whatever his or her origin, regarding the *yes* which must be given to the Lord who calls and regarding the acceptance of his law, the total response to the demands of the Christian vocation and an ever greater participation in the life of the Church.

In the parable of the ten virgins "who took their lamps and went out to meet the bridegroom" (Mt 25:1), Jesus also used the wedding analogy to explain his idea of the kingdom of God and the Church in which this kingdom is made concrete. Here we also find his insistence on the need for that interior disposition without which one cannot attend the wedding banquet. In this parable Jesus calls us to be ready, vigilant and fervently committed in waiting for the bridegroom. Only five of the ten virgins made the effort to see that their lamps would be burning when the bridegroom arrived. The other careless ones lacked oil. "The bridegroom came and those who were ready went into the wedding feast with him. Then the door was locked" (Mt 25:10). This is a discreet but unmistakable reference to the lot of those who lack the interior disposition needed for meeting God, and thus lack fervor and perseverance in waiting. It refers to the threat of seeing the door closed in one's face. Once again we find an appeal being made to one's sense of responsibility concerning the Christian vocation.

Turning now from the parable to the Gospel account of the facts, we should recall the wedding feast at Cana in Galilee, where Jesus was invited with the disciples (cf. Jn 2:1-11). According to John the evangelist, Jesus performed his first miracle there, the first sign proving his messianic mission. One may interpret his action as an indirect way of making it understood that the bridegroom announced by the prophets was present among his people, Israel. The entire setting of the wedding ceremony takes on special meaning in this case. In particular, we note that Jesus works his first "sign" at his Mother's request. It is pleasant here to recall what we said in the preceding catechesis: Mary is the beginning and the image of the Church as bride of the new covenant.

We will conclude by rereading those final words of John's text: "Jesus did this as the beginning of his signs in Cana in Galilee and so revealed his glory, and his disciples began to believe in him" (Jn 2:11). The words "did this" state that the bridegroom was already at work. At his side the figure of the bride of the new covenant was already beginning to take shape: the Church, present in Mary and those disciples at the wedding feast.

General audience of December 11, 1991

Christ Loves His Bride, the Church

St. Paul writes to the Ephesians: "Christ loved the Church and handed himself over for her" (Eph 5:25). As you can see, the analogy of married love, which was inherited from the prophets of the old covenant, reappeared in the preaching of John the Baptist. It was taken up again by Jesus and passed into the Gospels, and was proposed again by the Apostle Paul. The Baptist and the Gospels present Christ as the bridegroom; we saw this in the preceding catechesis. He is the bridegroom of the new People of God, which is the Church. From the lips of Jesus and his precursor, the analogy received from the old covenant was used to announce that the time had come for its real fulfillment. The paschal events gave it its full significance. Precisely in reference to these events, the Apostle can write in Ephesians, "Christ loved the Church and handed himself over for her." These words echo the prophets, who used this analogy in the old covenant to speak of the spousal love God had for his chosen people, Israel. There is at least an implicit reference to the application Jesus makes of it in presenting himself as this bridegroom, as it must have been said by the apostles to the first communities where the Gospels arose. There is a deepening of the saving dimension of Christ Jesus' love, which is both spousal and redemptive: "Christ handed himself over for the Church," the Apostle recalls.

This teaching is even more evident if one considers that Ephesians directly relates Christ's spousal love for the Church to the sacrament which unites man and woman in marriage, thereby consecrating their love. We read: "Husbands, love your wives, even as Christ loved the Church and handed himself over for her to sanctify her, cleansing her by the bath of water with the word [a reference to Baptism], that he might present to himself the Church in splendor, without spot or wrinkle or any such thing, that she might be holy and without blemish" (Eph 5:25-27). A little farther on in the letter the Apostle himself emphasizes the great mystery of this marital union, because he is speaking "in reference to Christ and the Church" (Eph 5:32). The essential meaning of his discourse is that the spousal love of the Redeemer for his Church is reflected in Christian marriage and married love: a redemptive love, full of saving power, at work in the mystery of grace by which Christ shares new life with the members of his body.

This is why the Apostle, in developing his discourse, refers to the passage of Genesis which speaks of the union of man and woman: "The two shall become one flesh" (Eph 5:31; Gen 2:24). Taking his inspiration from this statement, the Apostle writes: "So husbands should love their wives as their own bodies. He who loves his wife loves himself. For no one hates his own flesh but rather nourishes and cherishes it, even as Christ does the Church" (Eph 5:28-29).

It can be said that in Paul's thought married love comes under a law of equality, which man and woman fulfill in Jesus Christ (cf. 1 Cor 7:4). However, when the Apostle observes: "The husband is head of his wife just as Christ is head of the Church, he himself the Savior of the body" (Eph 5:23), the equality, the interhuman parity, is surpassed, because theirs is an order within love. The husband's love for his wife is a participation in Christ's love for the Church. Now Christ, the

Church's bridegroom, was the first to love, because he accomplished salvation (cf. Rom 5:6; 1 Jn 4:19). Therefore, he is also head of the Church, his body, which he saves, nourishes and cherishes with unspeakable love.

This relationship between head and body does not cancel marital reciprocity, but rather strengthens it. It is precisely the Redeemer's precedence over the redeemed (and so, over the Church) which makes this marital reciprocity possible, in the power of the grace which Christ himself bestows. This is the essence of the mystery of the Church as the bride of Christ the Redeemer, a truth repeatedly witnessed and taught by St. Paul.

The Apostle is not a detached and disinterested witness, speaking or writing as if he were a scholar or notary. In his letters he appears as one profoundly involved in the duty of inculcating this truth. As he writes to the Corinthians: "For I am jealous of you with the jealousy of God, since I betrothed you to one husband to present you as a chaste virgin to Christ" (2 Cor 11:2). In this text Paul presents himself as the best man, whose burning concern is to encourage the bride's complete faithfulness to the marriage union. In fact, he continues: "But I am afraid that, as the serpent deceived Eve by his cunning, your thoughts may be corrupted from a sincere and pure commitment to Christ" (2 Cor 11:3). This is the Apostle's jealousy!

In First Corinthians we also read the same truth found in Ephesians and Second Corinthians, which were cited above. The Apostle writes: "Do you not know that your bodies are members of Christ? Shall I then take Christ's members and make them members of a prostitute? Of course not!" (1 Cor 6:15). Here too it is easy almost to hear an echo of the old covenant prophets who accused the people of prostitution, especially for their lapses into idolatry. Unlike the prophets, who spoke of prostitution metaphorically to stigmatize any serious sin of infidelity to the law of God, Paul is really speaking of sexual relations with prostitutes and declares them absolutely incompatible with being a Christian. It is unthinkable to take the members of Christ and make them members of a prostitute. Paul then clarifies an important point. A man's relationship with a prostitute occurs merely on the level of the flesh and thus calls for a divorce between flesh and spirit. But Christ's union with the Church occurs on the level of the spirit and so corresponds to all the demands of genuine love. The Apostle writes: "Do you not know that anyone who joins himself to a prostitute becomes one body with her? For 'the two,' it says, 'will become one flesh.' But whoever is joined to the Lord becomes one spirit with him" (1 Cor 6:16-17). The analogy the prophets used so passionately to condemn the profanation and betrayal of Israel's marital love for her God, enables the Apostle here to call attention to the union with Christ which is the essence of the new covenant, and to clarify its demands for Christian behavior: "Whoever is joined to the Lord becomes one spirit with him."

The "experience" of Christ's Passover and the "experience" of Pentecost were necessary to give this meaning to the married love analogy inherited from the prophets. Paul was aware of this double experience of the early community, which had received from the disciples not only instruction, but also a living sharing in that mystery. He relived and deepened this experience, and now in turn, becomes its apostle to the faithful of Corinth, Ephesus, and all the churches to which he writes. It was a sublime translation of his experience of the marital relationship of Christ and the Church: "Do you not know that your body is a temple of the Holy Spirit within you, whom you have from God, and that you are not your own?" (1 Cor 6:19).

We conclude with this observation of faith, which makes us want this beautiful experience: the Church is the bride of Christ. She belongs to him as a bride, in virtue of the Holy Spirit, who, drawing on "the fountain of salvation" (Is 12:3), sanctifies the Church and allows her to respond to love with love.

General audience of December 18, 1991

The Spirit and the Bride Say "Come"

Paul the Apostle has told us that "Christ loved the Church and handed himself over for her" (Eph 5:25). This basic truth of Pauline ecclesiology regarding the mystery of the Redeemer's spousal love for his Church is taken up again and confirmed in the Book of Revelation, where John speaks about the bride of the Lamb: "Come here, I will show you the bride, the wife of the Lamb" (Rev 21:9). The author had already described the preparations: "For the wedding day of the Lamb has come, his bride has made herself ready. She was allowed to wear a bright, clean linen garment. (The linen represents the righteous deeds of the holy ones).... Blessed are those who have been called to the wedding feast of the Lamb" (Rev 19:7-9). Thus, the image of the wedding and the wedding banquet returns in this eschatological book in which the Church is considered in her heavenly state. But she is the same Church which Jesus spoke of when he presented himself as her spouse; the same Church which St. Paul spoke of when he recalled the sacrifice that Christ, her spouse, made for her; and the same Church which John now speaks of as the betrothed for whom Christ the Lamb offers himself. Earth and heaven, time and eternity, are united in this transcendent vision of the relationship between Christ and the Church.

The author of Revelation above all describes the Church-
bride in her descending phase, as a gift from on high. The bride
of the Lamb (cf. Rev 21:9) is identified as "the holy city
Jerusalem coming down out of heaven from God, gleaming
with the splendor of God" (Rev 21:10-11), as the "new
Jerusalem...prepared as a bride adorned for her husband" (Rev
21:2). If in Ephesians Paul presents Christ as the Redeemer
who bestows his gifts on the Church-bride, in Revelation John
describes the same Church-bride, the bride of the Lamb, as
receiving from him, as from her source, holiness and participation in God's glory. In Revelation, then, the descending aspect
of the Church's mystery predominates. The gift from on high
is expressed not only in her origin at Easter and Pentecost, but
also throughout her earthly pilgrimage in the state of faith.
Israel, the people of the old covenant, was also on pilgrimage.
Her principal sin was betraying that faith through infidelity to
God who chose her and loved her as a bride. For the Church,
the new People of God, the duty of fidelity is even stronger and
will perdure until the last day. As we read in Vatican II: "She
herself [the Church] is a virgin, who keeps the faith given to
her by her spouse whole and entire. Imitating the mother of her
Lord, and by the power of the Holy Spirit, she keeps with
virginal purity an entire faith, a firm hope and a sincere charity" (LG 64). Faith is the basic presupposition of the spousal
love with which the Church continues the pilgrimage begun by
the Virgin Mary.

Peter the Apostle, who in the neighborhood of Caesarea
Philippi professed a faith full of love for Christ, wrote in the
first letter to his disciples: "Although you have not seen him
[Christ] you love him; even though you do not see him now
you believe in him" (1 Pet 1:8). According to the Apostle
Peter, faith in Christ means not only accepting his truth, but
also being related to his Person in receptivity and love. In this
sense, fidelity comes from faith, and faithfulness is the proof
of love. This love is inspired by Christ and through him

reaches God, in order to love him "with all your heart, and with all your soul, and with all your strength," as the first and greatest commandment of the old law says (cf. Dt 6:4-5). Jesus himself confirmed and strengthened this commandment (cf., e.g., Mk 12:28-30).

In virtue of this love which she learned from Christ and the apostles, the Church is the bride "who keeps the faith given to her by her spouse whole and entire" *(LG* 64). Led by the Holy Spirit and moved by the power she receives from him, the Church cannot be separated from her spouse. She cannot become "non-faithful." Jesus Christ himself, in giving the Church his Spirit, established an indissoluble bond. We cannot fail to note here, with the Council, that this image of the Church, indissolubly united to Christ her spouse, finds particular expression in those who are bound to him by vows, such as religious and consecrated persons in general. For this reason they have such an essential place in the Church's life (cf. *LG* 44).

However, the Church is a society which also includes sinners. The Council is well aware of this fact and says: "The Church, embracing in its bosom sinners, at the same time holy and always in need of being purified, always follows the way of penance and renewal" *(LG* 8). Since the Church seeks to live in the truth, she certainly lives in the truth of the redemption wrought by Christ, and she also lives while confessing the human sinfulness of her children. In the midst of the trials and tribulations of her historical journey, the Church "is strengthened by the power of God's grace, which was promised to her by the Lord, so that in the weakness of the flesh she may not waver from perfect fidelity, but remain a bride worthy of her Lord, and moved by the Holy Spirit may never cease to renew herself, until through the cross she arrives at the light which knows no setting" *(LG* 9). In this way the apocalyptic image of the holy city coming down from heaven is being constantly realized in the Church, as the image of a people on the way.

The Church advances on this way toward an eschatological goal, toward the full realization of her marriage with
Christ described in the Book of Revelation, toward the final
stage of her history. As we read in *Lumen Gentium:* "While on
earth it journeys in a foreign land away from the Lord (cf. 2
Cor 5:6), [the Church] is like an exile. It seeks and experiences
those things which are above, where Christ is seated at the
right hand of God, where the life of the Church is hidden
with Christ in God until it appears in glory with its spouse (cf.
Col 3:1-4)" *(LG* 6).

The Church's earthly pilgrimage is thus a journey filled
with hope and is expressed succinctly in those words of the
Book of Revelation: "The Spirit and the bride say, 'Come!'"
(Rev 22:17). This text appears to be a confirmation, on the last
page of the New Testament, of the Church's spousal character
by reason of her relationship with Christ.

In this light we understand better what the Council says:
"The Church, 'like a stranger in a foreign land, presses forward
amid the persecutions of the world and the consolations of
God' (cf. St. Augustine, *De Civitate Dei,* XVIII, 51, 2: *PL* 41,
614), announcing the cross and death of the Lord until he
comes (cf. 1 Cor 11:26). By the power of the risen Lord it is
given strength that it might, in patience and in love, overcome
its sorrows and its challenges, both within itself and from
without, and that it might reveal to the world, faithfully though
darkly, the mystery of its Lord until, in the end, it will be
manifested in full light" *(LG* 8).

In this sense, "The Spirit and the bride say, 'Come!'"

General audience of January 8, 1992

The Church Is a *Communio* of Love

We begin this catechesis with a beautiful text from Ephesians, which says: "Blessed be the God and Father of our Lord Jesus Christ...as he chose us in him before the foundation of the world.... In love he destined us for adoption to himself through Jesus Christ, in accord with the favor of his will...to sum up all things in Christ, in heaven and on earth" (Eph 1:3-10). With a bird's-eye view and a profound sense of the Church's mystery, St. Paul is lifted up in contemplating God's eternal plan of reuniting everything in Christ the head. Men and women, eternally chosen by the Father in his beloved Son, find in Christ the way to reach their goal as adopted children. They are united to him by becoming his body. Through him they return to the Father as one whole, with everything on earth and in heaven.

This divine plan was historically realized when Jesus instituted the Church, which he first announced (cf. Mt 16:18), and then established by the sacrifice of his blood and the mandate conferred on the apostles to shepherd his flock. It is a historical fact as well as a mystery of communion in Christ, which the Apostle is not satisfied merely to contemplate. In its presence he feels compelled to express in a song of blessing the truth he has contemplated: "Blessed be the God and Father of our Lord Jesus Christ."

To accomplish this communion of human beings in Christ, which was eternally willed by God, the commandment which Jesus himself called "my commandment" has an essential importance (Jn 15:12). He called it "a new commandment." "I give you a new commandment: love one another. As I have loved you, so you also should love one another" (Jn 13:34). "This is my commandment: love one another as I have loved you" (Jn 15:12).

The commandment to love God above all things and to love one's neighbor as one's self is rooted in the Old Testament. But Jesus summarized it, formulated it in clear-cut terms and gave it a new meaning as the sign that his followers belong to him. "This is how all will know that you are my disciples, if you have love for one another" (Jn 13:35). Christ himself is the living model and constitutes the measure of the love he speaks of in his commandment: "as I have loved you," he says. He even presented himself as the source of that love, as "the vine" which bears the fruit of this love in his disciples, who are his branches. "I am the vine, you are the branches. Whoever remains in me and I in him will bear much fruit because without me you can do nothing" (Jn 15:5). So he exhorted them: "Remain in my love" (Jn 15:9). The community of disciples, rooted in that love with which Christ himself loved them, is the Church, the body of Christ, the one vine of which we all are the branches. It is the Church as a communion, the Church as a community of love, the Church as a mystery of love.

The members of this community love Christ and in him they love one another. It is a love with which Jesus himself loves them, and it is linked to the source of the God-Man's love—the communion of the Trinity. Its whole nature and its supernatural character derive from this communion and tend toward it as its definitive fulfillment. This mystery of trinitarian, Christological and ecclesial communion is revealed in John's text, which tells of the Redeemer's priestly prayer at the Last Supper. That evening Jesus said to the Father: "I pray not only for them, but also for those who will believe in me through their word, so that they may all be one, as you, Father, are in me and I in you, that they also may be one in us, that the world may believe that you sent me" (Jn 17:20-21). "I in them and you in me, that they may be brought to perfection as one, that the world may know that you sent me, and that you loved them even as you loved me" (Jn 17:23).

In his final prayer Jesus drew the complete picture of the interpersonal ecclesial relations which originate in him and in the Trinity. He proposed to his disciples, and to us all, the supreme model of that *communio* which the Church is called to be by reason of her divine origin: it is he himself in his intimate communion with the Father in the life of the Trinity. In his love for us Jesus showed the extent of that commandment which he left his disciples, as he said on another occasion: "So be perfect, just as your heavenly Father is perfect" (Mt 5:48). He said it during the Sermon on the Mount, when he urged them to love their enemies: "Love your enemies, and pray for those who persecute you, that you may be children of your heavenly Father, for he makes his sun rise on the bad and the good, and causes rain to fall on the just and the unjust" (Mt 5:44-45). Many other times, especially during his passion, Jesus confirmed that this perfect love of the Father was also his love, the love with which he himself loved his own until the end.

This love which Jesus taught his followers, as a likeness of the same love he has, is clearly related in the priestly prayer to the model of the Trinity. "That they also may be one in us," Jesus said, "that the love with which you loved me may be in them and I in them" (Jn 17:26). He emphasized that this is the love with which "You [O Father] loved me before the foundation of the world" (Jn 17:24).

It is precisely this love, on which the Church is founded and built up as a *communio* of believers in Christ, which is the condition of his saving mission. Jesus prayed, "May they be one as we are one, so that the world may know that you sent me" (Jn 17:23). This is the essence of the Church's apostolate: to spread and to make acceptable and believable the truth of Christ's and God's love, which is witnessed to, made visible and practiced by the Church. The Eucharist is the sacramental expression of this love. In a certain sense, in the Eucharist the Church is continually reborn and renewed as that *communio* which Christ brought to the world by fulfilling the Father's eternal plan (cf. Eph 1:3-10). Especially in the Eucharist and through the Eucharist, the Church contains in herself the seed of a truly universal and eternal communion, the definitive union in Christ of everything in heaven and on earth, as Paul told us (cf. Eph 1:10).

General audience of January 15, 1992

The Church: A *Communio* of Prayer

We read in the Acts of the Apostles that after the risen Lord's ascension into heaven, the disciples returned to Jerusalem. "When they entered the city they went to the upper room where they were staying, Peter and John and James and Andrew, Philip and Thomas, Bartholomew and Matthew, James son of Alphaeus, Simon the Zealot, and Judas son of James. All these devoted themselves with one accord to prayer, together with some women, and Mary the Mother of Jesus, and his brothers" (Acts 1:12-14). This is the first image of that community, the *communio ecclesialis,* which we see described in a detailed way in the Acts of the Apostles.

It was a community gathered by the will of Jesus himself, who, at the time he was returning to the Father, ordered his disciples to remain united in expectation of the other event he had announced: "I am sending the promise of my Father upon you. But stay in the city until you are clothed with power from on high" (Lk 24:49).

The evangelist Luke, who was also the author of the Acts of the Apostles, introduces us to that first community of the Church in Jerusalem by reminding us of Jesus' own exhortation: "Eating together with them, he enjoined them not to depart from Jerusalem, but to wait for 'the promise of the

Father about which you have heard me speak; for John baptized with water, but in a few days you will be baptized with the Holy Spirit'" (Acts 1:4).

These texts show that this first Church community, which was to be revealed in broad daylight on the day of Pentecost by the coming of the Holy Spirit, results from an order of Jesus himself, who gave the Church her own "form," so to speak. This last text reveals a detail which merits attention: Jesus made this arrangement while "eating together with them" (Acts 1:4). When he would return to the Father, the Eucharist would become for all time the expression of the Church's communion, in which Christ is sacramentally present. At this meal in Jerusalem Jesus was visibly present as the risen Lord, who celebrated with his friends the feast of the bridegroom who had come back among them for awhile.

After Christ's ascension, the little community continued its life. We read especially: "All these [the apostles] devoted themselves with one accord to prayer, together with some women, and Mary the mother of Jesus, and his brothers" (Acts 1:14). The first image of the Church is that of a community which is devoted to prayer. All were praying for the gift of the Holy Spirit who had been promised them by Christ even before his passion, and again, before his ascension into heaven.

Prayer—prayer in common—is the basic feature of that "communion" at the time when the Church began, and so it will always be. This is evidenced in every century—and today as well—by prayer in common, especially liturgical prayer, in our churches, religious communities and, may God increasingly grant us this grace, in Christian families.

The author of the Acts of the Apostles accentuates their being devoted to prayer, a constant and, one would say, regular prayer, well ordered and attended by the community. This is another feature of the ecclesial community, the heir to that beginning which remains an example for all generations to come.

Luke emphasizes the "unanimity" *(homothymadon)* of this prayer. This fact highlights the communal meaning of the prayer. The prayer of the early community—as would always be the case in the Church—expresses and serves this spiritual "communion," and at the same time it creates, deepens and strengthens it. In this communion of prayer the differences and divisions which come from other material and spiritual factors are overcome. Prayer produces the community's spiritual unity.

Luke also emphasizes the fact that the apostles devoted themselves with one accord "together with some women, and Mary the mother of Jesus, and his brothers." In this case, cousins related to Jesus are called brothers and are mentioned in the Gospels at certain moments in Jesus' life. The Gospels also speak of the presence and active participation of quite a few women in the Messiah's work of evangelization. Luke himself also attests in his Gospel: "Accompanying him [Jesus] were the Twelve and some women who had been cured of evil spirits and infirmities, Mary, called Magdalene, from whom seven demons had gone out, Joanna, the wife of Herod's steward Chuza, Susanna, and many others who provided for them out of their resources" (Lk 8:2-3). In Acts, Luke also describes how the situation in the Gospel continued at the beginning of the ecclesial community. These generous women gathered in prayer with the apostles. On the day of Pentecost they were to receive the Holy Spirit along with them. At that time there was already a lively experience of ecclesial community, in regard to which the Apostle Paul would say, "There is neither male and female; for you are all one in Christ Jesus" (Gal 3:28). At that time the Church was already being revealed as the seed of the new humanity which was called in its entirety to communion with Christ.

Luke wants us to note the presence of Mary, the mother of Jesus, in that first community (cf. Acts 1:14). We know that Mary did not participate directly in Jesus' public activity.

However, John's Gospel shows she was present at two decisive moments: at Cana in Galilee, when the "beginning of the messianic signs" took place through her intervention, and at Calvary. Luke in his Gospel highlights Mary's importance, especially at the annunciation, visitation, birth, presentation in the Temple and during Jesus' hidden life in Nazareth. In Acts, Luke teaches us how Mary, having given human life to the son of God, is now in turn present at the Church's birth: present in prayer, silence, communion and hope-filled waiting.

Gathering up the expressions of the 2000-year tradition which began with Luke and John, Vatican II, in the last chapter of the *Dogmatic Constitution on the Church,* highlighted the special importance of Christ's mother in the economy of salvation which takes concrete form in the Church. She is the figure of the Church *(typus ecclesiae),* principally in regard to union with Christ. This union is the source of the *communio ecclesialis,* as we said in the previous catechesis. Therefore, Mary is with her Son at the origin of this communion.

The presence of Christ's Mother in the apostolic community on the day of Pentecost was prepared for in a special way at the foot of the cross on Golgotha, where Jesus gave his life "to gather into one the dispersed children of God" (Jn 11:52). On the day of Pentecost this "gathering into one of the dispersed children of God" started occurring through the action of the Holy Spirit. Mary—whom Jesus gave as mother to the disciple whom he loved and through him to the apostolic community of the whole Church—was present in "the upper room where they were staying" (Acts 1:13), to obtain and serve the strengthening of that *communio* which by Christ's will his Church was meant to be.

This is valid for all time, for the present moment as well, when we are especially aware of the need for recourse to her who is the type and mother of the Church's unity. The Council urges us to this in a text which summarizes Christian doctrine and tradition, and with which we will conclude this catechesis.

We read: "The entire body of the faithful pours forth urgent supplications to the Mother of God and of men that she, who aided the beginnings of the Church by her prayers, may now, exalted as she is above all the angels and saints, intercede before her Son in the fellowship of all the saints, until all the families of people, whether they are honored with the title of Christian or whether they still do not know the Savior, may be happily gathered together in peace and harmony into one People of God, for the glory of the Most Holy and Undivided Trinity" *(LG* 69).

General audience of January 29, 1992

The Church Lives
in the Mystery of *Communio*

Before Pentecost we already find the first outline of the community which the Church was to become. The *communio ecclesialis* was formed according to the exhortations received directly from Jesus before his ascension into heaven in expectation of the Paraclete's coming. This community already possessed the basic elements which would be further strengthened and specified after the coming of the Holy Spirit. This is what we read in the Acts of the Apostles: "They devoted themselves to the teaching of the apostles and to the communal life, to the breaking of the bread and to the prayers" (Acts 2:42); and in another place: "The community of believers was of one heart and mind" (Acts 4:32). These final words express most incisively, perhaps because most concretely, the content of *koinonia,* or ecclesial communion. The teaching of the apostles, the common prayer—also in the temple of Jerusalem (cf. Acts 2:46)—contributed to that interior oneness of Christ's disciples—"one heart and mind."

To achieve this unity a particularly important element was prayer, the soul of communion, especially at difficult times. So we read that Peter and John, after being set free by the Sanhedrin, "...went back to their own people and reported what the chief priests and elders had told them. When they heard it, they raised their voices to God with one accord and said, 'Sovereign Lord, maker of heaven and earth and the sea and all that is in them...'" (Acts 4:23-24). "As they prayed, the place where they were gathered shook, and they were all filled with the Holy Spirit and continued to speak the word of God with boldness" (Acts 4:31). The Consoler immediately answered the apostolic community's prayer. It was almost a constant fulfillment of Pentecost.

Again we read: "Every day they devoted themselves to meeting together in the Temple area and to breaking bread in their homes. They ate their meals with exultation and sincerity of heart" (Acts 2:46). Though at the time their place of prayer was still the Temple in Jerusalem, they also celebrated the Eucharist "in their homes," joining it to a joyful meal in common.

This sense of communion was so intense that it spurred them to use each one's material possessions to serve the needs of all. "No one claimed that any of his possessions was his own, but they had everything in common." This does not mean that they made a principle of rejecting personal (private) property; it merely indicates a great fraternal sensitivity to the needs of others, as is proved by the words of Peter in the incident with Ananias and Sapphira (cf. Acts 5:4).

The clear conclusion we can draw from Acts and from other New Testament sources is that the early Church was a community which led its members to share with each other the goods they had available, especially for the benefit of the poorest.

This was even more the case with the treasury of truth they received and possessed. Here it is a question of spiritual goods which are to be shared—communicated, spread and preached—as the apostles taught by the witness of their word and example: "It is impossible for us not to speak about what we have seen and heard" (Acts 4:20). Therefore, they spoke and the Lord confirmed their witness. "Many signs and won-

ders were done among the people at the hands of the apostles"
(Acts 5:12).

The Apostle expressed this goal and endeavor of the
apostles by declaring in his first letter: "What we have seen
and heard we proclaim now to you, so that you too may have
fellowship with us; for our fellowship is with the Father and
with his Son, Jesus Christ" (1 Jn 1:3). This text enables us to
understand the awareness that the apostles (and the early community formed by them) had of the trinitarian communion
which gave the Church her impulse for evangelizing, and then
aided the further development of the community (the *communio ecclesialis*).

One finds Christ at the center of this communion and the
communion which it opens up. In fact, John writes: "What was
from the beginning, what we have heard, what we have seen
with our eyes, what we looked upon and touched with our
hands concerns the Word of life—for the life was made visible; we have seen it and testify to it and proclaim to you the
eternal life that was with the Father and was made visible to
us" (1 Jn 1:1-2). St. Paul, in turn, writes to the Corinthians:
"God is faithful, and by him you were called to fellowship with
his Son, Jesus Christ our Lord" (1 Cor 1:9).

St. John highlights communion with Christ in the truth.
St. Paul emphasizes "sharing in his sufferings," conceived of
and presented as a communion with Christ's Passover, a sharing in the paschal mystery, that is, a redemptive "passing over"
from the sacrifice of the cross to the manifestation of "the
power of his resurrection" (Phil 3:10).

In the early Church—and in every age—communion in
Christ's Passover becomes a source of reciprocal communion:
"If one part [of the community] suffers, all the parts suffer
with it" (1 Cor 12:26). This gives rise to a tendency toward
reciprocal giving, including the giving of temporal goods,
which Paul urges to be done for the poor, as if to realize a
certain compensation in the balance of love between the giving

of the well-off and the receiving of the needy: "Your surplus at the present time should supply their needs, so that their surplus may also supply your needs" (2 Cor 8:14). According to the Apostle, those who give, receive at the same time. This process does not only promote a leveling of society (cf. 2 Cor 8:14-15), but also the building up of the community of the Body-Church, which "joined and held together...receives strength to grow and build itself up in love" (Eph 4:16). Through this exchange the Church is also realized as a *communio.*

Christ in his paschal mystery always remains the source of everything. According to John's text, Jesus himself compared to the pains of childbirth this "passing over" from suffering to joy: "When a woman is in labor, she is in anguish because her hour has arrived; but when she has given birth to a child, she no longer remembers the pain because of her joy that a child has been born into the world" (Jn 16:21). This text can also be related to the pain of Jesus' mother on Calvary, as she who "precedes" and sums up the Church in her own person by "passing over" from the grief of the passion to the joy of the resurrection. Jesus himself applies this metaphor to his disciples and the Church: "So you also are now in anguish. But I will see you again, and your hearts will rejoice and no one will take your joy away from you" (Jn 16:22).

To achieve communion, to nourish the community gathered in Christ, the Holy Spirit continues to intervene so that in the Church there is a "participation in the Spirit" *(koinonia pneumatos),* as St. Paul says (cf. Phil 2:1). Precisely through this "participation in the Spirit," the giving of temporal possessions also enters the realm of mystery and promotes the institution of the Church, increases communion, and results in "growing in every way into him who is the head, Christ" (cf. Eph 4:15).

By him, through him, and in him—Christ—in virtue of the life-giving Spirit, the Church is realized as a body "joined and held together by every supporting ligament, with the proper functioning of each part" (Eph 4:16). From this experience of the first Christians' communion, perceived in all its depth, Paul derived his teaching about the Church as the body of Christ, the head.

General audience of February 5, 1992

The Call to Holiness
Is Essential for the Church

"The Lord said to Moses, 'Speak to the whole Israelite community and tell them: Be holy, for I, the Lord your God, am holy'" (Lev 19:1-2). The call to holiness thus belongs to the very essence of God's covenant with humanity in the Old Testament. "For I am God and not man, the Holy One present among you" (Hos 11:9). God, who in his essence is supreme holiness, the thrice holy (cf. Is 6:3), draws near to human beings, his Chosen People, so that they may share in the radiance of this holiness. From the beginning the call to holiness, and indeed, communion in the holiness of God himself, was written into God's covenant with man: "You shall be to me a kingdom of priests, a holy nation" (Ex 19:6). In this text from Exodus, communion in the holiness of God himself and the priestly nature of the chosen people are connected. It is an early revelation of the holiness of the priesthood, which would be fulfilled definitively in the new covenant, through the blood of Christ, when that "worship in Spirit and truth" would begin which Jesus spoke of in Sychar during his conversation with the Samaritan woman (cf. Jn 4:24).

The Church as a communion in God's holiness, and thus as a "communion of saints," is one of the key ideas in the First Letter of Peter. Jesus Christ is the source of this communion and the consecration of the human person, and all creation derives from his sacrifice. St. Peter writes: "For Christ also suffered for sins once, the righteous for the sake of the unrighteous, that he might lead you to God. Put to death in the flesh, he was brought to life in the Spirit" (1 Pet 3:18). Because of Christ's sacrifice, which in itself contains the power to sanctify the human person and all creation, the Apostle Peter can declare: "You were ransomed...with the precious blood of Christ, as of a spotless unblemished lamb" (1 Pet 1:18-19). In this sense he says: "You are 'a chosen race, a royal priesthood, a holy nation'" (1 Pet 2:9; cf. Ex 19:6). In virtue of Christ's sacrifice we can partake of God's holiness and achieve "communion in holiness."

St. Peter writes: "Christ also suffered for you, leaving you an example, that you should follow in his footsteps" (1 Pet 2:21). Following in the footsteps of Jesus Christ means reliving in ourselves his holy life which we have shared through the sanctifying and consecrating grace we received in Baptism; it means continuing to realize in our own lives the "appeal to God for a clear conscience, through the resurrection of Jesus Christ" (1 Pet 3:21); it means being able, through good works, to give glory to God before the world and especially before non-believers (cf. 1 Pet 2:12; 3:1-2). According to the Apostle Peter, this constitutes the "offering of spiritual sacrifices acceptable to God through Jesus Christ" (1 Pet 2:5). This is what it means to be "built into a spiritual house...like living stones...to be a holy priesthood" (1 Pet 2:5).

The "holy priesthood" is expressed in offering spiritual sacrifices which have their source and perfect model in Christ's own sacrifice. Peter adds: "For it is better to suffer for doing good, if that be the will of God, than for doing evil" (1 Pet 3:17). In this way the Church is realized as a communion in holiness. Because of Jesus and through the work of the Holy Spirit the communion of the new People of God fully responds to God's call: "Be holy, for I, the Lord, your God, am holy."

We also find the same teaching in the letters of St. Paul. He writes to the Romans: "I urge you, therefore, brothers, by the mercies of God, to offer your bodies as a living sacrifice, holy and pleasing to God, your spiritual worship" (Rom 12:1). "Present yourselves to God as raised from the dead to life and the parts of your bodies to God as weapons for righteousness" (Rom 6:13). The passage from death to life, according to the Apostle, is accomplished through the sacrament of Baptism. It is a baptism "into the death" of Christ. In fact, we have been buried "with him through baptism into death, so that, just as Christ was raised from the dead by the glory of the Father, we too might live in newness of life" (Rom 6:3-4).

Just as Peter speaks of "living stones" being "built into a spiritual house," so too Paul uses the image of a building: "You are God's building" (1 Cor 3:9), and then advises, "Do you not know that you are the temple of God, and that the Spirit of God dwells in you?" (1 Cor 3:16). Then he adds, almost as if answering his own question: "For the temple of God, which you are, is holy" (1 Cor 3:17).

The image of the temple calls attention to the participation of Christians in God's holiness, to their "communion" in holiness which is the result of the Holy Spirit's action. The Apostle speaks elsewhere of believers being "sealed with the Holy Spirit" (cf. Eph 1:13). God, who "has anointed us [that is, has confirmed us in Christ], has also put his seal upon us and given the Spirit in our hearts as a first installment" (2 Cor 1:21-22).

According to these texts of the two apostles, communion in God's holiness means the sanctification accomplished in us by the Holy Spirit, in virtue of Christ's sacrifice. This communion is expressed by offering spiritual sacrifice according to Christ's example. In this way it exercises "the holy priesthood." It is served by the apostolic ministry, the purpose of which, St. Paul writes, is "so that the offering up" of the faithful "may be acceptable [to God], sanctified by the Holy

Spirit" (Rom 15:16). Thus the "first installment of the Spirit" in the Church community bears fruit by the ministry of holiness. The communion in holiness is transformed for the faithful into an apostolic commitment to the salvation of all humanity.

The teaching of the Apostles Peter and Paul is repeated in the Book of Revelation. In this book, immediately after the opening greeting of "grace and peace" (Rev 1:4), we read the following acclamation addressed to Christ: "To him who loves us and has freed us from our sins by his blood, who has made us into a kingdom, priests for his God and Father, to him be glory and power forever and ever" (Rev 1:5-6). In this acclamation the Church expresses her grateful love and her rejoicing over the work of sanctification and priestly consecration which Christ has accomplished "with his blood." Another passage makes it clear that this consecration extends to men and women "from every tribe and tongue, people and nation" (Rev 5:9-10). This multitude is later portrayed as those who "stood before the throne [of God] and before the Lamb" (Rev 7:9), and "worship him day and night in his temple" (Rev 7:15).

If Peter's letter shows the communion in God's holiness through Christ as a basic task of the Church on earth, the Book of Revelation gives an eschatological vision of the communion of saints in God. It is the mystery of the heavenly Church, where all the holiness of earth converges, climbing up the path of innocence and repentance. Its point of departure is Baptism, along with the grace it imparts and the character it impresses on the soul, conforming it to the priesthood of Christ crucified and enabling it to share in that priesthood, as St. Thomas Aquinas writes (cf. *Summa Theol.,* III, q. 63, a. 3). In the heavenly Church the communion of holiness will be enlightened with the glory of the risen Christ.

General audience of February 12, 1992

The Church Is a Priestly Community

We saw in the preceding catechesis that, according to the letters of Peter and Paul and the Revelation of John, Christ the Lord, "a high priest taken from among men" (Heb 5:1), made [his new people] "a kingdom of priests for his God and Father" (Rev 1:6; cf. 5:9-10). In this way communion in God's holiness is achieved according to what he required of the old Israel and which is an even greater demand for the new one: "Be holy, for I, the Lord, your God, am holy" (Lev 19:2). The communion in God's holiness is achieved as the fruit of Christ's redemptive sacrifice, as a result of which we come to share in that love which "has been poured out into our hearts through the Holy Spirit that has been given to us" (Rom 5:5). The gift of the sanctifying Spirit realizes in us "a holy priesthood," which according to Peter makes us able "to offer spiritual sacrifices acceptable to God through Jesus Christ" (1 Pet 2:5). Therefore, there is a "holy priesthood." We can recognize in the Church, then, a priestly community in the sense that we are now going to explain.

We read in Vatican II, which cites the First Letter of Peter: "The baptized, by regeneration and the anointing of the Holy Spirit, are consecrated as a spiritual house and a holy priesthood, in order that through all those works which are those of the Christian man they may offer spiritual sacrifices and proclaim the power of him who has called them out of darkness into his marvelous light (cf. 1 Pet 2:4-10)" *(LG* 10).

In this text the Council links the prayer by which Christians glorify God with the sacrifice of themselves, "a living sacrifice, holy and pleasing to God" (cf. Rom 12:1), and with the witness to be given to Christ. Here we see summarized the vocation of all the baptized as a participation in the messianic mission of Christ, who is priest, prophet and king.

The universal participation in the priesthood of Christ, also called the priesthood of the faithful *(sacerdotium universale fidelium),* is considered by the Council in its special relationship with the ministerial priesthood: "Though they differ from one another in essence and not only in degree, the common priesthood of the faithful and the ministerial or hierarchical priesthood are nonetheless interrelated: each of them in its own special way is a participation in the one priesthood of Christ" *(LG* 10). The hierarchical priesthood as an "office" *(officium)* is a particular service, because of which the universal priesthood of the faithful can be realized so that the Church may be the fullness of the "priestly community" according to the measure of Christ's gift. "Those of the faithful who are consecrated by Holy Orders are appointed to feed the Church in Christ's name with the word and the grace of God" *(LG* 11).

The Council emphasizes that the universal priesthood of the faithful and the ministerial (or hierarchical) priesthood are ordered to one another. At the same time it states: "They differ from one another in essence and not only in degree" *(LG* 10). The hierarchical ministerial priesthood is not a "product" of the universal priesthood of the faithful. It does not come from a selection or delegation by the community of believers, but from a special divine call: "No one takes this honor upon himself but only when called by God, just as Aaron was" (Heb 5:4). A Christian obtains this office on the basis of a special sacrament, that of Orders.

According to the Council, "The ministerial priest, by the sacred power he enjoys, teaches and rules the priestly people; acting in the person of Christ, he makes present the Eucharistic sacrifice, and offers it to God in the name of all the people" *(LG* 10).

The Council discusses this point more extensively in the *Decree on the Ministry and Life of Priests:* "The same Lord, however, has established ministers among his faithful to unite them together in one body in which, 'not all the members have the same function' (Rom 12:4). These ministers in the society of the faithful are able by the sacred power of orders to offer sacrifice and to forgive sins, and they perform their priestly office publicly for men in the name of Christ.... Priests, by the anointing of the Holy Spirit, are signed with a special character and are conformed to Christ the Priest in such a way that they can act in the person of Christ the head" *(PO* 2; cf. St. Thomas, *Summa Theol.,* III, q. 63, a. 3). Along with the character they also receive the grace necessary for worthily fulfilling their ministry: "In the measure in which they participate in the office of the apostles, God gives priests a special grace to be ministers of Christ among the people. They perform the sacred duty of preaching the Gospel, so that the offering of the people can be made acceptable and sanctified by the Holy Spirit" *(PO* 2).

As we said, the hierarchical-ministerial priesthood was instituted in the Church to put into operation the resources of the universal priesthood of the faithful. The Council states this at various points and, in particular, when it discusses the gathering of the faithful at the celebration of the Eucharist. We read: "Taking part in the Eucharistic sacrifice, which is the fount and apex of the whole Christian life, they offer the divine victim to God, and offer themselves along with it. Thus both by reason of the offering and through Holy Communion all take part in this liturgical service, not indeed, all in the same way but each in that way which is proper to himself. Strengthened in Holy Communion by the Body of Christ, they then manifest in a concrete way that unity of the People of God which is suitably signified and wondrously brought about by this most august sacrament" *(LG* 11).

According to this doctrine, which belongs to the most ancient Christian tradition, the Church's "activity" is not confined to the hierarchical ministry of her pastors, as if the laity had to remain in a state of passivity. In fact, all the Christian activity of lay people at any time, and especially the modern apostolate of the laity, gives evidence of the Council's teaching. According to it the priesthood of the faithful and the priestly ministry of the ecclesiastical hierarchy are "ordered to one another."

The Council maintains, "For those ministers, who are endowed with sacred power, serve their brethren, so that all who are of the People of God, and therefore enjoy a true Christian dignity, working toward a common goal freely and in an orderly way, may arrive at salvation" *(LG* 18).

For this reason the priesthood of the hierarchy has a ministerial character. Precisely for this reason the bishops and priests are pastors in the Church. Their task is to serve the faithful like Jesus Christ, the good shepherd, the one universal pastor of the Church and all humanity, who says of himself: "The Son of Man did not come to be served but to serve and to give his life as a ransom for many" (Mt 20:28). In light of the teaching and example of the good shepherd, the entire Church, which shares in the grace of redemption poured out in the whole Body of Christ by the Holy Spirit, is and functions as a priestly community.

General audience of March 18, 1992

Baptism: Entry into the Life of Grace

We read in Vatican II's document *Lumen Gentium:* "It is through the sacraments and the exercise of the virtues that the sacred nature and organic structure of the priestly community is brought into operation" (11). This means that the exercise of the universal priesthood is connected with the sacraments, which certainly play a fundamental role in Christian life. But the Council joins "sacraments" with "virtues." This significant association shows, on the one hand, that the sacramental life cannot be reduced to a set of words and ritual gestures; the sacraments are expressions of faith, hope and love. On the other hand, it emphasizes that the development of these virtues and all others in the Christian life arises from the sacraments. So we can say that in the Catholic conception, sacramental worship has its natural continuation in the flourishing of Christian life.

The Council first of all refers to Baptism, the sacrament which constitutes the human person as a member of the Church and thus brings him into the priestly community. We read: "Incorporated in the Church through Baptism, the faithful are destined by the baptismal character for the worship of the Christian religion; reborn as sons of God they must confess before men the faith which they have received from God through the Church" *(LG* 11). This text is rich in doctrine derived from the New Testament and developed in the tradition of the Fathers and doctors of the Church. In this catechesis we want to grasp the essential points.

The Council begins by stating that Baptism brings us into the Church, the body of Christ. This echoes St. Paul, who wrote: "In one Spirit we were all baptized into one body" (1 Cor 12:13).

It is important to underscore the role and value of Baptism for entering the ecclesial community. Even today some refuse to recognize this role, avoiding or delaying Baptism, especially of children. According to the Church's established tradition, however, the Christian life does not simply begin with human dispositions, but with a sacrament endowed with divine efficacy. Baptism as a sacrament, that is, as a visible sign of invisible grace, is the door through which God acts in the human soul—even in the soul of a newborn—to unite it to himself in Christ and the Church. He infuses new life into it. He makes it part of the communion of saints. He opens the way to the other sacraments, which serve to develop the Christian life fully. For this reason Baptism is like a rebirth by which a child of man becomes a child of God!

The Council says that the baptized are reborn as children of God. In this we hear an echo of the Apostle Peter, who blessed God the Father because "in his great mercy he gave us a new birth" (1 Pet 1:3). Here we find the teaching of Jesus himself, recorded by St. John in his account of the conversation with Nicodemus: "Amen, amen, I say to you, no one can enter the kingdom of God without being born of water and Spirit" (Jn 3:5).

Jesus teaches us that the new birth is produced by the Spirit. The letter to Titus emphasizes this by saying that God has saved us "through the bath of rebirth and renewal by the Holy Spirit, whom he richly poured out on us through Jesus Christ our Savior" (Titus 3:5). The Baptist had already proclaimed Baptism in the spirit (cf. Mt 3:11). Jesus tells us that the Holy Spirit "gives life" (Jn 6:63). We profess our faith in this revealed truth when we say in the Nicene-Constantinopolitan Creed: "...and in the Holy Spirit, the Lord and Giver of life." It is a question of the new life by which we become children of God in the sense intended by the Gospel. Christ shares with believers his divine Sonship through the sacrament of Baptism, which he instituted as Baptism in the Spirit.

In this sacrament, the spiritual birth to new life which is the result of the redeeming Incarnation takes place. The sacrament enables human beings to live the same life of the risen Christ. This is the soteriological dimension of Baptism, about which St. Paul states: "We who were baptized into Christ Jesus were baptized into his death...so that just as Christ was raised from the dead...we too might live a new life" (Rom 6:3-4). This passage from Romans allows us to understand clearly the priestly aspect of Baptism. It demonstrates that receiving Baptism means being personally united to the paschal mystery of Jesus, the one priestly sacrifice which is truly perfect and pleasing to God. As a result of this union every baptized person is able to make his entire life a priestly offering united to that of Christ (cf. Rom 12:1; 1 Pet 2:4-5).

Along with Christ's life Baptism fills the soul with his holiness, as the new condition of belonging to God through liberation and purification, as St. Paul reminded the Corinthians: "You have had yourselves washed; you were sanctified; you were justified in the name of the Lord Jesus Christ and in the Spirit of God" (1 Cor 6:11).

Also according to the Apostle's teaching, Christ purifies the entire Church "by the bath of water with the Word." She becomes "holy and without blemish" in her members, since they receive Baptism (cf. Eph 5:26), which is deliverance and also benefits the entire community for which it is the basis of a continual process of spiritual growth (cf. Eph 2:21). It is clear that from baptismal sanctification Christians—as individuals and community—obtain the ability and obligation of leading a holy life. According to St. Paul, the baptized are "dead to sin," and must reject the life of sin (Rom 6:2). He says: "You must think of yourselves as being dead to sin and alive for God in Christ Jesus" (Rom 6:11). In this sense Baptism enables us to share in the death and resurrection of Christ, in his victory over the forces of evil.

This is the meaning of the baptismal rite, in which the candidate is asked: "Do you reject Satan?" He is asked to make a personal commitment to total freedom from sin, and thus, from the power of Satan: the commitment to fight, throughout his earthly life, against the seductions of Satan. It will be a "good fight," which will make the individual more worthy of his heavenly calling, but also more perfect as a human person. For this double reason, the request and acceptance of this obligation ought also to be made at the Baptism of an infant, who replies through his parents and godparents. In the power of this sacrament he is purified and sanctified by the Spirit, who fills him with new life as a participation in Christ's life.

In addition to the life-giving and sanctifying grace of the Spirit, one also receives in Baptism the seal which is called the character, about which the Apostle says to Christians: "You were sealed with the promised Holy Spirit" (Eph 1:13; cf. 4:30; 2 Cor 1:22).

The character (in Greek *sphragis)* is a sign of belonging. The baptized person becomes the property of Christ, the property of God, and in this belonging his fundamental and definitive holiness is put into effect. For this reason St. Paul called Christians "saints" (Rom 1:7; 1 Cor 1:2; 2 Cor 1:1; etc.). This is the holiness of the universal priesthood of the Church's members. In the Church the ancient promise is fulfilled in a new way: "You shall be to me a kingdom of priests, a holy nation" (Ex 19:6). This means a definitive and permanent consecration, effected by Baptism and secured by an indelible character.

The Council of Trent expressed Christian tradition in defining that the character is an "indelible and spiritual sign" impressed upon the soul by three sacraments: Baptism, Confirmation and Holy Orders (cf. *DS* 1609). This does not mean a visible sign, although in many baptized persons some of its effects are visible, such as the sense of belonging to Christ and the Church, which is shown in the words and deeds of truly faithful Christians, both priests and laity.

One of the ways this sense is shown is in zeal for divine worship. According to the beautiful Christian tradition mentioned and confirmed by the Second Vatican Council, the faithful are "appointed by their baptismal character to Christian religious worship," that is, to worship God in Christ's Church. St. Thomas Aquinas maintained this on the basis of that tradition. According to him, the character is a "spiritual power" (cf. *Summa Theol.,* III, q. 63, a. 2), which enables the baptized to participate in the Church's worship as her recognized and assembled members, especially in the Eucharistic sacrifice and by the entire sacramental life. This capacity is inalienable and cannot be taken away, since it arises from an indelible character. There is cause for joy in discovering this other aspect of the mystery of the new life begun in Baptism, the first sacramental source of the universal priesthood, whose fundamental duty is to worship God!

At this point, however, I must add that the capacity involved in the character entails a mission and, thus, a responsibility. Whoever has received the holiness of Christ must show it to the world "in every aspect of his conduct" (1 Pet 1:15). Therefore he must nourish it with the sacramental life, especially through participation in the Eucharistic banquet.

The grace of the Holy Spirit, infused by Baptism, makes the character alive. In its dynamism this grace brings about the entire development of the life of Christ the priest in us, of Christ who gives the Father perfect worship in the Incarnation, on the cross and in heaven, and allows the Christian to share his priesthood in the Church, which was established primarily to renew his sacrifice in the world.

Just as Christ conformed his entire life to the demands of his priestly sacrifice while on earth, so too his followers—as individuals and as a community—are called to translate this sacrificial capacity received with the character into a behavior which belongs to the spirit of the universal priesthood which they are part of through Baptism.

The Council especially underscores growth in giving witness to the faith: "Reborn as children of God, they must profess before all the faith they have received from God through the Church" *(LG* 11).

According to St. Paul, Baptism has the effect of enlightenment: "Christ will give you light" (Eph 5:14; cf. Heb 6:4; 10:32). The baptized, having left the ancient night, must live in this light: "For you were once darkness, but now you are light in the Lord. Live as children of light" (Eph 5:8).

This life in the light is also expressed in the public profession of faith demanded by Jesus: "Everyone who acknowledges me before others I will acknowledge before my heavenly Father" (Mt 10:32). This is a personal confession which the Christian makes in the power of baptismal grace, a profession of faith "received from God through the Church," as the Council says *(LG* 1). Therefore, it is part of the confession of the universal Church, which every day repeats in chorus her *I believe* "in deed and truth" (Jn 3:18).

General audience of March 25, 1992

Confirmation Perfects Baptismal Grace

On the basis of the Council's text which says: "It is through the sacraments and the exercise of the virtues that the sacred nature and organic structure of the priestly community is brought into operation" *(LG* 11), in today's catechesis we will continue to develop this truth about the Church, focusing our attention on the sacrament of Confirmation. We read in *Lumen Gentium:* "They are more perfectly bound to the Church by the sacrament of Confirmation, and the Holy Spirit endows them with special strength so that they are more strictly obliged to spread and defend the faith, both by word and by deed, as true witnesses of Christ" *(LG* 11).

Early evidence of this sacrament appears in the Acts of the Apostles. There it says that the deacon Philip (a different person from the Apostle Philip), one of the seven men "filled with the Holy Spirit and wisdom" who were ordained by the apostles, had gone down to a town in Samaria to preach the Good News. "With one accord, the crowds paid attention to what was said by Philip when they heard it and saw the signs he was doing.... Once they began to believe Philip as he preached the Good News about the kingdom of God and the name of Jesus Christ, men and women alike were baptized.... Now when the apostles in Jerusalem heard that Samaria had accepted the word of God, they sent them Peter and John, who went down and prayed for them, that they might receive the Holy Spirit, for it had not yet fallen upon any of them; they had only been baptized in the name of the Lord Jesus. Then they laid hands on them and they received the Holy Spirit" (Acts 8:6-17).

This episode shows us the connection which existed from the Church's earliest days between Baptism and an "imposition of hands," a new sacramental act to receive and confer the gift of the Holy Spirit. This rite is considered to be a completion of Baptism. It was thought to be so important that Peter and John were sent expressly from Jerusalem to Samaria for this purpose.

The role the apostles played in conferring the gift of the Holy Spirit is the origin of the role given to the bishop in the Latin rite of the Church. The rite consists in the imposition of hands, performed by the Church since the second century, as attested to by the *Apostolic Tradition* of Hippolytus of Rome (around the year 200), which speaks of a double rite: the anointing done by a presbyter before Baptism, followed by the imposition of the hand on the baptized, performed by a bishop who pours holy chrism on their heads. This shows the difference between the anointing at Baptism and that at Confirmation.

Over the Christian centuries different practices in the administration of Confirmation were followed in the East and West. In the Eastern Church Confirmation is conferred immediately after Baptism (Baptism is given with an anointing), while in the Western Church, in the case of infant Baptism, Confirmation is administered after the age of reason has been reached, or at a later time determined by the episcopal conference (cf. *CIC,* can. 891).

In the East the minister of Confirmation is the priest who baptizes. In the West, the ordinary minister is the bishop, but there are also presbyters who receive the faculty to administer the sacrament.

Moreover, in the East the essential rite consists in the anointing alone; in the West the anointing is done with the imposition of the hand (cf. can. 880).

In addition to these differences between the East and West there is also a variety of arrangements in the Western Church regarding the most appropriate age for Confirmation, depending on time, place or spiritual and cultural conditions. This is based on the freedom the Church maintains in determining the particular conditions for celebrating the sacramental rite.

The essential effect of the sacrament of Confirmation is to bring to perfection the gift of the Holy Spirit received in Baptism, so that the person who receives it is able to witness to Christ in speech and with his life.

Baptism achieves purification and liberation from sin, and confers new life. Confirmation highlights the positive aspect of sanctification and the strength which the Holy Spirit gives the Christian for an authentically Christian life and effective witness.

As with Baptism, a special character is also impressed on the soul by the sacrament of Confirmation. It brings to perfection the baptismal consecration and is conferred by two ritual acts, the imposition of hands and the anointing.

The ability to participate in worship, which was already received in Baptism, is strengthened by Confirmation. The universal priesthood is more deeply rooted in the person and can be exercised more effectively. The specific function of the character of Confirmation is to put into practice Christian witness and action, which St. Peter already pointed out as originating in the universal priesthood (cf. 1 Pet 2:11ff.). St. Thomas Aquinas explains that the confirmed give witness to the name of Christ and perform the acts of good Christians in the defense and spread of the faith, in virtue of the character's "special power" (cf. *Summa Theol.,* III, q. 72, a. 5, in c. and ad 1), inasmuch as they are entrusted with a special function and mandate. It is a "participation in the priesthood of Christ on the part of the faithful who are called to the divine worship which in Christianity derives from Christ's priesthood" *(Summa*

Theol., III, q. 63, a. 3). Public witness to Christ is also included in the universal priesthood of the faithful, to which they are called "almost *ex officio" (Summa Theol.,* III, q. 72, a. 5, ad 2).

The grace conferred by the sacrament of Confirmation is more specifically a gift of strength. The Council says that through "the sacrament of Confirmation...the Holy Spirit endows them [the baptized] with special strength" *(LG* 11). This gift corresponds to the need for greater zeal in facing the "spiritual battle" of faith and charity (cf. *Summa Theol.,* III, q. 72, a. 5), in order to resist temptation and give to the world the witness of Christian word and deed with courage, fervor and perseverance. In the sacrament, the Holy Spirit confers this zeal.

Jesus noted the danger of being ashamed to profess the faith: "Whoever is ashamed of me and of my words, the Son of Man will be ashamed of when he comes in his glory and in the glory of the Father and of the holy angels" (Lk 9:26; cf. Mk 8:38). Being ashamed of Christ is often expressed in those forms of "human respect" by which one hides one's own faith and agrees to compromises which are unacceptable for someone who wants to be Christ's true disciple. How many people, even Christians, make compromises today!

Through the sacrament of Confirmation, the Holy Spirit fills the individual with the courage to profess his faith in Christ. According to the Council text which we began with, professing this faith means "to spread the faith by word and deed" as consistent and faithful witnesses.

Since the Middle Ages, theology, which developed in a context of generous commitment of "spiritual combat" for Christ, has not hesitated to highlight the strength given by Confirmation to Christians who are called "to serve as soldiers for God." Theology continues to see in this sacrament the value of sacrifice and consecration which is included in its origin from the "fullness of Christ's grace" (cf. *Summa Theol.,* III. q. 72, a. 1, ad 4). St. Thomas Aquinas explains the fact that Confirmation is distinguished from Baptism and comes after:

"The sacrament of Confirmation is, as it were, the final completion of the sacrament of Baptism, in the sense that by Baptism (according to St. Paul) the Christian is built up into a spiritual dwelling (cf. 1 Cor 3:9), and is written like a spiritual letter (cf. 2 Cor 3:2-3); whereas by the sacrament of Confirmation, like a house already built, he is consecrated as a temple of the Holy Spirit, and as a letter already written, is signed with the sign of the cross" *(Summa Theol.,* III, q. 72, a. 11).

As we know, there are pastoral problems regarding Confirmation, especially concerning the appropriate age for receiving this sacrament. There has been a recent tendency to delay the time of conferral until the age of fifteen to eighteen, so that the recipient's personality may be more mature and he can consciously make a more serious and stable commitment to Christian life and witness.

Others prefer a younger age. In any case, there must be hope that there will be a thorough preparation for this sacrament, which will allow those who receive it to renew their baptismal promises with full awareness of the gifts they are receiving and the obligations they are assuming. Without a long and serious preparation, they run the risk of reducing the sacrament to a mere formality or external ritual, or even losing sight of the essential sacramental aspect by insisting exclusively on the moral commitment involved.

I will conclude by recalling that Confirmation is the sacrament capable of inspiring and supporting the commitment of the faithful who want to devote themselves to Christian witness in society. I hope that all young Christians—especially with the help that comes from the grace of Confirmation—will merit the acknowledgment given by the Apostle John: "I write to you, young men, because you are strong and the Word of God remains in you, and you have conquered the evil one" (1 Jn 2:14).

General audience of April 1, 1992

The Eucharist Is
the Source of the Church's Life

According to the Second Vatican Council the truth of the Church as a priestly community is realized through the sacraments; it comes to fulfillment in the Eucharist. Indeed, we read in *Lumen Gentium* that the faithful, "Taking part in the Eucharistic sacrifice, which is the fount and apex of the whole Christian life...offer the divine victim to God, and offer themselves along with it" *(LG* 11).

The Eucharist is the *source* of the Christian life because whoever shares in it receives the motivation and strength to live as a true Christian. Christ's sacrifice on the cross imparts to the believer the dynamism of his generous love. The Eucharistic banquet nourishes the faithful with the Body and Blood of the divine Lamb sacrificed for us and it gives them the strength to "follow in his footsteps" (cf. 1 Pet 2:21).

The Eucharist is the *summit* of the whole Christian life because the faithful bring to it all their prayers and good works, their joys and sufferings. These modest offerings are united to the perfect sacrifice of Christ. Thus they are completely sanctified and lifted up to God in an act of perfect worship which brings the faithful into the divine intimacy (cf. Jn 6:56-57). Therefore, as St. Thomas Aquinas writes, the Eucharist is "the culmination of the spiritual life and the goal of all the sacraments" *(Summa Theol.,* III, q. 66, a. 6).

The Angelic Doctor also notes that the "effect of this sacrament is the unity of the mystical body [the Church], without which there can be no salvation. Therefore it is necessary to receive the Eucharist, at least by desire *(in voto),* in order to be saved" (III, q. 73, a. 1, ad 2). These words echo everything Jesus himself said about the necessity of the Eucharist for the Christian life: "Amen, amen, I say to you, unless you eat the flesh of the Son of Man and drink his blood, you do not have life within you. Whoever eats my flesh and drinks my blood has eternal life, and I will raise him on the last day" (Jn 6:53-54).

According to these words of Jesus, the Eucharist is a pledge of the resurrection to come, but it is already a source of eternal life in time. Jesus does not say *"will have* eternal life," but *"has* eternal life." Through the food of the Eucharist, Christ's eternal life penetrates and flows within human life.

The Eucharist requires the participation of the Church's members. According to the Council, "Both by reason of the offering and through Holy Communion all take part in this liturgical service, not indeed, all in the same way but each in that way which is proper to himself" *(LG* 11).

Participation is common to the entire "priestly people," who have been allowed to unite themselves to the offering and the Communion. But this participation differs according to the condition of the Church's members, in accord with the sacramental institution. There is a specific role for the priestly ministry. However, it does not eliminate, but rather promotes the role of the common priesthood. It is a specific role willed by Christ when he charged his apostles with celebrating the Eucharist in his memory, by instituting for this function the sacrament of Holy Orders, conferred on bishops and priests (and on deacons as ministers of the altar).

The purpose of the priestly ministry is to gather the people of God: "All belonging to this people, since they have been sanctified by the Holy Spirit, can offer themselves as 'a sacrifice, living, holy, pleasing to God' (Rom 12:1)" *(PO* 2).

If, as I have mentioned in the preceding catecheses, the common priesthood is meant to offer spiritual sacrifices, the faithful can make this offering because they are "sanctified by the Holy Spirit." The Holy Spirit, who animated Christ's sacrifice on the cross (cf. Heb 9:14), will give life to the offering of the faithful.

According to the Council, because of the priestly ministry spiritual sacrifices can achieve their goal. "Through the ministry of the priests, the spiritual sacrifice of the faithful is made perfect in union with the sacrifice of Christ. He is the only mediator who in the name of the whole Church is offered sacramentally in the Eucharist and in an unbloody manner until the Lord himself comes" *(PO* 2).

In virtue of Baptism and Confirmation, as we stated in the preceding catecheses, the Christian is qualified to participate "as if *ex officio"* in divine worship, which has its center and culmination in the sacrifice of Christ made present in the Eucharist. But the Eucharistic offering entails the involvement of an ordained minister. The offering is fulfilled in the act of consecration carried out by the priest in Christ's name.

In this way the priestly ministry contributes to the full expression of the universal priesthood. As the Council states, citing St. Augustine, the ministry of priests tends to this, that "The entire commonwealth of the redeemed and the society of the saints be offered to God through the High Priest who offered himself also for us in his passion that we might be the body of so great a head *(De Civitate Dei,* 10, 6: *PL* 41, 284)" *(PO* 2).

After the sacrifice has taken place, the Eucharistic communion which follows is meant to provide the faithful with the spiritual force necessary for the full development of the "priesthood," and especially for offering all the sacrifices of their everyday life. We read in the Decree *Presbyterorum Or-*

dinis: "Priests must instruct their people to offer to God the Father the divine victim in the Sacrifice of the Mass, and to join to it the offering of their own lives" *(PO 5)*.

It can be said that according to Jesus' intention in formulating the new commandment of love at the Last Supper, Eucharistic communion enables those who receive it to put it into practice: "Love one another as I have loved you" (Jn 13:34; 15:12).

Participating in the Eucharistic banquet testifies to their unity, as the Council points out in writing that the faithful, "Strengthened in Holy Communion by the Body of Christ ...then manifest in a concrete way that unity of the People of God which is suitably signified and wondrously brought about by this most august sacrament" *(LG 11)*.

This is the truth which the Church's faith inherited from St. Paul, who wrote: "The bread that we break, is it not a participation in the body of Christ? Because the loaf of bread is one, we though many, are one body, for we all partake of the one loaf" (1 Cor 10:16-17). For this reason St. Thomas saw the Eucharist as the sacrament of the Mystical Body's unity *(Summa Theol.,* III, q. 72, a. 3). We conclude this ecclesiological-Eucharistic catechesis by emphasizing that, if Eucharistic communion is the efficacious sign of unity, it then gives the faithful a continually new impulse to mutual love and reconciliation, and the sacramental strength necessary for preserving good understanding in family and ecclesial relationships.

General audience of April 8, 1992

Penance in the Ecclesial Community

As the Second Vatican Council says: "It is through the sacraments and the exercise of the virtues that the sacred nature and organic structure of the priestly community is brought into operation" *(LG* 11). In today's catechesis we want to show how this truth is reflected in the sacrament of Reconciliation, which traditionally has been called the sacrament of Penance. In this sacrament there is a real exercise of the "universal priesthood," common to all the baptized, because a fundamental duty of the priesthood is to take away the obstacle of sin, which prevents a life-giving relationship with God. So, this sacrament was instituted for the remission of sins committed after Baptism and the baptized have an active role to play in it. They are not limited to receiving a ritual and formal pardon, as if they were passive subjects. On the contrary, with the help of grace they take the initiative in the struggle against sin by confessing their faults and seeking forgiveness of them. They know that the sacrament involves an act of conversion on their part. With this understanding they participate actively in the sacrament and fulfill their role, as is clear from the rite itself.

We have to acknowledge that lately there has been a crisis in many places regarding the reception of the sacrament of Penance by the faithful. The reasons, which concern the same spiritual and socio-cultural conditions of broad sections of humanity in our time, can be summarized in two points.

On the one hand, the sense of sin has been weakened in the consciences of a certain number of the faithful who, under the influence of an atmosphere current in today's world which claims total human freedom and independence, experience difficulty in acknowledging the reality and seriousness of sin, and even of their own guilt before God.

On the other hand, many faithful do not see the necessity and benefit of receiving the sacrament, and prefer to seek forgiveness from God more directly. In this case they find difficulty in accepting the Church's mediation in being reconciled to God.

The Council replied briefly to these two difficulties and considered sin in its twofold aspect as an offense against God and a wound to the Church. We read in *Lumen Gentium:* "Those who approach the sacrament of Penance obtain pardon from the mercy of God for the offense committed against him and are at the same time reconciled with the Church, which they have wounded by their sins, and which by charity, example and prayer seeks their conversion" *(LG* 11). Concise, well-thought out and enlightening, the Council's words offer various important points for our catechesis.

First and foremost, the Council recalls that sin's essential nature is that of an offense against God. This is an important fact which includes the perverse act of the creature who knowingly and freely opposes the will of his Creator and Lord, violating the law of good and freely submitting to the yoke of evil. It is an offense against the divine majesty, in regard to which St. Thomas Aquinas does not hesitate to say that "the sin committed against God has a certain infinity in virtue of the infinity of the divine majesty" *(Summa Theol.,* III, q. 1, a. 2, ad 2). We must say that it is also an act which offends the divine charity in that it is an infraction against the law of friendship and covenant which God has established for his people and every person in the blood of Christ. Therefore it is an act of infidelity, and in practice, a rejection of his love. Sin, therefore, is not a simply human error, nor does it cause damage only to the person. It is an offense against God in that the sinner disobeys the law of the Creator and Lord, and thus offends his paternal love. Sin cannot be considered merely from the point of view of its psychological consequences. Sin draws its significance from the person's relationship to God.

Especially in the parable of the prodigal son, Jesus makes us understand that sin is an offense against the love of the Father in his description of the son's outrageous scorn for his father's authority and house. The son is reduced to very tragic conditions, which reflect the situation of Adam and his descendants after the first sin. However, the great gift which Jesus gives us in this parable is the comforting and reassuring revelation of the merciful love of a Father. With his arms open wide, he awaits the prodigal son's return, hurries to embrace and pardon him, cancels all the consequences of sin and celebrates the feast of new life for him (cf. Lk 15:11-32). What hope this has enkindled in hearts. Throughout the Christian centuries, how many people have been helped to return to God by reading this parable narrated by Luke, who has rightfully been called the "scribe of Christ's meekness." The sacrament of Penance is part of the revelation of God's love and fatherly goodness which Jesus has given us.

The Council reminds us that sin is also a wound inflicted upon the Church. In fact, every sin harms the holiness of the ecclesial community. Since all the faithful are in solidarity in the Christian community, there can never be a sin which does not have an effect on the whole community. If it is true that the good done by one person is a benefit and help to all the others, unfortunately it is equally true that the evil committed by one obstructs the perfection to which all are tending. If every per-

son who seeks perfection lifts up the whole world as Blessed
Elisabeth Leseur said, it is also true that every act which betrays the divine love weighs down the human condition and
impoverishes the Church. Reconciliation with God is also reconciliation with the Church, and in a certain sense with all of
creation, whose harmony is violated by sin. The Church is the
mediatrix of this reconciliation. Her Founder assigned this role
to her and gave her the mission and power of "forgiving sins."
Every instance of reconciliation with God thus takes place in
an explicit or implicit, conscious or unconscious relationship
with the Church. St. Thomas writes about "the unity of the
Mystical Body, without which there can be no salvation; for
there is no entering into salvation outside the Church, just as in
the time of the deluge there was none outside the ark, which
denotes the Church, according to St. Peter (1 Pet 3:20-21)"
(Summa Theol., III, q. 73, a. 3; cf. *Suppl.,* III, q. 17, a. 1).
Without a doubt the power to pardon belongs to God, and the
forgiveness of sins is the work of the Holy Spirit. Nevertheless, forgiveness comes from the application to the sinner of
the redemption gained through the cross of Christ (cf. Eph 1:7;
Col 1:14, 20). He entrusted the Church with the mission and
ministry of bringing salvation to the whole world in his name
(cf. *Summa Theol.,* III, q. 84, a. 1). Forgiveness is asked of God
and granted by God, but not independently of the Church
founded by Jesus Christ for the salvation of all.

We know that in order to communicate the fruits of his
passion and death to people, the risen Christ conferred on the
apostles the power to forgive sins: "Whose sins you forgive are
forgiven them, and whose sins you retain are retained" (Jn
20:23). In the Church the priests, as heirs of the mission and
power of the apostles, forgive sins in Christ's name. However,
we can say that in the sacrament of Reconciliation the priest's
specific ministry does not exclude, but rather includes the
exercise of the "common priesthood" of the faithful who con-

fess their sins and ask for pardon under the influence of the
Holy Spirit who converts them intimately through the grace of
Christ, the Redeemer. In affirming this role of the faithful, St.
Thomas cites the famous words of St. Augustine: "He who
created you without your consent will not justify you without
your consent" (St. Augustine, *Super Ioannem,* serm. 169, c. 11;
St. Thomas, *Summa Theol.,* III, q. 84, aa. 5 and 7).

The Christian's active role in the sacrament of Penance
consists in recognizing his own faults with a "confession"
which, apart from exceptional cases, is made individually to
the priest; expressing his own repentance for his offense
against God (contrition); humbly submitting to the Church's
institutional priesthood to receive the "efficacious sign" of
divine forgiveness; offering the "satisfaction" imposed by the
priest as a sign of personal participation in the reparatory
sacrifice of Christ who offered himself to the Father as a
victim for our sins; last of all, giving thanks for the forgiveness
he has received.

It is good to recall that all that we have said is true of the
sin which breaks our friendship with God and deprives us of
"eternal life"; that is why it is called "mortal." Recourse to the
sacrament is necessary when even only one mortal sin has been
committed (cf. Council of Trent., *DS* 1707). However, the
Christian who believes in the effectiveness of sacramental
forgiveness has recourse to the sacrament with a certain fre-
quency, even when it is not a case of necessity. In it he finds
the path for an increasing sensitivity of conscience and an ever
deeper purification, a source of peace, a help in resisting temptation and in striving for a life that responds more and more to
the demands of the law and love of God.

The Church is at the side of each Christian as a community which, as the Council says, "by charity, example and
prayer seeks their conversion" *(LG* 11). The Christian is never
left alone, not even in the state of sin. He is always part of the
"priestly community" which supports him with the solidarity

of charity, fraternity and prayer to obtain for him the grace of being restored to God's friendship and the company of the "saints." The Church, the community of saints, in the sacrament of Penance shows that she is a priestly community of mercy and forgiveness.

General audience of April 15, 1992

Anointing Brings Spiritual Healing

The reality of the priestly community can be said to be fulfilled and revealed in an especially meaningful way in the sacrament of the Anointing of the Sick, about which St. James wrote: "Is anyone among you sick? He should summon the presbyters of the Church, and they should pray over him and anoint him with oil in the name of the Lord, and the prayer of faith will save the sick person, and the Lord will raise him up. If he has committed any sins, he will be forgiven" (Jas 5:14-15).

As we see, the Letter of James recommends initiative on the part of the sick person who, personally or through his loved ones, asks for the priests to come. It could be said that the common priesthood is already being exercised here in a personal act of participating in the community of life enjoyed by the "saints," that is, by those who have been consecrated in the Holy Spirit, whose anointing is sought. But the letter also shows us that giving help to the sick through anointing is a duty of the priestly ministry performed by "presbyters." This is another time when the priestly community is realized through harmonious and active participation in a sacrament.

The initial basis of this sacrament can be found in Jesus' care and concern for the sick. The evangelists tell us that from the very beginning of his public life Jesus showed great love and sincere compassion toward the sick and all the other needy and suffering who sought his help. St. Matthew states that he "cured every disease and illness" (Mt 9:35).

For Jesus the countless miraculous cures were the sign of the salvation which he wanted to bring to humanity. Frequently he showed the clear connection in meaning between them, as when he forgave the paralytic his sins and only afterward worked a miracle, in order to show that "the Son of Man has authority to forgive sins on earth" (Mk 2:10). His vision does not stop at mere bodily health; he also looks to the healing of the soul, to spiritual salvation.

Jesus' way of acting was part of the plan of his messianic mission, which the prophecy in the Book of Isaiah had described in terms of healing the sick and helping the poor (cf. Is 61:1ff; Lk 4:18-19). It is a mission which, even during his earthly life, Jesus wanted to entrust to his disciples so that they would give help to the needy and especially, healing to the sick. The evangelist Matthew tells us that Jesus "summoned his twelve disciples and gave them authority over unclean spirits to drive them out and to cure every disease and every illness" (Mt 10:1). Mark says that they "drove out many demons, and they anointed with oil many who were sick" (Mk 6:13). Significantly, in the early Church this aspect of Jesus' messianic mission was highlighted and many pages of the Gospels devoted to it, and also the work he entrusted to his disciples and apostles in connection with his mission was underscored.

The Church has made her own the special concern which Jesus had for the sick. On the one hand, she has promoted many endeavors of generous service to their care. On the other hand, with the sacrament of Anointing she has given and continues to give them the healing touch of Christ's own mercy.

In this regard it should be noted that sickness is never a mere physical evil; it is also a time of moral and spiritual testing. The sick person has great need of interior strength in order to triumph over this trial. Through sacramental anointing Christ reveals his love and bestows on the sick the interior strength they need. In the parable of the Good Samaritan, the oil poured in the wounds of the unfortunate man on the road to Jericho is a simple means of physical care. In the sacrament, the anointing with oil becomes the efficacious sign of grace and spiritual salvation, through the ministry of priests.

In the Letter of James we read that the anointing and the priestly prayer have the effects of salvation, comfort and the remission of sins. In commenting on the text of James, the Council of Trent says that this sacrament confers a grace of the Holy Spirit, whose internal anointing, on the one hand, frees the sick person's soul from sin and the remnants of sin, and on the other hand, gives him relief and strength, inspiring in him great trust in the merciful goodness of God (cf. *DS* 1696). Thus he is helped to bear more readily the discomfort and pain of illness, and to resist with great force the devil's temptations. In addition, the anointing sometimes obtains physical healing for the sick person as well, when that is advantageous for the salvation of his soul. This is the Church's doctrine, which the Council of Trent expounded.

Therefore, the sacrament of Anointing bestows a grace of strength which increases the sick person's courage and resistance. It causes spiritual healing, such as the forgiveness of sins, which is accomplished by the sacrament itself through the power of Christ, if there is no obstacle in the soul's disposition. Sometimes it brings physical healing. This is not the sacrament's essential purpose, but when it does take place it shows the salvation given by Christ in the abundance of his love and mercy for all the needy, which he already revealed during his earthly life. Even now his heart beats with that love which continues in his new life in heaven and is poured out upon his human creation through the power of the Holy Spirit.

The sacrament of Anointing is thus an effective presence of Christ in every instance of serious illness or physical weakness due to advanced age, in which the presbyters of the Church are called to administer it.

The traditional term for this sacrament was "Extreme Unction," because it was considered to be the sacrament of the dying. Vatican II no longer used this expression, so the Anointing could be better seen as the sacrament of the seriously ill, which it is. Therefore, it is not right to wait until the last moment to ask for this sacrament and thus deprive the sick person of the help which the Anointing gives the soul, and sometimes even the body. At the proper time, relatives and friends must express the sick person's desire to receive the sacrament in the case of serious illness. This desire is to be presumed, unless it was rejected, even when the sick person is no longer able to express it formally. It is part of his adherence to Christ through faith in his Word and acceptance of the means of salvation instituted by him and entrusted to the ministry of the Church. Experience also shows that the sacrament gives a spiritual strength which changes the way the sick person feels and gives him relief even in his physical condition. This strength is especially beneficial at the time of death, because it helps in the passage to the afterlife. Let us pray every day that at the end of our lives we may be given that supreme gift of sanctifying grace which, at least in anticipation, is already beatifying!

The Second Vatican Council emphasizes the Church's commitment to assist with this holy Anointing at the time of illness, old age and finally death. The Council says that the entire Church asks the Lord for a lessening of the sick person's sufferings, and in this way she shows Christ's love for all the infirm (cf. *LG* 11). The priest, the minister of the sacrament, expresses this commitment of the Church, "the priestly community," of which the sick person is still an active, participating member doing good works. For this reason, the Church exhorts the suffering to unite themselves to the passion and death of Jesus Christ in order to obtain from him salvation and

a more abundant life for the entire People of God. Indeed, the
purpose of this sacrament is not only the personal welfare of
the sick, but also the spiritual growth of the whole Church.
Seen in this light, the Anointing appears as it really is: a
supreme form of that participation in the priestly sacrifice of
Christ, of which St. Paul said: "Now I rejoice in my sufferings
for your sake, and in my flesh I am filling up what is lacking in
the afflictions of Christ on behalf of his body, which is the
Church" (Col 1:24).

Ever greater attention must be drawn to the contribution
which the sick make to the development of the Church's spiritual life. May everyone—the sick, their loved ones, their
doctors and others who care for them—always take into account the value suffering has as a way of exercising the
Church's universal priesthood, by offering spiritual sacrifice,
one's sufferings in union with the passion of Christ. May
everyone see in the sick the image of the suffering Christ
(Christus patiens), the Christ who, according to the prophecy
in the Book of Isaiah about the servant (cf. Is 53:4), bore our
infirmities.

We know, by faith and experience, that the sacrifice
made by the sick is very fruitful for the Church. The suffering
members of the Mystical Body are the ones who most greatly
contribute to the intimate union of the whole community with
Christ the Savior. The community should help the sick in all
the ways indicated by the Council, out of gratitude for the
benefits which it receives from them.

General audience of April 29, 1992

Christist Made Marriage a Sacrament

According to the Second Vatican Council, the Church is a "priestly community," whose "sacred and organic nature" is realized through the sacraments, among which a special place must be given to the sacraments of Holy Orders and Matrimony. Regarding Holy Orders, we read in the Constitution *Lumen Gentium:* "Those of the faithful who are consecrated by Holy Orders are appointed to feed the Church in Christ's name with the word and the grace of God." Regarding Matrimony we read: "Christian spouses, in virtue of the sacrament of Matrimony, whereby they signify and partake of the mystery of that unity and fruitful love which exists between Christ and his Church (cf. Eph 5:32), help each other to attain to holiness in their married life" *(LG* 11). We will devote today's catechesis exclusively to the sacrament of Matrimony and return to the ministerial priesthood at a later time.

In a previous catechesis we recalled that the first miracle Jesus worked took place in Cana during a wedding feast. Although the significance of this miracle, by which "Jesus revealed his glory" (Jn 2:11), goes far beyond the recorded event, we can also discover the Lord's appreciation for married love and the institution of marriage, as well as his intention to bring salvation to this fundamental aspect of human life and society. He gives new wine, the symbol of new love. The episode in Cana shows us how marriage is threatened when love is in danger of running out. With this sacrament Jesus Christ reveals his own help in an effective way, in order to save and strengthen the couple's love through the gift of theological charity, and to give them the strength of fidelity. We can also say that the miracle worked by Jesus at the beginning of his public life is a sign of the importance marriage has in God's saving plan and the formation of the Church.

Finally, we can say that Mary's initiative in asking and obtaining the miracle foretells her future role in the divine plan for Christian marriage: a benevolent presence, an intercession and a help in overcoming the inevitable problems.

In light of Cana we now want to call attention to the aspect of marriage which concerns us in this cycle of ecclesiological catecheses. It is a fact that in Christian marriage the common priesthood of the faithful is exercised in a remarkable way, because the married couple themselves are the ministers of the sacrament.

The human act, "by which," as the Council says, "the partners mutually surrender themselves to each other," has been raised to the dignity of a sacrament. The couple administer the sacrament to one another by their mutual consent. The sacrament shows the value of the man and woman's free consent, as a statement of their personality and an expression of mutual love.

The Council also said that through the sacrament Christian married couples "signify and partake of the mystery of that unity and fruitful love which exists between Christ and his Church (cf. Eph 5:32)" *(LG* 11).

"Authentic married love is caught up into divine love and is governed and enriched by Christ's redeeming power and the saving activity of the Church, so that this love may lead the spouses to God with powerful effect and may aid and strengthen them in the sublime office of being a father or a mother. For this reason Christian spouses have a special sacrament by which they are fortified and receive a kind of consecration in the duties and dignity of their state" *(GS* 48).

This last assertion of *Gaudium et Spes,* that spouses "have a special sacrament by which they are fortified and receive a kind of consecration" is very important. This shows precisely how they exercise their priesthood as those baptized and confirmed.

Through this special sharing in the common priesthood of the Church, couples can achieve holiness. Indeed, through the sacrament they receive the strength to fulfill their marital and family duties, and to advance in mutual holiness. The Council says that spouses "help each other to attain to holiness in their married life and in the rearing and education of their children. By reason of their state and rank in life they have their own special gift among the people of God (cf. 1 Cor 7:7)" *(LG* 11).

The sacrament of Matrimony is oriented toward fruitfulness. It is an inclination which is inborn in human nature. The Council says: "By their very nature, the institution of matrimony itself and conjugal love are ordained for the procreation and education of children, and find in them their ultimate crown" *(GS* 48).

The sacrament provides the spiritual strength of faith, love and generosity for fulfilling the duty of procreating and rearing offspring. It is a resource of divine grace which confirms and perfects this natural inclination and marks the very psychology of the couple, who have been made conscious of their own mission as those who "cooperate with the love of God the Creator," as the Council says *(GS* 50).

The realization that they are cooperating in the divine work of creation and the love which inspires it helps married couples to better understand the sacred character of procreation and procreative love, and strengthens the orientation of their love to transmitting life.

The Council also calls attention to the educational mission of the spouses. In fact, we read in *Gaudium et Spes:* "Graced with the dignity and office of fatherhood and motherhood, parents will energetically acquit themselves of a duty which devolves primarily on them, namely education and especially religious education" *(GS* 48). But *Lumen Gentium* sheds light on this exhortation where it says: "The family is, so to speak, the domestic church. In it parents should, by their word and example, be the first preachers of the faith to their children" *(LG* 11). The Council, then, casts an ecclesial light on the mission of married couples and parents, as members of the Church, the priestly and sacramental community.

Clearly, for believers Christian education is the most beautiful gift which parents can give their children, and it is the highest and truest sign of their love. It requires a sincere and consistent faith, and a life led in conformity with the faith.

The Council also says: "As a mutual gift of two persons, this intimate union and the good of the children impose total fidelity on the spouses and argue for an unbreakable oneness between them" *(GS* 48). Fidelity and unity come from the "special gifts of grace and love" *(GS* 49) given by the sacrament. They ensure that, in imitation of Christ who loved the Church, "spouses may love each other with perpetual fidelity through mutual self-bestowal" *(GS* 48). This too is a strength inherent in the grace of the sacrament.

Finally, we read in the Council that "The Christian family, which springs from marriage as a reflection of the loving covenant uniting Christ with the Church, and as a participation in that covenant, will manifest to all men Christ's living presence in the world, and the genuine nature of the Church. This the family will do by the mutual love of the spouses, by their generous fruitfulness, their solidarity and faithfulness, and by the loving way in which all members of the family assist one another" *(GS* 48).

Therefore, not only each Christian considered individually, but the whole family as such, consisting of Christian parents and children, is called to witness to the life, love and unity which the Church possesses as properties deriving from her nature as a sacred community, constituted and living in Christ's love.

General audience of May 6, 1992

The Church Is a Prophetic Community

In the previous catecheses we have spoken of the Church as a sacred and organic priestly community which is brought into operation through the sacraments and the exercise of virtues. It was a commentary on the Constitution *Lumen Gentium,* devoted to the identity of the Church (cf. *LG* 11). But in the same Constitution we read: "The holy People of God shares also in Christ's prophetic office *[munus];* it spreads abroad a living witness to him especially by a life of faith and charity and by offering to God a sacrifice of praise, the tribute of lips which praise his name (cf. Heb 13:15)" *(LG* 12). According to the Council, then, the Church has a prophetic character as sharing in the same prophetic office of Christ. We will discuss this character in today's catechesis and in the ones following, as we continue in the path laid out by the dogmatic constitution just cited, in which the Council explains this doctrine more explicitly (cf. *LG* 12). Today we will consider the presuppositions on which the Church's witness of faith is based.

In presenting the Church as a prophetic community, the Council's text highlights this feature in relation to the function of witnessing, for the sake of which she was desired and founded by Jesus. Indeed, the Council says that the Church "spreads abroad a living witness to Christ." The reference to Christ's words in the New Testament is obvious, primarily to

174

the words recorded in Acts which the risen Lord addressed to the apostles: "You will receive power when the Holy Spirit comes upon you, and you will be my witnesses" (Acts 1:8). With these words Jesus calls attention to the fact that the act of giving witness, which is the particular duty of the apostles, depends on the sending of the Holy Spirit whom he promised and who came on the day of Pentecost. In the power of the Paraclete, who is the Spirit of truth, the witness to Christ crucified and risen becomes a duty and responsibility for the other disciples, especially the women who were present with Christ's mother in the upper room in Jerusalem as members of the first ecclesial community. The women were already privileged, because they were the first to bring the message and were witnesses to Christ's resurrection (cf. Mt 28:1 10).

When Jesus said to the apostles: "You will be my witnesses" (Acts 1:8), he was speaking of the witness of faith which would certainly be fulfilled in them in a special way. They were eyewitnesses of Christ's works, and they heard with their own ears the words he spoke; they received directly from him the truths of divine revelation. They were the first to respond with faith to what they saw and heard. This is what Simon Peter did when, in the name of the Twelve, he professed that Jesus is "the Messiah, the Son of the living God" (Mt 16:16). Another time, near Capernaum, when some began to leave Jesus after he announced the mystery of the Eucharist, Simon Peter also did not hesitate to say: "Master, to whom shall we go? You have the words of eternal life. We have come to believe and are convinced that you are the Holy One of God" (Jn 6:68-69).

The apostles' particular witness of faith was a "gift from above" (cf. Jas 1:17). This was true not only of the apostles, but also of those who at that time and later were to hand on their testimony. Jesus said to them: "The mystery of the kingdom of God has been granted to you" (Mk 4:11). Looking ahead to a critical moment, he gave Peter this assurance:

"I have prayed that your own faith may not fail, and once you have turned back, you must strengthen your brothers" (Lk 22:32).

On the basis of these significant passages in the New Testament, we can say that, if the Church, as the People of God, shares in Christ's prophetic office by spreading abroad a living witness to him, as we read in the Council (cf. *LG* 12), then this witness of faith on the Church's part finds its basis and support in the witness of the apostles. This testimony is primordial and fundamental for the prophetic office of the entire People of God.

In another conciliar Constitution, *Dei Verbum,* we read that the apostles "by their oral preaching, by example, and by observances handed on what they had received from the lips of Christ, from living with him, and from what he did, or what they had learned through the prompting of the Holy Spirit" *(DV* 7). But others too, along with the Twelve, fulfilled the command of Christ about giving the witness of faith in the Gospel, that is, "those apostles [like Paul] and apostolic men who, under the inspiration of the same Holy Spirit, committed the message of salvation to writing" *(DV* 7). "What was handed on by the apostles includes everything which contributes toward the holiness of life and increase in faith of the People of God, and so the Church, in her teaching, life and worship, perpetuates and hands on to all generations all that she herself is, all that she believes" *(DV* 8).

According to the Council, then, this advance toward the fullness of divine truth under the protection of the Spirit of truth is fulfilled through insight, experience (such as a vivid sense of spiritual realities), and teaching (cf. *DV* 10).

In this regard, too, Mary is a model for the Church, because she was the first to "keep all these things, reflecting on them in her heart" (Lk 2:19, 51).

Under the Holy Spirit's influence, the community professes its faith and applies the truth of faith to daily life. On the one hand there is the whole Church's effort to gain a better understanding of revelation, the object of faith: a systematic study of Scripture and continuous reflection or meditation on the profound significance and value of God's word. On the other hand, in her own life the Church gives the witness of her faith, showing the consequences and implications of revealed doctrine and the superior value which human conduct derives from it. By teaching the precepts promulgated by Christ, she follows the way he opened and shows the excellence of the Gospel message.

Every Christian must "acknowledge Christ before others" (cf. Mt 10:32) in union with the whole Church and maintain "good conduct" among non-believers, so that they may arrive at faith (cf. 1 Pet 2:12).

In these ways indicated by the Council, that "sense of faith" by which the People of God share in the prophetic office of Christ, is developed and passed on through the "community" witness of the Church. We read in *Lumen Gentium:*

> That discernment in matters of faith is aroused and sustained by the Spirit of truth. It is exercised under the guidance of the sacred teaching authority, in faithful and respectful obedience to which the People of God accepts that which is not just the word of men but truly the Word of God (cf. 1 Thess 2:13). Through it, the People of God adheres unwaveringly to the faith given once and for all to the saints (cf. Jude 3), penetrates it more deeply with right thinking, and applies it more fully in its life *(LG* 12).

The Council text highlights the fact that this appreciation of the faith is "aroused and sustained by the Spirit of truth." Because of this "sense," in which the divine "anointing" bears fruit, the People of God, guided by the sacred Magisterium, "unwaveringly adheres to this faith" *(LG* 12). "The entire body of the faithful, anointed as they are by the Holy One, (cf. 1 Jn

2:20, 27) cannot err in matters of belief. They manifest this special property by means of the whole peoples' supernatural discernment in matters of faith when 'from the bishops down to the last of the lay faithful' they show universal agreement in matters of faith and morals" *(LG* 12).

It should be noted that a clear consequence of the conciliar text is that this "consent in faith and morals" does not derive from a referendum or plebiscite. It can only be understood properly to the extent that one continues to remember Christ's words: "I give praise to you, Father, Lord of heaven and earth, for although you have hidden these things from the wise and the learned you have revealed them to the childlike" (Mt 11:25).

General audience of May 13, 1992

The Church Bears Witness to Christ

The prophetic office which we spoke of in the previous catechesis is exercised by the Church through the witness of faith. This witness includes and highlights all the aspects of Christ's life and teaching. We find this stated in a text of Vatican II, in the Pastoral Constitution *Gaudium et Spes,* where it presents Jesus Christ as the new man who casts his light on the otherwise insoluble riddle of life and death. "Only in the mystery of the incarnate Word does the mystery of man take on light" *(GS* 22). The Council goes on to state that this is the help which the Church wants to offer people so that they may discover or rediscover in divine revelation their true and complete identity. We read: "Since it has been entrusted to the Church to reveal the mystery of God, who is the ultimate goal of man, she opens up to man at the same time the meaning of his own existence, that is, the innermost truth about himself. The Church truly knows that only God, whom she serves, meets the deepest longings of the human heart, which is never fully satisfied by what this world has to offer" *(GS* 41). This means that the Church's prophetic office, which consists in proclaiming divine truth, also entails revealing to the human person the truth about himself, the truth which is revealed in all its fullness only in Christ.

The Church shows the human person this truth not only in a theoretical or abstract way, but also in a way which we can call existential and very concrete, because her vocation is to give people the life which is in Christ crucified and risen, as Jesus himself foretold to the apostles, "...because I live and you will live" (Jn 14:19).

The bestowal of new life in Christ on a human person begins at the time of Baptism. St. Paul states this in an incomparable way in his Letter to the Romans: "Are you unaware that we who were baptized into Christ Jesus were baptized into his death? We were indeed buried with him through Baptism into death, so that, just as Christ was raised from the dead by the glory of the Father, we too might live in newness of life. For if we have grown into union with him through a death like his, we shall also be united with him in the resurrection.... Consequently, you too must think of yourselves as being dead to sin and living for God in Christ Jesus" (Rom 6:3-5, 11). This is the mystery of Baptism, which is an initiation into the new life that the "new man," Christ, shares with those who are sacramentally inserted into his one body which is the Church.

In Baptism and the other sacraments we truly can say that the Church "opens up to man...the meaning of his own existence" in a living and vital way. We can speak of a "sacramental evangelization" which belongs to the Church's prophetic office and enables us to understand better the truth about the Church as a "prophetic community."

The Church's prophetic ministry is expressed when she proclaims and sacramentally produces the "following of Christ," which becomes an imitation of Christ not only in a moral sense, but as a true and proper reproduction of Christ's life in the individual—a "newness of life" (Rom 6:4). It is a divine life, which through Christ is shared with man, as St. Paul states over and over: "And even when you were dead in transgressions...he brought you to life along with him

[Christ]" (Col 2:13); "So whoever is in Christ is a new creation" (2 Cor 5:17).

Christ, then, is the divine answer which the Church gives to basic human problems: Christ, who is perfect man. The Council says: "Whoever follows Christ...becomes himself more of a man" *(GS* 41). By giving witness to the life of Christ, the "perfect man," the Church shows every person the way to realize fully his or her own humanity. Through her preaching she offers everyone an authentic model of life, and with the sacraments she instills in believers the vital energy which allows the new life to develop and spread from member to member in the ecclesial community. For this reason, Jesus calls his disciples the "salt of the earth" and the "light of the world" (Mt 5:13-14)

In giving witness to Christ's life, the Church enables people to know him who, during his earthly life, most perfectly fulfilled "the greatest commandment" (Mt 22:38-40), which he himself proclaimed. He fulfilled it in its twofold dimension. In fact, through his life and death Jesus Christ showed what it means to love God "above all else" in that attitude of homage and obedience to the Father which led him to say: "My food is to do the will of him who sent me and to finish his work" (Jn 4:34). Jesus also confirmed and perfectly fulfilled the love of neighbor by which he defined and conducted himself as "the Son of Man [who] did not come to be served but to serve and to give his life as a ransom for many" (Mt 20:28).

The Church is a witness to the Beatitudes which Jesus proclaimed (cf. Mt 5:3-12). She strives to increase in the world the number of:

—"the poor in spirit," who do not seek the goal of life in material possessions or money;

—"the meek," who reveal Christ's "meek and humble heart" and reject violence;

—"the clean of heart," who live in truth and sincerity;

—"those who hunger and thirst for righteousness," that is, for the divine holiness which seeks to be established in individual and social life;

—"the merciful," who have compassion on the suffering and help them;

—"the peacemakers," who foster reconciliation and understanding among individuals and nations.

The Church is a witness and bearer of the sacrificial offering which Christ made of himself. She follows the way of the cross and always remembers the fruitfulness of suffering borne and offered in union with the Savior's sacrifice. Her prophetic office is exercised in recognizing the value of the cross. Therefore, the Church strives especially to live the Beatitudes of the suffering and the persecuted.

Jesus predicted persecution for his disciples (cf. Mt 24:9). Perseverance in persecution is part of the witness which the Church gives to Christ. It extends from the martyrdom of St. Stephen (cf. Acts 7:55-60), the apostles, their successors and so many Christians, to the sufferings of bishops, priests, religious and the faithful who in our day have also shed their blood and suffered torture, imprisonment and humiliations of every kind for their fidelity to Christ.

The Church is a witness to the resurrection, a witness to the joy of the Good News, a witness to eternal happiness and to that happiness which is already present in earthly life and which the risen Christ gives, as we shall see in the next catechesis.

In giving this multifaceted witness to the life of Christ, the Church fulfills the prophetic office proper to her. At the same time, through this prophetic witness she "reveals man to himself and makes his supreme calling clear," as the Council said *(GS 22)*.

It is a question of a prophetic mission which has a clearly Christocentric meaning and which, precisely for this reason, has a profound anthropological value, as a light and vital force coming from the incarnate Word. Today, more than ever, the Church is involved in this mission on behalf of human beings, for she knows that in human salvation the glory of God is achieved. For this reason, from my very first encyclical, *Redemptor Hominis,* I have said: "Man is the way for the Church" *(RH* 14).

General audience of May 20, 1992

The Church Witnesses to Gospel Hope

As we saw in the previous catechesis, the Church is a witness to the life of Christ. In Christ, the Church is also a witness of hope, of that gospel hope which finds its source in Christ. Indeed, in the Pastoral Constitution *Gaudium et Spes* Vatican II says of Christ: "The Lord is the goal of human history...the center of the human race, the joy of every heart and the answer to all its yearnings" *(GS* 45). In this text the Council quotes the words of Paul VI, who said in an address that Christ is "the focal point of the desires of history and civilization" *(Address* of February 3, 1965). As we see, the hope which the Church witnesses to has vast dimensions; we can even say it is immense.

It is primarily a question of hope for eternal life. This hope corresponds to the desire for immortality which the human person has in his heart in virtue of the soul's spiritual nature. The Church preaches that earthly life is the "passing" to another life, to life in God, where "there shall be no more death" (Rev 21:4). Because of Christ, who—as St. Paul says—is "the firstborn from the dead" (Col 1:18; cf. 1 Cor 15:20), because of his resurrection, human beings can live in expectation of the eternal life proclaimed and brought by him.

It is a question of hope for happiness in God. We are all

called to this happiness, as the command of Christ reveals to us: "Go into the whole world and proclaim the Gospel to every creature" (Mk 16:15). On another occasion Jesus assured his disciples: "In my Father's house there are many dwelling places" (Jn 14:2). He said he was leaving them on earth and going to heaven to "prepare a place for you...so that where I am you also may be" (Jn 14:3).

It is a question of hope in being with Christ "in the Father's house" after death. The Apostle Paul was full of this hope, to the point of saying, "I long to depart this life and be with Christ," and "that is far better" (Phil 1:23). "We are courageous," he also wrote, "and we would rather leave the body and go home to the Lord" (2 Cor 5:8). Christian hope also assures us that the "exile in the body" will not last and that our hope in the Lord will be fulfilled with the resurrection of the body at the end of the world. Jesus gives us this certitude and he relates it to the Eucharist: "Whoever eats my flesh and drinks my blood has eternal life, and I will raise him on the last day" (Jn 6:54). It is a true and proper resurrection of the body, with the full reintegration of individual persons into the new life of heaven. It is not a reincarnation understood as a return to life on the same earth in different bodies. In the revelation which Christ preached and to which the Church gives witness, the hope of resurrection is placed in the context of "a new heaven and a new earth" (Rev 21:1), in which the "new life" which people share with the incarnate Word will find its full realization.

If the Church gives witness to this hope—hope for eternal life, for the resurrection of the body, for eternal happiness in God—she does so as an echo of the apostles' teaching, especially that of St. Paul who said that Christ himself is the source and basis of this hope. "Christ Jesus our hope," the Apostle says (1 Tim 1:1). He also writes that in Christ "the mystery hidden from ages and from generations past...has been manifested to his holy ones, to whom God chose to make known the riches of the glory of this mystery; it is Christ...the hope for glory" (Col 1:26-27).

The prophecy of hope, then, is based on Christ, and on him depends the simultaneous growth of new life in him and of hope in eternal life.

Although the hope which comes from Christ has its ultimate goal beyond all temporal limits, it nevertheless permeates the life of Christians in time. St. Paul states: "In him [Christ] you also, who have heard the word of truth, the Gospel of your salvation, and have believed in him, were sealed with the promised Holy Spirit, which is the first installment of our inheritance toward redemption as God's possession, to the praise of his glory" (Eph 1:13-14). God is actually the one "who gives us security...in Christ and who anointed us.... He has also put his seal upon us and given the Spirit in our hearts as a first installment" (2 Cor 1:21-22).

Hope, therefore, is a gift of the Holy Spirit, the Spirit of Christ, because of whom the human person even now lives in eternity. He lives in Christ as a sharer in the eternal life which the Son receives from the Father and gives to his disciples (cf. Jn 5:26; 6:54-57; 10:28; 17:2). St. Paul says that this is the hope which "does not disappoint" because it draws on the power of God's love which "has been poured out into our hearts through the Holy Spirit that has been given to us" (Rom 5:5).

The Church is a witness to this hope. She proclaims it and brings it as a gift to individuals who accept Christ and live in him, and to the whole human race, to whom she must and wants to make known the "Gospel of the kingdom" (Mt 24:14), according to Christ's will.

Even in the face of the difficulties of this life and the painful experiences of misconduct and failure in human history, hope is the source of Christian optimism. Certainly, the

Church cannot close her eyes to the many kinds of evil in the world. Nevertheless, she knows how to rely on Christ's victorious presence and she inspires her long and patient activity with this certainty, ever mindful of what her Founder declared in his farewell speech to the apostles: "I have told you this so that you might have peace in me. In the world you will have trouble, but take courage; I have conquered the world" (Jn 16:33). From the certainty of this victory of Christ, which expands in history on a profound level, the Church draws that supernatural optimism in looking at the world and at life which the gift of hope translates into action. She is trained by history to resist and to continue in her work as the minister of Christ crucified and risen, but in virtue of the Holy Spirit whom she hopes will always bring new spiritual victories, instilling in souls and spreading through the world the Gospel leaven of grace and truth (cf. Jn 16:13). The Church wants to hand on to her members and, as much as possible, to all people, this Christian optimism, born of trust, courage and farsighted perseverance. She makes her own the words of the Apostle Paul in his Letter to the Romans: "May the God [the giver] of hope fill you with all joy and peace in believing, so that you may abound in hope by the power of the Holy Spirit" (Rom 15:13). The God of hope is "the God of endurance and encouragement" (Rom 15:5).

In fact, the Church in every age can make her own the memorable words of St. Francis Xavier, which were inspired by the grace at work in him: "I do not remember ever having had so many and such continual spiritual consolations, as on these islands [the Moluccas, where, amid great difficulties, the missionary saint was preaching the Gospel]. I walked at great length on these islands, which were surrounded by enemies and populated with friends who were not exactly sincere, in lands without any remedy for physical illness or any human help in preserving life. Those islands should not be called the 'Islands of the Moor,' but the 'Islands of Hope in God'" *(Epist.*

S. Francisci Xaverii, in *Monumenta Missionum Societatis Iesu,* vol. I [Rome, 1944], p. 380).

We can say that the world into which Christ has brought his paschal victory has become, through the power of his redemption, the "island of divine hope."

General audience of May 27, 1992

The Church Witnesses to Jesus' Love

Let us return to the Second Vatican Council's Dogmatic Constitution *Lumen Gentium* where we read: "The holy People of God shares also in Christ's prophetic office; it spreads abroad a living witness to him, especially by means of a life of faith and charity" *(LG* 12). We spoke about the witness to faith and hope in the preceding catecheses; today we move on to the witness of love. It is an especially important topic because, as St. Paul says of these three things, faith, hope and love, "The greatest of these is love" (1 Cor 13:13). Paul shows that he is aware of the value Christ placed on the commandment of love. Over the centuries the Church has never forgotten this teaching. She has always felt called to witness to the Gospel of love in word and deed, following the example of Christ, who—as we read in the Acts of the Apostles—"went about doing good" (Acts 10:38).

Jesus underscored the centrality of this commandment of love when he called it *his* commandment: "This is my commandment: love one another as I have loved you" (Jn 15:12). No longer is it merely the love of neighbor ordained by the Old Testament, but a "new commandment" (Jn 13:34). It is "new" because its model is Christ's love ("as I have loved you"), the perfect human expression of God's love for humanity. More especially, it is Christ's love in its supreme manifestation, that of sacrifice: "No one has greater love than this, to lay down one's life for one's friends" (Jn 15:13).

The Church, then, has the duty of giving witness to Christ's love for humanity, a love ready for sacrifice. Charity is not merely a demonstration of human solidarity; it is a sharing in the same divine love.

Jesus said: "This is how all will know that you are my disciples, if you have love for one another" (Jn 13:35). The love that Christ taught by word and example is the sign which must distinguish his disciples. He shows his heart's great desire when he confesses: "I have come to set the earth on fire, and how I wish it were already blazing!" (Lk 12:49). Fire means the intensity and strength of the love of charity. Jesus asks his followers to distinguish themselves by this form of love. The Church knows that in this form love becomes a witness to Christ. The Church is able to give this witness because, in receiving Christ's life, she receives his love. Christ has set hearts on fire with love (cf. Lk 12:49) and continues to light this fire in every time and place. The Church is responsible for spreading this fire throughout the world. All genuine witness to Christ entails charity; it requires the will to avoid inflicting any harm on love. So the whole Church must be distinguished by charity.

The charity kindled in the world by Christ is a limitless, universal love. The Church testifies to this love which overcomes every division among individuals, social classes, peoples and nations. She reacts against any national particularism which would limit charity to a people's borders. With her love open to all, the Church shows that the human person is called by Christ not only to shun all enmity among his own people but also to esteem and love the members of other nations and their peoples as such.

Christ's charity also overcomes differences in social class. It does not accept hatred or class struggle. The Church desires the union of all in Christ. She tries to live Gospel love, and exhorts and teaches everyone to live it, even for those whom some would like to consider enemies. In applying Christ's commandment of love, the Church seeks social justice, and thus an equitable distribution of material goods in society and help for the poorest and all the unfortunate. At the same time, however, she preaches and promotes peace and reconciliation in society.

The Church's charity essentially entails an attitude of forgiveness, in imitation of the kindness of Christ who condemned sin but showed himself "a friend of sinners" (cf. Mt 11:19; cf. Lk 19:5-10), and refused to condemn them (cf. Jn 8:11). In this way the Church strives to reproduce in herself, and in the hearts of her children, the generous spirit of Jesus, who forgave and asked the Father to forgive those who had handed him over to be put to death (cf. Lk 23:34).

Christians know that they can never take revenge, and according to the answer Jesus gave Peter, they must forgive all offenses without ceasing (cf. Mt 18:22). Every time they recite the Our Father they affirm their willingness to forgive. This witness to forgiveness, given and inculcated by the Church, is connected with the revelation of divine mercy. It is precisely because they are like the heavenly Father, according to Jesus' exhortation (cf. Lk 6:36-38; Mt 6:14-15; 18:33-35), that Christians are inclined to leniency, understanding and peace. This does not mean that they forego justice, but that justice must never be separated from mercy.

Charity is also shown through the respect and regard for every human person which the Church wants to practice and urges others to practice. She has received the task of spreading the truth of revelation and of making known the way of salvation established by Christ. In following Jesus Christ, she directs her message to individuals whom, as persons, she considers to be free, and the Church desires their full development as persons with the help of grace. In her work, therefore, she uses persuasion, dialogue, the common search for truth and the good. If the Church is firm in teaching the truths of the faith and the principles of morality, she addresses people by proposing these things, rather than imposing them, with respect and trusting their powers of judgment.

Charity also requires a willingness to serve one's neighbor. In the Church throughout history there have always been numerous people who have dedicated themselves to this service. We can say that no religious society has ever inspired as many works of charity as the Church has: service to the sick, the disabled, service to young people in schools, to people struck by natural disasters and other misfortunes, support for all kinds of poor and needy. Today we see a repetition of this phenomenon, which seems prodigious at times. Every new need which appears in the world is met with new endeavors of relief and assistance by Christians who live according to the spirit of the Gospel. It is a charity which is often witnessed to with heroism in the Church. She has many martyrs of charity. Here let us simply recall Maximilian Kolbe, who gave himself up to death to save the father of a family.

We must recognize that, since the Church is a community which is also composed of sinners, the precept of love has at times been transgressed over the centuries. It is a question of failures on the part of individuals and groups who bear the name Christian, failures on the level of reciprocal relations, both interpersonal as well as social and international. It is a sad reality which appears in the history of individuals and nations, and also in the Church's history. Conscious of their own vocation to love according to Christ's example, Christians confess these sins against love with humility and repentance, without, however, ceasing to believe in love. As St. Paul says, love "bears all things," and "never fails" (1 Cor 13:7-8). But if the history of humanity and of the Church herself abounds in sins against charity which cause sadness and pain, we must at the same time acknowledge with joy and gratitude that in every Christian age there have been marvelous acts of witness which confirm love, and that many times—as we have noted—this testimony has been heroic.

The heroic charity of individual persons goes hand in hand with the imposing witness of charitable works of a social nature. It is impossible to list them here or even give a summary. The Church's history is filled with them, from the first Christian centuries to the present day. Nevertheless, the dimension of human suffering and need always seems to outstrip and surpass the possibilities of aid. But love is and remains invincible *(amor vincit omnia),* even when it appears to have no other weapons than indestructible trust in Christ's truth and grace.

As a summary and conclusion, we can make an assertion which finds empirical confirmation, so to speak, in the history of the Church, her institutions and her saints. In her teaching and her striving for holiness, the Church has always kept alive the Gospel ideal of charity. She has inspired innumerable examples of charity, often to the point of heroism. She has spread love throughout humanity, and she is the more or less acknowledged source of the many institutions of solidarity and social cooperation which constitute the indispensable fabric of modern civilization. Finally, she has grown and continues to grow in her awareness of the demands of charity and in her fulfillment of the responsibilities which these demands entail. All this is under the influence of the Holy Spirit, who is eternal, infinite Love.

General audience of June 3, 1992

The Role of Charisms
in the Church's Life

"It is not only through the sacraments and the ministries of the Church that the Holy Spirit sanctifies and leads the people of God and enriches it with virtues, but, 'allotting his gifts to everyone according as he wills' (1 Cor 12:11), he distributes special graces among the faithful of every rank. By these gifts he makes them fit and ready to undertake the various tasks and offices which contribute toward the renewal and building up of the Church" *(LG* 12). This is the teaching of the Second Vatican Council.

Therefore, the People of God's sharing in the messianic mission is not obtained only through the Church's ministerial structure and sacramental life. It also occurs in another way, that of the spiritual gifts or charisms.

This doctrine, recalled by the Council, is based on the New Testament and helps to show that the development of the ecclesial community does not depend only on the institution of ministries and sacraments, but is also furthered by the free and unforeseeable gifts of the Spirit, who works outside established channels, too. Because of this bestowal of special graces it is apparent that the universal priesthood of the ecclesial community is led by the Spirit with a sovereign freedom that is often amazing—"as he wishes," St. Paul says (1 Cor 12:11).

St. Paul describes the variety and diversity of the charisms, which must be attributed to the work of the one Spirit (cf. 1 Cor 12:4).

Each of us receives from God many gifts which are appropriate for us personally and for our mission. Because of this diversity, no individual way of holiness or mission is ever identical to the others. The Holy Spirit shows respect for each person and wants to foster in each one an original development of the spiritual life and the giving of witness.

But we must keep in mind that spiritual gifts are to be accepted not only for one's personal benefit, but above all for the good of the Church. St. Peter writes: "As each one has received a gift, use it to serve one another as good stewards of God's varied grace" (1 Pet 4:10).

Because of these charisms the community's life is full of spiritual wealth and every kind of service. Diversity is necessary for a greater spiritual wealth; everyone makes a personal contribution which the others do not. The spiritual community lives on the contribution of all.

The diversity of charisms is also necessary for a better ordering of the entire life of the body of Christ. St. Paul emphasizes this when he explains the purpose and usefulness of the spiritual gifts: "You are Christ's body, and individually parts of it" (1 Cor 12:27).

In the one body each person must fulfill his own role in accord with the charism he has received. No one can claim to have received all the charisms, nor can he allow himself to be jealous of the charisms of others. Each person's charism must be respected and appreciated for the good of the body.

It should be noted that the charisms require discernment, especially in the case of extraordinary charisms. This discernment is given by the same Holy Spirit, who guides the intellect along the way of truth and wisdom. Since the whole ecclesial community has been placed by Christ under the leadership of the ecclesiastical authority, this latter is responsible for judging the value and authenticity of the charisms. The Council says: "Extraordinary gifts are not to be sought after, nor are the fruits of apostolic labor to be presumptuously expected from their use; but judgment as to their genuinity and proper use belongs to those who are appointed leaders in the Church, to whose special competence it belongs, not indeed to extinguish the Spirit, but to test all things and hold fast to that which is good (cf. 1 Thess 5:12, 19-21)" *(LG 12)*.

Some generally followed criteria of discernment can be indicated both by the ecclesiastical authority or by spiritual masters and directors:

a) *Agreement with the Church's faith in Jesus Christ* (cf. 1 Cor 12:3). A gift of the Holy Spirit cannot be contrary to the faith which the same Spirit inspires in the whole Church. "This is how," St. John writes, "you can know the Spirit of God: every spirit that acknowledges Jesus Christ come in the flesh belongs to God, and every spirit that does not acknowledge Jesus does not belong to God" (1 Jn 4:2).

b) *The presence of the "fruit of the spirit: love, joy, peace"* (Gal 5:22). Every gift of the Spirit fosters growth in love, both in the person himself and in the community, and thus it produces joy and peace.

If a charism causes trouble and confusion, this means either that it is not genuine or that it has not been used in the right way. As St. Paul says: "He is not the God of disorder but of peace" (1 Cor 14:33). Without love, even the most extraordinary charisms are not at all useful (cf. 1 Cor 13:1-3; cf. also Mt 7:22-23).

c) *Conformity with the Church's authority and acceptance of its directives.* After laying down very strict rules for using charisms in the Church of Corinth, St. Paul says: "If anyone thinks that he is a prophet or a spiritual person, he should recognize that what I am writing to you is a commandment of the Lord" (1 Cor 14:37). The authentic charismatic is recognized by his sincere docility to the pastors of the Church. A charism cannot cause rebellion or a rupture of unity.

d) *The use of charisms in the community is subject to a simple rule:* "Everything should be done for building up" (1 Cor 14:26). That is, charisms are accepted to the extent that they make a constructive contribution to the life of the community, a life of union with God and of fraternal communion. St. Paul insists firmly on this rule (1 Cor 14:4-5, 12, 18-19, 26-32).

Among the various gifts, St. Paul holds that of prophecy in such high esteem that he recommends: "Strive eagerly for the spiritual gifts, above all that you may prophesy" (1 Cor 14:1). It appears from the history of the Church and especially from the lives of the saints that the Holy Spirit often inspires prophetic words which are meant to foster the development or the reform of the Christian community's life. Sometimes these words are addressed especially to those who wield authority, as in the case of St. Catherine of Siena, who intervened with the Pope to obtain his return from Avignon to Rome. There have been many faithful and, above all, many saints who have given Popes and other pastors of the Church the light and strength necessary for fulfilling their mission, especially at difficult times for the Church.

This fact shows the possibility and usefulness of freedom of speech in the Church, a freedom which can also appear in the form of constructive criticism. The important thing is that what is said truly expresses a prophetic inspiration coming from the Spirit. As St. Paul says, "Where the Spirit of the Lord is, there is freedom" (2 Cor 3:17). The Holy Spirit fosters in the faithful a manner of acting characterized by sincerity and mutual trust (cf. Eph 4:25) and enables them "to admonish one another" (Rom 15:14; cf. Col 1:16).

Criticism is useful in the community, which must always be reformed and must try to correct its own imperfections. In many cases it helps the community to take a new step forward.

But if it comes from the Holy Spirit, criticism must be animated by the desire to advance in truth and love. It cannot be given with bitterness; it cannot be expressed in insults, in acts or judgments which offend the honor of individuals or groups. It must be filled with respect and with fraternal and filial affection, and it should avoid recourse to inappropriate forms of publicity by always adhering to the directions given by the Lord about fraternal correction (cf. Mt 18:15-16).

If this is the profile of freedom of speech, we can say that there is no opposition between charism and institution, because it is the one Spirit who enlivens the Church with the various charisms. The spiritual gifts also help in exercising the ministries. They are bestowed by the Spirit to help advance the kingdom of God. In this sense we can say that the Church is a community of charisms.

General audience of June 24, 1992

THE MINISTRY OF BISHOPS

The Church Is a Structured Society

The Church, a priestly, sacramental and prophetic community, was instituted by Jesus Christ as a structured, hierarchical and ministerial society, to provide pastoral governance for the continual formation and growth of the community. Chosen by Jesus Christ as the visible foundation of his Church, the twelve apostles were the first to exercise this ministerial and pastoral role. As Vatican II says: "Jesus Christ, the eternal shepherd, established his holy Church, having sent forth the apostles as he himself had been sent by the Father (cf. Jn 20:21), and he willed that their successors, namely the bishops, should be shepherds in his Church even to the consummation of the world" *(LG* 18).

This passage from *Lumen Gentium* first of all reminds us of the original and unique position of the apostles in the institutional aspect of the Church. From the Gospel story we know that Jesus called disciples to follow him and from among them he chose twelve (cf. Lk 6:13). The Gospel account informs us that for Jesus it was a decisive choice made after a night of prayer (cf. Lk 6:12); it was a choice made with sovereign freedom. Mark tells us that Jesus went up the mountain and summoned "those whom he wanted" (Mk 3:13). The Gospel texts list the names of the individuals called (cf. Mk 3:16-19), which is an indication that their importance was perceived and acknowledged in the early Church.

In forming the group of the Twelve, Jesus established the Church as a visible society organized to serve the Gospel and the coming of God's kingdom. The number twelve referred to the twelve tribes of Israel, and Jesus' use of it reveals his intention to create a new Israel, the new People of God established as a Church. Jesus' intention to create appears in the very word used by Mark to describe the foundation: "He appointed Twelve.... He appointed the Twelve." "Appointed" or "made" recalls the verb used in the Genesis account about the creation of the world and in Deutero-Isaiah (cf. 43:1; 44:2) about the creation of the People of God, the ancient Israel.

This creative will is also expressed in the new names given to Simon (Peter) and to James and John (sons of thunder), but also to the entire group or college considered as a whole. Indeed, St. Luke writes that Jesus "chose twelve, whom he also named apostles" (Lk 6:13). The twelve apostles thus became a special, distinct socio-ecclesial reality, one which in certain aspects cannot be repeated. In their group the Apostle Peter stood out. In his regard Jesus revealed most explicitly his intention of founding a new Israel by the name he gave to Simon: the "rock" on which Jesus chose to build his Church (cf. Mt 16:18).

Mark explains Jesus' purpose in establishing the Twelve: "He appointed twelve that they might be with him and he might send them forth to preach and to have authority to drive out demons" (Mk 3:14-15).

The first constitutive element of the Twelve, then, is their absolute adherence to Christ. They are persons called to "be with him," that is, to follow him by leaving everything. The second element is missionary, expressed in the model of Jesus' own mission of preaching and driving out demons. The mission of the Twelve is a sharing in Christ's mission on the part of men closely joined to him as disciples, friends and confidants.

In the apostles' mission the evangelist Mark emphasizes the "authority to drive out demons." It is an authority of power over evil, which means positively the authority to give people Christ's salvation, for he drives out "the ruler of this world" (Jn 12:31).

Luke confirms the meaning of this authority and the purpose of establishing the Twelve when he reports Jesus' words in conferring authority on the apostles in the kingdom: "It is you who have stood by me in my trials, and I confer a kingdom on you, just as my Father has conferred one on me" (Lk 22:28). In this declaration, perseverance in union with Christ is closely linked to the authority conferred in the kingdom.

This authority is pastoral, as we can see from the text on the mission specifically entrusted to Peter: "Feed my lambs.... Feed my sheep" (Jn 21:15-17). Peter personally received supreme authority in the pastoral mission. This mission is exercised as a participation in the authority of the one shepherd and teacher, Christ.

The supreme authority entrusted to Peter does not nullify the authority conferred on the other apostles in the kingdom. The pastoral mission is shared by the Twelve under the authority of a single, universal shepherd, who is the agent and representative of the good shepherd, Christ.

These are the specific duties which are inherent in the mission entrusted by Jesus Christ to the Twelve:

a) The mission and authority to evangelize all nations, as the three Synoptics clearly attest (cf. Mt 28:18-20; Mk 16:16-18; Lk 24:45-48). Among them, Matthew emphasizes the relationship established by Jesus himself between his messianic power and the mandate he conferred on the apostles: "All power in heaven and on earth has been given to me. Go, therefore, and make disciples of all nations" (Mt 28:18). The apostles can and must fulfill their mission because of Christ's power which will be manifested in them.

b) The mission and power to baptize as a fulfillment of

Christ's command, with a Baptism in the name of the holy Trinity (cf. Mt 28:29). Since it is tied to Christ's paschal mystery, it is also considered in the Acts of the Apostles as Baptism in the name of Jesus (cf. Acts 2:38; 8:16).

c) The mission and power to celebrate the Eucharist: "Do this in memory of me" (Lk 22:19; 1 Cor 11:24-25). The charge to do again what Jesus did at the Last Supper by consecrating bread and wine implies a power of the highest degree. To say in Christ's name: "This is my Body," "This is my Blood," is to be identified with Christ, as it were, in the sacramental act.

d) The mission and power to forgive sins (Jn 20:22-23). The apostles share in the power which the Son of Man has to forgive sins on earth (cf. Mk 2:10), that power which in Jesus' public life astonished the crowd. The evangelist Matthew tells us that they "glorified God who had given such authority to human beings" (Mt 9:8).

To fulfill this mission the apostles received, in addition to authority, the special gift of the Holy Spirit (cf. Jn 20: 21-22), which was manifested at Pentecost as Jesus had promised (cf. Acts 1:8). In virtue of this gift, from Pentecost on they began to fulfill the command to evangelize all nations. In the Constitution *Lumen Gentium* the Second Vatican Council tells us: "By preaching the Gospel everywhere, and it being accepted by their hearers under the influence of the Holy Spirit, the apostles gather together the universal Church, which the Lord established on the apostles and built upon blessed Peter, their chief, Christ Jesus himself being the supreme cornerstone (cf. Rev 21:14; Mt 16:18; Eph 2:20)" *(LG 19)*.

The mission of the Twelve included a foundational role reserved to them which would not be inherited by others: being eyewitnesses of Christ's life, death and resurrection (cf. Lk 24:28), handing on his message to the early community as the link between divine revelation and the Church, and for that very reason, initiating the Church in the name and power of Christ under the action of the Holy Spirit. Because of their function the twelve apostles represent a uniquely important group in the Church which is defined by the Nicene-Constantinopolitan Creed as *apostolic (Credo unam, sanctam, catholicam et apostolicam Ecclesiam),* due to this unbreakable link with the Twelve. This is also why the Church has introduced into the liturgy and reserved special, solemn celebrations in honor of the apostles.

Nevertheless, Jesus conferred on the apostles a mission to evangelize all nations, and this takes a very long time, a time which indeed will last "until the end of the age" (Mt 28:20). The apostles understood that it was Christ's will that they provide for successors, who, as their heirs and representatives, would continue their mission. Thus they set up "bishops and deacons" in the various communities "and arranged that after their death these other approved men would be successors in their ministry" *(1 Clem.* 44:2, cf. 42:1-4).

In this way Christ established a hierarchical and ministerial structure in the Church, one formed by the apostles and their successors. This structure did not originate from an antecedent, already established community, but was created directly by him. The apostles were at one and the same time the seeds of the new Israel and the origin of the sacred hierarchy, as we read in the Council's Constitution *Ad Gentes* (n. 5). Therefore, this structure belongs to the Church's very nature, according to the divine plan fulfilled by Jesus. According to the same plan, this structure has an essential role in the whole development of the Christian community, from the day of Pentecost until the end of time, when in the heavenly Jerusalem all the elect will fully share in the new life forever.

General audience of July 1, 1992

Bishops Are Successors of the Apostles

The Acts of the Apostles and the epistles document what we read in Vatican II's Constitution *Lumen Gentium,* namely, that the apostles "had various helpers in their ministry" *(LG* 20). In fact, as the Christian communities which were quickly formed after the day of Pentecost began to spread, the community of the apostles was certainly prominent, especially the group of those who in the Jerusalem community were "reputed to be pillars: James and Cephas and John," as St. Paul attests in Galatians (2:9). These are Peter, set up by Jesus as head of the apostles and supreme pastor of the Church; John, the beloved apostle; and James, "the brother of the Lord," acknowledged as the head of the Jerusalem Church.

However, along with the apostles, Acts mentions "presbyters" (cf. Acts 11:29-30; 15:2, 4), who with them constitute the first subordinate rank of the hierarchy. The apostles sent a representative named Barnabas to Antioch because of the progress made in evangelizing that region (cf. Acts 11:22). Acts also speaks of Saul (St. Paul), who, after his conversion and first missionary effort, went with Barnabas (to whom the name "apostle" was also given; cf. Acts 14:14) to Jerusalem, as the center of ecclesial authority, to confer with the apostles. At the same time he brought material aid to the local community (cf. Acts 11:29). In the Church of Antioch, alongside Barnabas and Saul, there were also "prophets and teachers...Symeon who was called Niger, Lucius of Cyrene, Manaen" (Acts 13:1). From there Barnabas and Saul were sent out on an apostolic mission, "after they [the apostles] had laid hands on them" (cf. Acts 13:2-3). From the time of that mission on, Saul began to be called Paul (cf. Acts 13:9). As communities gradually arose, we hear that "they appointed presbyters" (Acts 24:23). The responsibilities of these presbyters are defined in detail in the pastoral letters to Titus and Timothy, whom Paul appointed as heads of the community (cf. Ti 1:5; 1 Tim 5:17).

After the Council of Jerusalem the apostles sent two more leaders to Antioch along with Barnabas and Paul: Silas and Judas, who was called Barsabbas. They were considered as "leaders among the brothers" (Acts 15:22). In the Pauline letters other "co-workers" and "companions" of the Apostle are mentioned in addition to Titus and Timothy (cf. 1 Thess 1:1; 2 Cor 1:19; Rom 16:1, 3-5).

At a certain point the Church needed new leaders, successors of the apostles. The Second Vatican Council says in this regard that the apostles, "in order that the mission assigned to them might continue after their death...they passed on to their immediate cooperators, as it were, in the form of a testament, the duty of confirming and finishing the work begun by themselves, recommending to them that they attend to the whole flock in which the Holy Spirit placed them to shepherd the Church of God (cf. Acts 20:28). They therefore appointed such men, and gave them the order that, when they should have died, other approved men would take up their ministry (cf. St. Clement of Rome, *Ep. ad Cor.*, 44, 2)" *(LG 20)*.

This succession is attested to by the first non-biblical Christian authors, such as St. Clement, St. Irenaeus and Tertullian. It constitutes the foundation for handing on the authentic apostolic testimony from generation to generation. The Council says: "Thus, as St. Irenaeus testifies, through those who were appointed bishops by the apostles, and through their successors down in our own time, the apostolic tradition is manifested and preserved (St. Irenaeus, *Adv. Haer.*, III, 3, 1; cf. Tertullian, *De Praescr.*, 20, 4-8: *PL* 2, 32; *CC* 1, 202)" *(LG* 20).

From these same texts it is evident that the apostolic succession has two correlative aspects: the pastoral and the doctrinal, in continuity with the mission of the apostles themselves. In this regard a clarification must be made, on the basis of the texts, as to what is sometimes said of the apostles, namely, that they could not have successors because they enjoyed a unique experience of friendship with Christ during his earthly life and a unique role in initiating the work of salvation.

Now it is certainly true that the apostles had an exceptional experience, which as a personal experience could not be shared with others, and that they had a unique role in forming the Church—that of witnessing and handing on Christ's word and mystery on the basis of their direct knowledge, and of establishing the Church in Jerusalem. At the same time, however, they also received a mission of authoritative teaching and pastoral leadership for the Church's growth. According to Jesus' intention, this mission can and must be handed on to successors so as to complete the work of universal evangelization. In this second sense, therefore, the apostles had co-workers and later successors. The Council states this several times (cf. *LG* 18, 20, 22).

Bishops fulfill the pastoral mission entrusted to the apostles and have all the powers which this mission entails. Moreover, like the apostles, they fulfill it with the help of co-workers. We read in *Lumen Gentium:* "Bishops, therefore, with their helpers, the priests and deacons, have taken up the service of the community, presiding in place of God over the flock (cf. St. Ignatius of Antioch, *Philad.,* Praef.; 1, 1), whose shepherds they are, as teachers for doctrine, priests for sacred worship, and ministers for governing" *(LG* 20).

The Council stressed this apostolic succession of the bishops by stating that the succession is of divine institution. We read again in *Lumen Gentium:* "The Sacred Council teaches that bishops by divine institution have succeeded to the place of the apostles, as shepherds of the Church, and he who hears them, hears Christ, and he who rejects them, rejects Christ and him who sent Christ (cf. Lk 10:16)" *(LG* 20).

In virtue of this divine institution the bishops represent Christ in such a way that listening to them is listening to Christ. Therefore, the Successor of Peter is not the only one who represents Christ the shepherd, but so do the other successors of the apostles. The Council teaches: "In the bishops, therefore, for whom priests are assistants, our Lord Jesus Christ, the Supreme High Priest, is present in the midst of those who believe" *(LG* 21). The words of Jesus, "Whoever listens to you listens to me" (Lk 10:16), quoted by the Council, have an even broader application because they were addressed to the seventy-two disciples. We saw in the texts from the Acts of the Apostles, cited in the first two paragraphs of this catechesis, the abundance of co-workers gathered around the apostles, a hierarchy which was quickly differentiated into presbyters (bishops and their co-workers) and deacons, but not without the assistance of the ordinary faithful, helpers in the pastoral ministry.

General audience of July 8, 1992

Bishops Are Consecrated by a Sacrament

In talking about the bishops as successors of the apostles, we have noted that this succession entails their participation in the mission and powers that Jesus conferred on the apostles themselves.

In treating this subject, the Second Vatican Council highlighted the sacramental nature of the episcopacy, which reflects the priestly ministry of those who were appointed apostles by Jesus himself. This determines the specific nature of the responsibilities which bishops have in the Church.

We read in *Lumen Gentium* that Jesus Christ, "sitting at the right hand of God the Father, is not absent from the gathering of his high priests," for through their sublime ministry:

a) He first of all "preaches the word of God to all nations" *(LG* 21). Thus, it is the glorious Christ who acts with his sovereign power of salvation through the bishops, whose ministry of evangelization is rightly called "sublime." The bishop's preaching not only prolongs the Gospel preaching of Christ, but is the preaching of Christ himself in his ministry.

b) Furthermore, through the bishops (and their co-workers), Christ is "constantly administering the sacraments of faith to those who believe; by their paternal functioning (cf. 1 Cor 4:15) he incorporates new members in his body by a heavenly regeneration" *(LG* 21). All the sacraments are administered in the name of Christ. In a special way the spiritual paternity signified and realized in the sacrament of Baptism is tied to the rebirth which comes from Christ.

c) Lastly, Christ, "through the wisdom and prudence [of the bishops], directs and guides the people of the New Testament in their pilgrimage toward eternal happiness" *(LG* 21). Wisdom and prudence belong to the bishops, but they come from Christ who governs the People of God through them.

At this point we should note that the Lord, when he acts through the bishops, does not remove the limitations and imperfections of the human condition, which find expression in temperament, character, behavior and the influence of the historical factors of culture and life. In this regard we can also refer to what the Gospel tells us about the apostles chosen by Jesus.

These men certainly had flaws. During Jesus' public life they argued about the first place, and they all abandoned their Master at the time of his arrest. After Pentecost, with the grace of the Holy Spirit, they lived in a communion of faith and love. But that does not mean that all the weaknesses inherent in the human condition disappeared. We know that Paul rebuked Peter for being too accommodating toward those who wanted to retain in Christianity the observance of the Jewish law (cf. Gal 2:11-14). Paul himself did not have an easy disposition and there was a serious disagreement between him and Barnabas (cf. Acts 15:39), even though the latter was a "good man, filled with the Holy Spirit and faith" (Acts 11:24).

Jesus knew the imperfections of those he had chosen and he kept to his choice even when imperfections appeared in serious ways. Jesus wanted to act through imperfect and at times reprehensible men, because the power of grace given by the Holy Spirit would triumph over their weaknesses. It can happen that with their imperfections, or even their faults, bishops too can fail to fulfill the demands of their mission and bring harm to the community. Therefore, we must pray for bishops so that they will always strive to imitate the good shepherd. Indeed, the face of Christ the shepherd has been apparent in many of them and is so in an obvious way.

It is not possible here to list the holy bishops who have guided and formed their churches in ancient times and later ages, even most recently. Let a brief mention of the spiritual greatness of some eminent figures suffice. Think of the apostolic zeal and martyrdom of St. Ignatius of Antioch, the doctrinal wisdom and pastoral fervor of St. Ambrose and St. Augustine, the commitment of St. Charles Borromeo to true reform of the Church, the spiritual teaching of St. Francis de Sales and his struggle to maintain the Catholic faith, the dedication of St. Alphonsus Liguori to the sanctification of his people and to spiritual direction, the unblemished fidelity of St. Anthony Mary Gianelli to the Gospel and the Church! However, so many other pastors of the People of God should be remembered and celebrated, who belong to all the nations and churches of the world! Let us be content to express our homage and gratitude to the many bishops of the past and present who by their actions, prayer and martyrdom (often that of the heart and sometimes that of blood) have continued the witness of Christ's apostles.

Certainly, their responsibility as "servants of Christ and stewards of the mysteries of God" (1 Cor 4:1) corresponds to the greatness of the "sublime ministry" they received from Christ as successors of the apostles. As stewards who are responsible for the mysteries of God in order to dispense them in the name of Christ, bishops must be closely united and steadfast in fidelity to their Master, who did not hesitate to give them, as he gave the apostles, a decisive mission for the life of the Church in every age—the sanctification of God's people.

After affirming Christ's active presence in the ministry of bishops, the Second Vatican Council taught the sacramentality of the episcopacy. For a long time this point was the subject of doctrinal controversy. The Council of Trent asserted the superiority of bishops over presbyters; this superiority appears in the power reserved to bishops of confirming and ordaining *(DS* 1777). But it did not assert the sacramentality of episcopal ordination. Therefore, we can see the doctrinal progress made on this point by the last Council, which declared: "The Sacred Council teaches that by episcopal consecration the fullness of the sacrament of Orders is conferred, that fullness of power, namely, which both in the Church's liturgical practice and in the language of the Fathers of the Church is called the high priesthood, the supreme power of the sacred ministry" *(LG* 21). Moreover, the liturgical rite of ordination is sacramental: "By means of the imposition of hands and the words of consecration, the grace of the Holy Spirit is so conferred, and the sacred character so impressed" *(LG* 21).

In the Pastoral Letters (cf. 1 Tim 4:14) all of this was already considered as an effect of the sacrament which bishops receive and, in turn, presbyters and deacons from the hands of bishops. On this sacramental basis the hierarchical structure of the Church, the body of Christ, is formed.

The Council attributes to bishops the sacramental power to "admit newly elected members into the episcopal body by means of the sacrament of Orders" *(LG* 21). This is the greatest expression of hierarchical power, inasmuch as it concerns the nerve centers of the body of Christ, the Church: the establishment of leaders and shepherds to continue and perpetuate the work of the apostles in union with Christ and under the action of the Holy Spirit.

Something similar can be said about the ordination of presbyters. This is reserved to bishops on the basis of the traditional concept connected with the New Testament, which endows them, as successors of the apostles, with the power to "lay on hands" (cf. Acts 6:6; 8:19; 1 Tim 4:14; 2 Tim 1:6), to establish in the Church ministers of Christ closely joined to those who rightfully exercise the hierarchical mission. This means that the activity of priests finds its meaning in one, sacramental, priestly and hierarchical whole, within which that activity is meant to take place in the communion of ecclesial charity.

At the summit of this communion is the bishop, who exercises the power conferred on him by the "fullness" of the sacrament of Orders, which he received as a service of love, in his own way sharing in the love poured out in the Church by the Holy Spirit (cf. Rom 5:5). Moved by his awareness of this love, the bishop, and the priest in a similar fashion, will not act in an individualistic and absolutist way, but "in hierarchical communion with the head and members of the [episcopal] college" *(LG* 21). It is certain that the communion of the bishops, united among themselves and with the Pope, and analogously that of the presbyters and deacons, shows in the highest way the unity of the whole Church as a community of love.

General audience of September 30, 1992

Bishops Express the Unity of the Church

In the Constitution *Lumen Gentium,* the Second Vatican Council makes an analogy between the college of the apostles and that of the bishops in union with the Roman Pontiff: "Just as in the Gospel, the Lord so disposing, St. Peter and the other apostles constitute one apostolic college, so in a similar way the Roman Pontiff, the Successor of Peter, and the bishops, the successors of the apostles, are joined together" *(LG* 22). This is the doctrine regarding the collegiality of the episcopate in the Church. Its basic foundation lies in the fact that in establishing his Church, Christ the Lord called the Twelve, whom he appointed apostles and entrusted with the mission of preaching the Gospel and of giving pastoral governance to the Christian people. In this way he established the Church's "ministerial" structure. We see the twelve apostles as a *corpus* and a *collegium* of persons united one to the other by the love of Christ who placed them under Peter's authority when he said to him: "You are Peter, and upon this rock I will build my Church" (Mt 16:18). But that original group, having received the mission of preaching the Gospel until the end of time, had to have successors, who are precisely the bishops. According to the Council, this succession reproduces the original structure of the college of the Twelve united among themselves by the will of Christ under Peter's authority.

The Council does not present this doctrine as something new, except perhaps in its formulation, but as the content of a historical reality which receives and fulfills the will of Christ, as it comes to us in Tradition.

a) The Council speaks of "the very ancient practice whereby bishops duly established in all parts of the world were in communion with one another and with the Bishop of Rome in a bond of unity, charity and peace" *(LG* 22).

b) "...also the councils assembled together, in which more profound issues were settled in common, the opinion of the many having been prudently considered, both of these factors are already an indication of the collegiate character and aspect of the episcopal order, and the ecumenical councils held in the course of centuries are also manifest proof of that same character" *(LG* 22).

c) Collegiality is also indicated "in the practice, introduced in ancient times, of summoning several bishops to take part in the elevation of the newly elected to the ministry of the high priesthood. Hence, one is constituted a member of the episcopal body in virtue of sacramental consecration and hierarchical communion with the head and members of the body" *(LG* 22).

The college, we read again, "insofar as it is composed of many, expresses the variety and universality of the People of God, but insofar as it is assembled under one head, it expresses the unity of the flock of Christ" *(LG* 22). In union with the Successor of Peter the entire college of bishops exercises supreme authority over the universal Church. In later catecheses we will discuss the "Petrine ministry" in the Church. However, it must also be kept in mind when we speak of the collegiality of the episcopate.

Without a doubt, according to *Lumen Gentium,* "The supreme power in the universal Church, which this college enjoys, is exercised in a solemn way in an ecumenical council" *(LG* 22). But we also see that "It is the prerogative of the

Roman Pontiff to convoke these councils, to preside over them and to confirm them" *(LG* 22). A council cannot be truly ecumenical unless it has been confirmed, or at least accepted, by the Roman Pontiff. Otherwise, it would lack the seal of unity guaranteed by the Successor of Peter. When unity and catholicity are insured, an ecumenical council can also infallibly define truths in the area of faith and morals. Historically, ecumenical councils have had a very important and decisive role in clarifying, defining and developing doctrine. One need only think of the councils of Nicea, Constantinople, Ephesus and Chalcedon.

In addition to ecumenical councils, "This same collegiate power can be exercised together with the Pope by the bishops living in all parts of the world, provided that the head of the college calls them to collegiate action, or at least approves of or freely accepts the united action of the scattered bishops, so that it is thereby made a collegiate act" *(LG* 22).

Episcopal synods, established after Vatican II, are meant to realize concretely the participation of the episcopal college in the universal government of the Church. These synods study and discuss pastoral and doctrinal subjects of notable importance for the universal Church. The results of their work, produced in agreement with the Apostolic See, are collected in documents which are disseminated everywhere. The documents resulting from recent synods are expressly called "post-synodal."

We read again: "This collegial union is apparent also in the mutual relations of the individual bishops with particular churches and with the universal Church.... Each bishop represents his own Church, but all of them together and with the Pope represent the entire Church in the bond of peace, love and unity" *(LG* 23).

For this reason, "Each of them, [the bishops] as a member of the episcopal college and legitimate successor of the apostles, is obliged by Christ's institution and command to be solicitous for the whole Church, and this solicitude, though it is not exercised by an act of jurisdiction, contributes greatly to the advantage of the universal Church. For it is the duty of all bishops to promote and to safeguard the unity of faith and the discipline common to the whole Church, to instruct the faithful to love for the whole Mystical Body of Christ, especially for its poor and sorrowing members and for those who are suffering persecution for justice's sake, and finally to promote every activity that is of interest to the whole Church, especially that the faith may take increase and the light of full truth appear to all men" *(LG* 23).

At this point the Council recalls: "By divine Providence it has come about that various churches, established in various places by the apostles and their successors, have in the course of time coalesced into several groups, organically united, which, preserving the unity of faith and the unique divine constitution of the universal Church, enjoy their own discipline, their own liturgical usage, and their own theological and spiritual heritage. Some of these churches, notably the ancient patriarchal churches, as parent stocks of the Faith, so to speak, have begotten others as daughter churches, with which they are connected down to our own time by a close bond of charity in their sacramental life and in their mutual respect for their rights and duties" *(LG* 23).

We see, then, that the Council also calls attention (in the context of the doctrine on the collegiality of the episcopate) to the fundamental truth about the mutual interpenetration and integration of both the particular reality and the universal dimension in the Church's structure. The role of episcopal conferences must also be considered from this standpoint. *Lumen Gentium* states: "The episcopal bodies of today are in a position to render a manifold and fruitful assistance, so that this collegiate feeling may be put into practical application" *(LG* 23).

A more detailed statement on this subject was made in the Decree on the Pastoral Office of Bishops in the Church

(Christus Dominus). We read there: "An episcopal conference is, as it were, a council in which the bishops of a given nation or territory jointly exercise their pastoral office to promote the greater good which the Church offers mankind, especially through the forms and methods of the apostolate fittingly adapted to the circumstances of the age" *(CD* 38, 1).

The conclusion to be drawn from these texts is that episcopal conferences are able to deal with problems in the territory of their responsibility, beyond the boundaries of the individual dioceses, and to offer them answers of a pastoral or doctrinal nature. They can also give opinions on problems concerning the universal Church. Above all they can authoritatively provide for the needs of the Church's development according to what is required by or suitable to the national mentality and culture. They can make decisions, with the consent of the member bishops, which will have great impact on pastoral activities.

Episcopal conferences have their own responsibility within the territory of their competence, but their decisions have inevitable repercussions on the universal Church. The Petrine ministry of the Bishop of Rome guarantees the coordination of the conferences' activities with the life and teaching of the universal Church. In this regard the Council's decree establishes: "Decisions of the episcopal conference, provided they have been approved legitimately and by the votes of at least two-thirds of the prelates who have a deliberative vote in the conference, and have been recognized by the Apostolic See, are to have juridically binding force only in those cases prescribed by the common law or determined by a special mandate of the Apostolic See, given either spontaneously or in response to a petition of the conference itself" *(CD* 38, 4). Lastly, the decree establishes: "Wherever special circumstances require and with the approbation of the Apostolic See, bishops of many nations can establish a single conference" *(CD* 38, 5).

Something similar can also occur in regard to councils and meetings of bishops on the continental level, as for example, the Council of Latin American Conferences (C.E.L.A.M.) or that of European Churches (C.C.E.E.). All this is a vast range of new groups and organizations by which the one Church tries to respond to the spiritual needs and problems of the world today. This is a sign that the Church lives, reflects and is committed to working as an apostle of the Gospel in our day. In every case she is aware of the need to present herself, to work and to live in fidelity to the two basic features of the Christian community of every age and, in particular, of the apostolic college: unity and catholicity.

General audience of October 21, 1992

Bishops Teach, Sanctify and Govern

As successors of the apostles, bishops are called to share in the mission which Jesus Christ himself entrusted to the Twelve and the Church. The Second Vatican Council reminds us of this: "Bishops, as successors of the apostles, receive from the Lord, to whom was given all power in heaven and on earth, the mission to teach all nations and to preach the Gospel to every creature, so that all men may attain to salvation by faith, baptism and the fulfillment of the commandments" *(LG* 24).

According to the Council's text, this mission is one which the bishops "receive from the Lord" and which has the same scope as that of the apostles. It is the responsibility of the episcopal college as a whole, as we saw in the previous catechesis. We must add, however, that the apostles' inheritance—as mission and as sacred power—is handed on to each individual bishop within the context of the episcopal college. We want to explain this reality in today's catechesis, especially by turning to texts of the Council. They offer the most authoritative and competent lessons on this topic.

The mission of individual bishops is fulfilled within a strictly defined sphere. We read in the conciliar text: "The individual bishops, who are placed in charge of particular churches, exercise their pastoral government over the portion of the People of God committed to their care, and not over other churches nor over the universal Church" *(LG* 23). This matter is regulated by the canonical mission conferred on every bishop (cf. *LG* 24).

In every case the involvement of the supreme authority guarantees that the assignment of the canonical mission is done not only for the benefit of the local community, but for the welfare of the whole Church, in relation to the universal mission common to the episcopate in union with the Supreme Pontiff. This is a fundamental element of the "Petrine ministry."

The majority of bishops exercise their pastoral mission in dioceses. What is a diocese? The Council's Decree *Christus Dominus* answered this question in the following way: "A diocese is a portion of the people of God which is entrusted to a bishop to be shepherded by him with the cooperation of the presbytery. Thus by adhering to its pastor and gathered together by him through the Gospel and the Eucharist in the Holy Spirit, it constitutes a particular church in which the one, holy, catholic, and apostolic Church of Christ is truly present and operative" *(CD* 11).

According to the Council, then, each particular church lives the life of the universal Church, which is the fundamental reality of the Church. The latter is the most important and distinctive hallmark of the diocese, which is part of the universal Church, not only as a portion of the People of God, usually determined territorially, but also as one having particular features and characteristics that deserve respect and esteem. In some cases these values are very significant and widespread among individual peoples and even in the universal Church, as history attests. We can also say, however, that always and everywhere the variety of dioceses adds to the Church's spiritual wealth and to the fulfillment of her pastoral mission.

We read again in the Council: "Individual bishops who have been entrusted with the care of a particular church—under the authority of the Supreme Pontiff—feed their sheep in the name of the Lord as their own ordinary and immediate pastors, performing for them the office of teaching, sanctifying and governing" *(CD* 11). Bishops' jurisdiction over the flocks entrusted to them is thus proper, ordinary and immediate. Nevertheless, the Church's good order and unity require that this authority be exercised in strict communion with the authority of the Supreme Pontiff. For the same reasons bishops should "recognize the rights which legitimately belong to patriarchs or other hierarchical authorities" *(CD* 11), according to the historical development of the Church's structure in various places. As the Council points out, however, what really matters and is most decisive is that the bishops exercise their pastoral mission "in the name of the Lord."

Seen in this light, the mission of bishops is presented in its institutional, spiritual and pastoral value, in relation to the various conditions and states of the people entrusted to them, as follows: "Bishops," the Council states, "should dedicate themselves to their apostolic office as witnesses of Christ before all men. They should not only look after those who already follow the prince of pastors but should also wholeheartedly devote themselves to those who have strayed in any way from the path of truth or are ignorant of the Gospel of Christ and his saving mercy, until finally all men walk 'in all goodness and justice and truth' (Eph 5:9)" *(CD* 11).

Bishops, therefore, are called to imitate the "Son of Man," who "came to seek and to save what was lost" (Lk 19:10), as Jesus said during his visit to Zacchaeus' house. It is the very essence of their missionary vocation.

The Council continues in the same vein: "Special concern should be shown for those among the faithful who, on account of their way of life, cannot sufficiently make use of the common and ordinary pastoral care of parish priests or are quite cut off from it. Among this group are the majority of migrants, exiles and refugees, seafarers, air-travelers, gypsies, and others of this kind. Suitable pastoral methods should also be promoted to sustain the spiritual life of those who go to other lands for a time for the sake of recreation" *(CD* 18). All these groups and social strata, especially individuals belonging to old and new forms of societal life, belong to the pastoral mission of bishops, within or beyond the fixed structures of their dioceses, just as they are included in the Church's universal embrace.

In fulfilling their mission, bishops find that they must face social structures and the powers that control them. In this area they are committed to acting according to the Gospel norms of freedom and love that the apostles themselves followed. What Peter and John said before the Sanhedrin is valid in every case: "Whether it is right in the sight of God for us to obey you rather than God, you be the judges. It is impossible for us not to speak about what we have seen and heard" (Acts 4:19). These words clearly formulate the principle of action for the Church's pastors in relation to various earthly authorities and it is valid for all ages.

On this matter the Council teaches:

> In discharging their apostolic office, which concerns the salvation of souls, bishops *per se* enjoy full and perfect freedom and independence from any civil authority. Hence, the exercise of their ecclesiastical office may not be hindered, directly or indirectly, nor may they be forbidden to communicate freely with the Apostolic See, or ecclesiastical authorities, or their subjects.

> Assuredly, while sacred pastors devote themselves to the spiritual care of their flock, they also in fact have regard for their social and civil progress and prosperity. According to the nature of their office and as behooves bishops, they collaborate actively with public authorities for this purpose and advocate obedience to just laws and reverence for legitimately constituted authorities *(CD* 19).

In speaking of the bishops' mission and responsibilities, the Council also discussed the question of bishops who have been appointed as auxiliaries of the diocesan bishop. "Auxiliary bishops will frequently be appointed because the diocesan bishop cannot personally fulfill all his episcopal duties as the good of souls demands, either because of the vast extent of the diocese or the great number of its inhabitants, or because of the special nature of the apostolate or other reasons of a different nature. Sometimes, in fact, a particular need requires that a coadjutor bishop be appointed to assist the diocesan bishop" *(CD* 25). As a rule, the coadjutor bishop is appointed with the right to succeed the diocesan bishop in office. But over and above canonical distinctions stands the principle which the conciliar text refers to: the good of souls. Everything must always be arranged and done in accord with that "supreme law" which is "the salvation of souls."

The following conciliar laws can also be explained in relation to this good: "Since pastoral needs require more and more that some pastoral undertakings be directed and carried forward as joint projects, it is fitting that certain offices be created for the service of all or many dioceses of a determined region or nation. These offices can be filled by bishops" *(CD* 42). Anyone who observes the Church's pastoral and structural situation today in the various countries of the world can easily see that these laws have been implemented in the many offices created by bishops or by the Holy See itself before and after the Council, especially for missionary, charitable and cultural activities. A typical, well-known example is the spiritual care of military personnel, for which the Council provided the establishment of special Ordinaries, according to the Holy See's long-standing practice: "Since, because of the unique conditions of their way of life, the spiritual care of military personnel requires special consideration, there should be established in every nation, if possible, a military vicariate" *(CD* 43).

In these new areas of activity, which are often complex and difficult, as well as in the ordinary fulfillment of the pastoral mission in the individual dioceses entrusted to them, bishops need unity and cooperation with each other in a spirit of fraternal charity and apostolic solidarity as members of the episcopal college in the concrete fulfillment of their great and small tasks every day. The Council also said in this regard: "In these days especially bishops frequently are unable to fulfill their office effectively and fruitfully unless they develop a common effort involving constant growth in harmony and closeness of ties with other bishops" *(CD* 37).

Obviously, unity and cooperation are always recommended as the keystone of pastoral work. This is a principle of ecclesiology to which we must be ever more faithful, if we want to "build up the body of Christ," as St. Paul wanted (cf. Eph 4:12; Col 2:19; 1 Cor 12:12ff.; Rom 12:4-5; etc.), and together with him, every other genuine pastor of the Church over the centuries.

General audience of October 28, 1992

Bishops Are Heralds of the Gospel

Having discussed how the Second Vatican Council described the mission of bishops, both as a college and as pastors personally assigned to various dioceses, we now want to consider the essential elements of this mission, as the same Council explained them. The first element is to preach authoritatively the Word of God. The Council says: "Among the principal duties of bishops the preaching of the Gospel occupies an eminent place" *(LG 25)*.

The pastoral mission of proclaiming the Word of God is the first function entrusted to the bishops, as it was to the apostles. Today more than ever the Church is very aware of the necessity of proclaiming the Good News, both for the salvation of souls and for spreading and establishing her own social and community organization. She recalls St. Paul's words: "For 'everyone who calls on the name of the Lord will be saved.' But how can they call on him in whom they have not believed? And how can they believe in him of whom they have not heard? And how can they hear without someone to preach? And how can people preach unless they are sent? As it is written, 'How beautiful are the feet of those who bring the Good News!'" (Rom 10:13-15).

For this reason the Council says that "Bishops are heralds of the faith," and that as such they make the faith of God's people grow and bear fruit (cf. *LG* 25). The Council then lists the responsibilities of bishops in relation to this primary function of theirs as "heralds": to provide religious instruction for young people and adults; to preach revealed truth, the mystery of Christ, whole and entire; to remind people of the Church's teaching, especially on points most open to doubt or criticism. We read in *Christus Dominus:* "In exercising their duty of teaching—which is conspicuous among the principal duties of bishops—they should announce the Gospel of Christ to men, calling them to a faith in the power of the Spirit or confirming them in a living faith. They should expound the whole mystery of Christ to them, namely, those truths the ignorance of which is ignorance of Christ. At the same time they should point out the divinely revealed way to give glory to God and thereby to attain to eternal happiness" *(CD* 12).

At the same time, however, the Council urges bishops to present this doctrine in a way suited to the needs of the times: "The bishops should present Christian doctrine in a manner adapted to the needs of the times, that is to say, in a manner that will respond to the difficulties and questions by which people are especially burdened and troubled. They should also guard that doctrine, teaching the faithful to defend and propagate it" *(CD* 13).

In the context of preaching, it is also necessary, in the light of the mystery of Christ, to teach the true value of man, the human person and also of "earthly things." The Council recommends that bishops:

> ...should show, moreover, that earthly goods and human institutions according to the plan of God the Creator are also disposed for man's salvation and therefore can contribute much to the building up of the body of Christ.
>
> Therefore, they should teach, according to the doctrine of the Church, the great value of these things: the human

person with his freedom and bodily life, the family and its unity and stability, the procreation and education of children, civil society with its laws and professions, labor and leisure, the arts and technical inventions, poverty and affluence. Finally, they should set forth the ways by which are to be answered the most serious questions concerning the ownership, increase, and just distribution of material goods, peace and war, and brotherly relations among all countries *(CD* 12).

The foregoing is the historical and social dimension of preaching and of the very Gospel of Christ handed on by the apostles in their preaching. We should not be surprised that the historical and social nature of man abound in preaching today, even though this preaching should be done on the religious and moral level that is proper to it. Concern for the human condition, which today is troubled and often distressed on the economic, social and political level, is translated into a constant effort to bring individuals and peoples the help that comes from the light and love of the Gospel.

The faithful should respond to the bishops' teaching by adhering to it in a spirit of faith. The Council says: "Bishops, teaching in communion with the Roman Pontiff, are to be respected by all as witnesses to divine and Catholic truth. In matters of faith and morals, the bishops speak in the name of Christ and the faithful are to accept their teaching and adhere to it with a religious assent" *(LG* 25).

Obviously, the Council specifies that an essential condition for the value and obligatory quality of the bishops' teaching is that they are in communion with the Roman Pontiff and speak as such. Certainly each bishop has his own personality and presents the Lord's teaching by using the talents at his disposal. But precisely because it is a question of preaching the Lord's teaching entrusted to the Church, he must always remain in communion of mind and heart with the visible head of the Church.

When a doctrine of faith or morals is universally and definitively taught by the Church's bishops, their Magisterium enjoys an infallible authority. The Council also states:

> Although the individual bishops do not enjoy the pre-rogative of infallibility, they nevertheless proclaim Christ's doctrine infallibly whenever, even though dispersed through the world, but still maintaining the bond of communion among themselves and with the Successor of Peter, and authentically teaching matters of faith and morals, they are in agreement on one position as definitively to be held. This is even more clearly verified when, gathered together in an ecumenical council, they are teachers and judges of faith and morals for the universal Church, whose definitions must be adhered to with the submission of faith *(LG* 25).

The Roman Pontiff, as head of the college of bishops, personally enjoys this infallibility. (We will discuss this in a future catechesis.) For now let us finish reading the conciliar text regarding bishops: "The infallibility promised to the Church resides also in the body of bishops, when that body exercises the supreme Magisterium with the Successor of Peter. To these definitions the assent of the Church can never be wanting, on account of the activity of that same Holy Spirit, by which the whole flock of Christ is preserved and progresses in unity of faith" *(LG* 25).

The Holy Spirit, who guarantees the truth of the episcopal body's infallible teaching, also ensures the Church's assent of faith through his grace. Communion in the faith is the work of the Holy Spirit, the soul of the Church.

The Council says further:

> And this infallibility with which the divine Redeemer willed his Church to be endowed in defining doctrine of faith and morals, extends as far as the deposit of revelation extends.... But when either the Roman Pontiff or the

body of bishops together with him defines a judgment, they pronounce it in accordance with revelation itself, which all are obliged to abide by and be in conformity with, that is, the revelation which as written or orally handed down is transmitted in its entirety through the legitimate succession of bishops and especially in care of the Roman Pontiff himself, and which under the guiding light of the Spirit of truth is religiously preserved and faithfully expounded in the Church *(LG* 25).

Lastly, the Council advises: "The deposit of revelation...must be religiously guarded and faithfully expounded" *(LG* 25).

The entire body of bishops in union with the Roman Pontiff is responsible for constantly and faithfully guarding the patrimony of truth Christ entrusted to his Church. "Guard what has been entrusted to you," St. Paul urged his disciple Timothy (1 Tim 6:20), to whom he had entrusted the pastoral care of the church in Ephesus (cf. 1 Tim 1:3). As bishops of the Catholic Church, we must all be aware of this responsibility. We all know that, if we are faithful in guarding this "deposit," we will always be able to maintain the faith of the People of God in its integrity and to ensure that its content will be spread throughout the world today and in generations to come.

General audience of November 4, 1992

Bishops Are Stewards of God's Grace

In speaking of the bishop's functions, the Second Vatican Council attributes to the bishop himself a beautiful title taken from the prayer of episcopal consecration in the Byzantine rite: "The bishop, marked with the fullness of the sacrament of Orders, is 'the steward of the grace of the supreme priesthood'" *(LG* 26). Today's catechesis will treat this topic. It is related to that of the preceding catechesis on bishops as "heralds of the faith." Indeed, the service of proclaiming the Gospel is ordered to the service of grace in the Church's holy sacraments. As a minister of grace, the bishop exercises in the sacraments the service of sanctification *(munus sanctificandi)* which is the aim of the service of teaching *(munus docendi)* he fulfills among the People of God entrusted to him.

At the center of this sacramental service of the bishop is the Eucharist "which he offers or causes to be offered" *(LG* 26). The Council teaches: "Every legitimate celebration of the Eucharist is regulated by the bishop, to whom is committed the office of offering the worship of Christian religion to the divine majesty and of administering it in accordance with the Lord's commandments and the Church's laws, as further defined by his particular judgment for his diocese" *(LG* 26).

The bishop thus appears to his people primarily as the

man of the new and eternal worship of God that was instituted
by Jesus Christ through the sacrifice of the cross and of the
Last Supper; as the *sacerdos et pontifex,* in whom is seen
the figure of Christ himself, the principal agent of the Eucharistic sacrifice, which the bishop, and the priest with him, offer
in persona Christi (cf. St. Thomas, *Summa Theol.,* III, q. 78, a.
1; q. 82, a. 1); as the *hierarch,* concerned with celebrating the
sacred mysteries of the altar, which he proclaims and explains
in his preaching (cf. Dionysius, *De ecclesiastica hierar-
chia,* p. III, 7; *PG* 3, 513; St. Thomas, *Summa Theol.,* II-II,
q. 184, a. 5).

In his function of celebrating the sacred mysteries, the
bishop builds the Church as a communion in Christ. The Eucharist is the essential principle of life not only for the
individual members of faithful, but also for the community in
Christ itself. The faithful, gathered together by the preaching
of the Gospel of Christ, form communities in which the
Church of Christ is truly present, because they find and show
forth their full unity in celebrating the Eucharistic sacrifice.
We read in the Council:

> In any community of the altar, under the sacred ministry
> of the bishop, there is exhibited a symbol of that charity
> and "unity of the Mystical Body, without which there
> can be no salvation" (cf. *Summa Theol.,* III, q. 73, a. 3).
> In these communities, though frequently small and poor,
> or living in the Diaspora, Christ is present, and in virtue
> of his presence there is brought together one, holy, catho-
> lic and apostolic Church. For "the partaking of the Body
> and Blood of Christ does nothing other than make us be
> transformed into that which we consume" (St. Leo the
> Great, *Serm.* 63, 7; *PL* 54, 357C) *(LG* 26).

Consequently, among the bishop's basic tasks is that of
providing the various communities of his diocese with the
celebration of the Eucharist, according to the circumstances of
time and place, in recalling Jesus' statement: "Amen, amen, I

say to you, unless you eat the flesh of the Son of Man and
drink his blood, you do not have life within you" (Jn 6:53).

We know the difficulties that are encountered in many
regions of both the ancient and the new Christian churches in
satisfying this need, due to a shortage of priests and for other
reasons. But this fact makes the bishop, who is aware of his
own duty to organize worship in his diocese, even more attentive to the problem of vocations and the wise distribution of
available clergy. It is necessary to enable the largest number of
the faithful to receive the Body and Blood of Christ in the
Eucharistic celebration, which culminates in Communion. It is
the bishop's responsibility also to care for the sick and the
disabled who can receive the Eucharist only at home or wherever they are being cared for. Among all the demands of the
pastoral ministry, diligent concern for the celebration and for
what we might call the "apostolate of the Eucharist" is the
most compelling and important.

What we said in regard to the Holy Eucharist can also be
said of the whole sacramental service and sacramental life of
the diocese. As we read in *Lumen Gentium,* the bishops "direct
the conferring of Baptism, by which a sharing in the kingly
priesthood of Christ is granted. They are the original ministers
of Confirmation, dispensers of sacred Orders and the modera-
tors of penitential discipline, and they earnestly exhort and
instruct their people to carry out with faith and reverence their
part in the liturgy and especially in the holy sacrifice of the
Mass" *(LG* 26).

This conciliar text distinguishes between Baptism and
Confirmation, two sacraments that are differentiated on the
basis of the account in the Acts of the Apostles. This book says
that the Twelve, still gathered together in Jerusalem, on hearing "that Samaria had accepted the word of God," sent them
Peter and John, who "went down and prayed for them that they
might receive the Holy Spirit, for it had not yet fallen upon any
of them; they had only been baptized in the name of the Lord

Jesus. Then they laid hands on them and they received the Holy Spirit" (Acts 8:14-17; cf. 1:5, 2:38).

The imposition of hands by the two apostles for conferring the "gift of the Spirit," which Acts also calls the "gift of God" (Acts 8:20; cf. 2:38; 10:45; 11:17; Lk 11:9-13), is the basis for the Western Church's tradition which preserves and reserves the ministerial role in Confirmation to the bishop. As a successor of the apostles, the bishop is the ordinary minister of this sacrament and he is also its original minister, because chrism (the matter), which is an essential element of the sacramental rite, can be consecrated only by a bishop.

In regard to Baptism, which the bishop usually does not administer personally, it should be remembered that this sacrament too comes under his effective direction.

Another duty of bishops is to confer sacred Orders and regulate the discipline of Penance, as the Council says in describing their pastoral responsibilities (cf. *LG* 26). According to this conciliar text, the bishop confers Holy Orders in the sense that he has the power to ordain. However, since this power is linked with the bishop's pastoral mission, he consequently has the responsibility, as we said, of promoting the development of priestly vocations and of providing good discipline for candidates to the priesthood.

In regulating the discipline of Penance, the bishop oversees the conditions for administering the sacrament of forgiveness. We mention especially that he is supposed to enable the faithful to receive this sacrament by making confessors readily available.

Finally, the Council shows bishops the need of being examples and models of Christian life: "By the example of their way of life they must be an influence for good to those over whom they preside, refraining from all evil and, as far as they are able with God's help, exchanging evil for good, so that together with the flock committed to their care they may arrive at eternal life" *(LG* 26).

This example of life is guided completely by the theological virtues of faith, hope and charity. It is a way of living and acting based on the power of divine grace. It is a contagious, attractive and persuasive model that truly corresponds to the recommendations in the First Letter of Peter: "Tend the flock of God in your midst, overseeing not by constraint but willingly, as God would have it, not for shameful profit but eagerly. Do not lord it over those assigned to you, but be examples to the flock" (1 Pet 5:2-3).

This last point is especially important in regard to selflessness, concern for the poor, total dedication to the good of souls and that of the Church. It is the example which, according to the Acts of the Apostles, was given by Paul, who said of himself: "In every way I have shown you that by hard work of that sort we must help the weak, and keep in mind the words of the Lord Jesus who himself said, 'It is more blessed to give than to receive'" (Acts 20:35). In the Second Letter to the Thessalonians he also wrote: "In toil and drudgery, night and day we worked, so as not to burden any of you. Not that we do not have the right. Rather, we wanted to present ourselves as a model for you, so that you might imitate us" (2 Thess 3:8-9). Lastly, he urged the Corinthians: "Be imitators of me, as I am of Christ" (1 Cor 11:1).

The bishop's mission as a "steward of grace" is great but arduous. He cannot fulfill it without prayer. We conclude, then, by saying that the bishop's life is made of prayer. He does not give merely a "witness of prayer," but of an interior life invigorated by the spirit of prayer as the source of all his ministry. No one is as aware as the bishop of the meaning of Christ's words to the apostles and through them to their successors: "Without me you can do nothing" (Jn 15:5).

General audience of November 11, 1992

Bishops Govern Their Local Churches

In addition to the prophetic and sacramental service of bishops, to which we devoted the previous catecheses, there is a pastoral service, regarding which the Second Vatican Council said: "Bishops, as vicars and ambassadors of Christ, govern the particular churches entrusted to them by their counsel, exhortations, example, and even by their authority and sacred power, which indeed they use only for the edification of their flock in truth and holiness, remembering that he who is greater should become as the lesser and he who is the chief become as the servant (cf. Lk 22:26-27)" *(LG 27)*.

This wonderful teaching hinges on this basic principle: in the Church authority is meant to be upbuilding. St. Paul considered it as such when he wrote to the Corinthians, speaking of "our authority, which the Lord gave for building you up and not for tearing you down" (2 Cor 10:8). To the members of this Church that was very dear to him he always expressed the hope of not having to act harshly "in virtue of the authority that the Lord has given me to build up and not to tear down" (2 Cor 13:10).

The aim of building up requires patience and leniency from bishops. This means the spiritual development of their flock in truth and holiness, as the Council says: the truth of the

237

Gospel teaching and holiness as it was lived, willed and taught by Christ.

It is necessary to insist on the concept of service, which applies to every ecclesiastical ministry, beginning with that of bishops. Indeed, the episcopate is more a service than an honor. If it is also an honor, it is so when the bishop, a successor of the apostles, serves in a spirit of gospel humility, following the example of the Son of Man who admonished the Twelve: "Let the greatest among you be as the youngest, and the leader as the servant" (Lk 22:26). "Whoever wishes to be first among you will be the slave of all. For the Son of Man did not come to be served but to serve and to give his life as a ransom for many" (Mk 10:44-45; cf. Mt 20:27-28).

In *Christus Dominus* the Council adds: "In exercising their office of father and pastor, bishops should stand in the midst of their people as those who serve. Let them be good shepherds who know their sheep and whose sheep know them. Let them be true fathers who excel in the spirit of love and solicitude for all and to whose divinely conferred authority all gratefully submit themselves. Let them so gather and mold the whole family of their flock that everyone, conscious of his own duties, may live and work in the communion of love" *(CD* 16).

It is in the light of this service "as a good shepherd" that the authority which the bishop possesses *in proprio* must be understood, although it is always subject to that of the Supreme Pontiff. We read in *Lumen Gentium:* "This power, which they [the bishops] personally exercise in Christ's name, is proper, ordinary and immediate, although its exercise is ultimately regulated by the supreme authority of the Church, and can be circumscribed by certain limits, for the advantage of the Church or of the faithful. In virtue of this power, bishops have the sacred right and the duty before the Lord to make laws for their subjects, to pass judgment on them and to moderate everything pertaining to the ordering of worship and the apostolate" *(LG* 27).

Certainly it is a question of a true authority, which must be treated with respect and to which both the clergy and the faithful should be docile and obedient in the area of Church governance. However, it is always an authority with a pastoral function.

In regard to this pastoral care for their flock, which entails a corresponding personal responsibility for developing the Christian life of the people entrusted to them, the Council says of bishops: "The pastoral office or the habitual and daily care of their sheep is entrusted to them completely; nor are they to be regarded as vicars of the Roman Pontiffs, for they exercise an authority that is proper to them, and are quite correctly called 'prelates,' heads of the people whom they govern" *(LG 27)*.

Obviously, the Council does not hesitate to assert that every bishop has true authority over his own diocese, or local church. But it forcefully underscored another point that is basic to the unity and catholicity of the Church, that is, the communion of every bishop and the whole *corpus episcoporum "cum Petro,"* which is also communion *"sub Petro."* This is in virtue of the ecclesiological principle (which tends to be overlooked sometimes) according to which the ministry of Peter's successor belongs to the essence of every particular church "from within," or as a requirement of the Church's very constitution, and not as something added on from without, for historical, sociological or practical reasons. It is not a question of adapting to the circumstances of the times, but of fidelity to Christ's will for his Church. The Church's foundation on Peter the rock, the assigning of a primacy to Peter, which continues in his successors as bishops of Rome, entails a connection with the universal Church and its center in the church of Rome as a constitutive element of the particular church and a condition for its being a church at all. This point is fundamental to a good theology of the local church.

On the other hand, the power of bishops is not threatened by that of the Roman Pontiff. As the Council says: "Their power, therefore, is not destroyed by the supreme and universal power, but on the contrary it is affirmed, strengthened and vindicated by it, since the Holy Spirit unfailingly preserves the form of government established by Christ the Lord in his Church" *(LG* 27).

Consequently, the relationship among bishops and the Pope cannot fail to be a relationship of cooperation and mutual aid, in an atmosphere of friendship and fraternal trust, as can be observed—and even experienced—in the Church's life today.

To the bishop's authority there is the corresponding responsibility of a pastor, because of which he feels committed to giving his own life each day for the good of his flock, following the example of the good shepherd. Sharing in the cross of Christ, he is called to make many personal sacrifices for the Church. These sacrifices are the concrete expression of that commitment of perfect love to which he is called by the status he has received through episcopal consecration. Therein lies the specifically episcopal spirituality, as the supreme imitation of Christ, the good shepherd, and as the greatest sharing in his love.

The bishop, then, is called to imitate Christ the shepherd, allowing himself to be led by charity in regard to everyone. The Council especially recommends a listening attitude: "Let him not refuse to listen to his subjects, whom he cherishes as his true sons and exhorts to cooperate readily with him" *(LG* 27). The bishop should be distinguished by all the qualities necessary for communication and communion with his children and brethren: understanding and compassion for their spiritual and physical suffering; a desire to help and aid, to encourage and promote cooperation; and above all, universal love, with no exceptions, restrictions or reservations.

According to the Council, all of the above should find special expression in the bishop's attitude toward his brothers in the ministerial priesthood: "Bishops should always embrace priests with a special love since the latter to the best of their ability assume the bishops' anxieties and carry them on day by day so zealously. They should regard the priests as sons and friends and be ready to listen to them. Through their trusting familiarity with their priests they should strive to promote the whole pastoral work of the entire diocese" *(CD* 16).

However, the Council also mentions the duties of the pastor regarding the laity: "In exercising this pastoral care they should preserve for their faithful the share proper to them in Church affairs; they should also respect their duty and right of actively collaborating in the building up of the Mystical Body of Christ" *(CD* 16).

The Council also adds a note on the universal dimension of the love which should inspire the episcopal ministry: "They should deal lovingly with the separated brethren, urging the faithful also to conduct themselves with great kindness and charity in their regard and fostering ecumenism as it is understood by the Church. They should also have a place in their hearts for the non-baptized so that upon them too there may shine the charity of Christ Jesus, to whom the bishops are witnesses before all men" *(CD* 16).

The image of the bishop that emerges from the Council's texts, then, shows that he is distinguished in the Church by the greatness of his ministry and the nobility of his spirit as a good shepherd. His status obliges him to demanding and arduous duties and to lofty sentiments of love for Christ and his brothers and sisters. It is a difficult mission and life, and so for this reason too all those in the bishop's diocese should show him love and docility, and work with him for the coming of God's kingdom. In this regard the Council concludes: "The faithful must cling to their bishop, as the Church does to Christ, and Jesus Christ to the Father, so that all may be of one mind through unity, and abound to the glory of God (cf. 2 Cor 4:15)" *(LG* 27).

General audience of November 18, 1992

Christt Builds His Church on Peter

We have seen that according to the Council's teaching, which is a summary of the Church's traditional doctrine, there exists an "order of bishops which is the successor to the college of the apostles in their role as teachers and pastors." Indeed this episcopal college "gives this apostolic body continued existence, [and] is also the subject of supreme and full power over the universal Church, provided we understand this body together with its head the Roman Pontiff and never without this head. This power can be exercised only with the consent of the Roman Pontiff" *(LG* 22).

This text of Vatican II tells us about the Petrine ministry exercised in the Church by the Bishop of Rome as the head of the episcopal college. We will devote the set of catecheses that we are beginning today to this important and significant point of Catholic doctrine. We intend to give a clear, reasoned exposition of this teaching, in which the feeling of personal inadequacy is joined to that of the responsibility which stems from Jesus' mandate to Peter, and in particular, from the divine teacher's response to this profession of faith in the region of Caesarea Philippi (cf. Mt 16:13-19).

Let us again examine the text and context of the important dialogue handed down to us by the evangelist Matthew.

After asking: "Who do people say that the Son of Man is?" (Mt 16:13), Jesus asked his apostles a more direct question: "But who do you say that I am?" (Mt 16:15). It is already significant that Simon answered in the name of the Twelve: "You are the Messiah, the Son of the living God" (Mt 16:13-16). One might think that Simon made himself the spokesman for the Twelve by force of his own more vigorous and impulsive personality. Possibly this factor came into play to some extent. However, Jesus attributed his answer to a special revelation from the heavenly Father: "Blessed are you, Simon son of Jonah. For flesh and blood has not revealed this to you, but my heavenly Father" (Mt 16:17). Above and beyond factors of temperament, character, ethnic background or social status ("flesh and blood"), Simon was the beneficiary of an illumination and inspiration from on high that Jesus identified as "revelation." In virtue of this revelation Simon made a profession of faith in the name of the Twelve.

Here is Jesus' declaration, which in the very solemnity of its form manifests the binding and constitutive meaning that the Teacher intends to give it: "And so I say to you, you are Peter" (Mt 16:18). The declaration is indeed solemn: "I say to you." It involves Jesus' sovereign authority. It is a word of revelation, of effective revelation in that it accomplishes what it says.

A new name was given to Simon, the sign of a new mission. That this name was given is confirmed by Mark (3:16) and Luke (6:14) in their accounts of the choice of the Twelve. John also speaks of it, indicating that Jesus used the Aramaic word *Kephas,* which in Greek is translated as *Petros* (Jn 1:42).

We should remember that the Aramaic word *Kephas* which Jesus used, as well as the Greek word *Petros* which translates it, means "rock." In the Sermon on the Mount Jesus gave the example of the "wise man who built his house on rock" (Mt 7:24). Addressing Simon, Jesus declared to him that because of his faith, a gift from God, he had the solidity of rock upon which an unshakable edifice could be built. Jesus then stated his own decision to build on this rock just such a building—his Church.

In other passages of the New Testament we find similar although not identical images. In some texts Jesus himself is not called the "rock" on which something is built, but the "stone" which is used in building, the "cornerstone" which ensures the solidity of the structure. The builder then is not Jesus, but God the Father (cf. Mk 12:10-11; 1 Pet 2:4-7). Thus the viewpoints are different.

The Apostle Paul expresses yet another perspective when he reminds the Corinthians that "like a wise master builder" he "laid the foundation" of their Church and then indicates that this foundation is "Jesus Christ" (cf. 1 Cor 3:10-11).

Through the diversity of particular viewpoints one can nevertheless notice a basic relationship allowing us to conclude that by giving him a new name, Jesus made Simon Peter a sharer in his own capacity as foundation. Between Christ and Peter there is a foundational relationship rooted in the profound reality where the divine vocation is translated into a specific mission conferred by the Messiah.

Jesus went on to say: "Upon this rock I will build my Church, and the gates of the netherworld shall not prevail against it" (Mt 16:18). These words attest to Jesus' will to build his Church with an essential reference to the specific mission and power that in due time he would confer on Simon. Jesus described Simon Peter as the foundation on which the Church would be built. The Christ-Peter relationship is thus reflected in the Peter-Church relationship. It imbues it with value and discloses its theological and spiritual meaning, which is objectively and ecclesially the basis of its juridical significance.

Matthew is the only evangelist who records these words for us. But it must be remembered that Matthew is also the only one who collected the recollections concerning Peter specifically (cf. Mt 14:28-31). Perhaps this was with reference to the communities for which he wrote his Gospel and in which he wanted to instill the new idea of the "assembly called together" in the name of Christ present in Peter.

On the other hand, the "new name" of Peter which Jesus gave to Simon is confirmed by the other evangelists, without any difference in meaning attributed to it than that given by Matthew. Moreover, there is no other meaning it could possibly have.

The text of the evangelist Matthew (16:15-18) which presents Peter as the foundation of the Church has been the subject of many debates, too lengthy to repeat here. It is also the subject of denials which do not derive so much from proofs based on the biblical texts and Christian Tradition as much as from difficulty in understanding the mission and power of Peter and his successors. Without going into detail, here we simply point out that Jesus' words as recorded by Matthew have an unquestionable Semitic tone to them, noticeable even in the Greek and Latin translations. Furthermore, they involve an inexplicable innovation precisely in the Jewish cultural and religious context in which the evangelist presents them. In contemporary Judaism the role of foundation stone was not attributed to any religious leader; however, Jesus attributed it to Peter. This is the great innovation introduced by Jesus. It could not be the product of human invention, neither in Matthew nor in later authors.

We must also point out that the "Rock" of which Jesus spoke is properly the person of Simon. Jesus said to him: "*You are Kephas.*" The context of this statement enables us to understand better the sense of that "you-person." After Simon said who Jesus is, Jesus said who Simon is, according to his own plan for building the Church. It is true that Simon is called rock after the profession of faith, and that implies a relationship between faith and the role of rock conferred on Simon. However, the role of rock is attributed to the person of Simon, not to an act of his, however noble and pleasing to Jesus. The word "rock" expresses a permanent, subsisting being; therefore, it applies to the person, rather than to one of his necessarily transitory acts. Jesus' subsequent words confirm this when he said that the gates of the netherworld, the powers of death, will not prevail "against it." This expression can refer to the Church or to the rock. In any case, according to the logic of the discourse, the Church founded on the rock cannot be destroyed. The Church's permanence is connected with the rock. The Peter-Church relationship in itself reproduces the link between the Church and Christ. Jesus in fact said *"my* Church." This means that the Church will always be the Church of Christ, the Church which belongs to Christ. She does not become Peter's Church. However, as the Church of Christ she is built on Peter, who is *Kephas* in the name and by the power of Christ.

The evangelist Matthew records another metaphor which Jesus used to explain to Simon Peter, and to the other apostles, what he wanted to do with him: "I will give you the keys to the kingdom of heaven" (Mt 16:19). Here too we immediately note that, according to biblical tradition, the Messiah possesses the keys of the kingdom. The Book of Revelation repeats the expressions of the prophet Isaiah and presents Christ as "the holy one, the true, who holds the key of David, who opens and no one shall close, who closes and no one shall open" (Rev 3:7). The text of Isaiah (22:22) which concerns a certain Eliakim was seen as a prophetic expression of the messianic age when the "key" would not be for opening or closing the house of David (as a building or as a dynasty), but for opening the "kingdom of heaven," this new, transcendent reality proclaimed and ushered in by Jesus.

Jesus is the one who, according to the Letter to the Hebrews, "entered the heavenly sanctuary" (cf. 9:24) through his sacrifice. He possesses its keys and opens its gates. Jesus handed these keys over to Peter, who thus received power over the kingdom, power which he will exercise in Christ's name, as his steward and the head of the Church, the house which gathers together those who believe in Christ, the children of God.

Jesus indeed said to Peter: "I will give you the keys to the kingdom of heaven. Whatever you bind on earth shall be bound in heaven, and whatever you loose on earth shall be loosed in heaven" (Mt 16:19). This is another simile Jesus used to show his will to confer on Simon Peter a universal and complete power guaranteed and authenticated by heavenly approval. This does not mean only the power to formulate points of doctrine or general norms of action. According to Jesus, it is the power of "binding and loosing," that is, of doing whatever is necessary for the life and development of the Church. The opposing terms "binding-loosing" serve to show the totality of the power.

It should be immediately added, however, that the aim of this power is to open the entrance to the kingdom, not to close it: "open," that is, to make it possible to enter the kingdom of heaven and not to place obstacles that would be equivalent to "closing" it. This is the proper purpose of the Petrine ministry, rooted in the redemptive sacrifice of Christ who came to save and to be the gate and shepherd of all in the communion of the one fold (cf. Jn 10:7, 11, 16). Through his sacrifice Christ became "the gate for the sheep," the symbol of which was that built by Eliashib, the high priest, who with his priestly brothers worked to rebuild the walls of Jerusalem in the middle of the fifth century before Christ (cf. Neh 3:1). The Messiah is the true gate of the New Jerusalem built through his blood shed upon the cross. He entrusted the keys of this gate to Peter so that he might be the minister of his saving power in the Church.

General audience of November 25, 1992

Peter Strengthens His Brothers in Faith

At the Last Supper Jesus said something to Peter that deserves special consideration. Doubtlessly it refers to the dramatic situation at that time, but it has a fundamental value for the Church of all times, inasmuch as it belongs to the patrimony of the last exhortations and teachings which Jesus gave to the disciples during his earthly life.

In foretelling the triple denial which Peter would make out of fear during the passion, Jesus also predicted that he would overcome the crisis of that night: "Simon, Simon, behold Satan has demanded to sift all of you like wheat, but I have prayed that your own faith may not fail, and once you have turned back, you must strengthen your brothers" (Lk 22:31-32).

With these words Jesus guaranteed Simon a special prayer for the perseverance of his faith, but he also announced the mission entrusted to him of strengthening his brothers in the faith.

The authenticity of Jesus' words is seen not only in Luke's care in collecting positive information and setting it out in a critically sound narrative, as can be seen in the prologue of his Gospel, but also in the type of paradox which this information implies. Jesus lamented Simon Peter's weakness and at the same time entrusted him with the mission of strengthening the others. The paradox shows the grandeur of grace at work in human beings—Peter in this case—far beyond the possibilities afforded by their talents, virtues or merits. It also shows Jesus' awareness and firmness in choosing Peter. The evangelist Luke, wise and attentive to the meaning of words and things, did not hesitate to record that messianic paradox.

The context in which Jesus' words to Peter at the Last Supper are found is also very significant. He had just said to the apostles: "It is you who have stood by me in my trials, and I confer a kingdom on you, just as my Father has conferred one on me" (Lk 22:28-29). The Greek verb *diatithemai* (to prepare, arrange) has a strong meaning—to arrange in a causative way—and speaks of the reality of the messianic kingdom established by the heavenly Father and shared with the apostles. Jesus' words doubtlessly refer to the eschatological dimension of the kingdom, when the apostles will be called to "judge the twelve tribes of Israel" (Lk 22:30). However, they also have a value for its present phase, for the time of the Church here on earth, and this is a time of trial. Therefore, Jesus assured Simon Peter of his prayer so that in this trial the prince of this world would not prevail: "Satan has demanded to sift all of you like wheat" (Lk 22:31). Christ's prayer is especially necessary for Peter in view of the trial awaiting him and in view of the task Jesus entrusted to him. The words "strengthen your brothers" refer to this task (Lk 22:32).

The perspective in which Peter's responsibility—like the Church's whole mission—must be considered is therefore both historical and eschatological. It is a responsibility in the Church and for the Church in history, where there are trials to overcome, changes to face, cultural, social and religious situations in which to work. However, everything is in relation to the kingdom of heaven, already prepared and conferred by the Father as the terminus of the entire historical journey and of all personal and social experiences. The "kingdom" transcends the Church in her earthly pilgrimage; it transcends her duties and her powers. It also transcends Peter and the apostolic college, and therefore, their successors in the episcopacy. Nevertheless, it is already in the Church, already at work and developing in its historical phase and the earthly situation of its existence. In the Church there is more than an institutional and societal structure. There is the presence of the Holy Spirit, the essence of the new law according to St. Augustine (cf. *De spiritu et littera,* 21) and St. Thomas Aquinas (cf. *Summa Theol.,* I-II, q. 106, a. 1). However, this presence does not exclude, but rather demands on the ministerial level the visible, the institutional, the hierarchical.

The whole New Testament, preserved and preached by the Church, is a function of grace, of the kingdom of heaven. The Petrine ministry is situated in this perspective. Jesus announced to Simon Peter this task of service following the professions of faith he made as the spokesman of the Twelve: faith in Christ, the Son of the living God (cf. Mt 16:16), and in the words which foretold the Eucharist (cf. Jn 6:68). On the road to Caesarea Philippi, Jesus publicly approved of Simon's profession of faith, called him the fundamental rock of the Church and promised to give him the keys to the kingdom of heaven, with the power of binding and loosing. In that context it is understood that the evangelist especially highlights the aspect of mission and power concerning the faith, although other aspects are included, as we will see in the next catechesis.

It is interesting to note that the evangelist, although speaking of the human frailty of Peter who was not sheltered from difficulties and was tempted like the other apostles, emphasizes that he was the beneficiary of a special prayer for his perseverance in the faith: "I have prayed for you." Peter was not preserved from his denial, but after experiencing his own weakness, he was strengthened in faith by virtue of Jesus' prayer so that he could fulfill the mission of strengthening his brothers. This mission cannot be explained on the basis of purely human considerations.

The Apostle Peter, the only one to deny his Master—

three times!—was always Jesus' chosen one, charged with strengthening his companions. The human pretensions to fidelity that Peter professed failed, but grace triumphed.

The experience of falling enabled Peter to learn that he could not put his trust in his own strength or any other human factor, but only in Christ. It also enables us to see Peter's mission and power in light of the grace of election. What Jesus promised and entrusted to him comes from heaven and belongs—must belong—to the kingdom of heaven.

According to the evangelist, Peter's service to the kingdom consists primarily in strengthening his brothers, in helping them to keep the faith and develop it. It is interesting to point out that this mission is to be exercised *in trial*. Jesus was well aware of the difficulties in the historical phase of the Church, called to follow the way of the cross that he took. Peter's role, as head of the apostles, would be to support his "brothers" and the whole Church in faith. Since faith is not maintained without struggle, Peter must help the faithful in their struggle to overcome whatever would take away or lessen their faith. The experience of the first Christian communities is reflected in Luke's text. He was well aware of how that historical situation of persecution, temptation and struggle is explained in Christ's words to the apostles and principally to Peter.

The basic elements of the Petrine mission are found in those words: first of all, that of strengthening his brothers by expounding the faith, exhorting to faith, as well as all the measures necessary for the development of the faith. This activity is addressed to those whom Jesus, speaking to Peter, calls "your brothers." In context the expression applies first of all to the other apostles, but it does not rule out a wider sense embracing all the members of the Christian community (cf. Acts 1:15). It suggests the purpose of Peter's mission as the one who strengthens and supports faith: fraternal community in virtue of the faith.

Peter, and like him all his successors and heads of the

Church, has the mission of encouraging the faithful to put all their trust in Christ and the power of his grace, which Peter personally experienced. This is what Innocent III wrote in the Letter *Apostolicae Sedis Primatus* (November 12, 1199), citing the text of Luke 22:32 and commenting on it as follows: "The Lord clearly intimates that Peter's successors will never at any time deviate from the Catholic faith, but will instead recall the others and strengthen the hesitant" *(DS 775)*. That medieval Pope felt that Jesus' statement to Simon Peter was confirmed by the experience of 1,000 years.

The mission Jesus entrusted to Peter concerns the Church down through the centuries and human generations. That mandate "strengthen your brothers" means: teach the faith in every age, in different circumstances and amid all the difficulties and contradictions which preaching the faith will encounter in history; by teaching instill courage in the faithful; you yourself experienced that the power of my grace is greater than human weakness; therefore spread the message of faith, preach sound doctrine, reunite the "brethren," putting your trust in the prayer that I promised you; in virtue of my grace, try to help non-believers accept the faith and to comfort those who are in doubt. This is your mission, this is the reason for the mandate I entrust to you.

These words of the evangelist Luke (22:31-33) are very significant for all who exercise the *munus Petrinum* in the Church. They continually remind them of the kind of original paradox that Christ himself placed in them, with the certitude that in their ministry, as in Peter's, a special grace is at work which supports human weakness and allows him to "strengthen his brothers." "I have prayed"—Jesus' words to Peter, which re-echo in his ever poor, humble successors—"I have prayed that your own faith may not fail, and once you turned back, you must strengthen your brothers" (Lk 22:32).

General audience of December 2, 1992

Peter Is Charged
with Feeding the Sheep

The promise Jesus made to Peter to establish him as the foundation stone of his Church was confirmed in the mandate Christ entrusted to him after the resurrection: "Feed my lambs.... Feed my sheep" (Jn 21:15-17). There is an objective relationship between the conferral of the mission attested to in John's account and the promise recorded by Matthew (cf. Mt 16:18-19). In Matthew's text there is an announcement; in John's the announcement is fulfilled. The words, "Feed my sheep" show Jesus' intention to guarantee the future of the Church he founded under the direction of a universal shepherd—Peter—to whom he said that by his grace he will be "rock" and will have "the keys to the kingdom of heaven" with the power of "binding and loosing." After the resurrection Jesus gave a concrete form to the announcement and the promise made in Caesarea Philippi, establishing Peter's authority as a pastoral ministry of the Church on a universal scale.

We immediately note that this pastoral mission includes the duty to "strengthen his brothers" in the faith, which we discussed in the preceding catechesis. "Strengthening his brothers" and "feeding the sheep" together represent Peter's mission; it could be called the *proprium* of his universal ministry. As the First Vatican Council states, the Church's constant

Tradition has rightly maintained that Peter's apostolic primacy "also includes the supreme power of Magisterium" (cf. *DS* 3065). Both the primacy and the power of Magisterium are directly conferred by Jesus on Peter as a unique individual, although both prerogatives are ordered to the Church, without however being derived from the Church, but only from Christ. The primacy was given to Peter (cf. Mt 16:18) as *"totius ecclesiae figuram gerenti"* (St. Augustine, *Epist.* 53, 1, 2), that is, inasmuch as he personally represents the entire Church. The duty and power of Magisterium is conferred on him as confirmed faith so that it may strengthen all the "brothers" (cf. Lk 22:31f.). But all this is in the Church and for the Church, whose foundation is Peter, the keeper of the keys and the shepherd in the visible structure, in Christ's name and by his mandate.

Jesus had foretold this mission to Peter not only in Caesarea Philippi, but also at the first miraculous catch of fish, when he said to Simon, who had acknowledged that he was a sinner: "Do not be afraid; from now on you will be catching men" (Lk 5:10). On that occasion Jesus reserved this announcement to Peter personally, distinguishing him from his companions and colleagues, among whom were the "sons of Zebedee," James and John (cf. Lk 5:10).

At the second miraculous catch of fish following the resurrection, the person of Peter stands out from the other apostles, as John describes the event (21:2ff.). He hands on a record of it, as it were, in the prophetic symbolism of the fruitfulness of the mission Christ entrusted to those fishermen.

When Jesus was about to confer the mission on Peter, he addressed him officially as "Simon, son of John" (Jn 21:15), but he then assumed a familiar, friendly tone: "Do you love me more than these?" This question expresses his interest in the person of Simon Peter and stands in relationship to his choice for a personal mission. Jesus asked the question three times, with an implicit reference to the threefold denial. Peter gave an answer not based on trust in his own strength, personal abilities or merits. By now he was well aware that he must put all his trust in Christ alone: "Lord, you know everything; you know that I love you" (Jn 21:17).

Obviously the task of shepherd requires a special love for Christ. However, it is he, it is God who gives everything, including the ability to respond to one's vocation, to fulfill one's own mission. Indeed, we must say "all is grace," especially at that level!

After Simon Peter had given the desired answer, Jesus conferred on him the pastoral mission: "Feed my lambs.... Feed my sheep." It is a prolongation of Jesus' mission. He had said of himself: "I am the good shepherd" (Jn 10:11). Jesus, who shared with Simon his quality as "rock," also communicated to him his mission as "shepherd." It is a communication which implies an intimate communion, as can also be seen in Jesus' expression: "Feed my lambs...my sheep," as he had already said: "Upon this rock I will build my Church" (Mt 16:18). The Church is Christ's property, not Peter's. The lambs and sheep belong to Christ, and to no one else. They belong to him as the "good shepherd" who "lays down his life for the sheep" (Jn 10:11). Peter must take up the pastoral ministry for those redeemed "with the precious blood of Christ" (1 Pet 1:19).

The nature of the service which distinguishes the power connected to the mission conferred on Peter is based on the relationship between Christ and human beings, who have become his property through the redemption. It is a service to him who alone is "the shepherd and guardian of our souls" (1 Pet 2:25), as well as to all whom Christ, the good shepherd, has redeemed at the cost of his sacrifice on the cross.

The content of this service is also clear: as a shepherd leads his sheep to where they can find food and safety, so the shepherd of souls must offer them the food of God's word and of his holy will (cf. Jn 4:34), ensuring the unity of the flock and defending it from every hostile attack.

Certainly this mission entails a power, but for Peter—and for his successors—it is a power ordered to service, to a specific service, a *ministerium*. Peter receives it in the community of the Twelve. He is one of the community of the apostles. However, it is certain that Jesus, both by the announcement (cf. Mt 16:18-19) and by the conferral of the mission after his resurrection, assigned in a particular way to Peter everything he transmitted as mission and power to all the apostles. To him alone did Jesus say, "Feed," repeating it three times. Consequently, within the common task of the Twelve a mission and a power are defined for Peter which belong to him alone.

Jesus addressed Peter as a unique individual among the Twelve, not only as a representative of them: "Do *you* love me more than these?" (Jn 21:15). He asked this subject—the *you* that is Peter—for a declaration of love and on him this unique mission and authority were conferred. Peter was thus distinguished from the other apostles. The threefold repetition of the question about Peter's love, probably in relation to his triple denial of Christ, also highlights the fact that a particular *ministerium* is conferred on him, as a decision of Christ himself, independently of any quality or merit on the apostle's part, and even despite his temporary infidelity.

Communion in the messianic mission established by Jesus with Peter in that mandate, "Feed my lambs..." cannot fail to include the apostle-shepherd's participation in the sacrificial condition of Christ, the good shepherd, "who lays down his life for the sheep." This is the interpretative key for many events found in the history of the pontificate of Peter's successors. Throughout this history echoes the prediction Jesus made: "When you grow old, you will stretch out your hands, and someone else will dress you and lead you where you do not want to go" (Jn 21:18). This was a prediction of the confirmation Peter would give to his pastoral ministry by dying as a martyr. As John says, by such a death Peter "would glorify

God" (Jn 21:9). The pastoral service entrusted to Peter in the Church would be consummated by his sharing in the sacrifice of the cross offered by Christ to redeem the world. The cross, which redeemed Peter, would thus become for him the privileged way of totally fulfilling his duty as "servant of the servants of God."

General audience of December 9, 1992

Peter Ranks First among the Apostles

The texts which I have presented and explained in the previous catecheses directly concern Peter's mission of strengthening his brothers in the faith and of shepherding the flock of Christ's followers. They are the basic texts on the Petrine ministry. However, they must be seen in the larger context of the entire New Testament discussion of Peter, beginning with the place of his mission in the whole New Testament. In the Pauline letters, he is mentioned as the first witness of the resurrection (cf. 1 Cor 15:3ff.) and Paul says that he went to Jerusalem "to confer with Kephas" (cf. Gal 1:18). The Johannine tradition records a strong presence of Peter, and there are numerous references to him in the Synoptics as well.

The New Testament discussion also concerns Peter's position among the Twelve. The trio of Peter, James and John emerges; think, for example, of the transfiguration, the raising of Jairus' daughter, and Gethsemane. Peter is always first on all the lists of the apostles (in Matthew 10:2 he is even called "first"). Jesus gave him a new name, Kephas, which is translated into Greek (so it was considered significant), to designate the office and position that Simon would have in Christ's Church.

These facts enable us better to grasp the historical and ecclesiological meaning of Jesus' promise contained in Matthew's text (16:18-19), and the conferral of the pastoral mission described by John (21:15-19): the primacy of authority in the apostolic college and the Church.

At issue is a matter of fact, recounted by the evangelists as those who recorded Christ's life and teaching, but also as witnesses of the belief and practice of the first Christian community. It is clear from these writings that from the Church's beginning Peter exercised decisive authority at the highest level. This exercise, accepted and recognized by the community, is historical confirmation of the words Christ spoke regarding the mission and power of Peter.

It is easy to admit that Peter's personal qualities in themselves were not sufficient to obtain the recognition of a supreme authority in the Church. Although he had a leader's temperament, already apparent in the little fishing concern he had at the lake with his "partners," John and Andrew (cf. Lk 5:10), he could not assert his authority over the others on his own, given his well-known limitations and defects. On the other hand, we know that during Jesus' earthly life the apostles discussed who among them would be first in the kingdom. The fact, then, that Peter's authority was calmly recognized in the Church is due exclusively to Christ's will. It shows that the words with which Jesus assigned to the apostle his unique pastoral authority were understood and accepted without difficulty in the Christian community.

Let us briefly review the facts. According to Acts, the apostles came together immediately after the ascension. In their list Peter is mentioned first (cf. Acts 1:13), as in the lists of the Twelve provided for us in the Gospels and in the references to the three privileged ones (cf. Mk 5:37; 9:2; 13:3; 14:33 and parallels).

Peter spoke with authority: "During those days Peter

stood up in the midst of the brothers" (Acts 1:15). It was not the assembly which designated him. He acted as one possessing authority. At that meeting Peter presented the problem created by Judas' betrayal and death, which reduced the number of apostles to eleven. In fidelity to Jesus' will, filled with symbolism about passing from the old to the new Israel (twelve constitutive tribes—twelve apostles), Peter indicated the necessary solution: appoint a replacement who, with the Eleven, would become "a witness to his [Christ's] resurrection" (cf. Acts 1:21-22). The assembly accepted and implemented this solution, casting lots so that the choice would come from on high. Thus "the lot fell upon Matthias, and he was counted with the eleven apostles" (Acts 1:26).

It should be pointed out that among the witnesses to the resurrection by virtue of Christ's will, Peter was first. The angel who announced Jesus' resurrection to the women said to them: "But go and tell his disciples and Peter..." (Mk 16:7). John let Peter enter the tomb first (cf. Jn 20:1-10). To the disciples returning from Emmaus the others said: "The Lord has truly been raised and has appeared to Simon!" (Lk 24:34). That the risen Christ appeared to Peter first was an early tradition received by the Church and recorded by St. Paul: "He appeared to Kephas, then to the Twelve" (1 Cor 15:5). This priority corresponds to the mission assigned to Peter of strengthening his brothers in the faith as the first witness to the resurrection.

On the day of Pentecost Peter acted as the leader of the witnesses to the resurrection. He speaks on a spontaneous impulse: "Peter stood up with the Eleven, raised his voice, and proclaimed..." (Acts 2:14). Remarking about what happened, he declared: "God raised this Jesus; of this we are all witnesses" (Acts 2:32). All the Twelve were witnesses of this; Peter proclaimed it in the name of them all. He was the official spokesman, we could say, of the first community and the group of apostles. He told his listeners what they were to do: "Repent and be baptized, every one of you, in the name of Jesus Christ..." (Acts 2:38).

It was also Peter who worked the first miracle, astonishing the crowd. According to the account in Acts he was accompanied by John when he looked at the cripple begging for alms. He was the one to speak. "But Peter looked intently at him, as did John, and said, 'Look at us.' He paid attention to them, expecting to receive something from them. Peter said, 'I have neither silver nor gold, but what I do have I give you: in the name of Jesus Christ the Nazarene, rise and walk.' Then Peter took him by the right hand and raised him up, and immediately his feet and ankles grew strong. He leaped up, stood and walked around..." (Acts 3:3-8). In his words and deeds Peter was the instrument for this miracle, convinced that he had power given him by Christ in this area as well.

This is precisely the way he explained the miracle to the people, showing that the healing manifests the power of the risen Christ: "God raised him from the dead; of this we are witnesses" (Acts 3:15). Consequently, he urged his listeners: "Repent, therefore, and be converted" (Acts 3:19).

During the questioning by the Sanhedrin, Peter, "filled with the Holy Spirit," spoke to proclaim the salvation won by Jesus Christ (cf. Acts 4:8f.), crucified and risen (cf. Acts 7:10).

Later on Peter was the one who "with the apostles," said in reply to the prohibition against teaching in the name of Jesus: "We must obey God rather than men" (Acts 5:29).

In the painful case of Ananias and Sapphira too, Peter showed his authority as the one responsible for the community. Rebuking that Christian couple for their lie about the purchase price of some property, he accused the two guilty parties of having lied to the Holy Spirit (cf. Acts 5:1-11).

Peter responded in the same way to Simon the magician, who had offered money to the apostles in order to receive the Holy Spirit by the laying on of hands: "May your money perish with you, because you thought that you could buy the gift of

God with money.... Repent of this wickedness of yours and pray to the Lord that your intention may be forgiven" (Acts 8:20, 22).

Moreover, Acts tells us that the crowd thought of Peter as the one who worked marvels, even more than the other apostles. Certainly he was not the only one to perform miracles: "Many signs and wonders were done among the people at the hands of the apostles" (Acts 5:12). However, cures were expected above all from him: "They even carried the sick out into the streets and laid them on cots and mats so that when Peter came by, at least his shadow might fall on one or another of them" (Acts 5:15).

One thing is clearly evident in this first stage of the Church's beginning: under the power of the Spirit and in conformity with Jesus' command, Peter acted in communion with the other apostles, but took the initiative and decided personally as the head.

This explains the fact that when Peter was imprisoned by Herod ardent prayer was offered by the Church for him: "Peter was being kept in prison, but prayer was fervently being made to God on his behalf" (Acts 12:5). This prayer arose from the common conviction of Peter's unique importance. It was the beginning of the uninterrupted sequence of prayers which the Church would offer in every age for Peter's successors.

The angel's intervention and the miraculous release from prison (cf. Acts 12:6-17), moreover, show the special protection which Peter enjoyed, a protection which allowed him to fulfill the pastoral mission assigned to him. The faithful will always ask for this protection and assistance for the successors of Peter in the sufferings and persecutions they will inevitably encounter in their ministry as "servants of the servants of God."

We can conclude by recognizing that truly at the Church's beginning Peter acted as one who possessed the primary authority within the college of the apostles, and for this reason spoke in the name of the Twelve as a witness to the resurrection.

Therefore, he worked miracles which resembled Christ's and performed them in his name. He assumed responsibility for the moral behavior of the members of the first community and for its future development. He was the focus of concern for the new People of God and of the prayer they made to heaven to obtain his protection and deliverance.

General audience of December 16, 1992

Peter Allowed Gentiles to Be Baptized

The premier authority of Peter among the apostles was especially apparent in resolving the basic problem which the early Church had to face: the relationship with the Jewish religion and, thus, the constitutive basis of the new Israel. It was necessary to decide to draw the consequences of the fact that the Church was neither an offshoot of the Mosaic regime, nor some religious current or sect of ancient Israel.

Concretely, when the problem was posed to the apostles and the first Christian community with the case of the centurion Cornelius requesting Baptism, Peter's intervention was decisive. The Acts of the Apostles describes how the event unfolded. In a vision the pagan centurion received from an "angel of the Lord" the order to call on Peter: "Summon one Simon who is called Peter" (Acts 10:5). The angel's order included and confirmed the authority possessed by Peter. His decision would be needed for allowing pagans to be baptized.

Peter's decision, moreover, was clarified by a light given him in an exceptional way from on high: in a vision, Peter was invited to eat foods forbidden by the Jewish law. He heard a voice saying to him: "What God has made clean, you are not to call profane" (Acts 10:15). This enlightenment, given to him three times, as previously three times he had received the power to shepherd Christ's flock, showed Peter that he had to move beyond the demands of dietary laws and, in general, beyond Jewish ritual observances. It was an important religious achievement for the acceptance and treatment reserved for pagans, of whose arrival he had a presentiment.

The decisive step was taken immediately after the vision, when the men sent by the centurion Cornelius presented themselves to Peter. Peter could have hesitated to follow them, since Jewish law forbade contact with pagan foreigners, considered to be impure. But the new awareness he had as a result of the vision compelled him to overcome this discriminatory law. In addition, the impulse of the Holy Spirit made him understand that he should accompany these men without delay, for they had been sent to him by the Lord. He abandoned himself completely to fulfilling God's plan for his life. It is easy to suppose that, without the light of the Spirit, Peter would have continued to observe the prescriptions of Jewish law. It was that light, given to him personally so that he would make a decision in conformity with the Lord's views, which guided and supported him in his decision.

Now for the first time, in front of a group of pagans gathered around the centurion Cornelius, Peter gave his testimony about Jesus Christ and his resurrection: "In truth, I see that God shows no partiality. Rather, in every nation whoever fears him and acts uprightly is acceptable to him" (Acts 10:34-35). It was a decision which seemed revolutionary, because of its relationship to the Jewish mentality regarding the current interpretation of Mosaic law. God's plan, kept hidden from preceding generations, foresaw that the pagans would be "co-heirs in the promise of Jesus Christ" (Eph 3:5-6), without first having to be incorporated into the religious and ritual structure of the old covenant. This was the newness brought by Jesus, which by his gesture, Peter made his own and applied concretely.

It should be pointed out that the opening began by Peter

bore the seal of the Holy Spirit, who came down upon the group of pagan converts. There is a connection between Peter's word and the action of the Holy Spirit. We read: "While Peter was still speaking these things, the Holy Spirit fell upon all who were listening to the word" (Acts 10:44). A witness to this gift of the Holy Spirit, Peter saw the consequences and said to his brethren: "'Can anyone withhold the water for baptizing these people, who have received the Holy Spirit even as we have?' He ordered them to be baptized in the name of Jesus Christ" (Acts 10:47).

This formal resolution of Peter's, obviously illumined by the Spirit, took on decisive importance for the Church's development by eliminating the obstacles stemming from the observance of the Jewish law.

Not everyone was prepared to accept this great innovation and make it his own. In fact, Peter's decision was criticized by the so-called "Judaizers," who formed an important nucleus in the Christian community. It was a prelude to the reservations and opposition which would occur in the future against those who would have the task of exercising supreme authority in the Church (cf. Acts 11:1-2). However, Peter responded to those criticisms by relating what had occurred when Cornelius and the other pagans had been converted and by explaining the descent of the Holy Spirit upon that group of converts with these words of the Lord: "John baptized with the Holy Spirit" (Acts 11:16). Since the proof came from God— from Christ's words and the signs of the Holy Spirit—it was judged to be convincing, and the criticisms died down. Peter thus appeared as the first apostle of the Gentiles.

We know that later the Apostle Paul, the *Doctor Gentium,* would be especially called to proclaim the Gospel among the Gentiles. However, he himself recognized the authority of Peter as a guarantor of the rightness of his own mission of evangelization. Having begun to preach the Gospel to Gentiles, he relates: "After three years I went up to Jerusalem to confer with Kephas" (Gal 1:18). Paul was acquainted with Peter's role in the Church and recognized its importance.

Fourteen years later he again went to Jerusalem for verification: "...so that I might not be running, or have run, in vain" (Gal 2:2). This time he spoke not only to Peter but "to those of repute" (Gal 2:2). He shows, however, that he regarded Peter as the supreme head. In fact, although in the geo-religious distribution of work Peter was entrusted with the Gospel to the circumcised (Gal 2:7), he still was the first to preach the Gospel to the pagans, as seen in Cornelius' conversion. On that occasion Peter opened the door to all the Gentiles who could be reached at the time.

The incident that occurred in Antioch does not imply that Paul denied Peter's authority. Paul reproved his way of acting, but did not question his authority as head of the apostolic college and the Church. Paul wrote in Galatians:

> And when Kephas came to Antioch, I opposed him to his face because he clearly was wrong. For, until some people came from James, he used to eat with the Gentiles, but when they came, he began to draw back and separated himself, because he was afraid of the uncircumcised. And the rest of the Jews also acted hypocritically along with him, with the result that even Barnabas was carried away by their hypocrisy. But when I saw that they were not on the right road in line with the truth of the Gospel, I said to Kephas in front of all, "If you, though a Jew, are living like a Gentile and not like a Jew, how can you compel the Gentiles to live like Jews?" (Gal 2:11-14).

Paul did not exclude in an absolute way every concession to certain demands of the Jewish law (cf. Acts 16:3; 21:26; 1 Cor 8:13; Rom 14:21; cf. also 1 Cor 9:20). In Antioch, however, Peter's behavior had the disadvantage of compelling Christians of Gentile origin to submit to Jewish law. Precisely because he acknowledged Peter's authority, Paul protested and reprimanded him for not acting in accordance with the Gospel.

Later on, the problem of freedom regarding the Jewish law was finally resolved at a meeting of the apostles and elders in Jerusalem, during which Peter played a decisive role. A long discussion set Paul and Barnabas against a certain number of converted Pharisees, who asserted that all Christians had to be circumcised, even those coming from paganism.

After the discussion Peter stood up to explain that God did not want any discrimination and that he had given the Holy Spirit to Gentile converts to the faith. "We believe that we are saved through the grace of the Lord Jesus, in the same way as they" (Acts 15:11). Peter's intervention was decisive. Then, according to Acts: "The whole assembly fell silent, and they listened while Paul and Barnabas described the signs and wonders God had worked among the Gentiles through them" (Acts 15:12). This showed that Peter's position was confirmed by the facts. James too adopted it (cf. Acts 15:14), adding the confirmation of inspired Scripture to the testimonies of Barnabas and Paul: "The words of the prophets agree with this" (Acts 15:15), and citing an oracle of Amos. The assembly's decision was thus in conformity with the position enunciated by Peter. His authority thus played a decisive role in resolving an essential question for the Church's development and for the unity of the Christian community.

The person and mission of Peter in the early Church are situated in this light.

General audience of January 13, 1993

The Bishop of Rome
Is Peter's Successor

Jesus' intention to make Simon Peter the foundation "rock" of his Church (cf. Mt 16:18) has a value that outlasts the apostle's earthly life. Jesus actually conceived his Church and desired her presence and activity in all nations until the ultimate fulfillment of history (cf. Mt 26:14; 28:19; Mk 16:15; Lk 24:47; Acts 1:8). Therefore, as he wanted successors for the other apostles in order to continue the work of evangelization in the various parts of the world, so too he foresaw and desired successors for Peter. They would be charged with the same pastoral mission and equipped with the same power, beginning with the mission and power of being Rock—the visible principle of unity in faith, love and the ministry of evangelization, sanctification and leadership entrusted to the Church.

This was defined by the First Vatican Council: "What Christ the Lord, prince of pastors and great shepherd of the sheep, established in the blessed Apostle Peter for eternal salvation and for the everlasting welfare of the Church, must always perdure, by the will of the same Christ, in the Church which, founded on rock, will remain indestructible until the end of time" *(DS* 3056).

The same Council defined as a truth of the faith: "It is by the institution of Christ the Lord, that is, by divine right, that blessed Peter has endless successors in his primacy over the whole Church" *(DS* 3058). This is an essential element of the Church's organic and hierarchical structure, which no one has the power to change. For the Church's entire duration, there will be successors of Peter in virtue of Christ's will.

The Second Vatican Council accepted and repeated this teaching of Vatican I. It gave greater emphasis to the link between the primacy of Peter's successors and the collegiality of the apostles' successors, without weakening the definition of the primacy justified by the most ancient Christian tradition, in which St. Ignatius of Antioch and St. Irenaeus of Lyons stand out primarily.

On the basis of this tradition, Vatican I also defined: "The Roman Pontiff is the successor of blessed Peter in the same primacy" *(DS* 3058). The definition binds the primacy of Peter and his successors to the See of Rome, which cannot be replaced by any other see. However, it can happen that, due to circumstances of the times or for particular reasons, the bishops of Rome take up residence temporarily in places other than the Eternal City. Certainly, a city's political condition can change extensively and profoundly over centuries. But it remains, as is the case with Rome, a determinate space to which an institution such as an episcopal see is always referred—in the case of Rome, the See of Peter.

In truth, Jesus did not specify the role of Rome in Peter's succession. Doubtless he wanted Peter to have successors, but the New Testament does not state his specific desire to choose Rome as the primatial See. He preferred to entrust that to historical events in which the divine plan for the Church, the determination of the concrete conditions of Peter's succession, would appear.

The decisive historical event is that the fisherman of Bethsaida came to Rome and suffered martyrdom in this city. This fact is rich in theological significance, because it shows the mystery of the divine plan which arranges the course of human events to serve the Church's beginnings and development.

Peter's coming to Rome and his martyrdom here are part of a very ancient tradition expressed in basic historical documents and archeological discoveries regarding devotion to Peter on the site of his tomb, which early on became a place of veneration. Among the written documents we must first of all recall Pope Clement's *Letter to the Corinthians* (ca. 89-97), where the Church of Rome is considered as the Church of blessed Peter and Paul, whose martyrdom during Nero's persecution is mentioned by the Pope (5, 1-7). In this regard it is interesting to underscore the reference of tradition to the two apostles associated in their martyrdom with this Church. The Bishop of Rome is the Successor of Peter; however, he can also be called the heir of Paul, the greatest representative of the early Church's missionary efforts and of the wealth of her charisms. The bishops of Rome have generally spoken, taught, defended Christ's truth, celebrated pontifical rites and blessed the faithful in the name of Peter and Paul, the "princes of the apostles," the *olivae binae pietatis unicae* (twofold branch of the one piety), as is sung in the hymn for their feast on June 29. The Fathers, the liturgy and iconography often depict this association in martyrdom and glory.

Nevertheless, the Roman Pontiffs have exercised their authority in Rome and, according to the conditions and opportunities of the times, have done so in wider and even universal areas, by virtue of their succeeding Peter. Written documents do not tell us how this succession occurred in the first link connecting Peter with the series of the bishops of Rome. It can be deduced, however, by considering everything that Pope Clement states in the letter cited above regarding the appointment of the first bishops and their successors. After recalling that the apostles, "preaching in the countryside and the cities, experienced their first fruits in the Spirit and appointed them bishops and deacons of future believers" (42, 4), St. Clement says in detail that, in order to avoid future conflicts regarding the episcopal dignity, the apostles "appointed those whom we said and then ordered that, after they had died, other proven men would succeed them in their ministry" (44, 2). The historical and canonical means by which that inheritance is passed on to them can change, and have indeed changed. But over the centuries, an unbroken chain links that transition from Peter to his first successor in the Roman See.

This method of historical investigation (which could be called genetic) into the Petrine succession in the Church of Rome is confirmed by two other considerations. There is a negative one which, beginning with the need of a succession to Peter by virtue of Christ's very institution (and so *iure divino,* as is usually said in theological-canonical language), confirms that there are no signs of such a succession in any other Church. Moreover, there is another consideration we could call positive: it consists in showing the convergence of signs that in every age point to the See of Rome as that of Peter's successor.

Regarding the link between the papal primacy and the Roman See, significant testimony is given by Ignatius of Antioch, who extols the excellence of the Church of Rome. In his Letter to the Romans this authoritative witness of the Church's organizational and hierarchical development in the first half of the second century addressed the Church "which presides in the land of the Romans, worthy of God, worthy of honor, deservedly blessed, worthy of happy success, worthily chaste, which presides over charity" (Introduction). Charity *(agápe)* in St. Ignatius' language refers to the ecclesial community. Presiding over charity expresses the primacy in that communion of charity which is the Church, and necessarily includes the service of authority, the *ministerium Petrinum.* In fact, Ignatius acknowledges the Church of Rome's teaching authority: "You have never been jealous of anyone; you have taught the others. So I want those lessons that you give and enjoin in your teaching to be steadfast too" (3, 1).

The origin of this privileged position is indicated by those words regarding the significance of his authority as bishop of Antioch, which is also quite venerable because of its antiquity and relationship to the apostles: "Not as Peter and Paul do I command you" (4, 3). Rather, Ignatius entrusts the Church of Syria to the Church of Rome: "In your prayer remember the Church of Syria, which in my stead has God for its shepherd. Only Jesus Christ, and your charity, will rule it as a bishop" (9, 1).

In seeking to determine the apostolic succession of the churches, St. Irenaeus of Lyons in turn refers to the Church of Rome as the example and criterion *par excellence* of this succession. He writes:

> Since in this work it would take too long to list the successions of all the churches, we will consider the great and very ancient church known to all, the church founded and established in Rome by the two glorious apostles Peter and Paul. By showing the tradition received from the apostles and the faith proclaimed to men, which comes to us through the succession of bishops, we refute all who in any way, whether from madness or vainglory or blindness and mistaken thought, gather together beyond what is right. In fact, it is with this church, by reason of her more excellent origin, that every church [that is, the faithful who come from every area] must necessarily be in agreement—with this Church in which the tradition that comes from the apostles has always been preserved by everyone *(Adv. Haer.,* 3, 2).

The Church of Rome is acknowledged as having a "more excellent origin," which is that of Peter and Paul, the greatest representatives of the authority and charism of the apostles: the "keybearer of the Church" and the "Doctor of the Gentiles." The other churches can live and work only in agreement with her; agreement entails unity of faith, teaching and discipline, precisely what is contained in the apostolic tradition. The See of Rome is thus the criterion and measure of the apostolic authenticity of the various churches, the guarantee and principle of their communion in universal "charity," the foundation *(kephas)* of the visible organism of the Church established and ruled by the risen Christ as the eternal shepherd of the entire sheepfold of believers.

General audience of January 27, 1993

The Pope Exercises
Supreme Jurisdiction

In an earlier catechesis we spoke of the Bishop of Rome as the Successor of Peter. This succession has fundamental importance for fulfilling the mission that Jesus Christ handed on to the apostles and the Church.

The Second Vatican Council teaches that the Bishop of Rome, as Vicar of Christ, has supreme and universal power over the whole Church (cf. *LG* 22). This power, as well as that of all bishops, has a ministerial character *(ministerium* means service), as the Fathers of the Church had already observed.

The conciliar definitions on the Bishop of Rome's mission must be understood and explained in the light of this Christian tradition. It should be kept in mind that the traditional language used by the councils, especially the First Vatican Council, in regard to the powers of both the Pope and the bishops, uses terms proper to the world of civil law, which in this case must be given their correct ecclesial meaning.

Inasmuch as the Church is a group of human beings called to carry out in history God's plan for the salvation of the world, *power* in her appears as an indispensable requirement of *mission.* Nevertheless, the analogical value of the language used allows power to be conceived in the sense provided by Jesus' maxim on "power in order to serve" and by the Gospel idea of the pastoral leader. The power required by the mission of Peter and his successors is identified with this authoritative leadership guaranteed of divine assistance, which Jesus himself called the ministry (service) of a shepherd.

Having said that, we can reread the definition of the Council of Florence (1439), which stated: "We define that the Holy Apostolic See—and the Roman Pontiff—has primacy over the whole world, and that the same Roman Pontiff is the successor of blessed Peter, prince of the apostles and true Vicar of Christ, head of the whole Church, and father and teacher of all Christians, and that upon him, in blessed Peter, our Lord Jesus Christ conferred the full power of shepherding, ruling and governing the universal Church, as is also stated in the acts of the ecumenical councils and the sacred canons" *(DS* 1307).

We know that historically the problem of the primacy was posed by the Eastern Church separated from Rome. The Council of Florence, trying to foster reunion, expressed the precise meaning of the primacy. It is a mission of service to the universal Church, which necessarily entails a corresponding authority precisely because of this service: the full power of shepherding, ruling and governing, without prejudice to the privileges and rights of the Eastern patriarchs, according to the order of their dignity (cf. *DS* 1308).

For its part, Vatican I (1870) cited the Council of Florence's definition (cf. *DS* 3060) and, after mentioning the Gospel texts (Jn 1:42; Mt 16:16f.; Jn 21:15f.), expresses the meaning of this power in further detail. The Roman Pontiff "does not only have the office of inspection and direction," but enjoys "full and supreme power of jurisdiction, not only in matters of faith and morals, but also in those which concern the discipline and governance of the Church dispersed throughout the world" *(DS* 3064).

Attempts were made to reduce the Roman Pontiff's power to an "office of inspection and direction." Some proposed that the Pope be simply an arbiter of conflicts between local churches or that he merely give a general direction to the autonomous activities of the churches and of Christians with his counsel and exhortation. This limitation, however, did not conform to the mission Christ conferred on Peter. Therefore, Vatican I emphasized the fullness of papal power and defined that it is not enough to recognize that the Roman Pontiff "has the principal role." One must admit instead that he "has all the fullness of this supreme power" *(DS* 3064).

In this regard it would be well to clarify immediately that this "fullness" of power attributed to the Pope in no way detracts from the "fullness" also belonging to the body of bishops. On the contrary, one must assert that both the Pope and the episcopal body have "all the fullness" of power. The Pope possesses this fullness *personally,* while the body of bishops, united under the Pope's authority, possesses it *collegially.* The Pope's power does not result from simply adding numbers, but is the episcopal body's principle of unity and wholeness.

For this reason the Council underscores that the Pope's power "is ordinary and immediate over all the churches and over each and every member of the faithful" *(DS* 3064). It is *ordinary,* in the sense that it is proper to the Roman Pontiff by virtue of the office belonging to him and not by delegation from the bishops; it is *immediate,* because he can exercise it directly without the bishops' permission or mediation.

Vatican I's definition, however, does not assign to the Pope a power or responsibility to intervene daily in the local churches. It means only to exclude the possibility of imposing norms on him to limit the exercise of the primacy. The Council expressly states: "This power of the Supreme Pontiff does not at all impede the exercise of that power of ordinary and immediate episcopal jurisdiction with which the bishops, appointed by the Holy Spirit (cf. Acts 20:28) as successors of the apostles, shepherd and govern the flock entrusted to them as true pastors..." *(DS* 3061).

Indeed, we should keep in mind a statement of the German episcopate (1875) approved by Pius IX that said: "The episcopate also exists by virtue of the same divine institution on which the office of the Supreme Pontiff is based. It enjoys rights and duties in virtue of a disposition that comes from God himself, and the Supreme Pontiff has neither the right nor the power to change them." The decrees of Vatican I are thus understood in a completely erroneous way when one presumes that because of them "episcopal jurisdiction has been replaced by papal jurisdiction"; that the Pope "is taking for himself the place of every bishop"; and that the bishops are merely "instruments of the Pope: they are his officials without responsibility of their own" *(DS* 3115).

Now let us listen to the full, balanced and serene teaching of Vatican II, which states that "Jesus Christ, the eternal shepherd...willed that their successors, namely the bishops, should be shepherds in his Church even to the consummation of the world. And in order that the episcopate itself might be one and undivided, he placed blessed Peter over the other apostles, and instituted in him a permanent and visible source and foundation of unity of faith and communion" *(LG* 18).

In this sense Vatican II speaks of the Bishop of Rome as "pastor of the entire Church," having "full, supreme and universal power" *(LG* 22). That power is "primacy over all, both pastors and faithful" *(LG* 22). "The individual bishops, insofar as their own discharge of their duty permits, are obliged to enter into a community of work among themselves and with the Successor of Peter, upon whom was imposed in a special way the great duty of spreading the Christian name" *(LG* 23).

According to the same council, the Church is also catholic in the sense that all Christ's followers must work together in the overall mission of salvation, each in his own apostolate. The pastoral work of all, however, and especially that collegial activity of the whole episcopate, attains unity through the Bishop of Rome's *ministerium Petrinum.* The Council again says: "The bishops, faithfully recognizing the primacy and pre-eminence of their head, exercise their own authority for the good of their own faithful" *(LG* 22). We should also add from the Council that, if the collegial power over the whole Church attains its particular expression in an ecumenical council, it is "the prerogative of the Roman Pontiff to convoke these councils, to preside over them and to confirm them" *(LG* 22). Everything, then, depends on the Pope, the Bishop of Rome, as the principle of unity and communion.

At this point we should again note that, if Vatican II adopted the tradition of the ecclesiastical Magisterium on the topic of the Bishop of Rome's *ministerium Petrinum* previously expressed at the Council of Florence (1439) and at Vatican I (1870), to its credit, when it repeated this teaching, it brought out the correlation between the primacy and the collegiality of the episcopate in the Church. Because of this new clarification the erroneous interpretations often made of Vatican I's definition are rejected and the full significance of the Petrine ministry is shown in its harmony with the doctrine of episcopal collegiality. Also confirmed was the Roman Pontiff's right "within the exercise of his own office to communicate freely with the pastors and flock of the entire Church," and this in regard to all rites (cf. *DS* 3060, 3062).

This does not mean claiming for the Successor of Peter powers like those of the earthly "rulers" of whom Jesus spoke (cf. Mt 20:25-28), but being faithful to the will of the Church's Founder, who established this type of society and this form of governance to serve the communion in faith and love.

To fulfill Christ's will, the Successor of Peter must assume and exercise the authority he has received in a spirit of humble service and with the aim of ensuring unity. Even in the various historical ways of exercising that authority, he must imitate Christ in serving and bringing into unity those called to be part of the one fold. He will never subordinate what he has received for Christ and his Church to his own personal aims.

He can never forget that the universal pastoral mission must entail a very profound participation in the Redeemer's sacrifice, in the mystery of the cross.

Regarding his relationship with his brothers in the episcopate, he must remember and apply the words of St. Gregory the Great: "My honor is the honor of the universal Church. My honor is the solid strength of my brothers. I am truly honored, then, when each of them is not denied the honor due him" *(Epist. ad Eulogium Alexandrinum, PL 77, 993).*

General audience of February 24, 1993

The Roman Pontiff
Is the Supreme Teacher

The New Testament passages we have seen several times in the preceding catecheses show that Jesus revealed his intention to give Peter the keys to the kingdom in response to a profession of faith. In it Peter spoke in the name of the Twelve and by virtue of a revelation coming from the Father. He expressed his faith in Jesus as "the Messiah, the Son of the living God." This assent of faith in the person of Jesus was not a simple attitude of trust, but clearly included the affirmation of a Christological doctrine. The role of foundation stone conferred on Peter by Jesus thus has a doctrinal aspect (cf. Mt 16:18-19). The mission of "strengthening his brothers" in faith, also entrusted to him by Jesus (cf. Lk 22:32), has the same meaning. Peter is the beneficiary of the Master's special prayer in carrying out this role and helping his brothers to believe. The words "Feed my lambs.... Tend my sheep" (Jn 21:15-17) do not express a doctrinal mission explicitly, but rather imply it. Tending the flock means providing it with the solid food of the spiritual life, and this food imparts revealed doctrine to nourish the faith.

The Gospel texts demonstrate that the universal pastoral mission of the Roman Pontiff, the Successor of Peter, entails a doctrinal mission. As universal pastor, the Pope has the mission to proclaim revealed doctrine and to promote true faith in Christ throughout the Church. This is the integral meaning of the Petrine ministry.

The value of the doctrinal mission entrusted to Peter stems from the fact that, according to the Gospel sources, he shares in Christ's pastoral mission. Peter is the first of those apostles to whom Jesus said: "As the Father has sent me, so I send you" (Jn 20:21; cf. 17:18). As universal pastor, Peter must act in Christ's name and in harmony with him throughout the broad human area in which Jesus wants his Gospel preached and the saving truth brought: the entire world. The Successor of Peter in the mission of universal pastor is thus the heir of a doctrinal *munus* in which he is closely related, with Peter, to Jesus' mission.

This relationship in no way detracts from the pastoral mission of the bishops, who have among their principal duties that of preaching the Gospel. According to the Second Vatican Council, they are "preachers of the faith...who preach to the people committed to them the faith they must believe and put into practice" *(LG* 25).

Nevertheless, the Bishop of Rome, as head of the episcopal college by the will of Christ, is the first herald of the faith. It is his task to teach revealed truth and to show how it should be applied in human conduct. He has primary responsibility for spreading the faith in the world. The Second Council of Lyons (1274) asserted this about the Bishop of Rome's primacy and fullness of power, when it stressed: "He has the duty to defend the truth of the faith, and it is his responsibility to resolve all disputed matters in the area of faith" *(DS* 861). Along the same lines the Council of Florence (1439) acknowledged the Roman Pontiff as the "father and teacher of all Christians" *(DS* 1307).

The Successor of Peter fulfills this doctrinal mission in a continual series of oral and written interventions that represent the ordinary exercise of the Magisterium as the teaching of truths to be believed and put into practice *(fidem et mores)*.

The acts expressing this Magisterium can be more or less frequent and take various forms according to the needs of the time, the requirements of concrete situations, the opportunities and means available, and the methods and systems of communication. However, given that they derive from an explicit or implicit intention to make pronouncements on matters of faith and morals, they are linked to the mandate received by Peter and enjoy the authority conferred on him by Christ.

The exercise of this Magisterium can also take place in an extraordinary way when the Successor of Peter (alone, or with the college of bishops as successors of the apostles) makes an *ex cathedra* pronouncement on a particular point of doctrine or Christian morals. However, we shall speak of this in future catecheses. Now we must concentrate on the usual, ordinary form of the papal Magisterium, which has a broader extent and an essential importance for the thought and life of the Christian community.

In this regard the first point to be stressed is the positive value of this mission to proclaim and spread the Christian message, to make the authentic teaching of the Gospel known, to respond to old and new human questions about the basic problems of life with the eternal words of revelation. To think that the papal Magisterium consists merely in condemning errors against the faith would be reductive and erroneous. This somewhat negative aspect is doubtless part of his responsibility for spreading the faith, since it is also necessary to defend it against error and deviation. However, the essential task of the papal Magisterium is to explain the doctrine of the faith, and to promote knowledge of the mystery of God and the work of salvation, bringing out all the aspects of the divine plan as it unfolds in human history under the action of the Holy Spirit. This is the service to the truth that has been primarily entrusted to Peter's Successor, who in the ordinary exercise of his Magisterium is already acting not as a private person, but as the supreme teacher of the universal Church, according to the precise statement of Vatican II regarding definitions *ex cathe-dra* (cf. *LG* 25).

In carrying out this task, the Successor of Peter expresses in a personal way, but with institutional authority, the "rule of faith" which the members of the universal Church (the ordinary faithful, catechists, religion teachers, theologians) must adhere to in investigating the meaning of the permanent content of the Christian faith. This is true also in relation to the discussions arising within and outside the ecclesial community on various points or on the whole of doctrine. Everyone in the Church, especially the theologians, are called to perform this task of continually making it clear and explicit. However, the mission of Peter and his successors is to establish and authoritatively confirm what the Church has received and believed from the beginning, what the apostles taught, what Sacred Scripture and Christian Tradition have determined as the object of faith and the Christian norm of life. The Church's other pastors, the bishops as successors of the apostles, are "strengthened" by the Successor of Peter in their communion of faith with Christ and in properly fulfilling their mission. In this way the Bishop of Rome's Magisterium indicates to everyone the way of clarity and unity, which seems indispensable especially in times of great communication and discussion such as ours.

The mission of Peter's Successor is exercised in three basic ways: first of all, by *word*. As universal pastor, the Bishop of Rome addresses all Christians and the whole world, carrying out in a full and supreme way the mission Christ conferred on the apostles: "Make disciples of all nations" (Mt 28:19). Since today the communications media allow his words to reach all nations, he fulfills that divine mandate in a way never before possible. Because the means of transportation allow him personally to visit the most distant regions, he can bring Christ's message to the people of every country, thus carrying out the divine command to "go" in a new and previ-

ously unimagined way: "Go...and make disciples of all nations...."

The Successor of Peter also fulfills his mission by *writing:* beginning with his addresses that are published so that his
teaching is known and documented, up to all the documents
issued directly—and here the encyclicals, which formally have
the value of universal teaching, should be mentioned first—or
those issued indirectly by the departments of the Roman Curia
which operate under his mandate.

Lastly, the Pope carries out his task as pastor *with authoritative initiatives and institutions of a scholarly and
pastoral nature:* for example, by initiating or fostering activities of study, sanctification, evangelization, charity and
assistance, etc., throughout the Church; by promoting authorized and accredited institutes for teaching the faith (seminaries, faculties of theology and religious studies, theological
associations, academies, etc.). This is a broad range of initiatives for formation and action under the auspices of Peter's
successor.

In conclusion, we can say that the teaching of Peter's
successor (as that of the other bishops) contains, in its essence,
a witness to Christ, to the event of the Incarnation and the
redemption, to the Holy Spirit's presence and action in the
Church and in history. In its form of expression it can vary
according to the person who exercises it, his interpretation of
the needs of the time, his style of thought and communication.
However, its relationship to the living truth, Christ, has been,
is and will always be its vital force.

This relationship to Christ definitively explains the difficulties and opposition that the Church's Magisterium has
always encountered from Peter's day to our own. For all the
bishops and pastors of the Church, and especially for the Successor of Peter, Jesus' words are valid: "No disciple is above
his teacher" (Mt 10:24; Lk 6:40). Jesus himself exercised his
Magisterium amid the struggle between darkness and light,

which was the context for the Incarnation of the Word (cf. Jn 1:1-14). That struggle was intense during the apostolic period, as the Master had warned: "If they persecuted me, they will also persecute you" (Jn 15:20). Unfortunately, it took place too in some Christian communities, so much so that St. Paul felt it necessary to urge Timothy, his disciple: "Proclaim the Word; be persistent whether it is convenient or inconvenient; convince, reprimand, encourage through all patience and teaching...[even] when people will not tolerate sound doctrine" (2 Tim 4:2-3).

What Paul recommended to Timothy also applies to bishops today, and especially to the Roman Pontiff, who has the mission of protecting the Christian people from errors in faith and morals, and the duty of guarding the deposit of faith (cf. 2 Tim 4:7). Woe to him if he should be frightened by criticism and misunderstanding. His charge is to give witness to Christ, to his word, his law, his love. However, in addition to being aware of his responsibility for doctrine and morals, the Roman Pontiff must, like Jesus, be committed to being "meek and humble of heart" (Mt 11:29). Pray that he may be so and will become ever more so.

General audience of March 10, 1993

The Successor of Peter Teaches Infallibly

The Magisterium of the Roman Pontiff, which we explained in the preceding catechesis, belongs to and marks the high point of the mission to preach the Gospel that Jesus entrusted to the apostles and their successors. We read in Vatican II's Constitution *Lumen Gentium:*

> Among the principal duties of bishops the preaching of the Gospel occupies an eminent place. For bishops are preachers of the faith, who lead new disciples to Christ, and they are authentic teachers, that is, teachers endowed with the authority of Christ, who preach to the people committed to them the faith they must believe and put into practice.... Bishops, teaching in communion with the Roman Pontiff, are to be respected by all as witnesses to divine and Catholic truth. In matters of faith and morals, the bishops speak in the name of Christ and the faithful are to accept their teaching and adhere to it with a religious assent *(LG* 25).

The magisterial function of bishops, then, is strictly tied to that of the Roman Pontiff. Therefore, the conciliar text goes on aptly to say:

> This religious submission of mind and will must be shown in a special way to the authentic Magisterium of

the Roman Pontiff, even when he is not speaking *ex ca-thedra;* that is, it must be shown in such a way that his supreme Magisterium is acknowledged with reverence, the judgments made by him are sincerely adhered to, according to his manifest mind and will. His mind and will in the matter may be known either from the character of the documents, from his frequent repetition of the same doctrine, or from his manner of speaking *(LG* 25).

This supreme authority of the papal Magisterium, to which the term *apostolic* has been traditionally reserved, even in its ordinary exercise derives from the institutional fact that the Roman Pontiff is the Successor of Peter in the mission of teaching, strengthening his brothers, and guaranteeing that the Church's preaching conforms to the "deposit of faith" of the apostles and of Christ's teaching. However, it also stems from the conviction, developed in Christian tradition, that the Bishop of Rome is also the heir to Peter in the charism of special assistance that Jesus promised him when he said: "I have prayed for you" (Lk 22:32). This signifies the Holy Spirit's continual help in the whole exercise of the teaching mission, meant to explain revealed truth and its consequences in human life.

For this reason the Second Vatican Council states that all the Pope's teaching should be listened to and accepted, even when it is not given *ex cathedra* but is proposed in the ordinary exercise of his Magisterium with the manifest intention of declaring, recalling and confirming the doctrine of faith. It is a consequence of the institutional fact and spiritual inheritance that completes the dimensions of the succession to Peter.

As you know there are cases in which the papal Magisterium is exercised solemnly regarding particular points of doctrine belonging to the deposit of revelation or closely connected with it. This is the case with *ex cathedra* definitions, such as those of Mary's Immaculate Conception, made by Pius IX in 1854, and of her Assumption into heaven, made by Pius

XII in 1950. As we know, these definitions have provided all Catholics with certainty in affirming these truths and in excluding all doubt in the matter.

The reason for *ex cathedra* definitions is almost always to give this certification to the truths that are to be believed as belonging to the "deposit of faith" and to exclude all doubt, or even to condemn an error about their authenticity and meaning. This is the greatest and also the formal concentration of the doctrinal mission conferred by Jesus on the apostles and, in their person, on their successors.

Given the extraordinary greatness and importance that this Magisterium has for the faith, Christian tradition has recognized in the Successor of Peter, who exercises it personally or in communion with the bishops gathered in council, a charism of assistance from the Holy Spirit that is customarily called "infallibility."

Here is what Vatican I said on the matter:

> When the Roman Pontiff speaks *ex cathedra,* that is, when in exercising his office as shepherd and teacher of all Christians he defines with his supreme apostolic authority that a doctrine on faith and morals is to be held by the whole Church, through the divine assistance promised him in the person of St. Peter, he enjoys that infallibility with which the divine Redeemer wished to endow his Church in defining a doctrine on faith and morals. Therefore, these definitions of the Roman Pontiff are unreformable *per se,* and not because of the Church's consent *(DS* 3074).

This doctrine was taken up again, confirmed and further explained by Vatican II, which states:

> And this is the infallibility which the Roman Pontiff, the head of the college of bishops, enjoys in virtue of his office, when, as the supreme shepherd and teacher of all the faithful, who confirms his brethren in their faith

(cf. Lk 22:32), by a definitive act he proclaims a doctrine of faith or morals. And therefore his definitions, of themselves, and not from the consent of the Church, are justly styled irreformable, since they are pronounced with the assistance of the Holy Spirit, promised to him in blessed Peter, and therefore they need no approval of others, nor do they allow an appeal to any other judgment. For then the Roman Pontiff is not pronouncing judgment as a private person, but, as the supreme teacher of the universal Church, in whom the charism of infallibility of the Church itself is individually present, he is expounding or defending a doctrine of Catholic faith (LG 25).

It should be noted that the Second Vatican Council also calls attention to the Magisterium of the bishops in union with the Roman Pontiff, stressing that they too enjoy the Holy Spirit's assistance when they define a point of faith in conjunction with the Successor of Peter:

The infallibility promised to the Church resides also in the body of Bishops, when that body exercises the supreme Magisterium with the Successor of Peter.... But when either the Roman Pontiff or the body of bishops together with him defines a judgment, they pronounce it in accordance with revelation itself, which all are obliged to abide by and be in conformity with, that is, the revelation which as written or orally handed down is transmitted in its entirety through the legitimate succession of bishops...which under the guiding light of the Spirit of truth is religiously preserved and faithfully expounded in the Church (LG 25).

The Council also says:

Although the individual bishops do not enjoy the prerogative of infallibility, they nevertheless proclaim Christ's doctrine infallibly whenever, even though dispersed through the world, but still maintaining the bond of communion among themselves and with the Successor of Peter, and authentically teaching matters of faith and morals, they are in agreement on one position as definitively to be held. This is even more clearly verified when, gathered together in an ecumenical council, they are teachers and judges of faith and morals for the universal Church, whose definitions must be adhered to with the submission of faith. And this infallibility with which the divine Redeemer willed his Church to be endowed in defining doctrine of faith and morals, extends as far as the deposit of revelation extends *(LG* 25).

These conciliar texts codify as it were the awareness which the apostles already had when they assembled in Jerusalem: "It is the decision of the Holy Spirit, and ours too..." (Acts 15:28). This awareness confirmed Jesus' promise to send the Spirit of truth to the apostles and the Church once he had returned to the Father after offering the sacrifice of the cross: "He will teach you everything and remind you of all I told you" (Jn 14:26). That promise was fulfilled at Pentecost and the apostles continued to feel its life. The Church inherited that awareness and memory from them.

General audience of March 17, 1993

The Holy Spirit Assists
the Roman Pontiff

The infallibility of the Roman Pontiff is a very important topic for the Church's life. For this reason a further reflection on the conciliar texts seems appropriate in order to state in greater detail the meaning and extent of this prerogative.

First of all the councils assert that the infallibility attributed to the Roman Pontiff is personal, in the sense that it falls to him by virtue of his personal succession to Peter in the Roman Church. This means, in other words, that the Roman Pontiff does not enjoy merely an infallibility that really belongs to the Roman See. He exercises the Magisterium and, in general, the pastoral ministry as *vicarious Petri:* thus he was often called in the first Christian millennium. He personifies, as it were, Peter's mission and authority, exercised in the name of him on whom Jesus himself conferred them.

It is clear, however, that infallibility was not given to the Roman Pontiff as a private person, but inasmuch as he carries out the office of shepherd and teacher of all Christians. Furthermore, he does not exercise this office as one having authority in himself and from himself, but "with his supreme apostolic authority" and "through the divine assistance promised him in the person of blessed Peter." Lastly, he does not possess it as if it were available or he could count on it in every circumstance, but only "when he speaks *ex cathedra,*" and only in a doctrinal matter limited to truths of faith and morals and to those closely connected to them.

According to the conciliar texts, the infallible Magisterium is exercised in "doctrine concerning faith and morals." This refers to the matter of explicitly or implicitly revealed truths that require an assent of faith, which the Church guards in the deposit entrusted to her by Christ and handed on by the apostles. She would not guard them properly if she did not defend their purity and integrity. These are truths about God in himself and in his creative and redeeming work; the human person and the world in their creaturely status and destiny according to the design of Providence; eternal life and earthly life itself in its basic demands regarding truth and goodness.

It is a question, therefore, of "truths for life" and of applying them in human conduct. In the mandate to evangelize, the divine Master ordered the apostles: "Go, therefore, and make disciples of all nations...teaching them to observe all that I have commanded you" (Mt 28:20). The area of truths that the Magisterium can definitively teach includes those principles of reason that are not contained in the truths of faith but are closely related to them. In actual fact, both in the past and today, the Church's Magisterium, especially the Roman Pontiff's, preserves these principles and continually rescues them from the obfuscation and distortion they suffer under pressure from partisan viewpoints and bad habits well established in cultural models and currents of thought.

In this regard the First Vatican Council said that the object of the infallible Magisterium is the "doctrine on faith and morals to be held by the whole Church" *(DS* 3074). In the new formula of the profession of faith recently approved (cf. *AAS* 81 [1989]: 105, 1169), a distinction was made between divinely revealed truths and truths definitively taught but not as divinely revealed, which therefore require a definitive assent that nevertheless is not an assent of faith.

The conciliar texts also indicate the conditions for the Roman Pontiff's exercise of the infallible Magisterium. They can be summarized in this way: the Pope must act as "the shepherd and teacher of all Christians," pronouncing on truths regarding "faith and morals," in terms clearly showing his intention to define a certain truth and to require definitive assent of all Christians. That occurred, for example, in the definition of Mary's Immaculate Conception, about which Pius IX stated: "It is a doctrine revealed by God and for this reason it must be firmly and constantly believed by all the faithful" *(DS* 2803), or in the definition of the Assumption of Mary most holy, when Pius XII said: "By the authority of our Lord Jesus Christ, of the blessed Apostles Peter and Paul, and our own authority, we declare and define as divinely revealed dogma...etc." *(DS* 3903).

With these conditions one can speak of the extraordinary papal Magisterium, whose definitions are unreformable *per se,* and not "from the consent of the Church" *(ex sese, non autem ex consensu ecclesiae).* This means that these definitions do not need the consent of the bishops in order to be valid, neither an antecedent consent, nor a consequent consent, "since they are pronounced with the assistance of the Holy Spirit, promised to him in blessed Peter, and therefore they need no approval of others, nor do they allow an appeal to any other judgment" *(LG* 25).

The Supreme Pontiffs can exercise this form of Magisterium, and in fact they have done so. Many Popes, however, have not exercised it. But it must be noted that in the conciliar texts we are explaining, a distinction is made between the "ordinary" and "extraordinary" Magisterium, emphasizing the importance of the first, which is permanent and ongoing, while the second, which is expressed in definitions, could be called exceptional.

Alongside this infallibility of *ex cathedra* definitions, there is the charism of the Holy Spirit's assistance, granted to

Peter and his successors so that they would not err in matters of faith and morals, but rather shed great light on the Christian peoplc. This charism is not limited to exceptional cases, but embraces in varying degrees the whole exercise of the Magisterium.

The conciliar texts also point out how serious is the Roman Pontiff's responsibility in exercising both his extraordinary and ordinary Magisterium. He thus feels the need, one could say even the duty, to explore the *sensus ecclesiae* before defining a truth of faith, in the clear awareness that his definition "expounds or defends the teaching of the Catholic faith" *(LG* 25).

This occurred prior to the definitions of Mary's Immaculate Conception and Assumption through a broad and prccisc consultation of the whole Church. In the Bull *Munificentissimus* on the Assumption (1950), Pius XII mentioned among the arguments in favor of the definition that of the faith of the Christian community: "The universal consent of the Church's ordinary Magisterium provides a certain, solid argument to prove that the Blessed Virgin Mary's bodily assumption into heaven...is a truth revealed by God" *(AAS* 42 [1950]: 757).

Furthermore, in speaking of the truth to be taught, the Second Vatican Council states: "The Roman Pontiff and the bishops, in view of their office and the importance of the matter, by fitting means diligently strive to inquire properly into that revelation and to give apt expression to its contents" *(LG* 25). It is a sign of wisdom that finds confirmation in the experience of the procedures followed by the Popes and the offices of the Holy See assisting them in carrying out the duties of the Magisterium and governance of Peter's successors.

We will close by noting that the exercise of the Magisterium is a concrete expression of the Roman Pontiff's contribution to the development of the Church's teaching. The Pope (who not only plays a role as head of the college of bishops in the definitions on faith and morals that the latter make, or as the notary of their thoughts, but also a more personal role both in the ordinary Magisterium and in his definitions) carries out his task by applying himself personally and encouraging study on the part of pastors, theologians, experts in different areas of doctrine, experts in pastoral care, spirituality, social life, etc.

In this way he fosters a cultural and moral enrichment at all levels of the Church. In organizing this work of consultation and study too, he appears as the Successor of the "rock" on which Christ built his Church.

General audience of March 24, 1993

THE MINISTRY OF PRIESTS
AND DEACONS

Presbyters Share in Christ's Priesthood

Today we are beginning a new series of catecheses dedicated to the presbyterate and to presbyters, who, as we know, are the closest co-workers of the bishops, in whose consecration and priestly mission they share. I will talk about this by adhering strictly to the New Testament texts and by following the approach of the Second Vatican Council, which has been the style of these catecheses. I begin my development of this theme with deep affection for these close co-workers of the episcopal order, to whom I feel close and whom I love in the Lord, as I have said since the beginning of my pontificate, especially in my first letter to priests of the whole world, written for Holy Thursday, 1979.

It must immediately be pointed out that the priesthood, in every degree, and thus in both bishops and presbyters, is a participation in the priesthood of Christ. According to the Letter to the Hebrews, Christ is the one high priest of the new and eternal covenant, who "offered himself once for all" in a sacrifice of infinite value that remains unchangeable and unceasing at the very heart of the economy of salvation (cf. Heb 7:24-28). There is no further need or possibility of other priests in addition to or alongside the one Mediator, Christ (cf. Heb 9:15; Rom 5:15-19; 1 Tim 2:5). He is the point of union and reconciliation between mankind and God (cf. 2 Cor 5:14-20), the

Word made flesh, full of grace (cf. Jn 1:1-18), the true and definitive *hiereús,* or priest (Heb 5:6; 10:21). On earth he "took away sin by his sacrifice" (Heb 9:26) and in heaven he continues to intercede for his faithful (cf. Heb 7:25), until they attain the heavenly inheritance won and promised by him. No one else in the new covenant is *hiereús* in the same sense.

The participation in Christ's one priesthood, which is exercised in several degrees, was instituted by Christ, who wanted differentiated functions in his Church as in a well-organized social body. For the function of leadership he established ministers of his priesthood (cf. *CCC* 1554). He conferred on them the sacrament of Orders to constitute them officially as priests who would work in his name and with his power by offering sacrifice and forgiving sins. The Council notes: "Therefore, having sent the apostles just as he himself had been sent by the Father, Christ, through the apostles themselves, made their successors, the bishops, sharers in his consecration and mission. The office of their ministry has been handed down, in a lesser degree indeed, to the priests. Established in the order of the priesthood they can be co-workers of the episcopal order for the proper fulfillment of the apostolic mission entrusted to priests by Christ" *(PO* 2; cf. *CCC* 1562).

This will of Christ clearly appears in the Gospel, from which we know that Jesus assigned to Peter and the Twelve a supreme authority in his Church, but Jesus also wanted co-workers for their mission. What the evangelist Luke attests is significant, namely, that after Jesus sent the Twelve on mission (cf. 9:1-6), he sent a still larger number of disciples, to indicate that the mission of the Twelve was not enough for the work of evangelization. "After this the Lord appointed seventy-two others whom he sent ahead of him in pairs to every town and place he intended to visit" (Lk 10:1).

Doubtless this step only prefigures the ministry that Christ would formally institute later on. However, it already shows the divine Master's intention to introduce a sizable number of co-workers into the "vineyard." Jesus chose the Twelve from among a larger group of disciples (cf. Lk 6:12, 13). These "disciples," in the sense of the term used in the Gospel texts, were not only those who believed in Jesus but those who followed him and wanted to accept his teaching as the Master and devote themselves to his work. And Jesus involved them in his mission. According to Luke, it was precisely on this occasion that Jesus said: "The harvest is abundant but the laborers are few" (Lk 10:2). Thus he indicated that, in his mind, relative to the experience of the first ministry, the number of workers was too small. That was true not only then, but for all times, including our own, when the problem has become especially acute. We have to deal with it, feeling spurred on and at the same time comforted by these words and—so to speak—by Jesus' gaze on the fields where laborers are needed for harvesting the grain. Jesus gave the example by his initiative, which could be called "vocation promotion." He sent seventy-two disciples in addition to the twelve apostles.

According to the Gospel, Jesus assigned to the seventy-two disciples a mission like that of the Twelve; the disciples were sent to proclaim the coming of God's kingdom. They were to carry out this preaching in the name of Christ and with his authority: "Whoever listens to you listens to me. Whoever rejects you rejects me. And whoever rejects me rejects the one who sent me" (Lk 10:16).

Like the Twelve (cf. Mk 6:7; Lk 9:1), the disciples received the power to expel evil spirits, so much so that after their first experiences they said to Jesus: "Lord, even the demons are subject to us because of your name." This power was confirmed by Jesus himself: "I have observed Satan fall like lightning from the sky. Behold I have given you the power to tread upon serpents and upon the full force of the enemy..." (Lk 10:17-19).

This also means that they participated with the Twelve in the redemptive work of the one priest of the new covenant,

Christ, who wanted to confer on them too a mission and powers like those of the Twelve. The establishment of the presbyterate, therefore, not only answers one of the practical necessities of bishops, who feel the need for co-workers, but derives from an explicit intention of Christ.

In the early Christian era presbyters *(presbýteroi)* were present and functioning in the Church of the apostles and of the first bishops, their successors (cf. Acts 11:30; 14:23; 15:2, 4, 6, 22, 23, 41; 16:4; 20:17; 21:18; 1 Tim 4:14; 5:17, 19; Ti 1:5; Jas 5:14; 1 Pet 5:1, 5, 15; 2 Jn 1; 3 Jn 1). In these New Testament books it is not always easy to distinguish between "presbyters" and "bishops" regarding the duties assigned to them. But very early on, already in the Church of the apostles, the two categories of those sharing in Christ's mission and priesthood appear to take shape. They are found again later and more clearly described in the works of the subapostolic writers (like Pope St. Clement's *Letter to the Corinthians,* the *Letters* of St. Ignatius of Antioch, the *Shepherd of Hermas,* etc.). In the common terminology of the Church in Jerusalem, Rome and the other communities of the East and West, the word *bishop* was finally reserved for the one head and pastor of the community, while the term *presbyter* designated a minister who worked in dependence on a bishop.

Following Christian Tradition and in conformity with Christ's will as attested in the New Testament, the Second Vatican Council speaks of presbyters as ministers who do not have "the supreme degree of the priesthood" and who, in exercising their power, depend on bishops. On the other hand, they are "united with the bishops in sacerdotal dignity" *(LG* 28; cf. *CCC* 1564). This association is rooted in the sacrament of Orders: "The office of priests, since it is connected with the episcopal order, also, in its own degree, shares the authority by which Christ builds up, sanctifies and rules his body" *(PO* 2; cf. *CCC* 1563). Presbyters too bear "the image of Christ, the supreme and eternal Priest" *(LG* 28); therefore they participate in Christ's pastoral authority. This is the characteristic note of their ministry, based on the sacrament of Orders conferred on them. We read in *Presbyterorum Ordinis:* "Wherefore the priesthood, while indeed it presupposes the sacraments of Christian initiation, is conferred by that special sacrament; through it priests, by the anointing of the Holy Spirit, are signed with a special character and are conformed to Christ the priest in such a way that they can act in the person of Christ the head" *(PO* 2; cf. *CCC* 1563).

This character, in those who receive it through the sacramental anointing of the Holy Spirit, is a sign of:

—*a special consecration,* in relation to Baptism and Confirmation;

—*a deeper configuration to Christ the priest,* who makes them his active ministers in the official worship of God and in sanctifying their brothers and sisters;

—*the ministerial powers* to be exercised in the name of Christ, the head and shepherd of the Church (cf. *CCC* 1581-1584).

In the presbyter's soul the character is also a sign and vehicle of the special graces for carrying out the ministry, graces related to the sanctifying grace that Holy Orders imparts as a sacrament both at the time it is conferred and throughout his exercise of and growth in the ministry. It thus surrounds and involves the presbyter in an economy of sanctification, which the ministry itself implies both for the one who exercises it and for those who benefit from it in the various sacraments and other activities performed by their pastors. The whole Church garners the fruit of the sanctification resulting from the ministry of presbyter-pastors: both diocesan priests and those who, having received Holy Orders under any title or in any form, carry out their activity in communion with the diocesan bishops and the Successor of Peter.

The profound ontology of the consecration received in Orders and the dynamism of sanctification that it entails in the ministry certainly exclude any secularized interpretation of the priestly ministry, as if the presbyter were simply dedicated to establishing justice or spreading love in the world. The presbyter participates ontologically in the priesthood of Christ. He is truly consecrated, a "man of the sacred," designated like Christ to the worship that ascends to the Father and to the evangelizing mission by which he spreads and distributes sacred realities—the truth, the grace of God—to his brothers and sisters. This is the priest's true identity; this is the essential requirement of the priestly ministry in today's world too.

General audience of March 31, 1993

Priests Exercise a Ministry of Preaching

In the Church we all are called to proclaim the Good News of Jesus Christ, to communicate it ever more fully to believers (cf. Col 3:16), and to make it known to non-believers (cf. 1 Pet 3:15). No Christian can be excused from this task stemming from the sacraments of Baptism and Confirmation and working under the impulse of the Holy Spirit. Thus it must be stated immediately that evangelization is not reserved to only one category of the Church's members. Nevertheless, bishops are its principal agents and leaders for the entire Christian community, as we saw in discussing them. In this work they are assisted by presbyters, and to a certain degree by deacons, according to the Church's norms and practice, both in ancient times and in those of the "new evangelization."

For presbyters, it can be said that proclaiming the word of God is the first task to be carried out (cf. *LG* 28; *CCC* 1564), because the basis of personal and communal Christian life is faith, which results from the Word of God and is nourished on this word. The Second Vatican Council emphasized this evangelizing mission and related it to the formation of the People of God and to everyone's right to receive the Gospel message from priests (cf. *PO* 4).

The need for this preaching is highlighted by St. Paul, who adds to Christ's command his own experience as an apostle. In his work of evangelization, carried out in many regions and contexts, he noted that people did not believe because no one as yet had proclaimed the Good News to them. Although the way of salvation was now open to all, he observed that everyone had not yet been able to take advantage of it. Thus, he also explained the need for preaching because of Christ's command: "But how can they call on him in whom they have not believed? And how can they believe in him of whom they have not heard? And how can they hear without someone to preach? And how can people preach unless they are sent?" (Rom 10:14-15).

The Apostle was concerned to communicate the Word of God in abundance to those who had become believers. He himself said to the Thessalonians: "We treated each one of you as a father treats his children, exhorting and encouraging you and insisting that you conduct yourselves as worthy of the God who calls you..." (1 Thess 2:11-12). The Apostle urgently exhorted his disciple Timothy to carry out this ministry: "I charge you in the presence of God and of Christ...proclaim the word; be persistent whether it is convenient or inconvenient; convince, reprimand, encourage through all patience and teaching" (2 Tim 4:1-2). "Presbyters who preside well deserve double honor, especially those who toil in preaching and teaching" (1 Tim 5:17).

The preaching of presbyters is not a mere exercise of the word that answers a personal need to express oneself and to communicate one's own thought, nor can it consist solely in sharing one's personal experience. This psychological element, which can have a didactic-pastoral role, is neither the reason for nor the principal element in preaching. As the Fathers of the 1971 Synod of Bishops said: "The experiences of life, whether of men in general or of priests, which must be kept in mind and always interpreted in the light of the Gospel,

cannot be either the sole or the principal norm of preaching"
(Ench. Vat., IV, 1186).

The mission of preaching is entrusted by the Church to
presbyters as a sharing in Christ's mediation, to be exercised
by virtue of and according to the demands of his mandate.
Priests, "in their degree of ministry, share in the office of the
one Mediator, Christ (1 Tim 2:5), and proclaim to all the
divine word" *(Ench. Vat.,* IV, 1186).

This expression cannot fail to make us reflect: it is a
"divine word," which therefore is not "ours" and cannot be
manipulated, changed or adapted at will, but must be proclaimed in its entirety. Since the "divine word" has been
entrusted to the apostles and the Church, "Each priest shares in
the special responsibility of preaching the whole of the Word
of God and of interpreting it according to the faith of the
Church," as the Fathers also said at the 1971 Synod *(Ench.
Vat.,* IV, 1183).

The proclamation of the word takes place in close connection with the sacraments, through which Christ imparts and
develops the life of grace. In this regard it must also be noted
that a good part of preaching, especially today, takes place
during the celebration of the sacraments and especially during
holy Mass. It should also be observed that the proclamation
already occurs through the administration of the sacraments,
both because of the theological and catechetical richness of the
liturgical texts and readings, given today in the vernacular and
understandable by the people, and because of the ritual's pedagogical procedure.

Doubtless, however, preaching must precede, accompany
and crown the administration of the sacraments, in relation to
the preparation necessary to receive them and to their fruitfulness in faith and life.

The Council recalled that proclaiming the divine word
has the effect of producing and nourishing faith, and of contributing to the Church's development. It said: "Through the

saving word the spark of faith is lit in the hearts of unbelievers, and fed in the hearts of the faithful. This is the way that the congregation of faithful is started and grows" *(PO* 4).

This principle must always be kept in mind: the goal of spreading, strengthening and increasing the faith must remain fundamental for everyone who preaches the Gospel, and thus for the priest who is especially and so often called to exercise the ministry of the word. A preaching which would be a tissue of psychological themes related to the person, or taken up with raising problems without resolving them, or causing doubts without indicating the source of Gospel light that can illumine the way for individuals and society, would not achieve the essential objective desired by the Savior. It would instead result in a source of disorientation for public opinion and of damage for believers themselves, whose right to know the true content of revelation would thus be ignored.

Moreover, the Council has shown the breadth and variety of forms that the authentic proclamation of the Gospel can take, according to the Church's teaching and mandate to preachers: "To all men, therefore, priests are debtors that the truth of the Gospel which they have may be given to others. And so, whether by entering into profitable dialogue they bring people to the worship of God, whether by openly preaching they proclaim the mystery of Christ, or whether in the light of Christ they treat contemporary problems, they are relying not on their own wisdom, for it is the word of Christ they teach, and it is to conversion and holiness that they exhort all men" *(PO* 4).

These then are the ways to teach the divine word according to the Church: the witness of one's life, which makes it possible to discover the power of God's love and gives persuasive force to the preacher's word; explicitly preaching the mystery of Christ to non-believers; catechesis and the ordered, organic exposition of the Church's doctrine; application of revealed truth to judging and solving practical cases.

Under these conditions preaching shows its beauty and attracts people who want to see the glory of God today too.

This requirement of authentic and complete proclamation is not opposed to the principle of adapting preaching, which was especially stressed by the Council (cf. *PO* 4). Clearly, the priest must above all ask himself, with a sense of responsibility and realistic evaluation, whether what he says in his preaching is understood by his listeners and whether it has an effect on the way they think and live. He should also strive to take stock of his own preaching, the various needs of his listeners and the different reasons they come together and seek his help. Clearly he should know and recognize his talents and use them to good advantage, not to show off (which would simply destroy his credibility with his listeners), but the better to bring the divine word to human minds and hearts.

More than to natural talents, however, the preacher must have recourse to those supernatural charisms that the history of the Church and of sacred eloquence presents in so many holy preachers. He will feel compelled to ask the Holy Spirit for the most appropriate effective way to speak, act and dialogue with his audience.

All this is true as well for everyone who exercises the ministry of the word by writing, publishing, and by radio and television broadcasting. The use of these communications media also requires the preacher, lecturer, writer, religious entertainer and especially the priest to call upon and have recourse to the Holy Spirit, the light who gives life to minds and hearts.

According to the Council's directives, the divine word should be proclaimed in all areas and at all levels of society, also taking non-believers into account—this means true atheists or, as is more often the case, agnostics, the indifferent or the heedless. In order to interest them it will be necessary to devise more appropriate measures. Here once again one need only point out the problem, which is serious and must be addressed with intelligent zeal and a calm attitude. It can be useful for the priest to remember the wise words of the 1971 Synod of Bishops, which said: "By evangelization the minister of the word prepares the ways of the Lord with great patience and faith, conforming himself to the various conditions of individuals and peoples' lives" *(Ench. Vat.,* IV, 1184). The ever necessary calling upon the Lord's grace and on the Holy Spirit, its divine steward, will be felt even more intensely in all those cases of (at least practical) atheism, agnosticism, ignorance and religious indifference, sometimes hostile prejudice and even animosity, which show the priest how inadequate are all human means for opening souls to God. Then, more than ever, he will experience the "mystery of empty hands," as it has been called. But for this very reason he will remember that St. Paul, almost crucified by similar experiences, always found new courage in the "power of God and the wisdom of God" present in Christ (cf. 1 Cor 1:18-29), and he reminded the Corinthians: "When I came among you it was in weakness and fear, and with much trepidation. My message and my preaching had none of the persuasive force of 'wise' argumentation, but the convincing power of the Spirit. As a consequence, your faith rests not on the wisdom of men but on the power of God" (1 Cor 2:3-5). Perhaps this is the important *viaticum* for today's preacher.

General audience of April 21, 1993

Priests Sanctify
through the Sacraments

In speaking of the evangelizing mission of presbyters, we already saw that *in* the sacraments and *through* the sacraments a methodical and effective instruction on the Word of God and the mystery of salvation can be imparted to the faithful. In fact, the priest's evangelizing mission is essentially related to the ministry of sanctification through the sacraments (cf. *CCC* 893).

The ministry of the word cannot be limited merely to the immediate, proper effect of the word. Evangelization is the first of those "apostolic endeavors" which, according to the Council, have as their goal "that all who are made children of God by faith and Baptism should come together to praise God in the midst of his Church, to take part in the sacrifice and to eat the Lord's Supper" *(SC* 10). And the 1971 Synod of Bishops stated: "The ministry of the word, if rightly understood, leads to the sacraments and to the Christian life, as it is practiced in the visible community of the Church and in the world" (cf. *Ench. Vat.,* IV, 1179).

Any attempt to reduce the priestly ministry to preaching alone or to teaching would misunderstand an essential aspect of this ministry. The Council of Trent had already rejected the proposal to make the priesthood consist merely of the ministry of preaching the Gospel (cf. *DS* 1771). Since some, even recently, have too one-sidedly extolled the ministry of the word, the 1971 Synod of Bishops stressed the unbreakable covenant between word and sacrament. It said: "The sacraments are celebrated in conjunction with the proclamation of the Word of God and thus develop faith by strengthening it with grace. They cannot be considered of slight importance, since through them the word is brought to fuller effect, namely communion in the mystery of Christ" (cf. *Ench. Vat.,* IV, 1180).

Regarding this unitary nature of the evangelizing mission and the sacramental ministry, the 1971 Synod did not hesitate to say that a division between evangelization and the celebration of the sacraments "would divide the heart of the Church to the point of imperiling the faith" (cf. *Ench. Vat.,* IV, 1181).

However, the Synod recognized that for each priest there can be different ways of concretely applying this principle of unity, "for the exercise of the priestly ministry in practice needs to take different forms in order to better meet special or new situations, in which the Gospel is to be proclaimed" *(Ench. Vat.,* IV, 1182).

A wise application of the principle of unity must also take into account the charisms each presbyter has received. If some have a particular talent for preaching or teaching they should use it for the good of the Church. It is helpful to recall here the case of St. Paul, who, although convinced of the need for Baptism and even having occasionally administered this sacrament, he thought of himself as having been sent to preach the Gospel and devoted his efforts primarily to this form of ministry (cf. 1 Cor 1:14, 17). In his preaching, however, he did not lose sight of the essential task of building the community (cf. 1 Cor 3:10), which this preaching must serve.

This means that today too, as throughout the history of the pastoral ministry, the division of labor can stress preaching or worship and the sacraments, according to the individual's abilities and the assessment of the situation. However, one can never doubt that for presbyters teaching and preaching, even at the highest academic and scholarly level, must always retain their purpose of serving the ministry of sanctification through the sacraments.

In any case, the important mission of sanctification entrusted to priests cannot be called into question. They can exercise this mission above all in the ministry of worship and the sacraments. Doubtless it is a work carried out primarily by Christ, as the 1971 Synod pointed out: "Salvation, which is effected through the sacraments, does not come from us but from God; this demonstrates the primacy of the action of Christ, the one priest and mediator, in his body, which is the Church" (cf. *Ench. Vat.,* IV, 1187; cf. also the Post-Synodal Apostolic Exhortation *Pastores Dabo Vobis* 12). In the present economy of salvation, however, Christ uses the presbyters' ministry to sanctify believers (cf. *PO* 5). Acting in the name of Christ, the priest achieves effective sacramental action through the Holy Spirit, the Spirit of Christ, the principle and source of the holiness of the "new life."

The new life that the priest imparts, nurtures, restores and increases through the sacraments is a life of faith, hope and love. Faith is the basic divine gift: "This makes clear the great importance of preparation and of a disposition of faith on the part of the person who receives the sacraments; it also makes clear the necessity for a witness of faith on the part of the ministry in his entire life and especially in the way he values and celebrates the sacraments themselves" (cf. *Ench. Vat.,* IV, 1188).

The faith communicated by Christ through the sacraments is unfailingly accompanied by a "living hope" (1 Pet 1:3), which instills in the hearts of the faithful a powerful dynamism of spiritual life, an impulse toward "what is above" (Col 3:1-2). On the other hand, faith "works through love" (Gal 5:6), the love of charity, which springs from the Savior's heart and flows into the sacraments to spread throughout Christian life.

The sacramental ministry of presbyters is thus endowed with a divine fruitfulness. The Council clearly recalled this. Thus, by Baptism "men are truly brought into the People of God" *(PO* 5). Therefore priests are responsible not only for worthily celebrating the rite, but also for providing a good preparation for it, by forming adults in the faith, and in regard to children, by educating the family to cooperate in the celebration.

Moreover, "In the spirit of Christ the shepherd, they must prompt their people to confess their sins with a contrite heart in the sacrament of Penance...mindful of his words, 'Repent for the kingdom of God is at hand' (Mt 4:17)" *(PO* 5). For this reason priests too must personally live with the attitude of men who acknowledge their own sins and their own need for forgiveness, in a communion of humility and repentance with the faithful. Thus they can more effectively show the greatness of the divine mercy and give heavenly comfort, as well as forgiveness, to those who feel oppressed by the weight of their guilt.

In the sacrament of Matrimony, the presbyter is present as the one responsible for the celebration, testifying to the faith and receiving the consent on behalf of God, whom he represents as the Church's minister. In this way he participates deeply and vitally not only in the rite, but in the deepest dimension of the sacrament.

Finally, by the Anointing of the Sick, priests "relieve those who are ill" *(PO* 5). It is a mission foreseen by St. James, who taught in his letter: "Is anyone among you sick? He should summon the presbyters of the Church, and they should pray over him and anoint him with oil in the name of the Lord" (Jas 5:14). Knowing then that the sacrament of Anointing is meant to "relieve" and to bring purification and spiritual strength, the presbyter will feel the need to make sure that his presence brings the sick person the effective compassion of Christ and witnesses to Jesus' kindness toward the sick, to whom he devoted such a large part of his evangelical mission.

This discussion of the dispositions which are necessary when one approaches the sacraments, celebrating them with awareness and a spirit of faith, will be completed in the catecheses that, please God, we shall devote to the sacraments. In the next catechesis we will discuss another aspect of the priest's mission in the sacramental ministry: the worship of God, which is carried out especially in the Eucharist. For now let us say that this is the most important element of his role in the Church, the principal reason for his ordination, the purpose that gives meaning and joy to his life.

General audience of May 5, 1993

Priests Are Ordained to Celebrate Mass

The complete dimension of the presbyter's mission in relation to the Eucharist is understood if one considers that this sacrament is primarily the renewal at the altar of the sacrifice of the cross, the central moment in the work of redemption. Christ, the priest and victim, is as such the artisan of universal salvation, in obedience to the Father. He is the one high priest of the new and eternal covenant, who by accomplishing our salvation offers perfect worship to the Father, a worship which ancient celebrations of the Old Testament merely prefigured. By the sacrifice of his own blood on the cross, Christ "entered once for all into the sanctuary, thus obtaining eternal redemption" (Heb 9:12). He abolished every ancient sacrifice in order to establish a new one by offering himself to the Father's will (cf. Ps 40:8). "By this 'will,' we have been consecrated through the offering of the body of Jesus Christ once for all.... For by one offering he has made perfect forever those who are being consecrated" (Heb 10:10, 14).

In sacramentally renewing the sacrifice of the cross, the presbyter reopens that source of salvation in the Church and the entire world (cf. *CCC* 1362-1372). For this reason the 1971 Synod of Bishops pointed out, in accord with the documents of Vatican II, that "The priestly ministry reaches its summit in the celebration of the Eucharist, which is the source and center of the Church's unity" *(Ench. Vat.,* IV, 1166; cf. *AG* 39).

The Dogmatic Constitution on the Church asserts: "They exercise their sacred function especially in the Eucharistic worship or the celebration of the Mass by which acting in the person of Christ and proclaiming his mystery, they unite the prayers of the faithful with the sacrifice of their head and renew and apply in the sacrifice of the Mass until the coming of the Lord the only sacrifice of the New Testament, namely that of Christ offering himself once for all a spotless victim to the Father" *(LG* 28; cf. *CCC* 1566).

In this regard, the Decree *Presbyterorum Ordinis* makes two fundamental assertions: a) the community is gathered by the proclamation of the Gospel so that all can make a spiritual offering of themselves; b) the spiritual sacrifice of the faithful is made perfect through union with Christ's sacrifice, offered in an unbloody, sacramental manner by the hands of the priests. Their whole priestly ministry draws its force from this one sacrifice (cf. *PO* 2; *CCC* 1566).

This shows the connection between the ministerial priesthood and the common priesthood of the faithful. It also shows how the priest, among all the faithful, is especially called to identify himself with Christ mystically as well as sacramentally, in order to be himself in some way *sacerdos et hostia,* according to the beautiful expression of St. Thomas Aquinas (cf. *Summa Theol.,* III, q. 83, a. 1, ad 3).

In the Eucharist the presbyter reaches the high point of his ministry when he pronounces Jesus' words: "This is my Body.... This is the cup of my Blood...." These words concretize the greatest exercise of that power which enables the priest to make present the sacrifice of Christ. Then the community is truly built up and developed in a sacramental way, and thus with divine efficacy. The Eucharist is indeed the sacrament of communion and unity, as was asserted by the 1971 Synod of Bishops and more recently by the letter of the Congregation for the Doctrine of the Faith *On Some Aspects of the Church Understood As Communion* (cf. *Communionis Notio* 11).

This is how one explains the piety and fervor with which saintly priests—about whom hagiography tells us abundantly—always celebrated Mass, not hesitating to make adequate preparation beforehand and afterward to make suitable acts of thanksgiving. In order to help with making these acts the Missal offers appropriate prayers, often laudably printed on special cards in sacristies. We also know that on the theme of *sacerdos et hostia* various works of priestly spirituality have been written and can always be recommended to priests.

Here is another essential point of Eucharistic priestly theology, the subject of our catechesis: the whole ministry and all the sacraments are directed toward the Eucharist, in which, "The Most Blessed Eucharist contains the entire spiritual good of the Church (cf. St. Thomas Aquinas, *Summa Theol.,* III, q. 65, a. 3, ad 1; q. 79, a. 1), that is, Christ himself, our Pasch and Living Bread, by the action of the Holy Spirit through his very flesh vital and vitalizing, giving life to men who are thus invited and encouraged to offer themselves, their labors and all created things, together with him" *(PO 5).*

In the celebration of the Eucharist, therefore, the greatest participation takes place in the perfect worship which Christ the high priest gives to the Father by representing and expressing the whole created order. The presbyter sees and recognizes that his life is thus deeply linked to the Eucharist. On the one hand he feels the horizons of his spirit broadened on a global scale, embracing even heaven and earth, and on the other, he is aware of the increased need and responsibility to impart this treasure—"the entire spiritual good of the Church"—to the community.

Therefore, in the projects and programs of his pastoral ministry, he keeps in mind that the sacramental life of the faithful is directed toward the Eucharist (cf. *PO 5*) and he will see to it that Christian formation aims at the active, conscious participation of the faithful in the Eucharistic celebration.

Today it is necessary to rediscover the central importance of this celebration in Christian life and in the apostolate. The data on the Mass attendance of the faithful is not encouraging. Although the zeal of many priests has led to a generally fervent and active participation, the attendance percentages remain low. It is true that in this area, more than in any other regarding the interior life, the value of statistics is quite relative; furthermore, it is not the structured, outward expression of worship that proves its real worth.

Nevertheless, one cannot ignore the fact that outward worship is normally a logical consequence of what is inside (cf. St. Thomas Aquinas, *Summa Theol.*, II-II, q. 81, a. 7). In the case of Eucharistic worship, it is a consequence of faith itself in Christ the priest and his redeeming sacrifice. Nor would it be wise to minimize the importance of the celebration of worship by citing the fact that the vitality of the Christian faith is shown by conduct in complete conformity with the Gospel, rather than by ritual gestures. In fact, the Eucharistic celebration is not a mere ritual gesture. It is a sacrament, that is, an intervention of Christ himself who communicates to us the dynamism of his love. It would be a pernicious illusion to claim that one is acting in accordance with the Gospel without receiving strength from Christ himself in the Eucharist, the sacrament he instituted for this purpose. Such a claim would be a radically anti-Gospel attitude of self-sufficiency. The Eucharist gives Christians greater strength to live according to the demands of the Gospel; it makes them more fully members of the ecclesial community to which they belong; it renews and enriches in them the joy of communion in the Church.

Therefore, by catechesis, pastoral exhortation and the excellent quality of the celebration in its liturgical and ceremonial aspect, the priest will make every effort to encourage participation in the Eucharist. He will thus succeed, as the

Council stresses (cf. *PO* 5), in teaching the faithful to offer the divine victim to God the Father in the sacrifice of the Mass and, in union with this victim, to make an offering of their own lives in service to their brothers and sisters. The faithful will also learn to seek pardon for their sins, to meditate on the Word of God, to pray with sincere hearts for all the needs of the Church and the world and to put all their trust in Christ the Savior.

Finally, I want to mention that the priest has the mission to promote the worship of the Eucharistic presence also outside of the celebration of Mass, by striving to make his own church a Christian "house of prayer," one in which, according to the Council, "The presence of the Son of God, our Savior, offered for us on the altar of sacrifice bestows strength and blessings on the faithful" *(PO* 5). This house must be a worthy place for prayer and sacred functions both for its good order, cleanliness, the neatness with which it is maintained, and for the artistic beauty of its environment, which has a great importance for the way it forms and inspires prayer. For this reason the Council recommends that the priest "properly cultivate liturgical knowledge and art" *(PO* 5).

I have called attention to these aspects because they too belong to the complex picture of a good "care of souls" on the part of priests, especially parish priests and all those responsible for churches and other places of worship. In any case, I stress the close connection between the priesthood and the Eucharist, as the Church teaches us. I reaffirm with conviction and deep spiritual joy that the presbyter is above all the man of the Eucharist: Christ's servant and minister in this sacrament, in which—according to the Council, summarizing the teaching of the ancient Fathers and doctors—"the entire spiritual good of the Church is contained" *(PO* 5). Every priest, at any level, in any area of work, is the servant and minister of the paschal mystery accomplished on the cross and lived anew on the altar for the redemption of the world.

General audience of May 12, 1993

The Priest Is a Shepherd
to the Community

In the previous catecheses we explained the presbyters' task as co-workers of the bishops in the area of teaching authority (instructing) and sacramental ministry (sanctifying). Today we will speak of their cooperation in the pastoral governance of the community. For priests as well as for bishops this is a sharing in the third aspect of Christ's three-fold *munus* (prophetic, priestly, royal): a reflection of the high priesthood of Christ, the one Mediator between God and men, the one Teacher, the one Shepherd. In an ecclesial perspective pastoral work consists principally in the service of unity, that is, in ensuring the union of all in the body of Christ which is the Church (cf. *PDV* 16).

In this perspective the Council says: "Exercising the office of Christ, the shepherd and head, and according to their share of his authority, priests, in the name of the bishop, gather the family of God together as a brotherhood enlivened by one spirit. Through Christ they lead them in the Holy Spirit to God the Father" *(PO* 6). This is the essential purpose of their activity as pastors and of the authority conferred on them so that they may exercise it at their level of responsibility: leading the community entrusted to them to the full development of its spiritual and ecclesial life. The presbyter-*pastor* (shepherd) must exercise this authority by modeling himself on Christ the good shepherd, who did not impose it with external coercion but by forming the community through the interior action of his Spirit. He wanted to share his burning love with the group of disciples and with all those who accepted his message, in order to give life to a "community of love," which at the right moment he also established visibly as the Church. As co-workers of the bishops, the successors of the apostles, presbyters too fulfill their mission in the visible community by enlivening it with charity so that it may live in the Spirit of Christ.

This is a demand intrinsic to the pastoral mission, whose inspiration is not governed by the priest's desires and personal opinions, but by the teaching of the Gospel, as the Council says: "They should act toward men, not as seeking to please them, but in accord with the demands of Christian doctrine and life" *(PO* 6).

The presbyter is responsible for the organic functioning of the community. To fulfill this task the bishop gives him a necessary share in his authority. It is his responsibility to ensure that the various services, indispensable for the good of all, are carried out harmoniously; to find appropriate assistance for the liturgy, catechesis and the spiritual support of married couples; to foster the development of various spiritual and apostolic associations or "movements" in harmony and cooperation; to organize charitable aid for the needy, the sick and immigrants. At the same time he must ensure and promote the community's union with the bishop and the Pope.

The community dimension of pastoral care, however, cannot overlook the needs of the individual faithful. As we read in the Council: "Priests therefore, as educators in the faith, must see to it either by themselves or through others that the faithful are led individually in the Holy Spirit to a development of their own vocation according to the Gospel, to a sincere and practical charity, and to that freedom with which Christ has made us free" *(PO* 6). The Council stresses the need to help each member of the faithful to discover his specific vocation, as a proper, characteristic task of the pastor who wants to respect and promote each one's personality. One could say that by his own example Jesus himself, the good shepherd who "calls his own sheep by name" (cf. Jn 10:3-4), has set the standard of individual pastoral care: knowledge and a relationship of friendship with individual persons. The presbyter's task is to help each one to utilize well his own gift, and rightly to exercise the freedom that comes from Christ's salvation, as St. Paul urges (cf. Gal 4:3; 5:1, 13; Jn 8:36).

Everything must be directed toward practicing "a sincere and practical charity." This means that "Christians should be taught that they live not only for themselves, but according to the demands of the new law of charity, as every man has received grace, he must administer the same to others. In this way, all will discharge in a Christian manner their duties in the community of men" *(PO* 6). Therefore, the priest's mission includes calling to mind the obligations of charity, showing the applications of charity in social life, fostering an atmosphere of unity with respect for differences, encouraging programs and works of charity, by which great opportunities become available to the faithful, especially through the new emphasis on volunteer work, consciously provided as a good use of free time, and in many cases, as a choice of life.

The presbyter is also called to be involved personally in works of charity, sometimes even in extraordinary forms, as has happened in the past and does so today as well. Here I especially want to underscore that simple, habitual, almost unassuming but constant and generous charity. This is manifested not so much in huge projects—for which many do not have the talent and vocation—but in the daily practice of goodness, which helps, supports and comforts according to each one's capacity. Clearly the principal concern, and one could say the preference, must be for "the poor and weak entrusted to them, for our Lord himself showed that he was united to them, and their evangelization is mentioned as a sign of messianic activity" *(PO* 6); for "the sick and dying," to whom the priest should be especially devoted, "visiting them and strengthening them in the Lord" *(PO* 6); for young people, who must be looked after "with special diligence"; as well as for "married couples and parents" *(PO* 6). In particular, the priest must devote his time, energy and talents to young people who are the hope of the community, in order to foster their Christian education and their growth in living according to the Gospel.

The Council also commends to the presbyter's care "catechumens and the newly-baptized who must be educated gradually to know and to live the Christian life" *(PO* 6).

Lastly, a too limited vision of the local community and every particularist and "parochial" attitude must be overcome, to foster instead the community spirit that is open to the horizons of the universal Church. The presbyter must devote his time and concern to the local community entrusted to him, as is the case especially for parish priests and their closest co-workers. But his heart must remain open to the "fields ripe for the harvest" beyond all borders, both as the universal dimension of the spirit and as the personal participation in the Church's missionary tasks, and as zeal in promoting the cooperation of his own community with the necessary spiritual and material aid (cf. *RM* 67; *PDV* 32).

"Through the sacrament of Holy Orders," the *Catechism of the Catholic Church* states, "priests share in the universal dimensions of the mission that Christ entrusted to the apostles. The spiritual gift they have received in ordination prepares them, not for a limited and restricted mission, 'but for the fullest, in fact, the universal mission of salvation "to the end of the earth"' *(PO* 10), 'prepared in spirit to preach the Gospel everywhere' *(OT* 20)" *(CCC* 1565).

In any case, everything depends on the Eucharist, which contains the vital principle of pastoral leadership. As the Council says: "No Christian community, however, is built up unless it has its basis and center in the celebration of the most Holy Eucharist; from this, therefore, all education to the spirit of community must take its origin" *(PO* 6). The Eucharist is the source of unity and the most perfect expression of the union of all the Christian community's members. It is the presbyters' task to ensure that this is really so. Unfortunately, it sometimes happens that Eucharistic celebrations are not expressions of unity. Each person attends individually, ignoring the others. With great pastoral charity, priests will remind everyone of St. Paul's teaching: "Because the loaf of bread is one, we, though many, are one body, for we all partake of the one loaf," which is "a participation in the Body of Christ" (1 Cor 10:16-17). Awareness of this union in the Body of Christ will encourage a life of charity and effective solidarity.

Therefore, the Eucharist is the vital principle of the Church as the community of Christ's members; here pastoral leadership finds its inspiration, strength and extent.

General audience of May 19, 1993

The Priesthood Requires Personal Holiness

All Christian Tradition, based on Sacred Scripture, speaks of the priest as a "man of God," a man consecrated to God. *Homo Dei:* this definition is valid for every Christian, but St. Paul refers it especially to Bishop Timothy, his disciple, when he recommends the use of Sacred Scripture to him (cf. 2 Tim 3:16). It is appropriate to the presbyter as well as to the bishop, by reason of his special consecration to God. In truth, a person already receives a first, basic consecration in Baptism, with deliverance from evil and entry into a special state of belonging ontologically and psychologically to God (cf. St. Thomas, *Summa Theol.,* II-II, q. 81, a. 8). Priestly ordination confirms and deepens this state of consecration, as the 1971 Synod of Bishops recalled when it referred to the priesthood of Christ shared by the presbyter through the anointing of the Holy Spirit (cf. *Ench. Vat.,* IV, 1200-1201).

Here the Synod took up again the teaching of Vatican II which, after reminding presbyters of their duty to strive for perfection by virtue of their baptismal consecration, added: "Priests are bound, however, to acquire that perfection in special fashion. They have been consecrated by God in a new manner at their ordination and made living instruments of Christ the eternal priest that they may be able to carry on in time his marvelous work whereby the entire family of man is again made whole by power from above" *(PO* 12). Pius XI recommended the same in his encyclical *Ad Catholici Sacerdotii* of December 20, 1935 (cf. *AAS* 28 (1936):10).

According to the faith of the Church, priestly ordination not only confers a new mission in the Church, a ministry, but a new "consecration" of the person. This consecration is linked to the character imprinted by the sacrament of Orders as a spiritual, indelible sign of a special belonging to Christ in being and, consequently, in acting. The perfection required of the presbyter is thus commensurate with his sharing in the priesthood of Christ as the author of redemption. The minister cannot be exempted from reproducing in himself the sentiments, the inner tendencies and intentions, and the spirit of sacrifice to the Father and of service to the brethren that is proper to the "principal agent."

As a result the priest has a sort of mastery of grace, which allows him to enjoy union with Christ and at the same time to be devoted to the pastoral service of his brothers and sisters. As the Council says, "Since, therefore, every priest in his own fashion acts in place of Christ himself, he is enriched by a special grace, so that, as he serves the flock committed to him and the entire People of God, he may the better grow in the grace of him whose tasks he performs, because to the weakness of our flesh there is brought the holiness of him who for us was made a high priest 'holy, guiltless, undefiled, not reckoned among us sinners' (Heb 7:26)" *(PO* 12; cf. *PDV* 20). In this condition the priest is bound to a special imitation of Christ the priest, which is the result of the special grace of Orders: the grace of union with Christ the priest and victim and, by virtue of this same union, the grace of good pastoral service to his brothers and sisters.

In this regard it is helpful to recall the example of St. Paul. He lived as an entirely consecrated apostle, he who was "taken possession of by Christ Jesus," and left everything to live in union with him (cf. Phil 3:7-12). He felt so filled with

Christ's life that he could say in complete sincerity: "Yet I live, no longer I, but Christ lives in me" (Gal 2:20). Nevertheless, after alluding to the extraordinary favors he had received as a "man in Christ" (2 Cor 12:2), he also suffered a thorn in the flesh, a trial from which he was never freed. Despite a triple request made to the Lord, Paul heard him respond: "My grace is sufficient for you, for power is made perfect in weakness" (2 Cor 12:9).

In the light of this example, the presbyter can better understand that he must strive to live fully his own consecration by remaining united to Christ and allowing himself to be imbued with Christ's spirit, despite the priest's experience of his own human limitations. These will not prevent him from carrying out his ministry, because he is favored with a "grace that is sufficient for him." The priest must put his trust in this grace; he must have recourse to it, knowing that he can thus strive for perfection in the hope of continually increasing in holiness.

His sharing in Christ's priesthood cannot fail to arouse in the presbyter a sacrificial spirit too, a type of *pondus crucis,* the burden of the cross, which is expressed especially in mortification. As the Council says:

> Christ, whom the Father sanctified, consecrated and sent into the world, "gave himself for us that he might redeem us from all iniquity and cleanse for himself an acceptable people, pursuing good works" (Ti 2:14), and thus through suffering entered into his glory. In like fashion, priests consecrated by the anointing of the Holy Spirit and sent by Christ must mortify the works of the flesh in themselves and give themselves entirely to the service of men. It is in this way that they can go forward in that holiness with which Christ endows them to perfect man *(PO* 12).

This is the ascetical aspect of the way of perfection, which for the priest cannot be lacking in renunciation and struggle against every sort of desire and yearning that would induce him to seek the good things of this world, thus compromising his interior progress. This is the "spiritual combat" of which the ascetical masters speak and which is required of every follower of Christ, but especially of every minister in the work of the cross, called to reproduce in himself the image of him who is *sacerdos et hostia*.

Obviously, one always needs to be open and responsive to the grace which itself comes from him who begets "any measure of desire or achievement" (Phil 2:13), but who also demands that one use the means of mortification and self-discipline without which one remains impervious soil. The ascetical tradition has always pointed out—and in a certain sense prescribed—to priests certain means of sanctification, especially the appropriate celebration of Mass, the punctual recitation of the Divine Office ("not to be mishandled," as St. Alphonsus de Liguori recommended), visits to the Blessed Sacrament, daily recitation of the rosary, daily meditation and periodic reception of sacramental Penance. These practices are still valid and indispensable. Particular importance must be given to the sacrament of Penance, the careful reception of which helps the presbyter to have a realistic image of himself, with the resulting awareness that he too is a poor, weak man, a sinner among sinners, one in need of forgiveness. He thus acquires "truth about himself" and is led to have confident recourse to the divine mercy (cf. *Reconciliatio et Paenitentia* 31; *PDV* 26).

In addition, it must always be remembered, as the Council says, that: "Priests who perform their duties sincerely and indefatigably in the Spirit of Christ arrive at holiness by this very fact" *(PO* 13). Thus, the proclamation of the word encourages them to achieve in themselves what they teach to others. The celebration of the sacraments strengthens them in faith and in union with Christ. The whole pastoral ministry develops their charity: "As they direct and nourish the People of God, may they be aroused by the example of the good shepherd that they may give their life for their sheep, ready for the supreme sacrifice" *(PO* 13). Their ideal will be to achieve unity of life in Christ, integrating prayer and ministry, contemplation and action, because they continually seek the Father's will and the gift of themselves for the flock (cf. *PO* 14).

Moreover, it is a source of courage and joy for the presbyter to know that his personal commitment to sanctification helps make his ministry effective. In fact, as the Council recalls: "Although divine grace could use unworthy ministers to effect the work of salvation, yet for the most part God chooses, to show forth his wonders, those who are more open to the power and direction of the Holy Spirit, and who can by reason of their close union with Christ and their holiness of life say with St. Paul: 'And yet I am alive; or rather, not I; it is Christ that lives in me' (Gal 2:20)" *(PO* 12).

When the priest recognizes that he is called to serve as the instrument of Christ, he feels the need to live in intimate union with Christ in order to be a valid instrument of the "principal agent." Therefore, he seeks to reproduce in himself the "consecrated life" (the sentiments and virtues) of the one, eternal priest who shares with him not only his power, but also his state of sacrifice for accomplishing the divine plan—*sacerdos et hostia.*

I will finish with a recommendation of the Council: "This holy Council, to fulfill its pastoral desires of an internal renewal of the Church, of the spread of the Gospel in every land and of a dialogue with the world of today, strongly urges all priests that they strive always for that growth in holiness by which they will become consistently better instruments in the service of the whole People of God, using for this purpose those means which the Church has approved" *(PO* 12). This is the greatest contribution we can make to building the Church as the beginning of God's kingdom in the world.

General audience of May 26, 1993

Priests Must Be Devoted to Prayer

Today we return to some ideas already mentioned in the preceding catechesis in order to underscore further the demands and repercussions stemming from the reality of being a man consecrated to God. In a word we can say that, consecrated in the image of Christ, the priest must be a man of prayer like Christ himself. This concise definition embraces the whole spiritual life that gives the presbyter a true Christian identity, defines him as a priest and is the motivating principle of his apostolate.

The Gospel shows Jesus in prayer at every important moment of his mission. His public life, inaugurated at his baptism, began with prayer (Lk 3:21). Even in the more intense periods of teaching the crowds, he reserved long intervals for prayer (cf. Mk 1:35; Lk 5:16). Before choosing the Twelve he spent a night in prayer (cf. Lk 6:12), and he prayed before asking his apostles for a profession of faith (cf. Lk 9:18). He prayed alone on the mountain after the miracle of the loaves (cf. Mt 14:23; Mk 6:46); he prayed before teaching his disciples to pray (cf. Lk 11:1); he prayed before the extraordinary revelation of the transfiguration, having ascended the mountain precisely to pray (cf. Lk 9:28); he prayed before performing some miracles (cf. Jn 11:41-42); he prayed at the Last

Supper to entrust his future and that of his Church to the Father (cf. Jn 17). In Gethsemane he offered the Father the sorrowful prayer of his afflicted and almost horrified soul (cf. Mk 15:35-39 and parallel passages), and on the cross he made his last invocations, full of anguish (cf. Mt 27:46), but also of trustful abandon (cf. Lk 23:46). It could be said that Christ's whole mission was animated with prayer, from the beginning of his messianic ministry to the supreme priestly act: the sacrifice of the cross, which was made in prayer.

Those called to share Christ's mission and sacrifice find in his example the incentive to give prayer its rightful place in their lives, as the foundation, root and guarantee of holiness in action. Indeed, we learn from Jesus that a fruitful exercise of the priesthood is impossible without prayer, which protects the presbyter from the danger of neglecting the interior life for the sake of action and from the temptation of so throwing himself into work as to be lost in it.

After stating that "the norm of priestly life" is found in Christ's consecration, the source of his apostles' consecration, the 1971 Synod of Bishops also applied the norm to prayer in these words:

> Following the example of Christ who was continually in prayer, and led by the Holy Spirit in whom we cry, "Abba, Father," priests should give themselves to the contemplation of the Word of God and daily take the opportunity to examine the events of life in the light of the Gospel, so that having become faithful and attentive hearers of the word they may become true ministers of the word. Let them be assiduous in personal prayer, in the Liturgy of the Hours, in frequent reception of the sacrament of Penance and especially in devotion to the mystery of the Eucharist (cf. *Ench. Vat.,* IV, 1201).

For its part, the Second Vatican Council did not fail to remind priests of the need to be habitually united to Christ, and to this end it recommended diligence in prayer: "In many ways, but especially through mental prayer and the vocal prayers which they freely choose, priests seek and fervently pray that God will grant them the spirit of true adoration whereby they themselves, along with the people committed to them, may intimately unite themselves with Christ the Mediator of the New Testament" *(PO* 18). As we see, among the possible forms of prayer the Council calls attention to mental prayer, which is a way to pray that is free from rigid formulas, does not require the recitation of words and responds to the Holy Spirit's lead in contemplating the divine mystery.

The 1971 Synod of Bishops insisted especially on "contemplation of the Word of God" (cf. *Ench. Vat.,* IV, 1201). One should not be frightened by the word "contemplation" and the spiritual commitment it entails. It could be said that, independently of forms and lifestyles, among which the contemplative life remains the most splendid jewel of Christ's bride, the Church, the call to hear and meditate on the Word of God in a contemplative spirit is valid for everyone, so that hearts and minds may be nourished on it. This helps the priest to develop a way of thinking and of looking at the world with wisdom, in the perspective of its supreme purpose—God and his plan of salvation. The Synod says: "To examine the events of life in the light of the Gospel" (cf. *Ench. Vat.,* IV, 1201).

Herein lies supernatural wisdom, above all as a gift of the Holy Spirit, who makes it possible to exercise good judgment in the light of the "ultimate reasons," the "eternal things." Wisdom thus becomes the principal factor in identifying with Christ in thought, judgment, the evaluation of any matter however large or small, so that the priest (like every Christian, only more so) reflects the light, practical zeal, obedience to the Father, rhythm of prayer and action and, one could almost say, the spiritual breath of Christ. This goal can be reached by allowing oneself to be guided by the Holy Spirit in meditating on the Gospel, which fosters a deeper union with Christ, helps one to enter ever further into the Master's thought and strengthens the personal attachment to him. If the priest is diligent in this he remains more easily in a state of conscious joy arising from his perception of the intimate, personal fulfillment of the Word of God, which he must teach others. In fact, the Council says of presbyters, "As they seek how they may better teach others what they have learned, they will better understand 'the unfathomable riches of Christ' (Eph 3:8) and the manifold wisdom of God" *(PO* 13). Let us pray the Lord to grant us a great number of priests who in their prayer life discover, assimilate and taste the wisdom of God, and like the Apostle Paul, sense the supernatural inclination to proclaim and bestow it as the true reason for their apostolate (cf. *PDV* n. 47).

In speaking of the priest's prayer, the Council also mentions and recommends the Liturgy of the Hours, which joins the priest's personal prayer to that of the Church. "In the recitation of the Divine Office, they offer the voice of the Church which perseveres in prayer in the name of the whole human race, together with Christ who 'lives on still to make intercession on our behalf' (Heb 7:25)" *(PO* 13).

By virtue of the mission of representation and intercession entrusted to him, the presbyter is formally obliged to this form of "official" prayer, delegated by the Church and made in the name not only of believers but of all mankind and, one could say, of the whole universe (cf. *CIC,* can. 1174, §1). Sharing in Christ's priesthood, he intercedes for the needs of the Church, the world and every human being, knowing that he represents and expresses the universal voice that sings the glory of God and seeks the salvation of mankind.

It is good to recall that, in order to give greater assurance to their prayer life and to strengthen and renew it by drawing on its sources, the Council asks priests to devote (in addition to time for the daily practice of prayer) longer periods to intimacy with Christ: "Spiritual retreats and spiritual direction are of great worth" *(PO* 18). This direction will serve as a friendly and fatherly hand to help them on the way. As they experience the benefits of this guidance, they will be all the more ready to offer this help, in turn, to those who are entrusted to their pastoral ministry. This will be a great resource for many people today, especially young people, and will play a decisive role in solving the problem of vocations, as the experience of so many generations of priests and religious show.

In the preceding catechesis we already mentioned the importance of the sacrament of Penance. The Council urges the presbyter to make "frequent use" of it. Obviously whoever exercises the ministry of reconciling Christians with the Lord through the sacrament of forgiveness must himself have recourse to this sacrament. He will be the first to acknowledge that he is a sinner and to believe in the divine pardon expressed by sacramental absolution. In administering the sacrament of forgiveness, this awareness of being a sinner will help him better to understand sinners. Does not the Letter to the Hebrews say of the priest, taken from among men: "He is able to deal patiently with the ignorant and erring, for he himself is beset by weakness" (Heb 5:2)? In addition, the personal use of the sacrament of Penance motivates the priest to make himself more available to administering this sacrament to the faithful who request it. This too is an urgent pastoral need in our day.

However, the presbyter's prayer reaches its apex in the Eucharistic celebration, his "greatest task" *(PO* 13). This is such an important point for the priest's prayer life that I want to devote the next catechesis to it.

General audience of June 2, 1993

The Eucharist Is at the Heart of the Priest's Spirituality

The catecheses which we are developing on the spiritual life of the priest especially concern presbyters, but they are addressed to all the faithful. It is indeed good that everyone should know the Church's doctrine on the priesthood and what she desires of those who, having received it, are conformed to the sublime image of Christ, the eternal priest and most pure victim of the salvific sacrifice. That image is developed in the Letter to the Hebrews and in other texts of the apostles and evangelists, and it has been handed on faithfully in the Church's Tradition of thought and life. Today too it is necessary for the clergy to be faithful to that image, which mirrors the living truth of Christ the priest and victim.

The reproduction of that image in priests is attained primarily through their life-giving participation in the Eucharistic mystery, to which the Christian priesthood is essentially ordered and linked. The Council of Trent emphasized that the bond between the priesthood and sacrifice comes from the will of Christ, who conferred upon his ministers "the power to consecrate, to offer and to distribute his Body and his Blood" (cf. *DS* 1764). In this there is a mystery of communion with Christ in being and doing, which must be translated into a spiritual life imbued with faith in and love for the Eucharist.

The priest is quite aware that he cannot count on his own efforts to achieve the purposes of his ministry. Rather, he is called to serve as an instrument of the victorious action of Christ whose sacrifice, made present on the altars, obtains for humanity an abundance of divine gifts. However, he also knows that, in order worthily to pronounce the words of consecration in the name of Christ—"This is my Body.... This is the cup of my Blood"—he must be profoundly united to Christ and seek to reproduce Christ's countenance in himself. The more intensely he lives in Christ, the more authentically he can celebrate the Eucharist.

The Second Vatican Council recalled: "Priests act especially in the person of Christ as ministers of holy things, especially in the Sacrifice of the Mass" *(PO* 13) and that without a priest there can be no Eucharistic sacrifice. However, it emphasized that those who celebrate this sacrifice must fulfill their role in intimate spiritual union with Christ, with great humility, as his ministers in the service of the community. "They are asked to take example from that with which they deal, and inasmuch as they celebrate the mystery of the Lord's death they should keep their bodies free of wantonness and lusts" *(PO* 13). In offering the Eucharistic sacrifice, presbyters must offer themselves personally with Christ, accepting all the renunciation and sacrifice required by their priestly life—again and always, with Christ and like Christ, *sacerdos et hostia.*

If the priest "hears" this truth proposed to him and to all the faithful as the voice of the New Testament and Tradition, he will grasp the Council's earnest recommendation: "The daily celebration of Mass is strongly urged, since even if there cannot be present a number of the faithful, it is still an act of Christ and of the Church" *(PO* 13). The tendency to celebrate the Eucharist only when there was an assembly of the faithful emerged in those years. According to the Council, although everything possible should be done to gather the faithful for the celebration, it is also true that, even if the priest is alone, the Eucharistic offering which he performs in the name of

Christ has the effectiveness that comes from Christ and always obtains new graces for the Church. Therefore I, too, recommend to priests and to all the Christian people that they ask the Lord for a stronger faith in this value of the Eucharist.

The 1971 Synod of Bishops took up the conciliar doctrine, declaring: "Even if the Eucharist should be celebrated without participation of the faithful, it nevertheless remains the center of the life of the entire Church and the heart of priestly existence" (cf. *Ench. Vat.,* 4, 1201).

This is a wonderful expression: "The center of the life of the entire Church." The Eucharist makes the Church, just as the Church makes the Eucharist. The presbyter, having been given the charge of building the Church, performs this task essentially through the Eucharist. Even when the participation of the faithful is lacking, he cooperates in gathering people around Christ in the Church by offering the Eucharist.

The Synod speaks further of the Eucharist as the "heart of priestly existence." This means that the presbyter, desiring to be and remain personally and profoundly attached to Christ, finds him first in the Eucharist, the sacrament which brings about this intimate union, open to a growth which can reach the heights of mystical identification.

At this level, too, which is that of so many holy priests, the priestly soul is not closed in on itself, because in a particular way in the Eucharist it draws on the love of him "who gives himself as food to the faithful" *(PO* 13). Thus he feels led to give himself to the faithful to whom he distributes the Body of Christ. It is precisely in being nourished by this Body that he is impelled to help the faithful to open themselves in turn to that same presence, drawing nourishment from his infinite charity, in order to draw ever richer fruit from the sacrament.

To this end the presbyter can and must provide the atmosphere necessary for a worthy Eucharistic celebration. It is the atmosphere of prayer: liturgical prayer, to which the people must be called and trained; the prayer of personal contemplation; the prayer of sound Christian popular tradition, which can prepare for, follow and to some extent also accompany the Mass; the prayer of holy places, of sacred art, of sacred songs, of sacred music, (especially on the organ). This is incarnated as it were in the formulas and rites, and continually inspires and uplifts everything so that it can participate in giving praise to God and in spiritually uplifting the Christian people gathered in the Eucharistic assembly.

To priests the Council also recommends, in addition to the daily celebration of the Mass, personal devotion to the Holy Eucharist, and especially that "daily colloquy with Christ, a visit to and veneration of the Most Holy Eucharist" *(PO* 18). Faith in and love for the Eucharist cannot allow Christ's presence in the tabernacle to remain alone (cf. *CCC* 1418). Already in the Old Testament we read that God dwelt in a "tent" (or "tabernacle"), which was called the "meeting tent" (Ex 33:7). The meeting was desired by God. It can be said that in the tabernacle of the Eucharist too Christ is present in view of a dialogue with his new people and with individual believers. The presbyter is the first one called to enter this meeting tent, to visit Christ in the tabernacle for a "daily talk."

Lastly, I want to recall that, more than any other, the presbyter is called to share the fundamental disposition of Christ in this sacrament, that is, the "thanksgiving" from which it takes its name. Uniting himself with Christ the priest and victim, the presbyter shares not only his offering, but also his feelings, his disposition of gratitude to the Father for the benefits he has given to humanity, to every soul, to the priest himself, to all those who in heaven and on earth have been allowed to share in the glory of God. *Gratias agimus tibi propter magnam gloriam tuam....* Thus, to counter the expressions of accusation and protest against God—which are often heard in the world—the priest offers the chorus of praise and blessing, which is raised by those who can recognize in man and in the world the signs of an infinite goodness.

General audience of June 9, 1993

Priests Must Foster Devotion to Mary

The biographies of saintly priests always document the great role they attributed in their spiritual life to Mary. To the "written lives" corresponds the experience of the "lived lives" of so many dear, venerable priests whom the Lord appointed as true ministers of divine grace among the people entrusted to their pastoral care, or as preachers, chaplains, confessors, professors, writers. Spiritual directors and masters insist on the importance of devotion to our Lady in the priest's life, as an effective support on the path of sanctification, a constant comfort during personal trials and a powerful strength in the apostolate.

The 1971 Synod of Bishops also passed on these expressions of Christian Tradition to priests today when it recommended: "With his mind raised to heaven and sharing in the communion of saints, the priest should very often turn to Mary, the Mother of God, who received the Word of God with perfect faith, and daily ask her for the grace of conforming himself to her Son" *(Ench. Vat.,* IV, 1202). The profound reason for the presbyter's devotion to Mary most holy is based on the essential relationship established in the divine plan between the Mother of Jesus and the priesthood of her Son's ministers. We want to reflect on this important aspect of priestly spirituality and draw practical conclusions from it.

340

Mary's relationship to the priesthood derives primarily from the fact of her motherhood. Becoming the Mother of Christ by her consent to the angel's message, Mary became the Mother of the high priest. This is an objective reality: by assuming a human nature in the Incarnation, the eternal Son of God fulfilled the necessary condition for becoming the one priest of humanity through his death and resurrection (cf. Heb 5:1). We can marvel at the perfect correspondence between Mary and her Son at the moment of the Incarnation. Indeed, the Letter to the Hebrews reveals to us that when he "came into the world," Jesus gave a priestly orientation to his personal sacrifice and said to God: "Sacrifice and offering you did not desire, but a body you prepared for me.... Then I said, 'Behold, I come to do your will, O God'" (Heb 10: 5-7). The Gospel tells us that at the same moment the Virgin Mary expressed the same attitude, saying: "Behold, I am the handmaid of the Lord. May it be done to me according to your word" (Lk 1:38).

This perfect correspondence shows us that a close relationship has been established between Mary's motherhood and Christ's priesthood. By that very fact a special bond exists between the priestly ministry and Mary most holy.

As we know, the Blessed Virgin fulfilled her role as mother not only in physically begetting Jesus but also in his moral formation. In virtue of her motherhood, she was responsible for raising the child Jesus in a way appropriate to his priestly mission, the meaning of which she learned from the message of the Incarnation.

In Mary's consent we can recognize an assent to the substantial truth of Christ's priesthood and the willingness to cooperate in fulfilling it in the world. This lays the objective basis for the role Mary was called to play also in the formation of Christ's ministers, sharers in his priesthood. I called attention to this in the Post-Synodal Apostolic Exhortation *Pastores Dabo Vobis:* every aspect of priestly formation can be referred to Mary (cf. n. 82).

We know further that our Lady fully lived the mystery of Christ, which she discovered ever more deeply through her personal reflection on the events of her Son's birth and childhood (cf. Lk 2:19; 2:51). With mind and heart she strove to fathom the divine plan in order consciously and effectively to cooperate in it. Who today better than she could enlighten the ministers of her Son, leading them to fathom the "unspeakable riches" of his mystery in order to act in conformity with his priestly mission?

Mary was uniquely associated with Christ's priestly sacrifice, sharing his will to save the world by the cross. She was the first to share spiritually in his offering as *sacerdos et hostia,* and did so most perfectly. As such, she can obtain and give grace to those who share in her Son's priesthood on the ministerial level, the grace moving them to respond ever more fully to the demands of spiritual oblation that the priesthood entails: in particular, the grace of faith, hope and perseverance in trials, recognized as a challenge to share more generously in the redemptive sacrifice.

On Calvary Jesus entrusted a new motherhood to Mary when he said to her: "Woman, behold your son!" (Jn 19:26). We cannot overlook the fact that when this motherhood was proclaimed, it was in regard to a "priest," the beloved disciple. In fact, according to the Synoptic Gospels, John too received from the Master at the supper on the previous night the power to renew the sacrifice of the cross in his memory. With the other apostles he belonged to the group of the first "priests"; now at Mary's side he replaced the one, supreme priest who was leaving the world. Certainly, Jesus' intention at that moment was to establish Mary's universal motherhood in the life of grace for every disciple, both then and for all ages. But we cannot ignore the fact that this motherhood took on a concrete, immediate form in relation to an apostle-priest. And we can think that Jesus' gaze extended beyond John to the long series of his priests in every age until the end of the world. As he did for the beloved disciple, he made that entrustment to Mary's motherhood for them in particular, taken one by one.

Jesus also said to John: "Behold, your mother!" (Jn 19:27). To the beloved disciple he entrusted the task of caring for Mary as his own mother, of loving her, venerating her and protecting her for the remaining years of her life on earth. But this was in the light of what was written for her in heaven, where she would be assumed and glorified. These words are the origin of Marian devotion; the fact that they were addressed to a priest is significant. Can we not then draw the conclusion that the priest is charged with promoting and developing this devotion and that he is the one primarily responsible for it?

In his Gospel John thought it important to stress that "from that hour the disciple took her into his home" (Jn 19:27). Thus he responded immediately to Christ's invitation and took Mary with him, with a reverence appropriate to the circumstances. I would like to say that in this respect too he appeared as a true priest, certainly a faithful disciple of Jesus.

For every priest, taking Mary into his own home means finding a place for her in his own life, remaining in habitual union with her in his thoughts, feelings, zeal for the kingdom of God and for devotion to her (cf. *CCC* 2673-2679).

What should we ask of Mary as "Mother of priests"? Today, perhaps more than at any other time, the priest must ask Mary especially for the grace of knowing how to accept God's gift with grateful love, fully appreciating it as she did in the *Magnificat*—the grace of generosity in self-giving, in order to imitate her example as a "generous Mother"; the grace of purity and fidelity in the obligation of celibacy, following her example as the "faithful Virgin"; the grace of burning, merciful love, in the light of her witness as the "Mother of mercy."

The presbyter must always remember that in the difficulties he will meet he can count on Mary's help. In her and to her he confides and entrusts himself and his pastoral ministry, asking her to make it yield abundant fruit. Finally, he looks to her as the perfect model of his life and ministry, because she is the one, as the Council says, who "was led by the Holy Spirit to dedicate herself totally to the mystery of man's redemption. Let priests love and venerate with filial devotion and veneration this mother of the eternal high priest, Queen of Apostles and protector of their own ministry" *(PO* 18).

I urge my brothers in the priesthood to nourish this "true devotion to Mary" and to draw its practical consequences for their life and ministry. I urge all the faithful to join us priests in entrusting themselves to our Lady and in invoking her graces for themselves and for the whole Church.

General audience of June 30, 1993

The Priest Is Called
to Be a Man of Charity

In the preceding catecheses devoted to presbyters, we have already mentioned several times the importance of fraternal charity in their lives. Now we want to discuss this more explicitly, beginning with the very root of this charity in the priest's life. This root is found in his identity as a "man of God." The First Letter of John teaches us that "God is love" (4:8). Since the priest is a "man of God" he must be a man of charity. He would have no true love for God (nor even true piety or true apostolic zeal) without love for his neighbor.

Jesus himself showed the connection between love for God and love for neighbor, since "loving the Lord, your God, with all your heart" cannot be separated from "loving your neighbor" (cf. Mt 22:36-40). Consistently, therefore, the author of the Letter cited above reasons: "This is the commandment we have from him: whoever loves God must also love his brother" (1 Jn 4:21).

Speaking of himself, Jesus described this love as that of a "good shepherd" who does not seek his own interest or his own advantage, like a hired hand. He noted that the good shepherd loves his sheep to the point of giving his own life (cf. Jn 10:11, 15). Thus it is a love to the point of heroism.

We know to what extent this was realized in the life and death of Jesus. Those who, in virtue of priestly ordination, receive the mission of shepherds are called to present anew in their lives and witness to with their actions the heroic love of the good shepherd.

In Jesus' life one can clearly see the essential features of the "pastoral charity" that he had for his brothers and sisters, and that he asks his brother "shepherds" to imitate. Above all, his love was humble: "I am meek and humble of heart" (Mt 11:29). Significantly, he urged his apostles to renounce their personal ambitions and any spirit of domination so as to imitate the example of the "Son of Man" who "did not come to be served but to serve and to give his life as a ransom for many" (Mk 10:45; Mt 20:28; cf. *PDV* 21-22).

As a result the mission of shepherd cannot be carried out with a superior or authoritarian attitude (cf. 1 Pet 5:3), which would irritate the faithful and perhaps drive them from the fold. In the footsteps of Christ the good shepherd, we must be formed in a spirit of humble service (cf. *CCC* 876).

Jesus also gave the example of a love filled with compassion—a sincere, active sharing in the sufferings and problems of the faithful. He felt compassion for the crowd without a shepherd (cf. Mt 9:36). For this reason he was concerned to guide them by his words of life and began to "teach them many things" (Mk 6:34). With this same compassion he healed many of the sick (Mt 14:14), as a sign of his intention to give spiritual healing. He multiplied the loaves for the hungry (Mt 15:32; Mk 8:2), which was an eloquent symbol of the Eucharist. He was moved by the sight of human misery (Mt 20:34; Mk 1:41), and wanted to bring healing; he shared the pain of those who mourned the loss of a dear relative (Lk 7:13; Jn 11:33-35). He showed mercy even to sinners (cf. Lk 15:1-2), in union with the Father who is full of compassion for the prodigal son (cf. Lk 15:20) and prefers mercy to ritual sacrifice (cf. Mt 9:10-13). In some cases Jesus rebuked his adversaries for not understanding his mercy (Mt 12:7).

In this regard it is significant that the Letter to the Hebrews, in the light of Jesus' life and death, again sees an essential feature of the authentic priesthood in solidarity and compassion. Indeed, it reaffirms that the High Priest, "taken from among men and made their representative before God...is able to deal patiently with the ignorant and erring" (Heb 5:1-2). Therefore, the eternal Son of God too "had to become like his brothers in every way, that he might be a merciful and faithful high priest before God to expiate the sins of the people" (Heb 2:17). As a result our great consolation as Christians is knowing that "we do not have a high priest who is unable to sympathize with our weaknesses, but one who has similarly been tested in every way, yet without sin" (IIcb 4:15).

The presbyter thus finds in Christ the model of a true love for the suffering, the poor, the afflicted and especially for sinners, because Jesus is close to human beings having lived a life like our own. He endured trials and tribulations like our own; therefore he is full of compassion for us and "is able to deal patiently with erring sinners" (Heb 5:2). Finally, he is able effectively to help those sorely tried: "Since he was himself tested through what he suffered, he is able to help those who are tempted" (Heb 2:18).

Continuing in this light of divine love, the Second Vatican Council presents priestly consecration as a source of pastoral charity:

> Priests of the New Testament, by their vocation and ordination, are in a certain sense set apart in the bosom of the People of God. However, they are not to be separated from the People of God or from any person, but they are to be totally dedicated to the work for which the Lord has chosen them. They cannot be ministers of Christ unless they be witnesses and dispensers of a life other than earthly life. But they cannot be of service to men if they remain strangers to the life and conditions of men *(PO 3)*.

At issue are two demands on which the two aspects of priestly behavior are based: for presbyters, "Their ministry itself, by a special title, forbids that they be conformed to this world, yet at the same time it requires that they live in this world among men. They are to live as good shepherds that know their sheep, and they are to seek to lead those who are not of this sheepfold that they, too, may hear the voice of Christ, so that there might be one fold and one shepherd" *(PO* 3). This explains Paul's intense activity in collecting aid for the poorest communities (cf. 1 Cor 16:1-4), and the recommendation made by the author of the Letter to the Hebrews to share possessions in supporting one another as true followers of Christ (cf. Heb 13:16).

According to the Council, the presbyter who wants to be conformed to the good shepherd and reproduce in himself his charity for his brothers and sisters will have to be committed to some very important tasks today, even more so than in other times. He must know his own sheep (cf. *PO* 3), especially by contact, visits, relations of friendship, planned or occasional meetings, etc., always for a reason and with the spirit of a good shepherd. As Jesus did, he must welcome the people who come to him, remaining ready and able to listen, wanting to understand, being open and genuinely kind, engaging in deed and activities to aid the poor and unfortunate. He must cultivate and practice those "virtues which in human affairs are deservedly esteemed [and] contribute a great deal: such as goodness of heart, sincerity, strength and constancy of mind, zealous pursuit of justice, affability, and others" *(PO* 3), as well as patience, readiness to forgive quickly and generously, kindness, affability, the capacity to be obliging and helpful without playing the benefactor. There are a myriad of human and pastoral virtues which the fragrance of Christ's charity can and must determine in the priest's conduct (cf. *PDV* 23).

Sustained by charity, the presbyter can, in the exercise of his ministry, follow the example of Christ, whose food was to do his Father's will. In loving submission to this will the priest will find the principle and source of unity in his life. The Council states that priests can achieve this unity "by joining themselves with Christ in the recognition of the Father's will.... In this way, by adopting the role of the good shepherd they will find in the practice of pastoral charity itself the bond of priestly perfection which will achieve unity in their life and activity" *(PO* 14). The source on which to draw this charity is always the Eucharist, which is "the center and root of the priest's whole life." His soul must strive to make his own what takes place on the altar of sacrifice (cf. *PO* 14).

The grace and charity of the altar are thus spread to the pulpit, the confessional, the parish office, the school, recreational activities, homes and streets, hospitals, public transportation and the communications media, wherever the priest has the opportunity to carry out his task as a shepherd. In every case it is his Mass which is spread. His spiritual union with Christ the Priest and Victim leads him to be, as St. Ignatius of Antioch said, "God's wheat in order to become pure bread" for the good of his brothers and sisters (cf. *Epist. ad Romanos,* IV, 1).

General audience of July 7, 1993

The Church Is
Committed to Priestly Celibacy

In the Gospels, when Jesus called his first apostles to make them "fishers of men" (cf. Mt 4:19; Mk 1:17; Lk 5:10), they "left everything and followed him" (Lk 5:11; cf. Mt 4:20, 22; Mk 1:18, 20). One day Peter remembered this aspect of the apostolic vocation and said to Jesus: "We have given up everything and followed you" (Mt 19:27; Mk 10:28; cf. Lk 18:28). Jesus then listed all the necessary detachments "for my sake," and "for the sake of the Gospel" (Mk 10:29). This did not only mean renouncing material possessions, such as "house" or "lands," but also being separated from loved ones: "brothers or sisters or mother or father or children," according to Matthew and Mark, and "wife or brothers or parents or children," according to Luke (18:29).

Here we note the difference in vocations. Jesus did not demand this radical renunciation of family life from all his disciples, although he did require the first place in their hearts when he said: "Whoever loves father or mother more than me is not worthy of me, and whoever loves son or daughter more than me is not worthy of me" (Mt 10:37). The demand for practical renunciation is proper to the apostolic life or the life of special consecration. Called by Jesus, "James, the son of Zebedee, and his brother John" left not only the boat on which they were "mending their nets," but also their father who was with them (Mt 4:22; cf. Mk 1:20).

These observations help us understand the reason for the Church's legislation on priestly celibacy. In fact, the Church has considered and still considers that it belongs to the logic of priestly consecration and to the total belonging to Christ resulting from it, in order to fulfill consciously his mandate of evangelization and the spiritual life.

Indeed, in the Gospel according to Matthew, shortly before the passage cited above about leaving loved ones, Jesus expressed in strong Semitic language another renunciation required "for the sake of the Gospel," that is, the renunciation of marriage. "Some have made themselves eunuchs for the sake of the kingdom of heaven" (Mt 19:12). They are committed to celibacy, that is, in order to put themselves entirely at the service of the "Gospel of the kingdom" (cf. Mt 4:23; 9:35; 24:34).

In First Corinthians, the Apostle Paul states that he had resolved to take this path and shows the coherence of his own decision, declaring: "An unmarried man is anxious about the things of the Lord, how he may please the Lord. But a married man is anxious about the things of the world, how he may please his wife, and he is divided" (1 Cor 7:32-34). It is certainly inappropriate for someone to be "divided," who, like the priest, has been called to be concerned about the things of the Lord. As the Council says, the commitment of celibacy, stemming from a tradition linked to Christ, "is held by the Church to be of great value in a special manner for the priestly life. It is at the same time a sign and a stimulus for pastoral charity and a special source of spiritual fecundity in the world" *(PO* 16).

It is quite true that in the Eastern Churches many presbyters are legitimately married in accordance with their own canon law. Even in those churches, however, bishops are celibate, as are a number of priests. The difference in discipline, related to conditions of time and place evaluated by the

Church, is explained by the fact that perfect continence, as the Council says, "is not demanded by the very nature of the priesthood" *(PO* 16). It does not belong to the essence of the priesthood as Holy Orders, and thus is not imposed in an absolute way in all the churches. Nevertheless, there is no doubt about its suitability and indeed its appropriateness to the demands of Sacred Orders. As was said, it belongs to the logic of consecration.

Jesus is the concrete ideal of this form of consecrated life, an example for everyone, but especially for priests. He lived as a celibate, and for this reason he could devote all his energy to preaching the kingdom of God and to serving people, with a heart open to all humanity, as the founder of a new spiritual family. His choice was truly "for the sake of the kingdom of heaven" (cf. Mt 19:12).

By his example Jesus gave an orientation that was followed. According to the Gospels, it appears that the Twelve, destined to be the first to share in his priesthood, renounced family life in order to follow him. The Gospels never speak of wives or children in regard to the Twelve, although they tell us that Peter was a married man before he was called by Jesus (cf. Mt 8:14; Mk 1:30; Lk 4:38).

Jesus did not promulgate a law, but proposed the ideal of celibacy for the new priesthood he was instituting. This ideal was increasingly asserted in the Church. One can understand that in the first phase of Christianity's spread and development a large number of priests were married men, chosen and ordained in the wake of Jewish tradition. We know that in the Letters to Timothy (1 Tim 3:2-3) and to Titus (1:6), one of the qualities required of the men chosen as presbyters is that they be good fathers of families, married only once (that is, faithful to their wives). This was a phase in the Church's process of being organized, and, one could say, of testing which discipline of the states of life best corresponds to the ideal and the "counsels" taught by the Lord.

On the basis of experience and reflection the discipline of celibacy gradually spread to the point of becoming the general practice in the Western Church as a result of canonical legislation. It was not merely the consequence of a juridical and disciplinary fact. It was the growth of the Church's realization of the appropriateness of priestly celibacy not only for historical and practical reasons, but also for those arising from an ever better awareness of the congruence of celibacy and the demands of the priesthood.

The Second Vatican Council gave the reasons for this "inner consonance" of celibacy and the priesthood: "Through virginity, then, or celibacy observed for the kingdom of heaven, priests are consecrated to Christ by a new and exceptional reason. They adhere to him more easily with an undivided heart; they dedicate themselves more freely in him and through him to the service of God and men, and they more expeditiously minister to his kingdom and the work of heavenly regeneration, and thus they are apt to accept, in a broad sense, paternity in Christ." They "evoke the mysterious marriage established by Christ, and fully to be manifested in the future, in which the Church has Christ as her only spouse. They give, moreover, a living sign of the world to come, by a faith and charity already made present, in which the children of the resurrection neither marry nor take wives" *(PO* 16; cf. *PDV* 29, 50; *CCC* 1579).

These lofty, noble spiritual reasons can be summarized in the following essential point: a more complete adherence to Christ, loved and served with an undivided heart (cf. 1 Cor 7:32-33); greater availability to serve Christ's kingdom and to carry out their own tasks in the Church; the most exclusive choice of a spiritual fruitfulness (cf. 1 Cor 4:15); leading a life more like that definitive one in the world to come, and therefore, more exemplary for life here below. This is a valid reason for all times, including our own, and is the supreme criterion of every judgment and every choice in harmony with Jesus' invitation to the disciples and especially to the apostles to "leave everything." For this reason the 1971 Synod of Bishops confirmed: "The law of priestly celibacy existing in the Latin Church is to be kept in its entirety" *(Ench. Vat.,* IV, 1219).

Today the practice of celibacy faces obstacles, sometimes grave ones, in the subjective and objective conditions in which priests happen to live. The Synod of Bishops considered them, but held that even today's difficulties can be overcome if "suitable conditions are fostered, namely: growth of the interior life through prayer, renunciation and fervent love for God and one's neighbor and by other aids to the spiritual life; human balance through well-ordered integration into the fabric of social relationships; fraternal association and companionship with other priests and with the bishop, through pastoral structures better suited to this purpose and with the assistance also of the community of the faithful" *(Ench. Vat.,* IV, 1216).

This is a challenge that the Church makes to the mentality, tendencies and charms of the world, with an ever new desire for consistency with and fidelity to the gospel ideal. Therefore, although the Supreme Pontiff can consider and decide what is to be done in certain cases, the Synod reaffirmed that in the Latin Church, "The priestly ordination of married men is not permitted, even in particular cases" *(Ench. Vat.,* IV, 1220). The Church holds that the awareness of total consecration, developed over centuries, continues to hold good and to be increasingly improved.

The Church also knows and reminds presbyters and all the faithful with the Council that "this gift of the Spirit so fitting for the priesthood of the New Testament, [is] freely given by the Father, provided that those who participate in the priesthood of Christ through the sacrament of Orders— and also the whole Church—humbly and fervently pray for it" *(PO* 16).

Perhaps, however, and even first, it is necessary to ask for the grace of understanding priestly celibacy, which doubtless includes a certain mystery—that of asking for boldness and trust in the absolute attachment to the person and redeeming work of Christ, with a radical renunciation that can seem confusing to human eyes. In suggesting it, Jesus himself observed that not everyone can understand it (cf. Mt 19:10-12). Blessed are they who receive the grace to understand it and remain faithful on this journey!

General audience of July 17, 1993

Christ Is the Model of Priestly Poverty

One of the renunciations Jesus requested of his disciples is that of earthly goods, especially wealth (cf. Mt 19:21; Mk 10:21; Lk 12:33; 18:22). This request is directed to all Christians in regard to the spirit of poverty, that is, the interior detachment from earthly goods which makes them generous in sharing these goods with others. Poverty is required of a life inspired by faith in Christ and by love for him. It is a spirit that also demands a practice, with each one's renunciation of these goods corresponding to his condition both in civil life and his state in the Church by virtue of the Christian vocation, both as an individual and as a determinate group of people. The spirit of poverty is valid for all; a certain practice of it in conformity with the Gospel is necessary for everyone.

The poverty Jesus requested of the apostles is a current of spirituality that could not end with them or be reduced to particular groups. The spirit of poverty is necessary for everyone, in every time and place; its lack would betray the Gospel. Faithfulness to the spirit, however, does not require of Christians in general or of priests the practice of a radical poverty with the renunciation of all property or even the abolition of this human right. The Church's Magisterium has often condemned those who claimed this was necessary (cf. *DS* 760; 930f.; 1097); she has sought to lead thought and practice on a course of moderation. It is comforting to note, however, that over the course of time and under the influence of ancient and modern saints, the clergy has acquired an increasing awareness of a call to Gospel poverty, both as a spirit and as a practice corresponding to the demands of priestly consecration. The social and economic situation in which the clergy of almost all the countries of the world live has helped to concretize the condition of real poverty for individuals and institutions, even when the latter by their very nature need many means to carry out their work. In many cases it is a difficult and distressing condition, which the Church strives to overcome in various ways. This is done mainly by appealing to the charity of the faithful to receive their necessary contribution, in order to provide for worship, works of charity, support for the pastors of souls and for missionary projects. However, achieving a new sense of poverty is a blessing for priestly life, as for that of all Christians, because it allows them to conform themselves better to Jesus' counsels and suggestions.

It should be made clear that Gospel poverty entails no disdain for earthly goods, which God has put at man's disposal for his life and his cooperation in the plan of creation. According to the Second Vatican Council, the presbyter, like every other Christian, having a mission of praise and thanksgiving, must acknowledge and glorify the generosity of the heavenly Father who is revealed in created goods (cf. *PO* 17).

Nevertheless, the Council goes on to say that priests, although living in the midst of the world, must always keep in mind that, as the Lord said, they do not belong to the world (cf. Jn 17:14-16). They must be freed from every disordered attachment in order to obtain "spiritual discretion in which is found the right relationship to the world and earthly goods" *(PO* 17; cf. *PDV* 30). It must be recognized that this is a delicate problem. On the one hand, "The mission of the Church is fulfilled in the midst of the world and...created goods are altogether necessary for the personal development of man" *(PO*

17). Jesus did not forbid his apostles from accepting the goods necessary for their earthly life. Rather he asserted their right in this matter when he said in a discourse on mission: "Eat and drink what is offered to you, for the laborer deserves his payment" (Lk 10:7; cf. Mt 10:10). St. Paul reminds the Corinthians: "The Lord ordered that those who preach the Gospel should live by the Gospel" (1 Cor 9:14). He himself insisted on the rule that "One who is being instructed in the word should share all good things with his instructor" (Gal 6:6). It is right then that presbyters have earthly goods and use them "only toward ends which are licit according to the doctrine of Christ and the direction of the Church" (PO 17). The Council did not fail to give practical directions in this regard.

Above all, the management of ecclesiastical property, properly so called, must be guaranteed "according to their nature and ecclesiastical law, [and] should be administered by priests with the help of capable laymen as far as possible" (PO 17). This property is always to be used "for the carrying out of divine worship, for the procuring of honest sustenance for the clergy, and for the exercise of the works of the holy apostolate or works of charity, especially in behalf of the needy" (PO 17).

The goods acquired by the exercise of any ecclesiastical office must be used primarily "for adequate support and the fulfillment of their office and status, excepting those governed by particular laws. That which is in excess they should be willing to set aside for the good of the Church or for works of charity" (PO 17). This must be especially stressed: neither for priests nor for bishops can ecclesiastical office be an occasion of personal enrichment or of profit for their own family. "In no way placing their heart in treasures...[priests] should avoid all greediness and carefully abstain from every appearance of business" (PO 17). In any case, it must be kept in mind that all possessions must be used in the light of the Gospel.

The same must be said about the priest's involvement in secular activities or those pertaining to the management of earthly affairs outside of a religious, sacred context. The 1971 Synod of Bishops stated: "As a general rule, the priestly ministry shall be a full-time occupation. Sharing in the secular activities of men is by no means to be considered the principal end, nor can such participation suffice to give expression to the priest's specific responsibility" *(Ench. Vat.,* IV, 1191). This was a stance taken in response to a tendency appearing here and there toward the secularization of the priest's activity, in the sense that he could be involved, as are lay people, in exercising a trade or secular profession.

In truth there are circumstances in which the only effective way for the Church to reestablish links with a workplace that ignores Christ can be the presence of priests who exercise a trade in that environment, for example, by becoming workers with the workers. The generosity of these priests deserves to be praised. It should be noted, however, that by taking on secular, lay tasks and positions the priest runs the risk of reducing his own sacred ministry to a secondary role or even of eliminating it. Because of this risk, confirmed by experience, the Council had already stressed the need for approval by the competent authority for engaging in manual labor and sharing the living conditions of workers (cf. *PO* 8). The 1971 Synod gave as a practical rule the appropriateness, or less, of a certain secular occupation with the purposes of the priesthood: "This is to be judged by the local bishop with his presbyterate, and if necessary in consultation with the episcopal conference" *(Ench. Vat.,* IV, 1192).

On the other hand, clearly there are special cases today, as in the past, in which some especially talented and well-trained presbyters can be involved in labor and cultural activities that are not directly Church-related. However, care must be taken that these cases remain exceptional. Even then the criterion determined by the Synod must always be applied, in order to be faithful to the Gospel and the Church.

We shall conclude this catechesis by turning once again

to the figure of Jesus Christ, the high priest, the good shepherd and supreme model for priests. He is the presbyter's example of being stripped of one's earthly goods, if he wants to be conformed to the demand of evangelical poverty. Jesus was indeed born in poverty and he lived in it. St. Paul admonished: "He made himself poor though he was rich" (2 Cor 8:9). To someone who wanted to follow him, Jesus said of himself: "The foxes have lairs, the birds of the sky have nests, but the Son of Man has nowhere to lay his head" (Lk 9:58). These words show a complete detachment from all earthly comforts. However, one should not conclude that Jesus lived in destitution. Other Gospel passages state that he received and accepted invitations to the homes of rich people (cf. Mt 9:10-11; Mk 2:15-16; Lk 5:29; 7:36; 19:5-6). He had women who helped support him in his financial needs (Lk 8:2-3; cf. Mt 27:55; Mk 15:40; Lk 23:55-56), and he was able to give alms to the poor (cf. Jn 13:29). Nevertheless, there is no doubt about the spirit and life of poverty that distinguished him.

The same spirit of poverty should inspire the priest's behavior, characterizing his attitude, life and very image as a pastor and man of God. It is expressed in disinterest and detachment toward money, in renunciation of all greed for possessing earthly goods, in a simple lifestyle, in the choice of a modest dwelling accessible to all, and in rejecting everything that is or appears to be luxurious, while striving to give himself more and more freely to the service of God and the faithful.

Finally, let us add that, having been called by Jesus to "preach the Good News to the poor" and in accordance with his example, "Priests, therefore, and also bishops, should avoid everything which in any way could turn the poor away" (PO 17). Instead, by fostering in themselves the Gospel spirit of poverty, they will be in a position to show their own preferential option for the poor, translating it into sharing, into personal and community works of assistance, including material aid, to the needy. It is a witness to the poor Christ, which is given today by so many priests, poor themselves and the friends of the poor. It is a great flame of love enkindled in the life of the clergy and the Church. If occasionally in the past the clergy could in some places appear among the ranks of the wealthy, today they feel honored, with the whole Church, in being found in the first row among the "new poor." This is great progress in following Christ on the path of the Gospel.

General audience of July 21, 1993

Priests Do Not Have a Political Mission

The discussion of the presbyter's detachment from earthly goods is connected with that of his relationship to political affairs. Today more than ever one observes a continual interaction between economics and politics. This occurs both in the vast framework of problems on the national level, as well as in the more limited areas of personal and family life. This happens in the choice of parties, in electing one's own parliamentary representatives and public officials, in supporting the list of candidates presented to the citizens, and in statements on individuals, programs and budgets in regard to handling public affairs. It would be a mistake for politics to depend exclusively or primarily on the economic context. However, high-level projects in service to the human person and the common good are influenced by it. They cannot fail to take into account questions concerning the possession, use, allocation and distribution of earthly goods.

All these points have an ethical aspect that concerns priests too, precisely because of their service to man and society according to the mission they received from Christ. He taught a doctrine and formulated precepts that shed light not only on the life of individuals but also on that of society. In particular, Jesus formulated the precept of mutual love, which implies respect for every person and his rights. It implies rules of social justice aiming at recognizing what is each person's due and at harmoniously sharing earthly goods among individuals, families and groups. In addition, Jesus stressed the universal quality of love, above and beyond the differences of race and nationality constituting humanity. In calling himself the "Son of Man," he wanted to state, by the very way he presented his messianic identity, that his work was meant for every human person, without discrimination of class, language, culture, or ethnic and social group. Proclaiming peace for his disciples and for all people, Jesus laid the foundation for the precept of fraternal love, solidarity and reciprocal help on a universal scale. For him this clearly was and is the aim and principle of good politics.

Nevertheless, Jesus never wanted to be involved in a political movement, and fled from every attempt to draw him into earthly questions and affairs (cf. Jn 6:15). The kingdom he came to establish does not belong to this world (cf. Jn 18:36). For this reason he said to those who wanted him to take a stand regarding the civil power: "Give to Caesar what belongs to Caesar and to God what belongs to God" (Mt 22:21). He never promised the Jewish nation, to which he belonged and which he loved, the political liberation that many expected from the Messiah. Jesus stated that he came as the Son of God to offer humanity, enslaved by sin, spiritual liberation and a calling to the kingdom of God (cf. Jn 8:34-36). He said that he came not to be served, but to serve (cf. Mt 20:28). He said that his followers, especially the apostles, should not think of earthly power and dominion over nations as do the rulers of this world. Instead, they should be the humble servants of all (cf. Mt 20:20-28), like their "Teacher and Master" (Jn 13:13-14).

Certainly this spiritual liberation brought by Jesus was to have decisive consequences in all areas of social and private life. It opened an era of new appreciation for man as a person and for relations between individuals according to justice.

However, the Son of Man's immediate concern was not in this direction.

It is easy to understand that this state of poverty and freedom is most fitting for the priest. He is the spokesman for Christ in proclaiming human redemption and in his ministry of applying its fruits to every area and at every level of life. As the 1971 Synod of Bishops said:

> Together with the entire Church, priests are obliged, to their utmost ability, to select a definite pattern of action when it is a question of the defense of fundamental human rights, the promotion of the full development of persons and the pursuit of the cause of peace and justice. The means must indeed always be consonant with the Gospel. These principles are all valid not only in the individual sphere, but also in the social field; in this regard priests should help the laity to devote themselves to forming their consciences rightly *(Ench. Vat.,* IV, 1194).

This text, which shows that priests are united with all the Church's members in serving justice and peace, allows us to see that the role of priests in social and political action is not identical to that of the laity. This is said more clearly in the *Catechism of the Catholic Church,* where we read: "It is not the role of the pastors of the Church to intervene directly in the political structuring and organization of social life. This task is part of the vocation of the lay faithful, acting on their own initiative with their fellow citizens" *(CCC* 2442).

The lay Christian is called to be directly involved in this activity to make his contribution so that Gospel principles may hold ever greater sway in society. Following Christ, the priest is more directly concerned with the growth of God's kingdom. Like Jesus, he must renounce involvement in political activity, especially by not taking sides (which almost inevitably happens). Thus he will remain a man for all in terms of brotherhood and, to the extent that he is accepted as such, of spiritual fatherhood.

Naturally in regard to individuals, groups and situations there can be exceptional cases in which it may seem opportune or even necessary to help or supplement public institutions that are lacking or in disarray, in order to support the cause of justice and peace. Ecclesiastical institutions themselves, even at the highest level, have provided this service in the past, with all the advantages, but also with all the burdens and difficulties that this entails. Providentially, modern political, constitutional and doctrinal development tends in another direction. Civil society has been progressively given institutions and resources to fulfill its own tasks autonomously (cf. *GS* 40, 76).

Thus the Church still has her own task: proclaiming the Gospel, limiting herself to cooperating in her own way in the common good, without aiming at or accepting a political role.

In this light one can better understand what was decided by the 1971 Synod of Bishops regarding the priest's conduct in political life. He certainly retains the right to have personal political opinions and to exercise his right to vote according to his conscience. As the Synod said: "In circumstances in which there legitimately exist different political, social and economic options, priests like all citizens have a right to make their own personal choices. But since political options are by nature contingent and never in an entirely adequate and perennial way interpret the Gospel, the priest, who is the witness of things to come, must keep a certain distance from any political office or involvement" *(Ench. Vat.,* IV, 1195). In particular, he will keep in mind that a political party can never be identified with the truth of the Gospel, and therefore, unlike the Gospel, it can never become an object of absolute loyalty. Thus the presbyter will take this relativity into account, even when citizens of the Christian faith laudably form parties explicitly inspired by the Gospel. He must strive to shed the light of Christ on other parties and social groups too.

It should be added that the presbyter's right to express his own personal choices is limited by the requirements of his priestly ministry. This limitation too can be an aspect of the poverty he is called to practice following Christ's example. In fact, he can sometimes be obliged to abstain from exercising his own right so that he can be a strong sign of unity, and thus proclaim the Gospel in its fullness. Even more, he must avoid presenting his own choice as the only legitimate one, and within the Christian community, he should respect the maturity of the laity (cf. *Ench. Vat.,* IV, 1196), and even work to help them achieve that maturity by forming their consciences (cf. *Ench. Vat.,* IV, 1194). He will do what is possible to avoid making enemies by taking political stands that cause distrust and drive away the faithful entrusted to his pastoral mission.

The 1971 Synod of Bishops especially stressed that the presbyter must abstain from all political activism: "Leadership or active militancy on behalf of any political party is to be excluded by every priest unless, in concrete and exceptional circumstances, this is truly required by the good of the community, and receives the consent of the bishop after consultation with the presbyteral council and, if circumstances call for it, with the episcopal conference" *(Ench. Vat.,* IV, 1197). Thus it is possible to derogate from the common norm, but this can be justified only in truly exceptional circumstances and requires due authorization.

In their generous service to the gospel ideal, some priests feel drawn to political involvement in order to help more effectively in reforming political life and in eliminating injustices, exploitation, and every type of oppression. The Church reminds them that on this road it is easy to be caught in partisan strife, with the risk of helping not to bring about the just world for which they long, but new and worse ways of exploiting poor people. In any case they must know that they have neither the mission nor the charism from above for this political involvement and activism.

Therefore, I pray and invite you to pray that priests may have ever greater faith in their own pastoral mission for the good of the society in which they live. May they recognize its importance in our age too and understand this statement of the 1971 Synod of Bishops: "The priority of the specific mission which pervades the entire priestly existence must therefore always be kept in mind so that with great confidence, and having a renewed experience of the things of God, priests may be able to announce these things effectively and joyfully to the people who await them" *(Ench. Vat.,* IV, 1198).

Yes, I hope and pray that my brother priests today and tomorrow may increasingly be given this gift of spiritual insight, which enables them to understand and to follow the life of poverty taught by Jesus in its political dimension as well.

General audience of July 28, 1993

Bishops and Priests Must Be United

In the previous catecheses we have reflected on the importance which the invitation to the evangelical counsels of virginity and poverty have in the priest's life, and on how and to what extent they can be practiced in accordance with the spiritual tradition and Christian asceticism, and with the Church's law. Today it is good to recall that Jesus did not hesitate to tell those who wanted to follow him as he carried out his messianic ministry that they had to "deny themselves and take up their cross" (Mt 16:24; Lk 9:23) to be truly his disciples. This is a great maxim of perfection, valid for the Christian life as the definitive criterion for the heroic virtue of the saints. It applies especially to the priestly life, in which it takes more rigorous forms justified by the particular vocation and special charism of Christ's ministers.

A primary aspect of this "self-denial" appears in the renunciations connected with the commitment to communion that priests are called to fulfill between them and their bishop (cf. *LG* 28; *PDV* 74). The institution of the ministerial priesthood took place within the context of a priestly community and communion. Jesus assembled the first group, that of the Twelve, and called them to form a union in mutual love. He wanted to join co-workers to this first "priestly" community.

By sending the seventy-two disciples on mission, as well as the twelve apostles, he sent them out two by two (cf. Lk 10:1; Mk 6:7), so that they could help each other in their life and work and develop a habit of common action in which no one would act alone, independently of the Church community and the community of the apostles.

This fact is confirmed by reflecting on Christ's call, which is the origin of each priest's life and ministry. All priest-hood in the Church begins with a vocation. This is addressed to a particular person, but is tied to the calls given to others within the framework of one and the same plan for the evange-lization and sanctification of the world. Like the apostles, bishops and priests too are called together, although in their various personal vocations, by him who wants to commit them fully to the mystery of redemption. This community of voca-tion doubtless implies an openness of one to the other and of each to all, so as to live and work in communion.

This does not occur without renouncing an ever real, recurring individualism, without achieving "self-denial" (Mt 16:24) in the victory of charity over selfishness. The mind of the vocation community, expressed in communion, must never-theless encourage each and every one to work harmoniously, to acknowledge the grace given individually and collectively to the bishops and presbyters. It is a grace granted to each one, not due to personal merits or abilities, and not only for personal sanctification, but for "building up the body" (Eph 4:12, 16).

Priestly communion is deeply rooted in the sacrament of Orders, in which self-denial becomes an even closer spiritual sharing in the sacrifice of the cross. The sacrament of Orders implies each one's free response to the call addressed to him personally. The response is likewise personal. However, in consecration, the sovereign action of Christ, at work in ordi-nation through the Holy Spirit, creates as it were a new personality, transferring the mentality, conscience and inter-ests of the one receiving the sacrament into the priestly community beyond the sphere of individual aims. It is a psychological fact based on acknowledging the ontological bond between each priest and every other. The priesthood conferred on each one should be exercised in the ontological, psychological and spiritual context of this community. Then there will truly be priestly communion: a gift of the Holy Spirit, but also the fruit of a generous response by the priest.

In particular, the grace of Orders creates a special bond between bishops and priests, because priestly ordination is received from the bishop. The priesthood is extended by him and he introduces the newly ordained into the priestly community, of which he himself is a member.

Priestly communion presupposes and implies that all, bishops and presbyters, are attached to the person of Christ. When Jesus wanted to share his messianic mission with the Twelve, the Gospel of Mark says that he called them and appointed them "as his companions" (Mk 3:14). At the Last Supper he addressed them as those who had stood loyally by him in his trials (cf. Lk 22:28), urged them to unity and asked the Father for this on their behalf. By remaining united in Christ they would all remain united among themselves (cf. Jn 15:4-11). A vivid awareness of this unity and communion in Christ continued among the apostles during the preaching that led them from Jerusalem to the various regions of the then known world, under the compelling yet unifying action of the Spirit of Pentecost. This awareness appears in their Letters, the Gospels and the Acts.

In calling new presbyters to the priesthood, Jesus Christ also asks them to offer their lives to his own person, thus intending to unite them to each other by a special relationship of communion with him. This is the true source of the profound harmony of mind and heart that unites presbyters and bishops in priestly communion.

This communion is fostered by collaborating in one and the same work: spiritually building the community of salvation. Certainly every priest has his own field of activity to which he can devote all his abilities and talents, but this field belongs to the broader work by which every local church strives to develop the kingdom of Christ. This work is essentially communitarian, so that each one must act in cooperation with the other works of the same kingdom.

We know how much the desire to work on the same task can support and spur the common effort of each one. It creates a feeling of solidarity and makes it possible to accept the sacrifices that cooperation requires, by respecting others and welcoming their differences. Henceforth it is important to note that this cooperation is structured around the relationship between the bishop and his presbyters; the subordination of the latter to the former is essential for the life of the Christian community. Work for the kingdom of Christ can be carried out and developed only in accordance with the structure he established.

Now I would like to call attention to the role of the Eucharist in this communion. At the Last Supper Jesus wanted to found, in the most complete way, the unity of the apostolic group, to whom he first entrusted the priestly ministry. In answer to their dispute about the first place, he gave an example of humble service by washing their feet (cf. Jn 13:2-15). This settled the conflicts caused by ambition and taught his first priests to seek the last place rather than the first. During the same supper Jesus gave his commandment of mutual love (cf. Jn 13:34; 15:12) and opened the source that would give the strength to observe it. Alone the apostles would not have been able to love one another as the Master had loved them. But with Eucharistic communion they received the ability to live ecclesial communion and, in it, their specific priestly communion. By the sacrament, Jesus offered them this superior capacity for love and could make a bold supplication to the Father that he accomplish in his disciples a unity like that existing between the Father and the Son (Jn 17:21-23). Finally, at the

Last Supper Jesus invested the apostles jointly with their mission and with the power to celebrate the Eucharist in his memory, thus further deepening the bond uniting them. Communion in the power of celebrating the one Eucharist had to be the sign and source of unity for the apostles and for their successors and co-workers.

It is significant that in the priestly prayer at the Last Supper Jesus prayed not only for the consecration of his apostles by means of truth (cf. Jn 17:17), but also for their unity, a unity reflecting the very communion of the divine Persons (cf. Jn 17:11). Although that prayer primarily concerned the apostles whom Jesus wanted especially to gather around himself, it is extended also to bishops and presbyters, in addition to believers, of every age. Jesus asked that the priestly community be a reflection and participation in Trinitarian communion: what a sublime ideal! Nevertheless, the circumstances in which Jesus offered his prayer show that sacrifices are required to achieve this ideal. At the moment when he was offering his life to the Father, Jesus asked for the unity of his apostles and followers. He established priestly communion in his Church at the price of his own sacrifice. Therefore, priests cannot be surprised at the sacrifices that priestly communion requires of them. Taught by the word of Christ, they discover in these renunciations a concrete spiritual and ecclesial sharing in the divine Master's redeeming sacrifice.

General audience of August 4, 1993

Priestly Obedience Is an Act of Charity

The communion desired by Jesus among all who share in the sacrament of Orders should appear in an altogether special way in priests' relations with their bishops. On this subject the Second Vatican Council speaks of a "hierarchical communion" deriving from the unity of consecration and mission. We read: "All priests, in union with bishops, so share in one and the same priesthood and ministry of Christ that the very unity of their consecration and mission requires their hierarchical communion with the order of bishops. At times in an excellent manner they manifest this communion in liturgical concelebration as joined with the bishop when they celebrate the Eucharistic sacrifice" *(PO* 7). Clearly, the mystery of the Eucharist also appears here as a sign and source of unity. The sacrament of Orders is connected with the Eucharist. Orders establishes the hierarchical communion between all those who share Christ's priesthood: "All priests," the Council adds, "both diocesan and religious, by reason of Orders and ministry, fit into this body of bishops and priests, and serve the good of the whole Church according to their vocation and the grace given to them" *(LG* 28).

This bond between priests of any type or rank and the bishops is essential to exercising the priestly ministry. Priests receive from the bishop sacramental power and hierarchical authorization for this ministry. Religious too receive this power and authorization from the bishop who ordains them and from the one who governs the diocese where they exercise their ministry. Even when they belong to orders that are exempt from the jurisdiction of the diocesan bishops in regard to their internal governance, they receive from the bishop, in accordance with the norm of canon law, the mandate and consent for their involvement and activity within the diocese. Exception must always be made of the authority by which the Roman Pontiff, as head of the Church, can confer on religious orders or other institutes the power to govern themselves according to their own constitutions and to work on a universal scale. In their turn bishops regard priests as their "necessary helpers and counselors in the ministry and in their role of teaching, sanctifying and nourishing the People of God" *(PO* 7).

Because of this bond of sacramental communion between priests and bishops, presbyters are a support and instrument of the episcopal order, as *Lumen Gentium* states (cf. n. 28). In each community they continue the bishop's action and in a certain way represent him as pastor in various areas.

By virtue of its same pastoral identity and sacramental origin, the ministry of priests is clearly exercised under the authority of the bishop. According to *Lumen Gentium,* it is under this authority that they lend their efforts to the pastoral work of the whole diocese by sanctifying and governing that portion of the Lord's flock entrusted to them (cf. *LG* 28).

It is true that presbyters represent Christ and act in his name, sharing in his office as the one Mediator, according to their degree of ministry. However, they can act only as the bishop's co-workers, thus extending the ministry of the diocesan pastor in the local communities.

Spiritually rich relationships between bishops and presbyters are based on this theological principle of sharing within the framework of hierarchical communion. *Lumen Gentium* describes these relationships as follows: "On account of this sharing in their priesthood and mission, let priests sincerely look upon the bishop as their father and reverently obey him. And let the bishop regard his priests as his co-workers and as sons and friends, just as Christ called his disciples now not servants but friends (cf. Jn 15:15)" *(LG* 28).

Here Christ's example is the rule of conduct for bishops and presbyters alike. If he who had divine authority did not want to treat his disciples as servants but as friends, the bishop cannot consider his priests as servants in his employ. They serve the People of God with him. For their part presbyters should respond to the bishop as demanded by the law of reciprocal love in ecclesial and priestly communion, that is, as friends and spiritual "sons." The bishop's authority and the obedience of his co-workers, the priests, should thus be exercised in an atmosphere of true, sincere friendship.

This duty is based not only on the brotherhood existing among all Christians by virtue of Baptism and on that arising from the sacrament of Orders, but also on the word and example of Jesus. Even in triumph as the resurrected one, he lowered himself from that incomparable height to his disciples and called them "my brothers," declaring that his Father was "theirs" too (cf. Jn 20:17; Mt. 28:10). Thus, following Jesus' example and teaching, the bishop should treat his co-workers, the priests, as brothers and friends, without diminishing his authority as their pastor and ecclesiastical superior.

An atmosphere of brotherhood and friendship fosters the presbyters' trust and their willingness to cooperate and work harmoniously in friendship and in fraternal and filial charity toward their bishops.

The Council spells out some of the bishop's duties toward presbyters. Here one need only mention them: bishops should take the greatest interest they are capable of in the temporal and spiritual welfare of their priests; they should foster their sanctification and be concerned for their ongoing formation, examining with them problems that concern the needs of their pastoral work and the good of the diocese (cf. *PO* 7).

Likewise, the presbyters' duties toward their bishops are summarized in these words: "Priests, never losing sight of the fullness of the priesthood which the bishops enjoy, must respect in them the authority of Christ, the supreme shepherd. They must therefore stand by their bishops in sincere charity and obedience" *(PO* 7).

Charity and obedience are two spiritual essentials which should guide their conduct toward their own bishop. It is an obedience motivated by charity. The presbyter's basic intention in his ministry can only be to cooperate with his bishop. If the priest has a spirit of faith, he recognizes the will of Christ in his bishop's decisions.

Understandably, obedience can sometimes be more difficult, especially when different opinions clash. However, obedience was Jesus' fundamental attitude in sacrificing himself, and it bore fruit in the salvation that the whole world has received. The presbyter who lives by faith knows that he too is called to an obedience which, by fulfilling Jesus' saying about self-denial, gives him the power and the glory of sharing the redemptive fruitfulness of the sacrifice of the cross.

Lastly it should be added that, as everyone knows, today more than in the past, priests' cooperation and thus their union with the bishops are required by the pastoral ministry because of its complexity and vastness. As the Council says: "This union of priests with their bishops is all the more necessary today since in our present age, for various reasons, apostolic undertakings must necessarily not only take on many forms but frequently extend even beyond the boundaries of one parish or diocese. No priest, therefore, can on his own accomplish his mission in a satisfactory way. He can do so only by joining forces with other priests under the direction of the Church authorities" *(PO* 7).

For this reason "presbyteral councils" too have tried to structure and organize the consultation of priests by their bishops (cf. 1971 Synod of Bishops, *Ench. Vat.,* IV, 1224). On their part, presbyters participate in these councils in a spirit of enlightened and loyal cooperation, with the intention of helping to build up the "one body." Individually too, in their personal relations with their own bishop they should remember and keep in mind one thing above all: the growth in charity of each and every one, which is the fruit of self-sacrifice in the light of the cross.

General audience of August 25, 1993

Priestly Fraternity Means Cooperation

The "priestly community" or presbyterate that we have spoken of in the preceding catecheses establishes among those who belong to it a network of reciprocal relationships that are situated within the ecclesial communion arising from Baptism. The most specific foundation of these relationships is the common sacramental and spiritual sharing in the priesthood of Christ, from which a spontaneous sense of belonging to the presbyterate stems.

The Council pointed this out clearly: "Priests, by virtue of their ordination to the priesthood, are united among themselves in an intimate sacramental brotherhood. In individual dioceses, priests form one priesthood under their own bishop" *(PO* 8). Because of mutual knowledge, closeness and habits of life and work, this relationship with the diocesan presbyterate further develops that sense of belonging, which creates and nurtures fraternal communion and opens it to pastoral cooperation.

The bonds of pastoral charity are expressed in the ministry and the liturgy, as the Council goes on to note: "Each one, therefore, is united in special bonds of apostolic charity, ministry and brotherhood with the other members of this priesthood. This has been manifested from ancient times in the liturgy when the priests present at an ordination are invited to impose hands together with the ordaining bishop on the new candidate, and with united hearts concelebrate the Sacred Eucharist" *(PO* 8). These cases represent sacramental communion, and also that spiritual communion which in the liturgy finds the *una vox* to proclaim to God unity of spirit and to testify about it to the brothers and sisters.

Priestly fraternity is also expressed in the unity of pastoral ministry, in the wide variety of tasks, offices and activities to which presbyters are assigned. "Even though priests are assigned to different duties, nevertheless they carry on one priestly ministry" *(PO* 8).

The variety of duties can be considerable, for example: parish ministry and inter-parish and multi-parish ministry; diocesan, national and international activities; education, research, analysis; teaching in the various areas of religious and theological doctrine; every apostolate of giving witness, sometimes by studying and teaching various branches of human knowledge; in addition, spreading the Gospel message through the media; religious art in its many forms; the variety of charitable services; moral guidance to different categories of people involved in research or other work; and lastly, ecumenical activities, which are very timely and important today. This variety cannot create classes or inequalities, because for priests these tasks always fall within the scope of evangelization. We say with the Council: "All, indeed, are united in the building up of the body of Christ which, especially in our times, requires manifold duties and new methods" *(PO* 8).

Therefore, it is important for every priest to be willing—and properly trained—to understand and value the work performed by his brothers in the priesthood. It is a question of a Christian and ecclesial spirit, as well as an openness to the signs of the times. He will have to understand, for example, that there is a variety of needs in building the Christian community, as there are a diversity of charisms and gifts. There is also a variety of ways to plan and carry out apostolic projects, since new work methods can be proposed and employed in the pastoral sphere, while always remaining within the Church's communion of faith and action.

Reciprocal understanding is the basis of mutual help in the various areas. Let us repeat what the Council said: "It is very important that all priests, whether diocesan or religious, help one another always to be fellow workers in the truth" *(PO 8)*. Reciprocal help can be given in many ways, from being willing to assist a confrère in need, to accepting a work plan in a spirit of pastoral cooperation. This seems ever more necessary among the different agencies and groups and in the overall coordination of the apostolate.

It should be kept in mind that the parish itself (as sometimes the diocese too), although having its autonomy, cannot be an island. This is especially so at a time like our own, which abounds with means of communication, population mobility, the popularity of various attractions, a new uniformity of tendencies, attitudes, fashions and schedules. Parishes are the living organs of the one body of Christ, the one Church. They welcome and serve both the members of the local communities and all those who for any reason come there at a given moment, which could mean that God has become visible in a conscience, in a life. Naturally, this should not become a source of disorder or confusion in regard to canon law, which is also at the service of pastoral care.

A particular effort of mutual understanding and reciprocal help is desirable and should be fostered especially in the relationships between older and younger priests. Both are so necessary for the Christian community and so dear to bishops and to the Pope. The Council itself urged older priests to have understanding and sympathy for the projects of the younger ones, and advised the latter to have respect for the experience of their elders and to trust them. It recommended that both groups treat each other with sincere affection, in accordance with the example given by so many priests, past and present (cf. *PO* 8).

How many things spring from the heart to the lips on

these points, concretely showing the "priestly communion" that links presbyters! Let us be content to mention some things suggested by the Council: "In a fraternal spirit, priests should extend hospitality (cf. Heb 13:1-2), cultivate kindliness and share their goods in common (cf. Heb 13:16). They should be especially solicitous for the sick, the afflicted, those overburdened with work, the lonely, those exiled from their homeland, and those who suffer persecution (cf. Mt 5:10)" *(PO* 8).

When every pastor, every priest, looks back over his life, he finds it strewn with experiences when he needed understanding, help and the cooperation of so many brothers. The other faithful also find themselves with the various kinds of needs listed above, as do so many others! Who knows whether it would be possible to do more for all those "poor," loved by the Lord and entrusted by him to the Church's charity, and also for those who could be facing moments of crisis as the Council reminds us (cf. *PO* 8). Indeed, conscious of having followed the voice of the Lord and the Gospel, we must strive each day to do ever more and better for everyone.

The Council also suggests some community projects to foster mutual help in cases of need, which can be done in a permanent and almost institutional way on behalf of the brethren.

First of all, it mentions periodic fraternal gatherings for rest and relaxation, in order to answer the human need for restoring one's physical, mental and spiritual strength, which Jesus, the "Teacher and Lord," in his careful attention to the condition of others, already had in mind when he invited the apostles: "Come by yourselves to an out-of-the-way place and rest a little" (Mk 6:31). This invitation also applies to priests in every age, in ours more than ever, given the urgent tasks and their complexity in the pastoral ministry too (cf. *PO* 8).

The Council thus encourages projects that are meant to provide and facilitate a common life for presbyters in a permanent way, including wisely established and organized arrangements for living together, or at least for an easily accessible and practical common table in appropriate places. The reasons for these provisions are not only economic and practical, but also spiritual and in harmony with the institutions of the early Jerusalem community (cf. Acts 2:46-47). They are obvious and urgent in the modern condition of many presbyters and prelates, who must be offered attention and care to alleviate their difficulties and labors (cf. *PO* 8).

"One should hold also in high regard and eagerly promote those associations which, having been recognized by competent ecclesiastical authority, encourage priestly holiness in the ministry by the use of an appropriate and duly approved rule of life and by fraternal aid, intending thus to do service to the whole order of priests" *(PO* 8).

In many places and in the past as well, holy priests have experienced this. The Council zealously desires that it be as widespread as possible; new institutions providing great benefit for the clergy and Christian people are not wanting. Their growth and effectiveness vary in proportion to their fulfillment of the conditions laid down by the Council: the goal of priestly sanctification, fraternal help between priests, communion with ecclesiastical authority at the level of the diocese or the Apostolic See, according to the circumstances. This communion implies approved statutes as a rule of life and work, without which the members would almost inevitably be condemned to disorder or to the arbitrary impositions of some stronger personalities. It is an old problem for every type of association, and also occurs in the religious and ecclesiastical sphere. The Church's authority also fulfills its mission of service to priests and all the faithful when it exercises this function of discerning authentic values, protecting people's spiritual freedom and guaranteeing the validity of associations as well as the whole life of the community.

Here too it is a question of realizing the holy ideal of "priestly communion."

General audience of September 1, 1993

The Priest Must Serve Christ's Flock

The "priestly community," of which we have spoken several times in previous catecheses, is not isolated from the ecclesial community. It belongs to its very essence and is its very heart, in a constant interchange with all the other members of Christ's body. Presbyters serve this vital communion as pastors in virtue of sacramental Orders and the mandate that the Church confers on them.

At the Second Vatican Council the Church sought to reawaken in priests this awareness of belonging and sharing. It did this so that each of them would keep in mind that, although he is a pastor, he continues to be a Christian who must conform himself to all the demands of his Baptism and live as a brother with all the baptized, in service to "the same body of Christ which all are required to build up" *(PO* 9). It is significant that, on the basis of the ecclesiology of the body of Christ, the Council stressed the fraternal nature of the priest's relations with the other faithful, as it had already underscored the fraternal nature of the bishop's relations with his presbyters. In the Christian community, relationships are essentially fraternal, as Jesus requested in "his" commandment, recalled with such insistence by the Apostle St. John in his Gospel and

Letters (cf. Jn 13:14; 15:12, 17; 1 Jn 4:11, 21). Jesus himself said to his disciples: "You are all brothers" (Mt 23:8).

According to Jesus' teaching, presiding over the community means serving it, not domineering over it. He himself gave us the example of a shepherd who cares for and serves his flock, and he proclaimed that he came not to be served but to serve (cf. Mk 10:45; Mt 20:28). In the light of Jesus, the good shepherd and the one Teacher and Lord (cf. Mt 23:8), the priest understands that he cannot seek his own honor nor his own interests. He must seek only what Jesus Christ wanted, putting himself at the service of his kingdom in the world. Thus, he knows—and the Council reminds him—that he must act as the servant of all, with sincere and generous self-giving, accepting all the sacrifices required by this service. He must always remember that Jesus Christ, the one Teacher and Lord, came to serve and did so to the point of giving "his own life as a ransom for the many" (Mt 20:28).

The problem of the presbyter's relationship with the other faithful in the Christian community is especially significant with regard to the so-called lay apostolate. This has taken on special importance in our day because of the new awareness of the essential role which the lay faithful exercise in the Church.

Everyone knows that the same historical circumstances have fostered the cultural and organizational rebirth of the lay apostolate, especially in the 19th century. A theology of the lay apostolate developed in the Church between the two world wars. This led to the special conciliar Decree *Apostolicam Actuositatem,* and even more fundamentally, to the vision of the Church as community, which we find in *Lumen Gentium,* and the place for the lay apostolate it recognizes.

The Council considers priests' relationship with the laity in the light of the living, active and organic community which the priest is called to form and lead. To this end, the Council recommends that presbyters recognize and sincerely promote the dignity of the laity: their dignity as human persons raised by

Baptism to divine adoption and endowed with their own gifts of grace. For each of them, the divine gift entails a special role in the Church's mission of salvation, also in places where presbyters ordinarily cannot exercise the laity's specific roles, such as the family, civil society, professional life, culture, etc. (cf. *PO* 9). Both the laity and priests must acquire an ever greater awareness of these specific roles, one based on a more complete sense of belonging to and participating in the Church.

The Council also says that presbyters should respect the just freedom of the laity, inasmuch as they are children of God enlivened by the Holy Spirit. In this atmosphere of respect for dignity and freedom, the Council's exhortation to priests is understandable: "They must willingly listen to the laity," taking into account their aspirations and utilizing their experience and competence in human activity, in order to recognize "the signs of the times." Presbyters will also seek to discern, with the Lord's help, the laity's charisms, "whether humble or exalted," and will want to "acknowledge them with joy and foster them with diligence" *(PO* 9).

What the Council notes and recommends is interesting and important: "Among the other gifts of God, which are found in abundance among the laity, those are worthy of special mention by which not a few of the laity are attracted to a higher spiritual life" *(PO* 9). Thanks be to God, we know that many faithful—in the Church today and often outside of her visible organizations—are devoted or want to devote themselves to prayer, meditation, penance (at least that of tiring, everyday work, done with diligence and patience, and that of difficult living situations), with or without direct involvement in an active apostolate. They often feel the need for a priest counselor or even a spiritual director, who welcomes them, listens to them and treats them with Christian friendship, humility and charity.

One could say that the moral and social crisis of our time, with the problems it brings to both individuals and families, makes this need for priestly help in the spiritual life more keenly felt. A new recognition of and a new dedication to the ministry of the confessional and of spiritual direction are to be strongly recommended to priests, also because of the new requests of lay people who more greatly desire to follow the way of Christian perfection set forth by the Gospel.

The Council advises priests to recognize, promote and foster the cooperation of the laity in the apostolate and in the same pastoral ministry within the Christian community. They should not hesitate to "entrust to the laity duties in the service of the Church" and to give them "freedom and room for action; in fact, they should invite them on suitable occasions to undertake works on their own initiative" *(PO* 9). This is consistent with respect for the dignity and freedom of the children of God, but also with Gospel service: "service to the Church," the Council says. It bears repeating that all this presupposes a deep sense of belonging to the community and of actively participating in its life. Even more deeply, it presumes faith and confidence in the grace at work in the community and in its members.

What the Council says could serve as a key to pastoral practice in this area, namely, that presbyters "have been placed in the midst of the laity to lead them to the unity of charity" *(PO* 9). Everything revolves around this central truth, in particular, openness and acceptance of everyone, the constant effort to maintain or restore harmony in order to encourage reconciliation, foster mutual understanding and create an atmosphere of peace. Yes, priests must always and everywhere be men of peace.

The Council entrusts this mission of community peace to priests: peace in truth and charity.

> It is their task, therefore, to reconcile differences of mentality in such a way that no one need feel himself a stranger in the community of the faithful. They are de-

fenders of the common good, with which they are charged in the name of the bishop. At the same time, they are strenuous assertors of the truth, lest the faithful be carried about by "every wind of doctrine" (Eph 4:14). They are united by a special solicitude with those who have fallen away from the use of the sacraments, or perhaps even from the faith. Indeed, as good shepherds, they should not cease from going out to them *(PO* 9).

Thus, they are concerned for everyone in and outside the flock, in accordance with the demands of the missionary dimension that pastoral work must have today. Against this background every presbyter will view the question of contact with non-believers, the non-religious and even those who call themselves atheists. He will feel spurred by charity toward all; he will strive to open the doors of the community to everyone. On this point the Council calls priests' attention to those fellow Christians "who do not enjoy full ecclesiastical union with us." This is the ecumenical horizon. Finally, the Council invites them to see that "They have entrusted to them all those who do not recognize Christ as their Savior" *(PO* 9). To make Christ known, to open the doors of minds and hearts to him, to cooperate with his ever new coming into the world: this is the *raison d'être* of the pastoral ministry.

Through the Church priests have received a difficult charge from Christ. It is quite understandable that the Council asks all the faithful to cooperate as far as they can, to help them in their work and their problems, first of all with understanding and love. The faithful are the other element in the relationship of love linking priests to the whole community. The Church urges priests to care for and to look after the community, and calls the faithful in turn to solidarity toward their pastors: "The Christian faithful, for their part, should realize their obligations to their priests, and with filial love they should follow them as their pastors and fathers. In like manner, sharing their cares, they should help their priests by prayer and work" *(PO 9)*.

The Pope says this again, addressing to all the lay faithful an urgent request in the name of Jesus, our one Teacher and Lord: help your pastors by prayer and active work; love and support them in the daily exercise of their ministry.

General audience of September 22, 1993

The Harvest Is Great,
but the Workers Are Few

"It was not you who chose me, but I who chose you." The words Jesus spoke to the apostles are symbolic and refer not only to the Twelve, but to all the generations of those whom Jesus Christ has called down the centuries. They refer to some in a personal way. We are speaking of the priestly vocation, but we are also thinking of the vocations of men and women to the consecrated life. Vocations are a central problem for the Church, for the faith, for the future of the faith in this world.

Every vocation is a gift of God, according to these words of Jesus, "I chose you." Thus it is a choice, an election by Jesus, one that always concerns the person. However, this person lives in the given context of a family, a society, a culture, a Church. A vocation is a gift, but it is also the response to this gift. How each of us, how the one who is called and chosen can answer this divine call depends on many circumstances. It depends on a certain inner, personal maturity and on cooperation with God's grace.

This means to know how to cooperate, how to listen, how to follow. We know well what Jesus said to that young man in the Gospel: "Follow me." One must know how to follow, and when one follows, then the vocation is mature, fulfilled and realized. This is always for the good of the person and the community.

For its part, the community must know how to respond to the vocations that arise within it. They are born in the family, and the family must cooperate with a vocation. They are born in the parish, and the parish must cooperate with a vocation. These are the circumstances of human life and human existence: existential circumstances.

The response to a vocation depends to a very high degree on the witness of the whole community, the family and the parish. People help vocations to grow. By their example, priests can attract young men and help them respond to Jesus' words: "Follow me." Those who have received a vocation must give an example of how to follow it.

In the parish today it is increasingly apparent that movements and associations are contributing in a special way to the growth of vocations and to vocation work. One of the movements or associations that is typical of the parish is that of the altar servers. This fact is a great help to future vocations, as it was in the past. Many who first were altar boys later became priests. This is still useful today, but other ways must be tried: how to cooperate with the divine call, with the divine choice; how to fulfill the words of Jesus: "The harvest is great, but the workers are few." The harvest is always great; the workers are always few, especially in some countries.

However, Jesus urges us to pray for this to the Lord of the harvest. For us all, without exception, there remains above all the task of praying for vocations. If we feel involved in the redeeming work of Christ and the Church, we must always pray for vocations. The harvest is great!

General audience of September 29, 1993

Deacons Serve the Kingdom of God

In addition to presbyters, in the Church there is another category of ministers with specific tasks and charisms, as the Council of Trent recalls when it discusses the sacrament of Orders: "In the Catholic Church there is a hierarchy established by divine ordinance, which includes bishops, presbyters and ministers" *(DS* 1776). The New Testament books already attest to the presence of ministers, "deacons," who gradually formed a distinct category from the *presbýteroi* and *episcopoi.* One need only recall that Paul addressed his greeting to the bishops and ministers of Philippi (cf. Phil 1:1). The First Letter to Timothy lists the qualities that deacons should have, with the recommendation that they be tested before they are entrusted with their functions. They must be dignified and honest, faithful in marriage, and must manage their children and households well, "holding fast to the mystery of faith with a clear conscience" (cf. 1 Tim 3:8-13).

The Acts of the Apostles (6:1-6) speaks of seven "ministers" for service at table. Although the question of a sacramental ordination of deacons is not clear from the text, a long tradition has interpreted the episode as the first evidence of the institution of deacons. By the end of the first century or the beginning of the second, the deacon's place, at least in some churches, was already well established as a rank in the ministerial hierarchy.

An important witness is given especially by St. Ignatius of Antioch, according to whom the Christian community lives under the authority of a bishop, surrounded by presbyters and deacons. "There is only one Eucharist, one body of the Lord, one chalice, one altar, just as there is only one bishop with the college of presbyters and deacons, fellow servants" *(Ad Philad.,* 4, 1). In Ignatius' letters, deacons are always mentioned as a lower rank in the ministerial hierarchy. A deacon is praised for "being subject to the bishop as to the grace of God, and to the presbyter as to the law of Jesus Christ" *(Ad Magnes.,* 6, 1). As "ministers of the mysteries of Jesus Christ," deacons must "in every way be pleasing to all" *(Ad Trall.,* 2, 3). When Ignatius urges Christians to obey the bishop and the priests, he adds: "Respect the deacons as God's commandment" *(Ad Smyrn.,* 8, 1).

We find other witnesses in St. Polycarp of Smyrna *(Ad Phil.,* 5, 2), St. Justin *(Apol.,* I, 65, 5; 67; 5), Tertullian *(De Bapt.,* 17, 1), St. Cyprian *(Epist.,* 15 and 16), and later in St. Augustine *(De cat. rud.,* I, c. 1, 1).

In the early centuries the deacon carried out liturgical functions. In the Eucharistic celebration he read or chanted the epistle and the Gospel; he brought the offerings of the faithful to the celebrant; he distributed Communion and brought it to those absent; he was responsible for the orderliness of the ceremonies and at the end dismissed the assembly. In addition, he prepared catechumens for Baptism, instructed them and assisted the priest in administering this sacrament. In certain circumstances he himself baptized and preached. He also shared in the administration of ecclesiastical property and cared for the poor, widows, orphans and prisoners.

In Tradition there are witnesses to the distinction between the deacon's functions and those of the priest. For example, St. Hippolytus states (second to third century) that the deacon is ordained "not to the priesthood, but for service to the bishop, to do what he commands" *(SCh,* 11, p. 39; cf. *Constitutiones Aegypt.,* III, 2: ed. Funk, *Didascalia,* p. 103; *Statuta Ecclesiae Ant.,* 37-41; Mansi 3, 954). Actually, according to the Church's mind and practice, the diaconate belongs to the sacrament of Orders, but is not part of the priesthood and does not entail functions proper to priests.

With the passage of time, the presbyterate in the West assumed almost exclusive importance in relation to the diaconate, which was reduced to being merely a step on the way to the priesthood. This is not the place to retrace the historical process and explain the reasons for these changes. It is rather a question of pointing out that, on the basis of ancient teaching, the awareness of the diaconate's importance for the Church became greater and greater in theological and pastoral circles, as did the appropriateness of re-establishing it as an Order and permanent state of life. Pope Pius XII also referred to this in his address to the Second World Congress of the Lay Apostolate (October 5, 1957). He stated that although the idea of reintroducing the diaconate as a function distinct from the priesthood was not yet ripe, it could become such. In any case the diaconate was to be put in the context of the hierarchical ministry determined by the most ancient tradition.

The time was ripe at the Second Vatican Council, which considered the proposals of the preceding years and decided on its re-establishment (cf. *LG* 29). Pope Paul VI later implemented the decision, determining the complete canonical and liturgical discipline for this Order (cf. *Sacrum Diaconatus Ordinem,* June 18, 1967; *Pontificalis Romani Recognitio,* June 17, 1968; *Ad Pascendum,* August 15, 1972).

There were two main reasons for the theologians' proposals and the conciliar and papal decisions. First of all, it was considered fitting that certain charitable services, guaranteed in a stable way by laymen conscious of being called to the Church's Gospel mission, should be concretely expressed in a form recognized by virtue of an official consecration. It was also necessary to provide for the scarcity of priests, as well as to assist them in many responsibilities not directly connected to their pastoral ministry. Some saw the permanent diaconate as a bridge between pastors and the faithful.

Clearly, the Holy Spirit, who has the leading role in the Church's life, was mysteriously working through these reasons connected with historical circumstances and pastoral perspectives. He was bringing about a new realization of the complete picture of the hierarchy, traditionally composed of bishops, priests and deacons. Thus a revitalization of Christian communities was fostered, making them more like those founded by the apostles which flourished in the early centuries, always under the impulse of the Paraclete, as the Acts of the Apostles attest.

A deeply felt need in the decision to reestablish the permanent diaconate was and is that of a greater and more direct presence of Church ministers in the various spheres of the family, work, school, etc., in addition to existing pastoral structures. Among other things, this fact explains why the Council, while not totally rejecting the idea of celibacy for deacons, permitted this Order to be conferred on "mature married men." It was a prudent, realistic approach, chosen for reasons that can be easily understood by anyone familiar with different people's ages and concrete situations according to the level of maturity reached. For the same reason it was then decided, in applying the Council's provisions, that the diaconate would be conferred on married men under certain conditions: they would be at least thirty-five years of age and have their wife's consent, be of good character and reputation, and receive an adequate doctrinal and pastoral preparation given either by institutes or priests specially chosen for this purpose (cf. Paul VI, *SDO* 11-15: *Ench. Vat.,* II, 1381-1385).

However, it should be noted that the Council maintained the ideal of a diaconate open to younger men who would devote themselves totally to the Lord, with the commitment to celibacy as well. It is a life of "evangelical perfection," which can be understood, chosen and loved by generous men who want to serve the kingdom of God in the world, without entering the priesthood to which they do not feel called. Nevertheless, they receive a consecration that guarantees and institutionalizes their special service to the Church through the conferral of sacramental grace. These men are not lacking today. Certain provisions were given for them: for ordination to the diaconate they must be at least twenty-five years of age and receive formation for at least three years in a special institute, "where they are tested, trained to live a truly evangelical life and prepared to carry out effectively their own specific functions" (cf. *SDO* 5-9; *Ench. Vat*, II, 1375-1379). These provisions show the importance the Church puts on the diaconate and her desire that this ordination occur after due consideration and on a sound basis. But they are also a sign of the ancient yet ever new ideal of dedicating oneself to the kingdom of God, which the Church takes from the Gospel and raises as a banner especially before young people in our time too.

General audience of October 6, 1993

The Deacon Has Many Pastoral Functions

The Second Vatican Council determined the place deacons have in the Church's ministerial hierarchy in accordance with the most ancient tradition: "At a lower level of the hierarchy are deacons, upon whom hands are imposed 'not unto the priesthood, but unto a ministry of service.' For strengthened by sacramental grace, in communion with the bishop and his group of priests they serve in the diaconate of the liturgy, of the word, and of charity to the people of God" *(LG* 29). The formula "not unto the priesthood, but unto a ministry" is taken from a text of Hippolytus' *Apostolic Tradition,* and the Council sets it against a broader horizon. In this ancient text, the "ministry" is specified as a "service to the bishop"; the Council stresses the service to the People of God. Actually, this basic meaning of the deacon's service was asserted at the beginning by St. Ignatius of Antioch, who called deacons the "ministers of God's Church," recommending that for this reason they should be pleasing to everyone (cf. *Ad Trall.,* 2, 3). Down the centuries, in addition to being the bishop's helper, the deacon was also considered to be at the service of the Christian community.

In order to be allowed to carry out their functions, deacons receive before ordination the ministries of lector and acolyte. The conferral of these two ministries shows the essential twofold orientation of the deacon's functions, as Paul VI explains in his Apostolic Letter *Ad Pascendum* (1972):

> It is especially fitting that the ministries of lector and acolyte should be entrusted to those who, as candidates for the order of diaconate or priesthood, desire to devote themselves to God and to the Church in a special way. For the Church, which "does not cease to take the bread of life from the table of the Word of God and the Body of Christ and offer it to the faithful," considers it to be very opportune that both by study and by gradual exercise of the ministry of the word and of the altar candidates for sacred Orders should through intimate contact understand and reflect upon the double aspect of the priestly office *(Ench. Vat.,* IV, 1781)

This orientation is valid not only for the role of priests, but also for that of deacons.

It should be kept in mind that before Vatican II the lectorate and acolytate were considered minor Orders. In a letter to a bishop in 252, Pope Cornelius listed the seven ranks in the Church of Rome (cf. Eusebius, *Hist. Eccl.,* VI, 43: *PG* 20, 622): priests, deacons, subdeacons, acolytes, exorcists, lectors and porters. In the tradition of the Latin Church three were considered major Orders: those of the priest, deacon and subdeacon; four were minor Orders: those of the acolyte, exorcist, lector and porter. This arrangement of the ecclesiastical structure was due to the needs of Christian communities over the centuries and was determined by the Church's authority.

When the permanent diaconate was reestablished, this structure was changed. As to the sacramental framework, it was restored to the three Orders of divine institution: the diaconate, presbyterate and episcopate. In fact, in his Apostolic Letter on ministries in the Latin Church (1972), Pope Paul VI suppressed tonsure, which marked the entrance into the clerical state, and the subdiaconate, whose functions were given to lectors and acolytes. He kept the lectorate and the acolytate; however, they were no longer considered Orders, but ministries conferred by installation rather than by ordination. These ministries must be received by candidates to the diaconate and presbyterate, and are also open to laymen in the Church who want to assume only the responsibilities corresponding to them: the lectorate, as the office of reading the Word of God in the liturgical assembly, except for the Gospel, carrying out certain roles (such as leading the singing and instructing the faithful); and the acolytate, instituted to help the deacon and to minister to the priest (cf. *Ministeria quaedam, V, VI: Ench. Vat.,* IV, 1762-1763).

The Second Vatican Council lists the deacon's liturgical and pastoral functions: "to administer baptism solemnly, to be custodian and dispenser of the Eucharist, to assist at and bless marriages in the name of the Church, to bring *Viaticum* to the dying, to read the Sacred Scripture to the faithful, to instruct and exhort the people, to preside over the worship and prayer of the faithful, to administer sacramentals, to officiate at funeral and burial services" *(LG* 29).

Pope Paul VI laid down in addition that the deacon, "in the name of the parish priest or bishop, could legitimately lead dispersed Christian communities" *(SDO* 22, 10: *Ench. Vat.,* II, 1392). This is a missionary function to be carried out in territories, surroundings, social contexts and groups where a priest is lacking or not easily available. Especially in those places where no priest is available to celebrate the Eucharist, the deacon gathers and leads the community in a celebration of the Word with the distribution of the sacred species duly reserved. This is a supply function which the deacon fulfills by ecclesial mandate when it is a case of providing for the shortage of priests. This substitution, which can never be complete, reminds communities lacking priests of the urgent need to pray for priestly vocations and to do their utmost to encourage them as something good both for the Church and for themselves. The deacon too should foster this prayer.

Again, according to the Council, the functions assigned to the deacon can in no way diminish the role of lay people called and willing to cooperate in the apostolate with the hierarchy. On the contrary, the deacon's tasks include that of "promoting and sustaining the apostolic activities of the laity." To the extent that he is present and more involved than the priest in secular environments and structures, he should feel encouraged to foster closeness between the ordained ministry and lay activities, in common service to the kingdom of God.

The deacon has a charitable function as well, which also entails an appropriate service in the administration of property and in the Church's charitable works. In this area, the function of deacons is: "on behalf of the hierarchy, to exercise the duties of charity and administration in addition to social work" (Paul VI, *SDO* 22, 9: *Ench. Vat.,* II, 1392).

In this regard, the Council recommends to deacons what stems from the oldest tradition of Christian communities: "Dedicated to duties of charity and of administration, let deacons be mindful of the admonition of blessed Polycarp: 'Be merciful, diligent, walking according to the truth of the Lord, who became the servant of all'" *(LG* 29; cf. *Ad Phil.,* 5, 2).

According to the Council, the diaconate seems of particular value in the young churches. This is why the decree *Ad Gentes* establishes:

> Where episcopal conferences deem it opportune, the order of the diaconate should be restored as a permanent state of life according to the norms of the Constitution *Lumen Gentium.* For there are men who actually carry out the functions of the deacon's office, either preaching the Word of God as catechists, or presiding over scattered Christian communities in the name of the pastor and the bishop, or practicing charity in social or relief work. It is only right to strengthen them by the imposition of hands which has come down from the apostles, and to bind them more closely to the altar, that they may

carry out their ministry more effectively because of the sacramental grace of the diaconate *(AG* 16).

It is known that wherever missionary activity has led to the formation of new Christian communities, catechists often play an essential role. In many places they lead the community, instruct it, and encourage it to pray. The Order of the diaconate can confirm them in the mission they are exercising, through a more official consecration and a mandate that is more expressly granted by the authority of the Church through the conferral of a sacrament. In this sacrament, in addition to a sharing in the grace of Christ the Redeemer poured out in the Church through the Holy Spirit, the source of every apostolate, an indelible character is received which in a special way configures the Christian to Christ, "who made himself the 'deacon' or servant of all" *(CCC* 1570).

General audience of October 13, 1993

Deacons Are Called to a Life of Holiness

Among the catechetical topics on the diaconate the one about the spirit of the diaconate is especially important and attractive, for it concerns and involves all who receive this sacrament in order to carry out its functions in a Gospel perspective. This is the way that leads its ministers to Christian perfection and allows them to give truly effective service *(diakonia)* in the Church, so as "to build up the body of Christ" (Eph 4:12).

Here is the source of diaconal spirituality, which is rooted in what the Second Vatican Council calls the "sacramental grace of the diaconate" *(AG* 16). In addition to being a valuable help in carrying out various tasks, it deeply affects the deacon's heart, spurring him to offer his whole self to serving the kingdom of God in the Church. As the very word "diaconate" indicates, the spirit of service characterizes the interior mind and will of the one who receives the sacrament. In the diaconate an effort is made to carry out what Jesus stated about his mission: "The Son of Man has not come to be served but to serve—to give his life in ransom for many" (Mk 10:45; Mt 20:28).

Doubtless Jesus addressed these words to the Twelve whom he chose for the priesthood, to make them understand that, although endowed with authority conferred by him, they should act as he did, as servants. The advice applies to all ministers of Christ; however, it has particular meaning for deacons. For them, the aspect of service is stressed by virtue of their ordination. Although they do not exercise the pastoral authority of priests, in carrying out all their functions their particular aim is to show an intention to serve. If their ministry is consistent with this spirit, they shed greater light on that identifying feature of Christ's face—service. They are not only "servants of God," but also of their brothers and sisters.

This teaching of the spiritual life is of Gospel origin and entered the earliest Christian Tradition, as that ancient third-century text called the *Didascalia Apostolorum* confirms. It encourages deacons to take their inspiration from the Gospel incident of the washing of feet. "If the Lord did this," it says, "then you deacons should not hesitate to do it for the sick and infirm, since you are workers of the truth, who have put on Christ" (XVI, 36). The diaconate commits one to following Jesus with this attitude of humble service, which is expressed not only in works of charity, but shapes and embraces one's whole way of thinking and acting.

This perspective explains the condition set by the document *Sacrum Diaconatus Ordinem* for admitting young men to formation as deacons: "Only those young men should be enrolled to train for the diaconate who have shown a natural inclination for service to the hierarchy and the Christian community" *(SDO* 8: *Ench. Vat.,* II, 1378). The "natural inclination" should not be understood in the sense of a simple spontaneity of natural dispositions, although this too is a presupposition to be considered. It is rather an inclination of nature inspired by grace, with a spirit of service that conforms human behavior to Christ's. The sacrament of the diaconate develops this inclination. It makes the subject share more closely in Christ's spirit of service and imbues the will with a special grace, so that in all his actions he will be motivated by a new inclination to serve his brothers and sisters.

This service should first of all take the form of helping the bishop and the priest, both in liturgical worship and the apostolate. It scarcely needs remarking here that anyone whose dominant attitude was one of challenging or opposing authority could not properly carry out the functions of a deacon. The diaconate can only be conferred on those who believe in the value of the bishop's and priest's pastoral mission and in the Holy Spirit's assistance guiding them in their actions and their decisions. In particular, it must again be said that the deacon should "profess reverence and obedience to the bishop" *(SDO* 30: *Ench. Vat.,* II, 1400).

However, the deacon's service is also directed to his own Christian community and to the whole Church, to which he must foster a deep attachment, because of her mission and divine institution.

The Second Vatican Council also speaks of the duties and the obligations that deacons assume by virtue of their own sharing in the mission and grace of the high priesthood: "Inasmuch as they are dispensers of Christ's mysteries and servants of the Church, [deacons] should keep themselves free from every vice and stand before men as personifications of goodness and friends of God (cf. 1 Tim 3:8-10 and 12-13)" *(LG* 41). Theirs, then, is a duty of witness, which embraces not only their service and apostolate but also their whole life.

In the document cited above, *Sacrum Diaconatus Ordinem,* Paul VI called attention to this responsibility and the obligations it entails: "Deacons serve the mysteries of Christ and the Church, and must abstain from any vice, strive to please God, and be 'ready for any good work' for the salvation of men. Therefore, because of their reception of this Order, they should far excel others in their liturgical lives, in devotion to prayer, in the divine ministry, in obedience, charity and chastity" (n. 25: *Ench. Vat.,* II, 1395).

With particular regard to chastity, young men who are ordained deacons commit themselves to observing celibacy and to leading a life of more intense union with Christ. Here too, even those who are older and "have received ordination...may not, in accordance with traditional Church discipline, enter into marriage" *(SDO* 16: *Ench. Vat.,* II, 1386).

In order to fulfill these obligations and, even more deeply, to respond to the spiritual demands of the diaconate with the help of sacramental grace, the exercises of the spiritual life must be practiced, as described in Paul VI's Apostolic Letter. Deacons should: 1) apply themselves to reading carefully and to meditating attentively on the Word of God; 2) attend Mass frequently, even daily if possible, receive the Blessed Sacrament of the Eucharist and visit it out of devotion; 3) purify their souls frequently through the sacrament of Penance, having prepared for it worthily through a daily examination of conscience; 4) show a deep, filial love and veneration for the Virgin Mary, the Mother of God (cf. *SDO* 26: *Ench. Vat.,* II, 1396).

Moreover, Pope Paul VI adds: "It is very fitting for permanent deacons to recite daily at least some part of the Divine Office—to be specified by the episcopal conference" *(SDO* 27; *Ench. Vat.,* II, 1397). The episcopal conferences are also responsible for establishing more detailed norms for the lives of deacons in accordance with the circumstances of time and place.

Lastly, whoever receives the diaconate is obliged to ongoing doctrinal formation, which continually improves and updates the formation required before ordination: "Deacons should not slacken in their studies, especially of sacred doctrine; they should carefully read the Scriptures; they should devote themselves to ecclesiastical studies in such a way that they can correctly explain Catholic doctrine to others and day by day become better fitted to train and strengthen the souls of the faithful. With this in mind, deacons should be called to regular meetings at which matters concerning their life and sacred ministry will be treated" *(SDO* 29; *Ench. Vat.,* II, 1399).

The catechesis I have given on the diaconate, to complete the picture of the ecclesiastical hierarchy, highlights what is most important in this order, as in those of the presbyterate and the episcopate: a specific spiritual participation in the priesthood of Christ and the commitment to a life in conformity to him by the action of the Holy Spirit. I cannot conclude without recalling that deacons, like priests and bishops, who are committed to following Christ in the way of service, share most especially in his redeeming sacrifice. This is according to the principle Jesus formulated when speaking to the Twelve about the Son of Man, who came "to serve—to give his life in ransom for many" (Mk 10:45). Therefore, deacons are called to participate in the mystery of the cross, to share in the Church's sufferings, and to endure the hostility she encounters, in union with Christ the Redeemer. This painful aspect of the deacon's service makes it most fruitful.

General audience of October 20, 1993

THE ROLE OF THE LAITY

The Laity Have Full Membership in the Church

During our catecheses on ecclesiology, first we focused on the Church as the People of God, as a priestly and sacramental community, and then reflected on her various offices and ministries. We went from the apostles, chosen and sent by Christ, to the bishops, their successors; to the priests, the bishops' co-workers; and to the deacons. It is logical then for us to turn our attention to the status and role of the laity, who represent the vast majority of the *Populus Dei.* We shall do so by following the lead of the Second Vatican Council, but also by again considering the directives and guidelines in the Apostolic Exhortation *Christifideles Laici,* published on December 30, 1988, following the 1987 Synod of Bishops.

It is widely known that the word "lay" comes from the Greek term *laikós,* which in turn derives from *laós*—people. Thus "lay" means "belonging to the people." In this respect it is a beautiful word. Unfortunately, a long historical development has caused the word "lay," in secular and especially political usage, to acquire the meaning of opposition to religion and to the Church in particular. It thus expresses an attitude of separation and rejection, or at least, stated indifference. This development is certainly regrettable.

In Christian usage, however, the "laity" are those belonging to the People of God. More particularly, they are those who do not have functions and ministries related to the sacrament of Orders and do not belong to the "clergy," according to the traditional distinction between "clerics" and "lay people" (cf. *CIC,* can. 207 §1). Clerics are sacred ministers, that is, the Pope, bishops, priests and deacons; the laity are the other *Christifideles,* who, together with the pastors and ministers, constitute the People of God.

After making this distinction, the Code of Canon Law adds that from both groups—clergy and laity—there are faithful consecrated to God in a special way by a canonically recognized profession of the evangelical counsels (cf. *CIC,* can. 207, §2). In accordance with the distinction mentioned above, a certain number of religious or consecrated persons who take vows but do not receive sacred Orders are included, in this respect, among the laity. However, because of their consecrated state, they have a special place in the Church and so are distinguished from other lay people. For its part, the Council preferred to discuss them separately and considered as lay people those who are neither clerics nor religious (cf. *LG* 31). Without implying doctrinal complications or confusion, this further distinction is useful for simplifying and facilitating discussion of the various groups and categories in the Church's structure.

Here we adopt the threefold distinction mentioned, treating lay people as members of God's People who do not belong to the clergy and are not committed to the religious state or the profession of the evangelical counsels (cf. *CL* 9, and *CCC* 897, which repeat the Council's concept). After speaking of the status and role of this vast majority of those constituting the People of God, we will then be able to speak of the status and role of the religious *Christifideles* or those consecrated.

While noting that the laity are not the whole Church, the Council intended fully to recognize their dignity. If, from a ministerial and hierarchical standpoint, sacred Orders put the faithful receiving them in a particular position of authority by virtue of the role assigned them, the laity have full membership in the Church, as much as do sacred ministers or religious. In fact, according to the Council, "These faithful are by Baptism made one body with Christ" *(LG* 30) and have received the indelible sign of their belonging to Christ by virtue of the baptismal character. They belong to the Mystical Body of Christ.

On the other hand, the initial consecration through Baptism involves them in the mission of all God's people. "They are in their own way made sharers in the priestly, prophetic and kingly functions of Christ" *(LG* 30). Therefore, what we have said in preceding catecheses on the Church as a priestly and prophetic community also applies to the laity, who, together with the Church's members enjoying hierarchical functions and ministries, are called to develop their baptismal potential in communion with Christ the one head of the Mystical Body.

The recognition of lay people as full-fledged members of the Church excludes the identification of the latter with the hierarchy alone. It would be too narrow a concept and even an anti-evangelical, anti-theological error to think of the Church exclusively as the hierarchical body—a Church without people! According to the Gospel and Christian tradition, the Church is a community in which there is a hierarchy, indeed, but precisely because there is a people of "laity" who must be served and guided on the ways of the Lord. It is to be hoped that both clerics and lay people would be increasingly aware of this and never regard the Church from the outside, as an organization imposed on them without being their "body," their "soul." Clergy and laity, hierarchy and non-ordained faithful, are the one People of God, the one Church, the communion of Christ's followers, since the Church belongs to each and every one, and we are all responsible for her life and growth. Indeed, the words of Pius XII in a 1946 discourse *To the New Cardinals* are still famous: the laity "must have an ever clearer awareness of not only belonging to the Church, but of being the Church" *(AAS* 38 [1946], p. 149, cited in *CL* 9, and *CCC* 899). This is a memorable statement that marked a turning-point in pastoral psychology and sociology in the light of a better theology.

This same conviction was affirmed by the Second Vatican Council, as an awareness of the pastors (cf. *LG* 30). It must be said that in recent decades a clearer and richer awareness of this role has developed, with the contribution, in addition to that of pastors, of outstanding theologians and pastoral experts. Before and after Pius XII's address and the First World Congress for the Lay Apostolate (1951), they tried to clarify the theological questions about the lay state in the Church, writing as it were a new chapter of ecclesiology. Also helpful in this regard were meetings and conferences in which scholars and experts with practical, organizational experience compared the results of their reflections and the data obtained from their pastoral and social work. Thus they prepared valuable material for the papal and conciliar Magisterium. However, everything was in continuity with a tradition going back to the earliest Christian times, especially to Paul's exhortation quoted by the Council (cf. *LG* 30), which requested solidarity of the entire community and called to mind the responsibility of working to build up the body of Christ (cf. Eph 4:15-16).

In reality, as they have done in the past, countless lay people are working in the Church and the world in accordance with the recommendations and the requests of their pastors. They are quite worthy of admiration! Alongside those lay people who have a high-profile role, many, many more live their baptismal vocation without attracting attention. They spread throughout the Church the benefits of their charity. In silence, their apostolate flourishes, made effective and fruitful by the Spirit.

General audience of October 27, 1993

The Laity Fulfill Their Calling in the World

It is well-known that in distinguishing the Church's members between the laity and those belonging to the clergy and to religious institutes, the Second Vatican Council identified the lay state's secular character as its distinctive feature. It stated: "What specifically characterizes the laity is their secular nature" *(LG* 31). Thus it indicated a state of life that identifies the laity's vocation and mission on the basis of the baptismal consecration common to all. Similarly, Holy Orders and the priestly ministry specify the clerical state and the profession of the evangelical counsels specify that of religious.

It is a question of a special vocation. It further specifies the common Christian vocation by which we are all called to "work" according to the demands of our "being," that is, as members of the Mystical Body of Christ and, in him, as adopted children of God. Again according to the Council (cf. *LG* 31), the ordained are called to carry out sacred functions by concentrating their life on God in a particular way in order to obtain spiritual goods for humanity: the truth, life and love of Christ. Religious, in turn, witness to the search for the "one thing necessary" by renouncing temporal goods for the sake of God's kingdom. Thus they are witnesses of heaven. Lay people as such are called and destined to honor God by engag-

ing in temporal matters and by working together for the temporal progress of society. In this regard the Council speaks of the
secular character of the lay state in the Church. When it applies
this expression to the laity's vocation, the Council shows
its esteem for the temporal order and, we could say, for the
world. But the way in which it then defines this vocation
shows how the latter transcends temporal perspectives and
worldly matters.

According to the conciliar text, the lay Christian, as a
Christian, has a true vocation, which, for the lay person, has its
particular connotation. However, it always remains a vocation
to the kingdom of God! Lay Christians certainly live "in the
world," where they are concerned with temporal matters. They
must provide for their own needs, at the level of the individual,
the family and society. They must also work with others, to the
extent of their own possibilities and abilities, for the economic
and cultural development of the whole community, of which
they should feel living, active and responsible members. In this
type of life Christ calls and supports them, and the Church
acknowledges and respects them. By virtue of their being in
the world, they must "seek the kingdom of God" and "direct"
temporal affairs according to God's plan. The Council said:
"The laity, by their very vocation, seek the kingdom of God by
engaging in temporal affairs and by ordering them according to
the plan of God" *(LG* 31). The 1987 Synod reaffirmed this
(Propositio 4; cf. *CL* 15; *CCC* 898).

The Council goes on to say in further detail that lay
people "live in the world, that is, in each and in all of the
secular professions and occupations. They live in the ordinary
circumstances of family and social life, from which the very
web of their existence is woven" *(LG* 31). In this way they
witness to the fact that the Church, faithful to the Gospel, does
not consider the world essentially evil and unreformable, but
capable of receiving the saving strength of the cross.

The vocation of the laity and the secular character of

their state and mission raise a basic issue of evangelization: the Church's relationship with the "world," her judgment on it and the authentically Christian approach to salvation. Certainly, one cannot ignore the fact that in St. John's Gospel the phrase "the world" often means surroundings hostile to God and the Gospel. The human world does not accept the light (1:10); it does not recognize the Father (17:25) or the Spirit of truth (14:17); it is burning with hatred for Christ and his disciples (7:7; 15:18-19). Jesus refused to pray for this world (17:9) and drove out Satan, the "prince of this world" (12:31). In this respect the disciples did not belong to the world, just as Jesus himself did not belong to the world (17:14, 16; 8:23). The sharp opposition is also expressed in the First Letter of John: "We know that we belong to God, while the whole world is under the evil one" (5:19).

Nevertheless one must not forget that in John's Gospel the concept of "world" also refers to the whole human realm for which the message of salvation is meant: "God so loved the world that he gave his only Son, that whoever believes in him may not die but may have eternal life" (3:16). If God loved the world, where sin reigned, through the Incarnation and redemption this world receives a new value and should be loved. The world is destined for salvation: "God did not send his Son into the world to condemn the world, but that the world might be saved through him" (3:17).

Many Gospel texts show Jesus' attitude of kindness and mercy toward the world, inasmuch as he is its Savior. Jesus is the bread which comes down from heaven that "gives life to the world" (Jn 6:33); in the Eucharist, Christ's flesh is given "for the life of the world" (6:51). The world thus receives Christ's divine life. It also receives his light, for Christ is "the light of the world" (8:12; 9:5). His disciples too are called to be "the light of the world" (Mt 5:14). Like Jesus, they are sent "into the world" (Jn 17:18). The world is thus the sphere of evangelization and conversion. It is the realm where sin exercises its power and makes it felt, but where redemption is at work. The believer knows this tension is destined to be resolved by the victory of the cross, the victory whose signs have been seen in the world since the day of the resurrection.

This is the perspective found in the Second Vatican Council, especially in *Gaudium et Spes*. This document deals with the Church's relations with the world, understood as "the whole human family," where Christ's redeeming power is at work and God's plan is realized and gradually brought to fulfillment (cf. *GS* 2). The Council does not overlook the influence of sin on the world, but stresses that the world is good inasmuch as it was created by God and saved by Christ. It is understood, therefore, that the world, regarded in the positive value it receives from creation and redemption, constitutes "the place and the means for the lay faithful to fulfill their Christian vocation, because the world itself is destined to glorify God the Father in Christ" *(CL* 15). Thus, according to the Council, the laity's particular responsibility is to work so that the Redeemer's work is fulfilled in the world.

Instead of fleeing the world, lay people are called to sanctify it. We repeat this once again, citing a beautiful conciliar text that can serve as the conclusion for today's catechesis. Lay people "are called...by God that by exercising their proper function and led by the spirit of the Gospel they may work for the sanctification of the world from within as a leaven. In this way they may make Christ known to others, especially by the testimony of a life resplendent in faith, hope and charity" *(LG* 31).

General audience of November 3, 1993

Jesus' Earthly Life
Is a Model for the Laity

We have already noted that the secular character of the laity's life cannot be considered from a mere "worldly" standpoint, because it includes man's relationship with God in the community of salvation that is the Church. For the Christian, then, the lay state has a transcendent value stemming from Baptism, by which the human person becomes an adopted child of God and a member of the Mystical Body of Christ, the Church.

For this reason, from our first catechesis on the laity, we also said that it is wrong to understand and use the word "laity" in opposition to Christ or the Church, as if it meant an attitude of separation, independence or even mere indifference. In Christian usage a lay person is a member of the People of God who at the same time lives in the midst of the world.

The lay person's membership in the Church, as one of her living, active and responsible parts, originates from the will of Jesus Christ, who wanted his Church to be open to all. One need only recall the conduct of the vineyard owner in the meaningful and interesting parable recounted by Jesus. Seeing some men unemployed, the master says to them: "You go into the vineyard too" (Mt 20:4). The 1987 Synod of Bishops remarked that this call "never fails to resound in the course of history; it is addressed to every person who comes into this world. The call is a concern not only of pastors, clergy and men and women religious. The call is addressed to everyone: lay people as well are personally called by the Lord, from whom they receive a mission on behalf of the Church and the world" *(CL* 2). All are invited to "be reconciled to God" (2 Cor 5:20), to be saved and to work together for universal salvation, because God "wants all to be saved" (1 Tim 2:4). All are invited with their personal qualities to work in the Father's "vineyard," where each one has his own place and his own recompense.

The call of the laity involves their sharing in the Church's life and, consequently, an intimate communion with Christ's very life. It is a divine gift and, at the same time, it has a corresponding duty. Did not Jesus ask the disciples who followed him to remain in constant union with him and in him, and to allow his own zeal for life to penetrate their minds and hearts? "Live on in me, as I do in you. Apart from me you can do nothing" (Jn 15:4-5). As it is for priests, so it is for lay people—true fruitfulness depends on union with Christ.

"Apart from me you can do nothing" does not mean that without Christ they cannot use their talents and personal qualities in the realm of temporal affairs. However, Jesus' words, handed down in John's Gospel, warn us all—clergy and laity—that without Christ we cannot produce the most characteristic fruit of our Christian life. For lay people this fruit is specifically their contribution to transforming the world by grace, and to building a better society. Only with fidelity to grace can the ways of grace be opened in the world. This happens when the laity carry out their own family tasks, especially in raising children. It also involves their own work of service to society at every level and in every form of involvement for the sake of justice, love and peace.

This Gospel teaching was repeated by St. Paul (cf. Rom 9:16) and confirmed by St. Augustine (cf. *De Correptione et Gratia,* ch. 2). In harmony with it, the Council of Trent taught that, although it is possible to do "good works" even without being in the state of grace (cf. *DS* 1957), only grace gives saving value to these works (cf. *DS* 1551). Pope St. Pius V, in turn, while condemning the opinion of those who maintained that "all the works of non-believers are sins and the virtues of the [pagan] philosophers are mere vices" *(DS* 1925), rejected all naturalism and legalism as well. He asserted that the meritorious and saving good comes from the Holy Spirit who pours grace into the hearts of God's adopted children (cf. *DS* 1912-1915).

This was the balanced approach of St. Thomas Aquinas. To the question "whether without grace man can desire and accomplish what is good," he replied: "Because human nature is not altogether corrupted by sin, so as to be lacking all natural good, even in the state of corrupted nature it can, by virtue of its natural endowments, achieve some particular good, such as building dwellings, planting vineyards and the like [the sphere of values and activities in the realm of work, technology and the economy]. Yet it cannot do all the good natural to it...just as a sick man can of himself make some movements, yet he cannot move with the movements of one in health, unless he is cured with the help of medicine..." *(Summa Theol.,* I-II, q. 109, a. 2). Even less can he achieve the higher, supernatural good, which is the work of the infused virtues, especially of the charity due to grace. As you can see, this issue regarding the holiness of the laity also involves one of the basic theses of the theology of grace and salvation!

In their own lives lay people can be conformed to the mystery of the Incarnation precisely through the secular nature of their state. We know that the Son of God wanted to share our human condition, becoming like us in all things except sin (cf. Heb 2:17; 4:15). Jesus described himself as "he whom the Father consecrated and sent into the world" (Jn 10:36). The Gospel tells us that the eternal Son was fully involved in our condition, living his own consecration in the world. Jesus' fully human life in the world is the model that enlightens and inspires the life of all the baptized (cf. *GS* 32). The Gospel itself invites us to discover in Christ's life a perfect image of what can and should be the life of everyone who follows him as a disciple and shares in the mission and grace of the apostolate.

In choosing to live the common life of humanity, the Son of God conferred a new value on this life, raising it to the heights of the divine (cf. St. Thomas, *Summa Theol.,* III, q. 40, aa. 1-2). Since he is God, he introduced even the humblest activities of human existence to a participation in the divine life. In him we can and must recognize and honor God, who as man was born and lived like us. He ate, drank, worked and did what everyone must do, so that the mystery of the trinitarian life is reflected in all of life, in all human activities raised to a higher level. For whoever lives in the light of faith, as lay Christians, the mystery of the Incarnation also penetrates temporal activities, imbuing them with the leaven of grace.

In the light of faith, the laity who follow the logic of the Incarnation, which took place for our redemption, also share in the saving mystery of the cross. In Christ's life the Incarnation and the redemption are one mystery of love. The Son of God became incarnate to ransom humanity by his sacrifice: "The Son of Man has not come to be served but to serve—to give his life in ransom for the many" (Mk 10:45; Mt 20:28).

When the Letter to the Hebrews states that the Son became like us in all things except sin, it is speaking of a likeness and a sharing in the painful trials of this life (cf. Heb 4:15). We also read in Philippians that he who was born in the likeness of men obediently accepted even death on a cross (cf. Phil 2:7-8).

Just as the experience of daily difficulties in Christ's life culminated in the cross, so too in the life of the laity daily trials culminate in death united to that of Christ, who conquered death. In Christ and in all his followers, priests and lay people, the cross is the key to salvation.

General audience of November 10, 1993

The Laity Answer God's Call in a Variety of Ways

The Church is holy and all her members are called to holiness. Lay people participate in the Church's holiness as fully qualified members of the Christian community. This participation, which we could call ontological, also becomes for lay people a personal ethical commitment to sanctification. In this capacity and in this vocation to holiness, all the members of the Church are equal (cf. Gal 3:28).

The degree of personal holiness does not depend on the position occupied in society or in the Church, but solely on the degree to which charity is lived (cf. 1 Cor 13). A lay person who generously welcomes divine charity in his heart and in his life is holier than a priest or bishop who accepts it half-heartedly.

Christian holiness is rooted in adherence to Christ through faith and Baptism. This sacrament is at the origin of ecclesial communion in holiness, as is clear from Paul's text: "One Lord, one faith, one Baptism" (Eph 4:5). Vatican II quoted this text, and drew from it the statement on the commonality that links Christians in Christ and in the Church (cf. *LG* 32). The ontological, ecclesiological and ethical holiness of every believer, whether cleric or lay person, is connected to this participation in Christ's life through Baptism.

The Council asserts: "The followers of Christ are called by God, not because of their works, but according to his own purpose and grace. They are justified in the Lord Jesus, because in the Baptism of faith they truly become sons of God and sharers in the divine nature. In this way they are really made holy" *(LG* 40). Holiness means belonging to God. This belonging is realized in Baptism, when Christ takes possession of the human being, to make him "share in the divine nature" (cf. 2 Pet 1:4) which is in him by virtue of the Incarnation (cf. *Summa Theol.,* III, q. 7, a. 13; q. 8, a. 5). Thus Christ truly becomes, as has been said, "the life of the soul." The sacramental character imprinted on the person by Baptism is the sign and the bond of consecration to God. This is why Paul, speaking of the baptized, calls them "saints" (cf. Rom 1:7; 1 Cor 1:2; 2 Cor 1:1, etc.).

But as we have said, the commitment to ethical holiness derives from this ontological holiness. As the Council states, all must "hold on to and complete in their lives this holiness they have received" *(LG* 40). All must strive for holiness, because they already possess the seed in themselves. They must nurture this holiness which has been given them. Everyone must live "as is fitting among saints" (Eph 5:3), and put on, "as God's chosen ones, holy and beloved, heartfelt compassion, kindness, humility, gentleness and patience" (Col 3:12). In the baptized, the holiness that they possess shields them neither from temptation nor from every fault, because the weakness of human nature persists in this life. In this regard, the Council of Trent taught that no one is able to avoid even venial sin throughout his life without a special privilege from God, such as the Church believes was granted to the Blessed Virgin (cf. *DS* 1573). This leads to prayer to obtain an ever new grace from the Lord, perseverance in good, and the forgiveness of sins: "Forgive us our debts" (Mt 6:12).

According to the Council, all of Christ's followers, including the laity, are called to the perfection of love *(LG* 40).

To strive for perfection is not the privilege of some, but an obligation for all the members of the Church. The commitment to Christian perfection means persevering on the way of holiness. As the Council states: "The Lord Jesus, the divine Teacher and model of all perfection, preached holiness of life to each and every one of his disciples of every condition. He himself stands as the author and consummator of this holiness of life: 'Be you therefore perfect, even as your heavenly Father is perfect' (Mt 5:48)" *(LG* 40). Therefore, "all the faithful of Christ of whatever rank or status, are called to the fullness of the Christian life and to the perfection of charity" *(LG* 40). Precisely through the sanctification of each person, a new human perfection is introduced in earthly society. In the words of the Servant of God, Elizabeth Leseur, "Every soul that rises raises the world with it." The Council teaches that "by this holiness as such a more human manner of living is promoted in this earthly society" *(LG* 40).

At this point it is necessary to observe that the infinite richness of Christ's grace in which humanity participates is transformed into an abundance and variety of gifts with which each may serve and benefit others in the one body of the Church. When St. Peter exhorted Christians throughout Asia Minor to holiness, he recommended: "As each one has received a gift, use it to serve one another as good stewards of God's varied grace" (1 Pet 4:10).

Vatican II also states: "The classes and duties of life are many, but holiness is one—that sanctity which is cultivated by all who are moved by the Spirit of God" *(LG* 41). Thus it recalls the way of holiness for bishops, priests, deacons and clerics who aspire to become Christ's ministers, and those lay persons who, "chosen of God and called by the bishop spend themselves completely in apostolic labors" *(LG* 41). But it expressly considers the way of holiness for Christians committed to marriage: "Married couples and Christian parents should follow their own proper path (to holiness) by faithful love.

They should sustain one another in grace throughout the entire length of their lives. They should imbue their offspring, lovingly welcomed as God's gift, with Christian doctrine and the evangelical virtues. In this manner, they offer all men the example of unwearying and generous love; in this way they build up the brotherhood of charity; in so doing, they stand as the witnesses and cooperators in the fruitfulness of Holy Mother Church; by such lives, they are a sign and a participation in that very love with which Christ loved his bride and for which he delivered himself up for her" *(LG* 41).

The discussion can and must be extended to the circumstances of people who live alone, either by free choice or through events and special circumstances, such as unmarried men and women, widows and widowers, those who are separated or distant. The divine call to holiness is valid for all, realized in the form of charity. The discussion can and must be extended, as at the 1987 Synod (cf. *CL* 17), to those who in their ordinary professional life and daily work are working for the good of their brothers and sisters and the progress of society, imitating Jesus the worker. It can and must be extended, finally, to all those who, as the Council states, "are weighed down with poverty, infirmity and sickness, as well as those who must bear various hardships or who suffer persecution for justice sake—may they all know they are united with the suffering Christ in a special way for the salvation of the world" *(LG* 41).

Therefore many aspects and forms of Christian holiness are open to lay people in the various circumstances of their life. They are called to imitate Christ, and from him they can receive the necessary grace to fulfill their mission in the world. All are invited by God to walk the way of holiness and to attract to this path their companions in life and work in the world of temporal affairs.

General audience of November 24, 1993

Lay Spirituality Is Rooted in Christ

The specific role of lay people in the Church requires them to have a deep spiritual life. To help them to achieve this and to live it, theological and pastoral works have been published on spirituality for lay people. This is based on the assumption that every baptized person is called to holiness. The way this call is put into practice varies according to different factors: specific locations, living and working conditions, abilities and inclinations, personal preferences for a spiritual and apostolic director, or for a specific founder of an order or religious institute. This has happened and still happens in all the groups comprising the Church at prayer and at work, on her pilgrimage to heaven. The Second Vatican Council itself outlined a specific lay spirituality, in the context of a doctrine of life valid for everyone in the Church.

All Christian spirituality must be based on what Jesus said about the need for a vital union with him: "Remain in me.... Whoever remains in me and I in him will bear much fruit" (Jn 15:4-5). The distinction between the two aspects of the union to which the text refers is significant: Christ's presence in us, which we should welcome, recognize and increasingly desire, happy if we can sometimes experience it with particular intensity; and our presence in Christ, which we are invited to achieve through our faith and love.

This union with Christ is a gift of the Holy Spirit, who instills it in the soul. The soul accepts it and complies, both in contemplation of the divine mysteries and in the apostolate, and seeks to communicate its light in both personal and social action (cf. St. Thomas Aquinas, *Summa Theol.,* II-II, q. 45, a. 4). Lay people are called to this experience of communion just like any other member of the People of God. The Council recalled this, pointing out that: "While correctly fulfilling their secular duties in the ordinary conditions of life, they do not separate union with Christ from their life" *(AA* 4).

Since it is a gift of the Holy Spirit, union with Christ must be asked for in prayer. Doubtless, when work is performed according to God's will, something pleasing to the Lord is being done, and this is a form of prayer. Thus even the simplest actions become an offering that gives praise to God, and this pleases him. But it is equally true that this is not enough. Specific moments must be expressly devoted to prayer, following the example of Jesus, who even in the midst of the most intense messianic activity withdrew to pray (Lk 5:16).

This is true of everyone, and thus, for lay people too. These "pauses" for prayer can take many different forms. But in each case prayer remains indispensable for everyone, in both personal life and the apostolate. It is only through an intense life of prayer that lay people can find inspiration, energy, balance, the courage to face difficulties and obstacles, and a capacity for initiative, endurance and recovery.

The prayer life of every member of the faithful, including the laity, must involve participation in the liturgy, recourse to the sacrament of Reconciliation and above all the celebration of the Eucharist. Sacramental communion with Christ is the source of that kind of mutual immanence between the soul and Christ which he himself proclaimed: "Whoever eats my flesh and drinks my blood remains in me and I in him" (Jn 6:56). The Eucharistic banquet guarantees the spiritual nourishment that makes it possible to produce abundant fruit. The

Christifideles laici are also called and invited to an intense Eucharistic life. Sacramental participation in Sunday Mass should be the source of both their spiritual life and their apostolate. Blessed are they who, in addition to Sunday Mass and Communion, feel attracted and encouraged to receive Communion more frequently, as many saints recommended, especially in recent times with the ever greater development of the apostolate of the laity.

The Council wishes to remind lay people that union with Christ can and must involve all the aspects of their earthly life: "Neither family concerns nor other secular affairs should be irrelevant to their spiritual life, in keeping with the words of the Apostle, 'Whatever you do in word or work, do all in the name of the Lord Jesus Christ, giving thanks to God the Father through him' (Col 3:17)" *(AA* 4). All human activity takes on a deeper meaning in Christ. Here a broad and clear perspective of the value of earthly realities unfolds. Theology has stressed the positive nature of everything that exists and acts by virtue of its participation in the being, truth, beauty and goodness of God, the "Creator and Lord of heaven and earth," that is, of the whole universe and every small or great reality that is part of the universe. This was one of the fundamental theses of St. Thomas' vision of the cosmos (cf. *Summa Theol.,* I, q. 6, a. 4; q. 16, a. 6; q. 18, a. 4; q. 103, aa. 5-6; q. 105, a. 5, etc.). He based it on Genesis and many other biblical texts. It is widely confirmed by science with the marvelous results of research on microcosms and macrocosms. Everything has its own being; everything moves according to its own capacity for movement, but everything also declares its own limits, its dependence, its immanent finality.

A spirituality based on this authentic view of things, open to the infinite and eternal God who is sought, loved and served throughout life, is discovered and recognized like a light that clarifies the events of the world and history. Faith establishes and perfects this spirit of truth and wisdom and makes it possible to see Christ's presence in all things, even in so-called "temporal" things, which faith and hope reveal in their relationship with God, in whom we "live, move and have our being" (Acts 17:28; cf. *AA* 4). With faith, it is possible to discern the fulfillment of the divine plan of saving love, and in the development of one's own life the Father's constant solicitude revealed by Jesus—the interventions of Providence in response to human requests and needs (cf. Mt 6:25-34). In the lay state, this view of faith puts everyday things in the right light, in good and evil, in joy and sorrow, in work and rest, in reflection and action.

If faith provides a fresh outlook, hope also gives new energy to involvement in temporal affairs (cf. *AA* 4). Thus lay people can attest to the fact that spirituality and the apostolate do not paralyze commitment to perfection in the realm of temporal things. At the same time they demonstrate the surpassing greatness of the goals to which they aspire and the hope that animates them, which they desire to communicate to others. This is a hope that is not devoid of trouble and sorrow but can disappoint no one, because it is based on the paschal mystery, the mystery of Christ's cross and resurrection. Lay people know and witness to the fact that sharing in the sacrifice of the cross leads to sharing the joy proclaimed by Christ in glory. Thus in the very glance at external and temporal goods gleams the inner certainty of whoever sees them and deals with them, while respecting their proper purpose, as the means and the way to the perfection of eternal life. All this happens by virtue of the charity which the Holy Spirit pours out in the soul (cf. Rom 5:5), to enable it to participate in God's life already on earth.

General audience of December 1, 1993

The Laity Share in
the Priesthood of Christ

In the preceding catecheses on the laity we have alluded several times to their service of praising God and to the other duties of worship that are their responsibility. Today we wish to develop this theme more directly, taking as our starting point the texts of the Second Vatican Council, where we read: "The supreme and eternal priest, Christ Jesus, since he wills to continue his witness and service also through the laity, vivifies them in this Spirit and increasingly urges them on to every good and perfect work" *(LG* 34). Under this impulse of the Holy Spirit, the laity come to share in the priesthood of Christ, in the form we earlier defined as common to the whole Church, in which everyone, lay people included, are called to give God spiritual worship. "For besides intimately linking them to his life and his mission, he also gives them a sharing in his priestly function of offering spiritual worship for the glory of God and the salvation of men. For this reason the laity, dedicated to Christ and anointed by the Holy Spirit, are marvelously called and wonderfully prepared so that ever more abundant fruits of the Spirit may be produced in them" *(LG* 34).

We note that the Council does not merely describe the laity as sharing in the "priestly, prophetic and kingly functions of Christ" *(LG* 31), but specifies that Christ himself continues to exercise his priesthood in their lives. Hence their participation in the common priesthood of the Church occurs through the commission and action of Christ, the one eternal high priest.

Moreover, this priestly action of Christ in the laity takes place through the Holy Spirit. Christ "vivifies them with his Spirit." This is what Jesus had promised when he stated the principle that the Spirit gives life (cf. Jn 6:63). He who was sent on Pentecost to form the Church has the perennial task of developing Christ's priesthood and priestly activity in the Church, including the laity, who are fully-fledged members of the *corpus Christi* by virtue of Baptism. With Baptism, Christ's presence and priestly activity is initiated in every member of his body, in whom the Holy Spirit instills grace and on whom he impresses the character. This enables the believer to have a vital share in the worship given by Christ to the Father in the Church. In Confirmation he confers the ability to be committed adults in the faith, actively involved in the Church's mission of giving witness to and spreading the Gospel (cf. St. Thomas Aquinas, *Summa Theol.,* q. 63, a 3; q. 72, aa. 5-6).

By virtue of this sharing in his priesthood, Christ gives all his members, laity included (cf. *LG* 34), the capacity of offering in their lives that worship which he himself called "worshipping the Father in Spirit and truth" (Jn 4:23). By carrying out this worship the faithful, enlivened by the Holy Spirit, share in the incarnate Word's sacrifice and in his mission as high priest and universal Redeemer.

According to the Council, in this transcendent priestly reality of Christ's mystery the laity are called to offer their whole lives as a spiritual sacrifice, thus cooperating with the entire Church in the Redeemer's continual consecration of the world. This is the laity's great mission: "For all their works, prayers and apostolic endeavors, their ordinary married and family life, their daily occupations, their physical and mental relaxation, if carried out in the Spirit, and even the hardships of life, if patiently borne—all these become 'spiritual sacrifices acceptable to God through Jesus Christ.' Together with the offering of the Lord's body, they are most fittingly offered in the celebration of the Eucharist. Thus, as those everywhere who adore in holy activity, the laity consecrate the world itself to God" (cf. *LG* 34; *CCC* 901).

Spiritual worship implies the laity's participation in the Eucharistic celebration, the center of the whole network of relationships between God and human beings in the Church. In this regard, "the lay faithful [too] are sharers in the priestly mission, for which Jesus offered himself on the cross and continues to be offered in the celebration of the Eucharist for the glory of God and the salvation of humanity" *(CL* 14). In the Eucharistic celebration the laity share actively by offering themselves in union with Christ, priest and victim. Their offering has ecclesial value by virtue of the baptismal character that equips them to give the official worship of the Christian religion to God with Christ and in the Church (cf. St. Thomas, *Summa Theol.,* III, q. 63, a. 3). Sacramental participation in the Eucharistic banquet motivates and perfects their offering, instilling in them the sacramental grace that will help them to live and work in accord with the demands of the offering made with Christ and the Church.

At this point we must stress the importance of participating in the Sunday celebration of the Eucharist prescribed by the Church. For everyone it is the highest act of exercising the universal priesthood, as the sacramental offering of the Mass is for priests in exercising the ministerial priesthood. For everyone, participation in the Eucharistic banquet is a condition for vital union with Christ, as he himself said: "Let me solemnly assure you, if you do not eat the flesh of the Son of Man and drink his blood, you have no life in you" (Jn 6:53). The *Catechism of the Catholic Church* reminds all the faithful of the importance of participating in Sunday Mass (cf. *CCC* 2181-2182). Here I would like to conclude with the well-known words from the First Letter of Peter, which describe the image of the laity as sharers in the Eucharistic-ecclesial mystery: "You too are living stones, built as an edifice of spirit, into a holy priesthood, offering spiritual sacrifices acceptable to God through Jesus Christ" (1 Pet 2:5).

General audience of December 15, 1993

The Laity Witness to the Power of the Gospel

According to the Second Vatican Council, in the Church, the Mystical Body of Christ, everyone shares in the dignity and mission of Christ, the eternal high priest, as we saw in the catecheses on the "common priesthood." Everyone also shares in his dignity and mission as the great prophet, which we wish to consider in today's catechesis.

We begin by rereading the text of *Lumen Gentium,* which states that "Christ, the great prophet, who proclaimed the kingdom of his Father both by the testimony of his life and the power of his words, continually fulfills his prophetic office until the complete manifestation of glory. He does this not only through the hierarchy who teach in his name and with his authority, but also through the laity whom he made his witnesses and to whom he gave understanding of the faith *(sensus fidei)* and an attractiveness in speech so that the power of the Gospel might shine forth in their daily social and family life" *(LG* 35; cf. *CCC* 904).

As the text points out, this charge comes from Christ himself, who made the laity his witnesses, providing them with the "understanding of the faith" and the "attractiveness in speech," with a truly ecclesial and apostolic purpose. The objective of this witness and charge is to make the Gospel of

Christ shine out in the world, that is, in the various areas where the laity live and carry out their earthly tasks. The Council adds: "This evangelization, that is, this announcing of Christ by a living testimony as well as by the spoken word, takes on a specific quality and a special force in that it is carried out in the ordinary surroundings of the world" *(LG* 35; *CCC* 905). This, then, characterizes the laity's call to share in the prophetic mission of Christ, the true and faithful witness (cf. Rev 1:5). They must show that there is no opposition between following him and fulfilling the tasks that lay people must carry out in their "secular" condition, and that fidelity to the Gospel actually helps to enhance and improve earthly structures and institutions.

At this point, however, the nature of the laity's witness and, we could say, their "prophesying," as well as that of the whole Christian community, needs to be spelled out with the same Council. Jesus spoke of this when he said to his disciples before the ascension: "You will receive power when the Holy Spirit comes down on you; then you are to be my witnesses" (Acts 1:8). The Holy Spirit's intervention is needed for fulfilling the office of witness, as it is for exercising the universal priesthood. It is not only a question of a prophetic temperament linked to special "charisms" of the natural order, as they are sometimes understood in the language of modern psychology and sociology. It is rather a question of a supernatural prophesying, as foreshadowed in Joel's oracle (3:2), quoted by Peter on the day of Pentecost: "In the last days...your sons and daughters shall prophesy" (Acts 2:17). It means proclaiming, communicating and making resound in human hearts the revealed truths bringing the new life bestowed by the Holy Spirit!

For this reason the Council says that the lay faithful are appointed as witnesses, formed by "understanding of the faith and an attractiveness in speech" *(LG* 35). The Apostolic Exhortation *Christifideles Laici* adds that they are given the ability and responsibility "to accept the Gospel in faith and to proclaim it in word and deed, without hesitating to identify courageously and denounce evil" *(CL* 14). All this is possible because they receive from the Holy Spirit the grace to profess the faith and to find the most suitable way to express and communicate it to everyone.

Lay Christians, as "children of the promise," are also called to give witness in the world to the greatness and fruitfulness of the hope they bear in their hearts. This hope is based on the teaching and work of Jesus Christ, who died and rose for the salvation of all. Despite appearances, the world is often in anguish because of its ever new and disappointing experience of limitations, shortcomings and even the emptiness of many structures created for human happiness on earth. The witness of hope is especially necessary to direct minds in the search for the life to come, beyond the relative value of the things of this world. In this task the laity, as workers serving the Gospel through the structures of secular life, have an importance of their own. They show that Christian hope does not mean fleeing the world nor foregoing the fulfillment of earthly life, but the latter's openness to the transcendent dimension of eternal life which alone gives that life its true value.

Under the impulse of charity, faith and hope spread their witness throughout the living and working environment of the laity, who are called to make "the power of the Gospel...shine forth in their daily social and family life" *(LG* 35). The "power of the Gospel" is shown in the "continuous conversion" of one's soul to the Lord. It is shown in the struggle against the powers of evil at work in the world, working to remedy the damage caused by obscure or clearly visible powers that seek to turn people from their destiny. The "power of the Gospel" appears in everyday life when in every context or circumstance courageous Christians are not afraid to show their convictions, mindful of Jesus' words: "If a man is ashamed of me and my doctrine, the Son of Man will be ashamed of him when he comes in his glory and that of his Father and his holy angels"

(Lk 9:26; cf. Mk 8:38). "Whoever acknowledges me before men—the Son of Man will acknowledge him before the angels of God" (Lk 12:8). The "power of the Gospel" is shown in patiently enduring trials and giving witness to the cross of Christ.

The "power of the Gospel" is not required only of priests and religious in their mission as ministers of Christ's word and grace. The laity also need it to evangelize the secular surroundings and structures where they live their daily lives. In these areas of the world their witness is even more striking and can have an unexpected impact, beginning with marriage and family life, as the Council recalls (cf. *LG* 35). For them and for all Christ's followers—called to be prophets of faith and hope—we ask for the power that can only be received from the Holy Spirit through fervent, assiduous prayer.

General audience of January 26, 1994

The Laity Work to Spread the Kingdom

In the previous Christological catecheses, we described the kingly office, which is one of the offices proper to Christ. It is an office foreseen and foretold in the messianic tradition of the Old Testament. Christ gave the Church he founded a share in this kingship, as we explained in the ecclesiological catecheses. Now we can and should cast on the laity the light of that doctrine regarding the Church, the mystical and pastoral unity that continues the work of redemption in the world. If lay people are part of the Church, and indeed *are the Church,* as Pius XII said in his famous address in 1946, it follows that they too are incorporated in the kingship of the Church's supreme shepherd.

As the Second Vatican Council recalls in *Lumen Gentium,* Jesus Christ, the Son of God made man for our salvation, completed on earth the work of redemption, which culminated in the sacrifice of the cross and the resurrection. Before going up to heaven he said to his disciples: "Full authority has been given to me both in heaven and on earth" (Mt 28:18). He himself linked this assertion with his conferral on the disciples of the mission and authority to preach the Gospel to all nations, to all people, and to teach them to observe all his commandments (cf. Mt 28:20). Their sharing in his kingship consists in this. Indeed, Christ is a king inasmuch as he reveals the truth he has brought from heaven to earth (cf. Jn 18:37) and which he entrusted to the apostles and the Church that they might spread it in the world in every age. Living in the truth received from Christ and working to spread it in the world is thus the task and duty of all the Church's members, including the laity. The Council stated this (cf. *LG* 36) and the Exhortation *Christifideles Laici* emphasized it (n. 14).

The laity are called to exercise their "kingship as Christians" (cf. *CL* 14) by inwardly living the truth through faith and by their outward witness of charity. They work diligently so that through them as well faith and charity may become the leaven of new life for everyone. As *Lumen Gentium* states: "But the Lord wishes to spread his kingdom also by means of the laity, namely, a kingdom of truth and life, a kingdom of holiness and grace, a kingdom of justice, love and peace" *(LG* 36).

Again according to the Council, the laity's sharing in the growth of the kingdom is carried out especially by their direct, concrete activity in the temporal order. While priests and religious are dedicated to the more specifically spiritual, religious sphere for the conversion of individuals and the growth of Christ's Mystical Body, the laity are called to be involved in spreading Christ's influence in the temporal order, working directly in this order (cf. *AA* 7).

This fact presupposes that lay people, like the whole Church, have a vision of the world. In particular, they have an ability to evaluate human affairs that recognizes their positive value as well as the religious dimension already expressed in the Book of Wisdom: "In your wisdom you have established man to rule the creatures produced by you, to govern the world in holiness and justice" (Wis 9:2-3).

The temporal world cannot be considered as a self-contained system. This immanentist, "worldly" conception cannot be maintained at the philosophical level. It was radically rejected by Christianity, which learned from St. Paul, echoing Jesus, the order and purposeful dynamism of creation as the setting of the Church's very life: "All these are yours" the Apostle wrote to the Corinthians, as if to highlight the new dignity and power of Christians. However he immediately adds: "You are Christ's and Christ is God's" (1 Cor 3:22-23). This text can be accurately paraphrased by saying that the destiny of the entire universe is tied to this belonging.

This view of the world, beginning with Christ's kingship shared by the Church, is the foundation of an authentic theology of the lay state regarding the Christian role of lay people in the temporal order. As *Lumen Gentium* states:

> The faithful, therefore, must learn the deepest meaning and the value of all creation, as well as its role in the harmonious praise of God. They must assist each other to live holier lives even in their daily occupations. In this way the world may be permeated by the spirit of Christ and it may more effectively fulfill its purpose in justice, charity and peace. The laity have the principal role in the overall fulfillment of this duty. Therefore, by their competence in secular training and by their activity, elevated from within by the grace of Christ, let them vigorously contribute their effort, so that created goods may be perfected by human labor, technical skill and civic culture for the benefit of all men according to the design of the Creator and the light of his word. May the goods of this world be more equitably distributed among all men, and may they in their own way be conducive to universal progress in human and Christian freedom. In this manner, through the members of the Church, will Christ progressively illumine the whole of human society with his saving light....
>
> Moreover, let the laity also by their combined efforts remedy the customs and conditions of the world, if they

are an inducement to sin, so that they all may be conformed to the norms of justice and may favor the practice of virtue rather than hinder it. By so doing they will imbue culture and human activity with genuine moral values *(LG* 36; cf. *CCC* 909).

Each individual layman must stand before the world as a witness to the resurrection and life of the Lord Jesus and a symbol of the living God. All the laity as a community and each one according to his ability must nourish the world with spiritual fruits. They must diffuse in the world that spirit which animates the poor, the meek, the peace makers—whom the Lord in the Gospel proclaimed as blessed. In a word, "Christians must be to the world what the soul is to the body" *(LG* 38).

This program for enlightening and enlivening the world goes back to the earliest period of Christianity, as attested, for example, by the *Letter to Diognetus.* Today too this is the royal road to be followed by the heirs, witnesses and co-workers of Christ's kingdom.

General audience of February 9, 1994

The Laity Share in the Church's Saving Mission

The laity's participation in the growth of Christ's kingdom is a historical reality in every age—from the gathering in apostolic times; to the Christian communities of the early centuries; to the groups, movements, unions, fraternities and societies of the Middle Ages and the modern period; to the activities of individuals and associations that, in the last century and in ours, have supported the Church's pastors in defending faith and morals in families, societies, social contexts and classes. At times they have even paid for this witness with their blood. These activities, often promoted by saints and supported by bishops in the 19th and 20th centuries, have led to a deeper awareness of the laity's mission. They have also led to an ever clearer and more explicit conception of this mission as true and proper "apostolate."

Pius XI spoke of the "laity's cooperation in the apostolate of the hierarchy" with regard to "Catholic Action." This was a decisive period in the Church's life. It led to a remarkable development along two lines: the organizational, which especially took shape in Catholic Action, and that of theoretical, doctrinal reflection, culminating in the teaching of the Second Vatican Council. It presented the apostolate of the laity as "a participation in the salvific mission of the Church itself" *(LG* 33).

The Council could be said to have given a clearer doctrinal formulation to the ecclesial experience that began with Pentecost. All who then received the Holy Spirit felt they had been given a mission to proclaim the Gospel, to establish and develop the Church. In the centuries that followed sacramental theology made it clear that all who become members of the Church through Baptism are obliged, with the help of the Holy Spirit, to give witness to the faith and to spread Christ's kingdom. This task is strengthened by the sacrament of Confirmation, by which the faithful, as the Council says, "are more strictly obliged to spread and defend the faith, both by word and by deed, as true witnesses of Christ" *(LG* 11). In more recent times, advances in ecclesiology have developed the concept of lay involvement, not only in relation to the two sacraments of Christian initiation, but also as an expression of a more conscious participation in the Church's mystery in accordance with the spirit of Pentecost. This is another basic point of the theology of the laity.

The theological principle that "The apostolate of the laity derives from their Christian vocation and the Church can never be without it" *(AA* 1), clarifies in ever fuller and more transparent fashion the need for lay involvement in our age. This necessity is further emphasized by certain circumstances that characterize the present time. For example, there is the population growth in cities, where the number of priests is always insufficient; mobility because of work, school, recreation, etc., which is a feature of modern society; the autonomy of many areas of society which make ethical and religious conditions more difficult and action from within more necessary; the sociological distance of priests from many areas of work and culture. For these and other reasons a new work of evangelization is required of the laity. On the other hand, the growth of institutions and of the democratic mentality itself has made and is making the laity more sensitive to the demands of the ecclesial commitment. The spread and the rise in the average level of culture gives to many people greater abilities in working for the good of society and the Church.

From the historical point of view, then, one should not be surprised at the new forms that lay activity has assumed. Under the impulse of modern sociocultural conditions, greater attention has been paid to an ecclesiological principle, which had previously been left somewhat in the background: the diversity of ministries in the Church is a vital need of the Mystical Body. All its members are needed for it to develop, and it requires everyone's contribution in accord with each one's various abilities. "The whole body grows and, with the proper functioning of the members...builds itself up in love" (Eph 4:16). It is a "self-building" which depends on Christ, the head of the body, but requires the cooperation of each member. Hence the Church has a diversity of ministries in the unity of mission (cf. *AA* 2). Unity is not harmed but enriched by diversity.

There is an essential difference between ordained ministries and non-ordained ministries, as I explained in the catecheses on the priesthood. The Council teaches that the common priesthood of the faithful and the ministerial or hierarchical priesthood differ essentially and not only in degree (cf. *LG* 10). The Apostolic Exhortation *Christifideles Laici* notes that the ordained ministries are exercised in virtue of the sacrament of Orders. The non-ordained ministries, the offices and roles of the lay faithful "have their foundation in the sacraments of Baptism and Confirmation, and for a good many of them, in Matrimony" *(CL* 23). This last statement has great value, especially for married couples and parents, who are also called to carry out a Christian apostolate especially in their families (cf. *CCC* 902).

The same apostolic exhortation points out: "Pastors ought to acknowledge and foster the ministries, offices and roles of the lay faithful" (n. 23). A pastor of souls cannot expect to do everything in the community entrusted to him. He must put the laity's activity to the best possible use, with sincere esteem for their competence and availability. Although it is true that a lay person cannot replace the pastor in the ministries that require the powers given by the sacrament of Orders, it is also true that the pastor cannot replace the laity in areas where they have greater competence. Therefore he must promote their role and encourage their participation in the Church's mission.

In this regard what the Code of Canon Law prescribes must be kept in mind: "When the necessity of the Church warrants it," the laity can supply for certain of the clergy's activities (can. 230, §3). But as we read in *Christifideles Laici,* "The exercise of these tasks does not make pastors of the lay faithful." They derive their "legitimacy formally and immediately from the official deputation given by the pastors, as well as from its concrete exercise under the guidance of ecclesiastical authority" (n. 23).

However, it should be immediately added that the laity's activity is not limited to that of supplying "in situations of emergency and chronic necessity." There are areas of Church life in which, along with the tasks proper to the hierarchy, the active participation of the laity is also desired. The first is that of the liturgical assembly. Certainly the Eucharistic celebration requires the action of someone who has received from the sacrament of Orders the power to offer the sacrifice in Christ's name—the priest. However, according to *Christifideles Laici,* the liturgical celebration "is a sacred action not simply of the clergy, but of the entire assembly." It is a community action. "It is, therefore, natural that the tasks not proper to the ordained ministers be fulfilled by the lay faithful" *(CL* 23). How many lay people, children and adults, young and old, carry out these tasks extremely well in our churches, with prayers, readings, songs and various services inside and outside the sacred building! Let us thank the Lord for this reality of our time. We must pray that he will enable them continually to increase in number and quality.

In addition to the liturgy, lay people have their own duty to proclaim the Word of God, since they have a role in Christ's prophetic office and hence a responsibility for evangelization. To this end they can be given particular functions and even permanent mandates, for example, in catechesis, in education, in managing and editing religious periodicals, in Catholic publishing, in the mass media, in various works and projects that the Church sponsors for spreading the faith (cf. *CCC* 906).

In every case we are talking about a sharing in the Church's mission, in the ever new Pentecost whose goal is to bring the entire world the grace of the Spirit who descended on the upper room in Jerusalem so that the marvels of God might be proclaimed to all nations.

General audience of March 2, 1994

Lay Charisms Build up the Church

In the preceding catecheses we focused on the sacramental basis of the laity's ministries and roles in the Church: Baptism, Confirmation and, for many, the sacrament of Matrimony. It is an essential point in the theology of the lay state, linked to the Church's sacramental structure. However, now we must add that the Holy Spirit, the giver of every gift and the first principle of the Church's vitality, does not only work through the sacraments. According to St. Paul, he distributes to each his own gifts as he wills (cf. 1 Cor 12:11), pouring out into the People of God a great wealth of graces both for prayer and contemplation and for action. They are charisms. Lay people receive them too, especially in relation to their mission in the Church and society. The Second Vatican Council stated this in connection with St. Paul: "The Holy Spirit...distributes special graces among the faithful of every rank. By these gifts he makes them fit and ready to undertake the various tasks and offices which contribute toward the renewal and building up of the Church, according to the words of the Apostle: 'The manifestation of the Spirit is given to everyone for profit' (1 Cor 12:7)" *(LG 12)*.

St. Paul highlighted the multiplicity and variety of charisms in the early Church: some are extraordinary, such as healings, the gift of prophecy or that of tongues. Others are simpler, given for the ordinary fulfillment of the tasks assigned in the community (cf. 1 Cor 12:7-10).

As a result of Paul's text, charisms are often thought of as extraordinary gifts, which primarily marked the beginning of the Church's life. The Second Vatican Council called attention to charisms in their quality as gifts belonging to the ordinary life of the Church and not necessarily having an extraordinary or miraculous nature. The Apostolic Exhortation *Christifideles Laici* also spoke of charisms as gifts that can be "exceptional and great or simple and ordinary" (n. 24). In addition, it should be kept in mind that the primary or principal aim of many charisms is not the personal sanctification of those who receive them, but the service of others and the Church's welfare. Certainly they also aim at and serve the growth of personal holiness, but in an essentially altruistic and communitarian perspective. This belongs to the Church's organic dimension in that it concerns the growth of Christ's Mystical Body.

As St. Paul told us and the Council repeated, these charisms result from the free choice and gift of the Holy Spirit, in whose property as the first and substantial Gift within the trinitarian life they share. In a special way the Triune God shows his sovereign power in the gifts. This power is not subject to any antecedent rule, to any particular discipline or to a plan of interventions established once and for all. According to St. Paul, he distributes his gifts to each "as he wills" (1 Cor 12:11). It is an eternal will of love, whose freedom and gratuitousness is revealed in the action carried out by the Holy Spirit-Gift in the economy of salvation. Through this sovereign freedom and gratuitousness, charisms are also given to the laity, as the Church's history shows (cf. *CL* 24).

We cannot but admire the great wealth of gifts bestowed by the Holy Spirit on lay people as members of the Church in our age as well. Each of them has the necessary ability to carry out the tasks to which he is called for the welfare of the

Christian people and the world's salvation, if he is open, docile and faithful to the Holy Spirit's action.

However, we must also turn our attention to another aspect of St. Paul's teaching and that of the Church, an aspect that applies to every type of ministry and to charisms—their diversity and variety cannot harm unity. "There are different gifts but the same Spirit; there are different ministries but the same Lord" (1 Cor 12:4-5). Paul asked that these differences be respected because not everyone can expect to carry out the same role contrary to God's plan and the Spirit's gift, and contrary to the most elementary laws of any social structure. However, the Apostle equally stressed the need for unity, which itself answers a sociological demand, but which in the Christian community should even more be a reflection of the divine unity. One Spirit, one Lord, thus, one Church!

At the beginning of the Christian era extraordinary things were accomplished under the influence of charisms, both the extraordinary ones and those which could be called little, humble, everyday charisms. This has always been the case in the Church and is so in our era as well, generally in a hidden way, but sometimes in a striking way, when God desires it for the good of his Church. In our day, as in the past, a great number of lay people have contributed to the Church's spiritual and pastoral growth. We can say that there are many people who, because of their charisms, work as good, genuine witnesses of faith and love.

It is to be hoped that all will reflect on this transcendent value of eternal life already present in their work, if it is carried out in fidelity to their vocation and with docility to the Holy Spirit who lives and acts in their hearts. This realization can only serve as a stimulus, support and comfort especially for those who, out of fidelity to a holy vocation, are involved in serving the common good, in establishing justice, in improving the living conditions of the poor and needy, in taking care of the disabled, in welcoming refugees and in achieving peace throughout the world.

In the Church's community life and pastoral practice, charisms must be recognized but also discerned, as the Synod Fathers recalled in 1987 (cf. *CL* 24). Certainly, the Spirit "blows where he wills"; one can never expect to impose rules and conditions on him. The Christian community, however, has the right to be informed by its pastors about the authenticity of charisms and the reliability of those who claim to have received them. The Council recalled the need for prudence in this area, especially when it is a question of extraordinary charisms (cf. *LG* 12).

The Apostolic Exhortation *Christifideles Laici* stressed that "no charism dispenses a person from reference and submission to the Pastors of the Church" *(CL* 24). These norms of prudence are easily understandable and apply to all, both clerics and lay people.

That having been said, we would like to repeat with the Council and the exhortation cited above that "Charisms should be received in gratitude both on the part of the one who receives them, and also on the part of the entire Church" *(CL* 24). From these charisms there arises "for each believer the right and duty to use them in the Church and in the world for the good of men and the building up of the Church" *(AA* 3). This right is based on the Spirit's gift and the Church's validation. It is a duty stemming from the very fact of the gift received, which creates a responsibility and demands a commitment.

The history of the Church shows that whenever charisms are real, sooner or later they are recognized and can carry out their constructive, unifying role. It is a role, let us recall once again, that the majority of the Church's members, clerical and lay, effectively fulfill each day for the good of us all.

General audience of March 9, 1994

The Laity Witness
to Christ in the World

Today it is not difficult for Christians to admit that all the Church's members, including the laity, can and must share in her mission of bearing witness to, proclaiming and bringing Christ to the world. This requirement of Christ's Mystical Body has been reiterated by Popes, by the Second Vatican Council and by synods of bishops in harmony with Sacred Scripture and Tradition, the experience of the early Christians, the teaching of theologians and the history of pastoral life. In our century there has been no reluctance to speak of "apostolate," and this term and the idea it expresses are known to the clergy and faithful. However, one frequently has the feeling that there is still some uncertainty about the areas of concrete involvement and about the ways in which this involvement should be carried out. It would be helpful, then, to set forth some clearly established points on this subject, with the realization, though, that a more concrete, direct and developed formation can and should be sought locally from one's own parish priests, diocesan offices and centers for the lay apostolate.

The first area for the laity's apostolate within the ecclesial community is the parish. The Council insisted on this point in the Decree *Apostolicam Actuositatem,* which says: "The parish offers an obvious example of the apostolate on the community level" (n. 10). It is also stated that lay action is needed here so that the pastors' apostolate can achieve its full effect. This action, which must be developed in close union with their priests, is for "the laity with the right apostolic attitude" a form of direct, immediate participation in the Church's life (cf. *AA* 10).

Lay people can accomplish much in assisting with the liturgy, in teaching catechism, in pastoral and social projects, and on pastoral councils (cf. *CL* 27). They also contribute indirectly to the apostolate by helping with parish administration. The priest must not feel alone, but should be able to count on their competence and the support of their solidarity, understanding and generous devotion in the various ways of serving God's kingdom.

A second area of needs, concerns and possibilities was indicated by the Council when it urged the laity to "cultivate an ever-increasing appreciation of their own diocese'" (*AA* 10). The local church actually takes concrete shape in the diocese and makes the universal Church present for the clergy and faithful belonging to it. The laity are called to collaborate with a generous and lofty spirit on today's frequent diocesan projects in executive, consultative and at times directive roles, in accordance with the instructions and requests of the bishop and the agencies responsible. They also make a significant contribution by participating in diocesan pastoral councils, whose establishment was recommended by the 1987 Synod of Bishops as "the principal form of collaboration, dialogue and discernment at the diocesan level" (*CL* 27). We also expect from the laity specific help in spreading the teachings of the diocesan bishop, united with the other bishops and especially with the Pope, on religious and social issues that the ecclesial community faces; in a good formulation and resolution of administrative problems; in managing the catechetical, cultural and charitable activities that the diocese establishes and supports on behalf of their poor brothers and sisters, etc. How many other opportunities there are for fruitful labor for anyone who has goodwill, a desire for commitment and a spirit of sacrifice! May God inspire ever new and vigorous efforts to help bishops and dioceses, where many excellent lay people are showing their awareness that the local Church is everyone's home and family!

On a broader, even universal, scale the laity can and must feel that they are members of the Church and be committed to her growth, as the 1987 Synod of Bishops recalled (cf. *CL* 28). They should think of her as an essentially missionary community, whose members all have the duty and responsibility of preaching the Gospel to every nation, to all who need God, whether they know it or not. In this vast area of individuals and groups, of environments and social levels, there are also many who, although being registered as Christians, are spiritually distant, agnostic and indifferent to Christ. The new evangelization is aimed at these brothers and sisters, and lay people are called to give their valuable, indispensable cooperation to it. The 1987 Synod, after having said: "Without doubt a mending of the Christian fabric of society is urgently needed," added: "At this moment the lay faithful, in virtue of their participation in the prophetic mission of Christ, are fully part of this work of the Church" *(CL* 34). There are many places for the laity in the forefront of this new evangelization!

To carry out this task a suitable preparation in the doctrine of the faith and in pastoral methodology is indispensable, one which the laity too may receive in institutes of religious studies and special courses, in addition to their personal effort to study divine truth. The same degree of religious or even theological education will not be needed by everyone nor for every form of collaboration. But it cannot be neglected by those who must face the problems of science and human culture in relation to faith (cf. *CL* 34).

The new evangelization is aimed at forming mature ecclesial communities consisting of convinced Christians who are knowledgeable and persevering in faith and charity. They will be able to enliven the multitudes from within, even where Christ, the Redeemer of man, is unknown or forgotten (cf. *CL* 35), or where the bond linking him to thought and life is weak.

To this end old and new forms of association will be useful, such as confraternities, "companies," and pious unions, enriched when necessary with a new missionary spirit, and the various movements flourishing in the Church today. Traditional initiatives and popular exhibitions on the occasion of religious celebrations, while preserving certain features connected with local or regional customs, also could and should have an ecclesial impact, if prepared and carried out in a way that takes into account the needs of the new evangelization. It will be the task of the clergy and the laity who organize them to adapt them with wisdom, sensitivity and courage to the needs of the missionary Church, in every case fostering an instructive catechesis on the customs as well as sacramental practice, especially Penance and the Eucharist.

Eloquent examples of missionary endeavor in the above-mentioned fields or areas, and in so many others, are given to us by many lay people in our day. They have discovered the fullness of their Christian vocation and have accepted the divine mandate of universal evangelization, the gift of the Holy Spirit, who seeks to accomplish in the world an ever new Pentecost. The Church is grateful for these brothers and sisters of ours, both known and unknown, and they have certainly been blessed by God. May their example raise up an ever greater number of lay people committed to bringing Christ's message to every individual and to seeking to enkindle the missionary flame everywhere. For this reason too the Successor of Peter tries to visit every nation, on every continent, in order humbly to help spread the Gospel. In every country the bishops, successors of the apostles, are active as individual pastors and as an ecclesial body in the new evangelization.

General audience of March 16, 1994

Lay Groups Promote
the Church's Mission

In giving the lay apostolate a new impetus, the Second Vatican Council took care to declare that the first, basic and irreplaceable form of activity for building up the body of Christ is that undertaken by individual members of the Church (cf. *AA* 16). Every Christian is called to the apostolate; every lay person is called to give personal witness and to share in the Church's mission. This presupposes and involves personal conviction, arising from faith and the *sensus ecclesiae* that faith kindles in souls. If one believes and intends to be Church, one cannot fail to be convinced of one's "unique task which cannot be done by another and which is to be fulfilled for the good of all" *(CL* 28).

One can never do enough to inculcate in the faithful an awareness of their duty to cooperate in building the Church and advancing the kingdom. Lay people also have the task of imbuing temporal realities with the Gospel. There are many opportunities for involvement, especially in the family, at work, in professional life and with recreational and cultural groups, etc. Many people in the world today wish to do something to improve life, to make society more just, to contribute to the good of their fellow men and women. For them, the discovery of their Christian mission in the apostolate could be the highest development of the natural vocation to the common good, which would increase the validity, motivation, nobility and even perhaps the generosity of their activity.

But there is another natural vocation that can and must be expressed in the ecclesial apostolate: that of *association.* On the supernatural level, the human tendency to associate is enriched and raised to the level of fraternal communion in Christ. This "signifies the communion and unity of the Church in Christ, who said, 'Where two or three are gathered together in my name, there am I in the midst of them' (Mt 18:20)" *(AA* 18).

There is no doubt that this ecclesial tendency toward group apostolates has a supernatural origin in the charity that the Holy Spirit instills in hearts (cf. Rom 5:5) However, its theological value matches the sociological need that in the modern world leads to the organization of combined efforts in order to reach preestablished objectives. Even in the Church, the Council states, "Only the pooling of resources is capable of fully achieving all the aims of the modern apostolate and firmly protecting its interests" *(AA* 18). It is a question of combining and harmonizing the activities of those who aim at influencing the spirit and mentalities of people in various social conditions with the Gospel message. It is a question of putting into practice an evangelization that can exert an influence on public opinion and on institutions. To reach this aim, well-organized group action is required (cf. *AA* 19).

The Church encourages both individual and group apostolates. The Council declared the lay people's right to form associations for the apostolate: "Maintaining the proper relationship to Church authorities, the laity have the right to found and control such associations and to join those already existing" *(AA* 19).

The link with ecclesiastical authorities implies a fundamental desire for harmony and ecclesial cooperation. But it does not prevent the associations from having their own autonomy. In civil society the right to establish an association is recognized as an individual right based on man's freedom to join others to achieve a common aim. In the Church, the right to found an association for religious purposes, for the lay faithful too, springs from Baptism. For every Christian, Baptism entails the possibility, duty and strength of active participation in the Church's communion and mission (cf. *CL* 29). The Code of Canon Law speaks of this in the following way: "The Christian faithful are at liberty freely to found and to govern associations for charitable and religious purposes, or for the promotion of the Christian vocation in the world; they are free to hold meetings to pursue these purposes in common" (can. 215).

In the Church lay people are increasingly using this freedom. Truly, in the past there were many associations of the faithful, organized in the ways possible at the time. But there is no doubt that today the phenomenon has new breadth and variety. Along with the ancient fraternities, *Misericordiae,* pious sodalities, third orders, etc., we are witnessing the development everywhere of new kinds of associations. These groups, communities and movements pursue a great variety of aims, methods and fields of action. But they always act with a single fundamental purpose: the spread of Christian life and cooperation in the Church's mission (cf. *CL* 29).

Far from being an obstacle, the diversity of associations is rather an indication of the supreme freedom of the Holy Spirit, who respects and encourages the diversity of aspirations, temperaments, vocations and abilities that exist in people. However, it is certain that variety makes it necessary to preserve the concern for unity, avoiding rivalry, tension, and the tendency to monopolize the apostolate or to a superiority excluded by the Gospel itself. The spirit of participation and communion should always be fostered among the various associations in order truly to contribute to spreading the Gospel message.

The criteria that make it possible to recognize the ecclesial nature, that is, the genuinely Catholic character of various associations are:

a) the primacy given to the call of every Christian to holiness and to the perfection of charity as the goal of the Christian vocation;

b) the responsibility of professing the Catholic faith in communion with the Church's Magisterium;

c) participation in the Church's apostolic goals with a commitment to a presence in human society;

d) the witness to concrete communion with the Pope and one's own bishop (cf. *CL* 30).

These criteria should be followed and applied at local, regional and national levels, and even through international ties between cultural, social and political institutions. This is in conformity with the universal mission of the Church, which seeks to instill the spirit of truth, charity and peace in peoples, in states, and in the new communities of which these are composed.

The relations of lay associations with ecclesiastical authorities can also receive particular recognition and approval when this is deemed appropriate or even necessary by reason of their extension or their type of involvement in the apostolate (cf. *CL* 31). The Council pointed out this possibility and its fittingness for "associations and projects which have an immediately spiritual purpose" *(AA* 24). As regards cases of "ecumenical associations" with a Catholic majority and a non-Catholic minority, the Pontifical Council for the Laity determines the conditions for their approval (cf. *CL* 31).

Among the forms of group apostolate, the Council expressly and especially cites Catholic Action (cf. *AA* 20). Even in the various forms which this has taken in different countries and with the changes that have occurred over time, Catholic Action is distinguished by the extremely close link it maintains with the hierarchy. This is not the least of the reasons for the abundant fruit it has produced in the Church and in the world throughout the many years of its history.

The organizations known by the name of Catholic Action (but also by other names and of a similar type) have as their purpose to evangelize and sanctify one's neighbor, to form Christian consciences, to have an influence on morality, and to instill a religious spirit in society. The laity assumes responsibility in communion with the bishop and priests. They act "under the higher direction of the hierarchy itself, and the latter can sanction this cooperation by an explicit mandate" *(AA* 20). The degree of their capacity to build the body of Christ depends and will always depend on the extent of their fidelity to the hierarchy and their ecclesial harmony. At the same time, experience shows that, if on the basis of their own action dissent is sown and a conflicting attitude is taken almost as a general policy, the Church is not built up. Not only that, a self-destructive process is begun that frustrates the work and generally brings about its end.

The Church, the Council and the Pope hope and pray that in the group forms of the lay apostolate and especially in Catholic Action, the radiance of the ecclesial community in its unity, its charity and its mission to spread faith and holiness in the world may always be recognized.

General audience of March 23, 1994

The Laity Are Called
to Renew the Temporal Order

There is an order of reality—institutions, values, activities—which we are used to describing as "temporal" insofar as it directly concerns things that belong to the context of the present life, although they are also destined to eternal life. Today's world is not made up of appearances and deceptive shadows, nor can it be considered only in relation to the hereafter. As the Second Vatican Council declared: "All those things which make up the temporal order...not only aid in the attainment of man's ultimate goal but also possess their own intrinsic value" *(AA* 7). The biblical account of creation presents this value to us as recognized, desired and established by God. According to Genesis, God saw how good creation was (cf. Gen 1:12, 18, 21). Indeed, he "found it very good" after the creation of man and woman (cf. Gen 1:31). With the Incarnation and the redemption, the value of temporal things is not eliminated or diminished, as though the work of the Redeemer was opposed to the work of the Creator. Rather, it is restored and elevated, in accord with God's plan, "to sum up all things in Christ" (Eph 1:10) and "through him to reconcile all things for him" (Col 1:20). In Christ therefore all things hold together (cf. Col 1:17).

Nevertheless, we cannot overlook the historical experience of evil, and for man, of sin. This can only be explained by the revelation of the fall of his first parents and of the subsequent human falls from generation to generation. "In the course of history," the Council states, "the use of temporal things has been marred by serious vices" *(AA* 7). Today too, instead of having dominion over things in accord with God's plan and command, as scientific and technological progress would enable them to do, many people, through excessive confidence in their new powers, are enslaved by them and seriously harmed.

The Church's task is to help people to properly orientate the whole temporal order and direct it to God through Christ (cf. *AA* 7). Thus the Church makes herself the servant of mankind and lay people "participate in the mission of service to the person and society" *(CL* 36).

In this respect, it is necessary to remember first of all that lay people are called to help promote the human person, an especially urgent and necessary task today. It is a question of safeguarding—and often restoring—the pivotal value of the human being. Precisely because he is a person, a human being can never be treated "as an object to be used, or as a means, or as a thing" *(CL* 37).

All men are equal as regards their personal dignity. No racial, sexual, economic, social, cultural, political or geographical discrimination is permissible. It is a duty of solidarity to compensate for the differences stemming from the conditions of time and place in which each person is born and lives. This involves an active human and Christian support, expressed in concrete forms of justice and charity, as St. Paul explained and advised the Corinthians: "Not that others should have relief while you are burdened, but that as a matter of equality your surplus at the present time should supply their needs, so that their surplus may also supply your needs, that there may be equality" (2 Cor 8:13-14).

Promotion of the person's dignity is linked with "the respect, the defense and the promotion of the rights of the human person" *(CL* 38). First of all, this means recognition of the inviolability of human life. The right to life is essential and can be considered "the most basic and fundamental right and the condition for all other personal rights" *(CL* 38). As a result, "Whatever is opposed to life itself...whatever violates the integrity of the human person...whatever insults human dignity...all these things and others of their like...are a supreme dishonor to the Creator" *(GS* 27), who wanted man to be made in his image and after his likeness (cf. Gen 1:26), and placed under his dominion.

A special responsibility in this defense of personal dignity and the right to life belongs to parents, educators, healthcare workers and all those who wield economic and political power (cf. *CL* 38). In particular, the Church urges lay people to face bravely the challenges of the new bioethical problems (cf. *CL* 38).

The individual rights to be defended and promoted include the right to religious freedom, as well as to freedom of conscience and freedom of worship (cf. *CL* 39). The Church maintains that society has the duty to ensure the individual's right to profess his convictions and to practice his religion within the due limits established by the just requirements of public order (cf. *DH* 2, 7). There has been no lack of martyrs in every age to defend and to promote this right.

Lay people are called to be involved in political life according to their capacities and the conditions of time and place, to promote the common good in all its needs and especially to implement justice in service to citizens as persons. As we read in *Christifideles Laici:* "A political policy on behalf of the person and society finds its continuous line of action in the defense and promotion of justice" (n. 42). It is clear that in this activity, which belongs to all the members of the earthly city, lay Christians are called to give the example of honest political conduct. This does not aim for personal advantage or seek to serve the causes of groups and parties by illegal means, which lead to the collapse of even the noblest and most sacred ideals.

Lay Christians will not fail to join in society's efforts to re-establish peace in the world. For them it is a question of realizing the peace given by Christ (cf. Jn 14:27; Eph 2:14) in its social and political dimensions, in individual countries and in the world, as people's awareness increasingly demands. To this end, it is their task to carry out a thoroughgoing work of education in order to defeat the old culture of selfishness, hate, revenge and hostility, and thereby to develop the culture of solidarity and love of neighbor at every level (cf. *CL* 42).

It is also the task of lay Christians to be committed to economic and social development. This is a requirement of respect for the individual, of justice, solidarity and fraternal love. It is up to them to work together with all people of goodwill to find ways to guarantee the universal purpose of goods, whatever social regime is in force (cf. *CL* 43). It is also up to them to defend the rights of workers, seeking satisfactory solutions to the most serious problems of increasing unemployment, while striving to overcome all injustices. As lay Christians, they express in the world the Church's application of her own social doctrine. Nevertheless, they must be aware of their personal freedom and responsibility in matters of opinion, in which their choices, though always inspired by Gospel values, should not be presented as the only alternative for Christians. Respect for legitimate opinions and choices different from one's own is also a requirement of love.

Finally, lay Christians have the task of helping to develop human culture with all its values. Present in the various areas of science, artistic creation, philosophical thought, historical research, etc., they will contribute the necessary inspiration deriving from their faith. The development of culture increasingly implies the involvement of the mass media, a vital means for the formation of mentalities and behavior. So they will have a keen sense of responsibility in their involvement in the press, cinema, radio, television and theater, always carrying out their work in the light of the mandate to proclaim the Gospel to the ends of the earth. This has particular relevance in today's world, which urgently needs the ways of salvation that Jesus Christ has opened to everyone (cf. *CL* 44).

General audience of April 13, 1994

Human Work Involves
Sharing in Christ's Mission

Among the lay faithful, workers deserve special mention. The Church is aware of the importance of work in human life and recognizes it as an essential component of society at the socio-economic, political and religious level. She considers this latter aspect a primary expression of the "secular character" of the laity (cf. *LG* 31), most of whom are workers and can find in work the path to holiness. Because of this conviction, the Second Vatican Council considers work from the perspective of the task of salvation, and calls workers to collaborate in the apostolate (cf. *LG* 41).

I dedicated the Encyclical *Laborem Exercens* and other documents and addresses to this topic, thus seeking to shed light on the value, dignity and dimensions of work in all its exceptional greatness. Here I will only recall that the first reason for this greatness and dignity is that work is a cooperation in God's creative activity. The biblical account of creation teaches us this when it says: "The Lord God then took the man and settled him in the garden of Eden, to cultivate and care for it" (Gen 2:15), thus referring to the preceding order to subdue the earth (cf. Gen 1:28). As I wrote in *Laborem Exercens:* "Man is the image of God partly through the mandate received from his Creator to subdue, to dominate, the earth. In carrying out this mandate, man, every human being, reflects the very action of the Creator of the universe" *(LE* 4).

According to the Second Vatican Council (cf. *LG* 41), work is a path to holiness, because it provides the opportunity:

a) *to perfect oneself.* Work actually develops man's personality, cultivating his qualities and abilities. We understand this better in our era, with the drama of so many unemployed people who feel their dignity as human persons is diminished. The greatest attention must be paid to this personalist dimension for the sake of all workers. The attempt must be made in every case to ensure working conditions worthy of man.

b) *to help one's fellow citizens.* Here is the social dimension of work, which is a service for the good of all. This orientation should always be stressed. Work is not a selfish but an altruistic activity; one does not work exclusively for oneself, but also for others.

c) *to promote the progress of all society and creation.* Work thus attains a historical-eschatological and, one could say, cosmic dimension. Its purpose is to help improve the material conditions of life and the world, aiding humanity in this way to reach the higher goals to which God is calling it. The orientation of work to universal betterment is made more obvious by today's progress. However, much remains to be done in adapting work to these ends desired by the Creator himself.

d) *to imitate Christ with active love.* We will return to this point.

In the light of Genesis, according to which God established and enjoined work in addressing the first human couple (cf. Gen 1:27-28), the intention of so many men and women who work for the good of their families finds its meaning. The love of spouse and children, which inspires and motivates the majority of human beings to work, confers greater dignity on this work and makes it easier and more pleasant to perform, even when it is very toilsome.

In contemporary society too, where the principle of the right of men and women to paid labor holds sway, recognition and appreciation must always be given to the value of the not directly profitable work of many women who devote themselves to the needs of home and family. This work today also has a basic importance for family life and the good of society.

Here let it suffice to note this aspect of the issue, in order to move on to a point discussed by the Council which mentions the often toilsome labors (cf. *LG* 41) that are involved in work, which even today verifies the biblical words: "By the sweat of your face shall you get bread to eat" (Gen 3:19). As I wrote in *Laborem Exercens:* "Toil is something that is universally known, for it is universally experienced. It is familiar to those doing physical work under sometimes exceptionally laborious conditions.... It is likewise familiar to those at an intellectual workbench.... It is familiar to women, who, sometimes without proper recognition on the part of society and even of their own families, bear the daily burden and responsibility for their homes and the upbringing of their children" (n. 9).

Here we find not only the ethical but the ascetical dimension, which the Church teaches us to recognize in work. Precisely due to the effort it imposes, work requires the virtues of courage and patience, and thus can become a path to holiness.

Precisely because of the toil it implies, work appears more clearly as a task of cooperation with Christ in his redemptive work. Its value, already established by sharing in God's creative work, receives new light when considered as a sharing in Christ's life and mission. We cannot forget that in the Incarnation, God's Son, who became man for our salvation, did not fail to work hard at common labor. Jesus Christ learned the carpenter's trade from Joseph and practiced it until the beginning of his public mission. At Nazareth Jesus was known as "the carpenter's son" (Mt 13:55) or as "the carpenter" himself (Mk 6:3). For this reason too it seems so natural for him to refer in his parables to men's professional work or to women's domestic work, as I noted in *Laborem Exercens* (n. 26), and to show his esteem for the humblest tasks. It is an important aspect of the mystery of his life. As the Son of God, Jesus could and did confer a supreme dignity on human work. With human hands and human abilities the Son of God worked like us and with us, men of need and daily toil!

In the light of Christ's example, work takes on for believers its highest purpose, one connected with the paschal mystery. After giving the example of work similar to that of so many other workers, Jesus accomplished the highest work for which he was sent—redemption, culminating in the saving sacrifice of the cross. On Calvary, Jesus offered himself for the salvation of all in obedience to the Father.

Well then, workers are invited to unite themselves with the Savior's work. As the Council says: "They should imitate by their lively charity, in their joyous hope and by their voluntary sharing of each others' burdens, the very Christ who plied his hands with carpenter's tools and who in union with his Father, is continually working for the salvation of all men" *(LG* 41). Thus the salvific value of work, in some way perceived also in recent centuries by philosophy and sociology, is revealed at a very high level as sharing in the sublime work of redemption.

For this reason the Council states that all can, "by their daily work...climb to the heights of holiness and apostolic activity" *(LG* 41). Here lies the high mission of workers, called to cooperate not only in building a better material world, but also in the spiritual transformation of human and cosmic reality, made possible by the paschal mystery.

Hardship and suffering, stemming from both the toil of work itself and from the social conditions in which it is performed, thus acquire, because of their sharing in Christ's redeeming sacrifice, a supernatural fruitfulness for the entire human race. The words of St. Paul apply to this case too: "Yes, we know that all creation groans and is in agony even until now. Not only that, but we ourselves, although we have the Spirit as first fruits, groan inwardly while we await the redemption of our bodies" (Rom 8:22-23). This certainty of faith, in the Apostle's historical and eschatological vision, is the basis of his hope-filled assertion: "I consider the sufferings of the present to be as nothing compared with the glory to be revealed in us" (Rom 8:18).

General audience of April 20, 1994

The Lord Sanctifies Those Who Suffer

The reality of suffering is ever before our eyes and often in the body, soul and heart of each of us. Apart from faith, pain has always been a great riddle of human existence. However, ever since Jesus redeemed the world by his passion and death, a new perspective has been opened. Through suffering one can grow in self-giving and attain the highest degree of love (cf. Jn 13:1), because of him who "loved us and gave himself for us" (Eph 5:2). As a sharing in the mystery of the cross, suffering can now be accepted and lived as a cooperation in Christ's saving mission. The Second Vatican Council expressed the Church's awareness that all who are troubled and oppressed are specially united with the suffering Christ for the salvation of the world (cf. *LG* 41).

In proclaiming the Beatitudes, Jesus himself considered every manifestation of human suffering: the poor, the hungry, the afflicted, those who are scorned by society or unjustly persecuted. Looking at the world, we too discover so much misery in a variety of ancient and new forms. The signs of suffering are everywhere. Let us then speak of them in this catechesis, seeking better to discover the divine plan guiding humanity on so painful a path and the saving value that suffering, like work, has for the whole human race.

In the cross the "Gospel of suffering" has been revealed

to Christians *(SD* 25). Jesus recognized in his sacrifice the way established by the Father for the redemption of humanity, and he followed this way. He also told his disciples that they would be associated with this sacrifice: "I tell you truly, you will weep and mourn while the world rejoices" (Jn 16:20). This prediction, however, is not the only one, nor is it the final word, because it is completed by the announcement that their pain will be changed into joy: "You will grieve for a time, but your grief will be turned into joy" (Jn 16:20). In the perspective of redemption, Christ's passion is oriented toward the resurrection. Human beings too are thus associated with the mystery of the cross in order to share joyfully in the mystery of the resurrection.

For this reason Jesus did not hesitate to proclaim the blessedness of those who suffer: "Blest are the sorrowing; they shall be consoled.... Blest are those persecuted for holiness' sake; the reign of God is theirs. Blest are you when they insult you and persecute you and utter every kind of slander against you because of me. Be glad and rejoice, for your reward is great in heaven" (Mt 5:4, 10-12). This blessedness can only be understood if one admits that human life is not limited to the time spent on earth, but is wholly directed to perfect joy and fullness of life in the hereafter. When accepted in love, earthly suffering is like a bitter kernel containing the seed of new life, the treasure of divine glory to be given man in eternity. The sight of a world burdened with evil and misfortunes of every sort is often so wretched; nevertheless the hope of a better world of love and grace is hidden within it. Hope is nourished on Christ's promise. With this support, those who suffer united in faith with him already experience in this life a joy that can seem humanly unexplainable. Heaven begins on earth; beatitude is anticipated, so to speak, in the Beatitudes. "In holy people," St. Thomas Aquinas said, "there is a beginning of future happiness..." (cf. *Summa Theol.,* I-II, q. 69, a. 2; cf. II-II, q. 8, a. 7).

Another basic principle of the Christian faith is the fruitfulness of suffering and, hence, the call of all who suffer to unite themselves with Christ's redemptive sacrifice. Suffering thus becomes an offering, an oblation. This has happened and still does in so many holy souls. Especially those who are oppressed by apparently senseless moral suffering find in Jesus' moral suffering the meaning of their own trials and they go with him into Gethsemane. In him they find the strength to accept pain with holy abandon and trusting obedience to the Father's will. They feel rising from within their hearts the prayer of Gethsemane: "But let it be as you would have it, Father, not as I" (Mk 14:36). They mystically identify with Jesus' resolve when he was arrested: "Am I not to drink the cup the Father has given me?" (Jn 18:11). In Christ they also find the courage to offer their pain for the salvation of all. They have learned the mysterious fruitfulness of every sacrifice from the offering on Calvary, according to the principle set forth by Jesus: "I solemnly assure you, unless the grain of wheat falls to the earth and dies, it remains just a grain of wheat. But if it dies, it produces much fruit" (Jn 12:24).

Jesus' teaching is confirmed by the Apostle Paul, who had a very vivid awareness of sharing in Christ's passion in his own life and of the cooperation he could thus offer for the good of the Christian community. Because of union with Christ in suffering, he could speak of completing in himself what was lacking in the sufferings of Christ for the sake of his body, the Church (cf. Col 1:24). Convinced of the fruitfulness of his union with the redeeming passion, he stated: "Death is at work in us, but life in you" (2 Cor 4:12). The tribulations of his life as an apostle did not discourage Paul, but strengthened his hope and trust, because he realized that the passion of Christ was the source of life: "As we have shared much in the suffering of Christ, so through Christ do we share abundantly in his consolation. If we are afflicted it is for your encouragement and salvation" (2 Cor 1:5-6). Looking at this model, the disciples of Christ better understand the Master's lesson, the vocation to the cross, for the full growth of the life of Christ in their personal lives and of the mysterious fruitfulness that benefits the Church.

The disciples of Christ have the privilege of understanding the "Gospel of suffering," which at all times has a salvific value, at least implicitly, because "down through the centuries and generations it has been seen that in suffering there is concealed a particular power that draws a person interiorly close to Christ, a special grace" *(SD* 26). Whoever follows Christ, whoever accepts St. Paul's theology of pain, knows that a precious grace, a divine favor, is connected with suffering, even if it is a grace that remains a mystery to us, because it is hidden under the appearances of a painful destiny. It is certainly not easy to discover in suffering the genuine divine love that wishes, through the acceptance of suffering, to raise human life to the level of Christ's saving love. However, faith enables us to cling to this mystery and despite everything, brings peace and joy to the soul of the one suffering. At times he even says with St. Paul: "I am filled with consolation, and despite my many afflictions my joy knows no bounds" (2 Cor 7:4).

Whoever relives the spirit of Christ's sacrifice is also moved to imitate him by helping others who are suffering. Jesus relieved the countless human sufferings around him. In this respect too he is a perfect model. He prescribed the command of mutual love that implies compassion and reciprocal aid. In the parable of the Good Samaritan, Jesus taught generous initiative on behalf of the suffering! He revealed his presence in all who are in need and pain, so that every act of helping the poor is done to Christ himself (cf. Mt 25:35-40).

In conclusion, I would like to leave you with Jesus' own words: "I assure you, as often as you did it for one of my least brothers, you did it for me" (Mt 25:40). This means that suffering, intended to sanctify those who suffer, is also meant to sanctify those who help and comfort them. We are always within the heart of the mystery of the saving cross!

General audience of April 27, 1994

The Church Sees Christ's Face in the Sick

In an earlier catechesis we discussed the dignity of those who suffer and their apostolate in the Church. Today, let us consider more specifically the sick and infirm, because the trials to which health is subjected, today as in the past, stand out clearly in human life. The Church must take to heart the need to be close to and to share in this painful mystery that links so many people of every era to Jesus Christ's state during his passion.

Everyone has some health problems. But some have more than others, such as those who suffer from a permanent affliction or who are subjected, by some irregularity or physical weakness, to many ailments. One need only go into a hospital to discover the world of the sick, the face of human pain and suffering. It is impossible for the Church not to see and help others to see in this face the features of the *Christus patiens,* and not to remember the divine plan that leads these lives in precarious health to a higher order of fruitfulness. There has to be an *ecclesia compatiens* with Christ, and with all those who suffer.

Jesus showed his compassion for the sick and the infirm, revealing his great kindness and tenderness of heart. He was also prepared to save those suffering in soul and body by means of his power to work miracles. He therefore worked many cures, so many that the sick flocked to him to benefit from his miraculous power. As the evangelist Luke said, numerous crowds assembled not only to hear him, but also "to be cured of their ailments" (Lk 5:5). In his dedication to freeing those who approached him from the burden of sickness or infirmity, Jesus allows us to glimpse the special intention of God's mercy in their regard. God is not indifferent to the sufferings caused by disease and offers his help to the sick through the saving plan that the incarnate Word reveals and fulfills in the world.

Indeed Jesus considered and treated the sick and infirm in the light of the saving work he was sent to accomplish. Bodily cures are part of this work of salvation and at the same time, they are signs of the great spiritual healing he brings humanity. This loftier intention of his emerged clearly when he first forgave the sins of a paralytic, brought before him to be cured. Aware of the unstated objections of some of the Scribes and Pharisees about the exclusive power of God in this regard, he declared: "'But that you may know that the Son of Man has authority to forgive sins on earth,' he said to the paralytic, 'I say to you, rise, pick up your mat and go home'" (Mk 2:10-11).

In this case and in many others, Jesus wanted to show by a miracle his power of freeing the human soul from its sins and purifying it. He cured the sick in view of this superior gift, which he offers to all men, in other words, spiritual salvation (cf. *CCC* 549). The sufferings of illness cannot cause us to forget the overriding importance of spiritual salvation for everyone.

Therefore in this perspective of salvation, Jesus asks for faith in his power as Savior. In the case of the paralytic just mentioned, Jesus responded to the faith of the four people who had brought him the sick man: "Jesus saw their faith," says Mark (2:5).

He asked for faith from the father of the epileptic, saying:

"Everything is possible to one who has faith" (Mk 9:23). He was deeply impressed by the centurion's faith: "You may go; as you have believed, let it be done for you" (Mt 8:13), and the Canaanite woman's: "O woman, great is your faith! Let it be done for you as you wish" (Mt 15:28). The miracle worked for the blind Bartimaeus was attributed to his faith: "Your faith has saved you" (Mk 10:52). He spoke similar words to the woman with a hemorrhage: "Daughter your faith has saved you" (Mk 5:34).

Jesus wished to inculcate the idea that faith in him, inspired by the desire to be healed, is meant to bring about spiritual salvation, which counts even more. From the gospel episodes cited, we know that in the divine plan, sickness can prove to stimulate faith. The sick are spurred to live the time of their illness as a more intense period of faith, and thus as a time for sanctification and for a more complete and conscious acceptance of the salvation that comes from Christ. It is a great grace to receive this light about the profound truth of illness!

The Gospel attests that Jesus associated his apostles with his power to heal the sick (cf. Mt 10:1). Thus, when he took leave of them before the ascension, he indicated the cures they were to work as one of the signs of the truth of the Gospel preaching (cf. Mk 16:17-20). The Gospel had to be brought to the world, to all peoples, amid humanly insurmountable difficulties. This explains why in the early days of the Church many miraculous healings occurred, emphasized in the Acts of the Apostles (cf. 3:1-10; 8:7; 9:33-35; 14:8-10; 28:8-10). In later periods, there have always been cures considered "miraculous." This is attested in authoritative historical and biographical sources and in the documentation of causes for canonization. We know that the Church is very demanding in this respect. This corresponds to her duty to be prudent. However, in the light of history, one cannot deny many cases which in every age prove the Lord's extraordinary intervention on behalf of the sick. Nevertheless, although the Church always relies on this kind of intervention, she does not feel dispensed from her daily obligation to comfort and care for the sick, both with her traditional charitable institutions and with the modern network of health-care services.

Indeed, in the perspective of faith, sickness assumes a greater nobility and proves especially effective in helping the apostolic ministry. In this regard, the Church does not hesitate to state her need for the sick and their sacrifice to the Lord in order to obtain more abundant graces for all humanity. If in the light of the Gospel illness can be a time of grace, a time when divine love more deeply penetrates those who suffer, there is no doubt that by their self-offering, the sick and the infirm sanctify themselves and contribute to the sanctification of others.

This is especially true for those who are dedicated to the service of the sick and the infirm. This service is a way of sanctification like illness itself. Down the centuries it has been a manifestation of the love of Christ, who is precisely the source of holiness.

This service requires dedication, patience and sensitivity, together with a great capacity for compassion and understanding. This is all the more so because, in addition to medical care in the strict sense, the sick also need moral comfort, as Jesus advises: "I was...ill and you cared for me" (Mt 25:36).

All this contributes to building up the body of Christ in charity, both through the effectiveness of the sacrifice of the sick, and through the practice of virtue in those who care for them or visit them. Thus the mystery of the Church, mother and minister of charity, is realized. Artists such as Piero della Francesca have painted it. In the *Polyptych of Mercy*, painted in 1448 and preserved in Borgo San Sepolcro, he shows the Virgin Mary as an image of the Church in the act of spreading her mantle to protect the faithful. They are the weak, the poor, the disheartened, the people, the clergy and consecrated virgins, as Bishop Fulbert of Chartres listed them in a homily written in 1208.

For an effective exercise of the therapy of love, we should strive to make our humble and loving service to the sick share in that of the Church our Mother, of which Mary is the perfect example (cf. *LG* 64-65).

General audience of June 15, 1994

Woman's Dignity Must Be Respected

In the catecheses on the dignity and the apostolate of lay people in the Church, we have explained the Church's thought and plans, applicable to all the faithful, both men and women. We would now like to consider more especially the role of the Christian woman, because of the importance that women have always had in the Church, and because of the hopes for the present and the future which can and must be placed in them. In our era, many voices have spoken demanding respect for woman's personal dignity and recognition of her real equality of rights with man, so as to offer her the full opportunity to fulfill her role in all sectors and at all levels in society.

The Church considers this movement, described as the emancipation, liberation or promotion of woman, in light of the revealed teaching on the dignity of the human person, on the value of individual persons—men and women—in the Creator's sight, and on the role attributed to woman in the work of salvation. The Church therefore holds that the recognition of woman's value has its ultimate source in the Christian awareness of the value of every person. This awareness, encouraged by the development of socio-cultural conditions and enlightened by the Holy Spirit, is gradually achieving a better understanding of the intentions of God's plan contained in revelation. We should seek to study these "divine intentions," especially in the Gospel, and to deal with the value of the life of lay people and in particular that of women. This is to foster their contribution to the Church's work for the spread of the Gospel message and for the coming of God's kingdom.

In the perspective of Christian anthropology, every human person has his own dignity; as a person, woman has no less a dignity than man. All too often woman, on the contrary, is considered as an object because of male selfishness, which has appeared in so many contexts in the past and is still being seen today. In today's situation many cultural and social reasons for this intervene and should be considered with serene objectivity. It is nonetheless not difficult to discover the influence of a tendency to domination and arrogance, which has found and is finding its victims especially in women and children. Moreover, the phenomenon was and is more general. It originated, as I wrote in *Christifideles Laici,* "in that unjust and deleterious mentality which considers the human being as a thing, as an object to buy and sell, as an instrument for selfish interests or for pleasure only" (n. 49).

Lay Christians are called to combat all forms of this mentality, even when transferred to films and advertising in order to intensify unrestrained consumerism. But women themselves have the duty to demand respect for their nature as persons, not descending to any form of complicity with what demeans their dignity.

Still on the same anthropological basis, the Church's doctrine teaches that the principle of woman's equality with man, in personal dignity and in fundamental human rights, should be consistently brought to all its consequences. The Bible itself reveals this equality. Although in the earliest mention of the creation of Adam and Eve (cf. Gen 2:4-25) woman was created by God "from the rib" of man, she was put next to man as another "self" with whom he could converse on an equal level, differently from any other creature. The other creation account belongs in this perspective (cf. Gen 1:26-28). It immediately declares that man created in God's image is "male and female." "God created man in his own image, in the image of God he created him; male and female, he created them" (Gen 1:27; cf. *MD* 6). This expresses the difference between the sexes, but especially their essential complementarity. One could say that the sacred author was eager to assert, once and for all, that woman bears within her a likeness with God no less than man does, and that she was created in God's image in her own personal characteristics as a woman, and not only because of what she has in common with man. This is equality in diversity (cf. *CCC* 369). Therefore perfection for woman is not to be like man, making herself masculine to the point of losing her specific qualities as a woman. Her perfection—which is also a secret of affirmation and of relative autonomy—is to be a woman, equal to man but different. In civil society and also in the Church, the equality and diversity of women must be recognized.

Diversity does not mean a necessary and almost implacable opposition. In the same biblical account of creation, the cooperation of man and woman is said to be a condition for the development of humanity and its work of exercising dominion over the universe: "Be fertile and multiply, fill the earth and subdue it" (Gen 1:28). In the light of the Creator's mandate, the Church maintains that "The first and basic expression of the social dimension of the person, then, is the married couple and the family" *(CL* 40). On a more general level, let us say that the renewal of the temporal order depends on the cooperation of man and woman.

But the subsequent Genesis text likewise shows that in the divine plan the cooperation of man and woman must be realized on a higher level, within the perspective of the association of the new Adam and the new Eve. In the Protoevangelium (cf. Gn 3:15), enmity is established between the devil and the woman. The first enemy of the evil one, woman is God's first ally (cf. *MD* 11). In the light of the Gospel, we can recognize the Virgin Mary in this woman. But in this text, we can also interpret a truth which concerns women in general. They were promoted, by God's gratuitous choice, to a primary role in the divine covenant. Indeed, this can be discerned in the figures of many women saints, true heroines of God's kingdom. But the work of woman in serving the good has also been demonstrated in history and in human culture.

The value attributed to the person and mission of woman is fully revealed in Mary. One need only reflect on the anthropological value of the basic aspects of Mariology to be convinced of this. "Mary is full of grace" from the very first moment of her existence, and thus is preserved from sin. Divine favor was manifestly granted to her with abundance—"blessed among all women"—and it was reflected from Mary onto the very condition of woman, excluding any inferiority (cf. *RMt* 7-11).

Furthermore, Mary was committed to God's definitive covenant with humanity. She has the task of consenting, in the name of humanity, to the Savior's coming. This role surpasses all claims of women's rights, even the most recent. Mary intervened in a supereminent and humanly unthinkable way in the history of humanity, and with her consent, contributed to the transformation of all human destiny.

In addition, Mary cooperated in the development of Jesus' mission, both by giving birth to him, raising him, and being close to him in his hidden life. Then, during the years of his public ministry, she did this by discreetly supporting his activities, beginning with Cana when she obtained the first demonstration of the Savior's miraculous power. As the Council says, Mary "brought about by her intercession the beginning of the miracles of Jesus the Messiah" *(LG* 58).

Above all, Mary cooperated with Christ in his work of

redemption, not only preparing Jesus for his mission, but also joining in his sacrifice for the salvation of all (cf. *MD* 3-5).

Today too, Mary's light can spread throughout the world of woman, to embrace woman's old and new problems, helping everyone to understand her dignity and to recognize her rights. Women receive a special grace; they receive it to live in covenant with God, at the level of their dignity and mission. They are called to be united in their own way—in an excellent way—with Christ's redeeming work. Women have a great role in the Church. This can be clearly understood in the light of the Gospel and of the sublime figure of Mary.

General audience of June 22, 1994

Women Bear an
Effective Witness to Faith

When speaking of the dignity and mission of woman according to the teaching and spirit of the Church, one must always look to the Gospel. The Christian sees, examines and judges everything in its light.

In the preceding catechesis we cast the light of revelation on woman's identity and destiny, presenting the Virgin Mary as the symbol according to what is indicated in the Gospel. However, in that same divine source we find other signs of Christ's will toward women. He speaks of them with respect and goodness, showing by his attitude his willingness to accept women and to seek their involvement in establishing God's kingdom in the world.

First we can recall the many cases in which women were healed (cf. *MD* 13), and those others in which Jesus revealed his Savior's heart, full of tenderness in his encounters with the suffering, be they men or women. "Do not weep!" he said to the widow of Nain (Lk 7:13). Then he gave her back the son he raised from the dead. This episode allows us to glimpse what must have been Jesus' personal feelings toward his mother Mary, in the dramatic setting of her sharing in his own passion and death. Jesus said tenderly to the deceased daughter of Jairus: "Little girl, I say to you, arise!" Having raised her, he "told them to give her something to eat" (Mk 5:41, 43). He showed his sympathy for the stooped woman whom he healed. In this case, by referring to Satan he also called to mind the spiritual salvation he was bringing that woman (cf. Lk 13:10-17).

On other pages of the Gospel we find Jesus expressing his admiration for the faith of some women. For example, in the case of the woman with a hemorrhage, he told her: "Your faith has made you well" (Mk 5:34). This praise has all the more value because the woman was subject to the segregation imposed by the old law. Jesus freed women from this social oppression too. In her turn, the Canaanite received this recognition from Jesus: "O woman, great is your faith!" (Mt 15:28). This praise has an altogether special meaning, if one considers that it was addressed to a stranger to Israel's world. We can also recall Jesus' admiration for the widow who gave her mite to the temple treasury (cf. Lk 21:1-4), and his appreciation of the service he received from Mary of Bethany (cf. Mt 26:6-13; Mk 14:3-9; Jn 12:1-8). He announced that her action would be known throughout the world.

In his parables too Jesus did not hesitate to draw examples and comparisons from the feminine world, unlike the rabbis' *midrash,* where only male figures appear. Jesus referred to both women and men. If one wishes to make a comparison, it could perhaps be said that women have the advantage. This at least means that Jesus avoided even appearing to attribute inferiority to women.

Again, Jesus allowed women as well as men to enter his kingdom. In opening it to women, he wanted to open it to children. When he said: "Let the children come to me" (Mk 10:14), he was reacting to the watchfulness of the disciples, who wanted to prevent the women from bringing their children to the Teacher. It could be said that he agreed with the women and their love for children!

In his ministry Jesus was accompanied by many women,

who followed him and assisted him and the community of disciples (cf. Lk 8:1-3). It was something new with respect to Jewish tradition. Having drawn those women to following him, Jesus thus showed how he went beyond the widespread prejudices in his surroundings, as in much of the ancient world, regarding the inferiority of women. This rejection of discrimination between men and women in his Church is part of his struggle against injustice and arrogance (cf. *MD* 13).

We must add that the Gospel also shows Jesus' kindness to several women sinners. He asked for their repentance, but without acting harshly toward them because of their mistakes, all the more so because the latter involved man's coresponsibility. Several episodes are very significant: the woman who went to the house of Simon the Pharisee (cf. Lk 7:36-50) was not only forgiven her sins, but was also praised for her love; the Samaritan woman became a messenger of her new faith (cf. Jn 4:7-37); the woman caught in adultery received with her pardon the simple exhortation not to sin again (cf. Jn 8:3-11; *MD* 14). Doubtless Jesus did not acquiesce in the face of evil, of sin, regardless of who commits it. But what understanding of human weakness he had and what goodness he showed toward those who were suffering from their own spiritual misery and more or less seeking in him a Savior!

Lastly, the Gospel attests that Jesus expressly called women to collaborate in his saving work. He not only allowed them to follow him to assist him and his community of disciples, but he asked for other forms of personal commitment. Thus he asked Martha for a faith commitment (cf. Jn 11:26-27). Responding to the Teacher's invitation, she made her profession of faith before Lazarus was raised. After the resurrection, he entrusted Mary Magdalene and the devout women who had gone to the tomb with the task of conveying his message to the apostles (cf. Mt 28:8-10; Jn 20:17-18). "Thus the women were the first messengers of Christ's resurrection for the apostles themselves" *(CCC* 641). These are rather eloquent signs of his desire to involve women too in the service of the kingdom.

Jesus' behavior is explained theologically by his intention to unify humanity. As St. Paul says, he wished to reconcile all men through his sacrifice "in one body" and make everyone "one new man" (Eph 2:15, 16), so that now "There is neither Jew nor Greek, there is neither slave nor free, there is neither male nor female; for you are all one in Christ Jesus" (Gal 3:28).

This is the conclusion of our catechesis—if Jesus Christ reunited man and woman in their equal status as children of God, he engaged both of them in his mission, not indeed by suppressing their differences, but by eliminating all unjust inequality and by reconciling all in the unity of the Church.

The history of the first Christian communities shows the great contribution women made to evangelization, beginning with "our sister Phoebe," as St. Paul calls her, "a deaconess of the Church at Cenchreae." He says: "She has been a helper of many and of myself as well" (Rom 16:1-2). Here I would like to pay homage to her memory and to the many other women who assisted the apostles at Cenchreae, in Rome and all Christian communities. With them we remember and extol all the other women—religious and lay—who down the centuries have witnessed to the Gospel and handed on the faith, exercising a great influence on the flourishing of a Christian atmosphere in the family and in society.

General audience of July 6, 1994

Women Are Essential
to the Church's Mission

All of Christ's followers can and must be active members in the Church by virtue of Baptism and Confirmation, and for married couples, by virtue of the sacrament of Matrimony. Today however, I would like to stress several points regarding the role of women, who are certainly called to their own most worthy and important collaboration in the Church's mission.

As do all the faithful, they share in the priestly, prophetic and kingly office of Christ. They express specific aspects which correspond and are suited to the feminine personality. Precisely for this reason they receive charisms that open concrete ways for their mission.

I cannot repeat here all that I wrote in the Apostolic Letter *Mulieris Dignitatem* (August 15, 1988) and in the Apostolic Exhortation *Christifideles Laici* (December 30, 1988) on the dignity of woman and the anthropological and theological foundations of the feminine state. There I spoke of her sharing in the life of human and Christian society and in the Church's mission with regard to the family, culture, the various states of life, the various areas of human activity, the various experiences of joy and sorrow, health and illness, and success and failure, which are part of everyone's life.

According to the principle enunciated by the 1987 Synod

and taken up in *Christifideles Laici:* "Without discrimination women should be participants in the life of the Church, and also in consultation and the decision-making process" (n. 51). Consequently, women have the possibility of participating in various diocesan and parish pastoral councils, as well as in diocesan synods and particular councils. According to the Synod's proposition, women "ought to be associated in the preparation of pastoral and missionary documents and ought to be recognized as co-workers in the mission of the Church in the family, in professional life and in the civil community" *(CL* 51). These are all areas where the involvement of qualified women can make a great contribution of wisdom and moderation, courage and dedication, and spirituality and fervor, for the good of the Church and society.

The whole ecclesial involvement of women can and should reflect the light of Gospel revelation, according to which a woman, as the representative of the human race, was called to give her consent to the Incarnation of the Word. The account of the annunciation suggests this truth when it tells us that only after the *fiat mihi* of Mary, who consented to be the mother of the Messiah, did "the angel depart from her" (Lk 1:38). The angel had completed his mission; he could bring to God humanity's "yes," spoken by Mary of Nazareth.

By following the example of Mary, whom Elizabeth shortly afterward called blessed for her having believed (cf. Lk 1:45), and recalling that Jesus also requested a profession of faith from Martha before he raised Lazarus (cf. Jn 11:26), the Christian woman will feel called in a unique way to profess and give witness to the faith. The Church needs resolute, consistent and faithful witnesses, who, in the face of the widespread doubts and disbelief on many levels in society today, will show in word and deed their commitment to the ever living Christ.

We cannot forget that, according to the Gospel account, on the day of Jesus' resurrection, the women first gave witness to this truth. They encountered doubt and perhaps a certain skepticism on the part of the disciples, who did not want to believe but in the end shared the women's faith. That moment too revealed the more intuitive nature of woman's mind, which makes her more open to revealed truth, more able to grasp the meaning of events and to accept the Gospel message. Down the centuries there have been countless proofs of this ability and this readiness.

Women have a very particular approach to handing on the faith and thus Jesus himself summoned them to evangelize. This happened with the Samaritan woman, whom Jesus met at Jacob's well and chose for the first expansion of the new faith into non-Jewish territory. The evangelist notes that, after personally expressing her faith in Christ, the Samaritan woman hastened to share it with others, enthusiastically but also with that sincerity which encourages the assent of faith: "Come, see a man who told me all that I ever did. Can this be the Christ?" (Jn 4:29). The Samaritan woman limited herself to asking a question and to drawing her fellow townsfolk to Jesus by the sincere humility that accompanied her account of the wondrous discovery she had made.

In her behavior we can glimpse the characteristic features of the feminine apostolate in our times too: humble initiative, respect for individuals without seeking to impose a way of seeing things, the invitation to repeat the same experience as a way of reaching the same personal conviction of faith.

It should be pointed out that in the family women have the opportunity and the responsibility to transmit the faith in the early training of their children. They are especially responsible for the joyful task of leading them to discover the supernatural world. The deep communion uniting her with them allows her to guide them effectively to Christ.

Nevertheless, for woman this task of handing on the faith is not meant to be carried out only in the family, but as we read in *Christifideles Laici,* "also in the various educational environments and, in broader terms, in all that concerns embracing the Word of God, its understanding and its communication, as well as its study, research and theological teaching" (n. 51). These are all indications of the role women have in the field of catechesis, which today has spread into broad and diverse areas, some of which were unthinkable in times past.

Woman has an understanding, sensitive and compassionate heart that allows her to give a delicate, concrete style to charity. We know that in the Church there have always been many women—religious and lay, mothers of families and single—who have been dedicated to relieving human suffering. They have written a marvelous record of attention to the needs of the poor, the sick, the infirm, the disabled and all those who in the past and often today as well have been abandoned or rejected by society. How many names spring from the heart to the lips when just a simple mention is made of those heroic figures of a charity exercised with utterly feminine tact and skill, both in families and institutes, in cases of physical illness and toward people suffering moral anguish, oppression or exploitation. None of this escapes the divine sight. The Church too bears in her heart the names and exemplary experiences of so many noble representatives of charity; sometimes she enrolls them among her saints.

Lastly, a significant area of women's apostolate in the Church is liturgical involvement. Women's participation in the celebrations, which they generally attend in larger numbers than men, shows faith commitment, spiritual sensitivity, attraction to piety and an attachment to liturgical prayer and the Eucharist.

In this cooperation of women with the priest and the other faithful in the Eucharistic celebration, we see reflected the light of the Virgin Mary's cooperation with Christ in the Incarnation and redemption. *Ecce ancilla Domini:* "Behold, I am the handmaid of the Lord; let it be to me according to your word" (Lk 1:38). Mary is the model of the Christian woman in the spirit and work of spreading across the world the mystery of the incarnate and redeeming Word.

In the Church, Jesus has entrusted the continuation of his redeeming work to the ministry of the Twelve and of their co-workers and successors. However, he wanted women to work at their side, as already appears from his associating Mary in his work. More specifically, he showed this intention by choosing Mary Magdalene as the first messenger of the risen one to the apostles. This cooperation appears from the very outset of evangelization. It is later repeated countless times from the first Christian centuries as an educational or scholastic activity, as involvement in the cultural apostolate or in social action, as collaboration with parishes, dioceses and various Catholic institutions. In every case the light of the *ancilla Domini* and of the other exemplary women immortalized by the Gospel shines on the ministry of woman. Even if many of them remain unknown, none is forgotten by Christ. In referring to Mary of Bethany, who had poured perfumed oil over his head, he said: "Wherever this Gospel is preached in the whole world, what she has done will be told..." (cf. Mt 26:13).

General audience of July 13, 1994

Mothers Share in God's Creative Work

Whatever professional opportunities women enjoy in society and the Church's apostolate, nothing can ever compare to the preeminent dignity that is theirs through motherhood lived in all its dimensions. We see that Mary, the model woman, fulfilled the mission to which she was called in the economy of the Incarnation and redemption by way of motherhood.

In the Apostolic Letter *Mulieris Dignitatem,* I emphasized that Mary's motherhood was united in an exceptional manner with her virginity, in such a way that it is also a model for women who consecrate their virginity to God (cf. n. 17). When we discuss the consecrated life we will return to this theme of virginity consecrated to the Lord. Continuing our reflection on the laity's role in the Church, in this catechesis I would like to consider woman's contribution to the human and Christian community through motherhood.

The value of motherhood was raised to the highest level in Mary, the Mother of God the eternal Word, made man in her virginal womb. Because of this motherhood, Mary is an essential part of the mystery of the Incarnation. In addition, by her union with Christ's redeeming sacrifice, she became the Mother of all Christians and of all people. In this respect too there shines the value attributed in God's plan to motherhood, which finds its unique, sublime expression in Mary, but whose reflection from that highest summit is seen in all human motherhood.

Today, perhaps more than ever, the idea of motherhood has had to be reevaluated. It is not an archaic concept, belonging to the mythological dawn of civilization. However much woman's roles can be multiplied and broadened, everything in her—physiology, psychology, almost connatural habit, moral, religious and even aesthetic sentiment—reveals and exalts her aptitude, ability and mission in bringing forth from herself a new being. She is much more disposed than man to the generative task. In virtue of pregnancy and childbirth, she is more intimately bound to the child, close to its whole development, more immediately responsible for its growth, more intensely sharing in its joy, sorrow, and risk in life. Although the mother's task must be coordinated with the father's presence and responsibility, the woman plays the most important role at the beginning of every human being's life. This role highlights an essential characteristic of the human person, who is not meant to remain closed within self but to be open and self-giving to others. *Gaudium et Spes* stated: "Man...cannot fully find himself except through a sincere gift of himself" *(GS* 24). This orientation toward others is essential to the person by virtue of the highest source of trinitarian love, from which man takes his origin. Motherhood represents an apex of this personalistic and community orientation.

Unfortunately, the value of motherhood has been contested and criticized. The greatness traditionally attributed to it has been presented as a backward idea, a social fetish. From an anthropological and ethical standpoint, some have thought that it limits the development of the female personality, and restricts women's freedom and their desire to take up and engage in other activities. Hence many women feel compelled to forgo motherhood not for other reasons of service and, ultimately, of spiritual motherhood, but to be able to devote themselves to professional work. Many even claim the right to suppress the life of their own child through abortion, as if the right they possess over their own body implied ownership rights over the unborn child. If some mothers have preferred to risk losing their life, they are accused of folly or selfishness, and in any case, of being socially backward. These aberrations show the fearful effects of abandoning the Christian spirit, which can guarantee and re-establish human values as well.

The concept of human personhood and communion derived from the Gospel does not allow us to approve the voluntary rejection of motherhood out of a mere desire to gain material advantages or satisfaction from performing certain activities. This is actually a distortion of the female personality, which is destined to unfold connaturally in motherhood.

The marriage union itself cannot be consumed in a selfishness for two. The love that unites the spouses seeks to extend itself in the child and to become the love of parents for their child. This is proven by the experience of so many couples in past centuries and in our times as well. These couples have found in the fruit of their love the way to strengthen and orient themselves and, in certain cases, to recover and be renewed.

On the other hand, the person of the child, even when just conceived, already enjoys rights that must be respected. The baby is not an object that the mother can dispose of at will, but a person to whom she is obliged to devote herself, with all the sacrifices that motherhood entails, but also with the joys it provides (cf. Jn 16:21).

Even in the psychosocial conditions of the world today, woman is thus called to be aware of the value of her vocation to motherhood as an affirmation of her own personal dignity, as the capacity and acceptance of extending herself to new lives, and in the light of theology, as a sharing in God's creative activity (cf. *MD* 18). This sharing is more intense in woman than in man by virtue of her specific role in procreation. Awareness of this privilege led Eve to say after her first childbirth, as we read in Genesis: "I have brought a man into being with the help of the Lord" (Gen 4:1). Since motherhood is a contribution *par excellence* to the propagation of life, the biblical text calls Eve "the mother of all the living" (Gen 3:20). This name makes us think of the realization in Eve—as in every mother—of the image of God, who, as Jesus proclaimed, "is not God of the dead, but of the living" (Mk 12:27).

In the light of biblical and Christian revelation, motherhood is seen as a sharing in God's love for men, a love which, according to the Bible, also has a maternal aspect of compassion and mercy (cf. Is 49:15; Dt 32:11; Ps 86:15; etc.).

Along with the motherhood lived in the family, there are many other marvelous forms of spiritual motherhood. These exist not only in the consecrated life, of which we will speak in due course, but wherever we see women working with maternal devotion on behalf of orphaned, sick or abandoned children, on behalf of the poor and unfortunate, and in many works and projects inspired by Christian charity. In these examples the basic principle of the Church's pastoral work, that of humanizing contemporary society, is magnificently fulfilled. Truly "woman in virtue of her special experience of motherhood seems to have a specific sensitivity toward the human person and all that constitutes the individual's true welfare, beginning with the fundamental value of life" *(CL* 51). Hence it is not an exaggeration to define woman's place in the Church and in society as a key position.

General audience of July 20, 1994

Women and the Ministerial Priesthood

Woman shares in the common priesthood of the faithful (cf. *LG* 10) in many ways, but especially through motherhood, not only spiritual motherhood, but also what many women choose as their own natural role with regard to conceiving, giving birth to and raising children: "A child is born into the world!" In the Church this task includes a lofty vocation and becomes a mission through woman's sharing in the common priesthood of the faithful.

Quite recently some women, even among Catholics, have asserted a claim to the ministerial priesthood. This demand is based on an untenable assumption. The priestly ministry is not a function one approaches on the basis of sociological criteria or legal procedures, but only in obedience to the will of Christ. Now, Jesus has entrusted the task of the ministerial priesthood only to males. Although he invited some women to follow him and even sought their cooperation, he did not call or allow any of them to be part of the group he entrusted with the ministerial priesthood in his Church. His will is seen in his behavior as a whole, as well as in significant actions which Christian tradition has constantly interpreted as directions to be followed.

Thus the Gospels indicate that Jesus never sent women on preaching missions, as he did with the group of the

Twelve, all of whom were male (cf. Lk 9:1-6), and also with the seventy-two, among whom no feminine presence is mentioned (cf. Lk 10:1-20).

Jesus gave authority over his kingdom to the Twelve alone: "As my Father appointed a kingdom for me, so do I appoint for you" (cf. Lk 22:29). He conferred only on the Twelve the mission and power of celebrating the Eucharist in his name (cf. Lk 22:19)—the essence of the ministerial priesthood. After his resurrection he gave to the apostles alone the power to forgive sins (cf. Jn 20:22-23) and to undertake the work of universal evangelization (cf. Mt 28:18-20; Mk 16: 16-18).

Christ's will was followed by the apostles and the other leaders of the first communities. They gave rise to the Christian tradition which since then has remained ever in force in the Church. I felt it my duty to confirm this tradition with the recent Apostolic Letter *Ordinatio Sacerdotalis* (May 22, 1994), declaring that "The Church has no authority whatsoever to confer priestly ordination on women and that this judgment is to be definitively held by all the Church's faithful" (n. 4). At issue here is fidelity to the pastoral ministry as Christ instituted it. Pius XII had already asserted this when he pointed out: "The Church has no power over the substance of the sacraments, that is, over anything that Christ the Lord, as attested by the sources of revelation, wanted to be maintained in the sacramental sign." He concluded that the Church is obliged to accept as normative "his practice of conferring priestly ordination on men alone" (cf. *AAS* 40 [1948], p. 5).

The permanent and normative value of this practice cannot be contested by saying that Christ's manifest will was due to the mentality of his time and to prejudice against women then and later. In reality, Jesus never conformed to a mentality unfavorable to women and indeed reacted against inequalities based on sexual differences. By calling women to follow him he showed that he went beyond the customs and outlook of his environment. If he reserved the ministerial priesthood to men, he did so with full freedom, and in his provisions and choices he took no stance unfavorable to women.

If a reason is sought as to why Jesus reserved admission to the ministerial priesthood to men, it can be discovered in the fact that the priest represents Christ himself in his relationship to the Church. Now, this relationship is spousal in nature: Christ is the bridegroom (cf. Mt 9:15; Jn 3:29; 2 Cor 11:2; Eph 5:25); the Church is the bride (cf. 2 Cor 11:2; Eph 5:25-27, 31-32; Rev 19:7; 21:9). Because the relationship between Christ and the Church is validly expressed in sacramental Orders, it is necessary that Christ be represented by a man. The distinction between the sexes is very significant in this case and cannot be disregarded without undermining the sacrament. Indeed, the specific nature of the sign used is essential to the sacraments. Baptism has to be performed with water that washes; it cannot be done with oil, which anoints, even though oil is more expensive than water. Analogously, the sacrament of Orders is celebrated with men, without questioning the value of persons. Thus, we can understand the Council's teaching that priests are ordained "in such a way that they can act in the person of Christ the head" *(PO* 2), "exercising the office of Christ, the shepherd and head, and according to their share of his authority" *(PO* 6).

Mulieris Dignitatem also explains the reason for Christ's decision, which has been faithfully preserved by the Catholic Church in her laws and discipline (cf. *MD* 26-27).

We should also point out that woman's true advancement consists in promoting what is proper and fitting to her as woman, that is, as a creature different from man and called herself, no less than man, to be a model of human personhood. This "emancipation" corresponds to the indications and instructions of Jesus, who wished to give woman a mission of her own in conformity with her natural difference from man. Carrying out this mission opens the way to the development of woman's personality, which can offer humanity, and the Church in particular, a service conforming to her own qualities.

We can close then by saying that Jesus, in not assigning the ministerial priesthood to women, did not put them in an inferior position, nor deprive them of a right that might be theirs, nor violate woman's equality with man. Rather, he acknowledged and respected their dignity. By instituting the ministerial priesthood for men, he did not intend to make them superior but to call them to a humble service modeled on that of the Son of Man (cf. Mk 10:45; Mt 20:28). By assigning woman a mission corresponding to her personality, he elevated her dignity and confirmed the right to her own originality in the Church too.

The example of Mary, the Mother of Jesus, completes the demonstration of respect for woman's dignity in the mission entrusted to her in the Church. Mary was not called to the ministerial priesthood. But the mission she received had no less value than a pastoral ministry; indeed, it was quite superior. She received a maternal mission at the highest level—to be the mother of Jesus Christ, and thus *Theotókos,* the Mother of God. This mission would broaden into a motherhood for all men and women in the order of grace.

The same can be said of the mission of motherhood that many women accept in the Church (cf. *MD* 27). They are placed by Christ in the wondrous light of Mary, which shines at the summit of the Church and creation.

General audience of July 27, 1994

Married Life Is a True Way of Holiness

We have stressed woman's role in the Church. Obviously, the task of man is no less important. The Church needs the collaboration of both to carry out her mission. The basic context where this cooperation is shown is married life, the family, which is "the first, primordial expression of the social dimension of the person" *(CL 40)*.

The Second Vatican Council acknowledged: "The classes and duties of life are many, but holiness is one," and expressly cited married life as a way of holiness:

> Married couples and Christian parents should follow their own proper path (to holiness) by faithful love. They should sustain one another in grace throughout the entire length of their lives. They should imbue their offspring, lovingly welcomed as God's gift, with Christian doctrine and the evangelical virtues. In this manner, they offer all men the example of unwearying and generous love; in this way they build up the brotherhood of charity; in so doing, they stand as the witnesses and cooperators in the fruitfulness of Holy Mother Church; by such lives, they are a sign and a participation in that very love, with which Christ loved his bride and for which he delivered himself up for her *(LG 41)*.

Thus the path of the married couple and the family has two essential aspects: sanctification in a union of faithful love, and sanctification in fruitfulness, by fulfilling the task of raising their children as Christians.

Today we wish to reflect on the way of holiness proper to Christian married people, and therefore, to most of the faithful. It is an important way, but one badly shaken today by certain intellectual trends fueled by the rampant hedonism in society as a whole.

We go back to the Council's beautiful statement that the way of marriage is a way of holiness, because it is meant to be a "sign and a participation in that very love with which Christ loved his bride and for which he delivered himself up for her."

In this ecclesiological view, Christ's love is the source and foundation of the love uniting the spouses. It should be stressed that true conjugal love is meant, and not a mere spontaneous impulse. Today sexuality is often exalted to the point of obscuring the profound nature of love. Certainly, sexual life too has its own genuine value, which can never be underestimated. But it is a limited value that is an insufficient basis for the marriage union, which by its nature depends on total personal commitment. Every sound psychology and philosophy of love agrees on this point. Christian teaching also emphasizes the qualities of the individuals' unitive love and casts a higher light on it, raising it—by virtue of a sacrament—to the level of grace and of sharing in the divine love of Christ. Along these lines St. Paul says of marriage: "This is a great mystery" (Eph 5:32), in reference to Christ and the Church. For the Christian, this theological mystery is at the root of the ethics of marriage, conjugal love and sexual life itself: "Husbands, love your wives, as Christ loved the Church and gave himself up for her" (Eph 5:25).

Grace and the sacramental bond enable conjugal life, as a sign of and share in the love of Christ the bridegroom, to be a way of holiness for Christian spouses. At the same time, it is an effective incentive for the Church to invigorate the communion of love that distinguishes her. The Council stated that married couples "build up the brotherhood of charity" *(LG* 41).

The Council states and explains the demands of this noble love of Christian couples. In asserting that they must support each other, it underscores the altruistic nature of their love, a love which finds concrete expression in mutual support and generous devotion. By speaking of a faithful love all through life, the Council calls attention to fidelity as an obligation based on the absolute fidelity of Christ the bridegroom. The appeal to this duty is more necessary than ever, especially with regard to one of the great evils of contemporary society, the widespread plague of divorce. This has serious consequences for married couples themselves and their children. With divorce, husband and wife inflict a deep wound on each other, fail to keep their own word and break a vital bond. At the same time they harm their children. How many children suffer over the departure of one or the other parent! It must be said over and over again to everyone that, with his absolutely faithful love, Jesus Christ gives Christian spouses the strength of fidelity and enables them to resist the temptation to separate, which today is so widespread and seductive.

We must remember that, since the love of Christ the bridegroom for the Church is a redemptive love, the love of Christian spouses becomes an active participation in redemption. Redemption is tied to the cross. This helps us understand and appreciate the meaning of the trials that the couple's life is certainly not spared, but which in God's plan are meant to reinforce their love and bring greater fruitfulness to their married life. Far from promising his married followers an earthly paradise, Jesus Christ offers them the opportunity and the vocation to make a journey with him which, through difficulties and suffering, will strengthen their union and lead them to a greater joy, as proven by the experience of so many Christian couples, in our day as well.

Fulfilling the task of procreation contributes to the sanctification of married life, as we noted in regard to motherhood. The love of husband and wife, which is not turned in on itself, but according to the impulse and law of nature is open to new life, becomes with the help of God's grace an exercise of holy and sanctifying charity, in which the spouses contribute to the Church's growth.

The same thing occurs in carrying out the task of education, which is a duty connected with procreation. As the Second Vatican Council said, Christian married couples "should imbue their offspring, lovingly welcomed as God's gift, with Christian doctrine and the evangelical virtues" *(LG* 41). It is the most essential apostolate of family life. This work of giving their children moral and spiritual formation also sanctifies the parents, who are themselves blessed with a deeper, renewed faith, as the experience of Christian families often shows.

Once again we can conclude that married life is a way of holiness and apostolate. This catechesis thus serves to deepen our view of the family, which is so important for the Church and the world.

General audience of August 3, 1994

Single People Contribute
to the Church's Holiness

From earliest times in the Christian tradition, particular attention was given to women who, after losing their husbands, were alone in life and were often poor and defenseless. Already in the Old Testament, widows were often mentioned because of their poverty and recommended to the fraternal care and solidarity of the community and in particular, of those responsible for the law (cf. Ex 22:21; Dt 10:18; 24:17; 26:12; 27:19).

A spirit of charity toward widows fills the Gospels, the Acts of the Apostles and the Letters. Jesus repeatedly showed them thoughtful attention. For example, he publicly praised a poor widow's offering for the Temple (cf. Lk 21:3; Mk 12:43); he was moved to compassion at the sight of the widow in Nain as she accompanied her dead son's funeral procession. He approached her, saying gently: "Do not weep," and gave her back the young man he had restored to life (cf. Lk 7:11-15). The Gospel also reminds us of Jesus' words on the "need to pray always, without becoming weary," taking as an example the widow who obtained justice from the dishonest judge by her persistence (Lk 18:5), and Jesus' other words, severely reprimanding the scribes who "devour the houses of widows," but make a hypocritical show of reciting long prayers (cf. Mk 12:40; Lk 20:47).

Christ's attitude, which fulfills the true spirit of the old covenant, is at the root of the pastoral exhortations of St. Paul and St. James concerning spiritual and charitable aid to widows: "Honor widows who are truly widows" (1 Tim 5:3); "Religion that is pure and undefiled before God is this: to care for widows and orphans in their affliction..." (Jas 1:27).

However, in Christian communities the widows' lot was not only to be cared for. They also had an active role, an almost distinctive sharing in the universal vocation of Christ's disciples to the life of prayer.

The First Letter to Timothy indicates that a basic duty entrusted to widows was "to continue in supplications and prayers night and day" (5:5). Luke's Gospel introduces a model of holy widowhood in the person of "Anna, daughter of Phanuel," widowed after only seven years of marriage. The Gospel states that she "never left the Temple, but worshipped night and day with fasting and prayer" (Lk 2:36-37). She had the great joy of being in the Temple when the Child Jesus was presented. In their distress, widows can and must similarly rely on the valuable graces of the spiritual life, to which they are asked to respond generously.

In the pastoral and spiritual framework of the Christian community, there was also a "roll" to which a widow could belong. To use the words of the Letter quoted above, she was to be "no less than sixty years old [in other words, elderly], married only once, with a reputation for good works, namely, that she has raised children, practiced hospitality, washed the feet of the holy ones [an ancient rite of hospitality adopted by Christianity], helped those in distress, involved herself in every good work..." (1 Tim 5:9-10).

In all this, the early Church was offering an example of charitable solidarity (cf. Acts 6:1), which we find again in many other periods of Christian history. This was especially so when, for social and political reasons, wars and epidemics, etc., the phenomenon of widowhood or other forms of solitary

life assumed alarming dimensions. The Church's charity cannot be passive.

Today there are many other cases of people on their own,
to whom the Church cannot fail to show sensitivity and concern. First of all there are the "separated" and "divorced," to
whom I devoted special attention in the Apostolic Exhortation
Familiaris Consortio (cf. n. 83). Then there are "unwed mothers," who are subject to particular moral, financial and social
difficulties. I would like to say to all these people that whatever
their personal responsibility for the tragic situation they are in,
they continue to belong to the Church. Pastors, who know
about their trials, should not abandon them to themselves. On
the contrary, they should do all they can to help and comfort
them, and to make them still feel part of Christ's flock.

Even when the Church cannot allow practices that would
contradict the demands of truth and the common good of families and society itself, she should never give up loving,
understanding and being close to all those in difficulty. The
Church feels especially close to people with a broken marriage
in their past, who persevere in fidelity, foregoing a second
marriage and dedicating themselves as best they can to raising
their children. They deserve support and encouragement from
everyone. It would be impossible for the Church and the Pope
not to praise them for their beautiful witness of Christian consistency, lived generously in the midst of trial.

However, since this catechesis, like the others in our
series, is dedicated to the lay apostolate, I would once more
like to mention the large numbers of single people, and especially widows and widowers. Having fewer family obligations,
they willingly devote themselves to promoting Christian activities in parishes or in more extensive projects. Their own
lives are thus raised to a higher level of participation in the
Church's life as the fruit of a higher degree of charity. Consequently, the Church and the world benefit from the generous
dedication of people who thus find the way to attain a higher

quality of life, expressing themselves fully in service to their brothers and sisters.

We close then by reaffirming what we read in the Second Vatican Council, that the example of charitable good works should be given not only by Christian married couples and parents. "A like example, but one given in a different way, is that offered by widows and single people, who are able to make great contributions toward holiness and apostolic endeavor in the Church" *(LG* 41). Whatever the cause of their state in life, many of these people can recognize the higher plan of God's wisdom directing their lives and leading them to holiness on the way of the cross, a cross which in their circumstances proves especially fruitful.

General audience of August 10, 1994

Children Are a
Special Gift to the Church

We cannot overlook the role of children in the Church, but must speak of them with great affection. They are heaven's smile entrusted to earth. They are the true gems of the family and society and the Church's delight. They are like the "lilies of the field," of which Jesus said that "not even Solomon in all his splendor was arrayed like one of these" (Mt 6:28-29). They are Jesus' favorites, and the Church, the Pope, cannot fail to hear beating in their own heart the feelings of love for them in Christ's heart.

To tell the truth, we already find in the Old Testament signs of special concern for children. The First Book of Samuel (1-3) describes the call of a child to whom God entrusted a message and mission for his people. Children participate in the worship and prayers of the assembly of the people. As we read in the prophet Joel (2:16): "Gather the children and the infants at the breast." In the Book of Judith (4:10f.) we find the penitential prayer raised by all "with their wives and children." At the Exodus God already showed a special love for orphans, who are under his protection (Ex 22:21f.; cf. Ps 68:6).

In Psalm 131 a child is the image of abandonment to God's love: "I have stilled and quieted my soul like a weaned child. Like a weaned child on its mother's lap, so is my soul within me" (v. 2).

It is significant that later in salvation history the powerful voice of the prophet Isaiah (7:14f.; 9:1-6) announced the fulfillment of messianic hope in the birth of Emmanuel, a child destined to reestablish the kingdom of David.

Here the Gospel tells us that the child born of Mary is the foretold Emmanuel (cf. Mt 1:22-23; Is 7:14). This child was then consecrated to God during the presentation in the temple (cf. Lk 2:22), blessed by the prophet Simeon (cf. Lk 2:28-35) and welcomed by the prophetess Anna, who praised God and "talked about the child to all who looked forward to the deliverance of Jerusalem" (Lk 2:38).

In his public life Jesus showed great love for children. The evangelist Mark attests: "He embraced them and blessed them, placing his hands on them" (10:16). It was a "tender and generous love" *(CL* 47) by which he attracted children and their parents, about whom we read: "They were bringing their little children to him to have him touch them" (Mk 10:13). In *Christifideles Laici,* I recalled that the little ones "are the eloquent symbol and splendid image of those moral and spiritual conditions that are essential for entering the kingdom of God and for living the logic of total confidence in the Lord" (n. 47). These conditions are simplicity, sincerity and receptive humility.

The disciples were called to become like children. The "little ones" accepted revelation as a gift of the Father's gracious will (cf. Mt 11:25f.). For this reason too children should be welcomed like Jesus himself: "Whoever welcomes one such child for my sake welcomes me" (Mt 18:5).

For his part Jesus professed deep respect for children, and warned: "See that you never despise one of these little ones. I assure you, their angels in heaven constantly behold my heavenly Father's face" (Mt 18:10). When the children shouted "Hosanna to the Son of David," Jesus appreciated and justified their attitude as praise given to God (cf. Mt 21:15-16). Their homage contrasted with his enemies' disbelief.

Jesus' love and esteem for children are a light for the Church, which imitates her Founder. She cannot fail to welcome children as he did. It should be noted that this welcome can already be seen in the Baptism administered to children, even if they are infants. By this sacrament they become members of the Church. From the beginning of their human development, Baptism fosters their growth in the life of grace. The Holy Spirit's influence gives direction to their first inner inclinations, even if they are not capable yet of making an act of faith. They will do so later as a confirmation of that early influence.

Here we see the importance of infant Baptism, which frees them from original sin, makes them children of God in Christ and gives them a share in the Christian community's life of grace.

The presence of children in the Church is also a gift for us adults. It makes us better understand that the Christian life is first and foremost a gratuitous gift of divine sovereignty: "Children are a continual reminder that the missionary fruitfulness of the Church has its life-giving basis not in human means and merits, but in the absolute gratuitous gift of God" *(CL 47)*.

Children are an example of innocence, which discloses the simplicity of holiness. They live a holiness appropriate to their age and thus contribute to building the Church.

Unfortunately, there are many children who suffer: the physical sufferings of hunger, want, disease or illness; moral sufferings resulting from mistreatment by their parents, from their discord, from the exploitation to which the cynical selfishness of adults sometimes subjects them. How can our hearts not be moved by certain situations of unspeakable pain involving defenseless creatures guilty of nothing other than being alive? How can we not protest on their behalf, lending our voices to those who cannot make their own interests known? The only comfort in this great wretchedness is the word of faith, which assures us that God's grace transforms these sufferings into an opportunity for mysterious union with the sacrifice of the innocent Lamb. They contribute to enhancing the value of these children's lives and to the spiritual progress of humanity (cf. *CL* 47).

The Church feels zealously committed to promoting the Christian formation of children, something that is frequently inadequate. It is a question of forming them in the faith by teaching Christian doctrine, in charity toward all, in prayer according to the most beautiful traditions of the Christian family, which for many of us are unforgettable and ever blessed!

From the psychological and pedagogical standpoint, we know that a child easily and willingly begins to pray when encouraged to do so, as the experience of so many parents, educators, catechists and friends shows. The responsibility of the family and the school for these matters should be pointed out continually.

The Church urges parents and educators to see that their little ones are formed in the sacramental life, especially in using the sacrament of forgiveness and in participating in the Eucharistic celebration. She advises all her pastors and those who work with them to make a serious effort to adapt to children's abilities. As far as possible, especially when religious celebrations are planned exclusively for children, the adaptations provided for by the liturgical norms are advisable. If wisely used, they can have a very significant effect.

In this catechesis devoted to the "apostolate of the laity," it is natural for me to close with an incisive expression of my predecessor, St. Pius X. In explaining why he lowered the age for First Communion, he said: "There will be saints among the children." And indeed, there have been saints. But today we can add: "There will be apostles among the children."

Let us pray that this prediction, this wish, will be increasingly fulfilled, as was Pius X's.

General audience of August 17, 1994

Young People's Involvement in the Lay Apostolate

Affirming the need for Christian education and reminding pastors of their gravest duty to provide it for all, the Second Vatican Council observed that the young "...are the hope of the Church" *(Gravissimum Educationis* 2). What are the reasons for this hope?

One could say that the first is of a demographic order. Young people, "in a great many countries of the world...represent half the entire population, and often constitute in number half of the People of God living in those countries" *(CL* 46).

But there is another even stronger reason of a psychological, spiritual and ecclesiological kind. The Church today observes the generosity of many young people, their desire to make the world a better place and to make the Christian community advance (cf. *CL* 46). Thus she focuses her attention on them, seeing in them a privileged participation in the hope which comes to her from the Holy Spirit. The grace operating in young people paves the way for the Church's progress as regards both her expansion and her quality. Very rightly we can speak of the Church of the young, remembering that the Holy Spirit renews in everyone—even in the elderly, provided they remain open and receptive—the vibrance of grace.

This conviction stems from the reality of the Church's origins. Jesus began his ministry and the work of founding the Church when he was about thirty. To give life to the Church, he chose at least some young people. With their cooperation he wished to inaugurate a new age, to give new direction to the history of salvation. He chose them and trained them with a spirit that could be called youthful, spelling out the principle: "No one pours new wine into old wineskins" (Mk 2:22). This is a metaphor of the new life which springs from the eternal and merges with the desire for change and novelty, characteristic of young people. Even the radicality of dedication to a cause, typical of a youthful age, must have been present in those persons whom Jesus chose as future apostles. We can deduce this from his conversation with the rich young man, who did not have the courage to follow his proposal (cf. Mk 10:17-22), and from Peter's subsequent appraisal (cf. Mk 10:28).

The Church was born from those youthful impulses that came from the Holy Spirit, dwelling in Christ and communicated by him to his disciples and apostles, and then to the communities which they gathered from the days of Pentecost.

The sense of trust and friendship with which the Church viewed youth right from the start derives from these same impulses. This can be deduced from the words of the Apostle John, who was young when Christ called him, even though he was already old when he wrote. "I write to you, children, because you know the Father.... I write to you, young men, because you are strong and the word of God remains in you, and you have conquered the evil one" (1 Jn 2:14).

This reference to youthful vitality is interesting. It is known that young people appreciate physical strength, which is expended in sports, for example. But St. John wished to recognize and praise the spiritual vigor shown by the young people of the Christian community to whom he addressed his letter. This force comes from the Holy Spirit and obtains the victory in struggles and temptation. Young people's moral victory is a manifestation of the power of the Holy Spirit, which Jesus promised to his disciples. It urges the young Christians of today, like those in the first century, to participate actively in the life of the Church.

It is a constant factor, not only of psychology, but also of the spirituality of youth that they are not satisfied with passive adherence to the faith. Young people feel the desire to contribute actively to the Church's development, as well as to that of civil society. This is especially evident in many fine girls and boys of today, who wish to be "leading characters in evangelization and participants in the renewal of society. Youth is a time of an especially intensive discovery of one's 'self' and one's 'choice of life'" *(CL* 46). Today, more than ever, it is necessary to help young people to get to know themselves with regard to what is beautiful and promising within them. Their qualities and creative capacity should be oriented to the highest aim that can attract and infect them with enthusiasm: the good of society, solidarity toward all their brothers and sisters, the spread of the Gospel ideal of life and concrete commitment to neighbor, participation in the Church's efforts to encourage the advent of a better world.

In this light, let us say that today we need to encourage young people to dedicate themselves in particular to promoting the values that they themselves most appreciate and want to assert. As the Fathers of the 1987 Synod said, "The sensitivity of young people profoundly affects their perceiving of the values of justice, non-violence and peace. Their hearts are disposed to fellowship, friendship and solidarity. They are greatly moved by causes that relate to the quality of life and the conservation of nature" *(Ench. Vat.,* 2206).

These values certainly conform to the teaching of the Gospel. We know that Jesus proclaimed a new order of justice and love. In defining himself as "meek and humble of heart" (Mt 11:29), he rejected all violence, and desired to give man his peace, which is more genuine, consistent and permanent than that of the world (cf. Jn 14:27). These are interior and spiritual values. But we know that Jesus himself encouraged his followers to express them in mutual love, fellowship, friendship, solidarity, respect for persons and for nature itself, which is the work of God and the area of man's collaboration with him. Thus young people find in the Gospel a most worthwhile, sincere support, which they feel corresponds to their aspirations and plans.

On the other hand, it is true that young people are also "troubled by anxieties, by disappointment, by anguish and fear of the world, as well as by the temptations that come with their state" *(CL* 46). This is the other facet of the reality of youth which cannot be ignored. But while being wisely demanding with youth, a sincere affection for them will lead to discovering the most appropriate ways to help them overcome their difficulties. Perhaps the best way is in commitment to the lay apostolate, as a service to their own brothers and sisters, near and far, in communion with the evangelizing Church.

I hope that young people will find ever wider openings in the apostolate. The Church must introduce them to the message of the Gospel with its promises and demands. In turn, young people must express their aspirations and their plans to the Church. "This mutual dialogue, by taking place with great cordiality, clarity and courage, will provide a favorable setting for the meeting and exchange between generations, and will be a source of richness and youthfulness for the Church and for civil society" *(CL* 46).

The Pope will never tire of repeating the invitation to dialogue, and of urging the involvement of youth. He has done so in a great many texts addressed to them, and in particular in the *Letter on the Occasion of the International Youth Year* proclaimed by the United Nations (1985). He has done so and does it in numerous meetings with youth groups in parishes, associations, movements, and especially in the Palm Sunday liturgies and his world youth meetings, as at Santiago de Compostela, Czestochowa and Denver.

This is one of the most comforting experiences of my pontifical ministry, as it is that of the pastoral activities of my brother bishops throughout the world. Like the Pope, they see the Church advancing with the youth in prayer, at the service of humanity, in evangelization. We all yearn to conform increasingly to the example and teaching of Jesus, who called people to follow him in the manner of "children" and "young people."

General audience of August 31, 1994

The Elderly Can Devote
Themselves to the Community or Parish

In today's society, with its cult of productivity, elderly people risk being considered unproductive and a burden to others. The prolongation of life itself aggravates the problem of assisting the growing number of elderly who need looking after. Perhaps even more, they need affectionate, caring presences to fill their loneliness. The Church is aware of this problem and seeks to help resolve it, even at the level of assistance, despite the difficulty caused her by the lack of personnel and means, today more than in the past. She does not cease to promote the interventions of religious institutes and voluntary lay groups to meet this need for assistance. The Church reminds all, young people and adults, of their duty to think of their dear ones who, generally, have done so much for them.

The Church stresses with particular joy that senior citizens also have their place and use in the Christian community. They continue to be full members of the community and are called to contribute as far as they can to its development with their witness, prayer and activities.

The Church knows well that many people draw close to God especially in the so-called "third age." Precisely in this period, they can be helped to rejuvenate their spirit through reflection and sacramental life. The experience accumulated in the course of the years leads the elderly to understand the limits of worldly things and to feel in their earthly lives a deeper need for the presence of God. The disappointments they have known in some circumstances have taught them to trust in God. Their acquired wisdom can be a great advantage not only to their relatives, but to the whole Christian community.

On the other hand, the Church recalls that in the Bible the older person is presented as the man of wisdom, judgment, discernment and counsel (cf. Sir 25:4-6). This is why the sacred authors recommend associating with the elderly, as we read especially in Sirach (6:34): "Frequent the company of the elders; whoever is wise, stay close to them." The Church also repeats the double warning. "Insult no man when he is old, for some of us, too, will grow old" (Sir 8:6). "Reject not the tradition of old men which they have learned from their fathers" (Sir 8:9). She regards with admiration the tradition of Israel which bound the new generations to listen to the old. "Our fathers" chants the Psalm, "have declared to us the deeds you did in their days, in days of old" (Ps 44:2).

The Gospel also proposes the ancient precept of the Law: "Honor your father and your mother" (Ex 20:12; Dt 5:16). Christ called attention to this, protesting against the expedients used to avoid it (cf. Mk 7:9-13). In the tradition of her Magisterium and her pastoral ministry, the Church has always taught and demanded respect and honor for parents, as well as material help in their need. This recommendation to respect elderly parents and to give them material help retains all its value in our age too. Today more than ever, the atmosphere of community solidarity which must reign in the Church, can lead to the practice—in old and new ways—of filial charity, in the concrete application of this duty.

In the context of the Christian community, the Church honors the elderly, recognizing their qualities and abilities and inviting them to carry out their mission. This mission is not

linked to certain times and conditions of life only, but can be
carried out in different forms according to the circumstances of
each individual. For this reason they should resist the "temptation of taking refuge in nostalgia, in a never-to-return past, or
fleeing from present responsibility because of difficulties encountered in a world of one novelty after another" *(CL* 48).

Even when they are struggling to understand the evolution of the society in which they live, elderly people must not
retreat into a state of voluntary withdrawal, accompanied by
pessimism and reluctance to "interpret" the reality approach-
ing. It is important that they make the effort to look to the
future with confidence, supported by Christian hope and faith,
and growing in the grace of Christ which spreads throughout
the world.

In the light of this faith and with the fortitude of this
hope, the elderly can better discover that they are destined to
enrich the Church with their qualities and the wealth of their
spirituality. Indeed, they can offer a witness of faith enriched
by a long experience of life, a judgment full of wisdom about
the things and situations of the world, a clearer vision of the
demands of mutual love, a more serene conviction of the divine love, which directs every life and all the world's history.
As Psalm 92 already promised to the "just" of Israel: "They
shall bear fruit even in old age; vigorous and sturdy shall they
be, declaring how just is the Lord..." (vv. 14-15).

Moreover, a serene view of contemporary society can
make us recognize that it favors a new development of the
mission of older people in the Church (cf. *CL* 48). Today a
number of senior citizens retain good health, or regain it more
easily than in the past. They can therefore be of service to the
parish or in other sectors.

In fact, some elderly people make themselves very useful, where their competence and concrete possibilities can be
employed. Age does not prevent them from devoting themselves to the needs of the community, for example, in worship,

in visiting the sick, in helping the poor. Even when advancing age imposes the reduction or suspension of these activities, older persons retain the commitment to offer the Church the contribution of their prayer and to accept possible discomforts for love of the Lord.

Finally, we should remember, as old people, that with health problems and the decline of our physical strength, we are especially associated with Christ in his passion and on the cross. It is therefore possible to penetrate ever more deeply into this mystery of the redeeming sacrifice and to give the witness of faith to this mystery, of the courage and hope that derive from it in the various difficulties and trials of old age. Everything in the life of the elderly may serve to fulfill their earthly mission. Nothing is in vain. On the contrary, their cooperation, precisely because it is hidden, is yet more valuable for the Church (cf. *CL* 48).

We should add that old age is also a gift for which we are called to give thanks. It is a gift for the person on in years, for society and for the Church. Life is always a great gift. Indeed, for the faithful followers of Christ, we can speak of a special charism granted to older persons that they may use their talents and physical strength appropriately, for their own joy and for the good of others.

May the Lord wish to grant all our brothers and sisters who are getting on in years the gift of the Spirit, foretold and invoked by the Psalmist when he sang: "Send forth your light and your fidelity; they shall lead me on and bring me to your holy mountain, to your dwelling place. Then will I go in to the altar of God, the God of my gladness and joy.... Why are you so downcast, O my soul? Why do you sigh within me? Hope in God! For I shall again be thanking him, in the presence of my savior and my God" (Ps 43:3-5). How is it possible not to remember that in the Greek version of the so-called Septuagint, followed by the Latin Vulgate, the original Hebrew of verse 4 was interpreted and translated as an invocation to God "who brings joy to my youth" *(Deus, qui laetificat iuventutem meam)?* We older priests have repeated these words of the Psalm which introduced the Mass for so many years. Nothing prevents us in our prayers and personal aspirations from continuing, even as elderly people, to invoke and to praise God who brings joy to our youth!

General audience of September 7, 1994

The Spirit Bestows
Abundant Lay Charisms

A great hope enlivens the Church on this eve of the third millennium of the Christian era. She is preparing to enter it with an intense effort to renew all her forces, among which is the Christian laity.

The more vivid awareness that lay people have been acquiring of their own mission in the Church's life, in conjunction with a notable development of ecclesiology, is a positive reality in the history of the last century. Too often in the past the Church seemed to lay people to be identified with the hierarchy, so that their attitude was rather that of someone who must receive and not of someone called to action and a specific responsibility. Fortunately, today many realize that, in union with those who exercise the ministerial priesthood, lay people too *are* the Church and have challenging tasks in her life and growth.

The Church's pastors themselves invited the laity to assume this responsibility. In particular, Pius XI's promotion of Catholic Action opened a decisive chapter in the development of the laity's work in the religious, social, cultural, political and even economic fields. The historical experience and doctrinal development of Catholic Action provided new incentives, opened new perspectives, and kindled new fires. The hierarchy proved more and more favorable to lay action, even to that kind of apostolic mobilization Pius XII often sought. In his 1952 Easter message, he urged and invited: "At the priests' side let the laity speak, who have learned to penetrate hearts and minds with words and love. Yes, bearers of life, permeate every place: factories, workshops, fields, wherever Christ has a right to enter" *(Discorsi e radiomessaggi de Sua Santità Pio XII,* vol. XIV, p. 64). Pius XII's appeals invigorated many initiatives of Catholic Action and of other associations and movements, which increasingly spread the activity of lay Christians in the Church and in society.

The subsequent interventions of Popes and bishops, especially at Vatican II (cf. the Decree *Apostolicam Actuositatem),* at the synods and in many post-conciliar documents, increasingly confirmed and promoted a reawakening of the laity's ecclesial awareness, which today is a source of hope for the Church's growth.

It is possible to speak of a new lay life, rich in immense human potential, as fact. The true value of this life comes from the Holy Spirit, who abundantly bestows his gifts on the Church, as he has done since the beginning on the day of Pentecost (cf. Acts 2:3-4; 1 Cor 12:7f.). In our day too, many signs and great witness have been given by individuals, groups and movements generously dedicated to the apostolate. They show that the marvels of Pentecost have not ceased, but are renewed abundantly in the Church today. It is obvious that in addition to a considerable development in the doctrine of the charisms, there has also been a new flowering of active lay people in the Church. It is not by chance that the two facts have occurred at the same time. It is all the work of the Holy Spirit, the effective and vital source of everything in the Christian life that is really and authentically evangelical.

As everyone knows, the Holy Spirit's action is not displayed only in impulses and charismatic gifts, but also in the sacramental life. From this aspect too we can joyfully recognize that many signs of progress have been noted in the value put on the sacramental life of lay Christians.

There is a trend to appreciate Baptism better as the source of the whole Christian life. Further progress must be made in this direction, in order better and better to discover and exploit the riches of a sacrament whose effects extend throughout one's whole life.

It will also be appropriate to put greater stress on the value of the sacrament of Confirmation, which, by a special gift of the Holy Spirit, bestows the ability to give an adult witness of faith in Christ and to take up one's own responsibilities more consciously and deliberately in the Church's life and apostolate.

Making the most of the sacrament of Marriage is of primary importance for the sanctification of the spouses themselves and for the formation of Christian homes, on which the future of God's people and of all society depends. Groups and associations for deepening marital spirituality are working in this direction. Tireless and unceasing progress must also be made along these lines.

A more intense, conscious and active participation by the laity in the Eucharistic celebration allows us to see a vigorous affirmation of witness and apostolic involvement in Christian communities. Here one always finds the living source of union with Christ, of ecclesial communion and of zeal in evangelizing.

Perhaps in recent years less attention has been paid to the sacrament of Reconciliation. We must hope that more intense efforts will be made once again to esteem the reception of this sacrament. The gift of spiritual healing that comes from God, a new fervor in one's interior life, a new clearness of vision and a sincere commitment to Church service derive from this sacrament. However, we must not forget that in the case of serious sin, sacramental confession is necessary for receiving the Eucharist.

As these simple observations on the situation for the laity

in the Church today show, promoting the apostolate of the laity requires a corresponding development in their formation (cf. *CL* 60). This primarily means cultivating the spiritual life. It is a joy to observe in this regard that the laity increasingly have at their disposal suitable means to grow in this way—from prayer groups and spiritual associations in many parishes, to meetings for reading and discussing the word of God, days of recollection and courses of spiritual exercises. Religious radio and television broadcasts are also an effective tool for faith enrichment and for giving direction to the Christian people in their spiritual life and worship.

In our world, marked by widespread growth in the cultural level of various classes of people, lay persons involved in Church-related tasks have an ever greater need of good doctrinal formation (cf. *CL* 60). Here too it is a pleasure to see notable progress. Many lay people are seeking a greater understanding of the doctrine of the faith. The increased number of institutes for religious studies is significant. Theology courses and conferences, which were once reserved to those preparing for the priesthood, have become more and more open to the laity. These courses and conferences are attended not only by those who must be certified in religious education, but by many others who desire a more complete formation, which will benefit their family, friends and acquaintances. Another sign of hope is the deep interest with which the *Catechism of the Catholic Church* has been received in various parts of the world.

Progress in the doctrinal formation of the laity has also been made with regard to a better knowledge of the Church's social teaching. Those who are involved in economic and political life at all levels must be inspired by the principles of this teaching in their programs of action. We would like to see the progress achieved thus far continue to increase. Unfortunately the Church's social teaching is too little known. It is the responsibility of today's socially and spiritually well-trained

Christian laity to seek appropriate ways to apply these principles, thus effectively contributing to building a society of greater justice and solidarity.

While arousing a feeling of gratitude to the Lord, who is ever wondrous in his gifts, the promotion of the laity's life in the Church also justifies an outburst of new hope. Christian lay people are also sharing more and more actively in the Church's missionary effort. The prospects for preaching the Gospel in the world today depend considerably on their contribution. In the laity the face of God's people is revealed in all its splendor, a people on the way to their own salvation. Precisely for this reason, they are committed to spreading the light of the Gospel and bringing Christ to life in the minds and hearts of their brothers and sisters. We are sure that the Holy Spirit, who has developed the spirituality and mission of lay people in the Church today, will continue his activity for the greater good of the Church tomorrow and forever.

General audience of September 21, 1994

CONSECRATED LIFE

Religious Intensely Live Their Baptismal Vows

In the ecclesiological catecheses we have been giving for some time, we have often presented the Church as a "priestly" people, that is, comprising persons who share in Christ's priesthood as a state of consecration to God and of offering the perfect, definitive worship he gives to the Father in the name of all humanity. This is a result of Baptism, which inserts the believer into Christ's Mystical Body and appoints him— almost *ex officio* and, one could say, in an institutional way—to reproduce in himself the condition of priest and victim *(sacerdos et hostia)* of the head (cf. St. Thomas, *Summa Theol.,* III, q. 63, a. 3 in c. and ad 2; a. 6).

Every other sacrament—especially Confirmation—completes this spiritual state of the believer. The sacrament of Orders also confers the power to act ministerially as Christ's instrument in proclaiming the word, renewing the sacrifice of the cross and forgiving sin.

To explain better this consecration of God's people, we now would like to discuss another basic chapter of ecclesiology, which in our day has become increasingly important from the theological and spiritual standpoint. We are speaking of the consecrated life, which many of Christ's followers embrace as an especially elevated, intense and demanding way of living out the consequences of Baptism with a lofty charity leading to perfection and holiness.

Heir to the theological and spiritual tradition of two millennia of Christianity, the Second Vatican Council has highlighted the value of the consecrated life. According to what the Gospel indicates, this life "is expressed in the practice of chastity consecrated to God, poverty and obedience," which are called precisely the "evangelical counsels" (cf. *LG* 43). The Council speaks of them as a spontaneous manifestation of the sovereign action of the Holy Spirit, who from the beginning has produced an abundance of generous souls moved by the desire for perfection and self-giving for the good of all Christ's body (cf. *LG* 43).

We are speaking of individual experiences, which have never been lacking and even today continue to blossom in the Church. However, since the first centuries a tendency has been noted to move from the personal and—one could almost say—"private" practice of the evangelical counsels to a state of public recognition by the Church. This has happened both in the solitary life of hermits and ever increasingly in the formation of monastic communities or religious families, which are meant to assist in attaining the objectives of the consecrated life: stability, better doctrinal formation, obedience, mutual help and progress in charity.

Thus, from the first centuries down to our day, "a wondrous variety of religious communities" has emerged. In them, the "manifold wisdom of God" is displayed (cf. *PC* 1) and the Church's extraordinary vitality is expressed, but in the unity of Christ's body, according to the words of St. Paul: "There are different gifts but the same Spirit" (1 Cor 12:4). The Spirit pours out his gifts in a great variety of forms to enrich the one Church, which in her multicolored beauty reveals in time "the unfathomable riches of Christ" (Eph 3:8), as all creation manifests "in many forms and in each individual part" *(multipliciter et divisim),* as St. Thomas says *(Summa Theol.,* I, q. 47, a. 1), what in God is absolute unity.

In every case, it is a question of one basic "divine gift," although expressed in the multiplicity and variety of spiritual gifts or charisms bestowed on individuals and communities (cf. *Summa Theol.,* II-II, q. 103, a. 2). Charisms can be individual or collective. The individual ones are widespread in the Church and vary so much from person to person that they are difficult to categorize and in each case require the Church's discernment. Collective charisms are generally bestowed on men and women who are destined to establish ecclesial works, especially religious institutes, which receive their distinctive mark from their founders' charisms. These men and women live and work under their influence and, to the extent of their fidelity, receive new gifts and charisms for each individual member and for the community as a whole. The latter can thus discover new forms of activity in accordance with the needs of time and place, without breaking the line of continuity and development going back to the founder, or by easily recovering its identity and vigor.

The Council observes: "The Church gladly welcomed and approved [religious families] by her authority" *(PC* 1). This was in harmony with her own responsibility for charisms, because it is her "special competence...not indeed to extinguish the Spirit, but to test all things and hold fast to that which is good (cf. 1 Thess 5:12, 19-21)" *(LG* 12). This explains why, with regard to the evangelical counsels, "Church authority has the duty, under the inspiration of the Holy Spirit, of interpreting these evangelical counsels, of regulating their practice and finally to build on them stable forms of living" *(LG* 43).

It should always be kept in mind, however, that the state of consecrated life does not belong to the hierarchical structure of the Church. The Council notes this: "From the point of view of the divine and hierarchical structure of the Church, the religious state of life is not an intermediate state between the clerical and lay states. But, rather, the faithful of Christ are called by God from both these states of life so that they might enjoy this particular gift in the life of the Church and thus each in one's own way, may be of some advantage to the salvific mission of the Church" *(LG* 43).

The Council immediately adds, however, that the religious state, "which is constituted by the profession of the evangelical counsels, though it does not belong to the hierarchical structure of the Church, nevertheless, undeniably belongs to its life and holiness" *(LG* 44). This adverb "undeniably" means that all the blows that can disturb the Church's life will never be able to eliminate the consecrated life characterized by the profession of the evangelical counsels. This state of life will endure as an essential element of the Church's holiness. According to the Council, this is an "unshakable" truth.

That having been said, it must still be stated clearly that no particular form of consecrated life is sure to last forever. Individual religious communities can die out. History shows that some have in fact disappeared, just as certain particular churches have also come to an end. Institutes that are no longer suited to their age, or which have no more vocations, can be forced to close or to be consolidated with others. The guarantee of lasting until the end of the world, which was given to the Church as a whole, has not necessarily been granted to individual religious institutes. History teaches that the charism of the consecrated life is always on the move. This shows that it can discover and "invent," so to speak, new forms that more directly answer the needs and aspirations of the time, while remaining faithful to the founder's charism. However, communities that have existed for centuries are also called to adapt to these needs and aspirations so as not to condemn themselves to disappearing.

Nevertheless, the practice of the evangelical counsels, in whatever forms it may take, is guaranteed to last throughout history. This is because Jesus Christ himself desired and established it as a definitive feature of the Church's economy of holiness. The idea of a Church consisting only of lay people involved in marriage and secular professions does not correspond to Christ's intentions as we find them in the Gospel. All this shows us—also from looking at history and even current events—that there will always be men and women (and boys and girls) who will want to give themselves totally to Christ and his kingdom by the way of celibacy, poverty and submission to a rule of life. Those who take this way will continue, in the future as in the past, to play an important role for the Christian community's growth in holiness and for its evangelizing mission. Indeed, today more than ever, the way of the evangelical counsels offers great hope for the future of the Church.

General audience of September 28, 1994

The Spirit Continues
Giving New Charisms

Consecrated life, which has marked the Church's development over the centuries, has experienced and still experiences different expressions. This variety must be kept in mind while reading the chapter of *Lumen Gentium* dedicated to the profession of the evangelical counsels. Its bears the title "Religious," but the range of its doctrinal considerations and pastoral intentions covers the much wider and diversified area of consecrated life as it has developed in recent years.

Many people today also choose the way of consecrated life in religious institutes and congregations that have long been active in the Church, which continues to find new enrichment in the spiritual life from their living, fruitful presence.

In the Church today, however, there are also new visible associations of consecrated persons, recognized and regulated from the canonical standpoint. First of all, there are the secular institutes, in which, according to the Code of Canon Law, "The Christian faithful living in the world strive for the perfection of charity and work for the sanctification of the world especially from within" (can. 710). The members of these institutes are obliged to follow the evangelical counsels, but they harmonize them with a life of involvement in the world of secular activity and institutions. For many years, even before the Council, there were some gifted pioneers in this form of consecrated life, which externally is more like that of "seculars" than of "religious." For some this choice was perhaps based on necessity, in that they were not able to enter a religious community because of certain family obligations or other obstacles. But for many it was the commitment to an ideal: to combine an authentic consecration to God with a life lived amid the affairs of the world, and this too as a vocation. It is to Pope Pius XII's credit to have recognized the legitimacy of this form of consecration in the Apostolic Constitution *Provida Mater Ecclesia* (1947).

In addition to secular institutes, the Code of Canon Law recognizes societies of apostolic life, "whose members without religious vows pursue the particular apostolic purpose of the society, and leading a life as brothers or sisters in common according to a particular manner of life, strive for the perfection of charity through the observance of the constitutions" (can. 731, §1). Among these societies, which are "assimilated" to the institutes of consecrated life, there are some whose members are committed to practicing the evangelical counsels by a bond defined in the constitutions. This too is a form of consecration.

In more recent times, a certain number of "movements" or "ecclesial associations" have appeared. I spoke of them appreciatively on the occasion of a convention sponsored by the Italian Episcopal Conference on *The Christian Community and Associations of the Laity:* "The phenomenon of ecclesial associations," I said, "is a fact characterizing the present historical moment of the Church. And it must also be noted, with true consolation, that the range of these associations covers the entire span of the forms of the Christian's presence in current society" *(Insegnamenti,* VII, 2, 1984, 290; *L'Osservatore Romano* English edition, Sept. 17, 1984, p. 8). Now as then, I hope that these lay associations will live "in full ecclesial communion with the bishop" *(Insegnamenti,* p. 292). This is in order to avoid the risk of a certain self-satisfaction on the part of those who tend to absolutize their own experience, and of an isolation from the community life of the local churches and their pastors.

Although consisting of lay people, these "movements" or "associations" often steer their members—or some of their members—toward practicing the evangelical counsels. Consequently, even if they are defined as lay people, groups or communities of consecrated life arise among them. What is more, this form of consecrated life can be accompanied by an openness to the priestly ministry, when some communities accept priests or guide young men to priestly ordination. As a result, some of these movements reflect the image of the Church according to the three directions that the development of her historical composition can take: those of lay people, of priests and of consecrated souls within the context of the evangelical counsels.

One need only refer to this new situation without having to describe the various movements in detail, in order to emphasize the significance of their presence in the Church today.

It is important to see them as a sign of the charisms given to the Church by the Holy Spirit in ever new and at times unforeseeable ways. The experience of recent years allows us to state that, in harmony with the foundations of the faith, the charismatic life is far from being spent. It is finding new expressions in the Church, especially in the forms of consecrated life.

A very particular and, in a certain sense, new aspect of this experience is the importance that the lay character generally has in it. It is true that there can be some misunderstanding about the word "lay," even in the religious sphere. When lay people are committed to the way of the evangelical counsels, doubtless to a certain extent they belong to a state of consecrated life that is very different from the more common state of other believers who choose marriage and secular professions. "Consecrated" lay people, however, intend to maintain and strengthen their attachment to the title "lay," since they wish to be and to be known as members of the People of God, in accordance with the origin of the word "lay" (from *laós* = people). They wish to witness to the fact that they belong to this people, without distancing themselves from their brothers and sisters even in civil life.

Also of considerable importance and interest is the ecclesial vision of movements which show a firm intention to live the life of the whole Church, as a community of Christ's followers, and to reflect it in deep union and cooperation between "lay people," religious and priests in their personal decisions and in the apostolate.

It is true that these three characteristics—charismatic vitality, the desire to witness to one's membership in the People of God, and the requirement of communion for consecrated persons with lay people and priests—are features common to all forms of consecrated religious life. But we must acknowledge that they are expressed more intensely in contemporary movements, which are generally distinguished by a deep commitment of dedication to the mystery of the Church and of skilled service to her mission.

In addition to movements and communities of a "lay-ecclesial" orientation, we must now mention other types of recent communities, which put greater stress on the traditional elements of religious life. Some of these new communities have a strictly monastic orientation, with a notable development of liturgical prayer. Others follow in the "canon" tradition, which along with the more strictly "monastic" tradition, was so active in the Middle Ages, having particular care for parishes and later, for a more extensive apostolate. Even more radical today is the new "eremitical" tendency, with the foundation or rebirth of both old and new style hermitages.

At a superficial glance some of these forms of consecrated life could seem out of step with the current direction of ecclesial life. However, the Church—which certainly needs consecrated persons who turn more directly to the world in order to evangelize it—also needs, and perhaps even more so, those who seek, cultivate and give witness to God's presence and intimacy, with the intention of working for the sanctification of the world. These are the two aspects of consecrated life seen in Jesus Christ, who reached out to men to bring them light and life, but also sought solitude to devote himself to prayer and contemplation. Neither of these two requirements can be neglected in the Church's life today. We must be grateful to the Holy Spirit who enables us to understand this continually through the charisms he abundantly distributes and the often surprising initiatives he inspires.

General audience of October 5, 1994

Jesus' Will Is the
Origin of Consecrated Life

What counts the most in the old and new forms of "consecrated life" is that one perceives in them a basic conformity with the will of Christ, who instituted the evangelical counsels. In this sense, he is the founder of religious life and of every similar state of consecration. As the Second Vatican Council said, the evangelical counsels are "based upon the words and examples of the Lord" *(LG* 43).

Some have doubted this basis by considering the consecrated life as a purely human institution that arose from the initiative of Christians who wanted to live the Gospel ideal more deeply. Now, it is true that Jesus did not directly found any of the religious communities that gradually grew up in the Church, nor did he determine the particular forms of consecrated life. However, what he wanted and established is the state of consecrated life in its overall value and essential elements. There is no historical evidence that can explain this state as a later human initiative. Nor can one readily conceive that consecrated life—which has played so large a role in the growth of the Church's holiness and mission—did not stem from the founding will of Christ. If we carefully explore the Gospel testimonies, we will discover that this will can be seen very clearly.

The Gospel shows that from the beginning of his public life Jesus called men to follow him. This call was not necessarily expressed in words. It could result merely from the attraction Jesus' personality held for those he met, as in the case of the first two disciples according to the account of John's Gospel. Formerly disciples of John the Baptist, Andrew and his companion (who seems to have been the evangelist himself) were fascinated and almost carried away by the one presented to them as "the Lamb of God." They immediately began to follow Jesus, even before he had said a word to them. When Jesus asked: "What are you looking for?" they answered with another question: "Teacher, where do you stay?" Then they received the invitation that would change their lives: "Come and see" (cf. Jn 1:38-39).

In general, however, the most characteristic expression of the call are the words: "Follow me" (Mt 8:22; 9:9; 19:21; Mk 2:14; 10:21; Lk 9:59; 18:22; Jn 1:43; 21:19).

It shows Jesus' initiative. Before that time, those who wanted to embrace a master's teaching chose the person whose pupils they wished to become. However, with the words "Follow me," Jesus showed that he is the one who chooses the companions and disciples he wishes to have. In fact, he said to the apostles: "It was not you who chose me, it was I who chose you" (Jn 15:16).

In Jesus' initiative a sovereign will appears, but also intense love. The account of the call addressed to the rich young man reveals this love. There we read that, when the rich young man stated that he had observed the commandments of the law since his childhood, Jesus "looked at him with love" (Mk 10:21). This penetrating, loving gaze accompanied the invitation: "Go and sell what you have and give to the poor; you will then have treasure in heaven. After that, come and follow me" (Mk 10:21). Jesus' divine and human love, so burning as to be recalled by a witness to the scene, is repeated in every call to total self-giving in the consecrated life. As I wrote in the Apostolic Exhortation *Redemptionis Donum:* "This love reflects the eternal love of the Father, who 'so loved the world that he gave his only Son, that whoever believes in him should not perish but have eternal life' (Jn 3:16)" (n. 3).

The Gospel also attests that the call to follow Jesus makes many broad demands. The account of the invitation to the rich young man stresses the renunciation of material possessions; in other cases the renunciation of one's family is more expressly emphasized (cf. for example, Lk 9:59-60). In general, following Jesus means renouncing everything in order to be united with him and to accompany him on the paths of his mission. That is the renunciation to which the apostles agreed, when Peter declared: "Here we have put everything aside to follow you" (Mt 19:27) Precisely in his response to Peter, Jesus indicated the renunciation of human possessions as the basic component in following him (cf. Mt 19:29). The Old Testament shows that God asked his people to follow him by observing the commandments, but without ever making such radical demands. Jesus revealed his divine sovereignty, on the other hand, by requiring absolute devotion to himself, to the point of total detachment from earthly possessions and affections.

It should be noted, however, that although he made new demands in the call to follow him, Jesus offers them for the free choice of those he calls. They are not precepts, but invitations or "counsels." The love with which Jesus addressed the call did not take away the rich young man's power to decide freely, as shown by his refusal to follow Jesus because he preferred his possessions. The evangelist Mark notes that the young man "went away sad, for he had many possessions" (Mk 10:22). Jesus did not condemn him for this. But he remarked in turn, and not without some sadness, that it is difficult for the rich to enter the kingdom of heaven and that only God can bring about certain detachments, a certain interior freedom that makes it possible to answer the call (cf. Mk 10:23-27).

On the other hand, Jesus promised that the renunciations required by the call to follow him will receive their recompense, "treasure in heaven," that is, an abundance of spiritual goods. He even promised eternal life in the world to come and a hundredfold in this present age (cf. Mt 19:29). This hundredfold refers to a higher quality of life, a superior happiness. Experience teaches that consecrated life, according to Jesus' plan, is a deeply happy life. This happiness is measured according to fidelity to Jesus' plan. This is true even though, as the reference to persecution recorded by Mark in the same episode (10:30) suggests, the "hundredfold" does not spare one from sharing in Christ's cross.

Jesus also called women to follow him. A gospel witness says that a group of women accompanied Jesus, and there were many of them (cf. Lk 8:1-3; Mt 27:55; Mk 15:40-41). This was a great novelty with respect to Jewish custom. Only Jesus' innovative will, which included the advancement and, in a certain way, the liberation of women, can explain this fact. No account of the call of any woman has come down to us in the Gospel. However, the presence of many women with the Twelve around Jesus presupposes a call on his part, a choice whether silent or expressed.

Jesus showed that the state of consecrated life which consists in following him is not necessarily connected with the goal of priestly ministry, and that this state includes both women and men, each in his or her own area and with the role determined by the divine call. In the group of women following Jesus we can see a sign and even the initial nucleus of the enormous number of women who would be dedicated to religious life or other forms of consecrated life over the Church's centuries down to our day. This applies to "consecrated" women, but also to many other sisters of ours. In new ways they follow the authentic example of Jesus' collaborators, for example as lay "volunteers" in many apostolic tasks and in many offices and ministries of the Church.

We conclude this catechesis by recognizing that, in calling men and women to abandon everything in order to follow him, Jesus inaugurated a state of life which would gradually develop in the Church in the various forms of consecrated life expressed in religious life, or also—for those chosen by God—in the priesthood. From gospel times to our own day, Christ's founding will has continued to be at work, the will expressed in that very beautiful and holy invitation addressed to so many souls: "Follow me!"

General audience of October 12, 1994

Prayer Is the Answer
to the Vocation Shortage

In discussing the foundation of consecrated life on the part of Jesus Christ, we mentioned the calls he extended from the beginning of his public life, generally expressed in the words: "Follow me." Jesus' care in making these appeals shows the importance he attributed to Gospel discipleship for the life of the Church. He linked that discipleship with the "counsels" of consecrated life, which he desired for his disciples as that conformation to himself which is the heart of gospel holiness (cf. *Veritatis Splendor* 21). In fact, history confirms that consecrated persons—priests, men and women religious, members of other institutes and similar movements—have played an essential role in the Church's expansion, as they have in her growth in holiness and love.

In the Church today, vocations to religious life have no less importance than in centuries past. Unfortunately, in many places we see that their number is insufficient for meeting the needs of communities and their apostolate. It is no exaggeration to say that for some institutes this problem has become critical, to the point of threatening their survival. Even without wishing to share the dire predictions for the not-too-distant future, it is already apparent today that, for lack of members, some communities are forced to give up works usually destined to produce abundant spiritual fruit. More generally, fewer vocations lead to a decline in the Church's active presence in society, with considerable losses in every field.

The present vocation shortage in some parts of the world is a challenge to be met with determination and courage. It is certain that Jesus Christ, who during his earthly life called many to consecrated life, is still doing so in today's world and often receives a generous, positive response, as daily experience proves. Knowing the Church's needs, he continues to extend the invitation, "Follow me," especially to young people, whom his grace makes responsive to the ideal of a life of total dedication.

In addition, the lack of workers for God's harvest was already a challenge in gospel times for Jesus himself. His example teaches us that the shortage of consecrated persons is a situation inherent in the world's condition and not only an accidental fact due to contemporary circumstances. The Gospel tells us that as he roamed through towns and villages, Jesus was moved with pity for the crowds which "were lying prostrate from exhaustion, like sheep without a shepherd" (Mt 9:36). He tried to remedy that situation by teaching them at great length (cf. Mk 6:34), but he wanted the disciples to join him in solving the problem. So he invited them, first of all, to pray: "Beg the harvest master to send out laborers to gather his harvest" (Mt 9:38). According to the context, this prayer was intended to provide people with a greater number of pastors. However, the expression "laborers for the harvest" can have a wider application, indicating everyone who works for the Church's growth. The prayer, then, also seeks to obtain a greater number of consecrated persons.

The stress put on prayer is surprising. Given God's sovereign initiative in calling, we might think that only the harvest master, independently of other intervention or cooperation, should provide a sufficient number of workers. On the contrary, Jesus insisted on the cooperation and responsibility of his followers. He also teaches us today that with prayer we can and must influence the number of vocations. The Father welcomes this prayer because he wants it and expects it, and he himself makes it effective. Whenever and wherever the vocation crisis is more serious, this prayer is all the more necessary. But it must rise to heaven in every time and place. In this area the whole Church and every Christian always have a responsibility.

This prayer must be joined to efforts to encourage an increase in the responses to the divine call. Here too we find the prime example in the Gospel. After his first contact with Jesus, Andrew brought his brother Simon to him (cf. Jn 1:42). Certainly, Jesus showed himself sovereign in his call to Simon, but on his own initiative Andrew played a decisive role in Simon's meeting with the Master. "In a way this is the heart of all the Church's pastoral work on behalf of vocations" *(PDV* 38).

Encouraging vocations can come from personal initiative, like Andrew's, or from collective efforts, as is done in many dioceses that have developed a vocation apostolate. This promotion of vocations does not at all aim at restricting the individual's freedom of choice regarding the direction of his own life. Therefore, this promotion avoids putting any kind of constraint or pressure on each person's decision. But it seeks to shed light on everyone's choice and to show each individual, in particular, the way opened in his or her life by the Gospel's "Follow me." Young people especially need and have a right to receive this light. On the other hand, the seeds of a vocation, especially in young people, must certainly be cultivated and strengthened. Vocations must develop and grow, which usually does not occur unless conditions favorable to this development and growth are guaranteed. This is the purpose of institutions for vocations and the various programs, meetings, retreats, prayer groups, etc., that promote the work of vocations. One can never do enough in the vocations apostolate, even though every human initiative must always be based on the conviction that, in the end, each person's vocation depends on God's sovereign decision.

A basic form of cooperation is the witness of consecrated persons themselves, which exercises a healthy, effective attraction. Experience shows that often the example of a man or woman religious has a decisive impact on the direction of a young personality which has been able to discover in that fidelity, integrity and joy the concrete example of an ideal way to live. In particular, religious communities can only attract young people by a collective witness of authentic consecration, lived in the joy of self-giving to Christ and to their brothers and sisters.

Lastly, the importance of the family should be stressed as the Christian environment in which vocations can develop and grow. Once again I invite Christian parents to pray that Christ will call one of their children to the consecrated life. The task of Christian parents is to form a family in which Gospel values are honored, cultivated and lived, and where an authentic Christian life can elevate the aspirations of the young. Because of these families the Church will continue to produce vocations. Therefore, she asks families to collaborate in answering the harvest master, who wants us all to be committed to sending new "laborers into the harvest."

General audience of October 19, 1994

Consecrated Life Is Rooted in Baptism

Several times in the preceding catecheses I have spoken of the "evangelical counsels," which in consecrated life are expressed as the vows—or at least commitments—of chastity, poverty and obedience. They find their full meaning in the context of a life totally dedicated to God in communion with Christ. The adverb "totally," used by St. Thomas Aquinas to indicate the essential value of religious life, is most expressive. "Religion is a virtue whereby a man offers something to the service and worship of God. Therefore, those are called religious by antonomasia, who consecrate themselves totally to the divine service, as offering a holocaust to God" *(Summa Theol.,* II-II, q. 186, a. 1). It is an idea drawn from the tradition of the Fathers, especially from St. Jerome (cf. Epist. 125, *Ad Rusticum),* and from St. Gregory the Great (cf. *Super Ezech.,* Hom. 20). The Second Vatican Council, which quotes St. Thomas Aquinas, made his teaching its own and speaks of a complete, interior "consecration to God." As a development of the baptismal consecration, it takes place in the religious state through the bonds of the evangelical counsels (cf. *LG* 44).

It should be noted that in this consecration human endeavor does not have the priority. The initiative comes from Christ, who asks for a freely accepted covenant in following him. It is he who, by taking possession of a human person, "consecrates" him.

According to the Old Testament, God himself consecrated persons or objects by imparting his holiness in some way to them. This should not be understood in the sense that God inwardly sanctified people, much less objects, but in the sense that he took possession of them and set them apart for his direct service. The sacred objects were intended for the worship of the Lord, and thus could only be used in the temple and during worship, and not for what was profane. This sacredness was attributed to things that could not be touched by profane hands (for example, the Ark of the Covenant, the cups of the temple in Jerusalem which Antiochus Epiphanes profaned, as we read in 1 Mc 1:22). In turn, the people of Israel were "holy" as the "Lord's possession" *(segullah* = the sovereign's personal treasury), and thus had a sacred character (cf. Ex 19:5; Dt 7:6; Ps 135:4; etc.). To communicate with this *segullah,* God chose "spokesmen," "men of God," "prophets," who were to speak in his name. He sanctified them (morally) through the relationship of trust and special friendship he reserved for them, so much so that some of these persons were called "God's friends" (cf. Wis 7:27; Is 41:8; Jas 2:23).

However, there was no individual, means or institution that by its inner force could communicate God's holiness to men, however well-disposed. This would be the great newness of Christian Baptism, by which believers have their "hearts sprinkled clean" (Heb 10:22), and are inwardly "washed, consecrated, justified in the name of our Lord Jesus Christ and in the Spirit of our God" (1 Cor 6:11).

The essential element of the Gospel law is grace, which is a power of life that justifies and saves, as St. Thomas explains (cf. *Summa Theol.,* I-II, q. 106, a. 2), following St. Augustine (cf. *De Spiritu et Littera,* ch. 7). Christ already takes possession of the person from within through Baptism, in which he begins his sanctifying action. He consecrates him and instills in him the need for a response that Christ himself makes possible by his grace, to the extent of the subject's physical, psychological, spiritual and moral capacity. The sovereign power exercised by the grace of Christ in consecration does not at all diminish the freedom of the response to the call, nor the value and importance of human effort. This is made especially clear in the call to practice the evangelical counsels. Christ's call is accompanied by a grace that elevates the human person and gives him abilities of a higher order to follow these counsels. This means that in consecrated life there is a development of the human personality itself, which is not frustrated but elevated and enhanced by the divine gift.

The person who accepts the call and follows the evangelical counsels performs a basic act of love for God, as we read in the Constitution *Lumen Gentium* (cf. n. 44) of the Second Vatican Council. The purpose of religious vows is to scale the heights of love, a complete love, dedicated to Christ under the impulse of the Holy Spirit and, through Christ, offered to the Father. Hence there is the value of the obligation and consecration of religious profession which in the Eastern and Western Christian tradition is considered as a *baptismus flaminis* (baptism of the Spirit), inasmuch as "a person's heart is moved by the Holy Spirit to believe in and love God, and to repent of his sins" *(Summa Theol.,* III, q. 66, a. 11).

I explained this idea of an almost new Baptism in the Letter *Redemptionis Donum.*

> Religious profession is a new "burial in the death of Christ": new, because it is made of love and vocation; new, by reason of unceasing "conversion." This "burial in death" causes the person "buried together with Christ" to "walk like Christ in newness of life." In Christ crucified is to be found the ultimate foundation both of baptismal consecration and of the profession of the evangelical counsels, which—in the words of the Second

Vatican Council—"constitutes a special consecration." It is at one and the same time both death and liberation. St. Paul writes: "Consider yourselves dead to sin." At the same time he calls this death "freedom from the slavery of sin." Above all, though, religious consecration, through its sacramental foundation in holy Baptism, constitutes a new life "for God in Jesus Christ" *(RD* 7).

This life is all the more perfect and produces more abundant fruits of baptismal grace (cf. *LG* 44), inasmuch as the intimate union with Christ received in Baptism develops into a more complete union. Indeed, the commandment to love God with all one's heart, which is enjoined on the baptized, is observed to the full by the love vowed to God through the evangelical counsels. It is a "special consecration" *(PC* 5); a closer consecration to the divine service "by a new and special title" *(LG* 44); a new consecration, which cannot be considered an implication or logical consequence of Baptism. Baptism does not necessarily imply an orientation toward celibacy and the renunciation of material possessions in the form of the evangelical counsels. Religious consecration, instead, means the call to a new life that implies the gift of an original charism not granted to everyone, as Jesus stated when he spoke of voluntary celibacy (cf. Mt 19:10-12). Hence, it is a sovereign act of God, who freely chooses, calls and opens a way that is certainly connected with the baptismal consecration, but is distinct from it.

In a similar way, it can be said that the profession of evangelical counsels further develops that consecration received in the sacrament of Confirmation. It is a new gift of the Holy Spirit, conferred for the sake of an active Christian life in a closer bond of collaboration and service to the Church. This produces, through the evangelical counsels, new fruits of holiness and apostleship in addition to the demands of the consecration received in Confirmation. The sacrament of Confirmation—and the character of Christian soldiering and Christian apostleship that it entails—is also at the root of consecrated life.

In this regard it is correct to see effects of Baptism and Confirmation in the consecration implied by accepting the evangelical counsels and to situate religious life, which by its nature is charismatic, in the sacramental economy. Along these lines, we can also note that, for religious priests, the sacrament of Orders also bears fruit in the practice of the evangelical counsels, requiring a closer attachment to the Lord. The vows of chastity, poverty, and obedience aim at the concrete realization of this attachment.

The connection between the evangelical counsels and the sacraments of Baptism, Confirmation and Holy Orders helps to show the essential value that consecrated life represents for the growth of the Church's holiness. For this reason I wish to close by inviting you to pray—to pray a great deal—that the Lord will increasingly bestow the gift of consecrated life on the Church that he himself willed and established as "holy."

General audience of October 26, 1994

Gospel Counsels
Are a Way of Perfection

The way of evangelical counsels has often been called a "way of perfection," and the state of consecrated life the "state of perfection." These terms are also found in *Lumen Gentium* (cf. n. 45), while the decree on the renewal of religious life is entitled *Perfectae Caritatis* and has as its theme the "pursuit of perfect charity through the evangelical counsels" *(PC* 1).

A way of perfection obviously means a way of perfection to be acquired, and not of a perfection already acquired, as St. Thomas Aquinas explains clearly (cf. *Summa Theol.,* II-II, q. 184, aa. 5, 7). Those who are committed to the practice of the evangelical counsels do not at all claim to possess perfection. They acknowledge that they are sinners like all men, sinners who have been saved. But they feel and are more expressly called to strive for perfection, which consists essentially in charity (cf. *ibid.,* q. 184, aa. 1, 3).

It cannot be forgotten that all Christians are called to perfection. Jesus Christ himself referred to this call: "Be perfect as your heavenly Father is perfect" (Mt 5:48). In discussing the Church's universal call to holiness, the Second Vatican Council says that this holiness "is expressed in many ways in individuals, who in their walk of life, tend toward the perfection of charity, thus causing the edification of others"

(LG 39; cf. 40). Nevertheless, the universality of this call does not prevent others from being called in a particular way to a life of perfection. According to Matthew's account, Jesus addressed his call to the rich young man by saying: "If you wish to be perfect..." (Mt 19:21). This is the Gospel source of the idea of a "way of perfection." The rich young man had asked Jesus about "what is good," and in reply he received a list of commandments. But at the time of the call, he was invited to a perfection that goes beyond the commandments. He was called to renounce everything in order to follow Jesus. Perfection consists in the most complete gift of self to Christ. In this sense the way of the evangelical counsels is a "way of perfection" for those who are called to it.

It should again be noted that the perfection Jesus offered the rich young man does not mean harm to one's person but rather its enrichment. Jesus invited the young man to renounce a plan of life in which concern about having is the focal point, in order for him to discover the true value of personal fulfillment in giving oneself to others and especially in generous devotion to the Savior. Thus we can say that the real and considerable renunciations demanded by the evangelical counsels do not have a "depersonalizing" effect. But they are aimed at perfecting personal life, as the result of a supernatural grace corresponding to the human being's deepest and noblest aspirations. In this regard St. Thomas speaks of *spiritualis libertas* and *augmentum spirituale:* spiritual freedom and growth (cf. *Summa Theol.,* II-II, q. 184, a. 4).

What are the main elements of freedom and growth involved in the evangelical counsels for whoever professes them?

First of all, there is a conscious striving for the perfection of faith. The response to the call: "Follow me," with the renunciations it entails, requires an ardent faith in the divine person of Christ and absolute trust in his love. Both will have to grow and be strengthened along the way to avoid yielding to adversity.

Nor can a conscious striving for the perfection of hope be lacking. Christ's request must be viewed in the perspective of eternal life. Those who commit themselves to it are called to a firm, solid hope both at the time of their profession and throughout their life. This will allow them to witness to the everlasting value of the goods of heaven, amid the relative, fleeting goods of this world.

The profession of the evangelical counsels especially develops a conscious striving for the perfection of one's love for God. The Second Vatican Council speaks of the consecration produced by the evangelical counsels as the gift of self to God who is "supremely loved" *(LG* 44). It is the fulfillment of the first commandment: "You shall love the Lord your God with all your heart, and with all your soul, and with all your strength" (Dt 6:5; cf. Mk 12:30 and par.). Consecrated life genuinely grows by the continual deepening of this initial gift and by an ever stronger and more sincere love in its trinitarian dimension. It is love for Christ, who calls us to intimacy with him; for the Holy Spirit, who seeks and helps us to become completely open to his inspirations; for the Father, the original source and ultimate goal of consecrated life. This takes place especially in prayer, but also in every action, which receives a decidedly vertical dimension from the infused virtue of religion.

Obviously faith, hope and love arouse and increasingly heighten the striving for perfection of one's love of neighbor, as an expansion of one's love of God. The "gift of self to God who is supremely loved" implies an intense love of neighbor— love that strives to be as perfect as possible, in imitation of the Savior's charity.

The truth of consecrated life as union with Christ in divine charity is expressed in certain basic attitudes, which should increase throughout one's life. In a general way they can be described as follows: the desire to pass on to others the love that comes from God through the Heart of Christ, and thus, the universality of a love that cannot be stopped by the barriers human selfishness erects in the name of race, nationality, cultural tradition, social or religious status, etc.; an effort to show goodwill and esteem toward all, most especially toward those who, humanly speaking, tend to be more neglected or despised; the desire to show special solidarity to the poor and the victims of persecution and injustice; care in helping the suffering, such as the many today who are handicapped, forsaken, exiled, etc.; the witness of a meek and humble heart, which refrains from condemning, renounces all violence and revenge, and forgives joyfully; the desire to foster reconciliation everywhere and to welcome the gospel gift of peace; generous dedication in every apostolic endeavor that seeks to spread the light of Christ and bring salvation to mankind; assiduous prayer according to the principal intentions of the Holy Father and the Church.

There are many vast fields that today more than ever call for the work of consecrated persons, as an expression of divine charity in the concrete forms of human solidarity. In many cases, perhaps, they can accomplish, humanly speaking, only little, or at least quiet, low-key things. But even small contributions are effective, if imbued with true love (the truly great and powerful "thing"), especially if it is the same trinitarian love poured out in the Church and the world. Consecrated persons are called to be these humble, faithful collaborators in the Church's progress in the world along the path of charity.

General audience of November 9, 1994

Chastity for the Sake of the Kingdom

According to the Second Vatican Council, the precious gift of "perfect continence, out of desire for the kingdom of heaven," is outstanding among the evangelical counsels. This is a gift of divine grace, "given by the Father to certain souls, (cf. Mt 19:11; 1 Cor 7:7), whereby they may devote themselves to God alone the more easily, due to an undivided heart (cf. 1 Cor 7:32-34).... Perfect continence for the love of God is an incentive to charity, and is certainly a particular source of spiritual fecundity in the world" *(LG 42)*.

Traditionally, three vows are usually spoken of—poverty, chastity and obedience—beginning with the discussion of poverty as detachment from external goods, ranked on a lower level with regard to the goods of body and soul (cf. St. Thomas, *Summa Theol.,* II-II, q. 186, a. 3). The Council, instead, expressly mentions consecrated chastity before the other two vows (cf. *LG* 43; *PC* 12, 13, 14), because it considers chastity as the determining commitment of the state of consecrated life. It is also the evangelical counsel that most obviously shows the power of grace, which raises love beyond the human being's natural inclinations.

Its spiritual greatness stands out in the Gospel, because Jesus himself explained the value he placed on commitment to the way of celibacy. According to Matthew, Jesus praised voluntary celibacy after he asserted the indissolubility of marriage. Since Jesus forbade husbands to divorce their wives, the disciples reacted: "If such is the case of a man with his wife, it is not expedient to marry." Jesus answered by giving a deeper meaning to the phrase, "It is not expedient to marry": "Not all can receive this precept, but only those to whom it is given. For there are eunuchs who have been so from birth, and there are eunuchs who have been made eunuchs by men, and there are eunuchs who have made themselves eunuchs for the sake of the kingdom of heaven. He who is able to receive this, let him receive it" (Mt 19:10-12).

In stating this possibility of understanding a new way, which was that practiced by him and the disciples, and which perhaps led those around them to wonder or even to criticize, Jesus used an image that alluded to a well-known fact, the condition of "eunuchs." They could be such because of a congenital imperfection or because of human intervention. But Jesus immediately added that there was a new category— his!— "eunuchs for the sake of the kingdom of heaven." It was an obvious reference to the choice he made and recommended to his closest followers. According to the Mosaic law, eunuchs were excluded from worship (Dt 23:2) and the priesthood (Lv 21:20). An oracle in the Book of Isaiah had foretold the end of this exclusion (Is 56:3-5). Jesus opened an even more innovative horizon: the voluntary choice "for the sake of the kingdom of heaven" of this situation considered unworthy of man. Obviously, Jesus' words did not mean an actual physical mutilation, which the Church has never permitted, but the free renunciation of sexual relations. As I wrote in the Apostolic Exhortation *Redemptionis Donum,* this means a "renunciation therefore—the reflection of the mystery of Calvary—in order 'to be' more fully in the crucified and risen Christ; renunciation in order to recognize fully in him the mystery of one's own human nature, and to confirm this on the path of that wonderful process of which the same apostle writes in another place: 'Though our outer nature is wasting away, our inner nature is being renewed every day' (2 Cor 4:16)" *(RD* 10).

Jesus was aware of the values renounced by those who live in perpetual celibacy. He himself had affirmed them shortly before when he spoke of marriage as a union of which God is the author and which therefore cannot be broken. Being committed to celibacy does indeed mean renouncing the goods inherent in married life and the family, but never ceasing to appreciate them for their real value. The renunciation is made in view of a greater good, of higher values, summed up in the beautiful Gospel expression of the "kingdom of heaven." The complete gift of self to this kingdom justifies and sanctifies celibacy.

Jesus called attention to the gift of divine light needed to understand the way of voluntary celibacy. Not everyone can understand it, in the sense that not everyone is "able" to grasp its meaning, to accept it, to practice it. This gift of light and decision is only granted to some. It is a privilege granted them for the sake of a greater love. We should not be surprised then if many, who do not understand the value of consecrated celibacy, are not attracted to it, and often are not even able to appreciate it. This means that there is a variety of ways, charisms and roles, as St. Paul recognized. He spontaneously wished to share his ideal of virginal life with everyone. He wrote: "I wish that all were as I myself am. But each," he adds, "has his own special gift from God, one of one kind and one of another" (1 Cor 7:7). Moreover, as St. Thomas observed, "The Church derives a certain beauty from the variety of states" *(Summa Theol.,* II-II, q. 184, a. 4).

For his part, the individual is required to make a deliberate act of will conscious of the duty and the privilege of consecrated celibacy. This does not mean simply abstaining from marriage, nor an unmotivated and almost passive observance of the norms imposed by chastity. The act of renunciation has a positive aspect in the total dedication to the kingdom, which implies absolute devotion to God "who is supremely loved" and to the service of his kingdom. Therefore, the choice must be well thought out and stem from a firm, conscious decision that has matured deep within the individual.

St. Paul states the demands and advantages of this dedication to the kingdom: "The unmarried man is anxious about the affairs of the Lord, how to please the Lord, but the married man is anxious about worldly affairs, how to please his wife, and his interests are divided. The unmarried woman or girl is anxious about the affairs of the Lord, how to be holy in body and spirit, but the married woman is anxious about worldly affairs, how to please her husband" (1 Cor 7:32-34). The Apostle does not mean to condemn the married state (cf. 1 Tim 4:1-3), nor "to lay restraint" on anyone, as he said (1 Cor 7:35). But with the realism of experience enlightened by the Holy Spirit, he speaks and counsels—as he wrote—"for your own benefit...to promote good order and to secure your undivided devotion to the Lord" (1 Cor 7:35). This is the purpose of the evangelical counsels. Faithful to the tradition of the counsels, the Second Vatican Council states that chastity is "the most suitable means by which religious dedicate themselves with undivided heart to the service of God and the works of the apostolate" *(PC* 12).

Consecrated celibacy has been criticized over and over again in history, and many times the Church has had to call attention to the excellence of the religious state in this regard. One need only recall the declaration of the Council of Trent (cf. *DS* 1810), which Pius XII cited in the Encyclical *Sacra Virginitas* because of its magisterial value (cf. *AAS* 46 [1954], 174). This does not mean casting a shadow on the married state. Instead we must keep in mind what the *Catechism of the Catholic Church* states: "Both the sacrament of Matrimony and virginity for the kingdom of God come from the Lord himself. It is he who gives them meaning and grants them the grace which is indispensable for living them out in conformity with his will. Esteem of virginity for the sake of the kingdom and the Christian understanding of marriage are inseparable, and they reinforce each other" (n. 1620; cf. *RD* 11).

The Second Vatican Council warns that accepting and observing the evangelical counsel of consecrated virginity and celibacy requires sufficient "psychological and emotional maturity" *(PC* 12). This maturity is indispensable.

Hence, the conditions for faithfully following Christ on this point are: trust in God's love, and prayer to him stirred by the awareness of human weakness; prudent and humble behavior; and above all, a life of intense union with Christ.

This last point, which is the key to all consecrated life, contains the secret of fidelity to Christ as the one bridegroom of the soul, the only reason to live.

General audience of November 16, 1994

A Witness to Spousal Love for the Church

According to *Perfectae Caritatis,* religious "recall to the minds of all the faithful that wondrous marriage decreed by God and which is to be fully revealed in the future age in which the Church takes Christ as its only spouse" *(PC* 12). In this marriage the basic value of virginity or celibacy in relation to God is discovered. It is for this reason that one speaks of "consecrated chastity."

The truth of this marriage is revealed by many statements in the New Testament. We remember that the Baptist called Jesus the bridegroom who has the bride, that is, the people who rushed to his baptism. John saw himself as the "groom's best man who waits there listening for him and is overjoyed to hear his voice" (Jn 3:29). This marriage imagery was already used in the Old Testament to indicate the close relationship between God and Israel. Especially after Hosea (cf. 1:2ff.), the prophets used it to exalt that relationship and to call the people back to it if they had betrayed it (cf. Is 1:21; Jer 2:2; 3:1; 3:6-12; Ez 16, 23). In the second part of the Book of Isaiah, the restoration of Israel is described as the reconciliation of an unfaithful wife with her husband (cf. Is 50:1; 54:5-8; 62:4-5). The presence of this imagery in the religious faith of Israel also appears in the Song of Songs and in Psalm 45, wedding songs prefiguring the marriage with the Messiah King, as they were interpreted by Jewish and Christian tradition.

Within the context of his people's tradition, Jesus used the imagery to say that he himself is the bridegroom foretold and awaited—the Messiah bridegroom (cf. Mt 9:15; 25:1). He also insisted on this analogy and terminology to explain what the "kingdom" is that he had come to bring. "The reign of God may be likened to a king who gave a wedding banquet for his son" (Mt 22:2). He compared his disciples to the bridegroom's friends, who rejoice at his presence and will fast when the bridegroom is taken away from them (cf. Mk 2:19-20). There is also the well-known parable of the ten virgins waiting for the bridegroom to arrive for the wedding feast (cf. Mt 25:1-3), as well as that of the servants who must be watching to welcome their master when he returns from a wedding (cf. Lk 12:35-38). In this regard it could be said that the first miracle Jesus performed at Cana, precisely at a wedding banquet, is significant (cf. Jn 2:1-11).

By calling himself the bridegroom, Jesus expressed the meaning of his entrance into history. He came to bring about God's marriage with humanity, in accordance with what the prophets foretold, in order to establish Yahweh's new covenant with his people, and to fill human hearts with the new gift of divine love, enabling them to taste its joy. As the bridegroom, he invites everyone to respond to this gift of love. All are called to answer love with love. He asks some to give a fuller, stronger and more radical response: that of virginity or celibacy "for the kingdom of heaven."

We also know that St. Paul accepted and developed the imagery of Christ the bridegroom suggested by the Old Testament and taken up by Jesus in his preaching and in teaching the disciples whom he would establish as the first community. The apostle urges those who are married to consider the example of the messianic marriage: "Husbands, love your wives as Christ loved the Church" (Eph 5:25). In addition to this special application, he looks on the Christian life in the perspective of a spousal union with Christ: "I have given you in marriage to one husband, presenting you as a chaste virgin to Christ" (2 Cor 11:2).

Paul wishes to make this presentation to Christ the bridegroom for all Christians. However, there is no doubt that the Pauline imagery of the chaste virgin finds its full realization and its greatest meaning in consecrated chastity. The most splendid model of this fulfillment is the Virgin Mary, who accepted in her being the best of her people's marital tradition. She did not limit herself to the awareness of her special belonging to God on the socio-religious level, but applied the idea of Israel as a bride to the complete giving of her soul and body "for the kingdom of heaven," in her sublime form of consciously chosen chastity. Hence the Council could state that in the Church the consecrated life is lived in deep harmony with the Blessed Virgin Mary (cf. *LG* 41), who is presented by the Church as "the one most fully consecrated" (cf. *RD* 17).

In the Christian world a new light was shed by Christ's word and Mary's example of oblation, a light soon to be known by the first communities. The reference to the nuptial union of Christ and the Church gives marriage itself its highest dignity. In particular, the sacrament of Matrimony introduces the spouses into the mystery of Christ's union with the Church. However, the profession of virginity or celibacy enables consecrated persons to share more directly in the mystery of this marriage. While conjugal love goes to Christ the bridegroom through a human union, virginal love goes directly to the person of Christ through an immediate union with him, without intermediaries—a truly complete and decisive spiritual espousal. Thus in the person of those who profess and live consecrated chastity, the Church expresses her union as bride with Christ the bridegroom to the greatest extent. For this reason it must be said that the virginal life is found at the heart of the Church.

In line with the evangelical and Christian concept, it must also be said that this immediate union with the bridegroom is an anticipation of the life of heaven, which will be characterized by a vision or possession of God without intermediaries. As the Second Vatican Council said, consecrated chastity will "recall to the minds of all the faithful that wondrous marriage decreed by God and which is to be fully revealed in the future age" *(PC* 12). In the Church the state of virginity or celibacy thus has an eschatological meaning. It is an especially expressive foretaste of the possession of Christ as the one bridegroom, as will occur in the fullness of the life to come. This is the meaning of what Jesus said about the state of life which will belong to the elect after the resurrection of the body. They "neither marry nor are given in marriage. They become like angels and are no longer liable to death. Sons of the resurrection [= raised up], they are sons of God" (Lk 20:35-36). Despite the obscurities and difficulties of earthly life, the state of consecrated chastity foreshadows the union with God, in Christ, which the elect will have in heavenly happiness, when the spiritualization of the risen man will be complete.

The profound happiness of consecrated life is understood from a consideration of this goal of heavenly union with Christ the bridegroom. St. Paul refers to this happiness when he says that the unmarried man is busy with the Lord's affairs and is not divided between the world and the Lord (cf. 1 Cor 7:32-35). But this is a happiness from which sacrifice is neither excluded nor dispensed with, since consecrated celibacy involves renunciations by which one is called to be more closely conformed to Christ crucified. St. Paul expressly states that in his bridegroom's love, Jesus Christ offered his sacrifice for the holiness of the Church (cf. Eph 5:25). In the light of the cross, we understand that every union with Christ the bridegroom is a loving commitment to the One who was crucified. Those who profess consecrated chastity know they are destined to a deeper sharing in Christ's sacrifice for the redemption of the world (cf. *RD* 8, 11).

The permanent nature of the nuptial union of Christ and the Church is expressed in the definitive value of the profession of consecrated chastity in religious life. "This consecration will be the more perfect, inasmuch as the indissoluble bond of the union of Christ and his bride, the Church, is represented by firm and more stable bonds" *(LG* 44). The indissolubility of the Church's covenant with Christ the bridegroom, shared in the pledge of self-giving to Christ in the virginal life, is the basis for the permanent validity of perpetual profession. It could be said that it is an absolute gift to him who is the Absolute. Jesus himself made this clear when he said: "Whoever puts his hand to the plow but keeps looking back is unfit for the reign of God" (Lk 9:62). Permanence, fidelity in the commitment to religious life, is clarified in the light of this Gospel saying.

With their witness of fidelity to Christ, consecrated persons support the fidelity of couples themselves in their marriage. The task of giving this support underlies Jesus' statement about those who become eunuchs for the sake of the kingdom of heaven (cf. Mt 19:10-12). By this statement the Master wished to show that the indissolubility of marriage—which he had just enunciated—is not impossible to observe, as the disciples were implying, because there are people who, with the help of grace, live outside marriage in perfect continence.

Hence we see that, far from being opposed to one another, consecrated celibacy and marriage are joined in the divine plan. Together they are meant to make the union of Christ and the Church more visible.

General audience of November 23, 1994

How Blest Are the Poor in Spirit!

In the contemporary world, with its blatant contrast between ancient and new forms of greed and the situations of unheard-of misery in which enormously broad strata of society live, the value of poverty freely chosen and consistently practiced is seen ever more clearly at the sociological level. From the Christian point of view, poverty has always been experienced as a state of life that makes it easier to follow Christ in contemplation, prayer and evangelization. It is important for the Church that many Christians have a deeper awareness of Christ's love for the poor and of the urgent need to come to their aid. But it is equally true that conditions in contemporary society point ever more harshly to the distance between the Gospel of the poor and a world often absorbed in pursuing interests connected with the craving of wealth, which has become an idol holding sway over all of life. This is why the Church is ever more intensely aware of the Spirit's prompting to be poor among the poor, to remind everyone of the need to conform to the ideal of poverty which Christ preached and practiced and to imitate his sincere, active love for the poor.

In particular, there is in the Church a revitalized and consolidated awareness of the front-line position occupied in this area of gospel values by religious and all those who seek to follow Christ in consecrated life. They are called to reflect in their own person and to witness before the world to the Master's poverty and his love for the poor. He himself linked the counsel of poverty both to the need for being personally stripped of the burden of earthly belongings so as to possess heavenly goods, and to charity toward the poor: "Go and sell what you have and give to the poor; you will then have treasure in heaven. After that, come and follow me" (Mk 10:21).

In asking for the renunciation, Jesus set for the rich young man a prior condition for following him: that of sharing most closely in the renunciation of the Incarnation. Paul reminded the Christians of Corinth of this, to encourage them to be generous with the poor, imitating the example of Christ, who "made himself poor though he was rich, so that you might become rich by his poverty" (2 Cor 8:9). St. Thomas comments that Jesus "endured material poverty to give us spiritual riches" *(Summa Theol.,* III, q. 40, a. 3). Everyone who accepts his invitation and voluntarily follows the way of poverty he inaugurated is led to enrich the human race spiritually. Far from simply adding their poverty to that of the other poor who fill the world, they are called to bring them true wealth, which is spiritual in nature. As I wrote in *Redemptionis Donum,* Christ "is the teacher and spokesman of poverty who makes us rich" (n. 12).

If we look at this teacher, we learn from him the true meaning of gospel poverty and the greatness of the call to follow him on the path of this poverty. First of all, we see that Jesus really lived like the poor. According to St. Paul, Christ, the Son of God, embraced the human condition as one of poverty, and in this human condition he lived a life of poverty. His birth was that of a poor person, as shown by the hut in which he was born and the manger in which his Mother placed him. For thirty years he lived in a family in which Joseph earned his daily bread by working as a carpenter, work he himself later shared (cf. Mt 13:55; Mk 6:3). In his public life he could say of himself: "The Son of Man has nowhere to lay his head" (Lk 9:58), as if to show his total dedication to his messianic mission in conditions of poverty. He died as a slave and poor man on the cross, literally stripped of everything. He chose to be poor to the very end.

Jesus proclaimed the blessedness of the poor: "Blest are you poor; the reign of God is yours" (Lk 6:20). In this regard we should remember that the Old Testament already spoke of the "Lord's poor" (cf. Ps 74:19; 149:4f.), the object of God's good will (Is 49:13; 66:2). This does not mean simply the destitute, but rather the lowly who sought God and trustfully put themselves under his protection. This attitude of humility and trust clarifies the expression used in Matthew's version of the Beatitudes: "How blest are the poor in spirit" (Mt 5:3). The poor in spirit are all those who do not put their trust in money or material possessions, and are open instead to the kingdom of God. However, it is precisely this value of poverty that Jesus praised and recommended as a life choice, which can include a voluntary renunciation of belongings, and precisely so on behalf of the poor. It is the privilege of some who are chosen and called to this way by him.

However, Jesus affirmed for everyone the need to make a basic decision regarding earthly goods—to be freed of their tyranny. No one, he said, can serve two masters. One either serves God or serves mammon (cf. Lk 16:13; Mt 6:24). The idolatry of mammon, or money, is incompatible with serving God. Jesus noted that the rich are more easily attached to money (called *mamôna'* in Aramaic, meaning "riches"), and have difficulty in turning to God. "How hard it will be for the rich to enter the kingdom of God! Indeed, it is easier for a camel to go through a needle's eye than for a rich man to enter the kingdom of heaven" (Lk 18.24-25, and par.).

Jesus warned against the twofold danger of earthly possessions—that with wealth one's heart is closed to God and is closed to one's neighbor, as we see in the parable of the rich man and Lazarus (cf. Lk 16:19-31). Nevertheless, Jesus did not condemn the possession of earthly goods absolutely. Instead, he was anxious to remind those who own them of the two-fold commandment of love of God and love of neighbor. But he asks much more of anyone who can and wishes to understand this.

The Gospel is clear on this point: Jesus asked those he called and invited to follow him to share his own poverty by renouncing their possessions, however great or few they may be. We already quoted his invitation to the rich young man: "Sell what you have and give to the poor" (Mk 10:21). It was a fundamental requirement, repeated many times, which meant giving up home and property (cf. Mk 10:29; and par.), or boat (cf. Mt 4:22), or even everything: "None of you can be my disciple if he does not renounce all his possessions" (Lk 14:33). To his "disciples," that is, those called to follow him by totally giving of themselves, Jesus said: "Sell what you have and give alms" (Lk 12:33).

This poverty is asked of those who are willing to follow Christ in consecrated life. Their poverty is expressed concretely in a juridical way, as the Council recalls. It can take various forms: the radical renunciation of owning property, as in the ancient "mendicant orders," and as practiced today by the members of other religious congregations, and other possible forms which the Council encourages to be sought (cf. *PC* 13). What matters is that poverty be really lived as a sharing in Christ's poverty: "With regard to religious poverty it is not enough to use goods in a way subject to the superior's will, but members must be poor both in fact and in spirit, their treasures being in heaven (cf. Mt 6:20)" *(PC* 13).

Institutes themselves are called to a collective witness to poverty. Giving new authority to the voice of so many teachers of spirituality and religious life, the Council especially stressed that institutes "should avoid every appearance of luxury, excessive wealth and the accumulation of goods" *(PC* 13).

Again, their poverty should be animated by a spirit of sharing between provinces and houses, and of generosity "for the needs of the Church and the support of the poor" *(PC* 13).

Another point, which is emerging again and again in the recent development of the forms of poverty, is seen in the Council's recommendation concerning "the common law of labor" *(PC* 13). In the past, there was the choice and practice of begging, a sign of poverty, humility and beneficial charity toward the needy. Today it is rather by their labor that religious "procure what is required for their sustenance and works" *(PC* 13). It is a law of life and a practice of poverty. Embracing it freely and joyfully means accepting the counsel and believing in the gospel blessedness of poverty. It is the greatest service that religious can give to the Gospel in this respect: witnessing to and practicing the spirit of trusting abandonment into the Father's hands as true followers of Christ, who lived and taught that spirit and left it as an inheritance to his Church.

General audience of November 30, 1994

Religious Offer Their Own Wills to God

When Jesus called disciples to follow him, he taught them the need for an obedience devoted to his person. This was not only a question of the common observance of the divine law and the dictates of a true and upright human conscience, but of a much greater commitment. Following Christ meant being willing to do all that he personally commanded and putting oneself under his direction in serving the Gospel for the coming of God's kingdom (cf. Lk 9:60, 62).

Therefore, in addition to the commitment to celibacy and poverty, with his "Follow me" Jesus also asked for one of obedience. This extended to the disciples his own obedience to the Father in the condition of the incarnate Word who became the "servant of Yahweh" (cf. Is 42:1; 52:13-53; Phil 2:7). Like poverty and chastity, obedience thus marked the fulfillment of Jesus' mission and indeed was its basic principle, expressed in the very intense feeling that led him to say: "My food is to do the will of him who sent me, and to accomplish his work" (Jn 4:34; cf. *RD* 13). We know from the Gospel that in virtue of this attitude, Jesus went so far as the sacrifice of the cross with total self-dedication, when—as St. Paul wrote—he who was divine in nature "humbled himself and became obedient unto death, even death on a cross" (Phil 2:8). The Letter to the

Hebrews stresses that Jesus Christ, "although he was Son, learned obedience through what he suffered" (Heb 5:8).

Jesus himself revealed that his heart's desire was to sacrifice himself totally, as it were through a mysterious *pondus crucis,* a sort of law of gravity of immolated life. This would find its greatest ·expression in the prayer of Gethsemane: "Abba, Father, all things are possible to you; remove this cup from me; yet not what I will, but what you will" (Mk 14:36).

Religious are heirs of the disciples directly called by Jesus to follow him in his messianic mission. The Council says: "In professing obedience, religious offer the full surrender of their own will as a sacrifice of themselves to God and so arc unitcd pcrmanently and securely to God's salvific will" *(PC* 14). Their response to God's saving will justifies the renunciation of their own freedom. As openness to God's saving plan against the limitless horizon in which the Father embraces all creation, evangelical obedience goes far beyond the disciple's personal destiny. It is a sharing in the work of universal redemption.

St. Paul underscored this salvific value in regard to Christ's obedience. If sin came into the world through an act of disobedience, universal salvation was obtained by the Redeemer's obedience: "For as by one man's disobedience many were made sinners, so by one man's obedience many will be made righteous" (Rom 5:19). In the patristic literature of the early centuries the parallel St. Paul made between Adam and Christ was taken up and developed, as was the reference to Mary in relation to Eve, from the aspect of obedience. St. Irenaeus wrote: "The knot of Eve's disobedience was loosed by Mary's obedience.... As the former was seduced into disobeying God, so the latter was convinced to obey God" *(Adv. Haer.,* III, 22, 4). For this reason Mary became the cooperator of salvation: *causa salutis.* By their obedience religious are also deeply involved in the work of salvation.

St. Thomas sees in religious obedience the most perfect

form of imitating Christ, who, as St. Paul says "...became obedient unto death, even death on a cross" (Phil 2:8). Obedience thus holds the chief place in the holocaust of religious profession (cf. *Summa Theol.,* II-II, q. 186, aa. 5, 7, 8).

Following this strong, beautiful Christian tradition, the Council states: "After the example of Jesus Christ...religious, under the motion of the Holy Spirit, subject themselves in faith to their superiors who hold the place of God. Under their guidance they are led to serve all their brothers in Christ, just as Christ himself in obedience to the Father served his brethren and laid down his life as a ransom for many" *(PC* 14). Jesus lived obedience to the Father without excluding human intermediaries. As a child Jesus obeyed Joseph and Mary: St. Luke says that he "was obedient to them" (Lk 2:51).

Thus Jesus is the model for those who obey human authority by perceiving in this authority a sign of God's will. By the evangelical counsel of obedience religious are called to obey their superiors as God's representatives. For this reason, in explaining a text (ch. 68 of St. Benedict's *Rule),* St. Thomas asserts that religious must abide by the judgment of the superior (cf. *Summa Theol.,* I-II, q. 13, a. 5, ad 3).

It is easy to understand that the difficulty of obedience often lies in perceiving this divine representation in a human creature. But if the mystery of the cross appears here, it should be kept in view. It should always be remembered that religious obedience is not simply a human submission to a human authority. Whoever obeys, submits himself to God, to the divine will expressed in the will of the superiors. It is a matter of faith. Religious must believe in God who communicates his will to them through their superiors. Even when the superiors' faults are apparent, their will, if not contrary to the law of God or to the rule, expresses the divine will. Even when from the standpoint of human judgment the decision does not seem wise, a faith judgment accepts the mystery of God's will: *mysterium crucis.*

Moreover, human mediation, though imperfect, bears a stamp of authenticity: that of the Church, which by her authority approves religious institutes and their laws as sure ways of Christian perfection. In addition to this reason of an ecclesial nature there is another stemming from the purpose of religious institutes: "They are contributing to building up the body of Christ according to God's plan" *(PC* 14). For the religious who regards and practices obedience in this way, it becomes the secret of true happiness given by the Christian certitude of having followed God's will instead of his own, with an intense love for Christ and the Church.

In addition, the Council urges superiors first to be docile to God's will, to be aware of their responsibility, to foster a spirit of service, to show charity to their brethren, to respect their subjects as human persons, to create an atmosphere of cooperation, and to listen to their brethren willingly, while retaining their authority to make decisions (cf. *PC* 14).

Love for the Church was at the origin of the rules and constitutions of religious families, which sometimes expressly declared their pledge of submission to Church authority. This explains the example of St. Ignatius of Loyola. In order to better serve Christ and the Church, he gave the Society of Jesus the famous "fourth vow" of "special obedience to the Pope concerning the missions." This vow states explicitly a norm that was and is implicit in any religious profession. Other institutes have also made this norm explicit in one way or another. Today the Code of Canon Law emphasizes it, in accord with the best tradition of gospel teaching and spirituality: "Institutes of consecrated life, inasmuch as they are dedicated in a special way to the service of God and of the entire Church, are subject to the supreme authority of this same Church in a special manner" (can. 590, §1). "Individual members [of institutes] are also bound to obey the Supreme Pontiff as their highest superior by reason of the sacred bond of obedience" (can. 590, §2). These are norms of life, which, when embraced and followed in faith, lead religious far beyond a juridical idea of structural organization in the Christian community. They feel the need to be as involved as possible in the Church's spiritual propensities and apostolic endeavors, in the various moments of her life, by their actions or at least by their prayer, and always with their filial affection.

General audience of December 7, 1994

Common Life Is
Modeled on the Early Church

Regarding the essential aspects of consecrated life, after discussing the evangelical counsels of chastity, poverty and obedience in the Decree *Perfectae Caritatis*, the Second Vatican Council speaks of life in common with reference to the example of the first Christian communities and in the light of the Gospel.

The Council's teaching on this point is very important, although it is true that a life in common, strictly understood, does not exist or is greatly reduced in some forms of consecrated life, such as the eremetic, while it is not necessarily required in secular institutes. However, it exists in the great majority of institutes of consecrated life and has always been considered by founders and by the Church as a basic observance for the good progress of religious life and the effective organization of the apostolate. As a confirmation of this, the Congregation for Institutes of Consecrated Life and Societies of Apostolic Life recently published a special document on *Fraternal Life in Community* (February 2, 1994).

If we look at the Gospel, it could be said that life in common is a response to Jesus' teaching on the connection between the two precepts of love of God and love of neighbor. In a state of life in which God is supremely loved, one cannot but strive to love one's neighbor with particular generosity, beginning with those who are closest because they belong to the same community. This is the state of life of consecrated persons.

Moreover, it is clear from the Gospel that Jesus' calls were addressed to individuals, but usually in order to invite them to join and to form a group. This was the case with the group of disciples and with that of the women.

The Gospel indicates the importance of fraternal charity as the soul of the community, and thus as an essential value of the common life. There is a reference to the disputes which took place on several occasions between the apostles themselves. In following Jesus, they did not cease to be men, children of their time and their people. They were anxious to establish ranks of greatness and authority. Jesus' response was a lesson in humility and willingness to serve (cf. Mt 18:3-4; 20:26-28, and par.). Then he gave them "his" commandment of mutual love according to his example (cf. Jn 13:34; 15:12, 17). In the history of the Church, especially in that of religious institutes, the question of the relationship between individuals and groups has often been raised. It has no other valid answer than that of Christian humility and fraternal love, which unites in the name and power of Christ's love, as the ancient song of the *"agapes"* says over and over: *Congregavit nos in unum Christi amor,* the love of Christ has gathered us together.

Certainly, the practice of fraternal love in the common life requires considerable effort and sacrifice, and demands generosity no less than the practice of the evangelical counsels. Hence, joining a religious institute or community implies a serious commitment to living fraternal love in all its aspects.

An example of this is found in the first Christian community. They came together immediately after the ascension to pray in unity of heart (cf. Acts 1:14) and to persevere in fraternal "communion" (Acts 2:42), going so far as to share their possessions: "They shared all things in common" (Acts

2:44). The unity desired by Christ found at the time of the
Church's beginning a fulfillment worthy of being recorded:
"The community of believers were of one heart and one mind"
(Acts 4:32).

The Church has always retained a deep memory of and
perhaps even a nostalgia for that early community. Basically,
religious communities have always sought to produce that
ideal of communion in charity as a practical rule of life in
common. Their members, gathered by the love of Christ, live
together because they intend to abide in this love. Thus they
can witness to the Church's true countenance, which reflects
her soul: charity.

"One heart and one mind" does not mean a rigid, fea-
tureless uniformity, but a deep communion in mutual understanding and reciprocal respect.

It cannot only be a matter, however, of a union of like-
mindedness and human affection. Echoing the Acts of the
Apostles, the Council speaks of a "sharing of the same spirit"
(PC 15). It is a question of a unity that has its deepest root in
the Holy Spirit, who pours out his love into hearts. He spurs
different people to help one another on the path of perfection
by creating and maintaining an atmosphere of good understanding and cooperation among themselves. As the guarantee
of unity in the whole Church, the Holy Spirit establishes it and
causes it to abide in an even more intense way in communities
of consecrated life.

What are the ways of this charity infused by the Holy
Spirit? The Council calls particular attention to mutual esteem
(cf. *PC* 15). It applies to religious two of St. Paul's exhortations to Christians: "Love one another with mutual affection;
anticipate each other in showing respect" (Rom 12:10), and
"Help carry one another's burdens" (Gal 6:2).

Mutual esteem is an expression of mutual love, which is
opposed to the widespread tendency to judge one's neighbor
harshly and criticize him. Paul's exhortation urges us to dis-

cover other people's qualities and, as far as the poor human eye can tell, the marvelous work of grace and—ultimately—of the Holy Spirit. This esteem means accepting the other with his characteristics and his way of thinking and acting. Thus, despite many obstacles, harmony among what are often very different dispositions can be achieved.

"Help carry one another's burdens" means sympathetically bearing with the true or apparent defects of others, however irksome, and willingly accepting all the sacrifices required by living together with those whose mentality and temperament are not fully in accord with one's own way of seeing and judging.

In this regard, the Council recalls that charity is the fulfillment of the law (cf. Rom 13:10), the bond of perfection (cf. Col 3:14), the sign of having passed from death to life (cf. 1 Jn 3:14), the manifestation of Christ's coming (cf. Jn 14:21, 23) and the source of great apostolic power (cf. *PC* 15). We can apply to the common life the excellence of charity described by St. Paul in First Corinthians (13:1-13) and attribute to it what the Apostle calls the fruits of the Spirit: "love, joy, peace, patient endurance, kindness, generosity, mildness and chastity" (Gal 5:22). The Council says that these are fruits of "the love of God which is poured into their hearts" *(PC* 15).

Jesus said: "Where two or three are gathered in my name, there am I in their midst" (Mt 18:20). Christ is present wherever there is unity in charity, and Christ's presence is the source of deep joy, which is renewed each day until the definitive meeting with him.

General audience of December 14, 1994

Prayer Is the One Thing Necessary

In the Christian tradition a prominent place has always been given to contemplation as the highest expression of the spiritual life and the culminating moment in the process of prayer. The contemplative act gives the fullness of meaning to religious life of whatever form, as a consequence of the special consecration resulting from the profession of the evangelical counsels. By virtue of this consecration, religious life is—and cannot but be—a life of prayer and thus of contemplation, even when in the form of spirituality and in practice, the time devoted to prayer is not exclusive or predominant.

This is why the Council states: "The members of every community, seeking God solely and before everything else, should join contemplation, by which they fix their minds and hearts on him, with apostolic love..." *(PC 5)*.

Thus the Council stresses that contemplation is not only obligatory in institutes that are purely contemplative but in all institutes, even those which are dedicated to very demanding apostolic work. Commitment to prayer is essential in every consecrated life.

This is what we learn from the Gospel, to which the Council itself refers. A Gospel episode recalled in particular (cf. *PC 5*) is that of Mary of Bethany, "who sat beside the Lord at his feet listening to him speak." To Martha, who wanted her sister to help her do the serving and so asked Jesus to intervene to urge her to work, the Master replied: "Mary has chosen the better part, which will not be taken from her" (Lk 10:38-41).

The meaning of this reply is self-evident. The "better part" is listening to Christ, remaining close to him, adhering to him in spirit and heart. This is why in the Christian tradition inspired by the Gospel, contemplation enjoys undisputed priority in religious life. Furthermore, in his reply the Master made Martha understand that adhering to his person, to his words, to the truth which he reveals and offers on God's behalf is "the only thing that is [truly] needed." It is as if to say that God—and also the Son made man—desires the homage of the heart before that of activity, and that the purpose of the religion Jesus instituted in the world is to adore the Father "in spirit and truth" (Jn 4:24). He himself desires this, according to the teaching given to the Samaritan woman.

In this priority of the homage of the heart, the Council teaches us to see also the proper response to the love of God who has first loved us (cf. *PC* 6). Sought in a privileged way by the Father, religious are called in turn to "seek God," to direct their desires to the Father, to maintain contact with him through prayer and to give him their hearts with ardent love.

They realize this intimacy with God in a life with Christ and in Christ. The Council says: "Let them strive to foster in all circumstances a life hidden with Christ in God (cf. Col 3:3)" *(PC* 6). St. Paul states the basic law of this hidden life: "Think of what is above, not of what is on earth" (Col 3:2). This hidden aspect of the intimate union with Christ will be revealed to us in its profound truth and beauty in the world to come.

On the basis of this essential meaning of consecrated life the Council recommends: "Members of religious communities should resolutely cultivate both the spirit and practice of prayer" *(PC* 6). Here it is sufficient for us to explain that "the spirit of prayer" is identified with the attitude of the soul that thirsts for divine intimacy and strives to live in this intimacy with total self-dedication. This attitude is expressed in concrete prayer to which a certain period is devoted each day of one's life. This too is an imitation of Jesus. Even during the most intense period of his ministry he set aside moments exclusively for dialogue with the Father in solitary prayer (cf. Mk 1:35; Lk 5:16; 6:12).

It is known that in the Christian tradition there are various forms of prayer, especially prayer "in common" and "private" prayer. Both are necessary and are generally prescribed. Prayer in common should never cause one to become unaccustomed to private prayer, nor should the latter become so prevalent that community prayer is eliminated or disparaged. A genuine spirit of gospel prayer regulates both forms in a beneficial balance for the soul, a balance which the founders and legislators of religious institutes establish in harmony with the authority of the Church.

Jesus recommended humble, sincere prayer: "Pray to your Father in secret" (Mt 6:6). He warned that it is not the quantity of words which insures that prayers will be heard (cf. Mt 6:7). But it is likewise true that interior prayer tends by human nature itself to be expressed and extended in words and gestures, in a series of acts of so-called external worship, whose soul is always the prayer of the heart.

The Council also indicates "the authentic sources of Christian spirituality" and prayer *(PC* 6). They are reading and meditating on Sacred Scripture, so as to enter more deeply into the mystery of Christ; and the liturgy, especially the celebration of the Eucharist, with its wealth of readings, sacramental participation in the redemptive sacrifice of the cross, and living contact with Christ as our food and drink in Communion. Some institutes also promote the practice of Eucharistic adoration, which fosters contemplation and attachment to the person of Christ, and witnesses to the attraction his presence exercises on humanity (cf. Jn 12:32). They cannot but be praised and held up for imitation.

We know that today, as always in the past, there are institutes "entirely dedicated to contemplation" *(PC* 7). They have their place in the Church's life even "no matter how pressing the needs of the active apostolate may be" *(PC* 7), which are felt in the world today. This is the concrete recognition of Christ's words about the "one thing that is necessary." The Church needs the prayer of contemplatives to grow in her union with Christ and to obtain the necessary graces for her development in the world. Contemplatives, monks and nuns, and cloistered monasteries are thus also witnesses to the priority which the Church gives to prayer and of the fidelity she wishes to reserve to the reply Jesus gave Martha about the "better part" chosen by Mary.

At this point it is necessary to remember that the response to the contemplative vocation implies great sacrifices, especially that of giving up direct apostolic activity, which today especially seems connatural to the majority of Christian men and women. Contemplatives are dedicated to the worship of the Eternal and "offer to God a sacrifice of praise which is outstanding" *(PC* 7) in a state of personal oblation so lofty as to require a special vocation, which must be verified before admission or final profession.

However, it should be noted that contemplative institutes also have an apostolic function in the Church. Indeed, prayer is a service to the Church and to souls. It yields "abundant fruits of holiness" and obtains for the People of God "a hidden apostolic fruitfulness" *(PC* 7). Indeed, we know that contemplatives pray and live for the Church. They often obtain for her support and progress those heavenly graces and assistance that are far superior to those achieved by activity.

In this respect it is beautiful to end this catechesis by recalling St. Thérèse of the Child Jesus. By her prayers and sacrifices she furthered the preaching of the Gospel as much as and more than if she had been totally dedicated to missionary activity, so much so that she was proclaimed patroness of the missions. This highlights the essential importance of institutes of contemplative life. It recalls the need for all these institutes of religious life, even those dedicated to the busiest and most varied apostolates, to remember that activity—even the holiest and the most beneficial to our neighbor—can never dispense with prayer as the homage of one's heart, mind and whole life to God.

General audience of January 4, 1995

Religious Serve the Growth of God's Reign

The Second Vatican Council sheds light on the ecclesiological dimension of the evangelical counsels (cf. *LG* 44). In the Gospel, Jesus himself let it be understood that establishing the kingdom is the objective of his call to the consecrated life. Voluntary celibacy must be practiced for the kingdom of heaven (cf. Mt 19:12), and total renouncement in order to follow the Master is justified by the "kingdom of God" (Lk 18:29).

Jesus established a very close connection between the mission he entrusted to the apostles and his request that they leave everything to follow him—their secular activities and their possessions *(ta idia),* as we read in Luke 18:28. Peter realized this, which is why he declared to Jesus, also on behalf of the other apostles: "We have given up everything and followed you" (Mk 10:28; cf. Mt 19:27).

All that Jesus demanded of his apostles, he also asks of those who, in the various ages of the Church's history, are willing to follow him in the apostolate on the path of the evangelical counsels—the total gift of self and of every effort to promote the kingdom of God on earth, a development for which the Church has the main responsibility. It should be said that, according to Christian tradition, personal sanctification is never exclusively the aim of a vocation. On the contrary, an exclusively personal sanctification would not be authentic because Christ has closely linked holiness and charity. Therefore, those who strive for personal holiness must do so in the context of a commitment of service to the Church's life and holiness. Even purely contemplative life involves this ecclesiological orientation, as we have seen in a previous catechesis.

According to the Council, the task and duty of religious who work "to implant and strengthen the kingdom of Christ in souls and to extend that kingdom to every clime" *(LG* 44) stems from this fact. In the wide variety of services which the Church needs there is room for everyone. Every consecrated person can and should concentrate his or her whole strength to establish and spread Christ's kingdom on earth, according to the gifts and charisms with which each is endowed, in constructive harmony with the mission of each one's religious family.

Missionary activity seeks to spread Christ's kingdom (cf. *LG* 44). Indeed, history confirms that religious have played an important part in the Church's missionary expansion. Called and vowed to total consecration, religious show their generous dedication by bringing the proclamation of the Good News of their Lord and Master everywhere, even in regions furthest from their own countries, as happened with the apostles. Side by side with the institutes in which some members are devoted to missionary activity *ad gentes,* there are others founded expressly for the evangelization of peoples who have not or had not yet received the Gospel.

The Church's missionary nature thus becomes concrete in a "special vocation" (cf. *RM* 65), which makes her work extend beyond all geographical, ethnic and cultural boundaries, *"in universo mundo"* (Mk 16:5).

The Second Vatican Council's Decree *Perfectae Caritatis* recalls: "There are in the Church very many institutes,

both clerical and lay, which devote themselves to various apostolic tasks. The gifts which these communities possess differ
according to the grace which is allotted to them" *(PC* 8). The
Holy Spirit distributes charisms in relation to the growing
needs of the Church and the world. It is impossible not to
recognize in this fact one of the clearest signs of divine generosity, which inspires and stimulates human generosity. We
must indeed rejoice when this sign is as frequent as it is in our
time, precisely because it demonstrates that the sense of service to the kingdom of God and to the Church's development
is spreading and intensifying. According to the Council's
teaching, the activity of religious, at both the more directly
apostolic and the charitable level, is not an obstacle to their
sanctification, but helps promote it. This is because it increases
their love of God and neighbor, and enables those who carry
out the apostolate to share in the grace granted to those who
receive the benefits of this activity.

But the Council adds that all apostolic activity should be
motivated by union with Christ, to which religious cannot fail
to aspire by virtue of their profession itself. "The whole religious life of their members should be inspired by an apostolic
spirit and all their apostolic activity formed by the spirit of
religion" *(PC* 8). Religious must be the first in the Church to
show that they know how to resist the temptation to sacrifice
prayer to activity. It is incumbent on them to show how action
draws its apostolic fruitfulness from an interior life rich in
faith and the experience of divine things: *"ex plenitudine
contemplationis, "* as St. Thomas Aquinas says *(Summa Theol.,*
II-II, q. 288, a. 6; III, q. 40, a.1, ad 2).

The problem of how to combine apostolic activity with
prayer has arisen at various times down the centuries as it does
today, especially in monastic institutes. The Council pays tribute to "the monastic life, that venerable institution which in the
course of a long history has won for itself notable renown in
the Church and in human society" *(PC* 9). It recognizes the

possibility of stressing different aspects of the "principal duty of monks," which is "to offer a service to the divine majesty at once humble and noble within the walls of the monastery, whether they dedicate themselves entirely to divine worship in the contemplative life, or have legitimately undertaken some apostolate or work of Christian charity" *(PC 9)*.

More generally, the Council recommends that all institutes suitably adapt their observances and customs to the needs of their particular apostolate. They should nevertheless take into account the many forms of the active religious life and thus their diversity, and also the need that "the lives of religious dedicated to the service of Christ in these various communities be sustained by special provisions appropriate to each" *(PC 8)*. Moreover, in this work of adaptation it should never be forgotten that it is first and foremost a work of the Holy Spirit, docility to whom is thus necessary for seeking the means of a more effective and fruitful activity.

By this many-faceted contribution which religious, in accordance with the variety of their vocations and charisms, give through prayer and activity to spreading and strengthening Christ's kingdom, the Council states: "The Church preserves and fosters the special character of her various religious institutes" *(LG 44)*. "The Church not only raises the religious profession to the dignity of a canonical state by her approval, but even manifests that this profession is a state consecrated to God by the liturgical setting of that profession. The Church...accompanies their self-offering by the Eucharistic sacrifice" *(LG 45)*.

In particular, according to the Council, the Roman Pontiff looks to the welfare of religious institutes and their individual members "in order to more fully provide for the necessities of the entire flock of the Lord" *(LG 45)*. The scope of this objective includes the exemption by which some institutes are directly subject to papal authority. This exemption does not dispense religious from showing "reverence and obedience to bishops" *(LG* 45). Its only purpose is to ensure the opportunity for an apostolic activity which is better oriented to the good of the whole Church. In the service of the Church, consecrated life is more especially available for the concerns and programs of the Pope, the visible head of the universal Church. Here the ecclesial dimension of consecrated life reaches a summit which belongs not only to the canonical order but also the spiritual. This is a concrete expression of the profession of obedience which religious make to the authority of the Church, in the vicarious role assigned to her by Christ.

General audience of January 11, 1995

A Witness to the World's True Destiny

After describing the religious vocation, the Second Vatican Council states: "The profession of the evangelical counsels, then, appears as a sign which can and ought to attract all the members of the Church to an effective and prompt fulfillment of the duties of their Christian vocation" (LG 44). This means that the radical commitment of religious to follow Christ encourages all Christians to have a keener awareness of their own calling and to appreciate better its beauty. It helps them to accept joyfully the commitments that are part of their vocation and inspires them to take on tasks which meet the concrete needs of apostolic and charitable work. The consecrated life is therefore a sign which strengthens all in their service to the kingdom.

We seek to understand more deeply the meaning of this conciliar teaching. Indeed, we can say that the religious state makes the form of life assumed by the incarnate Son of God present in this age just as it has done throughout Christian history. Thus it reveals more clearly the Christ of the Gospel (cf. LG 44).

Those who now follow Jesus, leaving everything for his sake, call to mind the apostles who gave up everything in answer to his invitation. As a result, it has become traditional to speak of religious life as an *apostolica vivendi forma*. Indeed, after the example of Peter, John, James, Andrew and the other apostles, religious imitate and reproduce the form of evangelical life lived and taught by the divine Master. They witness to the Gospel as an ever living reality in the Church and in the world. In this way they too fulfill the words of Jesus Christ to his apostles: "You will be my witnesses" (Acts 1:8).

The Council added: "The religious state clearly manifests that the kingdom of God and its needs, in a very special way, are raised above all earthly considerations. Finally it clearly shows all men both the unsurpassed breadth of the strength of Christ the King and the infinite power of the Holy Spirit marvelously working in the Church" *(LG* 44). In other words, life according to the evangelical counsels manifests the supernatural and transcendent majesty of the Triune God and, in particular, the sublime plan of the Father, who desires the complete gift of the human person as a filial response to his infinite love. It reveals the attractive power of Christ, the Incarnate Word, who takes over the whole of life to ennoble it by the highest participation in the mystery of Trinitarian life. At the same time, it is a sign of the transforming power of the Holy Spirit, who infuses in all souls the gifts of eternal Love, who works all the marvels of redemption and spurs the human response of faith and obedience in filial love to its peak.

For these same reasons, for believers who are called to a secular commitment, consecrated life is a sign and witness of the world's true destiny, which goes well beyond all immediate and visible perspectives however legitimate or proper. According to the Council, by their state, "Religious give splendid and striking testimony that the world cannot be transformed and offered to God without the spirit of the Beatitudes" *(LG* 31).

The religious state seeks to put the gospel Beatitudes into practice and helps one to discover and love them, showing the deep happiness attained through renouncement and sacrifice.

This is a striking witness, as the Council says, because it reflects a ray of the divine light that pervades the words, the call, the "counsels" of Jesus. It is also an outstanding witness, because the evangelical counsels, such as voluntary celibacy or gospel poverty, represent a particular way of life which has an irreplaceable value for the Church. It also has an unparalleled effectiveness for all those who, in the world, are more or less directly and consciously seeking God's kingdom. Lastly, it is a witness connected with the religious state as such. So it is natural that it should shine in noble religious figures who, with total dedication of soul and life, respond faithfully to their vocation.

The consecrated life is also a reminder of the value of the heavenly goods that Christianity teaches us to consider already present in view of the mystery of Christ, the Son of God who came down to earth from heaven and ascended into heaven as "the new Adam," the head of the new humanity called to share in God's glory. It is the doctrine of the Council explained in a beautiful passage: "The People of God have no lasting city here below, but look forward to one that is to come. Since this is so, the religious state, whose purpose is to free its members from earthly cares, more fully manifests to all believers the presence of heavenly goods already possessed here below. Furthermore, it not only witnesses to the fact of a new and eternal life acquired by the redemption of Christ, but it foretells the future resurrection and the glory of the heavenly kingdom" *(LG* 44).

The evangelical counsels thus have an eschatological meaning. In particular, consecrated celibacy proclaims the life to come and union with Christ the bridegroom. Poverty brings treasure in heaven; the commitment to obedience opens the way to possessing the perfect freedom of God's children, in conformity with the will of the heavenly Father.

Thus consecrated persons are symbols and witnesses that anticipate heavenly life here on earth. Earthly life cannot find its own perfection in itself but must be increasingly directed toward eternal life—a future already present, in germ, in the grace that begets hope.

For all these reasons, the Church desires that consecrated life should continue to flourish in order to reveal better Christ's presence in his Mystical Body, where today he lives and renews in his followers the "mysteries" revealed to us in the Gospel. The witness of consecrated chastity has shown itself to be of particular importance for today's world. It is the testimony of a love for Christ which is greater than any other love, of a grace that overcomes the forces of human nature, of a lofty spirit which is unflinching when confronted with the illusions and ambiguities caused by the demands of sensuality.

The testimony of both poverty, which religious offer as the secret and guarantee of greater spiritual wealth, and obedience, professed and practiced as an element of true freedom, is as important today as it was in the past.

The crowning virtue is charity, even in religious life— charity toward God, first of all. With it, consecrated life becomes a sign of the world "offered to God" *(LG* 31). In their total gift, including the conscious and loving association with Christ's redeeming sacrifice, religious show the world the way to true happiness, that is, the gospel Beatitudes.

This requires charity to one's neighbor, shown both in mutual love among those who live in community and in the practice of openness and hospitality, in aiding the poor and all the unfortunate, and in dedication to the apostolate. This is a witness of essential importance, which gives the Church her true gospel face. Consecrated persons are called to witness to and spread the "message...heard from the beginning: we should love one another" (1 Jn 3:11), thus becoming pioneers of the desired civilization of love.

General audience of February 8, 1995

Religious Life Can
Greatly Assist Priests

There are deep affinities between the priesthood and religious life. Actually, down the centuries the number of religious priests has increased. In most cases these are men who, having entered a religious institute, were ordained priests within it. Less frequent, but still numerous, are the cases of priests incardinated in a diocese who subsequently join a religious institute. Both cases show that in male consecrated life the vocation to a religious institute is often associated with a vocation to the priestly ministry.

We ask ourselves what the religious life contributes to the priestly ministry and why, in God's plan, so many men are called to this ministry within the framework of religious life. Let us answer that, if it is true that priestly ordination itself entails a personal consecration, entering religious life predisposes the subject to accept the grace of priestly ordination better and to live its requirements more completely. The grace of the evangelical counsels and of community life has been shown to foster the acquisition of the holiness required by the priesthood because of the priest's function with respect to the Eucharistic and Mystical Body of Christ.

Furthermore, the striving for perfection that marks and characterizes religious life encourages the ascetic effort to

597

make progress in virtue, to grow in faith, hope and especially charity, and to live a life that conforms to the Gospel ideal. To this end, institutes offer formation so that religious may be firmly guided from their youth in a life of holiness and acquire solid convictions and habits of life that are evangelically austere. In these spiritual conditions, they can draw greater benefit from the graces which accompany priestly ordination.

Nevertheless, before religious vows become obligations assumed in connection with Holy Orders and the ministry, they have an inherent value as a response of oblative love to the one who with infinite love "offered himself freely" for our sake (cf. Is 53:12; Heb 9:28). Thus the commitment to celibacy is not primarily a requirement for the diaconate or the priesthood, but adherence to an ideal that requires the total gift of self to Christ.

Let us add that with this commitment prior to ordination, religious can help diocesan priests to understand better and further appreciate the value of celibacy. It is to be hoped that, far from casting doubt on the validity of such a decision, they will encourage diocesan priests to be faithful in this area. This is a beautiful and holy ecclesial role carried out by religious institutes outside their confines for the benefit of the entire Christian community.

Belonging to a religious institute enables the priest to live evangelical poverty more radically. Indeed, community life permits the members of an institute to give up their personal belongings, while the diocesan priest normally has to provide for himself. Thus an increasingly visible witness of evangelical poverty is to be hoped for and expected from religious priests. In addition to sustaining them on their way to the perfection of love, this witness can encourage diocesan priests to seek practical ways of living a life of greater poverty, especially by pooling some of their resources.

Lastly, the vow of obedience taken by religious is intended to exercise a beneficial influence on their attitude in the priestly ministry. It spurs them to submission toward the superiors of the community helping them, to communion in the spirit of faith with those who represent God's will for them, and to respect for the authority of the bishops and the Pope in the fulfillment of their sacred ministry. Therefore, not only is formal obedience to the Church's hierarchy expected and hoped for from religious priests, but also a spirit of loyal, friendly and generous cooperation with it. By their formation in evangelical obedience, they can more easily overcome the temptations of rebellion, systematic criticism or distrust, and can recognize in the pastors the expression of divine authority. This is also a useful aid that, as we read in the Decree *Christus Dominus* of the Second Vatican Council, religious priests can and must bring the sacred pastors of the Church. This is true today as in the past and even more in the future, "in view of the greater needs of souls...the increasing demands of the apostolate" *(CD* 34).

Again, religious priests can show through their community life the charity which must motivate the presbyterate. According to the intention Christ expressed in the upper room, the precept of mutual love is linked to priestly consecration. In relations of communion established in view of the perfection of love, religious can witness to the fraternal charity that binds those who, in Christ's name, exercise the priestly ministry. Clearly, this fraternal love should also characterize their relations with diocesan priests and with the members of institutes other than their own. This is the source of that organized cooperation recommended by the Council (cf. *CD* 35, 5).

Again according to the Council, religious are more deeply committed to serving the Church by virtue of their consecration based on the profession of the evangelical counsels (cf. *LG* 44). This service consists above all in prayer, in acts of penance and in the example given by their own life. Also, "With due consideration for the special character of each religious institute, they should also enter more vigorously into the external works of the apostolate" *(CD* 33). By their participation in the care of souls and the works of the apostolate under the authority of the sacred pastors, religious priests "can be said in a real sense to belong to the clergy of the diocese" *(CD* 34). They must therefore "discharge their duties as active and obedient helpers of the bishops" *(CD* 35, 1) while at the same time preserving "the spirit of their religious community" and remaining faithful to the observance of their rule *(CD* 35, 2).

It is to be hoped that through the work of religious priests, the unity and harmony Jesus requested for all those who agree to be, like him, "consecrated in the truth" (Jn 17:19), will become more and more a reality in dioceses and in the whole Church, and thus radiate the *imago ecclesiae caritatis* throughout the world!

General audience of February 15, 1995

The Role of Lay Religious in the Church

In religious institutes which consist mainly of priests, there are many "brothers" who are full-fledged members although they have not received Holy Orders. They sometimes have the title of "cooperators," or an equivalent term. In the ancient mendicant orders they were generally known as "lay brothers." In this expression, the term "brothers" means "religious," and the qualification "lay" means "those not ordained priests." If it is then considered that in several of the ancient orders such religious were called *conversi,* in most cases it is easy to perceive the historical reference to their vocation—in other words, to the conversion which originally impelled them to give themselves to God in service to the "priest brothers," after years of life spent in various secular careers: administrative, civil, military, commercial, etc.

However, the words of the Second Vatican Council remain decisive. They state: "The religious life, undertaken by lay people, either men or women, is a state for the profession of the evangelical counsels which is complete in itself" *(PC* 10). Commitment to the priestly ministry is not required by the consecration which is proper to the religious state, and therefore even without priestly ordination a religious may live his consecration to the full.

In looking at the historical development of consecrated

life in the Church, a significant fact is clear: the members of the first religious communities were called "brothers" without distinction, and the great majority of them did not receive priestly ordination because they did not have a vocation to the ministry. A priest could join these communities but could not claim privileges because of Holy Orders. When priests were needed, one of the "brothers" was ordained in order to meet the community's sacramental needs. Over the centuries, the proportion of monks who were priests or deacons in comparison to the number of those who were not priests continued to grow. Gradually a division was established between clerical members and lay brothers or *conversi*. The ideal of a consecrated life without the priesthood lives on in St. Francis of Assisi. He did not feel personally called to the priestly ministry, although he later agreed to be ordained a deacon. Francis can be considered as an example of the holiness of a "lay" religious life. His witness demonstrates the perfection that can be reached by this way of life.

Lay religious life has continued to flourish down the centuries. In our age too it has endured and has developed in two directions. On the one hand, we have a certain number of lay brothers who have joined various clerical institutes. With regard to them, the Second Vatican Council makes one recommendation: "That all the members be more closely knit by the bond of brotherly love, those who are called lay brothers, assistants, or some similar name should be drawn closely into the life and work of the community" *(PC* 15).

Then there are lay institutes which, recognized as such by the authority of the Church, have their own proper role by virtue of their nature, character and aim. This is defined by their founder or by a legitimate tradition, and does not include the exercise of Holy Orders (cf. *CIC,* can. 588, §3). These "institutes of brothers," as they are called, do indeed carry out a precise function which is valuable in itself and especially useful in the Church's life.

The Second Vatican Council was thinking in particular of these secular institutes when it showed its appreciation for the state of lay religious life: "While holding in high esteem therefore this way of life so useful to the pastoral mission of the Church in educating youth, caring for the sick and carrying out its other ministries, the sacred synod confirms these religious in their vocation and urges them to adjust their way of life to modern needs" *(PC* 10). The Church's recent history confirms the important role played by the religious who belong to these institutes, especially in educational or charitable works. It can be said that in many places they have given the young a Christian education, founding schools of every kind and for all levels. They have created and administered institutions offering social assistance to the sick and the physically and mentally handicapped, for whom they have also provided the necessary buildings and equipment. Thus their witness to the Christian faith, their dedication and their sacrifice should be admired and praised. It is to be hoped that the aid of benefactors—in the best Christian tradition—and subsidies provided by modern social legislation may increasingly enable them to care for the poor.

The "great esteem" the Council expressed shows that the Church's authority highly appreciates the gift offered by "brothers" to Christian society through the ages, and their collaboration in evangelization and in the pastoral and social care of peoples. Today more than ever, we can and must recognize their historical role and their ecclesial function as witnesses and ministers of Christ's kingdom.

The Council made provision for brothers' institutes to benefit from the pastoral ministry necessary for the development of their religious life. This is the meaning of the statement which resolved a problem frequently discussed inside and outside these worthy institutes: "There is nothing to prevent some members of religious communities of brothers being admitted to Holy Orders by provision of their general

chapter in order to meet the need for priestly ministrations in
their own houses, provided that the lay character of the community remains unchanged" *(PC* 10). This is a possibility to be
evaluated in accordance with the needs of time and place, but
in harmony with the most ancient tradition of monastic institutes, which are thus able to flourish again. The Council
recognized this possibility and stated that there was no impedi-
ment to its implementation. But it lets the highest governing
assembly of these institutes—the general chapter—decide,
without offering explicit encouragement in this regard. This is
precisely because it is concerned that these institutes of brothers continue in line with their vocation and mission.

I cannot bring this discussion to a close without stressing
the rich spirituality suggested by the term "brothers." These
religious are called to be brothers of Christ, deeply united with
him, "the firstborn among many brothers" (Rom 8:29); brothers to one another, in mutual love and working together in the
Church in the same service to what is good; brothers to every
man, in their witness to Christ's love for all, especially the
lowliest, the neediest; brothers for a greater brotherhood in the
Church.

Unfortunately in recent times a decreased number of vocations to the lay religious life is becoming apparent in both
clerical and secular institutes. A new effort must be made to
foster these important and noble vocations so they may thrive
anew—a fresh effort to promote vocations, with a new commitment to prayer. The possibility of a lay consecrated life
must also be presented as a way of true religious perfection in
both the old and new male institutes.

At the same time, it is most important that in clerical
institutes whose members also include lay brothers, the latter
should play a suitable role so as to cooperate actively in the
institute's life and apostolate. Then there is a need to encourage lay institutes to persevere on the path of their vocation,

adapting to a changing society but constantly retaining and deepening the spirit of total self-giving to Christ and to the Church as expressed in their individual charism. I ask the Lord that an ever growing number of brothers may enrich the Church's holiness and mission.

General audience of February 22, 1995

Women Religious
Faithfully Serve Christ

The life of consecrated women has a very important place in the Church. It is enough to think of the deep influence of the contemplative life and prayer of women religious. We think of their work in education and health care, of their collaboration in many places in parish life, of the important services that they provide at diocesan or interdiocesan levels and of the specialized tasks which they are increasingly assuming even in the Holy See.

Let us also remember that in some countries the proclamation of the Gospel, catechetical activities and even the conferring of Baptism are largely entrusted to women religious, who have direct contact with the people in schools and families. Neither should we forget the other women who, in various forms of individual consecration and ecclesial communion, give of themselves to Christ in service to his kingdom in the Church. This happens today in the order of virgins, which one enters through special consecration to God in the hands of the diocesan bishop (cf. *CIC,* can. 604).

Blessed be this multiform host of "handmaids of the Lord." Down the centuries they extend and renew the very beautiful experience of the women who followed Jesus and served him and his disciples (cf. Lk 8:1-3).

No less than the apostles, they experienced the overwhelming power of the divine Master's word and love, and began to help and serve him to the best of their ability on his missionary journeys. Jesus' pleasure is apparent in the Gospel. He could not fail to appreciate these expressions of generosity and kindness typical of feminine psychology, but inspired by a faith in his person beyond mere human explanation. Mary Magdalene was a significant example of this. A faithful disciple and minister of Christ in his life, she was also later a witness to and, one could almost say, the first messenger of his resurrection (cf. Jn 20:17-18).

It cannot be ruled out that her gesture of sincere and faithful adherence is a sublime reflection of the sense of total dedication that leads a woman to betrothal. Even more so, at the level of supernatural love, it leads to virginal consecration to Christ, as I pointed out in *Mulieris Dignitatem* (cf. n. 20).

In this following of Christ expressed as service, we can also discover the other feminine quality of self-giving, which the Virgin Mary so vividly expressed in her final words to the angel: "Behold, I am the handmaid of the Lord. May it be done to me according to your word" (Lk 1:38). It is an expression of faith and love, which is made concrete in obedience to the divine call, at the service of God and of our brothers and sisters. Thus it was with Mary; thus it was with the women who followed Jesus; thus it was with all those who, in their footsteps, were to follow him down the centuries.

Today spousal mysticism appears less pronounced in young aspirants to the religious life. This outlook is not fostered by the common mentality, by school or by reading. Besides, there are well-known saintly figures who found and followed other paths in their relationship of consecration to God. This includes service to the coming of his kingdom, the gift of themselves to him in order to serve him in their poor brothers and sisters, and a keen sense of his sovereignty ("My Lord and my God!"—cf. Jn 20:28). It also includes identification with the Eucharistic sacrifice, being a daughter of the Church, the vocation to works of mercy, the desire to be the least or the last in the Christian community, to be the heart of the Church or to offer in their own souls a little temple to the Blessed Trinity. These are some of the *leitmotifs* of a life—like that of St. Paul and especially that of Mary—grasped by Christ Jesus (cf. Phil 3:12).

In addition, it could be useful to underscore for all women religious the value of participating in the condition of the "servant of the Lord" (cf. Is 41:9; 42:1; 49:3; Phil 2:7, etc.), proper to Christ the priest and victim. The service that Jesus came to fulfill by giving his life "as a ransom for many" (Mt 20:28) becomes an example to be imitated and a redeeming participation, to be lived in fraternal service (cf. Mt 20:25-27). This does not exclude—on the contrary, it includes—special fulfillment of the Church's spousal dimension in union with Christ and in the constant application to the world of the fruits of the redemption wrought by the priesthood of the cross.

According to the Council, the mystery of the Church's spousal union with Christ is represented in every consecrated life (cf. *LG* 44), especially through the profession of the evangelical counsel of chastity (cf. *PC* 12). It is understandable that this representation is especially realized in the consecrated woman. To her the title *sponsa Christi* is frequently attributed, even in the liturgical texts. Tertullian applied the image of nuptials with God to men and women without distinction when he wrote: "How many men and women in the ranks of the Church have appealed to continence and preferred to be wedded to God..." *(De exhort. cast.,* 13; *PL* 2:930A; *Corp. Christ,* 2, 1035, 35-39). But it cannot be denied that the feminine soul has a particular capacity to live in a mystical spousal relationship with Christ and thus to reproduce in herself the face and heart of his bride, the Church. This is why, in the rite for the profession of women religious and consecrated virgins in the world, the singing or recitation of the antiphon *"Veni sponsa*

Christi..." fills their hearts with intense emotion, enveloping those concerned and the whole assembly in an aura of mysticism.

In the logic of the union with Christ as priest and spouse, the sense of spiritual motherhood is also developed in women. Virginity, or evangelical chastity, implies renouncement of physical motherhood, but so as to be expressed, according to God's plan, in a superior kind of motherhood on which the light of the Virgin Mary's motherhood shines. Every consecrated virgin is destined to receive from the Lord a gift which in a certain way reproduces the features of universality and spiritual fruitfulness of Mary's motherhood.

This is shown in the work accomplished by many women religious in educating young people in faith. It is well known that many female congregations were founded and have established numerous schools precisely to impart this education. Especially when it is a question of little ones, womanly qualities are valuable and indispensable for this. This is also the case with many works of charity and assistance to the poor, the sick, the handicapped, the abandoned, especially children and little girls, once described as waifs. These are all cases where dedication and compassion, the treasures of the feminine heart, are involved. It is finally found in the various forms of cooperation in the services provided by parishes and Catholic institutions, where a woman's capacities for collaboration in the pastoral ministry are being ever more clearly revealed.

However, among all the values in female religious life, prayer should always be recognized as having priority. This is the main form of achieving and expressing intimacy with the divine bridegroom. All women religious are called to be women of prayer, women of piety, women of interior life, of a life of prayer. If it is true that the witness to this vocation is more obvious in institutes of contemplative life, certainly it also appears in institutes of the active apostolate that carefully safeguard the times of prayer and contemplation which corre-

spond to the needs and demands of consecrated persons and to
the advice given in the Gospel. Jesus recommended prayer to
all his disciples. He wished to shed light on the value of a life
of prayer and contemplation with the example of a woman,
Mary of Bethany, whom he praised for choosing "the better
part" (Lk 10:42): listening to the divine word, assimilating it,
making it a secret of life. Was not this a light for the whole
future contribution of women to the Church's life of prayer?

In assiduous prayer, moreover, lies the secret of perseverance in that commitment of fidelity to Christ which must serve
as an example for everyone in the Church.

This unblemished witness to persevering love can be a
great help to other women in critical situations which in this
regard also afflict our society. We hope and pray that many
women religious, possessing the heart of a bride of Christ and
showing it in their lives, may also help reveal to all people the
Church's fidelity in her union with Christ her spouse and enable them to understand it better: fidelity in truth, in charity,
and in yearning for universal salvation.

General audience of March 15, 1995

The Holy Spirit Is
the Soul of Community Life

In *Lumen Gentium,* the Second Vatican Council states that in its many forms, consecrated life shows "the infinite power of the Holy Spirit marvelously working in the Church" *(LG* 44). Likewise, the Council's decree on the renewal of religious life emphasizes that it was under "the inspiration of the Holy Spirit" that many became hermits or founded religious families which "the Church gladly welcomed and approved by her authority" *(PC* 1).

The spirituality of religious commitment, which animates all institutes of consecrated life, is clearly centered on Christ. It is centered on his person, on his virginal and poor life, taken to the point of the supreme gift of self for his brothers and sisters in perfect obedience to the Father. However, such a spirituality, understood in the strongest sense of the term, is a direction given by the Holy Spirit. In fact, following Christ in poverty, chastity and obedience would be impossible without the impulse of the Holy Spirit, the author of all inner growth and giver of every grace in the Church. "Driven by love with which the Holy Spirit floods their hearts," the Council continues, consecrated persons "live more and more for Christ and for his body which is the Church" *(PC* 1).

Indeed, in religious life and in every consecrated life, there is a sovereign and decisive action of the Holy Spirit. This may be experienced in an ineffable way by attentive souls through a kind of connaturality created by divine love, as St. Thomas would say (cf. *Summa Theol.,* II-II, q. 45, a. 2).

When, in his Church, Jesus Christ calls men or women to follow him, he makes his voice heard and his fascination felt by the inner action of the Holy Spirit. He entrusts to the Spirit the task of making his call understood and of awakening the desire to respond to it with a life entirely dedicated to Christ and his kingdom. The Holy Spirit nurtures the grace of vocation in the depths of the soul, making way for his grace to achieve its aim. He takes the lead in fostering vocations and guides consecrated souls on the way of perfection. He is the author of the generosity, patience and fidelity of one and all.

In addition to carrying out his role in individual souls, the Holy Spirit is also at the origin of communities of consecrated persons. The Second Vatican Council itself pointed this out (cf. *PC* 1). This is how it was in the past and it is the same today. The Holy Spirit has always granted the founding charism to some in the Church. He has always surrounded the founder or foundress with people who share the direction of his or her form of consecrated life, teaching, ideals and the attraction of his or her charity, knowledge or pastoral apostolate. The Holy Spirit has always created and fostered harmony among consecrated persons, and helped them to develop a community life enlivened by charity, in accordance with the specific direction of the founder's charism and of his faithful followers. It is comforting to note that in recent times too the Holy Spirit has caused new types of communities to arise in the Church, as well as new experiences of consecrated life.

Moreover, it is important to remember that in the Church, the Holy Spirit guides the responsible authorities in accepting and canonically recognizing communities of consecrated persons. This happens after examining, possibly improving and eventually approving their Constitutions (cf. *LG* 45), in order to encourage, sustain and often inspire their choice of activity. How many initiatives, how many newly-founded institutes and parishes, how many missionary expeditions have been more or less known to originate in the request or recommendations made by the Church's pastors to the founders and major superiors of institutes!

Often it is through the hierarchy that the Holy Spirit's action develops and even awakens charisms in religious. In any case he uses the hierarchy to guarantee religious families an orientation in conformity with the divine will and the teaching of the Gospel.

Again, the Holy Spirit exercises his influence on the formation of candidates for the consecrated life. He establishes in Christ the harmonious union of all the spiritual, apostolic, doctrinal and practical elements that the Church considers necessary for good formation (cf. *Directives on Formation in Religious Institutes).*

The Holy Spirit enables us especially to understand the value of the evangelical counsel of chastity, through an inner enlightenment which transcends ordinary human intelligence (cf. Mt 19:10-12). He inspires souls to give themselves radically to Christ in celibacy. Through his work, "persons consecrated by the vows of religion place at the center of their affective life a 'more immediate' relationship with God through Christ *in the Spirit" (Directives on Formation* 13), as an effect of the evangelical counsel of chastity.

The Holy Spirit also makes his active, creative power felt in the other two evangelical counsels. He not only provides the strength to renounce earthly goods and their advantages, but forms a spirit of poverty in the soul, instilling a preference for heavenly treasure, far beyond material goods. He also grants the necessary enlightenment to the judgment of faith in order to recognize God's mysterious will in the will of superiors, and to discern in the exercise of obedience a humble but generous cooperation in fulfilling the plan of salvation.

As the soul of the Mystical Body, the Holy Spirit is the soul of all community life. He develops all the priorities of charity which can contribute to unity and peace in community life. He ensures that Christ's word and example regarding the love of one's brothers and sisters is the active force in hearts, as St. Paul said (cf. Rom 5:5). With his grace he imbues the behavior of consecrated persons with the love of Jesus' meek and humble heart, his attitude of service and his heroic forgiveness.

No less necessary is the Holy Spirit's permanent influence on the perseverance of consecrated persons in prayer and in a life of intimate union with Christ. He instills the desire for divine intimacy, fosters a taste for prayer, and inspires a growing attraction toward the person of Christ, his word and the example of his life.

The breath of the Holy Spirit also animates the missionary apostolate of consecrated persons as individuals and in community. The history of the development of religious life, marked by a growing dedication to the evangelizing mission, confirms this action of the Spirit in support of the missionary involvement of religious families in the Church.

For their part, consecrated persons must cultivate a great docility to the inspirations and movements of the Holy Spirit, a constant communion with him and unceasing prayer to obtain his gifts in ever greater abundance, accompanied by a holy abandon to his initiative. This is the way increasingly discerned by the saints who were pastors and doctors of the Church, in harmony with the teaching of Jesus and the apostles. This is the way of the holy founders and foundresses who have opened up so many different types of community in the Church, giving rise to a variety of spiritualities: Basilian, Augustinian, Benedictine, Franciscan, Dominican, Carmelite, and many more. They are all experiences, ways and schools that witness to the wealth of the Holy Spirit's charisms and lead by diverse routes to the one, total Christ, in the one Church.

General audience of March 22, 1995

Mary Shows the Nobility of Virginity

The relationship with Mary most holy, which for every believer stems from his union with Christ, is even more pronounced in the life of consecrated persons. It is an essential aspect of their spirituality, more directly expressed in the very titles of some institutes which take the name of Mary and call themselves her "sons" or "daughters," "servants," "handmaids" or "apostles," etc. Many of them acknowledge and proclaim their link with Mary as specifically rooted in their tradition of doctrine and devotion from their foundation. They are all convinced that Mary's presence is of fundamental importance both for the spiritual life of each consecrated person, and for the solidity, unity and progress of the whole community.

There are sound reasons for this in Sacred Scripture itself. In the annunciation, Mary is described by the angel Gabriel as *gratia plena (kécharitôménê*—Lk 1:28), in an explicit reference to the sovereign and gratuitous action of grace (cf. *RMt* 7). Mary was chosen by virtue of a unique divine love. If she belongs totally to God and lives for him, it is because she first "had found favor" with God, who wished to make her the privileged place of his relationship with humanity in the Incarnation. Mary thus reminds consecrated persons that the grace of a vocation is an unmerited favor. God has loved them first (cf. 1 Jn 4:10, 19), by virtue of a gratuitous love which should move them to give thanks.

Mary is also the model of the acceptance of grace by the human creature. In her, grace itself brought about the "yes" of her will, her free adherence, the conscious docility of her *fiat,* which led her to a holiness that continued to develop throughout her life. Mary never hindered this development. She always followed the inspirations of grace and made God's intentions her own; she always cooperated with God. By her example, she teaches consecrated persons not to waste the graces they have received, to make an ever more generous response to the divine gift, to let themselves be inspired, moved and guided by the Holy Spirit.

Mary is the one "who believed," as her cousin Elizabeth recognized. This faith enabled her to collaborate in the fulfillment of the divine plan, which to human eyes appeared impossible (cf. Lk 1:37). This is how the mystery of the Lord's coming into this world was fulfilled. The Blessed Virgin's great merit is to have cooperated with his coming. She herself, like other human beings, did not know how it could come about. She believed, and "the Word became flesh" (Jn 1:14) by the power of the Holy Spirit (cf. *RMt* 12-14).

Those who answer the call to the consecrated life also need great faith. To be committed to the way of the evangelical counsels, they must believe in the God who calls them to live the counsels, and in the higher destiny he offers. In order to give oneself to Christ without reserve, one must recognize that he is the absolute Lord and Master, who can ask for everything because he can do everything to bring about what he asks. Therefore Mary, the model of faith, guides consecrated persons on the path of faith.

Mary is the Virgin of virgins *(Virgo virginum).* Since the earliest centuries of the Church she has been recognized as a model of consecrated virginity. Mary's will to preserve her virginity is surprising in a context where this ideal was not widespread. Her decision was the fruit of a special grace of the Holy Spirit, who opened her heart to the desire to offer herself totally to God, body and soul. This brought about in the loftiest and humanly inconceivable way Israel's vocation to a spousal relationship with God, to belonging totally and exclusively to him as the People of God.

The Holy Spirit prepared her for her extraordinary motherhood by means of virginity, because, according to God's eternal plan, a virginal soul was to welcome the Son of God in his Incarnation. Mary's example makes it possible to understand the beauty of virginity and encourages those called to the consecrated life to take this path. It is the time to reassess virginity in the light of Mary. It is the time to propose it once again to boys and girls as a serious plan of life. With her help, Mary sustains those who have undertaken this commitment, shows them the nobility of the total gift of the heart to God and constantly strengthens their fidelity even in difficult or dangerous moments.

For years and years, Mary was wholly dedicated to serving her Son. She helped him grow up and prepare himself for his mission at home and in the carpenter's workshop in Nazareth (cf. *RMt* 17). At Cana, she asked him to reveal his power as Savior and obtained his first miracle for a couple in difficulty (cf. *RMt* 18, 23). She has shown us the way of perfect docility to Christ, saying: "Do whatever he tells you" (Jn 2:5). On Calvary she was close to Jesus as his mother. In the upper room, she prayed with Jesus' disciples as they waited for the Holy Spirit he had promised.

Thus she shows consecrated persons the way of dedication to Christ in the Church as a family of faith, hope, and love. She obtains for them the wonders of the manifestation of the sovereign power of her Son, our Lord and Savior.

The new motherhood granted to Mary on Calvary is a gift which enriches all Christians, but its value is accentuated even more for consecrated persons. John, the beloved disciple, had offered his whole heart and all his strength to Christ. Hearing the words: "Woman, behold your son" (Jn 19:26), Mary accepted John as her son. She had understood too, that this new motherhood was open to all Christ's disciples. Her communion of ideals with John and with all consecrated people enables her motherhood to expand to the full.

Mary acts as a mother who is very attentive to helping those who have offered Christ all their love. She is full of concern for their spiritual needs. She also helps communities, as the history of religious institutes often attests. She who was present in the early community (Acts 1:14) is pleased to remain in the heart of all communities gathered in the name of her Son. In particular, she watches over the preservation and growth of their love.

The words of Jesus to the beloved disciple: "Behold your mother" (Jn 19:27), assume a particular depth in the life of consecrated persons. They are invited to consider Mary as their mother and to love her as Christ loved her. More especially, they are called to take her into their home, as John "took her into his home" (literally "among his possessions"—Jn 19:27). Above all, they must make room for her in their hearts and in their life. They must seek an ever greater development of their relationship with Mary, model and Mother of the Church, model and Mother of communities, model and Mother of all whom Christ calls to follow him.

Dearly beloved, how beautiful, venerable and in some ways enviable is this privileged position of consecrated persons beneath Mary's mantle and in Mary's heart! We pray that she may be close to them always and shine ever more as the star of their lives!

General audience of March 29, 1995

MISSIONARY ACTIVITY AND UNITY AMONG CHRISTIANS

The Apostles Were
Sent into the Whole World

In the progressive development of the catechesis on the Church, we started with the eternal plan of God who wanted her to be the sacrament, point of convergence and radiating center of the economy of salvation. Having considered the various aspects of the Church's mystery as the People of God, sacrament of the union between humanity and God, bride of Christ and priestly community, we explained the ministries she is called to carry out. Regarding these ministries, we considered the episcopal college's mission in the succession of the apostolic college; the mission of the Pope, Successor of Peter in the Roman episcopate and in his primacy over the universal Church; the mission of priests and its implications for their state of life; the mission of deacons, appreciated today as in early Christian times and rightly considered a fresh leaven of hope for the entire People of God. Further, we spoke of the laity, shedding light on their value and mission as "Christ's faithful" in general, and in their various conditions of personal, family and social life. Lastly, we focused on the consecrated life as a treasure of the Church, in its traditional forms and in its many expressions which are flourishing today.

During these talks we constantly referred to the mission of the Church and of each of her members. However, it is time to discuss them more systematically, to identify more clearly the essence of the Church's universal mission and at the same time to deal with the problems connected with it. Thus we will also have the opportunity to further clarify the significance of the catholicity that the Nicene-Constantinopolitan Creed attributes to the Church as an essential note, together with that of unity. In this way we will address topics of great timeliness and will analyze the problems posed by the growing commitment to ecumenism.

The Second Vatican Council recalled that the universality of the mission of the Church, which "strives ever to proclaim the Gospel to all men," is based on Christ's specific order and on the "inner necessity of her own catholicity" *(AG* 1).

Jesus entrusted a precise mandate to the apostles: "Go into the whole world and proclaim the Gospel to every creature" (Mk 16:15). "Make disciples of all nations" (Mt 28:19). Their preaching was destined to arouse "repentance, for the forgiveness of sins...." (Lk 24:47). At the time of the ascension the disciples limited their hope to the kingdom of Israel; in fact, they asked their Master: "Lord, are you at this time going to restore the kingdom to Israel?" (Acts 1:6). In his response, the Savior clearly showed them that they had to go beyond this viewpoint, that they themselves would become his witnesses not only in Jerusalem, but throughout Judea and Samaria, and "to the ends of the earth" (Acts 1:8).

The Redeemer did not rely merely on his disciples' docility to his word, but on the superior power of the Spirit whom he promised them: "You will receive power when the Holy Spirit comes upon you" (Acts 1:8). In this respect, the command to remain in Jerusalem was significant. In order to give a universal witness, the disciples were not to leave the city until they had received the promised divine power: "But stay in the city until you are clothed with power from on high" (Lk 24:49).

The universality of the mission entered the hearts of the disciples with the gift of the Holy Spirit. Thus the universal openness of the Church is not a characteristic imposed from without, but an expression of a property that belongs to her very essence. The Church is "catholic," "the universal sacrament of salvation" *(LG* 48), because by the power of the Holy Spirit, God's kingdom is anticipated in her.

Before quoting the disciples' question on the restoration of the kingdom of Israel, Luke tells how in the apparitions during the forty days after the resurrection, Jesus had spoken of "the kingdom of God." "God's kingdom" is the universal kingdom that reflects in itself the infinite being of God, without the borders and divisions which are typical of human kingdoms.

A trinitarian origin is present in Christian universalism. As we saw, Jesus attributed to the power of the Holy Spirit the work of the apostles, and therefore, of the Church in the universal evangelization. He spoke of the "Father's kingdom" (Mt 13:43; 26:29) and taught them to ask for the coming of this kingdom: "Our Father...your kingdom come" (Mt 6:9-10; cf. Lk 11:2). But he also said: "My kingdom" (Lk 22:30; Jn 18:36; cf. Mt 20:21; Lk 23:42), explaining that this kingdom had been prepared for him by his Father (cf. Lk 22:30) and did not belong to this world (cf. Jn 18:36).

For the disciples this meant going beyond the cultural and religious limits within which they were accustomed to thinking and living, to see themselves at the level of a kingdom of universal dimensions. In his conversation with the Samaritan woman, Jesus emphasized the need to overcome the cultural, national and ethnic conflicts historically associated with specific shrines, in order to establish the true worship of God: "The hour is coming when you will worship the Father neither on this mountain nor in Jerusalem.... But the hour is coming, and is now here, when true worshippers will worship the Father in Spirit and truth, and indeed the Father seeks such people to worship him" (Jn 4:21, 23). What Jesus asked of his disciples is his Father's will: to pass from God's kingdom in

Israel alone, to God's kingdom in all nations. The Father has a universal heart and, through the Son and in the Spirit, he establishes a universal worship. As I said in the Encyclical *Redemptoris Missio,* the Church emerges from the Father's universal heart, and she is catholic because the Father extends his fatherhood to all humanity (cf. *RM* 12).

The universality of the Father's eternal plan shines forth concretely in the messianic work of his only Son made man, which is at the origin of Christianity.

In accordance with the Father's mandate, Jesus' preaching was limited to the Jewish people, "to the lost sheep of the house of Israel," as he himself declared (cf. Mt 15:24). However, this preaching was only a prelude to the universal evangelization and the entry of all nations into the kingdom proclaimed by Christ himself, in harmony with the deep meaning of the prophets' preaching: "I say to you, many will come from the East and the West, and will recline with Abraham, Isaac and Jacob at the banquet in the kingdom of heaven..." (Mt 8:11). This universalist vision is brought to light by Jesus' presentation of himself as "Son of Man" and not only "Son of David," since he himself was David's Lord (cf. Mt 22:45; Mk 12:37; Lk 20:44).

The title "Son of Man" in the language of Jewish apocalyptic literature, inspired by the prophet Daniel (7:13), is a reference to the heavenly figure who would receive the eschatological kingdom from God. Jesus used it to express the true nature of his Messianism as a mission fulfilled at the level of true humanity, but transcending all ethnic, national and religious particularism.

The universality which proceeds from the Father and the incarnate Son was definitively transmitted to the Church on the day of Pentecost, when the Holy Spirit filled the first Christian community and made it universal. The apostles then witnessed to Christ, addressing people of all nations, who understood them as though they were speaking each one's native language (cf. Acts 2:7-8). From that day on, the Church with the "power of the Holy Spirit," as Jesus had promised, acted incisively "in Jerusalem, in the whole of Judea and Samaria and to the ends of the earth" (Acts 1:8).

Thus the Church's universal mission does not rise from below but descends from above, from the Holy Spirit, as if imbued with the universality of trinitarian love. The trinitarian mystery, through the mystery of the Redemption, by the influence of the Holy Spirit, communicates to the Church the property of universalism. Thus the mystery of the Church derives from the mystery of the Trinity.

General audience of April 5, 1995

The Church Is Missionary by Her Nature

Heir to and continuation of the apostles who were sent to witness to Christ and to preach the Gospel "to the ends of the earth" (Acts 1:8), the Church possesses the note of "catholicity" from which her "missionary" nature derives. This second characteristic, part of her mystery, comes "from on high." The Second Vatican Council notes this in the Decree *Ad Gentes,* according to which, "The pilgrim Church is missionary by her very nature, since it is from the mission of the Son and the mission of the Holy Spirit that she draws her origin, in accordance with the decree of God the Father" *(AG* 2). It is a mystery established by the divine trinitarian plan which is fulfilled in the Church and made manifest as permanently her own, since the day of Pentecost.

Being essentially missionary does not mean merely that the Church has a universal mission to all humanity. It means that in her constitutive reality, in her soul, and thus it could be said in her very "psychology," she possesses a dynamism that concretely unfolds in preaching the Gospel, in spreading the faith and in calling to conversion. All this is proclaimed "to the very ends of the earth." This interior drive, intimately linked to her mission, comes from the Holy Spirit and is therefore part of her mystery. The dynamism that comes from it is thus expressed as a distinctive characteristic of the whole Church. This is shown in a concrete and effective way especially in those who, starting with the apostles, go to regions far from their land for the sake of the Gospel. Even if all are not called personally to go to mission lands, each one in the Church and with the Church has the task of spreading the light of the Gospel, according to the saving mission passed on by the Redeemer to the ecclesial community. Indeed, all are called to cooperate in this mission.

We must insist on deepening the trinitarian origin of this missionary dynamism, to which the Decree *Ad Gentes* refers (cf. nn. 2, 3, 5). This dynamism flows from the "fountain-like love," that is, from the "love of God the Father," from "his great and merciful kindness." He is the God who creates us and "gratuitously calls us to share in his life and in his glory." He "pours out his divine goodness" in order to be "all in all" (1 Cor 15:28). It is from his infinite generosity destined for every creature that the Church's missionary movement stems as the Holy Spirit's gift, a movement committed to spreading the message of salvation in the world.

The dynamism of divine life was first communicated in the Incarnation of the eternal Son of God, sent by the Father to bring mankind revelation and salvation. The coming into the world of the Word made flesh (cf. Jn 1:14) can be considered a "type" or "archetype"—as the Fathers would say—of the Church's missionary drive. Going beyond the frontiers of ancient Israel, it extends the kingdom of heaven to all humanity. This drive is carried out in particular by the "leap" of missionaries, who, like the apostles, leave their native countries to proclaim the divine message to "all nations" (Mt 28:18).

The first missionary, the only begotten Son sent on earth by the Father to redeem the world, sends the apostles out to continue his mission (cf. Jn 20:21). The missionary typology of the "Word made flesh" also includes the self-emptying of the one who exists in the form of God and who assumed the form of a servant, becoming like men (cf. Phil 2:6-7). The Pauline concept of "kenosis" allows us to see in the Incarnation the first example of the self-emptying of those who accept Christ's mandate and leave everything to bring the Good News "to the very ends of the earth."

In affirming the transcendent origin of the missionary dynamism of his Incarnation, Jesus also reveals in it his purpose, which consists in opening to all the way back to God. Jesus marked this path out first. He declared: "I came from the Father and have come into the world. Now I am leaving the world and going back to the Father" (Jn 16:28). He explained that the aim of this "going" was to prepare a place "in his Father's house" for the disciples, to whom he said: "I will come back again and take you to myself, so that where I am you also may be" (Jn 14:3). Jesus' return to the Father was carried out through a sacrifice in which he showed his love for men "to the end" (Jn 13:1).

He wants men to participate in his ascent to the Father. To bring about this participation, he sends his apostles, and together with them, the whole Church, which extends his preaching and activities in all places and in all ages.

We have emphasized the fact that Christ's missionary activity culminated in the offering of his sacrifice. According to the Father's plan, Jesus spent only a short period of his earthly life preaching, which was limited to the "lost sheep of the house of Israel" (Mt 15:24). At the start, he also limited the ministry of the Twelve to this (cf. Mt 10:6). However, with the sacrifice of the cross he totally fulfilled the missionary purpose of his coming on earth: the salvation not only of the people of Israel or the Samaritans, but also the "Greeks" (cf. Jn 12:20-24), indeed, all humanity (Jn 12:32).

This fact sheds light on the Church's missionary activity, which must be marked by a sacrificial note foretold by Jesus:

"No disciple is above his teacher, no slave above his master" (Mt 10:24). "You will be hated by all because of my name" (Mt 10:22).

We must follow the divine Master on the way of the cross. This is the way of the Church and the way of missionaries, as the Council recalls: "The Church, prompted by the Holy Spirit, must walk in the same path on which Christ walked: a path of poverty and obedience, of service and self-sacrifice to the death, from which death he came forth a victor by his resurrection" *(AG 5)*.

On this way of the Church and her missionaries, Christ is not only the initiator and the perfect example. He is also the one who supplies the necessary energy to proceed, communicating the Holy Spirit to his Church in every age. As we read again in the Council, to achieve universal salvation, "Christ sent from the Father his Holy Spirit, who was to carry on inwardly his saving work and prompt the Church to spread out" *(AG 4)*. Let us return once again to the trinitarian source of the Church's missionary dynamism, which the Holy Spirit kindled at Pentecost. He continuously nourishes it in hearts, as the Love of the Father and the Son—*ignis, caritas*—which imparts to the Church the fire of eternal Charity.

Pentecost was not only a moment of intense emotion. It was the start of a dynamism of supernatural origin which developed throughout the Church's history (cf. *RM* 24). As on the day of Pentecost, so in our times the Holy Spirit continues inwardly to inspire missionary enthusiasm and to give hierarchical and charismatic gifts (cf. 1 Cor 12:4ff.), which make the Church "one in communion and in ministering" *(AG 4; cf. LG 4)*. This intimate unity of Jesus' disciples is expressed in "fraternal communion," in being "of one heart and mind" *(RM 26)*.

The Holy Spirit illumines and inflames the whole person with divine love, working effectively in minds and hearts. He intervenes deeply in the Church's missionary activity, which he himself at times "visibly anticipates...just as he unceasingly accompanies and directs it in different ways" *(AG 4)*. Thus the Church, moved "by the grace and love of the Holy Spirit," fulfills her mission, opening up for all men "a firm and free road to full participation in the mystery of Christ" *(AG 5)*.

General audience of April 19, 1995

The Church Preaches
the Gospel to the End of Time

The Church's universal mission unfolds in time and is fulfilled throughout the history of humanity. Before Christ's coming, the period of preparation (cf. Gal 3:23; Heb 1:1) and expectation (cf. Rom 3:26; Acts 17:30) ended with the coming of the "fullness of time," when the Son of God became incarnate for man's salvation (cf. Gal 4:4). With this event a new period began, which we cannot measure and which will extend to the end of history.

The evangelization of the world is therefore subject to the laws of the succession of centuries and human generations. It addresses every person, era and culture. The Gospel proclamation must always be renewed. It must become ever more complete and profound, even in regions and cultures evangelized long ago. In short, it must begin again every day, until the coming of the "last day" (Jn 12:48).

Evangelization should be seen in the perspective which Christ himself gave it. It will come to its fulfillment only at the end of the world: "And this Gospel of the kingdom will be preached throughout the world as a witness to all nations, and then the end will come" (Mt 24:14).

It has not been granted us to "know the times or seasons" (Acts 1:7) established by God's plan regarding the fulfillment of the work of evangelization, a premise for the coming of God's kingdom. Neither can we know how deep the mission will have to penetrate for "the end to come." We only know that evangelization progresses through history, to which the final meaning will be given when it has been fulfilled. Until that time, there is a mystery of evangelization which at the same time penetrates the very mystery of history.

It should be noted that we are still far from a complete evangelization of "all nations" (Mt 24:14; 28:19), and that the vast majority have not yet adhered to the Gospel or to the Church. Then, as I wrote in *Redemptoris Missio:* "Missionary activity is only beginning" (n. 30). This historical conclusion is not opposed to the heavenly Father's universal saving will to insure that, with the light of Christ and through the power of the Holy Spirit, the gift of redemption reaches the heart of every man. There is no doubt that for the Church's task of evangelization this mystery of presence and saving action is fundamental. The mandate Jesus entrusted to the apostles, and therefore to the Church, to "go," "baptize," "teach," and "proclaim the Gospel to every creature" (Mk 16:15), "to all nations" (Mt 28:19; Lk 24:47), "until the end of the age" (Mt 28:20), must be understood in this light.

At the end of Mark's Gospel we read that the apostles "went forth and preached everywhere, while the Lord worked with them and confirmed the word through accompanying signs" (Mk 16:20). It could be said that the mission entrusted to them by Christ had awakened a sort of urgent need to fulfill the mandate they had received to evangelize all nations. The first Christians shared this spirit and powerfully felt the need to take the Good News to every region of the world.

After 2000 years, the same task and the same responsibility remain unchanged in the Church. Today Christians are still asked to devote themselves, each in his own walk of life, to the important task of evangelization.

In an earlier catechesis I recalled the question the disciples asked Christ at the moment of the ascension: "Lord, are you at this time going to restore the kingdom to Israel?" (Acts 1:6). They had not yet understood what kingdom Christ had come to establish. The kingdom of God, which extends throughout the world and to every generation, is the spiritual transformation of humanity by a process of conversion, the times of which are known only to the heavenly Father. In fact, to the disciples, as yet incapable of understanding Christ's work, the risen one replied: "It is not for you to know the times or seasons that the Father has established by his own authority" (Acts 1:7).

The Father then has provided a succession of times and seasons for the fulfillment of his saving plan. These *kairoi,* these moments of grace that mark the stages of the fulfillment of his kingdom, belong to him. Although he is the Almighty, he has decided to work patiently within history, according to the rhythms of human development—personal and collective—taking into account human possibilities, resistance, willingness and freedom.

This divine pedagogy must be the model inspiring all the Church's missionary activity. Evangelizers must patiently accept the times of evangelization, sometimes slow, sometimes even very slow, aware that God, to whom "the times and seasons" belong, tirelessly guides the course of history with sovereign wisdom.

The time of expectation, as I have already pointed out, can be long before the favorable time comes. Although encountering resistance, deafness and delay astutely orchestrated by the "ruler of this world" (Jn 12:31), the Church knows that she must act with patience, with deep respect for each ethnic, cultural, psychological and sociological situation. Nevertheless, she can never lose heart if her efforts are not immediately crowned with success. Above all, she can never deviate from the basic task entrusted to her, that of proclaiming the Good News to all nations.

Knowing how to wait for the "times and seasons" of God implies a vigilant attitude. One must make the most of the opportunities and possibilities for Gospel proclamation in changing historical circumstances. The Council recommends this when it recalls: "These circumstances in turn depend sometimes on the Church, sometimes on the peoples or groups or men to whom the mission is directed. For the Church, although of itself including the totality or fullness of the means of salvation, does not and cannot always and instantly bring them all into action" *(AG* 6). "There are times when after a happy beginning, she must again lament a setback, or at least must linger in a certain state of unfinished insufficiency" *(AG* 6). This is also part of the mystery of the cross that pervades history.

It is well known that down the centuries, for various reasons, entire Christian communities have disappeared. This is the sad message of history, which warns about the possibilities of failure inherent in human activities. Not even the work of evangelization is preserved from this. But history also attests that through God's grace the setbacks, limited to certain places or to certain times, do not impede the general development of evangelization which, in accordance with Christ's words, will gradually spread to all humanity (cf. Mt 24:14). In fact, even amid varying circumstances, the Church continues her mission of evangelization with the same enthusiasm of the first centuries, and the kingdom of God continues to develop and spread.

Today too she is aware of the difficulties which arise on her long journey through history. Nevertheless she sincerely believes in the power of the Holy Spirit, who opens hearts to the Gospel and guides her in her mission. The Spirit draws to Christ every man, every culture and people, respecting their freedom and pattern of life and gently guiding all to the truth. However what could seem to human eyes a slow and uneven path, is actually God's method. This certainty sustains and strengthens Christ's followers—starting with pastors and missionaries—in the hope that their work is not in vain and will not be wasted. This hope is based on an eschatological perspective which is at the root of the Church's evangelizing activity as she makes her earthly pilgrimage to the end of time.

General audience of April 26, 1995

The Church Cannot
Abandon Mission Work

In traditional terms we speak of "missions" in the plural and of the "missionaries" who work there by a specific mandate. This form of expression does not contradict the unity of the Church's mission. Rather, it reveals more vividly the fundamental commitment to evangelization. Not only do missionaries not overshadow the principle that the whole Church is missionary but, on the contrary, they personally fulfill it.

What are the missions? According to the Council, they are "particular undertakings by which the heralds of the Gospel, sent out by the Church and going forth into the whole world, carry out the task of preaching the Gospel and planting the Church among peoples or groups who do not yet believe in Christ" *(AG 6)*. In *Redemptoris Missio* it is explained that these are established in territories where the Church "has not yet taken root" and with peoples "whose culture has not yet been influenced by the Gospel" *(RM 34)*.

We can state that these activities aim at building the local Church. Not only do they contribute to establishing structures and an ecclesial hierarchy, but they cooperate in forming communities of Christian life through the proclamation of God's Word and the administration of the sacraments. St. Thomas Aquinas already mentioned this implantation of the Church as the apostolic *munus* (cf. *I Sent.;* D. 16, q. 1, a. 2, ad 2 and 4; *Summa Theol.,* I, q. 43, a. 7, ad 6; I-II, q. 106, a. 4, ad 4). A concept which belongs to a solid ecclesiological tradition, it has been deepened by the Pontiffs of our century in various documents and taken up by the Second Vatican Council (cf. *AG* 34). Both my venerable predecessors and St. Thomas also use the other term: *dilatatio ecclesiae,* that is, the spread, the extension of the Church (cf. St. Thomas, *Comm. in Matth.* 16:28). The Council explained:

> From the seed which is the Word of God, particular autochthonous churches should be sufficiently established and should grow up all over the world.... The chief means of the planting referred to is the preaching of the Gospel of Jesus Christ. To preach this Gospel the Lord sent forth his disciples into the whole world, that being reborn by the Word of God (cf. 1 Pet 1:23), men might be joined to the Church through baptism—that Church which, as the body of the Word incarnate, is nourished and lives by the word of God and by the Eucharistic bread (cf. Acts 2:42) *(AG* 6).

These are churches with their own proper strength and maturity, endowed with their own hierarchy and the appropriate means for the Christian life of their own members, and they can contribute to the good of the whole Church (cf. *AG* 6).

This is the ideal to follow in missionary activity: the foundation of a church which on her own provides for her pastors and all the necessities for the life of faith, while remaining in communion with the other particular churches and with the See of Peter.

Various stages in missionary activity can be distinguished (cf. *AG* 6): the beginning or planting, with a preaching of the Gospel aimed at bringing men to Baptism; then follows a time of freshness and youthfulness, with education in faith and in the Christian way of life, with the formation of the local community, with the birth and development of priestly and religious vocations. In these formative moments the community is provided with a ministerial structure which helps it to develop in a perspective of openness and missionary co-operation.

There has been no lack of misunderstandings with regard to missionary activity and the value of missions, even in recent times. Due to contingent historical circumstances, a connection was established for a time between missionary activity and political colonization. Because of this, some have wished to conclude that the gradual disappearance of the historical phenomenon of colonies should coincide with the parallel disappearance of missions.

In addition to these uncertainties there is the consideration that in the churches of the first evangelization, from which came many missionaries working in "mission countries," there is an increasing awareness that their territory is becoming a mission land requiring a new evangelization. Thus the problem has arisen of choosing between missions in countries not yet evangelized and the urgent tasks of the apostolate in countries with an ancient Christian tradition.

The question cannot be solved by the choice of the second alternative, taken in the absolute, to the detriment of the former. It is true that the need for a new evangelization is making itself felt "in the ancient Christian countries" where "entire groups of the baptized have lost a living sense of the faith, or even no longer consider themselves members of the Church and live a life far removed from Christ and his Gospel" (RM 33). Specific missionary activity cannot be rejected and must be carried out in territories where the Church is not yet implanted or where the number of Christians is very small. The Gospel message must be brought to the knowledge of all, and Christian communities themselves, even if they are flourishing and exemplary, must be able to exercise a beneficial influence on customs and institutions, through a useful dialogue with the other groups and communities.

As I pointed out in the encyclical quoted, "The number of those who do not know Christ and do not belong to the Church is constantly on the increase. Indeed, since the end of the Council it has almost doubled" *(RM* 3). This results from the fact that as the world's population continues to grow, the numerical proportion of non-Christians has notably increased. This is due to well known demographic reasons and because of greater stability in the preservation of religious elements, almost connatural with culture.

With regard then to the relationship between missionary activity and the colonizing policies of some countries, it is necessary calmly and clearly to analyze the facts. These show that in some cases the coincidence led to reprehensible behavior on the part of missionaries. This happened in relation to their countries of origin or in collaboration with local authorities, whom it was not always possible to ignore. Nevertheless, considered overall, evangelizing activity has always been distinguished by a very different goal from that of earthly powers. It aims to promote the personal dignity of the evangelized, giving them access to the divine sonship obtained for every man by Christ and communicated to the faithful in Baptism. In fact, this generally encouraged the progress of those peoples toward their freedom and development even at the social and economic level. The missionaries acted out of the respect they felt for men as persons loved by God and redeemed by Jesus Christ.

Today as in the past, their activities with peoples or groups where the Church is not yet present and active does not respond to goals of human power or interest, nor is it inspired by the pride of cultural or social superiority. Rather it desires to be, and is in reality, a humble service of love to those who have not yet received the light and life of Christ within the context of the Church he desired and founded for the salvation of the world.

The Council also recognized that there are situations in which missionary activity must limit itself to a discreet presence, because it cannot develop in visibly organized and functional structures (cf. *AG* 6). Perhaps, in precisely such cases, missionaries represent even more clearly the Church founded by Christ to preach the Gospel and to build communities of salvation everywhere. Indeed, she is always well aware of the mystery of the cross, which sometimes involves silent and trusting expectation of the light of Easter, as history amply illustrates.

General audience of May 3, 1995

Missionary Activity Remains Urgent

Let us continue the reflection we began in our last catechesis on the objections and doubt about the value of missionary activity and in particular, about its evangelizing goal. There has been no lack of people who have wanted to interpret missionary activity as an attempt to impose one's own convictions and choices on others. This is contrasted with a certain modern spirit that boasts absolute freedom of thought and personal conscience as a definitive achievement.

According to this viewpoint, evangelizing activity should give way to interreligious dialogue, which would consist in an exchange of opinions and information in which each party makes known his own "creed" and is enriched by the others' thought, with no concern about reaching a conclusion. This would entail—it is said—that Christians renounce guiding non-Christians to the way of the Gospel, refrain from proposing or encouraging conversion, and exclude the prospect of Baptism. Thus the way of salvation followed by each according to his own education and religious background would be respected (cf. *RM* 4).

But such a concept appears incompatible with Christ's mandate to the apostles (cf. Mt 28:19-20; Mk 16:15) handed down to the Church, and with the authentic ecclesiology to which the Second Vatican Council referred in order to show the obvious need for missionary activity. It is a question of several basic truths. God desires salvation for all. Jesus Christ is the "only Mediator," the one who "gave himself as a ransom for all" (1 Tim 2:5), since "neither is there salvation in any other" (Acts 4:12). "All must be converted to him, made known by the Church's preaching, and all must be incorporated into him by baptism and into the Church which is his body. For Christ himself by stressing in express language the necessity of faith and baptism (cf. Mk 16:16; Jn 3:5), at the same time confirmed the necessity of the Church" *(AG* 7).

The Council mentions the words of Jesus Christ on the necessary missionary mandate entrusted to the apostles. Expressly inculcating the need for faith and Baptism (cf. Mk 16:16; Jn 3:5), at the same time he confirmed the role of the Church into which one ought to enter and persevere if he desires salvation (cf. *AG* 7). This necessity of faith, received by means of the Church's preaching, in relation to salvation, is not only a theological deduction but a doctrine the Lord revealed. The urgency of missionary activity through preaching the Gospel and conferring Baptism derives from it and guarantees entry into the communion of the Church. The Church's traditional teaching illustrates the inconsistency and superficiality of a relativist and irenic attitude regarding the way of salvation in a religion different from that based on faith in Christ.

Doubtless we must believe in the existence of hidden ways in God's plan of salvation for those who, through no fault of their own, cannot enter the Church. Nevertheless, one cannot, in the name of these ways, slow down or abandon missionary activity. On this topic the Council observes: "Though God in ways known to himself can lead those inculpably ignorant of the Gospel to find that faith without which it is impossible to please him (cf. Heb 11:6), yet a necessity lies upon the Church (cf. 1 Cor 9:16), and at the same time a sacred duty, to preach the Gospel. And hence missionary activity today as always retains its power and necessity" *(AG* 7).

The Council explains the ecclesiological reasons for the "power and necessity" of the missionary activity with regard to the Church's inner life. "By means of this activity, the Mystical Body of Christ unceasingly gathers and directs its forces toward its own growth (cf. Eph 4:11-16)." The members of the Church are "impelled to carry on such missionary activity by reason of the love with which they love God and by which they desire to share with all men the spiritual goods of both this life and the life to come.

"Finally, by means of this missionary activity, God is fully glorified, provided that men fully and consciously accept his work of salvation, which he has accomplished in Christ" *(AG* 7). Thus God's plan to which Christ submitted is realized: "...that the whole human race might form one people of God and be built up into one temple of the Holy Spirit" *(AG* 7).

Missionary activity fully responds to the plan of the Creator, which the patristic tradition cited by the Second Vatican Council drew attention to. It will be realized "when all who share one human nature, regenerated in Christ through the Holy Spirit and beholding the glory of God, will be able to say with one accord: 'Our Father.'" But at the same time, evangelization "corresponds with the inmost wishes of all men" *(AG* 7), who more or less consciously and—we could say—almost instinctively, seek God, fraternal harmony, peace, eternal life. Missionary activity aims precisely at all this.

Among man's fundamental aspirations to which the Church's missionary activity brings the light of Christ's revelation, there is the knowledge of the truth about oneself and one's own destiny. The Council states: "By manifesting Christ, the Church reveals to men the real truth about their condition and their whole calling, since Christ is the source and model of that redeemed humanity, imbued with brotherly love, sincerity and a peaceful spirit, to which they all aspire. Christ and the

Church, which bears witness to him by preaching the Gospel, transcend every peculiarity of race or nation and therefore cannot be considered foreign anywhere or to anybody" *(AG* 8).

What we have pointed out several times must be repeated here: the truth of the Gospel is not linked to a specific nation or culture. It is the truth of Christ that enlightens every man regardless of tradition or race. This is why it is essential that it be proclaimed to all humanity: "Christ himself is the way and the truth, which the preaching of the Gospel opens to all..." *(AG* 8).

We can conclude today's reflection by confirming the full validity of the missions and of missionary activity for our time, too. It is an excellent way to put into practice the Church's mission to preach Christ the incarnate Word, the Redeemer of man. Indeed, through missionary activity, the Church applies the Lord Jesus' saving power to the whole good of man, as she awaits his new coming into the world in the eschatological fullness of God's kingdom. Regarding missionaries, the words about Paul, who came to Rome as a missionary, can be repeated today: "From morning to evening he laid the case before them, bearing witness to the reign of God among men. He sought to convince them about Jesus" (Acts 28:23). The passage from the Acts of the Apostles refers to a meeting with the brothers of the Jewish community in Rome. On that occasion "some, indeed, were convinced by what he said; others would not believe" (Acts 28:24). The Apostle, however, made his great resolution in one final word: "Now you must realize that this salvation of God has been transmitted to the Gentiles—who will heed it!" (Acts 28:28).

We can say that on that day, in Paul's rented lodgings, a new phase began in the development of the history of Christianity: a history of faith, civilization and Gospel values, ever rich and fruitful for the good of humanity.

General audience of May 10, 1995

The Church Perseveres in Her Mission

In one of the previous catecheses on the theme of mission, we already referred to the immense work of evangelization to which the Church is called today, and to the difficulties she meets. We must especially remember once again that the demographic factor has given rise to a considerable numerical imbalance between Christians and non-Christians, in the face of which we cannot fail to be aware of the human inadequacy and weakness of our resources. Moreover, the complexity of social relations, even at the international and intercontinental level, and the spread of culture by schools and the whole range of social communications, create new problems for missionary activity. It can no longer rely on homogeneous and fundamentally religious popular traditions.

Nor should "the growth in the number of new churches in recent times" give rise to facile illusions in the faithful. In fact, there "remain vast regions still to be evangelized" *(RM* 37). Among the very peoples who have received the Christian faith a new evangelization, which is deeper and more attentive to new needs and demands, is required. Indeed, "there is a need not only for a new evangelization, but also, in some cases, for an initial evangelization" *(RM* 37).

This is what I wrote in the Encyclical *Redemptoris Missio,* stressing: "The mission *ad gentes* faces an enormous task, which is in no way disappearing. Indeed, both from the numerical standpoint of demographic increase and from the socio-cultural standpoint of the appearance of new relationships, contacts and changing situations, the mission seems destined to have ever wider horizons" *(RM* 35).

In certain countries evangelization encounters "obstacles...of a cultural nature: passing on the Gospel message seems irrelevant or incomprehensible, and conversion is seen as a rejection of one's own people and culture" *(RM* 35). In these cases the passage to Christianity can even lead to persecution, which shows intolerance and contrasts with man's basic rights to freedom of thought and worship. In such cases a sort of cultural withdrawal can be seen which is a precise obstacle to evangelization. But in itself it also demonstrates a deplorable lack of dialogue and openness to true spiritual, intellectual and moral enrichment.

In the mission encyclical I mentioned that sometimes the difficulties in missionary activity "seem insurmountable and could easily lead to discouragement, if it were a question of a merely human enterprise" *(RM* 35). However, we cannot shut our eyes to the human elements of this task. There are real shortcomings and deficiencies and I did not neglect to point them out (cf. *RM* 36).

These are primarily: a certain waning of missionary zeal; the sad experience of past and still present divisions among Christians; the drop in vocations; the counter-witness of all those who are not faithful to their missionary promises and commitments; the indifferentist mentality marked by religious relativism, which makes many of our contemporaries think and say that "one religion is as good as another."

But these difficulties serve to increase our understanding of the challenge that missionary commitment must face today more than ever. We can recall that from the start the Church's mission has always been a challenge. How did that little group of Christ's disciples commit themselves to the work of universal evangelization he had requested? How could that small group of fishermen from Galilee "make disciples of all the nations"? Jesus was well aware of the difficulties that the apostles would meet. This is why he offers us the same guarantee: "And know that I am with you always, until the end of the world!" (Mt 28:20).

They believed in him, in his presence and in his power over life and death. The early Church was nourished by this same faith. Although the Church today is aware of the limitations of human strength, she reacts to the difficulties of evangelization with the humility and faith of the first believers and of those who followed. She revives her faith in Christ's almighty presence.

A part of this faith is the certitude that the gifts of the Holy Spirit will never fail to renew the missionary zeal of believers for overcoming divisions with the unity of charity, for encouraging the increase and fervor of missionary vocations, for reinforcing the witness that stems from conviction and for avoiding all discouragement. The Church feels she can repeat without arrogance the words of the Apostle Paul: "In him who is the source of my strength I have strength for everything" (Phil 4:13).

Therefore strengthened by Christ, missionaries face the problems in missionary activity caused by the world's social and cultural conditions. The recent worldwide demographic evolution leads a large part of the population to be increasingly concentrated in metropolitan areas. Missionary activity is no longer carried out "in isolated regions which are far from centers of civilization." The Church does not hesitate to recognize that "efforts should be concentrated on the big cities, where new customs and styles of living arise, together with new forms of culture and communication," while she must not overlook "the most abandoned and isolated human groups" *(RM* 37).

The means for proclaiming the Gospel must be reexamined

and the use of the media must be constantly improved. "The first Aeropagus of the modern age is the world of communications, which is unifying humanity and turning it into what is known as a 'global village.' The means of social communication have become so important as to be for many the chief means of information and education, of guidance and inspiration in their behavior as individuals, families and within society at large" *(RM* 37). Up to now these means have not been sufficiently exploited, while everyone is aware of the power they possess and which could serve to extend missionary outreach.

It is also well known that the mass media contribute to the development of a new culture. The Church has the task of implanting the Gospel spirit in this culture. "Involvement in the mass media, however, is not meant merely to strengthen the preaching of the Gospel. There is a deeper reality involved here: since the very evangelization of modern culture depends to a great extent on the influence of the media, it is not enough to use the media simply to spread the Christian message and the Church's authentic teaching. It is also necessary to integrate that message into the 'new culture' created by modern communications" *(RM* 37). We must therefore make sure that in the hands of the new apostles, the means of social communication, especially radio and television because of their enormous influence on the masses, become a valuable tool for evangelization. In this area, lay people are called to play a most important role, which presupposes a serious professional competence and a genuine spirit of faith.

Today too, with divine help, following in St. Paul's footsteps, the Church must be committed to bringing the Gospel leaven to our constantly evolving cultures. They are also God's fields, where we must sow and cultivate the Gospel like good farmers, with steadfast trust in him who gives us strength.

General audience of May 17, 1995

All Salvation Comes through Christ

The difficulties that sometimes accompany the development of evangelization highlight a delicate problem, whose solution is not to be sought in purely historical or sociological terms. It is the problem of the salvation of those who do not visibly belong to the Church. We have not been given the possibility to discern the mystery of God's action in minds and hearts, in order to assess the power of Christ's grace as he takes possession, in life and in death, of all that "the Father gives him," and which he himself proclaims he does not want to "lose." We hear him repeat this in one of the suggested Gospel readings in the Mass for the dead (cf. Jn 6:39-40).

However, as I wrote in the Encyclical *Redemptoris Missio,* the gift of salvation cannot be limited "to those who explicitly believe in Christ and have entered the Church. Since salvation is offered to all, it must be made concretely available to all." And, in admitting that it is concretely impossible for many people to have access to the Gospel message, I added: "Many people do not have the opportunity to come to know or accept the Gospel revelation or to enter the Church. The social and cultural conditions in which they live do not permit this, and frequently they have been brought up in other religious traditions" *(RM* 10).

We must acknowledge that, as far as human beings can know and foresee, this practical impossibility would seem destined to last a long time, perhaps until the work of evangelization is finally completed. Jesus himself warned that only the Father knows "the exact time" set by him for the establishment of his kingdom in the world (cf. Acts 1:7).

What I have said above, however, does not justify the relativistic position of those who maintain that a way of salvation can be found in any religion, even independently of faith in Christ the Redeemer, and that interreligious dialogue must be based on this ambiguous idea. That solution to the problem of the salvation of those who do not profess the Christian creed is not in conformity with the Gospel. Rather, we must maintain that the way of salvation always passes through Christ, and therefore the Church and her missionaries have the task of making him known and loved in every time, place and culture. Apart from Christ "there is no salvation." As Peter proclaimed before the Sanhedrin at the very start of the apostolic preaching: "There is no other name in the whole world given to men by which we are to be saved" (Acts 4:12).

For those too who through no fault of their own do not know Christ and are not recognized as Christians, the divine plan has provided a way of salvation. As we read in the Council's Decree *Ad Gentes,* we believe that "God in ways known to himself can lead those inculpably ignorant of the Gospel" to the faith necessary for salvation *(AG 7)*. Certainly, the condition "inculpably ignorant" cannot be verified nor weighed by human evaluation, but must be left to the divine judgment alone. For this reason, the Council states in the Constitution *Gaudium et Spes* that in the heart of every man of good will, "Grace works in an unseen way.... The Holy Spirit in a manner known only to God offers to every man the possibility of being associated with this paschal mystery" *(GS 22)*.

It is important to stress that the way of salvation taken by those who do not know the Gospel is not a way apart from

Christ and the Church. The universal salvific will is linked to the one mediation of Christ. "God our Savior...wants all men to be saved and come to know the truth. And the truth is this: God is one. One also is the mediator between God and men, the man Christ Jesus, who gave himself as a ransom for all" (1 Tim 2:3-6). Peter proclaimed this when he said: "There is no salvation in anyone else" and called Jesus the "cornerstone" (Acts 4:11-12), emphasizing Christ's necessary role at the basis of the Church.

This affirmation of the Savior's "uniqueness" derives from the Lord's own words. He stated that he came "to give his own life in ransom for the many" (Mk 10:45), that is, for humanity, as St. Paul explains when he writes: "One died for all" (2 Cor 5:14; cf. Rom 5.18). Christ won universal salvation with the gift of his own life. No other mediator has been established by God as Savior. The unique value of the sacrifice of the cross must always be acknowledged in the destiny of every man.

Since Christ brings about salvation through his Mystical Body, which is the Church, the way of salvation is connected essentially with the Church. The axiom *extra ecclesiam nulla salus*—"outside the Church there is no salvation"—stated by St. Cyprian *(Epist.* 73, 21; *PL* 1123 AB), belongs to the Christian tradition. It was included in the Fourth Lateran Council *(DS* 802), in the Bull *Unam Sanctam* of Boniface VIII *(DS* 870) and the Council of Florence *(Decretum pro Jacobitis, DS* 1351). The axiom means that for those who are not ignorant of the fact that the Church has been established as necessary by God through Jesus Christ, there is an obligation to enter the Church and remain in her in order to attain salvation (cf. *LG* 14). For those, however, who have not received the Gospel proclamation, as I wrote in the Encyclical *Redemptoris Missio,* salvation is accessible in mysterious ways, inasmuch as divine grace is granted to them by virtue of Christ's redeeming sacrifice, without external membership in the Church, but nonetheless always in relation to her (cf. *RM* 10). It is a mysterious relationship. It is mysterious for those who receive the grace, because they do not know the Church and sometimes even outwardly reject her. It is also mysterious in itself, because it is linked to the saving mystery of grace, which includes an essential reference to the Church the Savior founded.

In order to take effect, saving grace requires acceptance, cooperation, a *yes* to the divine gift. This acceptance is, at least implicitly, oriented to Christ and the Church. Thus it can also be said that *sine ecclesia nulla salus*—"without the Church there is no salvation." Belonging to the Church, the Mystical Body of Christ, however implicitly and indeed mysteriously, is an essential condition for salvation.

Religions can exercise a positive influence on the destiny of those who belong to them and follow their guidance in a sincere spirit. However, if decisive action for salvation is the work of the Holy Spirit, we must keep in mind that man receives his salvation only from Christ through the Holy Spirit. Salvation already begins during earthly life. This grace, when accepted and responded to, brings forth fruit in the gospel sense for earth and for heaven.

Hence the importance of the Church's indispensable role. She "is not an end unto herself, but rather is fervently concerned to be completely of Christ, in Christ and for Christ, as well as completely of men, among men and for men." This role then is not "ecclesiocentric," as is sometimes said. The Church does not exist nor does she work for herself, but is at the service of a humanity called to divine sonship in Christ (cf. *RM* 19). She thus exercises an implicit mediation also with regard to those who do not know the Gospel.

What has been said, however, should not lead to the conclusion that her missionary activity is less needed in these situations—quite the contrary. In fact, whoever does not know Christ, even through no fault of his own, is in a state of darkness and spiritual hunger, often with negative repercussions at the cultural and moral level. The Church's missionary work can provide him with the resources for the full development of Christ's saving grace, by offering full and conscious adherence to the message of faith and active participation in Church life through the sacraments.

This is the theological approach drawn from Christian tradition. The Church's Magisterium has followed it in her doctrine and practice as the way indicated by Christ himself for the apostles and for missionaries in every age.

General audience of May 31, 1995

Local Churches Have a Missionary Task

The Church was founded by Jesus Christ as one and universal. As we have seen in previous catecheses, these two dimensions are based on the will of Jesus Christ himself. Nevertheless the Acts of the Apostles and the epistles show that the local churches were formed within the one, universal Church through the work of the apostles or their co-workers, and afterward by their successors. Thus a distinction appears between the universal Church entrusted to the apostles under the guidance of Peter, and the local churches with their own pastors. We recall that of Jerusalem, to which elders were appointed (cf. Acts 11:30) with James (cf. Acts 12:17; 21:18; that of Antioch, with prophets and doctors, and the other communities in which Paul and Barnabas were "elders" (cf. Acts 14:23; 20:17) or "guardians" (cf. Acts 20:28).

The composition of the one Church in a plurality of local churches corresponds to Christ's institution. It is also in conformity with the sociological and psychological law of her localization and coexistence in local communities in which links remain strong and fruitful. At the religious and Christian level, the existence of the local churches is essential to the universal Church's life. Christ's disciples need communities where they can live the Gospel, which is identical for all, in conformity with their specific culture. The Second Vatican Council recalls that the Church's two dimensions do not contradict one another. The universal Church subsists in the local churches, while they express the universal character of the Catholic Church in their life as individual communities. "Within the Church particular churches hold a rightful place; these churches retain their own traditions, without in any way opposing the primacy of the Chair of Peter, which presides over the whole assembly of charity" *(LG* 13).

Yet a third principle governs the mission of the local churches within the universal Church: that of the inculturation of the Good News. Evangelization takes place not only through its adaptation to the cultural expressions of the various peoples, but also through a vital integration of the Gospel into their thought, values, customs and prayer, thanks to research and respect for the core of truth, which can more or less be openly found there. This is the concept explained in *Redemptoris Missio* (cf. n. 52), in harmony with previous documents of the papal Magisterium and the Council, following the logic of the Incarnation.

The Incarnation is the model for every evangelization of culture. Jesus Christ, the incarnate Word, came into the world to redeem all humanity and to be "Lord of all" (Acts 10:36). Nonetheless, he was a part of and lived the religious tradition of Israel (cf. Lk 2:22-24, 39, 41; Mt 4:23; 17:27). He brought it to fulfillment however, in accordance with a new form of covenant which he inaugurated by surpassing some elements of the old law, as the New Testament writings state (cf. Mt 5:17-20; 15:1-6; Rom 8:1-4; Gal 4:4). However, Jesus also thought and spoke of the "other sheep" whom he, as the one shepherd, wanted to lead back to the one fold (cf. Jn 10:6). Further, St. Paul, called by Christ to be the "apostle to the Gentiles" (Rom 11:13; cf. Rom 1:5), established that the new Christians in "all the churches" should remain in the state in which they were at the time of their conversion (cf. 1 Cor 7:17,

20, 24). In other words, they were not to adopt the cultural practices of the Jews, but were to continue in their own culture and live their Christian faith within it.

This explains and justifies why Christian culture and civilization accepted the contributions of even pagan cultures and religious traditions belonging to peoples or nations foreign to Israel, but for which the spirituality of the Old Testament prepared the ground. This is a historical reality that should be considered in its profound religious dimension. The Gospel message, in its essence as the revelation of God through the life and teaching of Christ, should be presented to different cultures by fostering the development of the seeds, longings, expectations—it could be said, almost the presentiments of Gospel values—already present within them. Consequently a transformation can take place which does not result in the loss of peoples' cultural identity. On the contrary, precisely because this is a message of divine origin, it tends to enhance the local culture. It stimulates it and encourages it to yield new fruits at the highest level to which Christ's presence brings it, with the grace of the Holy Spirit and the light of the Gospel.

In fact this is an arduous undertaking and a "difficult process," as we read in the Encyclical *Redemptoris Missio,* "for it must in no way compromise the distinctiveness and integrity of the Christian faith" (n. 52). It will never be admissible to give up part of Christian teaching so that the truth proposed may be more easily assimilated. It will never be possible to embrace customs that contradict the decisions of the Gospel.

It would be an illusion to attempt a harmonization that would introduce foreign elements from other religions into Christ's teaching. This would be mere religious syncretism, an unacceptable solution. Instead, a true and elevating transformation is necessary. When it happens, it renews the cultures that receive Christian revelation and wish to be nourished by its life-giving content.

In this way, original expressions of Christian teaching and experiences of life can be produced, the variety of which is an enrichment for the universal Church. Thanks to inculturation in the local church, "The universal Church herself is enriched with forms of expression and values in the various sectors of Christian life, such as evangelization, worship, theology and charitable works. She comes to know and to express better the mystery of Christ, all the while being motivated to continual renewal" *(RM 52)*. Rightly understood and carried out, inculturation expresses better the meaning of the Church's universality. This takes up and assimilates all cultural manifestations, as it accepts and incorporates all human realities in order to sanctify and transform them according to the plan of God.

In the particular churches that arise and develop in areas where the Gospel is preached, this work can and must be carried out as a valid and fruitful missionary task. The criterion everyone must follow is that in every culture it is possible to find and to discern authentic values, but in none is there absolute truth nor an infallible rule of life or prayer.

Thus it is necessary to recognize these values, as the Fathers already did in the first centuries with Greek and Latin culture, and then, gradually, with those of the peoples evangelized. Today, too, the local churches are called to exercise their missionary vocation in fostering the meeting between the Gospel and cultures, in order to achieve the unity and universality of God's family.

General audience of June 14, 1995

The Church Shares the Hopes of the Human Family

The Church's evangelizing mission raises the question of her relationship with the world. The Second Vatican Council addressed this problem, especially in *Gaudium et Spes*. In previous catecheses dealing with the role of lay people in the Church's life, we have also mentioned several aspects of this relationship. Now, at the conclusion of the catechesis dedicated to the Church's missionary activity, we would like to formulate some guidelines, the better to illustrate the general framework of her mission. This is precisely in relation to the world in which she lives and to which she communicates divine grace and salvation.

First of all, it should be remembered that the Church "has a saving and an eschatological purpose which can be fully attained only in the future world" *(GS* 40). We cannot therefore expect her energies to be exclusively or principally absorbed by the needs and problems of the earthly world. Nor is it possible to assess properly her action in the world today, as it was in past centuries, by looking at it only from the perspective of temporal ends or the material well-being of society. Orientation toward the future world is essential to her. She knows she is surrounded by the visible world, but she realizes that she must be concerned with it in its relationship with the invisible, eternal kingdom that she already mysteriously makes present (cf. *LG* 3), and to whose full expression she ardently aspires. This fundamental truth is well expressed in the traditional motto *per visibilia ad invisibilia* (through visible realities to the invisible).

On earth the Church is present as the family of God's children, "constituted and organized in the world as a society" *(LG* 8). This is why she feels that she shares in human events in solidarity with all humanity. As the Council recalls, she "goes forward together with humanity and experiences the same earthly lot which the world does" *(GS* 40). This means that the Church experiences in her members the trials and difficulties of nations, families and individuals, as she shares in humanity's arduous journey down the paths of history. In dealing with the Church's relations with the world, the Second Vatican Council begins precisely with the Church's sharing in the "joys and the hopes, the griefs and the anxieties of the men of this age" *(GS* 1). Especially today, because of the new universal knowledge of the real conditions of the world, this sharing has become especially intense and profound.

The Council also states that the Church does not limit herself to sharing the lot that, in our time as in every other age in history, characterizes human experience. Indeed she knows that she "serves as a leaven and as a kind of soul for human society" *(GS* 40). Enlivened by the breath of the Holy Spirit, the Church wishes to implant a new striving in society, in order to make it a spiritually and, as far as possible, a materially well-ordered and happy community. As Thomas Aquinas said, it is a question of leading men to "live well," to live "in accordance with the virtues." This is the substance of the temporal common good at which all citizens should aim under the guidance of the state, but working with a view to their final end, to which the pastors and the whole Church direct individuals and peoples (cf. *De Regimine Principum,* ch. 1, 14, 15).

Precisely in the light of the "supreme good" which regulates all human existence, even with regard to "intermediate ends" (cf. *ibid.,* ch. 15), the Church "believes she can contribute greatly toward making the family of man and its history more human" *(GS* 40). She makes her own contribution by promoting the dignity of the person and the ties that bind individuals and peoples, as well as by emphasizing the spiritual significance of daily work in the great plan of creation and the proper development of human freedom.

The Council states clearly that the Church is a great help to men. In the first place she reveals to each person the truth about his existence and destiny. She then shows each one how God is the only true answer to the deepest longings of the heart, "which is never fully satisfied by what this world has to offer" *(GS* 41). Furthermore, she defends every person, by virtue of the Gospel entrusted to her, with the proclamation of "the basic rights of the person and the family" *(GS* 42) and with her beneficial influence on society, so that it will respect these rights and begin to change all those situations where they are obviously violated.

Lastly, the Church sheds light on and also proclaims the rights of the family, undeniably linked to those of individual persons and required by the human being as such. In addition to defending the dignity of the person at every stage of life, the Church never ceases to stress the value of the family, to which every man and woman belong by nature. In fact, a deep correlation exists between the rights of the person and those of the family. It is impossible to safeguard individuals effectively without a clear reference to their family context.

Although the Church has a mission which is not "in the political, economic or social order" but is "a religious one" *(GS* 42), she also carries out an activity which benefits society. This activity is expressed in different forms. She organizes projects at the service of all, especially the needy, and promotes "wholesome socialization and...association in civic and economic realms" *(GS 42)*. She urges men to overcome dissension between races and nations, encouraging unity at the international and world levels. As far as she can, she supports and sustains institutions whose purpose is the common good.

She guides and encourages human activity (cf. *GS* 43) and spurs Christians to devote their energies in every field for the good of society. She exhorts them to follow the example of Christ, the workingman of Nazareth, to observe the precept of love of neighbor, and to fulfill in their life Jesus' exhortation to make personal talents fruitful (cf. Mt 25:14-30). She also encourages people to make their own contribution to the scientific and technical efforts of human society, to be involved in their own situation as lay people in temporal activities (cf. *GS* 42). This will further the progress of culture, and the promotion of justice and true peace.

In her relations with the world, the Church not only offers but also receives aid and contributions from individual persons, groups and societies. The Council recognizes this openly: "Just as it is in the world's interest to acknowledge the Church as an historical reality, and to recognize her good influence, so the Church herself knows how richly she has profited by the history and development of humanity" *(GS 44)*. Thus a "living exchange between the Church and the diverse cultures of people" *(GS* 44) takes place. The missionary Church, especially in her task of evangelization, always uses the languages, concepts and cultures of different peoples. From the earliest centuries, she has found in the wisdom of philosophers those *semina verbi* which are a true and proper preparation for the explicit proclamation of the Gospel. Well aware that she receives a great deal from the world, the Church thus professes her gratitude, but without losing sight of the conviction of her missionary vocation and of her capacity to give humanity the greatest and highest gift it can receive: divine life in Christ, through the grace of the Holy Spirit, who leads it to the Father. This is the essence of the missionary spirit with which the Church goes to the world and seeks to be close to it in communion of life.

General audience of June 21, 1995

Unity Results from Legitimate Diversity

Ecumenism also belongs to the Church's missionary dimension. I am especially glad to address this topic while the official delegation of the Patriarchate of Constantinople is present in Rome, led by His Holiness Bartholomew I. I am sure that my venerable brother also feels intensely aware of this problem and that his visit will not fail to make an effective contribution to the progress of the ecumenical dialogue.

I recently published an Encyclical Letter *Ut Unum Sint* on this specific subject, inviting all those who call themselves disciples of Christ to redouble their commitment to achieving the full unity of all Christians. In fact, "This unity, which the Lord has bestowed on his Church and in which he wishes to embrace all people, is not something added on, but stands at the very heart of Christ's mission. Nor is it some secondary attribute of the community of his disciples. Rather, it belongs to the very essence of this community. God wills the Church, because he wills unity, and unity is an expression of the whole depth of his *agape*" (n. 9).

Down the centuries, unfortunately, there have been many ruptures between Christ's disciples. These divisions have nothing to do with the legitimate variety which distinguishes the local or particular churches, where the one Church of Christ is present and expressed.

In order to explain the historical diversity and variety of the Christian Churches, it is appropriate to observe that the unity Christ desired does not involve any external, stifling uniformity. In this regard, in the encyclical cited I pointed out: "Legitimate diversity is in no way opposed to the Church's unity, but rather enhances her splendor and contributes greatly to the fulfillment of her mission" *(UUS* 50). Many local or particular churches preserve their own way of living the Christian commitment, in accordance with institutions of apostolic origin, very ancient traditions or practices established in various periods on the basis of experiences that have proved apt for the inculturation of the Gospel. Thus, over the centuries a variety of local churches has developed, which has contributed and still contributes to the spiritual wealth of the universal Church, and does no harm to unity.

Therefore variety is a good that should remain. The Church's unity will have nothing to suffer from it especially if Christians, aware of its divine origin, implore it constantly in their prayers.

The Second Vatican Council fittingly recalls that the unity of the universal Church is neither the result nor the product of the union of local churches but one of her essential properties. From the beginning, the Church was founded by Christ as universal, and historically the local churches took shape as the presence and expression of this one universal Church. This Christian faith is therefore faith in the one Catholic Church (cf. *LG* 13).

Christ's words, handed down by the apostles and contained in the New Testament, leave no doubts as to his will, which is in conformity with the Father's plan: "I do not pray for these only, but also for those who believe in me through their word, that they may all be one; even as you, Father, are in me and I in you, that they also may be in us..." (Jn 17:20-21). The unity of the Father and the Son in the Holy Spirit is the supreme basis of the Church's unity. The perfection of that transcendent unity must be imitated, "that they may become perfectly one" (Jn 17:23). This divine unity is therefore the founding principle of the union of believers: "that they may all be one...in us" (Jn 17:21).

In the Gospels and in the other New Testament writings, it is also clearly stated that the unity of the Church was achieved by the redeeming sacrifice. For example, we read in John's Gospel: "Jesus should die...and not for the nation only, but to gather into one the children of God who are scattered abroad" (Jn 11:51-52). If their dispersion was the fruit of sin—this is the lesson that emerges from the tower of Babel episode—the reunification of God's dispersed children was the work of redemption. With his sacrifice Jesus created "one new man" and reconciled human beings with one another, breaking down the hostility that divided them (cf. Eph 2:14-16).

In accordance with Christ's word, St. Paul taught that the diversity of the body's members does not hinder their unity: "For just as the body is one and has many members, and all the members of the body, though many, are one body, so it is with Christ" (1 Cor 12:12). This unity in the Church derives first of all from Baptism and the Eucharist, through which the Holy Spirit is communicated and acts: "For by one Spirit we were all baptized into one body...and all were made to drink of one Spirit" (1 Cor 12:12, 13). "Because there is one bread, we who are many are one body, for we all partake of the one bread" (1 Cor 10:17).

St. Paul, apostle and doctor of unity, described its dimension in the life of the Church: "There is one body and one Spirit, just as you were called to the one hope that belongs to your call, one Lord, one faith, one Baptism, one God and Father of us all, who is above all and through all and in all" (Eph 4:4-6).

One body—the image expresses an organic whole, indissolubly united through a spiritual unity: *one Spirit*. This is a real unity, which Christians are called to live ever more deeply, fulfilling its demands "with perfect humility, meekness and patience, bearing with one another lovingly" (Eph 4:2).

The Church's unity thus expresses a twofold aspect: it is a property whose indestructible foundations are the divine unity of the Trinity itself, but it also demands of believers the responsibility of accepting it and concretely putting it into practice in their lives (cf. *UUS* 6).

It is first of all a question of preserving the *una fides,* the profession of the one faith of which the Apostle Paul speaks. This faith involves common adherence to Christ and to the whole truth revealed by him to humanity, attested in Scripture and preserved in the Church's living Tradition. Precisely in order to maintain and foster unity in the faith *(unitas fidei catholicae),* Jesus wanted to establish a specific authority in the apostolic college, linking its Magisterium to himself: "He who hears you hears me" (Lk 10:16; cf. Mt 28:18-20).

As a function of the *koinonia* of believers, the authority of the apostles and their successors is a service that is expressed sacramentally, doctrinally and pastorally as a function of a unity not only of doctrine but also of direction and governance. St. Paul confirms this: "His gifts were that some should be apostles, some prophets, some evangelists, some pastors and teachers...for building up the body of Christ, until we all attain to the unity of the faith and of the knowledge of the Son of God..." (Eph 4:11-13).

In this perspective the specific ministry assigned to Peter and his successors is easily understood. It was founded on Christ's very words, as they have been passed down in the Gospel tradition (cf. *UUS* 96).

It is a mystery of grace which the eternal Pastor of our souls has desired for his Church, so that by growing and working in charity and truth, she might remain in every age visibly united with the glory of God the Father.

We ask him for the gift of an ever deeper understanding between the faithful and their pastors, and as regards the Petrine ministry, we implore the necessary light in order to identify the best ways it can achieve a service of communion recognized by all *(UUS* 96).

General audience of June 28, 1995

All Must Strive for the Goal of Full Unity

The commitment to ecumenism is of primary importance for the Christian. It is known that Jesus prayed with heartfelt intensity at the Last Supper for the unity of his disciples: "...as you, Father are in me, and I in you, I pray that they may be one in us, that the world may believe that you sent me" (Jn 17:21).

Jesus did not hesitate to pray to the Father for his disciples "that their unity may be complete" (Jn 17:23), in spite of the difficulties and tensions he knew they would encounter. He himself had noticed the disagreements between the Twelve even during the Last Supper, and foresaw those which were shortly to appear in the life of the Christian communities, scattered throughout such a vast and varied world. Nonetheless, he prayed for the complete unity of his followers and for this end he offered the sacrifice of his own life.

Therefore, unity is a gift of the Lord to his Church, "a people gathered together by the unity of the Father, the Son and the Holy Spirit" as St. Cyprian effectively points out *(De Orat. Dom.,* 23, *PL* 4, 536). Indeed, the Church "is a mystery that finds its highest exemplar and source in the unity of the Persons of the Trinity: the Father and the Son in the Holy Spirit, one God" *(UR* 2).

In reality, in the first community that gathered after Pen-

tecost, we see that deep unity prevailed: "They devoted themselves to the apostles' instruction and the communal life, to the
breaking of the bread and the prayers" (Acts 2:42). "The
community of believers were of one heart and one mind"
(Acts 4:32).

Reading the pages of the Acts of the Apostles which
describe the early experiences of life in the apostolic community, one is struck by the observation that this union and
harmony owed much to Mary's presence (cf. Acts 1:13-14).
Among the women present at the first gathering, she is the only
one Luke mentioned by name. He did not fail to describe her as
"the Mother of Jesus," thus holding her up as a sign and an
intimate force of *koinonia*. This title conferred upon her a
singular position connected to her new maternity which Christ
proclaimed on the cross. Therefore, in this text it cannot be
ignored that the Church's unity is expressed as fidelity to
Christ, supported and protected by Mary's maternal presence.

The essential value of this unity achieved at the beginning of the Church's life will never disappear. The Second
Vatican Council repeated: "Christ the Lord founded one
Church and one Church only" *(UR* 1). However it must be
observed that this original unity has suffered deep lacerations
in the course of history. Love of Christ must spur his followers
today to reconsider together their past, to return to the way of
unity with renewed vigor.

The New Testament writings themselves tell us that from
the very beginning of the Church's life there have been divisions among Christians. Paul speaks of discord in the Church
in Corinth (cf. 1 Cor 1:10-12). John complains of those who
spread false teaching (cf. 2 Jn 10) or who claim the most
important place in the Church (cf. 3 Jn 9-10). It was the start of
a painful history, recorded in every age, with the formation of
particular groups of Christians who broke away from the
Catholic Church, the emergence of schisms and heresies, and
the birth of "separated" Churches. These were not in commu-

nion either with the other particular churches nor with the universal Church, constituted as "one flock" under the care of "one shepherd," Christ (Jn 10:16), represented by one universal vicar, the Supreme Pontiff.

The ecumenical movement arose from the painful confrontation of this historical situation with the Gospel law of unity. This movement aims at restoring even visible unity among all Christians, "that the world may be converted to the Gospel and so be saved, to the glory of God" *(UR* 1). The Second Vatican Council gave the greatest importance to this movement, pointing out how it implies, for those who work for it, a communion of faith in the Trinity and in Christ, and a common longing for the one and universal Church (cf. *UR* 1). But authentic ecumenical commitment likewise requires of all Christians who are motivated by a sincere desire for communion, freedom from prejudices which hinder the development of the dialogue of charity in truth.

The Council formulates a differentiated judgment on the historical evolution of the separations. It says: "Large communities became separated from full communion with the Catholic Church—for which, often enough, men of both sides were to blame" *(UR* 3). This was the initial moment of separation. Subsequently, the situation changed: "The children who are born into these communities and who grow up believing in Christ cannot be accused of the sin involved in the separation, and the Catholic Church embraces them as brothers, with respect and affection" *(UR* 3).

With the Second Vatican Council, the Catholic Church committed herself definitively to follow the path of ecumenical research, setting herself to listen to the Spirit of the Lord. The way of ecumenism has become the way of the Church.

We must note further that, according to the Council, those who are separated from the Catholic Church preserve with her a certain communion—incomplete but real. In fact, those who believe in Christ and have received Baptism are rightly recognized by the children of the Catholic Church "as brothers in the Lord," even if there are differences "whether in doctrine and sometimes in discipline, or concerning the structure of the Church" *(UR* 3). We can be united with them through several elements of great value, such as, "the written Word of God; the life of grace; faith, hope and charity, with the other interior gifts of the Holy Spirit, and visible elements too" *(UR* 3). All of this is the heritage of the one Church of Christ, which "subsists in the Catholic Church" *(LG* 8).

Even with regard to the work of evangelization and sanctification, the Council's attitude is sincere and respectful. It affirms that the Churches and ecclesial communities are not in fact deprived of significance and importance in the mystery of salvation. "For the Spirit of Christ has not refrained from using them as means of salvation" *(UR* 3).

All this contains the impelling appeal for full unity. It is not merely a matter of gathering all the spiritual riches scattered throughout the Christian communities, as if in so doing we might arrive at a more perfect Church, the Church which God would desire for the future. Instead, it is a question of bringing about fully that Church which God already manifested in her profound reality at Pentecost. This is the goal toward which all must strive, already united in hope, prayer, conversion of heart, and, as is often demanded of us, in suffering which draws its value from the cross of Christ.

General audience of July 12, 1995

Recognize the Importance of Prayer

The way of ecumenism is keenly felt to be an obligation by both Catholic believers and by the Christians of other Churches and ecclesial communities. The Second Vatican Council adopted this course of action and in the Decree *Unitatis Redintegratio,* established the principles of a healthy ecumenism. Today I would like to refer to the main points, recalling that they have been set out in great detail together with practical orientations in the *Directory for the Application of the Principles and Norms of Ecumenism* (1993).

In the face of the divisions which have afflicted the Christian world down the centuries, it is impossible to be passive. Catholics and non-Catholics cannot but suffer acutely when they see their separations, in such contrast with Christ's heartfelt words at the Last Supper (cf. Jn 17:20-23).

Of course, the constitutive unity of the Church desired by her Founder has never been lacking. It has remained unchanged in the Catholic Church, which came into being on the day of Pentecost with the gift of the Spirit to the apostles. The Church has stayed faithful to the principles of the doctrinal and community tradition which rests on the foundations of the legitimate pastors in communion with the Successor of Peter. It is a providential factor in which historical facts are intricately interwoven with theological foundations as a consequence of Christ's will. But it cannot be denied that historically, in the past as in the present, the unity of the Church does not fully show either the vigor or the extension which she could and must achieve in accordance with the requirements of the Gospel.

Thus, the fundamental attitude of Christians who have this unity at heart and who are aware of the gap that exists between the unity desired by Christ and what has concretely been achieved, cannot but be to turn their eyes to heaven and to implore God to provide ever new incentives to unity with the Holy Spirit's inspiration. According to the Council's instructions, we should first of all recognize the essential value of prayer for unity. Indeed, this is not reduced to a mere form of harmony of good human relations. Jesus asked the Father for unity among believers modeled on the divine communion in which he and his Father, in the unity of the Holy Spirit, are "one" (Jn 17:20-21). This is a goal that can only be reached with the help of God's grace. Hence the need for prayer.

Moreover, the daily observation that ecumenical commitment takes place in an area fraught with difficulties, makes human inadequacy and the urgent need for trusting recourse to God's omnipotence all the more keenly felt. This is what we express, especially during the week that is dedicated each year to prayer for Christian unity. It is first and foremost a period of most intense prayer. It is true that this important project also fosters studies, encounters, exchanges of ideas and experiences, but its priority is always prayer.

On many other occasions also, the union of believers is the object of the Church's prayers. Indeed, it should be recalled that at the culminating moment of every Eucharistic celebration, just before Communion, the priest addresses to the Lord the prayer for the Church's unity and peace.

The other contribution which the Council requested from every Christian is active commitment to unity, in the first place in their thoughts and words. Catholics are urged to make "every effort to avoid expressions, judgments and actions which do not represent the conditions of our separated brethren with truth and fairness and so make mutual relations with them more difficult" *(UR* 4). While I emphasize this important recommendation, I urge all to overcome their prejudices and to assume an attitude of effective charity and sincere esteem, accentuating the unitive rather than the divisive aspects, taking into account the defense of the whole inheritance handed down by the apostles.

Furthermore, for better mutual knowledge, it is necessary to cultivate dialogue. If this is undertaken by competent spokesmen (cf. *UUS* 81), it can encourage an increase of mutual esteem and understanding between the different Churches and communions and a "more intensive cooperation in carrying out any duties for the common good" *(UR* 4).

On the basis of dialogue and of every other ecumenical project, there should be loyal and consistent readiness to *recognize expressions of grace* in our brethren who are not yet in full communion with us. As the Council states: "Catholics must gladly acknowledge and esteem the truly Christian endowments from our common heritage which are to be found among our separated brethren" *(UR* 4). Nevertheless, "in this courageous journey toward unity, the transparency and the prudence of faith require us to avoid both false irenicism and indifference to the Church's ordinances" *(UUS* 79). To discover and to recognize the goodness, the virtue and the yearning for an ever greater grace which are present in the other Churches also serves for our own edification.

If it is to be authentic and fruitful, ecumenism demands from the Catholic faithful some basic attitudes. In the first place, it demands charity, with a gaze full of compassion and a sincere desire to cooperate, wherever possible, with our brothers and sisters in the other Churches or ecclesial communities. In the second place, it requires fidelity to the Catholic Church while neither disregarding nor denying the visible failings in the conduct of some of the members. In the third place, it demands the spirit of discernment, in order to appreciate what is good and praiseworthy. Lastly, it requires a sincere wish for purification and renewal, both through personal commitment oriented to Christian perfection and by contributing "each according to his station, playing his part that the Church may daily be more purified and renewed. For the Church must bear in her own body the humility and dying of Jesus (cf. 2 Cor 4:10; Phil 2:5-8), against the day when Christ will present her to himself in all her glory without spot or wrinkle (cf. Eph 5:27)" *(UR 4)*.

This is not a utopian prospect. It can and must be accomplished day after day, century after century, by person after person, however long history lasts and whatever the variety of its largely unforeseeable events. Ecumenism operates in this perspective. Thus it fits into a context broader than that of the problem of individual membership in the Catholic Church by single persons from other Christian communities whose preparation and reconciliation is not in contradiction to the ecumenical project, since "both proceed from the marvelous ways of God" *(UR 4)*.

Let us therefore conclude this catechesis with the hope and the exhortation that all in the Church may be able to safeguard unity in the essential things and enjoy their proper freedom in research, dialogue, comparison and collaboration with all those who profess Jesus Christ the Lord. May they all always preserve charity, which remains the best expression of the will to perfect the historical expression of the Church's unity and catholicity.

General audience of July 26, 1995

Unity Is Furthered
by Continual Renewal

In our previous catechesis, we stressed how the Second Vatican Council recommended prayer as the essential and principal task of Christians who truly intend to dedicate themselves to the full achievement of the unity Christ desired. The Council added that the ecumenical movement "is the concern of the whole Church, faithful and shepherds alike," according to each one's ability, whether it be exercised in daily Christian living or in theological and historical studies (cf. *UR* 5). This means that responsibility in this area can and must be examined at various levels. It involves all Christians, but understandably obliges some in a quite particular way, such as theologians and historians. Ten years ago I remarked: "We must take every care to meet the legitimate desires and expectations of our Christian brethren, coming to know their way of thinking and their sensibilities. The talents of each person must be developed for the utility and advantage of all" *(Address to the Roman Curia,* June 28, 1985, *AAS* 77, pp. 1151-1152; *L'Osservatore Romano* English edition, July 15, 1985, p. 3).

We can list the main paths which the Council proposed for ecumenical activity. First of all, it recalled the need for continuous renewal. "Christ summons the Church to continual reformation as she sojourns here on earth. The Church is always in need of this, insofar as she is an institution of men here on earth" *(UR* 6). The reform concerns behavior as well as Church discipline. It can be added that this need comes from above. That is, it is ordained by God himself, who puts the Church in a permanent state of development. This involves adjusting to historical circumstances, but also and above all, advancing in the fulfillment of her vocation as an ever more satisfactory response to the demands of God's plan of salvation.

Another basic point is the Church's commitment to becoming aware of the deficiencies and defects which, due to human frailty, have afflicted her pilgrim members throughout history. This is especially true with regard to sins against unity, even by Catholics. We must not forget St. John's warning: "If we say we have not sinned, we make him a liar, and his word is not in us" (1 Jn 1:10). Referring precisely to this warning, the Council exhorts: "So we humbly beg pardon of God and of our separated brethren, just as we forgive them that trespass against us" *(UR* 7).

In this journey the purification of our historical memory has proved highly important, since "each one therefore ought to be more radically converted to the Gospel, and without ever losing sight of God's plan, change his or her way of looking at things" *(UUS* 15).

It should also be remembered that harmony with our brethren in the other Churches and ecclesial communities, as well as with others in general, is rooted in the determination to lead a life that more closely conforms with Christ. Thus holiness of life, guaranteed by union with God through the grace of the Spirit, makes possible the union of all Christ's followers and causes it to advance, since unity is a gift which comes from on high.

Together with conversion of heart and holiness of life, ecumenical activity also includes private and public prayer for Christian unity. These are encouraged in various circumstances and especially at ecumenical gatherings. They are all the more necessary the more one perceives the obstacles on the way to full, visible unity. Thus it is understood that real progress toward the unity desired by Christ can only come from divine grace, and that any occasion when Christ's disciples meet to ask God for the gift of unity deserves praise.

The Council states that not only is this permitted but it is also desirable (cf. *UR* 8). Concrete action in various circumstances—of place, time and individuals—must be agreed to in harmony with the local bishop, in the context of the norms established by the episcopal conferences and the Holy See (cf. *UR* 8; *Ecumenical Directory* 28-34).

A special effort should be made to become more familiar with the state of mind and doctrinal, spiritual and liturgical position of our separated brethren in the other Churches or ecclesial communities. To this end, study conferences with the participation of both sides are a help, "especially for discussion of theological problems—where each can treat with the other on an equal footing—provided that those who take part in them are truly competent" *(UR* 9).

These study meetings must be motivated by the desire to share knowledge and the blessings of the Spirit through an effective exchange of gifts in the light of Christ's truth and with a spirit of goodwill (cf. *UR* 9). A methodology enlivened by passion for the truth in love requires from all participants the threefold commitment to explain their position clearly, to strive to understand others and to seek points of agreement.

The Council also recommended that, in view of this form of ecumenical activity, the teaching of theology and the other subjects, especially the historical disciplines, should also be carried out "from the ecumenical point of view" *(UR* 10). This will prevent a polemical attitude and will instead strive to show the convergences and divergences existing between the various parties in their way of receiving and presenting the truths of the faith. Obviously, firmness in the defined faith will not be shaken if sincere adherence to the Church is the basis of the ecumenical methodology followed in the work of formation.

Dialogue procedures should have the same basis. In this dialogue Catholic doctrine must be clearly explained in its integrity: "Nothing is so foreign to the spirit of ecumenism as a false irenicism, in which the purity of Catholic doctrine suffers loss and its genuine and certain meaning is clouded" *(UR* 11).

The task of theologians must therefore be to explain the Catholic faith more profoundly and precisely. They must proceed "with love for the truth, with charity, and with humility" *(UR* 11). Furthermore, when comparing doctrines with one another, as the Council recommends, they should remember "that in Catholic doctrine there exists a 'hierarchy' of truths, since they vary in their relation to the fundamental Christian faith" *(UR* 11). With regard to this important point, theologians should be well trained and be able to discern the relationship which the various positions and the articles of the Creed themselves have with the two fundamental truths of Christianity: the Trinity and the Incarnation of the Word, the Son of God *propter nos homines et propter nostram salutem.* Catholic theologians cannot set out on ways which oppose the apostolic faith as it has been taught by the Fathers and confirmed by the councils. They must always start with humble and sincere acceptance of the exhortation repeated by the Council itself on the subject of ecumenical dialogue: "Let all Christians confess their faith in the triune God, one and three, in the incarnate Son of God, our Redeemer and Lord" *(UR* 12).

General audience of August 2, 1995

Vatican II Praised Eastern Traditions

On the topic of ecumenism, what the Second Vatican Council says about relations between the Eastern Orthodox Churches and the Catholic Church is especially important: the current separation cannot make us forget the long way we have come together. "For many centuries the Church of the East and that of the West each followed their separate ways though linked in a brotherly union of faith and sacramental life; the Roman See by common consent acted as guide when disagreements arose between them over matters of faith or discipline" *(UR* 14). During that historical period, the Eastern Churches had their own way of celebrating and expressing the mystery of the common faith and their own discipline. Their legitimate differences did not prevent them from accepting the ministry entrusted to Peter and his successors.

On their journey together, the West received a great deal from the East in the area of liturgy, spiritual tradition and juridical order. Furthermore, "The ecumenical councils held in the East...defined the basic dogmas of the Christian faith, on the Trinity, on the Word of God who took flesh of the Virgin Mary" *(UR* 14). The doctrinal development which occurred in the East in the early centuries was decisive for the formulation of the Church's universal faith. Here I would like to remember with deep veneration the doctrine defined by several ecumenical councils in the first centuries: the consubstantiality of the Son with the Father, at Nicea in 325; the divinity of the Holy Spirit, at the First Council of Constantinople, celebrated in 381; the divine motherhood of Mary, at Ephesus in 431; the one person and two natures of Christ, at Chalcedon in 451. The thematic developments that make it possible to understand with increasing clarity the "unsearchable riches" of Christ's mystery (cf. Eph 3:8) must be based on this fundamental contribution which is definitive for the Christian faith.

The Second Vatican Council refrained from examining the circumstances of the separation, as well as from evaluating the mutual rebukes. It merely noted that the same inheritance received from the apostles was developed in different places and various ways in the East and in the West, "owing to diversities of genius and conditions of life" *(UR* 14). This created problems that, in addition to "external causes, prepared the way for decisions arising also from a lack of charity and mutual understanding" *(UR* 14). The memory of the painful pages of the past, instead of imprisoning us in recrimination and controversy, should spur us to mutual understanding and charity, in the present and in the future.

In this regard, I would like to stress the great consideration shown by the Council for the spiritual treasures of the Christian East, starting with those connected with the sacred liturgy. The Eastern Churches celebrate the liturgy with great love. This is especially true with regard to the Eucharistic celebration, where we are all called to an ever greater discovery of the "source of the Church's life and pledge of future glory" *(UR* 15). In it, "The faithful, united with their bishop, have access to God the Father through the Son, the Word made flesh, who suffered and has been glorified, and so, in the outpouring of the Holy Spirit, they enter into communion with the most holy Trinity, being made 'sharers of the divine nature' (2 Pet 1:4). Hence, through the celebration of the Holy Eucharist in each of these churches, the Church of God is built up and grows in stature" *(UR* 15).

Then the *Decree on Ecumenism* recalls the Eastern Churches' devotion to Mary, the Ever-Virgin Mother of God, who is extolled with splendid hymns. Devotion to the *Theotókos* highlights the essential importance of Mary in the work of redemption and also sheds light on the meaning and value of the veneration given to the saints. The decree puts special emphasis on the spiritual traditions, especially those of the monastic life, observing that they were the source "from which Latin monastic life took its rise and has drawn fresh vigor ever since" *(UR* 15).

The contribution of the East to the life of Christ's Church was and still is very important. Thus the Council exhorts Catholics: "The very rich liturgical and spiritual heritage of the Eastern Churches should be known, venerated, preserved and cherished by all. They must recognize that this is of supreme importance for the faithful preservation of the fullness of Christian tradition, and for bringing about reconciliation between Eastern and Western Christians" *(UR* 15). In particular, Catholics are invited "to avail themselves of the spiritual riches of the Eastern Fathers" in the tradition of a spirituality which "lifts up the whole man to the contemplation of the divine" *(UR* 15).

Concerning aspects of intercommunion, the recent *Ecumenical Directory* confirms and states precisely all that the Council said. A certain intercommunion is possible, since the Eastern Churches possess true sacraments, especially the priesthood and the Eucharist.

On this sensitive point, specific instructions have been issued, stating that, whenever it is impossible for a Catholic to have recourse to a Catholic priest, he may receive the sacraments of Penance, the Eucharist and the Anointing of the Sick from the minister of an Eastern Church *(Directory* 123). Reciprocally, Catholic ministers can licitly administer the sacraments of Penance, the Eucharist and the Anointing of the Sick to Eastern Christians who ask for them. However, any form of pastoral activity that does not give due consideration to the dignity and freedom of conscience should be avoided. In other specific cases, provisions have been made for forms of *communicatio in sacris* in particular concrete situations.

In this context, I would like to convey a cordial greeting to those Eastern Churches who live in full communion with the Bishop of Rome, while still preserving their ancient liturgical, disciplinary and spiritual traditions. They offer a special witness to that diversity in unity which adds to the beauty of Christ's Church. Today more than ever, the mission entrusted to them is one of service to the unity Christ desired for his Church, by sharing "in the dialogue of love and in the theological dialogue at both the local and international levels, and thus contributing to mutual understanding..." *(UUS* 60).

According to the Council, "The Churches of the East, while remembering the necessary unity of the whole Church, have the power to govern themselves according to the disciplines proper to them" *(UR* 16). There is also a legitimate diversity in handing on the one doctrine received from the apostles. The various theological formulas of the East and the West are frequently complementary rather than conflicting. The Council also notes that the authentic theological traditions of the Orientals are admirably rooted in Holy Scripture (cf. *UR* 17).

Therefore, we must grow in our knowledge of what the Council taught and recommended about respecting the practices, customs and spiritual traditions of the Eastern Churches. We must strive for relations of sincere charity and fruitful collaboration with them, in full fidelity to the truth. We can only share and repeat our wish that "friendly collaboration with them may increase, in the spirit of love, to the exclusion of all feeling of rivalry or strife" *(UR* 18). Yes, may the Lord truly grant this as a gift of his love to the Church of our time!

General audience of August 9, 1995

Dialogue with Reform Communities

With regard to the current ecumenical effort, we would like to turn our attention today to the numerous ecclesial communities which arose in the West from the period of the Reformation onward. The Second Vatican Council recalls that those ecclesial communities "make open confession of Jesus Christ as God and Lord and as the sole Mediator between God and men, to the glory of the one God, Father, Son and Holy Spirit" *(UR* 20). Recognition of Christ's divinity and profession of faith in the Trinity constitute a sound basis for dialogue, even while taking into account as the Council itself observed, "There exist considerable divergences from the doctrine of the Catholic Church concerning Christ himself, the Word of God made flesh, the work of redemption, and consequently, concerning the mystery and ministry of the Church, and the role of Mary in the plan of salvation" *(UR* 20).

Moreover, notable differences are found between the ecclesial communities mentioned here, to the point that "on account of their different origins, and different teachings in matters of doctrine on the spiritual life, [which] vary considerably not only with us, but also among themselves, the task of describing them at all adequately is extremely difficult" *(UR* 19). Indeed, within a single communion, it is not rare to notice differing doctrinal trends, with divergences concerning even the substance of the faith. However, these difficulties make even more necessary the persevering scarch of dialogue.

Another significant element that helps to foster ecumenical dialogue is "a love and reverence of Sacred Scripture which might be described as devotion" by which our brethren are led "to a constant meditative study of the sacred text" *(UR* 21). Here the opportunity of knowing and adhering to Christ, "the source and center of Church unity" is offered to each. "Their longing for union with Christ inspires them to seek an ever closer unity, and also to bear witness to their faith among the peoples of the earth" *(UR* 20).

We cannot but admire them for their spiritual attitude which, among other things, leads to valuable achievements in biblical research. However, at the same time we should recognize that serious divergences exist regarding their understanding of the relationship between Sacred Scripture, Tradition and the authentic Magisterium of the Church. They deny, in particular, the Magisterium's decisive authority in explaining the meaning of the Word of God, as well as in drawing from it ethical teachings for Christian life (cf. *UUS* 69). However, this different attitude to revelation and the truths based on it must not prevent but rather spur the common commitment to ecumenical dialogue.

The Baptism we share with these brethren is the "sacramental bond of unity which links all who have been reborn by it" *(UR* 22). Every baptized person is incorporated into Christ crucified and glorified, and is reborn so as to share in divine life. We know that "of itself Baptism is only a beginning, an inauguration wholly directed toward the fullness of life in Christ. Baptism, therefore, envisages a complete profession of faith, complete incorporation in the system of salvation such as Christ willed it to be, and finally complete ingrafting in Eucharistic communion" *(UR* 22).

Indeed, Holy Orders and the Eucharist are found within the logic of Baptism. These are two sacraments missing among those who, precisely because of the absence of the priesthood, "have not retained the proper reality of the Eucharistic mystery in its fullness" *(UR* 22), around which the new community of believers is built. It is nonetheless essential to add that when the post-Reformation communities "commemorate his death and resurrection in the Lord's Supper, they profess that it signifies life in communion with Christ and look forward to his coming in glory" *(UR* 22). These elements have some similarity with the Catholic doctrine.

On all these points of fundamental importance it is especially necessary to continue the theological dialogue, encouraged by the significant steps that have already been made in the right direction.

Indeed, many study meetings have taken place in recent years, with qualified representatives of the various ecclesial communities of the post-Reformation. The results were set out in documents of great interest, which have opened up new prospects and, at the same time, have shown the need to delve more deeply into certain topics (cf. *UUS* 70). It is nevertheless necessary to recognize that the broad doctrinal diversity existing in these communities makes the full reception of the results achieved somewhat difficult within the communities.

It is therefore necessary to continue with constancy and respect on the way of fraternal encounter, relying on prayer above all. "Precisely because the search for full unity requires believers to question one another in relation to their faith in the one Lord, prayer is the source of enlightenment concerning the truth which has to be accepted in its entirety" *(UUS* 70).

There is still a long way to go. We must proceed with faith and courage, abstaining from superficiality or rashness. The result of our greater mutual knowledge and doctrinal convergences has been a reassuring affective and effective growth in communion. But we must not forget that the "ultimate goal of the ecumenical movement is to re-establish full visible unity among all the baptized" *(UUS* 77). Encouraged by the results achieved thus far, Christians must redouble their efforts.

Despite the old and new problems on the ecumenical path, we place our steadfast hope entirely "on the prayer of Christ for the Church, on our Father's love for us, and on the power of the Holy Spirit" *(UR* 24), convinced with St. Paul that "hope does not disappoint us, because God's love has been poured into our hearts through the Holy Spirit who has been given to us" (Rom 5:5).

General audience of August 23, 1995

Full Christian Unity Can Be Achieved

In view of the present divisions among Christians, there might be a temptation to think that the unity of Christ's Church does not exist or that it is merely a beautiful ideal to strive for, but one which will only be achieved in eschatology. However, the faith tells us that the Church's unity is not only a future hope; it already exists. Jesus Christ did not pray for it in vain. Nevertheless, unity has not yet reached its visible achievement among Christians and indeed, as is well known, down the centuries it has been subject to various difficulties and trials.

Similarly, it should be said that the Church is holy, but her holiness requires a constant process of conversion and renewal by the faithful as individuals and by communities. This also includes the humble request for the forgiveness of sins committed. Moreover, the Church is catholic, but her universal dimension must increasingly be expressed in missionary activity, inculturation of the faith and ecumenical effort guided by the Holy Spirit, until the divine call to faith in Christ is fully achieved.

Thus the problem of ecumenism is not to bring about from nothing a unity that does not yet exist, but to live fully and faithfully, under the action of the Holy Spirit, that unity in which Christ constituted the Church. In this way the true meaning of prayer for unity and of the efforts made to further understanding among Christians becomes clear (cf. *UUS* 21). Creating agreements is not merely a question of gathering together people of goodwill; rather, it is necessary to accept fully the unity desired by Christ and continuously bestowed by the Spirit. This cannot be reached simply by convergences agreed on from below. Rather it is necessary for each to be open to sincerely accepting the impulse that comes from on high, docilely following the action of the Spirit who wants to unite men in one flock under one shepherd, Christ the Lord (cf. Jn 10:16).

The Church's unity must therefore be considered primarily as a gift that comes from on high. A redeemed people, the Church has a unique structure that differs from that which regulates human societies. When the latter have reached the necessary maturity, through their own procedures they give themselves a governing authority and seek to ensure the contribution of all to the common good.

The Church, instead, receives her institution and structure from Jesus Christ, the incarnate Son of God, who founded her. He founded her by his own authority, choosing twelve men and making them apostles, that is, messengers to continue his work in his name. Among these Twelve he chose one, the Apostle Peter, to whom he said: "Simon, Simon...I have prayed for you that your faith may not fail, and when you have turned again, strengthen your brethren" (Lk 22:31-32).

So Peter was one of the Twelve, with the same tasks as the other apostles. However, Christ wished to entrust him with an additional task: that of confirming his brethren in the faith and in the concern of mutual charity. The ministry of the Successor of Peter is a gift which Christ gave his bride, so that in every age the unity of the whole People of God would be preserved and fostered. The Bishop of Rome is therefore the *servus servorum Dei,* established by God as the "perpetual and visible principle and foundation of unity" *(LG* 23; cf. *UUS* 88-96).

The Church's unity will not be expressed to the full until Christians make Christ's desire their own, accepting among his gifts of grace the authority he gave to his apostles. That authority today is exercised by their successors the bishops, in communion with the ministry of the Bishop of Rome, the Successor of Peter. Around this divinely instituted "cenacle of apostolicity," that same unity of all the faithful in Christ, for which he prayed intensely, must be achieved at the visible level through the power of the Holy Spirit.

It would not be in keeping with Scripture and Tradition to hypothesize a type of authority in the Church modeled on the political systems that have developed throughout the history of humanity. On the contrary, according to her Founder's idea and example, those who are called to belong to the apostolic college are required to serve, as Christ did. In the upper room he began the Last Supper by washing the apostles' feet. "The Son of Man also came not to be served but to serve, and to give his life as a ransom for many" (Mk 10:45). To serve the People of God so that they might all have one heart and one mind!

This is the basis of the Church's structure. But history reminds us that this ministry has left in the minds of the Christians of other Churches and ecclesial communities painful memories which need to be purified. The human weakness of Peter (cf. Mt 16:23), of Paul (cf. 2 Cor 12:9-10) and the apostles emphasizes the value of God's mercy and the power of his grace. The Gospel traditions, in fact, teach us that it is precisely this power of grace that transforms those called to follow the Lord and unites them in him. The ministry of Peter and his successors, within the college of the apostles and their successors, is "a ministry of mercy, born of an act of Christ's own mercy" *(UUS* 93).

The good shepherd desired that down the centuries his voice of truth should be heard by the whole flock he purchased by his sacrifice. This is why he entrusted to the Eleven with Peter as head, and to their successors, the mission to watch like sentries so that the one, holy, catholic and apostolic Church might be realized in each of the particular churches entrusted to them. Thus in the communion of pastors with the Bishop of Rome there is achieved the witness to truth that is also a service to unity, in which the role of the Successor of Peter has a very special place.

At the dawn of the new millennium, how can we not invoke for all Christians the grace of that unity merited for them by the Lord Jesus at so high a price? The unity of faith, in adherence to revealed Truth; the unity of hope, in the journey toward the fulfillment of God's kingdom; the unity of charity, with its multiple forms and applications in all areas of human life. In this unity all conflicts can be resolved, and all separated Christians can find reconciliation, in order to reach the goal of full and visible communion.

"And should we ask if all this is possible, the answer will always be 'yes.' It is the same answer which Mary of Nazareth heard: with God, nothing is impossible" *(UUS* 102). At the end of this cycle of catecheses, the Apostle Paul's exhortation comes to mind: "Mend your ways, heed my appeal, agree with one another, live in peace, and the God of love and peace will be with you.... The grace of the Lord Jesus Christ and the love of God and the fellowship of the Holy Spirit be with you all" (2 Cor 13:11, 14).

Amen!

General audience of August 30, 1995

Index

A

Abraham, 82 83

Acts of the Apostles, 57, 125, 130–31, 149, 206, 671
    and Holy Spirit, 74–75

Ad Gentes, 43, 58, 205, 399, 628, 629, 652

Alphonsus de Liguori, Saint, 212, 329

Ambrose, Saint, 212

Andrew, 542, 594

Anointing of the Sick (sacrament), 164–68, 314, 684

Anthony Mary Gianelli, Saint, 212

Apostle Paul. *See* Paul, Saint

Apostolicam Actuositatem, 384, 450–51, 524

Apostolic Tradition, 150, 396

Augustine, Saint, 120, 156, 162, 212, 250, 254, 392, 418, 551

B

Baptism (sacrament), 59, 74, 77, 114, 137–38, 143–48, 150–53, 156,
    158, 180, 204, 211, 234–35, 303, 305, 311, 314, 411, 421–22,
    487, 498, 525, 531–32, 550–54, 687–88
    infant Baptism, 510
    new, 552–53

BOOKS & MEDIA

The Daughters of St. Paul operate book and media centers at the
following addresses. Visit, call or write the one nearest you
today, or find us on the World Wide Web, www.pauline.org

CALIFORNIA
3908 Sepulveda Blvd., Culver City, CA 90230; 310-397-8676
5945 Balboa Ave., San Diego, CA 92111; 619-565-9181
46 Geary Street, San Francisco, CA 94108; 415-781-5180

FLORIDA
145 S.W. 107th Ave., Miami, FL 33174; 305-559-6715

HAWAII
1143 Bishop Street, Honolulu, HI 96813; 808-521-2731

ILLINOIS
172 North Michigan Ave., Chicago, IL 60601; 312-346-4228

LOUISIANA
4403 Veterans Memorial Blvd., Metairie, LA 70006; 504-887-7631

MASSACHUSETTS
Rte. 1, 885 Providence Hwy., Dedham, MA 02026; 781-326-5385

MISSOURI
9804 Watson Rd., St. Louis, MO 63126; 314-965-3512

NEW JERSEY
561 U.S. Route 1, Wick Plaza, Edison, NJ 08817; 732-572-1200

NEW YORK
150 East 52nd Street, New York, NY 10022; 212-754-1110
78 Fort Place, Staten Island, NY 10301; 718-447-5071

OHIO
2105 Ontario Street, Cleveland, OH 44115; 216-621-9427

PENNSYLVANIA
9171-A Roosevelt Blvd., Philadelphia, PA 19114; 215-676-9494

SOUTH CAROLINA
243 King Street, Charleston, SC 29401; 803-577-0175

TENNESSEE
4811 Poplar Ave., Memphis, TN 38117; 901-761-2987

TEXAS
114 Main Plaza, San Antonio, TX 78205; 210-224-8101

VIRGINIA
1025 King Street, Alexandria, VA 22314; 703-549-3806

CANADA
3022 Dufferin Street, Toronto, Ontario, Canada M6B 3T5; 416-781-9131
1155 Yonge Street, Toronto, Ontario, Canada M4T 1W2; 416-934-3440

¡Libros en español!